THE MULTINATIONAL ENTERPRISE IN TRANSITION

(Third Edition)

THE MULTINATIONAL ENTERPRISE IN TRANSITION

Selected Readings and Essays

(Third Edition)

Edited by

Phillip D. Grub
Aryamehr Professor of Multinational Management
The George Washington University

Fariborz Ghadar
Professor of International Business
The George Washington University

Dara Khambata
Professor of International Business
The American University

THE DARWIN PRESS, INC.
Princeton, New Jersey USA

Library of Congress Cataloging-in-Publication Data
The Multinational enterprise in transition.

  Includes bibliographical references and index.
  1. International business enterprises—Management.
I. Grub, Phillip Donald. II. Ghadar, Fariborz.
III. Khambata, Dara, 1948–
HD62.4.M84   1986   338.8'8   86–13442

ISBN 0-87850-051-0 (clothbound)
ISBN 0-87850-052-9 (paperbound)

A Darwin® book published by
                    THE DARWIN PRESS, INC.
                    BOX 2202
                    PRINCETON, NJ 08540 USA

Printed in the United States of America

To the Managers of Multinational Enterprises and our students,
the future entrepreneurs and leaders of this global economy.

CONTENTS

CONTRIBUTORS
(and affiliation at the time article was written)

ALEX ANCKONIE III
George Washington University

JACK N. BEHRMAN
University of North Carolina

LYNN BRENNER
Institutional Investor

JOHN A. CICCO, JR.
Cicco and Associates

FAROK J. CONTRACTOR
Rutgers University

GEORGE W. COOMBE, JR.
Attorney

WILLIAM H. DAVIDSON
University of Virginia

YVES L. DOZ
Harvard University

DENNIS J. ENCARNATION
Harvard University

NATHAN FAGRE
University of North Carolina

WILLIAM A. FISCHER
University of North Carolina

FARIBORZ GHADAR
George Washington University

FREDERICK W. GLUCK
The McKinsey Quarterly

LEONARD GLYNN
Institutional Investor

S. J. GRAY
University of Glasgow

STEPHEN K. GREEN
Hong Kong and Shanghai
  Banking Corporation

PHILLIP D. GRUB
George Washington University

MICHAEL C. HARVEY
Southern Methodist University

PHILIPPE HASPESLAGH
European Institute of Business
  Administration (INSEAD)

DAVID A. HEENAN
University of Hawaii

JEAN E. HELLER
American Graduate School
  of International Management

WARREN J. KEEGAN
Pace University

IVOR KENNY
International Academy of
  Management

DARA KHAMBATA
American University

STEPHEN J. KOBRIN
New York University

DUANE KUJAWA
University of Miami

L. B. McSWEENEY
Association of Certified
  Accountants, U.K.

SAMER MECATTAF
Mecattaf Trading Co., S.A.L.

xi

ROBERT J. PELOSKY, JR.
European-American Bank

ANN ELIZABETH ROBINSON
Consultant

FRANKLIN R. ROOT
University of Pennsylvania

JOHN S. SCHWENDIMAN
Dow Chemical Corporation

SUZANNE R. SETTLE
National Association of
    Manufacturers

J. C. SHAW
University of Glasgow

IBRAHIM F. I. SHIHATA
The World Bank

RICHARD D. SNYDER
Cicco and Associates

HIROTAKA TAKEUCHI
Harvard University

ROSALIE L. TUNG
University of Pennsylvania

WILLIAM D. TURNER
The McKinsey Quarterly

RAYMOND VERNON
Harvard University

LOUIS T. WELLS, JR.
Harvard University

PREFACE

THE MULTINATIONAL ENTERPRISE has probably had the greatest impact on the flow of goods and services in world trade of any international institution during the past three decades. This is as true today as it was when stated in the first edition of this book, where it was noted that "one of the most significant changes in international economic institutions during the past two decades has been the emergence of the multinational enterprise. Policy formulation has not yet caught up with this change." Government officials and corporate executives alike are attempting to cope with this continuing phenomenon and to formulate appropriate guidelines for policy coordination and control.

The study of international business operations is not new. The earliest attempts were made in the 1800s by economists such as Ricardo and others, who illustrated the gains from trade through the exchange of wheat for cotton. However, it was not until the 1930s that the more pragmatic business aspects were considered. Early contributors included New York University professors Paul V. Horn and Henry Gomez in *International Trade Principles and Practices* (1935); Edward E. Pratt in *Modern International Commerce* (1956); and John Fayerweather in *Management of International Operations* (1960).

Building on these efforts, others continued to expand the knowledge of international business operations. Active in this endeavor were Professors John S. Ewing of Stanford University and Frank Meissner, San Francisco State College, in *International Business Management*; Lawrence P. Dowd, San Francisco State College, in *World Business*; Franklin R. Root, Roland L. Kramer, and Maurice Y. d'Arlin, University of Pennsylvania, in *International Trade and Finance*; Hal Martyn, The American University, in *International Business*; and Richard Robinson, Massachusetts Institute of Technology, in *International Business Management*. Subsequent contributors to our knowledge of international business operations from the late 1960s to the present are far too numerous to mention. However, another major force in creating a greater awareness of the scope and significance of international business and trade has been The Academy of International Business through its professional association, leadership, and direction.

The purpose of this (Third) edition of *The Multinational Enterprise in Transition* is to provide the business executive, government official, scholar and student with a better understanding of the changing context in which business is conducted on a global basis. Forty-one leading observers of the multinational enterprise have contributed to this book. Particular emphasis has been placed on creating an awareness of the evolving patterns which uniquely characterize the multinational enterprise in its current and future context. In so doing, the editors have endeavored to accomplish the following objectives:

1. To present many of the key characteristics of a major form of international business activity, the multinational enterprise;

2. To describe the circumstances leading to the emergence and continued growth of the multinational enterprise;

3. To discuss the ways in which various subject areas—management, finance and banking, marketing, personnel, accounting and control, manufacturing, and production—function within a multinational enterprise;

4. To present some of the major environmental factors which influence and are influenced by multinational enterprises, including host government/multinational corporate relations and political risk assessment;

5. To explore some of the issues that will influence multinational business operations in the future.

The multinational corporation *is* and *will continue to be* in transition. During a little more than two decades of existence as a major form of international economic entity, it has acquired tremendous economic power with far-reaching social, economic, and political implications that transcend national boundaries. These and other dimensions of the multinational enterprise will be the subject of continuing research and debate in the future by corporate and public policy makers as well as scholars in the field.

Understandably, key policy makers continue to raise fundamental questions such as: For what and for whose benefit does a multinational enterprise exist? Are those costs (political, social, legal, economic) borne by a country greater than the benefits it secures from a multi-national enterprise? To whom is the enterprise accountable? How does the enterprise affect the sovereignty of a nation? What will be the future role of the enterprise? Important questions are also being focused on a functional level: How does the multinationality of a company affect its management style? What are the implications of extending a company's corporate policies across national boundaries? Who should control information emanting to and from multinational enterprises in their global locations and pursuits?

The Multinational Enterprise in Transition does not pretend to offer ready-made answers to these and other complex problems. It does, however, provide the student and researcher, as well as government and business executives, with a wealth of information not presently available in current textbooks or journals—information from which a better understanding of the current and emerging characteristics may be gained.

The book is organized into ten chapters containing thirty-one articles. Appendix I is a cross-reference index that will assist the student in using this book as supplemental reading with key texts in the field.

The Multinational Enterprise in Transition is designed for both the student and the practitioner. Its primary usefulness, however, will be to upper-level undergraduates and graduate students in international business courses. Since the articles included in this book provide specific insights into many phases of multinational corporate activity, the book is particularly ideal for courses directed to the management of international operations. It may also be used as a companion book with many of the existing texts in international business, as illustrated in Appendix I, as well as an excellent group of readings for case-oriented policy courses.

The Multinational Enterprise in Transition provides the breadth necessary to broaden the horizons of a typically domestic business policy text and consequently offers a multinational perspective where either the text or other required readings are domestic in their orientation. This book may also be used in international economic or political science courses providing a pragmatic viewpoint that complements the more theoretically-oriented texts in the field. As such, the background information offered the student is far greater than if only a basic text or cases had been used.

In the preparation of this book, the authors are indeed indebted to many of their colleagues in academia, principally members of the Academy of International Business for their comments and suggestions and encouragement. It was indeed a formidable task to narrow the number of contributions to a degree that would be within the framework of a single volume. While we are grateful for the assistance given us, we bear the sole responsibility for the final selections made.

Many individuals contributed to this book and we appreciate the assistance of Mark Neal, Graduate Assistant, and Greta Hendrickson, International Business Program secretary, in the preparation of the manuscript. We would also like to express our sincere appreciation for the cooperation of the authors—particularly those whose contributions were written specifically for this book—and the publishers whose works have been herewith included.

> Phillip D. Grub, Fariborz Ghadar, and Dara Khambata
> June 1986

Chapter One:
The Multinational Enterprise in Perspective

ONE OF THE MOST significant developments of the post-World War II era has been the growth and proliferation of multinational enterprises (MNEs). Their impact has been extraordinary on both the investing country and the country receiving the investment. Joining such well established global companies from the developed world as Phillips, General Electric, Nestle, Goodyear, Mitsubishi, Hitachi, and Unilever, new entries range from the Beatrice Companies in the United States to Hyundai and Daewoo from South Korea. No longer is global competition just the territory of corporations from the developed world; corporations from the newly industrialized countries and from the developing world, ranging from Brazil to Turkey, are emerging as major forces in the global, world market for their products and services.

In this section, the reader is introduced to the nature and size of multinationals, with particular emphasis on their origins, growth, and the change that has taken place in the past two decades. It is important to analyze the significant motives for "Going International" as well as ways in which these multinational enterprises are managed in a world of change.

The structural and behavioral characteristics of multinational companies, particularly in relation to planning for global expansion, is a key facet in the rising influence of multinationals. The acquisition and development of resources on a global basis is a major task and necessitates detailed and pragmatic planning. Thus, the multinational can reap tremendous benefits from economies of scale as well as access to less expensive and more cost-efficient resources.

Owing to its global orientation, the multinational company is the beneficiary of many advantages. Setting realistic and practical objectives is a vital step in the investment process. Efficient planning, supplemented by effective communication and careful execution, can lead to profitable exploitation of global opportunities. Trends and problems in foreign expansion should be carefully considered. Cultural compatibility, extent of ownership, availability of trained and disciplined workers, and the availability of other productive resources need close analysis in

1

the planning stage before large sums of money are committed. There-fore, a study of the growth of multinationals and the problems they have faced are the optimal starting points.

As we approach the year 2000, the global marketplace will be faced by continuous change and enhanced competition. Managers of multi-national enterprises will find that they will be spending more time com-municating with and traveling to their subsidiaries and joint ventures throughout the world. It will be essential to place strong emphasis on human resources so that managers are capable of keeping up with the fast pace of technology, exchange rate fluctuations, product innovation, and market competition. It is important for managers of the future to grasp the changes that have taken place in the global business environ-ment in order to be prepared for the challenges ahead. Not only will they be concerned about competition in markets abroad, but a greater concern faces them in the domestic markets because of increasing man-agerial and technical competence of corporations from the newly-industrialized countries and the developing world.

The multinational corporation has evolved in response to human needs for products and services, requiring firms to organize their opera-tions on a world-wide scale. As the multinational corporation continues to evolve, it must re-define its role to meet the common goals of the markets it serves; if it is to continue and to grow in this ever-changing world of economic progress, it must be a leader in the field of managerial and technical innovations.

1

Gone Are the Cash Cows of Yesteryear

Raymond Vernon

The parochial approach to managing parent-subsidiary relations traditionally taken by U.S. MNCs has had the effect of reducing the firm's ability to respond to increasing competition worldwide. Foreign subsidiaries have been under-utilized as sources of information and strength. By improving the lines of communication between headquarters and subsidiaries, U.S. multinationals will be in a better position to adapt to the uncertainties and surprises of foreign markets.

SUDDENLY WE ARE told, the great American juggernaut has run out of steam. No longer can the United States generate the supply of Edisons, Fords, and Salks who for a century or more had given the country its formidable worldwide technological lead. The United States is the newest victim of the English disease—too much government, too little incentive, too little commitment. American industry, which only yesterday could think of the world as its succulent oyster, must now respond to the mounting tide of competitors from newer, more energetic lands.

Those who worry that the United States is drifting downhill in in its innovative or productive capacities base their case on more than surmise. They point to figures on the decline in the nation's output per worker, the number of patents issued to American inventors, and the amount spent on R&D. But those figures, studied in detail, convey a complicated and uncertain message. We cannot say that American workers have grown lazier over the past 10 years or that American engineers and scientists have lost their creative capabilities.* But U.S. companies are losing competitive ground. To reverse the trend, we must first understand why.

To that end, it helps to explore the origins of our vaunted role— dating back to the second half of the nineteenth century—as the world's leader in industrial technology. That role did not result from an unusual abundance of skills. Although the Americans of that period were relatively literate and skilled, so were the British, the French, and the Germans. Indeed, outstanding scientists and engineers were more commonly found in Europe than in the United States. Americans, however, had other advantages: cheap and abundant raw materials, a large internal market, and almost no governmental restraints on the pursuit of profits.

HOW DID IT ALL BEGIN?

Only one fly contaminated the economic ointment of the American entrepreneurs. Because opportunities in the United States were so rich, labor was scarce; farming, lumbering, and mining drew off some of the available skilled labor, including immigrant carpenters and metalworkers who had made their way to America from Europe. America's businessmen therefore faced a tantalizing opportunity. With a market there for the taking, they had to find new production methods that could overcome both the scarcity and high cost of skilled workers in the United States.

---

* What is so difficult about interpreting the meaning of *productivity*, especially in terms of output per worker? Until about 10 years ago, industrial plants increased their measured output while destroying the recreational value of lakes, rivers, and open spaces; reducing the potability of water; and increasing the health hazards from befouled air. Should we have reduced measured output in the past to reflect those unmeasured uses of our natural resources? Should we regard U.S. workers as less productive if some of their efforts are now used to reduce these hitherto unmeasured costs?

Next, there is the problem of defining a worker. Over the past decade, untrained youths and women of all ages have augmented the work force in unprecedented numbers. Does the entry of this untrained contingent mean that U.S. workers as a whole should be regarded as less productive?

Finally, there is the problem of combining different kinds of output in an overall measure that makes sense. The output of the United States increasingly takes the form of services, including contributions to health, safety recreation, and education. Most of these services do not come in measurable units, many have no market price. We measure this part of U.S. output in ways that say little or nothing about the diligence of energy of U.S. workers.

Driven by the extraordinary challenge, proprietors of textile plants, iron foundries, glass factories, and machine shops produced such devices as sewing machines, glass-blowing machines, automatic woodworking and metalworking machines, and automatic railway signaling devices. Having broken the skilled labor bottleneck, they went on to develop and market a new generation of products, including the electric light, the telephone, the low-priced automobile, and the vacuum cleaner—all appropriate to the tastes of the richest mass market in the world.

Americans have not monpolized industrial innovations over the past century. But their innovations have differed from those of the Europeans in some important respects. In industrial goods, Europeans tended to stress innovation that would conserve capital and raw materials, such as the use of oxygen in blast furnaces and fuel injection in automobile motors. Americans tended to concentrate on labor-saving innovations and were profligate with energy and raw materials. In consumer goods, the United States ground out a stream of new products that could satisfy an apparently unlimited appetite for novelty and comfort. On the other hand, Europe (and later Japan) concentrated on smaller, cheaper, and more durable versions of the same dishwashers and television sets that had first been produced in the United States.

American innovations continued to exhibit their labor-saving, income-serving characteristics during the three decades following World War II (see Exhibit 1). Through the end of the 1960s, many

*Exhibit I: Perceived Advantages of Innovations Introduced in the United States, Europe, and Japan, 1945-1974***

Perceived Advantage	United States		Europe (including Britain)		Japan	
	No.	Percent	No.	Percent	No.	Percent
Labor saving	331	40.1	120	12.7	6	6.4
Material saving	175	21.2	444	46.9	32	34.1
Capital saving	58	7.0	104	11.0	7	7.4
Novel function	106	12.8	83	8.8	12	12.8
Safety	50	6.1	83	6.3	7	7.4
Other	106	12.8	135	14.3	30	31.9
TOTALS	826	100.0	946	100.0	94	100.0

**Based on a sample of 1,916 innovations

SOURCE: Adapted from W.H. Davidson, "Patterns of Factor-Saving Innovation in the industrialized World," *European Economic Review*, vol. 8, 1976, p. 214.

American enterprises felt secure and well entrenched. Here and there, some industries like automobiles and steel evidenced a certain amount of uneasiness. But by and large, American companies were contentedly herding and milking their cash cows, convinced that they were the most innovative and efficient producers on the face of the earth.

THINNING THE HERD

The 1970s began to obliterate features that had distinguished the United States from other industrialized countries. For one thing, European and Japanese income levels were rising rapidly and no longer trailed far behind those of the Americans. Accordingly, foreign consumers' demands in food, household goods, transportation, recreation, safety, and health drew abreast of those in the United States. These foreign markets were no longer small or fragmented, and with the strengthening of the European Community, they began to rival the United States in size and buying power.

Gone, too, were the differences in cost structures that had distinguished the United States from the other countries. Labor was almost as expensive in Europe as in the United States. Capital, thanks partly to the burgeoning Euromoney market, was plentiful on both sides of the Atlantic. And as Americans began to rely increasingly on imported raw materials, their historic advantage in the prices of such materials was also evaporating. Therefore, American business no longer had the unique advantage of operating in the environment of the future in its home markets. For once, it was obliged to start off even with its European and Japanese competitors.

Indeed, in one critical respect, the conditions of the 1970s gave the rivals of the United States an edge. Long-time trends in production costs were reversed: for once, raw materials and capital became more expensive all over the world, outdistancing increases in labor costs. Now European and Japanese innovations were in demand, with their emphasis on conserving capital, raw materials, and fuel. Italian oil burners designed for fuel economy found markets in American homes and factories; and the cast-aluminum engines of the Japanese and Europeans, designed to reduce overall automobile weight, found American markets as well.

Alas for America's cash cows. The size and productivity of the herd had largely depended on America's technological lead. With good luck and the advantages of the experience curve, American innovators had been able to ride the crest of growing world demand, profiting from a product well into its senescence. Now, however, the experience curve offers Americans little advantage; indeed, in some cases, the advantage lies with their rivals. So the cash cows, we can be reasonably sure, will be fewer and not quite so plump.

WHAT OF OUR CALVING RATES?

America is losing its competitive edge partly because it can no longer count on the advantages of an experience curve. But the deeper worry is that the country may also be suffering from a falling off in the ability of its scientists and engineers to innovate as well as in the willingness of its business community to underwrite those innovative efforts. For instance, a larger proportion of the total patents issued each year by the U.S. Patent Office goes to foreigners, and a smaller proportion of the patents issued by foreign patent offices goes to U.S. inventors. Moreover, R&D expenditures in the United States, calculated as a percentage of the country's GNP, have drifted downward over the past five years or more, whereas the same ratios for other key countries such as Germany and Japan have remained more or less constant for the same period.

Nevertheless, it is not at all clear that America's scientists and engineers have lost their creative abilities.*** True, we have been diverting some of our innovative efforts in various ways: our capacity to make better battle tanks is increasing more rapidly than our ability to make better automobiles. Moreover, some U.S. companies have transferred their efforts to other countries, with some U.S. drug companies

---

*** If U.S. inventors are getting fewer patents relative to foreigners both at home and abroad, why is this not conclusive evidence of declining innovative capabilities? There are two main factors to consider:

1. Inventors take out patents in a foreign country only if they plan to exploit the invention there. Formerly, many of the European and Japanese innovations had little application to the U.S. market; meanwhile, U.S. innovations had strong promise in the markets of Europe and Japan. More recently, however, the characteristic lines of innovation stressed by the Europeans and Japanese have become more relevant to the U.S. market, while U.S. lines of innovation have lost some of their uniqueness in foreign markets. These trends could well be producing the observed shifts in patenting.

2. The number of patents issued is probably losing its value as an indicator of innovation. With a speeding up in technological change, some companies prefer to keep their innovations to themselves rather than publish their results. Moreover, the shift in innovation from creating novel products to developing cost-reducing products and processes also tends to reduce the innovators' willingness to patent. Another major change is the tendency to create innovations by putting together familiar systems in new configurations—for instance, attaching microchips and electric circuits to electric ovens or washing machines. Innovations of this sort, useful though they may be, are commonly not patentable.

moving their laboratories to England to escape FDA regulations and IBM shifting some of its development work to Europe to keep French ministers happy. But the most important difference in the position of U.S. companies is the increase in the relevance of the technological work being done in Europe and Japan.

LOOK TO FOREIGN MARKETS

Americans need to practice what the Japanese and Europeans have been doing all along—that is, making both cheaper and more durable goods to appeal to the tastes of foreign markets. In fact, the emphasis on the amount and quality of U.S. R&D threatens to be a red herring, diverting attention from more important factors that could boost U.S. industrial performance. History shows repeatedly that countries with an outstanding record in science and technology are not necessarily those that shine in productivity and competitiveness.

The United Kingdom is the outstanding case in point. Surrounded by industrial decay, British scientists continue to perform remarkably. And although Japan's scientific and technological efforts have been increasing, these efforts are still not very impressive when measured by normal quantitative yardsticks.

Clearly, the United Kingdom does not use effectively all the information it generates, while Japan manages to apply a lot of the world's information which it had no hand in generating. A good example of Japan's integrative capability is the Nikon camera. Nikon has absorbed technology from all over the world: it uses—imaginatively and well—shutter electronics developed by a Minneapolis company and a single lens reflex mechanism copied from the Germans.

In addition, we must consider that about half the world's present industrial output is generated by MNCs with widespread productive facilities. Accordingly, the flashes of genius produced by an engineer in Morristown, New Jersey could show up on an assembly line in Jakarta as readily as in nearby Newark. By the same token, the ideas first expressed in a laboratory in Fontainebleau can swiftly be brought across the Atlantic provided, of course, that American business has both the antennas to learn about those ideas and the wit to recognize their value.

Therein lie the basic lessons: no longer can we either suppose that the innovations of other countries are irrelevant to American needs or expect that American innovations will hold a lead for any length of time over foreign competition. The biggest challenge for U.S. business is to create a scanning capability to survey the advances taking place in other countries and a managerial capability to incorporate those advances wherever they are relevant to our needs.

SCANNING OUR NEIGHBORS' PASTURES

A visitor from a distant planet observing the great network of U.S. subsidiaries in foreign lands might readily assume that Americans already had a highly developed capability for scanning their foreign markets. These subsidiaries number in the thousands, carry millions of employees on their payrolls, and account for a substantial proportion of the profits of their American parents. No other country's overseas contingent amounts to more than a fraction of America's establishment.

There are signs, however, that these networks are wired mostly for one-way transmission—the center issues commands, but the periphery has trouble transmitting unsolicited data back to the center. Most U.S.-owned subsidiaries operating abroad manufacture a range of products conceived in Toledo or Kankakee. The main task of the subsidiary is to convince the local populace that these products are exactly what it needs.

Here and there, to be sure, U.S.-owned subsidiaries have adapted successfully to the foreign markets in which they operate. The special skills and knowledge of such subsidiaries, however, are rarely allowed to penetrate the main network of the company. Each of America's big three automobile companies, for example, contains in its network at least one European subsidiary that has long mastered the technology of small-car construction. But Detroit has been remarkably slow to absorb those hard-won skills.

WHY NOT LISTEN?

Several factors explain the American propensity for one-way transmission over its multinational networks. Most important, these subsidiaries were created during a period in which U.S.-based companies characteristically enjoyed a technological lead over their competitors, generating and selling products that would represent the market of the future. As long as U.S. companies were secure in their innovative leads, there was no great need to use foreign subsidiaries as listening posts.

A second factor has been the premature obliteration of international divisions in many U.S. companies. As the foreign interests of American companies grew and flourished in the postwar period, the international divisions were often the star performers. But the success was eventually their undoing. By the middle 1960s, one American company after another reorganized itself to acknowledge the increased importance of its foreign business. According to one study undertaken in the early 1970s, the typical pattern consisted of abolishing the international division and setting up a series of so-called global product divisions to do the worrying about foreign markets.

In a recent study covering a group of 57 large U.S.-based multinationals, a colleague and I ran into some disturbing indications suggesting that some of these reorganizations may have been wildly counterproductive. A subset of our sample, organized along global product lines, exhibited rather striking characteristics. This group of companies seemed to show decidedly less interest in its foreign operations than those with an international division. Ten years after they had introduced their new products into the United States, the global product companies were only producing about 50 percent of those products in overseas locations. By contrast, the other companies in the sample were manufacturing more than 80 percent of their new products in foreign plants. At least in the case of this sample, the demise of the international division and the creation of a global product division suggested a sharp decline in interest in foreign operations.[1]

That result may not be as surprising as it first seems. When managers of domestic product divisions in the United States assume responsibility for global product divisions, the change in perspective may go deeper than the title on their business cards. In training and outlook, they may still be as American as the Dallas Cowboys and apple pie. And unlike the international specialists that they have replaced, these managers may shrink from confronting unfamiliar problems, which can range anywhere from transacting business in pesos to wrestling with Belgian labor laws.

Some companies have recognized the danger in the newer organizational form and are returning to the old way of doing things. A prime example is Westinghouse, which went from an international to a global product division and back to an international division again.

GETTING OUT OF DAIRYING

It may seem paradoxical at first that the country with the world's most extensive network of foreign manufacturing subsidiaries should be so parochial in its approach to foreign environments. But the explanation for the apparent contradiction is obvious: very few U.S. companies actively study or understand the particular needs of their foreign markets.

Most U.S. companies were swept into those markets either on the strength of their domestic industrial innovations or by the desire to best their American competitors. Many European and practically all Japanese managers, on the other hand, have always believed that they must export to survive. That difference in viewpoint has produced a change in attitude toward studying the surprises and uncertainties of foreign markets.

But American manufacturers no longer have a choice of entering foreign markets or leaving them alone. Whether they go to foreigners or not, foreigners will come to them—if not through imports then through the output of manufacturing subsidiaries located in the United States.

When citizen band radios suddenly grew popular in the United States, the Japanese built better, cheaper models and now have almost captured the leadership in that market. Volkswagen's little Pennsylvania plant cannot keep up with the demand. Honda will soon be a prime competitor on these shores. And Hitachi also plans to conquer the color television market from a new manufacturing base in the West. There is no longer a place where American business can hide.

RESPONDING TO THE CHALLENGE

That ineluctable fact is just the beginning to dawn on many U.S. managers. Once it becomes crystal clear, American companies may also realize that they still operate from a position of considerable strength. Their foreign subsidiaries are grossly underused sources of such strength. U.S. business can turn those subsidiaries into two-way conduits, relaying back to the parent information about the latest developments in product, process, and market that bear on America's competitive position. And the challenge for headquarters is to learn how to listen, to incorporate the foreign advances that are succeeding, and to try to improve on those advances.

A few companies already are rising to the challenge. Du Pont is one enterprise adept at scanning its foreign subsidiaries and using the results in other parts of its organization. A miniplant in Argentina, for instance, generates process innovations that can be used for other small plants in Africa.

For most companies, developing the new capability will take some time, but it will be worth it. The efforts of Ford and General Motors to develop a "world car," for instance, reflect their realization that what other markets want may really matter. There are, to be sure, certain inherent dangers—for example, the so-called world model could turn out to be a sham effort to dress up the preferred U.S. product in another guise. Nevertheless, some part of the world product response will be worthwhile, especially if it represents a genuine effort to respond to the tastes and needs of other markets.

Another strength on which U.S. business can draw is its formidable scientific and technological establishment, still by all odds the world's largest and best. Some of its current efforts seem misdirected, and those developments that are on target are unlikely to provide the same degree of technological lead as in the past. But it remains a formidable resource, unmatched in total strength by any other country.

In the end, U.S. business will have to accept the fact that its competitive position in world markets has changed profoundly. After American businesses have carefully studied the world's markets, after they have absorbed and incorporated the best that can be gleaned from the rest of the world, that effort will do no more than keep them abreast of their nearest competitors.

At that point, the race will be won by those enterprises with the best price, the best quality, and the best after-sales service. This emphasis will be new to many Americans—accustomed to offering the newest, most unusual products and hoping to turn a few of them into the proverbial cash cow. Changes in attitude come slowly, but I am betting that many U.S. enterprises will be able to make the shift.

NOTES

1. Raymond Vernon and W. H. Davidson, "Foreign Production of Technology-Intensive Product by U.S.-Based-Multinational Enterprises," Working Paper 79-5, Harvard Business School, 1979.

2
Multinationals in the World of Nations

Leonard Glynn

Multinational corporations are large, powerful organizations that date from ancient times. These organizations are constantly changing and become successful by applying a number of valid business principles to their operations. And in contrast to the myths and criticism that surround these corporations, MNCs are actually courted by governments of varying political colors in order for those governments to reap the benefits and contributions the MNCs bestow on national economies.

INTRODUCTION

Whether they elicit respect and admiration or suspicions and hostility, multinational corporations (MNCs) are a salient feature of today's world economy—and of our everyday lives. Names like Sony, IBM, Coca-Cola, and Volkswagen have become household words across most of planet earth. Both in the developed countries of the "West"—a term embracing Japan, Europe, and the United States—and in fast-growing "newly industrialized countries" like Brazil, Korea, and Taiwan, multinational corporations play key roles in national economies. They employ substantial numbers of the work force and produce, in many cases, major shares of their host countries' Gross National Products (GNPs). Yet, while their neon logos light the night skies from New York to Singapore to Buenos Aires, these globe-girdling corporations remain shrouded in mystery. Their contribution to the world economy is little understood. They are subject to both polemical attack and exaggerated praise.[1]

This essay aims to dispel the myths that have grown up around multinational corporations and to answer a series of questions about them that continue to absorb businessmen, labor leaders, political scientists, economists, and citizens in both the MNCs' "home" countries and in the "host" countries where their overseas arms operate. What exactly are multinational corporations? How are they different from companies that do business in just one country? And how are they similar? How did they arise? How big a part do they play in the world economy? What criteria do they use in deciding to invest? How have their relations with the countries where they operate changed in recent years? Are they in some way a threat to national sovereignty? Finally, what are the prospects for multinationals and what contributions can they make to the growth of the world economy and to the national economies in which they are active?

Such a survey promises to take us far from a simple profile of the multinational company. But the multinationals can only be understood in a wider context. MNCs, after all, have evolved over nearly a century to their modern form. The ideas behind them actually run back to ancient times. What's more, the environment that multinationals work in is constantly changing—and so are the MNCs themselves. As we examine these companies, we will discuss issues like the nature of free enterprise capitalism, and the steady shift since World War II from a global economy dominated by the North Atlantic nations to an interdependent world with numerous concentrations of power. The main focus, though, will be on ways multinationals have shaped and adapted to these changes, and what they promise for the future. First we need to define what a multinational corporation really is.

SOME DEFINITIONS

Many companies, in every advanced nation, have widespread foreign sales of their goods or services. This is hardly new. As early as the second century A.D., goods were conveyed by Roman roads, galleys, and camel caravans for thousands of miles to China. From the ancient Phoenicians to the giant Sogo Shosa trading firms that handle much of Japan's foreign sales and purchases today, long-distance trade seems to have accompanied the development of civilization itself. That is because, by trading, nations acquire goods that either cannot be made at home, for lack of skills or raw materials, or can be made more economically abroad. In general, if the exchange is a free one, untainted by fraud or coercion, both sides benefit from trade.

The fact that a company's goods cross political boundaries before reaching their buyer does not make the firm a multinational corporation. Traditionally, that term was reserved for companies holding equity (or ownership) interests in production facilities in at least two nations. But that definition of a multinational is broader than the way the term is commonly understood today. A better description is that arrived at by the Harvard University Multinational Enterprise Project: "They are invariably large in size, they operate in a substantial number of countries, they have access to a common pool of human and financial resources, and they control their widespread activities rather than serving as mere exporters or licensers of technology."[2] This is how most people—most multinational executives themselves—understand the term.

By this definition, something like 1,000 companies around the world might be regarded as multinationals. According to a definition by the Bureau of Economic Analysis—10 percent or more foreign ownership of a business enterprise—there are more like 10,000. But they are hardly a homogeneous group. To begin with, they break down into four broad categories: Extractive or resource companies that develop oil, minerals, or other raw materials; manufacturing companies that design and build tangible, industrial goods; service companies engaged in anything from providing fast foods to financial expertise; and agribusiness, producing food or farm commodities.

Most MNCs are the large private companies from the U.S., Europe, and Japan that are familiar to consumers and citizens worldwide: companies like General Motors, Hitachi, and Bayer. But some multinational companies are owned by governments, not by private investors. Elf-Acquitaine is a case in point. It is one of France's two government-owned petroleum exploration and development companies. What's more, some "multinationals" are not really capitalist firms, though they generally do business by the yardstick of profits and losses. (In 1979, a directory listed 382 Soviet and East European companies.) The Soviet Union's state-owned Moscow Narodny Bank, for example, has more than 65 affiliates around the world. It holds assets of more than $2 billion. And it publishes a glossy annual report revealing the basic business statistics required under British laws, since Moscow Narodny's western headquarters is in London.[3] New MNCs are also emerging in the developing world.

THE GLOBAL SCALE OF MULTINATIONALS

Though there is no single, comprehensive statistic that shows the total share of world output produced by multinational corporations, it is clear that MNCs are the largest and most powerful businesses on earth. One study by the publication *European Report* gives some sense of the scale of their operations by comparing the worldwide revenues of the 200 largest multinationals based in the 24-nation Organization for Economic Cooperation and Development (OECD) with the total Gross Domestic Products (GDPs) of the OECD nations.[4] (These include the 19 largest non-Communist economies in Europe plus the U.S., Japan, Canada, Australia, and New Zealand.) The study shows that the 200 multinational companies' revenues were equal to roughly one-third of the OECD member nations' total output.

If we extended the list to include multinationals based outside the OECD, we would find that these companies play such a large role that it is hard to understand the course of the current global economy without considering their influence. Moreover, most studies indicate that the MNCs are among the fastest-growing companies both in their home and host countries. That means that their role is likely to be even more significant in the future.

THE EVOLUTION OF TODAY'S MULTINATIONALS

Surprisingly, in light of their sheer size, today's multinationals are a relatively recent phenomenon. Though similar firms had existed as early as the 1790s, their scale was incomparably smaller, and the two world wars severely limited international corporate growth. Indeed, the decade after World War II is really the period MNCs began to grow explosively, alongside an ever more interdependent global economy.

Five basic conditions made the MNCs' post-war expansion possible. First, most major countries agreed to move toward freer trade and investment, in an attempt to avoid the nationalistic economic policies of the 1930s that had contributed so much to global depression and to World War II itself. Second, international bodies like the World Bank and the International Monetary Fund were set up to make payments of debts and settlement of trade balances between countries more dependable. Third, the empires of Europe's colonial powers broke up as first the Asian region, then the African nations, gained independence. The quest for economic development by most newly independent nations and by the less-developed countries of Latin America helped spur overall demand for commodities, energy, and productive equipment. Fourth, the press of wartime development itself, especially in the undamaged United States, had produced and left intact vast new productive forces able to operate on a truly global scale. Means of transport, communication, and finance were greatly enhanced. And new lines of products and technologies, some of which were originally developed for war, were available for commercial, civilian use. Fifth, and perhaps most important, the rebuilding of the war-ravaged economies of Europe and Japan provided a major source of demand for goods and capital.[5]

The United States, by far the richest and most powerful in the nation in the world at the time, provided billions of dollars of aid to the reconstruction of both allies and former enemies. And many of the largest American corporations, which had achieved massive increases in capacity and output during World War II, began a huge wave of investment overseas. American firms had the capital to finance new construction, the advanced management and sales techniques, and the experience of producing for a continent-sized home market. That made them especially well-adapted to invest and operate in European markets. Many U.S. firms organized plants that worked together from bases in different countries before European businesses were able to overcome national hostilities and do the same. In large measure, American management saw foreign investment as the best way to secure lasting shares of markets that might later be lost as Europe's own industry recovered. They succeeded so well that, by the late 1960s, the French author and political figure Jean-Jacques Servan-Schreiber warned in *The American Challenge* that U.S. multinationals might become the dominant power in the world economy. Indeed, that prospect seemed very real at the time.

Fifteen years later, in 1983, it was clear that the "takeover" of the world economy by U.S. multinationals was out of the question. Despite American MNCs' initial successes in the post-war period, foreign firms have since done quite well at emulating—and sometimes bettering—their international structures and ways of doing business. American success bred imitation. Though it is hard to date exactly, somewhere in the mid-1970s the total overseas investments from firms outside the

United States surpassed the foreign holdings of American MNCs.[6] In succession, the major firms of a resurgent Europe and, more recently, Japan, matched and then overtook the foreign stake of U.S. MNCs. (U.S. overseas investment at the end of 1981 was $228 billion out of a total of more than $500 billion from all nations.) Moreover, there is now an upsurge of MNCs based in countries that were only recently regarded as "developing." Companies from Mexico, India, South Korea, and Taiwan—to name just some of the pioneering Third World MNCs —are also beginning to expand abroad.*

What emerges from this cursory survey of the recent history and evolution of multinational corporations is that they are a dynamic form of enterprise; that while the largest number of them used to come from the United States, other nations' firms have become successful MNCs (only about half of today's MNCs are American); and that the expansion of this form of enterprise is continuing as companies in many nations, including the developing world, move into international investment.

No nation has a patent on the MNC as a form of business, and as one recent study concluded: "The process of [multinational] de-concentration is continuing, with many of the oil- and mineral-producing nations now entering the lists, usually through state-owned corporations. At the same time, the market share of any single private-ly-owned firm or group of firms in such a rapidly expanding global market is declining. . . ."[7] Thus, for example, where the "Big Three" U.S. automakers—General Motors, Ford, and Chrysler—produced more than half of the world's automobiles in the late 1940s, their share of the total world auto market today—including their production from plants outside the U.S.—is less than 25 percent. A similar trend can be seen in the decline of the share of world oil marketed by the "Seven Sisters," the oil giants which once dominated petroleum production and sales. But if the market share of any single MNC or group of MNCs is declining, the number of multinational corporations is growing, and promises to continue to do so. To find out why, we'll need to examine the structure of multinationals in a bit more detail, and consider the economic reasons that continue to make this form of enterprise succeed, even during serious downturns in the world economy.

---

* A development first noted in detail by David A. Heenan and Warren J. Keegan in "The Rise of Third World Multinationals," *Harvard Business Review*, January/February, 1979, pp. 101- 9.

THE STRUCTURE OF MULTINATIONAL CORPORATIONS

Perhaps the best account of the development of the modern corporate management provided by MNCs is A. D. Chandler's 1961 study, *Strategy and Structure*.[8] In the initial small workshop, Chandler notes, the entrepreneur or capitalist directly oversees production. As the family-owned business grows into a large factory, the office of management might move to the second floor, concentrating more effort on bookkeeping and marketing, while delegating the supervision of production to foremen and a plant manager. As the firm spreads across its national market and establishes several factories, the importance of the central office will grow. Various departments emerge—finance, legal affairs, personnel, purchasing, marketing, manufacturing, quality control, and customer affairs. The greater the size of the firm, the larger and more subdivided the operations of this central "brain and cortex" of management can become.

By the 1920s, in fact, the growing size of business corporations had led to the creation of the multidivisional firm, a form pioneered by the General Motors Corporation. Each division of such a firm is, in theory, a multidepartment organization with its head office staff responsible for overall operations. Above the divisional heads, the fully-developed firm is directed by a general office. At this point in the firm's growth, executives at the company's center are principally engaged in overseeing various departments within their division. If one or more of the divisions has reached out to undertake production in several countries outside the company's home nation, then the company has evolved, in effect, into a multinational corporation.

Although this basic pattern of organizational growth has been experienced by thousands of growing companies, there are innumerable variations in the management styles (or "corporate culture") that can be found under it. Some companies are rigidly controlled from the central office, sometimes down to the very minor, "paperclip" details of day-to-day operations. Other firms have evolved a far looser, more decentralized style. In the second type of company, for example, a division chief might have considerable latitude in developing new products, marketing strategies, labor contracts, and other important elements of the operations.

Although this form of organization may seem cumbersome, it is actually far more flexible than that of smaller companies. That is because a multidivisional corporation—a structure virtually all multinationals have adopted—can enter a new market simply by establishing a new division. Although not so readily, it can also abandon an old market or downplay it either by selling off a division or by limiting the money it commits to it.

Large size, multidivisional organization confers other advantages on fully-developed corporations. Since such a company has presumably proven its ability to produce goods that customers want in ever-increasing volume, it has the ability, if it wishes, to gain greater "name recognition" than smaller firms, if only because its divided structure makes it less likely to fail rapidly and more likely to repay. That gives the large corporation access to greater amounts of loan money from banks at lower rates of interest ("prime rates") than smaller competitors.

Finally, the same principle of the division of labor that made group production in the early workshops more efficient than the manual labor of single artisans also applies to management itself. With a large cadre of experienced employees at its central office, a major corporation is more able to "detach" expert executives. They may spend long periods of time examining the risk or profitability of such corporate moves as acquiring another company, establishing the firm's money, staff, time, and reputation in a productive venture in a foreign nation.

In virtually all of the largest MNCs, the sheer size of central and affiliate office staffs enables firms to devote substantial top executive effort to the creation and adjustment of strategies for the firm as a whole. Expert analysis is devoted to studying the growth rate of various nations' populations and economies, the needs of consumers, the possible application of new technologies to products, the prospects for changes in various nations' currency values, interest rates, corporate laws, and even political structures. No individual could possibly attempt to grasp such a number of constantly-changing factors. But with their staff's help, frequently supplemented by outside experts, the chief executives of today's MNCs can and do manage the multiple and often countervailing dynamics of operations spanning scores of countries.

Obviously, these executives can make mistakes. They may be outwitted or defeated by competitors, and sometimes be caught unawares by economic or political developments that damage their businesses. But the general office-divisional structure gives MNCs the capacity to make informed business decisions that smaller firms could only make by guess-work. And the type of structure they operate in has proven its capacity to survive and grow, despite individual failures by some MNCs. In the most commonsense way, the view from the 42nd floor of an MNC headquarters is far more global than that from the second-floor window of the 19th-century factory. And despite the height, the chances of a fall are less as well.[9]

After cataloguing the qualitative advantages that multinationals —or any very large corporations—enjoy, it may seem odd to insist that their similarities to smaller, merely national, companies are, in many ways, greater than their differences. But in every significant respect, MNCs are essentially small companies that have grown very large. On the bottom line—where profit and loss are measured—their continued growth and survival depend on the same factors that keep a small bicycle plant running. To understand why, let's look again at the free enterprise principles which guide the operations of both MNCs and smaller companies. The real difference is that MNCs simply apply them on a far larger, indeed a worldwide, scale.

MULTINATIONALS AS BUSINESSES

Consider again the example of a small bicycle maker. To launch his business, the entrepreneur must assemble and coordinate a wide variety of factors. First, he must have some reasonable sense that the type of bicycles he wants to build will actually find buyers; in other words, that he will meet the felt needs of consumers. Secondly, he must possess or acquire the money (capital) to buy land for his plant, to hire workers, and to obtain raw materials and tools. Once he begins producing, he must arrange to get the bikes to wholesalers or stores that can sell them. Very few individual customers are likely to come directly to his small factory.

At every stage of his business debut, the entrepreneur must balance competing economic forces. He must pay enough in wages to attract workers, but not more than his expanded revenues will justify. He must search for reliable suppliers of frames, tires, saddlebags, and other items that will be used in manufacturing. As he does so, he must weigh varying levels of quality, price, financing terms, and re-liability. And as the business develops, he must constantly watch the actions of competitors—on price, quality, and design—to make sure that his product has a good chance to win both customer approval and the consumer's hard-earned cash.

Suppose the business is highly successful, its product is in high demand, and production must expand to meet fast-growing orders. At some point, probably early on, the original entrepreneur will need to hire assistants to help manage the firm. Perhaps one man will oversee a group of functions like dealing with the company's workers, keeping the books on revenues and costs, and so on. Ultimately, new lines of business may be added—first motorcycles, then cars and small trucks. Later, the construction of a local plant in another country might make sense—moving the original bicycle maker toward the status of a multinational corporation. As the firm's production, employees, management staff, and marketing range spreads more widely across its home-country market, and eventually abroad, those in charge of operations will have to take note of factors that were barely noticed by the original small bicycle maker.

In general, the more a company grows, the wider its field of vision about obtaining the basic "inputs"—land, labor, capital, raw materials, productive equipment, and so on—that it needs to keep growing. Its transition to becoming an MNC, then, is really not such a radical step, but a logical outgrowth of growth. If the bicycle maker's story sounds familiar, it is. Japan's Honda Motor Company grew from a family-owned motorcycle firm into a multinational auto producer, with plants in the U.S. and other countries along much the same lines. In the process, of course, such a company changes dramatically. But the principles by which MNCs operate are the same as those they began with at the local or national level. Obviously, to stay in business and grow, a firm must realize more revenues on its sales than it spends to produce, promote, and distribute its goods or services. Successful firms do so by applying a number of principles that remain valid guides even if they branch out into production and marketing in dozens of countries. Among them are:

The Division of Labor. This means breaking down the production process into distinct phases at which a worker or manager can become expert. If a single man, given all the materials, may be able to build a house in a year's time, the chances are that twelve men can build it in a lot less than a month. Some will prove more capable than others at roofing, plumbing, or other tasks, and so speed the overall project. In factory production, where workers and machines are combined, a detailed division of labor produces vastly more dramatic increases in productivity. Today's car plants, for example, produce one auto per worker every few days. Can you imagine building an entire car from its parts before the next weekend?

Economy of Scale. If a plant that can produce 100 bicycles in an eight-hour day is set up, it can probably produce 300 bicycles if new workers come in to keep it going around the clock. And each of those 300 bicycles will be cheaper to make than the first 100. That is because the plant's initial, or "start-up," costs are the same. And when a company can buy larger amounts of materials, it is generally able to get lower prices per unit.

Comparative Advantage. If a foreign country is able to produce the tube steel needed for bicycles more cheaply than any firm in the home country, it makes sense for our bicycle maker to buy from it. Perhaps the foreign country has more iron ore; perhaps its workers are willing to work for lower wages at a given stage in its development; perhaps its steel companies are larger and more efficient (because of economies of scale). Whatever the reason, buying its steel will probably add to the profits of our hypothetical company.

The last principle—comparative advantage—is perhaps the single most important reason why multinational corporations have outpaced the growth of companies based in single countries. Different regions and nations have varying endowments of soil, resources, population, skills, and so on. It is more profitable for nations to utilize these advantages to produce what they are best suited for and then exchange their surplus with other nations that lack their advantages.

In a famous example, the 19th-century English economist David Ricardo examined the relative ability of England and Portugal to produce wine and wool. Portugal has rich soil in its hills and a warm climate ideal for growing grapes. England's cooler, damper climate produces the lush grass that sheep thrive on. Both nations, Ricardo argued, would gain if England raised sheep and Portugal raised grapes and then the two nations traded their surpluses. Overall, there would be more wine and more wool for both, because neither country would waste efforts on what the other could do better, and both would "play to" their "comparative advantages."

THE POLITICAL COSTS OF SUCCESS

The multinationals' very success at assembling managerial skills and technology and applying basic business principles—division of labor, economies of scale, and comparative advantage by mobilizing capital, technology, and managerial skills—have given rise in recent years to a litany of polemics. Some of the radical criticism—mainly from socialist and Communist sources—is frankly hostile to all free enterprise. But multinationals have also been buffeted by charges from authors and politicians who believe in free enterprise but view MNCs as a unique type of firm which requires stricter government regulation than that imposed on national companies. Among the most frequently cited charges are that:

- MNCs "export jobs" from the industrial West by moving plants to low-wage Third World nations.
  Their sheer size gives them inordinate bargaining power in dealings with host-country governments, many of which have smaller GNPs than the annual sales of the larger MNCs.
- They avoid paying taxes to host-country governments by complex accounting methods designed to realize final profits in such "tax havens" as the Bahamas, Panama, or Hong Kong.
- They distort the economies of host countries—especially in the Third World—by building up a well-to-do urban elite, driving smaller domestic businesses into bankruptcy, and draining sources of finance that local companies need.
- MNCs harm less-developed economies and indigenous cultures by introducing "unnecessary" or "inappropriate" products, like carbonated soda, canned dog food, or powdered infant formula.
- They "dump" dangerous products like DDT, which are forbidden in the West for health reasons, on unsuspecting Third World customers.
- For all the reasons cited above, they are "out of control" of governments, a breed of corporation that poses a profound "threat to national sovereignty."[10]

MNCs are large and powerful entities. They are not charities, but businesses, interested in securing profits in exchange for their goods and services. But the by-now-familiar attacks on the MNCs have, in fact, lost touch with the new realities emerging in the world economy. Where they do not stem from bad faith—that is, when they are not really attacks on free enterprise disguised as critiques of MNCs—most anti-multinational arguments have reactionary, romantic, and xenophobic roots.

In the broadest sense, criticism of the MNCs rests on the decisions that any company operating on a global basis—not simply within single nations—must make. But the same economic forces that move MNCs to expand, reduce, or even close down their operations in a given nation would apply with equal force if the MNC subsidiary were, instead, a wholly domestic firm.

Consider a case of relocation. If the cost of labor, raw materials, and other factors make an MNC subsidiary in France no longer profitable, the company may indeed decide to cut costs and step up output in Mexico. But if the MNC subsidiary were a domestic French firm instead, the same economic forces could simply drive it into bankruptcy.[11] In a world of increasing interdependence, the idea that any national economy could be sheltered for long from the global economic forces that MNCs obey is itself a delusion. Like the messenger blamed for bringing bad news, MNCs are invariably rebuked when forces beyond their control require lay-offs, plant closings, or other painful decisions.

Yet, the available evidence indicates that when any nation's own MNCs do invest abroad, the net effect is to create more jobs inside their home countries as well. That is because many MNCs continue to rely on components and supplies both from their own plants at home and from their traditional domestic suppliers. Roughly one-third of all U.S. exports, for example, represent sales to the foreign affiliates of American multinationals.[12]

A similar pattern holds true for MNCs from other nations. There is a still deeper error in the "job-export" argument. That is because the world economy is not a "zero-sum game." Gains by one country or company do not come at the expense of others. When the world economy as a whole grows, the advantages of trade and cross-border investment are mutual.

To examine the charge that MNCs are somehow "out of control," acting beyond the reach of national law, and hence threats to national sovereignty, let's look briefly at the worldwide institutional framework in which MNCs operate.

A WORLD OF NATIONS

The most obvious feature of today's international "system" is the division of the planet into more than 150 nation-states, each with exclusive claims to sovereignty over specific territories and varying degrees of economic, political, and military strength. From the weakest and poorest to the most powerful, these nations possess several common features which multinational corporations cannot afford to ignore. Whatever their mode of government, there resides in sovereignty the right to develop a body of laws and regulations that conditions all economic activity within national boundaries.[13] These include taxes, tariffs on imports, regulations on working conditions, product quality, property rights—the entire array of economic law. Little short of armed invasion by another nation-state can force a determined government to alter such basic decisions about the structure of its home economy and the rules of the game for all participants in it.

In contrast to nations, multinational corporations are private economic organizations. They possess no sovereignty, no armed forces, and no state apparatus. Instead, as they survey the world scene for possible investments or sales, they must carefully weigh the laws and regulations established by any nation in which they wish to do business or invest.

That does not imply that MNCs are powerless in dealing with nation-states. A country intent on securing foreign capital and expertise to develop its otherwise idle resources, or to establish new lines of production, must take into account the basic concerns that any MNC is likely to raise: a reasonable chance for profit; security of property rights; the cost of local taxes; government regulations and restrictions. The need of many nations for the jobs, expertise, and tax revenues that come with foreign investment gives MNCs a certain degree of bargaining leverage.[14] But the MNC's power is essentially a negative one—to decline involvement. Once it has actually been established in a country, the MNC subsidiary becomes, for as long as it remains there, a subject of the local government, vulnerable to any future changes in the nation's policies and politics.

OPPORTUNITIES AND BARRIERS

From the perspective of a typical MNC, the world of nations is divided into a multitude of segments. From the Elbe River in Germany to Indochina, a wide stretch of the Eurasian land mass is governed by Communist regimes, theoretically committed to the eradication of private enterprise. Despite that ideological rift, many MNCs trade with Communist-state organs, and even supply extensive technical assistance. Italy's Fiat, for example, has built a huge automotive plant under contract in the Soviet Union—though once built, the plant is owned and operated by the U.S.S.R. In some other Communist states, notably Hungary and Yugoslavia, Western corporations actually own shares in joint ventures with state enterprises.

Even more significantly, Communist China is soliciting Western

MNCs to help develop its offshore oil and export industries. The recent contract between China and America's Atlantic Richfield Co. for oil drilling in the South China Sea was essentially the same as any ARCO might conclude with a non-Communist government such as Brazil's. Indeed, one recent report on MNCs stated that Communist "countries have, by and large, been able to offer the transnational companies firm and well-defined conditions without fear of being taken over or dominated."[15]

Though there is a clear tendency by Communist nations to permit, even encourage, MNC investment—a phenomenon that Lenin once denounced as inherently "imperialist"—only a small fraction of MNC capital has yet entered the Communist world. By far the largest share of MNC investment has taken place among the 24 affluent, industrialized nations that form the Organization of Economic Cooperation and Development. That group embraces most of the nations of Western Europe, the U.S., Canada, and Japan. Literally billions of dollars have been cross-invested in a vast web of linkages. Overall, more than two-thirds of all MNC investments have been made within the OECD region. There are two basic reasons:

- Developed nations have larger internal markets, better-educated workforces, more sophisticated infrastructures, and greater wealth. All of these factors facilitate the growth of MNC branches.
- Most OECD nations have generated their own MNCs and are thoroughly familiar with investment abroad. They have long agreed on basic rules of the game for foreign MNCs.** Expropriation without compensation of a Japanese company's holdings by, say, the Canadian government, would be extremely unlikely.

Overall, barely more than a quarter of all multinational investment has gone into the Third World. And what has been invested has been largely concentrated in nations that openly seek foreign investment or which attract it because of their strong potential for growth. MNCs have played a major role, for example, in the growth of Taiwan, South Korea, Brazil, Singapore, Hong Kong, and other "newly industrialized countries." By the late 1970s industries based in these nations were increasingly able to compete with those of the developed North. In the poorest nations of the Third World, though, the tiny scale of internal

---

** OECD Code for the Liberalization of Capital Movements: *OECD Declaration on International Investment and Multinational Enterprises*, 1976.

markets, the lack of a large and well-trained work force, and the risk of political upheaval have so far constrained MNC investment. Third World governments such as Burma's, have had no trouble at all keeping them out. Almost by definition, MNCs are only willing to invest in any nation with active encouragement from the host government.

MULTINATIONALS AND NATION STATES

Nothing refutes the argument that multinationals have the power to place national sovereignty "at bay" better than the actual history of relations between MNCs and even the weakest Third World governments. Since World War II the record is replete with examples of companies forced to bow to arbitrary acts of state power. For one thing, no MNC can any longer count on coercive support from its home government. With the emergence of independent nations in place of pre-war European empires, the era of "Gunboat Diplomacy" passed rapidly into legend. The 1956 expedition in which French, British, and Israeli troops struck back at Egypt for its seizure of the Suez Canal—owned by European investors—was the last debacle of that imperial era. Today, it is virtually inconceivable that Western governments would launch fleets or troops to secure payment on overdue loans or to punish nations for the takeover of multinational holdings.[16]

Indeed, the list of expropriations of multinationals by Third World nations—with or without compensation—could fill a sizable book. A short sampling of takeovers in the past decade is enough to indicate the MNCs' deep vulnerability.

- Virtually every member state of OPEC had by 1980 bought out foreign oil companies within its borders—generally at far less than the oil companies' holding would draw on the open market. In Saudi Arabia and other states, the oil majors' former ownership of the resources they discovered has been converted into "service contracts" under which the companies extract crude oil at prices and in quantities set by the host government.
- Many MNC investments in Iran were seized after the overthrow of the Shah in 1979. Compensation, if any, is still a matter to be resolved by litigation.
- In Malaysia, the foreign-owned share of British plantation companies and other foreign firms is being gradually reduced by sales—under intense state pressure—to indigenous investors.

● In France, after the election of François Mitterrand's Socialist government, two American-owned companies were taken over—with compensation—by the government. There was no protest from Washington, and the affected companies expected none. They simply sat down to bargain for as good a price as they could get.

In case after case, the concept of ruthless multinationals browbeating or threatening helpless governments dissolves on examination into fantasy. If anything, the record suggests that MNCs are far more susceptible to, and actually are subjected to, unreasonable government pressures than the other way around. To cite just one recent example, the government of Bangladesh in 1981 ordered off the local market hundreds of drugs produced by global pharmaceutical companies and granted local companies the exclusive right to produce the drugs, without having to bear or recompensate the MNCs' research costs to develop them. Other governments have employed the slower, but equally powerful tactic of "creeping nationalization," requiring MNCs to sell greater and greater shares of their businesses to host-country investors until foreign holdings reach a "ceiling" of, say, 40 percent.

The courses of action that MNCs can take in the face of such government hostility, or even takeovers not in accord with international law***
—suits in their home countries, appeals to the World Court or other global bodies, refusal to buy from or supply spare parts to the offending nation—are long-term and indirect remedies. Aside from sympathy, or in some cases investment insurance coverage, multinationals' home governments are less and less willing to jeopardize their relations with foreign governments on behalf of private corporate complaints. The real issue today is not whether MNCs' power can overawe host governments; rather it is whether many host governments have been so unpredictable in their dealings with MNCs that, in the long run, their access to the capital, technology, and management techniques that MNCs provide may be jeopardized.

The balance of power between MNCs and governments has, in short, changed in the past decade from a time when oil companies could intimidate a producer by not renewing contracts or companies could wield substantial power over the internal politics of developing nations.

*** International law requires that government takeovers of foreign private firms be for a public purpose and that compensation be prompt, effective, and adequate.

MNCS AND THE THIRD WORLD

Today, governments from Malaysia to Ceylon, Brazil to the Ivory Coast, rely on their own skilled negotiators to develop beneficial terms for investment by foreign companies. Most Third World governments have by now passed through a "learning curve" in dealings with MNCs much like that experienced by the developed nations long ago.[17] In cases where a country may still lack indigenous expertise in a specific industry, entire consulting firms have sprung up to assist them in negotiating.

Naïveté at best, condescending racism at worst, underlies the persistent assumption that Third World nations are unable to deal with multinationals on an equal footing. Literally thousands of ranking civil servants in developing nations have had advanced business training in Western universities. Thousands more have learned the intimate details of MNC operations and finance by working for the multinationals themselves. They make formidable negotiating partners for any foreign company. Growing Third World expertise, allied with the urge for economic development felt around the world, is encouraging multinationals to work even harder to structure investment accords in which both parties have clear stakes and mutual benefits in compliance.

Perhaps the clearest evidence of this trend is the increasing number of MNC affiliates that are now being set up as joint ventures with host-country partners, or even with majority ownership by host-country investors.

From 1950 to 1975, for example, a survey (see Table 1) of new overseas affiliates established by American MNCs in the Third World shows that those wholly-owned by the parent firm dropped from 58.4 percent of the total to 43.7 percent. Those either shared 50-50 with developing-country partners or majority-owned by host-country investors rose from 16.8 percent to 38.5 percent. The figures are even more pronounced among MNCs from Britain, Continental Europe, and Japan. By 1970, 48.7 percent of British and European investments in developing countries took the form of equal partnerships or minority stakes; more than 75 Japanese investments in the Third World fell into the same categories by the 1970s as well.[18]

THE SCRAMBLE TO ATTRACT MULTINATIONALS

In an ironic counterpoint to the criticisms leveled at multinational

Table 1: Developing Nations' Stake in the MNCs

Home Country and Type of Ownership	Number Established as Percent of Total		
	Before 1951	**1966-1970**	**1971-1975**
Affiliates of 180 U.S.-based corporations			
Wholly owned	58.4		43.7
Majority owned	12.2		17.3
Co-owned	5.6		10.4
Minority owned	11.2		28.1
Unknown	12.6		0.4
Total	100.0		100.0
Affiliates of 135 European- and U.K.-based corporations			
Wholly owned	39.1	18.9	
Majority owned	15.4	16.4	
Co-owned	5.3	6.6	
Minority owned	9.8	42.1	
Unknown	30.5	16.0	
Total	100.0	100.0	
Affiliates of 76 other transnational corporations			
Wholly owned	27.4	6.1	
Majority owned	8.2	8.2	
Co-owned	12.3	7.5	
Minority owned	16.4	74.2	
Unknown	35.6	3.9	
Total	100.0	100.0	

Distribution of Ownership Patterns of 1,276 Manufacturing Affiliates of 391 Transnational Corporations Established in Developing Countries, by Period of Establishment, 1951 to 1975 (percent).

Of these 76 corporations, 61 are based in Japan.

SOURCES: United Nations, *Transnational Corporations in World Development: A Reexamination* (New York: United Nations, 1978), Table III-25, p. 229, and data supplied by the Harvard Multinational Enterprise Project.

corporations, governments of vastly divergent political colors are actively competing for their participation in national economies. Business magazines with global circulations frequently bulge with advertisements proclaiming advantages to foreign enterprises of investing in the Philippines, Brazil, Singapore, Berlin, Britain's Midland, and other regions. A broad spectrum of governments has decided that

MNCs have an important contribution to make—one that inspired an intense international battle to attract their investments.

Governments' motives and the incentives they offer vary. The governments of the industrial North generally aim to bring MNCs into their economies to assist in programs for reviving depressed regions or launching new zones of economic development. In the current period of worldwide technical/industrial transition, many of even the richest nations have been sorely hurt. Jobs are universally desired, more jobs than local enterprise can provide. To cope with the unemployment crisis many developed nations' governments offer lucrative packages of land, infrastructure, tax "holidays," and even cash grants to make investing more attractive. MNCs are prime targets.

Similar programs are available in the "free trade zones" set up by many developing nations as export bases for MNCs. Several hundred foreign companies, for example, have established assembly or warehouse operations in the Philippines' Bataan industrial park, one of the best-known free zones. But most multinational executives contend that state-sponsored incentives are almost always secondary considerations in deciding where to locate. Nations with strong intrinsic attractions for investors—large domestic markets, bountiful resources, sound domestic economic policies, governments conducted with integrity and efficiency, and fast-growing economies—have far less need for special devices. Indeed, such nations often impose strict regulations on multinationals that choose to locate within their borders. A vast array of devices—from mandatory shares of national ownership to export quotas designed to improve host nations' balances of payments—has been developed to adapt multinational investment to developing countries' needs. Of course, such measures often inhibit other MNCs from investing.

The resulting global picture is a mélange of contradictions. While French socialists move to nationalize some MNC holdings, Chinese Communists attempt to lure foreign companies as partners in development. Ireland and the Philippines boast of the low to nonexistent taxes charged against MNCs that invest in their countries. Brazil, by contrast, regulates multinationals closely, encouraging them to export as much as possible and generally shaping the business environment affecting MNCs to serve Brazil's national goals. Some nations clearly hold stronger bargaining positions vis-à-vis MNCs than others; though, like any partner in a negotiation, they may damage their own interests by pressing advantages too hard.

A growing majority of countries, whatever their public rhetoric, seem to share the view of the benefits that MNCs bring, expressed in a 1981 report of Britain's Trade Policy Research Center:

Their activities have brought to developing countries part of the dynamic entrepreneurial spirit of the developed world. They have found opportunities for creating new and better products from the natural, human and capital resources of the country. They have assembled capital, particularly for the development of natural resources, on a scale beyond the capacity of the local governments and domestic entrepreneurs. Where labour used to the disciplines of a modern industry has been scarce, labour training at all levels has been one of their most important contributions to development. They have also brought management training and demonstrated techniques for combining capital and skills. They have enabled developing countries to market manufactured goods abroad by producing goods up to international quality standards and in adequate supply and, also, in providing distribution outlets in foreign markets.[19]

A similar view comes from recent research by the International Labor Organization: "Much of [the MNCs'] present formal and informal training efforts certainly make a contribution to development not only in terms of economic growth but also in terms of skills required for development."[20]

The quest for MNC investment is by no means limited to developing nations. In the late 1970s, for instance, when Ford Motor Co. announced that it intended to build a major new production line for its European operations, the governments of France, Austria, and Spain engaged in a prolonged competition to win the plant. They assembled "packages" of tax breaks, low-interest loans, worker training grants, and cash that ultimately ranged upwards of $400 million. In effect, governments unable to launch and manage such an enterprise on their own were willing to absorb the bulk of Ford's risk in exchange for jobs and balance of payments benefits. In the end, however, Ford's choice of Spain was not based on that country's incentive "package," but on other, more fundamental business considerations.

WHY MULTINATIONALS INVEST

With dozens of potential host countries—much of the world, in fact—as their arena, what factors determine multinationals' investment decisions? How do they weigh and choose between alternatives?

These questions will become elaborate as we unravel them. For starters, we should consider the shortest possible answers:

- Multinationals invest in order to serve markets or develop raw materials, thereby maximizing their profits and growth, especially in key foreign markets that might be denied them by high tariffs or import quotas or by high transportation costs relative to product value, unless they have plants there. In doing so, they employ the best strategies their managements can develop.
- They choose between alternatives by using a yardstick known as return on investment (ROI), the percent of an initial outlay that will be "returned" annually—or eventually—by a given capital commitment.

Naturally, the simple-sounding goal of profit and ROI breaks down into a vastly more complex series of decisions in the world of nations. At any given time, the values of various national currencies against each other are shifting in ways that are difficult or impossible to predict. So is the rate of inflation—or deflation—in each nation. Varying national economic policies and growth rates are changing, too, under the constant pressure of internal political forces. Technological change continuously revolutionizes both production and consumer needs. It cannot be ignored. Virtually every MNC also has to consider the actions of current and potential competitors. General Motors cannot afford to lose track of what Toyota or Volkswagen are doing; IBM must monitor developments at Fujitsu. The management of even the richest MNC has to balance finite resources against potential commitments over specific limited periods of time. MNCs must select among a variety of types of investment as well—a wholly-owned new plant, joint venture, or minority participation, often, if not always, within the constraints of individual national policy.

Those are only the beginnings of the options that MNC managements must juggle. Changing world trade patterns and regulations must also be weighed. A case in point is the way that the vast surge of Japanese automobile imports to the United States in the late 1970s generated a powerful political backlash as hundreds of thousands of American workers lost their jobs. Threats of high tariffs, "local content" laws, and even outright import bans mounted.[21] Partly as a result, both the Honda Motor Co. and Toyota have decided to invest in U.S.-based automotive plants. Neither company based its decision merely on short-term return on investment. Both have secured big enough market shares in the United States to worry about the risk of losing them. United States plants would enable the Japanese auto makers to keep on supplying customers even if Japanese auto exports to the United States were banned entirely.

A similar desire to leap over real or potential tariff walls helped spur the rush of American MNC investment in Europe in the 1950s and 1960s. An even greater lure, in that case, was the rapid growth of the European economies. For many companies, the establishment of a substantial, profitable share of a foreign market through exporting is likely to make management willing, sometimes eager, to invest there. The risk of being excluded from such a hard-won market by trade or other barriers can also be a powerful goad to investing in it and producing on the ground. Fast economic growth in a nation or region is another definite plus.

Companies invest abroad for other reasons as well. Access to raw materials not available at comparable prices at home is a key example. Most Europe-based oil companies have no choice but to focus on development prospects abroad. The known or likely resources available at home are just not large enough. Mining companies, too, frequently must search for resources overseas. Britain's Rio Tinto Zinc is considering what may prove as much as a $2.1 billion investment in a large copper mine in Cerro Colorado, Panama. Only a fraction of the production from the mine (assuming the world market demands the copper) will be sold to users in Britain. But RTZ's market is global, not national. No comparable source of ore exists in the United Kingdom.

MNCs frequently invest to test the water of a host country, venturing limited amounts of capital into a market that may eventually become a major part of their operations. They also establish ownership shares in foreign companies as a way of developing mutually profitable links of trade and supply. General Motors' 25 percent ownership of the Japanese automaker, Isuzu, means that the American firm shares in Isuzu's earnings and that it thus realizes part of the profits made by Isuzu on sales of engines and other components to G.M. itself. G.M.'s holdings thus bind the interests of the two companies. And its seat on the Japanese firm's board gives it a say in Isuzu's planning for the future.

The array of variables that MNCs must weigh in overseas investing resembles an algebra equation to which new and unknown elements are constantly being added. There simply are no permanently fixed values to guide decisions. Human judgment, intuition, and luck play major roles. Political, economic, and technological surprises abound. And if MNCs rarely go bankrupt, it is because of their sheer size, financial reserves, and global diversification. Their individual investments and subsidiaries, though, often fall short of management expectations. Sometimes they end in disaster.

LIMITING THE UNCERTAINTIES

Facing such striking, inherent uncertainties, multinationals understandably strive to limit risks almost as much as they seek to maximize gain. Their concerns increasingly focus on the stability of business conditions in host countries. An entire industry of political risk analysts has emerged to meet the demand by MNCs for accurate information on the currents of change in nations in which they invest or plan to invest.[22] Many MNCs also employ in-house political scientists.

After the Iranian upheaval, the risk of violent revolution is a salient worry. To a limited extent, overseas investment insurance provided by the home governments of some MNCs has somewhat reduced losses due to some risks. More worrisome these days are the hazards of subtler changes in host nations that erode MNC profits and are more difficult to ensure against. As one recent report put it:

With few exceptions, multinational companies today point to instability, not ideology, as the principal deterrent to investing and operating abroad. By instability, the companies do not necessarily mean political upheavals accompanied by changes in regime. Foreign investment does, of course, fall off during a crisis, but tends to recover as the new regime consolidates its position. Much more important are those forms of instability that need not result from internal political upheavals: threats of political action, changes in conditions of operation such as ownership and remittance regulations, complex and drawn out bureaucratic procedures, and, more generally, the prospect of arbitrary and unpredictable alterations in the rules of the game after investment decisions have been made. Although companies have come to expect and live with changes in government policy and regulation both at home and abroad, and to recognize that such changes often reflect legitimate responses to altered conditions, they nevertheless perceive the degree of instability and arbitrariness of government policies in many developing countries as especially acute. . . .[23]

One result has been steady scrutiny by MNC management of the business climates of potential host nations. Countries that adopt and adhere to clear rules for MNC investments stand to be favored over those that change abruptly, even if the more reliable nations' rules are initially tougher. Heightened concern by MNCs requires careful consideration by any government seeking foreign investment. The balance of mutuality between host country and MNC is crossed roughly at the point where the combination of national taxes, import duties, regulations, and other constraints on business weigh down the profitability of an MNC operation as against other, potential investments. If such changes come after an MNC has committed itself, the company in question may not be easily able to withdraw from the host country. But neither it nor other MNCs will be likely to deepen their investments, however promising the host nation's potential.

TENSIONS AND PROMISE

The tensions between MNCs and developing nations are easy to exaggerate. Multinationals, after all, continue to invest and to grow faster than the world economy as a whole. Most governments these days are also striving to strike equitable accords with overseas investors while maximizing benefits to themselves. Differences of opinion, even bitter ones, are normal in such a situation. And it is to be expected that they would break out most frequently in the Third World.

In many ways, MNCs face unavoidable dilemmas in investing in the Third World. As Isaiah Frank explains:

If multinationals repatriate the bulk of their profits, they are depriving the nation of the newly-created wealth; if, on the other hand, the firms reinvest the bulk of their profits locally, they are further increasing their ownership and control of the host country. If multinationals pay local workers the standard wage, they are exploiting cheap labor and garnering excess profits; if, on the other hand, they pay more than the prevailing wage, they are siphoning off the best of the labor supply and rendering local firms noncompetitive. If multinationals bring in the latest and best machinery and equipment, they are introducing inappropriate technology and diminishing job opportunities in the host country; if, on the other hand, earlier and simpler technologies are introduced, they are shortchanging the local economy. Resolving these dilemmas has entailed policy shifts and adaptations on the part of developing countries in response to their changing perceptions of how to maximize their gains from the foreign investment process.[24]

Today's advanced industrial nations long ago passed through the upheavals of development which nations like Brazil or the Ivory Coast are experiencing. For many Western nations, notably the United States, foreign investment was a key element in spurring the growth of the national economy. For several generations, it has ceased to be a phenomenon that industrial nations fear. They are used to it. They know how to regulate it and gain from it. By contrast, Third World nations retain a legacy of suspicion, born in earlier periods of colonial rule or economic dependency. But they are no longer potential victims; instead, the vulnerability of MNCs is widely evident.

So is the increasing variety of nations whose companies have outgrown domestic markets and branched out around the globe. As an economic form, the multinational corporation has been and will be widely copied. Its power depends not on political clout, military power, or secret agentry used by home governments, but on an astounding capacity to mobolize human and material resources and the resiliency to survive severe setbacks. Companies from Imperial Britain and the American superstate have no monopoly on that. Nations with no pretensions to global power are generating new multinational corporations every year.

Judging from current trends, MNCs will become even more crucial actors in a world economy linked by rapid change and instantaneous communications. Governments in most Third World nations will rely on MNCs as catalysts of their industrial development. The most advanced nations of the global South are already spawning their own MNCs.

As it was in the industrial West, the process of development will be wrenching, painful, sometimes halting. But the sheer productive capacity unleashed by the MNC is bringing with it the means of eradicating hunger, poverty, and disease. Harnessing that engine of wealth to realize those human dreams remains a vital, unfinished task of our time.

NOTES AND REFERENCES

1. See Barnet and Muller, *Global reach* (New York: Simon & Schuster, 1976) for a strong attack on MNCs. Raymond Vernon'a *Storm Over the Multinationals* (Boston: Harvard University Press, 1977) provides a more balanced view of the issues.
2. *Multinational Corporations in World Development*, United Nations Department of Economic and Social Affairs, ST/ECA/190, 1973.
3. McCormack, Arthur, *Multinational Investment: Boon or Burden for the Developing Countries?* (New York: W. R. Grace & Co. Publications Department, 1980).
4. Cited in Lloyd N. Cutler, *Global Interdependence and the Multinational Firm* (New York: Foreign Policy Association, April, 1979), Headline Series No. 239.
5. Nussbaum, Glynn et al., *The Decline of U.S. Power* (Boston: Houghton-Mifflin, 1980). Section 3, "The Embattled Multinationals," pp. 113-161, provides a survey of MNC growth.
6. *Decline,* op. cit., p. 132.
7. *Global Interdependence,* op. cit., p. 7.
8. Chandler, A. D., *Strategy and Structure* (New York: Doubleday, 1961).
9. See Steven Hymer's discussion of MNC strategies in "The Multinational Corporation and the Law of Uneven Development," in J. Bhagwati (ed.), *Economics and World Order from the 1970s to the 1990s* (New York: Collier-McMillan, 1972, pp. 113-140.
10. Barnet and Muller's *Gobal Reach,* op. cit., is an extended, one-sided review of such charges.
11. *Multinational Business*, No. 3 (London: The Intelligence Unit of *The Economist*, 1977), discusses the relocation issue in Malcolm Crawford's "The Intellectual Attack on the Multinationals," pp. 10-19.
12. See *The Effects of U.S. Corporate Foreign Investment: 1970-77* (New York: Business International Research Study, 1979).
13. See Lord McFadzean of Kelvinside, *Global Strategy for Growth* (London: Trade Policy Research Centre, 1981), pp. 34-46, for a survey of the international order by which MNCs' do business.
14. Raymond Vernon, "The Multinationals," *Foreign Affairs*, January, 1977.
15. Isaiah Frank, *Foreign Enterprise in Developing Countries* (Baltimore: Johns Hopkins University Press, 1980), p. 26.
16. *Decline,* op. cit., pp. 118-135.
17. See R. S. Bhatt, "The Role of Multinationals in Developing Countries," *Economic News Digest* (New York: India Investment Centre, November-December, 1979), Vol. 6, Nos. 11 and 12.
18. *Foreign Enterprise*, op. cit., p. 21.
19. *Global Strategy*, op. cit., p. 25.
20. Hans Gunter, *ILO Research on Multinational Enterprises and Social Policy: An Overview* (Geneva: International Labour office, 1982), p. 21.

21. See "Is Free Trade Dead?," *The Economist* (25 December, 1982 - 7 January, 1983), pp. 75-93.
22. Louis Kraar, "The Multinationals Get Smarter About Political Risk," *Fortune,* March 24, 1980.
23. *Foreign Enterprise*, op. cit., p. 26.
24. *Ibid.*, p. 29.

3
Meeting the Challenge of Global Competition

Frederick W. Gluck

Contrary to the negative expectations generated by the economic dislocations of the 1970s, the decade of the 1980s is likely to provide a favorable climate for international business. The nature of competition worldwide has changed, offering new markets and opportunities for multinational firms. MNC management may need to adjust operating and planning strategies to take advantage of the changing structure of global competition. Those firms that have the resources to become truly global in orientation will be in a better position to respond to the imperatives of global competition than will those firms that maintain the posture of domestic competitors. The dynamic nature of the world economy will require equally dynamic and flexible management responses on the part of MNCs.

WHICH IS A riskier investment: exploring for oil in the United States or setting up a joint manufacturing venture in Thailand? Are floating exchange rates simply a headache for corporate financial officers, or do they also offer a way to take some of the uncertainty out of international competition? Do you see the low-wage labor forces of the Third World primarily as a threat to your competitive position, or as a potential competitive resource?

Your answers to these questions indicate whether you are bearish or bullish about the climate for international business in the 1980s. Many, perhaps most, American businessmen would come out on the bearish side—understandably, in view of the painful lessons of the 1970s. From the formation of OPEC, we learned the cost of depending too heavily on foreign oil. From Iran, we learned the danger of taking the security of our overseas investments for granted. Recent nationalizations in France reminded us once again that even in Western Europe it may be unwise to count on universal belief in the sanctity of private property.

Closer to home, losses in the shipbuilding, textile, and footwear industries have convinced some American managers that protectionist

Reprinted with permission from *the McKinsey Quarterly* (Autumn 1982).

measures and/or total automation offer the only hope for their firms' survival. And massive currency losses caused by fluctuating exchange rates have persuaded many treasurers that the best earnings are dollar earnings. With such good reasons for pessimism about the future of international business, it seems only sensible for companies to focus their efforts on safe and familiar domestic markets.

Beyond the immediate problems, however, a case can be made for the bullish side. The dislocations of the 1970s were abrupt and painful, yes. But as I see it, they were essentially constructive in that they paved the way for the emergence of new global markets. Through those changes and dislocations, an elaborate international network of regulations and cartels was transformed into a world of free markets for energy, currency, labor, and other vital business resources.

The climate for international business in 1980s, I believe, is going to be much more favorable than in the recent past and much more rational than might be guessed from reading the papers. American companies in particular will need to operate more aggressively on the international scene. In an increasing number of industries, firms that stay close to home will find it hard to maintain a competitive edge.

To compete successfully on an international scale, however, management is likely to need some new skills in the 1980s. Even more, however, it will need strategies and management approaches that reflect the realities of global competition.

COMPETITIVE PROSPECTS

To see why international competition in the 1980s is likely to be more rational than many people expect, consider first what has happened to the oil industry. Back in the 1950s and 1960s, oil was a rather comfortable business to be in. Prices were low and stable. Production was regulated by the Railroad Commission in Texas, and by agreements between the so-called "Seven Sisters" in the Middle East. As a result of this heavy regulation, the energy supply had shifted by the early 1970s from abundance to scarcity without any noticeable change in the price of oil.

In 1974, however, OPEC tripled the price of oil and the old regulatory mechanisms were destroyed. For a while, it seemed that they had been replaced by another, more tightly disciplined cartel. But appearances were deceptive; OPEC has turned out to be nothing of the kind. With hindsight, we can see that both prices and production in the 1970s actually reflected oil shortages, the continued regulation of market forces in the Western world, and varying economic conditions and motives in individual OPEC countries.

Today OPEC is still with us, and many U.S. government energy regulations are still in place. On the whole, however, energy prices are now determined by the independent actions of the various market participants. OPEC now produces less than half the world's oil. And as global exploration and production proliferate, individual countries and companies are less and less able to call the tune. Oil is truly becoming a world commodity, and prices are coming down.

Now, the implications of a free or nearly free market in energy are not all bad by any means. The price of oil will continue to fluctuate, but probably no more than that of sugar or any other commodity traded on exchanges. The impact of its fluctuations will be cushioned by the same type of hedging mechanisms now used in the copper industry and elsewhere. Barring world-shaking events, we shouldn't have to worry about any major price shocks; the Rotterdam spot market is a fairly sensitive early warning device.

In industries that depend on petroleum as a raw material, a free market for oil means greater freedom for corporate strategists, who no longer have to expend so much time and effort assuring sources of supply. Chemical companies, for example, won't have to integrate backward into oil production; they can now focus on making chemicals. (Thus, DuPont's acquisition of Conoco probably makes less sense now as a strategic move than it would have done five years ago.)

For oil producers, the implications are more complex. On the one hand, since oil is becoming a freely traded world commodity, low-cost producers should prevail. On the other hand, the cheapest resources won't necessarily be found in the world's safest locations. So any oil producer has to weigh the costs against the risks. In doing so, the industry may currently be opting too strongly for security. Last year, 40 percent of the free world's exploration and development took place on U.S. soil—at a cost about $40 billion. Yet the United States has only 5 percent of the free world's reserves. And it costs almost 10 times as much to find a barrel of oil in America as in other parts of the world.

These huge investments in domestic exploration offer a hint as to why the market values of oil companies have fallen even more sharply than the stock market as a whole. Investors may be telling us that $40 billion a year is too much to spend on domestic exploration—that they don't agree with the strategic choice of safety over cost. If so, they probably have a point, for there are several reasons to expect that the governments of the oil-rich nations are likely to behave more reasonably than in the past.

REASONS FOR RATIONALITY

First, those governments haven't performed very well at the jobs that used to be handled by private companies. They're ready to admit, grudgingly to be sure, that there is real economic value in the extracting, refining, and marketing of raw resources. Second, local populations are more demanding than ever before. This means that governments will be under greater pressure to put foreign-exchange earnings ahead of nationalist sentiment. Third, deals are more likely to stick now that they are being made in an atmosphere of mutual respect. When the Thai government decided to develop the reserves in the Gulf of Siam the bidding was wide open. And the final contract will be largely the result of what economists call a "voluntary exchange" between two parties.

Resource companies, moreover, may be able to pass along the risk that remains. Today, U.S. government units like the Overseas Private Investment Corporation (OPIC), international development institutions like the World Bank, and even commercial banks are willing to assume most of the political risks of project development abroad. The fees they charge are far less than the 10-to-1 premium that companies pay for the privilege of exploring in the United States.

And, of course, there is always the possibility of simply selling expertise outright, instead of owning resources overseas. American resource companies have technology, skills, and experience that are in critically short supply in the nations rich in low-cost resources. And, as Sheikh Yamani has reminded us: "Aramco doesn't make a profit. It is paid a fee." There's no shame in being a service company.

American energy companies are now experiencing a situation that resource-short Japanese and European firms have lived with for decades. It's not necessarily a bad spot to be in, but it does require a different perspective and some different skills. American companies, too, must learn to negotiate, to transfer risks to financial institutions, and to spread their activities across the globe.

CURRENCY CONSIDERATIONS

We can observe much the same sort of pattern in world currency markets. The cartel of central bankers that had fixed prices for two decades collapsed after Nixon devalued the dollar in August 1971.

Gradually, a market mechanism of floating exchange rates emerged. These floating rates have created a whole new set of problems for financial officers. But, in the long run, they will be a boon to international competition.

Floating rates, in fact, moderate the risks of operations internationally. This may sound strange to financial executives who have been plagued in recent years by wild exchange-rate swings. But even the troubled U.S. auto industry would be in substantially worse shape than it is today if floating rates had not made the dollar cheaper relative to the yen in the late 1970s, providing some needed relief from Japanese competition.

In free-float countries like Germany, Japan, and Britain, capital controls have also been relaxed. So a multinational manager there can get on with the job of making a profit without having to worry about the accounting complications and dubious legality of remitting funds back home. And since he has free access to the local debt market, he can make long-term investments without being forced into a simultaneous gamble on the local currency.

Floating rates have also led to the development of forward markets and currency futures contracts. All these changes have, in fact, made it easier to make sound business decisions.

Consider the relative situations of two managers working for an American multinational, one in Germany and one in Brazil. In making investment decisions, both have reason to worry that inflationary government policies will lead to a depreciating currency. But the German manager can look to floating exchange rates and an active forward market for clues about the Deutschmark's future value. He can be confident, too, that there will be no overnight devaluation. The Brazilian manager is less fortunate. Since the currency rate in Brazil is fixed by the government, he has to rely on rumor to find out when and by how much the cruzeiro will fall.

The German manager can hedge his exposure simply by short-selling Deutschmark contracts. The Brazilian can only reduce his exposure by deferring capital expenditures, stretching out payables, or reducing receivables—all moves that may hurt his long-term business interests.

As they increase the scope of their international operations, many companies will have to develop new skills to take full advantage of these developments. They will need to become more familiar with the capital markets of Europe and Asia. They will need to become adept at trading currency futures. Those with large fixed investments abroad will need experience with long-term debt in the countries where they operate.

All this, of course, will be far from easy. Pitfalls abound. Think of Laker Airways. Two years ago, when Sir Freddie Laker borrowed $240 million from U.S. banks to finance his growing fleet of jets, British interests rates were far above the American. But since Laker was selling advance tickets to British travelers with fares fixed in pounds sterling, the borrower took Sir Freddie far from his primary business of providing low-cost transatlantic travel. In fact, he was speculating in currencies, and the speculation turned sour when U.S. interest rates rose and the U.S. dollar began to soar. During the summer of 1981, two-thirds of Laker's receipts were in sterling. The fares had been fixed in late 1980 when the pound stood at $2.40. But by August 1981, when Laker's U.S. bank loans had to be repaid in dollars, it had declined to $1.93. The loss represented more than a quarter of the company's net worth. By February, Laker Airways was bankrupt.

Side by side with the potential payoff, then, is the need for developing international money management skills. A strong, internationally-minded corporate financial officer can moderate the risks of currency fluctuations and free the time and energy of business managers for the problems of business strategy and execution that should be their primary concern.

WORLDWIDE WORKFORCE

Next, consider developments in the world labor market. In the years since World War II, labor markets have slowly but steadily become more international as more and more countries have welcomed foreign capital. East Asian countries became market leaders in labor-intensive industries. Then Ireland, Spain, Greece, and eventually even larger developing nations like Mexico and Brazil began to shift toward export-led, foreign-capital-based economies.

With lower growth rates projected for the world economy, it seems likely that in the near future the developing countries will be increasingly hospitable to foreign capital. Japan took the first step, but now, with manufacturing islands like Hong Kong, Taiwan, Korea, Ireland, and the Mexican-American border region, access to a low-wage labor pool is open to anyone.

Hewlett-Packard's manufacturing chain reaches halfway around the globe, from well-paid, skilled engineers in California to low-wage assembly workers in Malaysia. General Electric has survived as a manufacturer of inexpensive audio products by centralizing its world production in Singapore. Matsushita has a mind-boggling array of production facilities covering a multitude of product lines in over 25 countries. And these are not isolated examples. The other day a colleague of mine opened up a personal computer and, without looking too hard, found parts in it from 13 different countries!

Obviously, manufacturers like these perceived long ago that worldwide sourcing skills would carry a big competitive punch in their industries. They saw the opening up of the global labor market as a vital opportunity to gain and hold a competitive advantage.

COMPETITIVE NEWCOMERS

Two other current developments will leave many companies with very little choice about becoming more international.

First, more and more countries around the world are developing the capacity to compete aggressively in world markets. In the Far East or in certain parts of Latin America, the will to compete is in the air—it's almost tangible. Businessmen are aware of world market trends and confident that they can reach new markets. People are eager to improve their economic condition and their living standards. And they're willing to learn, adapt, innovate—to "do it, fix it, try it." A top-level Brazilian manager recently told me that his company, one of Brazil's largest, had purchased 2,000 personal computers and distributed them throughout its headquarters and field operations, just to make sure that its employees would become computer-literate.

Thirty years ago, most American companies were confident that they could beat foreign competitors with relative ease. After all, they reasoned, we have the best technology, the best management skills, and the famous American "can do" attitude. Today there are many competitive new technologies in Europe, Japan, and elsewhere. And it's far from clear that American companies hold the unchallenged lead in management skills, either. It may well be that the current fuss over Japanese management techniques is a bit overdone. But too many U.S. managers have been inclined to equate strategy with the buying and selling of businesses. Too many have neglected the more fundamental questions: how their industries are changing, especially with respect to global competition, and how they can successfully adapt to the changes—or, better still, seize the competitive initiative. The strength of the Japanese is that they never lose sight of fundamentals. They seldom forget that the only ways to guarantee long-term competitive success are by providing better value to customers or achieving superior cost performance.

SUPPLYING THE WORLD

The second development that makes it so imperative in many industries to compete internationally is the proliferation of global product markets. All the principal barriers to the growth of such markets have weakened in the last decade. Tariffs have been reduced by GATT agreements. Transportation costs have declined with the use of containerization and larger-capacity ships. Many products have emerged that pack very high value-added into very small packages. Consumer needs in the industrialized nations have become increasingly similar. And purchasing power in certain Third World and OPEC countries has sharply increased. In consequence, a multitude of distinct national markets are beginning to coalesce into a true world market. This development too can be a source of competitive advantage for companies that plan their strategies accordingly.

A few examples will suggest how extensive the global product phenomenon has already become. Kids everywhere are playing Pac-Man and bounding along the streets to the sound of a Sony Walkman. The video tape recorder (VTR) market took off simultaneously in Japan, Europe and the United States, but the most extensive use of VTRs today is probably in places like Riyadh and Caracas. Shopping centers from Düsseldorf to Rio sell Gucci shoes, Yves St. Laurent suits, and Gloria Vanderbilt jeans. Siemens and ITT telephones can be found almost everywhere in the world. Mercedes-Benz and the Toyota Corolla are as much objects of passion in Manila as in California.

Just about every gas turbine sold in the world has some General Electric technology or component in it, and what country doesn't need gas turbines? How many airlines around the world could survive without Boeing or McDonnell Douglas equipment? Third World markets for high-voltage transmission equipment and diesel-electric locomotives are bigger than those in the developed countries. And today's new industries—robotics, videodiscs, fiber optics, satellite networks, high-technology plastics, artificial diamonds—seem to be global at birth.

Obviously, industries become global for different reasons. Convergence of income levels and standardization of tastes made universal products out of Gucci bags and designer jeans. Aircraft became global because of the massive R&D investments required and the manufacturers' need to amortize these investments over many markets. Consumer electronics became global because producers discovered that they could drive further and faster down the learning curve by going after fast-growing overseas markets.

STRATEGIC ADJUSTMENT

But while the reasons for globalization have been different in different industries, its implications have been the same for all. Most important, companies in global industries have had to reshape their strategies in fundamental ways. In order to compete profitably, they have been obliged to redesign their whole system of doing business to take advantage of the fact of global markets.

- In choosing technological processes, they follow the example of the Japanese in plain paper copiers and search the world for the technology offering greatest promise for most markets.
- In planning a new product, they design it to be marketable in the maximum number of countries (as Caterpillar has done with its heavy equipment), to serve an identifiable world market segment (as Toyota did with the Corolla), or to be easily adaptable to slightly differing markets (as Ericsson has done in telecommunications equipment).
- In working out a manufacturing strategy, they pick the lowest-cost source—Malaysia for simple electronics, perhaps; Sri Lanka for textiles; Tokyo for advanced semiconductors; the United States for personal computers; Europe for precision machinery—and design a manufacturing system geared to the scale requirements of the world market.
- If scale is important to product economics, they design a marketing system that gives them the broadest coverage and quickest penetration of world markets—even if it means signing cross-marketing agreements with their competitors, selling under other manufacturers' names, or marketing through distributors and dealers they cannot really control.

In short, they have thought hard about what global operations mean to the economics of their businesses, about where the economic leverage points in the business will be, and about how they must shape their own business systems to take advantage of these leverage points. And they have acted accordingly.

The process of adjustment is illustrated by today's developments in the automobile industry. As usual, the Japanese have been the first to sense and respond to globalization. They have recognized that since components make up most of the cost of a car, the key to competitive advantage is to minimize the number of components, standardize the components used in different models, design models that will sell in many countries, and push for maximum scale. In doing so, they have established a phenomenal cost advantage over European and U.S. competitors (estimated at between $1,000 and $2,000 for a typical small car).

In consequence, their competitors are now being forced to respond in kind. Those who have the resources to become truly global themselves are doing so—witness General Motors' world car concepts, its massive investments in integrated production systems that include Japan, Australia, Austria, Spain, Brazil, Mexico, as well as the United States, and its sourcing of technology and product from Japan through tie-ups with Isuzu and Suzuki. Smaller competitors are globalizing through cooperation with other companies—British Leyland in joint design with Honda, Alfa in joint production with Nissan, the French through growing cooperation with U.S. producers. Hardly anyone can doubt that competitors who fail to respond adequately to globalization will be out of existence within a few years.

The example drives home a final point about global industries: Those competitors who are first to exploit the advantages of globalization reap very great rewards and put their competitors on the defensive, while those whose response is tardy or halfhearted often fall by the wayside.

It is no exaggeration to say that in a global industry, or one that is rapidly becoming so, the riskiest possible posture is to remain a domestic competitor. The domestic competitor will not participate in the world's fastest growth market areas. He will watch as more aggressive companies use this growth to capture economies of scale and learning. And he will then be faced with an attack on his domestic markets by competitors armed with different and possibly superior technology, product design, manufacturing, and marketing approaches.

THE GLOBAL IMPERATIVE

What this all adds up to in practical terms is the absolute necessity of understanding where your industry now stands in this process of globalization and how rapidly it is likely to evolve toward global status. The growing willingness to compete, and the diffusion of technologies and management capabilities, are accelerating the process of globalization. If you fail to recognize this, you are likely to be shocked out of your complacency one of these days by a foreign competitor you hadn't even heard of five years ago.

Obviously, if your company is not in an industry that is global or likely to become so, you can afford to breathe a little easier. Defense of your domestic markets will not require you to go global; like a Heinz, a Nabisco Brands, or a Unilever, you have some latitude in deciding the extent and pace of your internationalization. Even so, you will do well to remember that operating in a number of different national markets reduces a company's vulnerability to local sales stagnation or decline, or to unforeseen substitution by other technologies, products, or competitors.

Moreover, a company operating internationally is likely to come upon technologies, products, or marketing approaches arising in particular markets that turn out to be applicable, and profitable, elsewhere. Even though internationalization may not be critical for such a company, it can certainly benefit from developing the necessary skills to compete internationally: financial skills to match the new monetary order; production and logistical skills to take advantage of a freer labor market; and information systems skills to monitor new technologies and marketing approaches.

If, on the other hand, you are in a global, or soon-to-be global, industry, you should carefully evaluate your own company's stage of sophistication where these skills are concerned, and take the measure of the challenge that confronts you. If you are an AT&T or a Western Electric—a domestic competitor in a global industry, faced with the momentous challenge of transforming yourself rapidly into a global competitor—you will unquestionably have to launch on a major upgrading of your skills, a revamping of your management organization and systems, and a drastic change in your strategy.

If your company is one of the venerable multinationals like Philips, Siemens, Olivetti, Rhone-Poulenc, General Electric, or Westinghouse, the need is to distinguish the global businesses from the more local ones, to develop unique worldwide strategies for each global business, and to design organization structures and management systems that will permit the necessary coordination of worldwide technology, product, and manufacturing decisions without compromising your ability to adapt marketing and distribution approaches to the particular conditions of each national market. For any company whose values, structures, and systems were shaped at a time when each national or regional market could be dealt with separately without much concern for the interconnections among them, this is likely to be quite an assignment.

If yours is a company like IBM, already fairly global in orientation, you must face up to the prospect of competing against determined challengers who have expressly designed their business systems so as to become leaders in global competition. Finally, if you are a Japanese multinational, you can congratulate yourself on having been at the forefront of globalization but you should ask yourself how long your competitive edge can be sustained by exporting from Japan, and how soon you should take on the more difficult task of building a manufacturing and direct marketing presence in your major markets.

In a world rapidly evolving toward global markets, even a commanding competitive advantage will be difficult to sustain. Indeed, for corporations competing in industries that are globalizing at an ever-increasing pace, continuing strategic and organizational adjustments will be part of the price of success.

One executive I know whose company is currently challenging a huge and powerful competitor recently told me that he has had to change his management style so often in the contest that it's like running a succession of different companies that simply happen to be named alike. And his reward for each success is the need for yet another strategic shift. In the coming decade, I believe, that is the kind of challenge that will confront most companies doing business around the world.

Chapter Two:
International Management

THE READINGS IN this chapter focus on the management process in a multinational company. Emphasis is placed on the role of top management in the choice of strategies, taking into consideration the administrative process vis-à-vis markets, competition, technology resources, and so forth. Political considerations in the form of host-government demands will also be examined, since these have a direct and immediate impact upon the strategic planning process.

Conflict resolution and the analysis of communications and human-relations problems in multinational corporations also deserve attention. These areas can be dealt with through such techniques as organizational development. The objective is to identify human weaknesss and to strive for a harmonious atmosphere among employees.

The functions of planning, organizing, directing, and controlling in the context of multinationals form the crux of the management process. These functions are critical in the relationship between the parent and the subsidiary. Also, they have a major impact on the integration of the numerous activities and subsidiaries of a multinational corporation.

The process of decision-making, as well as planning techniques, are the primary functions within the management process. These activities serve as the foundations of managerial decision-making. Subsequently, organizing, which is the grouping of work and people into manageable units, is the next important step. The degree of decentralization of the organization structure will depend upon the nature of the company and the size of its far-flung operations.

Motivating employees and making them happy and productive workers are crucial and difficult tasks. The wide array of cultures in which a multinational corporation needs to operate often makes employee motivation exceedingly difficult. Superior-subordinate relationships, the types of fringe benefits, and the role of money—are among the important considerations.

Controlling workers and operations is the final function relevant to the managerial process. This entails checking to learn who has met pre-stated objectives and where corrective action needs to be taken. Setting standards and comparing output with pre-set standards comprise the control process. In concluding this chapter, the changing management trends in Europe are explored.

4

Strategic Management in Multinational Companies

Yves L. Doz

Multinational management response to the conflict between the economic imperatives of successful operations and the political imperatives of adjusting to host-government demands reflect a range of possible strategies and administrative processes. The choice of strategy is dependent upon such factors as the markets being served, competition and level of technology used by the firm. The success of the strategy selected is in turn dependent upon the nature of internal management processes.

THE EVOLUTION OF multinational companies (MNCs) over the last decade has been characterized by a growing conflict between the requirements for economic survival and success (the *economic* imperative) and the adjustments made necessary by the demands of host governments (the *political* imperative). The lowering of trade barriers and the substantial economies of scale still available in many industries combined with vigorous competition from low-cost exporters push the MNCs toward the integration and rationalization of their activities among various countries.[1] Yet, the very international interdependence created by freer trade and MNC rationalization make individual countries more vulnerable to external factors and their traditional domestic economic policies less effective.[2] As a result, most governments turn more and more to specific sectorial policies implemented through direct negotiations with the companies involved and through incentives tailored to them.[3] Both the economic and political imperatives thus take on increasing importance in the management of the multinationals.

Reprinted from "Strategic Management in Multinational Companies," *Sloan Management Review*, Vol. 21, pp. 27-46, by permission of the publisher. Copyright © 1980 by the Sloan Management Review Association. All rights reserved.

This article, based on intensive field research of the management processes in about a dozen MNCs analyzes strategies and administrative processes used by MNCs to reconcile the conflicting economic and political imperatives. Findings are presented in four sections. First, MNC strategies to respond to the dual imperatives are described and contrasted. Second, conditions under which MNCs are likely to find one or another strategy most suitable for individual businesses are reviewed. Third, the interaction between strategies and the nature of internal management processes is analyzed. Fourth, implications for the management of interdependencies between businesses in diversified multinationals are outlined. In the conclusion, means to increase the overall managerial capability of the company are explored.

MULTINATIONAL STRATEGIES

Faced with the conflict between the economic and political imperatives within a business, MNCs can respond in several ways. Some companies clearly respond first to the economic imperatives, and follow a worldwide (or regional)[4] business strategy where the activities in various countries are integrated and centrally managed. Other companies forgo the economic benefits of integration and let their subsidiaries adjust to the demands of their host government (as if they were national companies), thus clearly giving the upper hand to the political imperative. Finally, some companies try to leave their strategy unclear and reap benefits from economic integration and political responsiveness, in turn, or find compromises between the two. These three strategies are described in this section.

WORLDWIDE INTEGRATION STRATEGY

Some companies choose to respond to the economic imperative and improve their international competitiveness. For companies that already have extensive manufacturing operations in several countries, the most attractive solution is to integrate and rationalize their activities among these countries. Individual plants are to provide only part of the product range (but for sales in all subsidiaries), thereby achieving greater economies of scale.[5] Plants can also be specialized by stages in the production process, and can be located in various countries according to the cost and availability of production factors for each stage (energy, labor, raw materials, skills).[6] Texas Instruments's location of labor-intensive semiconductor finishing activities in Southeast Asia, or Ford's and GM's

Europe-wide manufacturing rationalization, as well as their investments in Spain, illustrate this integration strategy.

Extensive transshipments of components and finished products between subsidiaries located in different countries result from such a strategy. Integration also involves the development of products acceptable on a worldwide basis. The "world car" concept pushed by GM, Ford, and Japanese exporters is an example of this approach. The driving principle of this integration strategy is the reduction of unit costs and the capture of large sales volumes; in industries where economies of scale are significant and not fully exploited within the size of national markets, it can bring sizable productivity advantages. For instance, Ford's unit direct manufacturing costs in Europe were estimated to be well below those of national competitors supplying a comparable car range. In industries where dynamic economies of scale are very strong (such as semiconductors), the cost level differences between such leaders as Texas Instruments and smaller national firms were significant. Similarly, IBM was believed to have costs significantly lower than its competitors.[7]

Where integration brought substantial cost advantages over competitors, the integrated firms could allocate part of the benefits from their higher internal efficiency to incur "good citizenship" costs in the host countries, and still remain competitive with nonintegrated firms. Some companies had a policy of full employment, balanced internal trade among countries, and performance of R&D in various countries. Such a policy may lead to less than optimal decisions, in a short-term financial sense, as it has some opportunity costs (for instance, the location of new plants and research centers in countries where a company sells more than it buys, instead of in low-wage or low-manufacturing cost countries). However, such a policy may also be the key to host countries' long-term acceptance of companies as leading worldwide corporations.

The benefits of integration not only enable the MNC to be better tolerated thanks to its ability to incur higher good citizenship costs, but integration itself can be seen as making expropriation less likely in developing countries.[8] Integration provides more bargaining power to MNCs for ongoing operations and also makes extreme solutions to conflicts with host governments (such as expropriation) into outcomes where both the host country and the MNC stand to lose.

A well-articulated, worldwide integration strategy also simplifies the management of international operations by providing a point of view on the environment, a framework to identify key sources of uncertainties, and a purpose in dealing with them. The worldwide integration strategy can guide managers in adopting a *proactive* stance. The simplicity of the driving principle of the integration strategy also makes a consistent, detailed strategic planning process possible, as it provides a unifying focus to the various parts of the organization. This process both guides the implementation of strategy and provides for its refinement and evolution over time.

NATIONAL RESPONSIVENESS STRATEGY

Some companies forgo the potential benefits of integration and give much more leeway to their subsidiaries to respond to the political imperative by having them behave almost as if they were national companies. Yet, the affiliation of subsidiaries to a multinational company can bring them four distinct advantages over purely national competitors. These advantages are:

1. The pooling of financial risks.
2. The spreading of research and development costs over a larger sales volume (than that of local competitors) without the difficulties involved in licensing transactions;
3. The coordination of export marketing to increase overall success in export markets;
4. The transfer of specific skills between subsidiaries (e.g., process technology or merchandising methods).

In this approach, each subsidiary remains free to pursue an autonomous economic or political strategy nationally as its management sees fit, given the situation of the national industry. In industries where the government plays a key role (nuclear engineering and electrical power, for instance), national strategies are primarily political; in industries where other local factors are important sources of differentiation (e.g., food processing), but where government plays a less prominent role, strategies are economic.[9]

In a nationally responsive MNC, the resources, know-how, or services of the headquarters (or of other subsidiares) are called upon only when the subsidiary management finds them helpful. Little central influence is exercised on the subsidiaries. The nationally responsive MNC, as a whole, has no strategy, except in a limited sense (Brown Boveri's technical excellence, for instance), and the strategy is usually not binding: subsidiaries follow it only when they see it in their own interest.

Manufacturing is usually done on a local-for-local basis, with few inter-subsidiary transfers. Coordination of R&D and avoidance of duplications are often difficult, particularly when host governments insist upon R&D being carried on locally on specific projects for which government support is available (new telecommunication technologies or micro-electronics, for instance).

ADMINISTRATIVE COORDINATION STRATEGY

Rejecting both clear-cut strategic solutions to the conflict between the economic and political imperatives offered by world-wide integration and national responsiveness, MNCs can choose to live with the conflict and look for structural and administrative adjustments instead of strategic solutions. Such adjustments are aimed at providing some of the benefits of both worldwide (or regional) integration and national responsiveness.

The strategy (literally) is to have no set strategy, but to let each strategic decision be made on its own merits and to challenge prior commitments. Individual decisions thus do not fit into the logic of clear goals, the reasonableness of which is tested against a comprehensive analysis of the environment and an assessment of the organization's capabilities. Strategy is not the search for an overall optimal fit, but a series of limited adjustments made in response to specific developments, without an attempt to integrate these adjustments into a consistent comprehensive strategy.[10]

The need for such adjustments emerges when new uncertainties are identified. These uncertainties can offer opportunities (e.g., the possibility to invest in a new country) or threats (e.g., the development of new technologies by competitors), or lend themselves to conflicting interpretation (the willingness of a government to grant R&D subsidies, but with some local production requirements). Instead of taking a stable proactive stance vis-à-vis the environment and relying on the chosen strategy to provide a framework within which to deal with sources of uncertainties and to make specific decisions as the need arises, companies using administrative coordination absorb uncertainties and try to resolve conflicts internally each time new uncertainties question prior allocations of strategic resources. In short, strategy becomes unclear, shifting with the perceived importance of changes in the economic or political environment, and it may become dissolved into a set of incremental decisions with a pattern which may make sense only *ex post*. Administrative coordination does not allow strategic planning: we are farther from the "timed sequence of conditional moves" representing the usual goal of strategic planning and much closer to public administration where issues get shaped, defined, attended to, and resolved one at a time in a "muddling through" process that never gives analytical consideration to the full implications of a step.[11]

By adopting such an internally flexible and negotiable posture, administratively coordinated companies make themselves more accessible to government influence, and become Janus-faced. On certain issues and at certain points in time, a view consistent with worldwide rationalization will prevail, in other cases national responsiveness will prevail, and in many cases some uneasy blend of the two will result. Some of the central control of the subsidiaries so critical in multinational integration is abandoned, making it easier for subsidiaries to cooperate with powerful partners such as government agencies or national companies on specific projects. Because commitments of resources are not all made consistently over time, and as the company is not likely to be very rationalized (given the role accorded to host governments' demands), excess resources are not likely to allow for large costs of good citizenship. In short, compared with multinational integration, *administrative coordination trades off internal efficiency for external flexibility.* Whereas multinational integration seeks to provide the organization with enough economic power for success, administrative coordination seeks to provide the flexibility needed for a constantly adjusted coalignment of the firm with the more powerful factors in the environment and with the most critical sources of uncertainty.[12] Acceptability to host governments derives from flexibility.

THE THREE STRATEGIES COMPARED

Both the worldwide (or regional) integration strategy and the national responsiveness strategy correspond to clear tradeoffs between the economic and the political imperatives. Integration demonstrates a clear preference for the economic imperative; the MNC attempts to fully exploit integration's potential for economic performance and shows willingness to incur large citizenship costs in exchange for being allowed to be very different from national companies. Conversely, national responsiveness minimizes the difference between the MNC and national companies, and thus minimizes the acceptability problems. It expresses a clear sensitivity to the political imperative, at the expense of economic performance. The economic advantages of multinationality are confined to a few domains: financial risks, amortization of R&D costs, export marketing, and skill transfers among the subsidiaries.

Administrative coordination, because it aims at a constantly fluctuating balance between the imperatives, is an ambiguous form of management. There is a consistent tension within the organization between the drive for economic success based on clear economic strategy, and the need to consider major uncertainties springing from the political imperative. The following comment, made by a senior manager in an administratively coordinated MNC, illustrates the tension:

In the long run we risk becoming a collection of inefficient, government-subsidized national companies unable to compete on the world market. Yet, if we rationalize our operations, we lose our preferential access to government R&D contracts and subsidies. So we try to develop an overall strategic plan that makes some competitive sense, and then bargain for each part of it with individual governments, trying to sell them on particular programs that contribute to the plan as a whole. Often we have to revise or abandon parts of our plan for lack of government support.

MARKETS, COMPETITION, TECHNOLOGY, AND STRATEGY

In thinking about which type of strategy may suit a particular MNC or an individual business within a diversified MNC, it is important to consider the markets being served, the competition being faced, and the technology being used by the firm. The argument will focus on products and industries for which multinational integration pressures are significant, leaving aside products for which national taste differences (food), high bulk to value added ratio (furniture), dependence on perishable products (food), small optimal size (garments and leather goods), or other such factors usually make rationalization unattractive or unfeasible.

MARKET STRUCTURE AND COMPETITION

The range of possible multinational strategies depends upon the structure of the world market in terms of customers and barriers to trade. First, for some products (such as electrical power systems or telecommunications equipment), the technology and economies of production would very strongly suggest global rationalization, but political imperatives are so strong as to prevent it. The international trade volumes, either captive within MNCs or in toto, for telecommunications equipment or power systems are extremely low.[13] In developed countries theoretically committed to free trade, restrictions come through monopoly market power of government-controlled entities—Post, Telegraph, Telephone (PTT), for instance—or through complex legislation and regulation that create artificial market differentiation. EEC regulations on trucks, officially designed for safety and road degradation reasons, effectively create barriers to entry for importers. In a similar way, inspection regulations for equipment (including the parts and components) purchased by state agencies in many European countries, effectively make it difficult to incorporate imported components into end products sold to the state.

In developing countries, market access restrictions are more straightforward. Under such conditions of restricted trade and controlled market access, worldwide strategic integration is obviously difficult. Often, the very nature of the goods, their strategic importance, as well as characteristics such as bulky, massive equipment produced in small volumes for a few large customers, reinforce the desire on the part of governments to control suppliers closely.[14]

Second, at another extreme, there are some goods that are traded quite freely, whose sales do not depend on location of manufacture or nationality of the manufacturer, and for which economies of scale beyond the size of national markets are significant. In such industries the only viable strategy is worldwide (or regional) integration. This is the strategy followed by all volume car manufacturers in Europe, led by Ford and General Motors but also including such national champions as Fiat, Renault, or Volkswagen. Smaller companies are adopting a specialization strategy by moving out of the price-sensitive volume market and serving the world market from a single location (BMW, Daimler Benz).

Third, and most interesting, are businesses (such as computers or semiconductors) whose markets are partly government-controlled and partly internationally competitive. In such businesses the market is split between customers who select their suppliers on economic grounds and customers that are state-owned or state-influenced and evidence strong preference for some control over their suppliers. Products, such as computers or integrated circuits, are of sufficient strategic and economic importance for host governments to try to have some control over their technology and their production.[15] In such industries governments try to restrict the strategic freedom of all multinationals and show great willingness to reward flexibility. Honeywell, for instance, was liberally rewarded for agreeing to create a joint venture between its French subsidiary and Compagnie Internationale pour l'Informatique, the ailing leader of the French computer industry. In addition to favored access to the French state-controlled markets, the joint venture received substantial grants and research contracts.

In these industries where both the economic and political imperatives are critical, multinationals face the most difficult choice between various possible strategies. Some companies may choose to integrate their operations multinationally, and some may choose to decentralize their operations to better match the demands of individual governments and benefit from their support and assistance. Still others may not make a clear strategic commitment and may instead resort to administrative coordination.

Yet, this choice is likely to look significantly different to various MNCs according to their competitive posture within their industry. In broad terms, *firms with the largest overall shares of the world market are likely to find integration more desirable.* There are several reasons for this choice.

Benefits of Integration

First, still assuming that there are unexploited economies of scale, large firms can achieve lower costs through integration than can smaller firms. The company with the largest overall share of the world market can become the low-cost producer in an industry by integrating its operations, thus making life difficult for smaller competitors. Conversely, smaller firms (with significant market shares in only a few countries) can remain cost competitive so long as larger competitors do not move to regional or worldwide integration. Firms that integrate across boundaries in a market that is partly price competitive and partly government-controlled, can expect to gain a larger share of the price competitive market and confine smaller competitors to segments protected by governments that value flexibility and control more than lower prices.[16]

Influence

Second, one can hypothesize that larger firms can have more influence on their environment than smaller ones, and thus find it more suitable to centralize strategic decision making and ignore some of the uncertainty and variety in the environment.[17] In particular, larger firms can take a tougher stance vis-à-vis individual governments when needed, and woo them with higher costs of good citizenship. How much integrated firms may be willing to give to host governments as costs of citizenship to maintain strategic integration may vary substantially. One can argue that a leading integrated firm in a partly government-controlled market with no comparable direct competitor (IBM, for instance), may be willing to provide a lot to host countries in order to maintain its integration. Conversely, when keen worldwide competition takes place among integrated companies of comparable strength (e.g., Texas Instruments, Motorola, and Fairchild), the economic imperative becomes much more demanding for each of them, and none may be willing to be accommodating for fear that the others would not match such behavior. In short, the following proposition can be made: *the more one integrated firm is submitted to direct competition from other integrated companies, the less it will be willing to provide host governments, except in exchange for profitable nonmatchable moves.*

The implications of this proposition in terms of public policy toward industry structure are significant. At the regional or worldwide level it raises the issue of whether to encourage competition, or to favor the emergence of a single integrated leading MNC and then bargain with that company on the sharing of revenues. Similarly, a significant industrial policy issue at the national level is whether to encourage competition, or to provide a single multinational with the opportunity for a profitable nonmatchable move.[18]

Conversely, smaller firms (such as Honeywell in comparison with IBM) could draw only lesser benefits from rationalization and had to be extremely flexible in dealing with the uncertainties represented by host governments. Thus, *smaller firms are likely to find administrative coordination more suitable and will enlist host governments' support and subsidies to compete against leading MNCs.* Market access protection, financial assistance, or both can be the only way for these smaller firms—multinational or not—to keep a semblance of competitiveness. In the same way that firms in competitive markets can differentiate their products (or even their strategy) to avoid competing head on against larger firms, firms in these markets under partial government control differentiate their strategy by trading off central control over their strategy for government protection. The willingness of governments to trade off economic efficiency for some amount of political control, as well as the importance of short-term social issues (chiefly employment protection) make such strategic differentiation possible.[19]

For smaller MNCs such differentiation usually involves forgoing integration and letting host governments gain a say in strategic decisions affecting the various subsidiaries. Yet, because the MNC still attempts to maintain some competitiveness in market segments not protected by governments, it is likely to find administrative coordination—despite the ambiguity and managerial difficulty it involves—the least evil.

Finally, national companies can attempt to achieve some economies of scale through interfirm agreements for the joint manufacture of particular components (car engines) or product lines (Airbus A300). Over time, national companies can move to develop a globally integrated system. A case in point is Volkswagen, whose U.S.-assembled "Rabbits" incorporate parts from Brazil, Germany, and Mexico. Where free trade prevails among developed countries, as in the automobile industry, this may be the only suitable strategy for national companies.

In summary, one can hypothesize a relationship between the extent of government control over (and limits to) international trade in an industry, the relative international market share of a firm active in that industry, and the type of strategy it adopts. In industries where free trade prevails, all competitors are expected to have to follow a worldwide (or regional) integration strategy. In industries in which governments take a keen interest, but where they control the markets only partly, and where formal free trade prevails (computers, for instance), all three strategies are likely to coexist within an industry. Finally, in industries where the political imperatives prevail and whose markets are mostly state-controlled, all competitors can be expected to adopt a national responsiveness strategy.

Data supporting the relationship summarized above are presented graphically in Figure 1. It shows the results of the in-depth study of six industries where the economic and the political imperatives strongly conflict. However, one word of caution is necessary here: the patterns shown can only represent the *preferred* strategy of a company. Most companies will have deviant subsidiaries, because within a given industry trade restrictions vary among countries. The figure was built from data in Western Europe, and assumes that in a given industry, trade restrictions are about the same for all countries. That may be approximately true within Western Europe, but is obviously false in other regions. For instance, Ford's European operations achieve integration at the regional level; Ford's other international subsidiaries are much more nationally responsive and often isolated by tough local content restrictions (for instance, in Latin America). In passing, it may be hypothesized that companies with substantial operations in numerous countries (within the same industry) break them up into regional management units when they face wide differences in the conditions of trade among the regions. Obviously, the value added of products with respect to their

Figure 1: Customers, Market Shares, and Multinational Strategies.

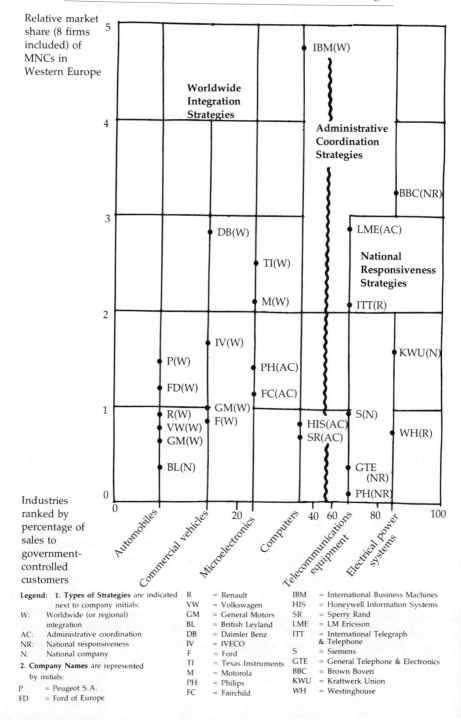

Relative market share (8 firms included) of MNCs in Western Europe

Worldwide Integration Strategies

Administrative Coordination Strategies

National Responsiveness Strategies

IBM(W), BBC(NR), DB(W), LME(AC), TI(W), M(W), ITT(R), IV(W), P(W), KWU(N), PH(AC), FD(W), FC(AC), GM(W), R(W), F(W), VW(W), GM(W), S(N), HIS(AC), SR(AC), WH(R), BL(N), GTE(NR), PH(NR)

Industries ranked by percentage of sales to government-controlled customers

Automobiles, Commercial vehicles, Microelectronics, Computers, Telecommunications equipment, Electrical power systems

0   20   40 60   80   100

Legend: 1. **Types of Strategies** are indicated next to company initials:
W: Worldwide (or regional) integration
AC: Administrative coordination
NR: National responsiveness
N: National company
2. **Company Names** are represented by initials:
P   = Peugeot S.A.
FD   = Ford of Europe

R   = Renault
VW   = Volkswagen
GM   = General Motors
BL   = British Leyland
DB   = Daimler Benz
IV   = IVECO
F   = Ford
TI   = Texas Instruments
M   = Motorola
PH   = Philips
FC   = Fairchild

IBM   = International Business Machines
HIS   = Honeywell Information Systems
SR   = Sperry Rand
LME   = LM Ericsson
ITT   = International Telegraph & Telephone
S   = Siemens
GTE   = General Telephone & Electronics
BBC   = Brown Boveri
KWU   = Kraftwerk Union
WH   = Westinghouse

weight or bulk also plays a role in limiting worldwide integration in a few industries where the value added per unit of weight is very high, and economies of scale and/or factor cost differences among regions are substantial (e.g., microelectronics).

TECHNOLOGY

Technology is usually seen as an important variable in the interface between MNCs and host governments. The introduction by MNCs of many innovative high technology products and the high market shares they still enjoy in their sales create much tension with host governments. Major industries, such as computers, microelectronics, or aerospace, remain dominated by U.S. multinationals. In tensions between economic and political imperatives within an industry, technology then plays a key role, MNCs that control the technology of specific industries have more power in bargaining with governments and also create technology barriers to competition from national firms. Often the minimal scale requirements increase so rapidly in high technology industries as to make it almost impossible for national firms to catch up.[20]

Technology, Trade, and Strategic Integration

Higher technology products are likely to correspond to freer trade. First, there is ample evidence that MNCs most often introduce their innovations in their home markets first.[21] So long as the new technology is not adopted by many countries, freer trade is likely to prevail for newer products than for older ones. Second, during the technology diffusion process within the MNC, the need to transfer the new technology quickly to subsidiaries creates pressures to increase coordination among them. Companies thus find it more desirable and easier to integrate regionally or to tilt their administrative coordination toward more integration. In terms of the graphics of Figure 1, a new higher technology can be represented by a move to the left. The move can affect a given industry as a whole if the technology is available to all MNCs but not to any national company, or more likely the move can be firm-specific.

In the study of the telecommunications industry, both moves were found. First, the shift to electronic switching and digital coding led the industry as a whole to be characterized by freer trade and by the opening of markets to new suppliers, as the various national PTTs were deciding upon their first orders for new equipment in the 1970s. Second, within the industry, L. M. Ericsson has always tried to be "one step ahead" of its competitors in technology, and to run its operations in a more integrated way than its competition. Conversely, ITT has most often been a technology follower, but let its subsidiaries be quite responsive to the demands of their host governments. It can be hypothesized that, *within an industry where the political imperatives are significant, higher technology firms (relative to their competitors) strive for integration, and can achieve some measure of it, and lower technology firms (relative to their competitors) strive for national responsiveness.*

Technology, Scale, and Government Intervention

It is also important to recognize that technological evolution can increase the minimal efficient scale of an industry and call to question the viability of national responsiveness. Even where restricted trade prevails, as the efficient scale increases in a high technology industry, pressures grow for domestic mergers and rationalization. Where multinational and national firms compete, the multinationals are unlikely to be the winners in a merger drive. Government interest is likely to prompt mergers into the "national champion" rather than to let the national industry be entirely controlled from outside. A national responsiveness strategy, i.e., a rather autonomous national subsidiary, makes such mergers into a national champion easier for the government to implement.

The examples of the French electrical power industry and telecommunications equipment in France and Great Britain tend to confirm the above analysis. In the case of electrical power systems, the transition from fossil fuel boilers to nuclear steam supply not only led to higher minimal efficient scale in the manufacture of turbogenerators, but also increased the interests of host governments in the industry. Two distinct effects were thus combined: minimal size increase and governments' greater interest in the technology itself.[22]

The Influence of Technology

This leaves us with less than a full understanding of the role of technology in the interface between MNCs and host governments in developed countries. On the one hand, for a given industry, a move to higher technology and new products can permit a firm (or all firms in an industry if they have access to the new technology) to be more multinationally integrated and centrally managed than it would otherwise be. There is some unclear causal relationship here, as integration is made possible by higher technology but is also required to facilitate technology transfer within the MNC.[23] On the other hand, it seems that very high technologies become extremely important in developed countries and prompt governments to try to narrowly control their development and use. Also, the move to higher technology often results in larger minimal efficient scale. This scale can be used by integrated multinationals to defend their market shares and attack smaller or less integrated firms, e.g., in microelectronics. In industries where trade is restricted, the government's usual responses are mergers into an emerging "national champion" first, and development of multinational government-sponsored programs second.

In both cases multinationals do not stand to benefit. This was clearly the case in electrical power systems. Telecommunications equipment was more ambiguous. Some countries were moving toward national consolidation (Brazil, France, the U.K.), and in others new electronic technology resulted in more open markets (Australia, South Africa, Spain, and several small European countries). Electronic technologies obviously increased the importance of the industry, yet provided opportunities to more integrated firms (e.g., L. M. Ericsson) or national firms with a distinctive technology (e.g., CIT Alcatel). When technology increases both the pressures to integrate within the industry and the interest governments take in the industry, either integration within MNCs across boundaries or integration within a country through government-directed mergers can prevail.

MANAGERIAL IMPLICATIONS

In practice, it is important to an MNC, or to executives running individual businesses in diversified multinationals, to recognize those changes in market openness, industry structure, and technology of an industry that foreshadow a need to change the overall strategy. Two simple examples are illuminating. Until the mid-1970s, General Motors ran its international operations as a collection of nationally responsive autonomous subsidiaries. With the globalization of the industry and the rationalization and integration of key competitors (mainly Ford), this posture became untenable. The strongest of the subsidiaries, Adam Opel in Germany, was able to hold its own in Europe, competing as a national company. But other subsidiaries, particularly Vauxhall in the U.K., were severely hurt. In 1975, General Motors started to bring the various subsidiaries together more closely through a series of administrative changes. By 1978, these moves resulted in an administrative coordination approach where numerous contradictions and ambiguities emerged. GM Overseas Operations' top management considered such administrative coordination as a transitional stage toward global integration. Many GMOO managers, however, felt that contradictions between the lingering desire for national subsidiaries' responsiveness and the emerging worldwide integration needs would not be easily resolved. In any case, the company had missed several precious years and had to struggle hard to remain competitive in Europe.

Conversely, in the late 1960s, Westinghouse was looking for acquisitions in the European electrical power system industry. It hoped to expand its business in Europe quickly, thanks to its light water nuclear reactor technology that was emerging as a clear technological winner over indigenous European technologies. To "better" manage its European operations, Westinghouse moved to a worldwide product group structure, aiming at multinational integration. At the same time, as we have seen, the increased minimal scale of the industry, the strategic importance of nuclear-related technologies, and the failure of Europe's own efforts in commercial reactors all combined to increase government sensitiveness about the industry. The discrepancy between the national responsiveness demanded by governments and what Westinghouse appeared willing to provide resulted in tensions in Belgium, France, and Germany, a substantial scale-down of Westinghouse's European expansion plans, and a shift in its strategy. In 1975, a former president of Westinghouse's Power Group commented to the author: "Our basic policy [for nuclear engineering and power plant sales] is to do it in whatever way a country would require." Yet, Westinghouse had probably lost the one opportunity to become a lasting factor in the European power system industry.

CHOICE OF STRATEGY AND MANAGEMENT PROCESS

We have seen that both worldwide (or regional) integration and national responsiveness lead to relatively straightforward management processes that are grounded in a clear strategy and a clear-cut delineation of headquarters' and subsidiaries' roles and responsibilities. Yet, the relative managerial simplicity both these strategies offer has an opportunity cost: it makes specific adjustment to the varying demands of governments difficult, and may prevent the company from entering certain businesses or certain countries. Such limitations make administrative coordination attractive as a way to increase the MNC's flexibility in finding balances between the economic and the political imperatives that match more closely the specific conditions of a given business in a given country. It is important to recognize that both worldwide integration and national responsiveness almost represent ideal polar opposites.

Some MNCs are likely not to wish (or be able) to exercise a clear choice, and thus find themselves improvising compromises through some process of administrative coordination.

In particular, when the political imperative is significant, its very nature makes clear-cut analytical choices impossible. Contrary to the economic imperative, information on the political imperative is most often indirect and not controllable centrally. When a subsidiary manager claims that his plans rest on the word of local intermediaries or on his relationships with national government officials, it is difficult, at best, for managers at headquarters to determine the soundness of his assumptions. The fact that the government's public logic is often quite different from the reality of the situation and from actual policy-making processes, makes it even more difficult for corporate or regional managers to understand the situation. As a result, top management's inability to reach an analytical choice on decisions involving the political imperative leads to adaptive coalitional decision making in which the firm internalizes tensions and uncertainties and tries to incorporate them into its decision-making process.

DECISION PROCESSES AND ADMINISTRATIVE COORDINATION

On any particular strategic decision, the company is trying to reach a satisfactory compromise given past decisions and past commitments of resources. Decisions cannot be left to either the subsidiary or the regional (or global) headquarters levels. They have to be reached by some group that collectively captures contradictions in the environment, internalizes them, and resolves them through contention, coalition, and consensus. Individual managers, representing different interests within the company and approaching questions from different points of view, are left to take sides on decisions according to how they perceive problems and how they prefer to deal with sources of uncertainty. In short, the question of deciding "what is right" becomes linked to that of "who is right" and "whose views are favored." Top management, instead of providing the inspiration for a strategic design and managing its implementation, shifts to a new role of deciding how to make decisions: who should be represented, with which voice, on which decisions. Top management can also provide some limits: would such decisions represent too wide a departure from the usual to be accepted? Choices on how to reach decisions can still be guided by a sense of which decisions, or which classes of decisions, should be made with integration as a priority, and which should be made with responsiveness as a priority.

The way to convey such sense of priority is not to decide in substance on specific decisions (except when irreconcilable conflicts occur) but to act on the way in which decisions are made, to influence the making and undoing of specific coalitions or to help the shift of coalitions among decisions.

Managing Dependencies

How can top management achieve such influence? Primarily by keeping control of dependencies between subunits competing for power and by regulating the game they pursue. Strategic and operational dependencies can be used to determine who, in the long run, has power over which class of decisions or what functions. For instance, the subsidiaries can be made dependent on the corporate headquarters or on domestic product divisions for key components or for process technology. Conversely, the domestic divisions can be dependent on subsidiaries for export sales. A central difficulty of this approach is the divisiveness introduced within the company by managing dependencies through arm's-length power relationships. Top management also has to develop some integrative forces (for instance, through training, career paths, and compensation) to balance these divisive forces and preserve some sense of corporate identity and loyalty.

Over the long run, successful administrative coordination thus hinges on the maintenance of a balance between divisive and integrative forces that reflects a structure of dependencies among subunits. Careful control of the dependencies between national subsidiary managers and product unit managers, through the use of functional managers and administrative managers, was found to provide top management tools for maintaining such a balance.

Functional Managers: The substantive expertise of functional managers is needed by supporters of multinational integration as well as by supporters of national responsiveness. Managers preferring multinational integration still depend upon functional managers and "the field" (in various countries) to achieve such integration. Conversely, national managers depend on support from functional and administrative headquarters staff and product divisions even though they try to pursue national responsiveness strategies. Because the power of functional managers is based on needed expertise, they may preserve a relatively uncommitted posture between multinational integration and national responsiveness.

Yet functional managers, over time, can develop a functional logic that is aligned to either national responsiveness or worldwide integration. Manufacturing staffs, for instance, can develop a logic that calls for integration and rationalization or for flexible local plants serving separate national markets. Within each function, of course, further distinctions can develop. For instance, rationalized component plants and local-for-local end-product plants can be favored, or distribution channels can be perceived as very different, whereas similar advertising can be used. By influencing corporate functional managers directly in the development of their preference for integration or responsiveness, and by then bringing them to throw their weight to particular issues and not to others, top management can develop a repertoire of intervention methods on the making of particular decisions.

Administrative Managers: Administrative procedures and the managers in charge of them can also be used by top management to maintain the tension between integration and responsiveness. To begin with, the formal structure usually provides a dominant orientation. Even when this structure is a matrix, it is usually complemented by fairly elaborate administrative procedures and guidelines that provide a dominant orientation by defining who is responsible for what and whether it is a primary or a secondary responsibility. Various devices, such as committees and task forces that cut across the formal structure, can be used to bring about changes in perception or to reach actual decisions. Planning processes can also be designed so that integration and responsiveness are considered. For instance, a contention process can exist between subsidiaries and product divisions (e.g., L. M. Ericsson). Interestingly, IBM had such a system very formalized and well developed among its regions and product groups, and between them and corporate functional staffs. Measurement systems can be set so that managers will see it as their duty to call to top management's attention "excessive" integration, autonomy, or responsiveness (e.g., GTE[24] or GM). Personal reward and punishment systems may be designed to reinforce tensions or ease them according to the measurement criteria and yardsticks used. Management of career paths can also be used to provide multiple views and facilitate coordination.

Administrative staff managers, and the way they design and run their administrative systems, provide top management with the same type of leverage as functional managers. One can expect the controller to strive for uniformity of accounting practices and comparability of results worldwide, opposing differentiation between subsidiaries. Personnel management, on the other hand, can either favor uniformity of pay scales and benefits worldwide, or leave this decision to subsidiaries. The way in which the administrative function develops its own operating paradigm[25] can be managed so that its specific procedures support responsiveness or integration.

DANGERS OF ADMINISTRATIVE COORDINATION

Even with the potential offered by functional and administrative managers for managing administrative coordination effectively, certain drawbacks are inescapable. In particular, administrative coordination may lead to strategic paralysis, fragmentation, or bureaucratization.

Strategic Paralysis

The willingness to respond to environmental changes when the environment is intrinsically ambiguous and contradictory is likely to lead to strategic paralysis. Students of ambiguous situations where several environments are relevant to decisions have stressed the danger of paralysis created by giving relatively equal power to managers most sensitive to different aspects of the environment.[26] Not using a stable pattern of resource commitment over time, according to spelled out goals, may lead to considerable waste and overall failure. It is fascinating to see that, in an environment where IBM is a strong leader, the agreements on the merger between C2I and Honeywell Bull in France spelled out a substantive strategy to avoid the risk of strategic paralysis. On the other hand, one could draw numerous examples of strategic paralysis from the very refined, stable administrative coordination processes.[27]

Strategic Fragmentation

Administrative coordination involves the use of dependencies and the management of power, which create divisive forces. In the absence of a strategic design, the management groups' loyalty must be maintained lest managers' frustrations lead to increasingly disjointed and partial decisions and to fragmentation. Cultural identity is often a means to circumvent these divisive forces. For instance, all top managers at L. M. Ericsson come from the same Stockholm telecommunications engineering school; the whole top management of Philips remains Dutch and has gone through the same formative experiences. Similarly, strong cultural identity facilitates the foreign expansion of Japanese companies.

Bureaucratization

Managers faced with very uncertain situations and power relationships may be tempted to reduce their perceived uncertainties. By developing bureaucratic procedure to cope with uncertainties, managers will gain power for themselves. Bureaucratic procedure also creates uncertainties for other members of the organization.[28] This leads to bureaucratization and lack of sensitivity to the outside environment. More time is spent on infighting than on external action.

Even assuming that administrative coordination does not lead to strategic paralysis, fragmentation, or bureaucracy, it remains an expensive way to run a business. The internal management process, with its multiple negotiations and complex coalitional processes, consumes much managerial energy and time, and can slow down decision processes considerably. It can also lead to "horse trading" and more suboptimal decisions than would be warranted by the situation at hand.

Should administrative coordination be avoided wherever possible, then? The answer is probably yes, but with the qualifications developed in the first part of this article. When free trade prevails and competitors follow a worldwide integration strategy, a clear choice should be made between committing enough resources to a business and divestment. In industries where governments evince interest, administrative coordination seems, at best, to be a way for the weaker, smaller international companies to stay in certain industries (Honeywell in data processing, Philips in integrated circuits). In industries where trade is restricted, the alternative is between national responsiveness and administrative coordination. For technology leaders within their industry, administrative coordination makes sense, as it can possibly provide for easier technology transfer, and host governments can accept such coordination as a price for receiving the technology.

STRATEGY IN THE DIVERSIFIED MULTINATIONAL[29]

So long as the several businesses of the multinational rely on the same strategy, the overall corporate management task is not greatly complicated by business diversity. Texas Instruments uses one extreme posture which applies the same semiconductor business logic and global integration framework across the board to all of its businesses.

Another extreme would be a multinational conglomerate adopting a purely financial approach and letting each business develop its own business logic independently. Yet, in most cases, such simple solutions as that of Texas Instruments or the multinational conglomerate are not applicable: the various businesses of the diversified multinational straddle several adaptation patterns and are interdependent. This raises the issues of strategic and administrative differentiation among the businesses, and of managing the interdependencies among differentiated businesses.

DIFFERENTIATION AND INTERDEPENDENCIES

Difficulties develop when the various businesses of a multinational straddle several adaptation patterns; some are most suitably managed through global strategic integration, others through administrative coordination, and still others through national responsiveness. It usually happens that, because of a history of dominance in one business, one pattern is preferred and applied across the board. For instance, Brown Boveri was slow to recognize that its industrial businesses, particularly small motors and breakers, would be faced with worldwide competition following the EEC trade liberalization. When competition came, Brown Boveri was even slower to react, because the logic of the whole organization and the energy of top management were geared to success in the government-controlled, restricted trade power system and heavy electrical equipment businesses.

In a similar vein, after World War II, Philips had strong national organizations and weak worldwide product groups coordinating its activities. With freer trade (following the development of the EEC), moves were made to increase the power of product divisions and to foster integration in similar businesses between national organizations. This led to a balanced product-geography-function matrix that faced great difficulties in businesses where administrative coordination did not fit well. Businesses, such as TV picture tubes or standard semiconductors, did not achieve full integration at a regional (color TV) or global (semiconductors) level, and telecommunications equipment did not enjoy sufficient national autonomy to achieve responsiveness comparable to that of competitors.

An obvious response to the difficulties faced by Brown Boveri or Philips is to differentiate the management among product lines, letting each find the appropriate balance between the economic and the political imperatives.

Yet, extensive interdependencies among businesses would usually make this management differentiation difficult. Interdependencies are of several types. They can involve common technologies among several businesses. For instance, magnetic tape technology at Philips served several product groups: data systems, instrumentation, medical products, professional recording, and audio consumer products. Interdependencies can also derive from vertical integration. The bulk of Philips's electronic component production was transferred internally to be incorporated into Philips's end products; still Philips also wanted to compete on the open market for semiconductors. Interdependencies are also market related, with different products sold to the same customers. IBM's Data Processing Complex's and General Business Group's system offerings overlap at the lower end of medium systems and compete against each other for the same orders. Finally, when products are sold to government-controlled customers, interdependencies may become political. Brown Boveri was commonly told: "We are willing to import your power stations, but what about you creating an export-oriented motor plant in one of our depressed areas to generate employment and offset the trade deficit that importing your power stations would create?"

It is important to recognize the difference in nature between internal interdependencies (common technology, joint production, vertical integration) and external ones (same customers, host governments, and so forth). When interdependencies are internal, the choice of how to relate businesses (from pure arm's length to joint administration) can be made by management. When interdependencies are external, such choice is usually imposed by external agents. The terms under which to coordinate component and TV set production could be decided internally in Philips. However, the Belgian Government's orders for Philips's computers were conditional upon the maintenance of Philips's employment levels in Belgium. The consumer product groups, whose internal interdependencies with the computer group were negligible, but who had high cost factories they wanted to close down in Belgium, suffered from the deal. Allegedly, this problem played some role in Philips's decision to withdraw from the mainframe computer business entirely.

MANAGING INTERDEPENDENCIES

The central tradeoff in the examples presented above is that between strategic and administrative clarity for individual businesses (i.e., enabling clear choices to be made between worldwide integration and national responsiveness), and the complexity of managing interdependencies.

Developing some clarity usually involves selectivity in the management of interdependencies. It is important to recognize that, within a diversified multinational, the relative importance of various interdependencies may change over time as the "critical factors"[30] in the strategy of a business evolve. ITT was able to revise frequently the formal structure of its European operations to respond to changes in the relative importance of interdependencies. The basic method used by ITT was to organize itself into several product groups worldwide. Each of these was managed somewhat differently: the Automotive Group (auto parts and accessories) and the Microelectronics Group, for instance, were pursuing worldwide integration strongly, whereas the Telecommunications Equipment Group stuck to its national responsiveness strategy. The Business Systems Group pursued regional integration in Europe. Individual businesses could be moved among these groups as warranted by competitive, technological, and government intervention changes. In the mid-1970s, ITT moved the private telephone exchange switching product line from the Telecommunications Equipment Group to the Business Systems Group, where it joined other office equipment. The successful adaptation of electronic switching technology to private exchange and the penetration of the private exchange market by such aggressive, integrated firms as IBM had shifted the key dependency from technology (Telecommunications Equipment Group) to marketing (Business Systems Group). In a similar vein, when ITT adopted worldwide strategic integration for its microelectronics business, it spun off the telecommunication-related components to the Telecommunications Equipment Group. Also ITT decreased the interdependencies between microelectronics and telecommunications in order to achieve a clear strategy for each business.

The development of clarity for Brown Boveri and Philips was more difficult than for ITT. Because they were less widely diversified (most of their products were related), they could not reduce any interdependencies easily. Yet some of their businesses were subject to worldwide product standardization and price competition (for instance, radios at Philips and motors at BBC), and others were more affected by regional or national differences (power systems at BBC, hi-fi at Philips). These different competitive conditions led to divergent strategic directions among businesses.

An approach to interbusiness coordination, under such circumstances, that is being tried by several companies, is the use of corporate functional staff in conjunction with planning committees. At Brown

Boveri, corporate marketing staffs coordinated the activities of the various national subsidiaries product line by product line. It was between various members of the corporate marketing staffs that tradeoffs between businesses could be made and the interdependencies could be managed. Assisting the corporate marketing staff in the strategic coordination of each business were several levels of committees. Some of these committees were functional and others were product-oriented. Functional committees could coordinate certain types of interdependencies among technologies and markets of several product groups. Other committees regrouped product division managers of the different subsidiaries and were in charge of managing the regional integration/ national responsiveness tradeoffs. Unfortunately, the committees often lacked the consensus necessary for action, as each member adopted a parochial view.

Faced with similar problems, IBM gave operating units the right to formally take issue with the plans of other operating units ("nonconcurrence" in IBM's internal language) that would impact their activities adversely. Through this approach IBM was able to force subunits to consider interdependencies in their planning and budgeting process and to reach a joint solution before their plans could be approved. Top management could also take the initiative of presenting key strategic issues that would require coordination between subunits as "focus issues" to be dealt with explicitly in the planning process.[31] Other companies also sometimes pulled key interdependencies of great strategic importance out of the regular structure: Brown Boveri, for instance, established a separate nuclear policy committee with the task of managing all interdependencies relating to nuclear energy.

Despite the efforts described above, the management of interdependencies raises difficult issues. Because costs and benefits of interdependencies lend themselves to ambiguous conflicting interpretations, interdependencies provide a rich arena for power plays and coalition bargaining. While particular coalition configurations seem endless in their variety, they add to the task of strategic management. Furthermore, coalitions often involve external agents. For instance, individual managers can rely on their government to establish linkages among product groups. It is not uncommon for alliances to develop, at least tacitly, between host governments and subsidiaries to decrease the dependence of the subsidiary on headquarters and to develop "binding" commitments with the government.

Faced with such difficulties, the MNC corporate management level is likely to strive for administrative uniformity across businesses. Yet, unless all businesses can be successful with the same strategic logic, some degree of differentiation between businesses remains necessary. In short, uniformity is impossible when businesses straddle several adaptation patterns. Uniformity is possible on some aspects (financial reporting and measurement at ITT, for instance), provided that great leeway for differentiation is left to other aspects. Yet, to avoid cognitive overload at the corporate management level, there are strong pressures toward administrative uniformity, thus making the substance of decisions at the business unit level accessible to the corporate level in a common format. Such administrative pressure for uniformity may prevent the appropriate strategic differentiation among businesses and the development of strategic clarity. These necessary strategic and administrative differentiations suggest that it is usually not possible to maintain unitary corporate office dealing with the substance of decisions. Similarly, a diversified multinational needs (beyond the divisionalized form) a corporate office that only manages selected aspects of the operations and influences decision processes while leaving room for differentiation among businesses—unless all follow the same worldwide integration strategy.

As a concluding note for this section, it may be hypothesized that the complex multinational structures, usually called matrix (or grid) and mixed types, represent an attempt by diversified MNCs to respond to the problems of combining the developing of a strategy for each business with the need to manage interdependencies between businesses. Thus, they are not aberrant or transitory structural stages only. Matrix structures correspond to the corporate desire to manage interdependencies among businesses while allowing strategic integration to develop. Mixed structures correspond to a clear differentiation and separation between businesses that follow different adaptation patterns.

CONCLUSION—COMBINING STRATEGIC CLARITY AND ADMINISTRATIVE COORDINATION?

The most difficult tradeoff for the diversified MNC is the one between clarity at the business level (multicountry integration or national responsiveness) and the benefits derived from operating and strategic interdependencies between businesses. The added complexity, compared to domestic diversified companies, of coping with broader environmental variety, makes the management of interdependencies less straightforward and more difficult.

Some simplification can be obtained by limiting and buffering interdependencies. For instance, at L. M. Ericsson, the national subsidiaries were dependent upon the center for components and technology, but the center could be severed from any subsidiary without great difficulty. Interdependencies between subsidiaries were negligible. Japanese companies usually adopted similar approaches to manage their joint ventures abroad. Philips was treating its semiconductor acquisition in the U.S., Signetics, differently from its European operations, leaving much strategic freedom to the company. So both operating and strategic interdependencies can be structured in such a way as to minimize the need for managing them. There is a tradeoff between the complexity of managing many interdependencies and the joint benefits they bring.

One way companies have tried to order the above tradeoff is to manage simultaneously along several dimensions. For instance, as the Dow Chemical matrix was becoming unbalanced, the operating responsibilities moved toward area executives, thus providing regional integration across vertically interdependent businesses at the area level (Europe, Far East, etc.). Yet, a Corporate Product Department was created with veto power over strategic resource allocation and control over interdependencies between areas.[32] Administrative systems were used by Dow to provide autonomy for regional strategic integration, except for the planning and resource allocation process that was used to check strategic integration and keep the autonomy of areas within bounds.

In an even more discriminating way, IBM's strategic planning process provided for functions, product lines, and areas (for countries) to be managed jointly in a cohesive process, inputs and control points were set up so that both the need for integration in relevant units (that differed between functions, businesses, and areas of the world), and the administrative coordination needed between interdependent businesses were recognized, in turn, and conflicts were resolved through a contention process.

ITT was not only letting different businesses develop their own strategies, but also used the various management levels differently. Regional headquarters controlled product and business strategies, but their weight, compared to that of national subsidiary managers, varied considerably from one business to another. The overall planning process was managed from worldwide product group headquarters in New York. Finally, measurement, control, and evaluation were corporate level responsibilities.

More research is needed to conceptualize adequately the responses of these companies. However, these companies illustrate very sophisticated methods for providing both strategic integration and administrative coordination according to the needs for strategic focus and operating or strategic interdependencies between subunits.

REFERENCES

1. See, for instance L. G. Franko, *The European Multinationals* (Stamford, CT: Greylock, Inc., 1976).
2. See, for instance: J. Dunning and M. Gilman, "Alternative Policy Prescriptions," in *The Multinational Enterprise in a Hostile World*, ed. Curzon and Curzon (London: Macmillan & Co., 1977); R. Vernon, *Storm over the Multinationals* (Cambridge, MA: Harvard University Press, 1977); R. Vernon, *Sovereignty at Bay* (New York: Basic Books, 1971).
3. See, for instance, C. Stoffaes, *La Grande Menace Industrielle* (Paris: Calmann-Levy, 1977).
4. Some authors have opposed worldwide and regional management within MNCs. See J. M. Stopford and L. T. Wells, Jr., *Managing the Multinational Enterprise* (New York: Basic Books, 1972). The evidence in the companies studied suggests that in either case a business strategy responding to the economic imperative underlies regional or worldwide management. Which strategy is preferred in a particular company depends upon cost analysis based primarily on difference in factor costs, freight rates, and barriers to trade between various countries and regions of the world. In terms of responsiveness to individual country policies, there is little difference between regional and worldwide management. See L. G. Franko, *Joint Venture Survival in Multinational Corporations* (New York: Praeger, 1972).
5. See Y. Doz, "Managing Manufacturing Rationalization within Multinational Companies," *Columbia Journal of World Business*, Fall 1978.
6. See R. Vernon, "The Location of Economic Activity," in *Economic Analysis and the Multinational Corporation*, ed. Dunning (London: Allen and Unwin, 1974).
7. Ford's costs are estimated by the author from various industry interviews. For many product families, experience curve models suggested unit cost levels in smaller European firms equal to several times the costs in such firms as Texas Instruments for integrated circuits or Motorola for discrete semiconductors. Exact figures are not public, but their significance can be deducted from the Boston Consulting Group and Mackintosh publications. Large losses among European national semiconductor companies and private communications about losses in Philips's or Siemens's semiconductor businesses support the same point. See P. Gadonneix, "Le Plan Calcul" (DBA diss., Harvard Business School, 1974).
8. See: D. G. Bradley, "Managing against Expropriation," *Harvard Business Review*, July-August 1977, pp. 75-83; B. D. Wilson, "The Disinvestment of

Foreign Subsidiaries by U.S. Multinational Companies" (DBA diss., Harvard Business School, 1979).

9. For political strategies see: J. Zysman, *Political Strategies for Industrial Order* (Berkeley, CA: University of California Press, 1976); Y. Doz, *Government Control and Multinational Strategic Management* (New York: Praeger, 1979). For economic strategies, see U. Wiechmann, "Integrating Multinational Marketing Activities," *Columbia Journal of World Business*, Winter 1974. Wiechmann studied intensively the food and beverage industries.

10. For a comprehensive treatment of strategy as an optimal fit between environmental opportunities and threats and the organizational strengths and weaknesses (consistent with the personal values of top management and the social responsibilities of the corporation), see: K. R. Andrews, *The Concept of Corporate Strategy* (Homewood, IL: Dow Jones Irwin, 1971); D. Braybrooke and C. E. Lindblom, *A Strategy of Decison* (New York: The Free Press, 1963).

11. On strategic planning, see, for example: G. A. Steiner, *Top Management Planning* (New York: Macmillan, 1966); H. I. Ansoff, *Corporate Strategy* (New York: McGraw-Hill, 1965); P. Lorange and R. F. Vancil, eds., *Strategic Planning Systems* (Englewood Cliffs, NJ: Prentice-Hall, 1977). On "muddling through," see: Braybrooke and Lindblom (1963); R. Cyert and J. March, *A Behavioral Theory of the Firm* (Englewood Cliffs, NJ: Prentice-Hall, 1963); J. D. Steinbruner, *The Cybernetic Theory of Decision* (Princeton: Princeton University Press, 1974).

12. For instance, see S. M. Davis and P. R. Lawrence, *Matrix* (Reading, MA: Addison-Wesley, 1977).

13. See: N. Jequier, *Les Télécommunications et l'Europe* (Geneva: Centre d'Etudes Industrielles, 1976); J. Surrey, *World Market for Electric Power Equipment* (Brighton, England: SPRI, University of Sussex, 1972).

14. See O. Williamson, *Markets and Hierarchies: Analysis and Antitrust Implications* (New York: The Free Press, 1975).

15. See: Y. S. Hu, *The Impact of U.S. Investment in Europe* (New York; Praeger, 1972); N. Jequier, "Computers," in *Big Business and the State*, ed. R. Vernon (Cambridge, MA: Harvard University Press, 1974).

16. There is ample evidence of this phenomenon in the computer and microelectronics industries. See: E. Sciberras, *Multinational Electronic Companies and National Economic Policies* (Greenwich, CT: JAI Press, 1977); "International Business Machines: Can the Europeans Ever Compete?," *Multinational Business*, 1973, pp. 37-46.

17. For a discussion of strategic decision making and environmental uncertainty, see E. Rhenman, *Organization Theory for Long-Range Planning* (New York: John Wiley & Sons, 1973).

18. See F. T. Knickerbocker, *Oligopolistic Reaction and Multinational Enterprise* (Boston: Harvard Business School Division of Research, 1973).

19. For a discussion of strategic differentiation and competition in a domestic oligopoly, see R. Caves and M. Porter, "From Barrier to Entry to Barrier to Mobility," *Quarterly Journal of Economics*, May 1977.

20. For instance, see Vernon (1977), chap. 3. The evolution of industries such as nuclear power or aerospace is revealing. As the technology for a given product (e.g., light water nuclear reactors or bypass turbofan jet engines) becomes more widespread, the bargaining power of MNCs is eroded. See H. R. Nau, *National Politics and International Technology* (Baltimore, MD: Johns Hopkins University Press, 1974); For lesser developed countries, see N. Fagre and L. T. Wells, "Bargaining Power of Multinationals and Host Governments" (Mimeo, 14 July 1978); On increasing economies of scale, for instance, see M. S. Hochmuth, "Aerospace," in *Big Business and the State,* ed. R. Vernon (Cambridge, MA: Harvard University Press, 1974).

21. Innovations in mature products are an occasional exception. They are sometimes introduced in the most competitive market. For instance, Sony introduced several innovations in the U.S. before introducing them in Japan. Yet many other Sony innovations were first introduced in Japan. For a summary, see Vernon (1977), chap. 3.

22. See Doz (1979). For recent evidence, see "ITT Fights U.K. Bid for Plessey Control of STC," *Electronic News,* 23 October 1978, p. 4. On electrical power, see: B. Epstein, *The Politics of Trade in Power Plants* (London: The Atlantic Trade Center, 1972): Central Policy Review Staff, *The Future of the United Kingdom Power Plant Manufacturing Industry* (London: Her Majesty's Stationery Office, 1976); Commission des Communautés Européenes, *Situation et Perspective des Industries des Gros Equipements Electromécaniques et Nucléaires liés à la Production d'Energie de la Communauté* (Brussels: CEE, 1976). For related data on the U.S., see I. Bupp, Jr. and J. C. Derian, *Light Water: How the Nuclear Dream Dissolved* (New York: Basic Books, 1978).

23. See J. Behrman and H. Wallender, *Transfers of Manufacturing Technology within Multinational Enterprises* (Cambridge, MA: Ballinger, 1976).

24. For a detailed analysis of GTE and L. M. Ericsson's administrative mechanisms, see Doz (1979).

25. Used here in the sense given by Steinbruner (1974), as the simplifying logic used by a particular function to reduce complexity in its environment by focusing on a few key parameters and taking cybernetic decisions based on them.

26. See: Davis and Lawrence (1977); C. K. Prahalad, "The Strategic Process in a Multinational Company" (DBA. diss., Harvard Business School, 1975).

27. See C. K. Prahalad and Y. Doz, "Strategic Change in the Multidimensional Organization" (Harvard Business School-University of Michigan Working Paper, October 1979).

28. See: M. Crozier, *The Bureaucratic Phenomenon* (Chicago: University of Chicago Press, 1964); D. J. Hickson et al., "A Strategic Contingencies Theory of Intraorganizational Power," *Administrative Science Quarterly 2* (1971): 216-229.

29. This section draws upon Y. Doz and C. K. Prahalad, "Strategic Management in Diversified Multinationals," in *Functioning of the Multinational Corporation in the Global Context,* ed. A. Negandhi (New York: Pergamon Press, forthcoming).

30. Taken here in the sense of Barnard's "strategic factors" or Selznick's "critical factor." See: C. L. Barnard, *The Functions of the Executive* (Cambridge, MA: Harvard University Press, 1938): P. Selznick, *Leadership in Administration* (New York: Harper & Row, 1957).

31. See A. Katz, "Planning in the IBM Corporation" (Paper submitted to the TIMS-ORSA Strategic Planning Conference, New Orleans, February 16-17, 1977).

32. See S. M. Davis, "Trends in the Organization of Multinational Corporations," *Columbia Journal of World Business,* Summer 1976, pp. 59-71. Information on Dow Chemical came from the 1976 *Annual Report* and the author's interviews.

5
American Workers and Japanese Direct Investment
Duane Kujawa

Along with international trade relations, Japanese direct investment in U.S. manufacturing is probably one of the most socially sensitive and significant issues in United States-Japan economic relationships. The reasons for this are several and may well differ depending upon which side of the Pacific one is on.

FOR MANY JAPANESE, direct foreign investment in U.S. manufacturing, which serves to displace exports from Japan, is felt to be contrary to comparative advantage and reduces global welfare. Kiyoshi Kojima, the highly regarded international economist, typifies this view. Kojima characterizes Japanese direct investment in Southeast Asia, which serves Japan and third markets, for example, as labor [low wage] oriented and trade-creating, and contrasts this to that which flows to the United States because of trade barriers, the threat of trade barriers, and/or pressures generated in oligopolistically structured markets—the home of most of the multinationals (Japanese, American, or otherwise). This latter investment flow is barrier-induced and anti-trade oriented. The former, that is, the trade-oriented Japanese model, is beneficial and to be preferred; the latter detrimental and to be discouraged.[1]

The Japanese are also concerned with the domestic employment effects of outward direct investment. As Japanese multinationals expand American-based production, what will happen to the jobs in Japan? Japanese employment concerns, reminiscent of those attendant to the growth of American multinational enterprises (MNEs) in the 1960s and 1970s, have spawned several studies, such as The Japan Institute of Labor's "Overseas Investment and Its Impacts on Domestic Employment," replete with crucial assumptions and tedious methodologies.[2]

This study is based on a report prepared by the author for the Council on Foreign Relations (New York) Study Group on U.S.-Japan Labor Issues, May 2, 1985.

The gut problem on the whole outward direct development issue, however, appears to be cultural adjustment. How does a society that has been historically deficient in natural resources and has successfully implemented a high-growth strategy necessarily dependent on product exports change?

From the U.S. perspective, foreign direct investment has been viewed (perhaps inaccurately) as an alternative to trade and as a method for reducing international commercial friction. The rationale here is that manufacturing automobiles in Tennessee takes the place of exporting them from Japan and dampens allegedly onerous domestic effects felt to be unacceptable. Japanese manufacturing in the United States carries important meaning from industry and consumer perspectives too. When a Japanese firm decides to invest in the United States, it does so to enhance its competitive presence and growth opportunities in the U.S. market. Other producers typically don't prefer added competition. Indeed, U.S.-owned firms in several industry segments, such as electronic components, high-tech ceramics, motorcycles and general-purpose pickup trucks have atrophied in the face of the competitive superiority of the U.S.-based subsidiaries of Japanese MNEs. Consumers, of course, value the benefits of this increased competition and traditionally reward the better performers, be they Japanese- or American-owned, with their purchase dollars.

American workers and Japanese direct investors have a special, two-way relationship. They share dependency. For the Japanese MNE there are concerns over whether or not competitive strategies based on local production can succeed. Successful workforce management seems quite important in this regard, as does the workplace culture. Can product quality be maintained? What about managing in a unionized environment? American workers have their concerns too. There is an employment impact—both in terms of the quantity and quality of jobs created. There are questions about employment stability and growth, and about personnel practices. There are questions too about Japanese approaches to union-management relations in the American industrial setting. These concerns were recently investigated by the present author in a case-study project sponsored by the U.S. Department of Labor. Highlights of the nine Japanese case studies included in the project will be discussed and analyzed subsequently and compared, when appropriate, with highlights of the U.S. company case studies, with special attention being paid to three distinct topics:

1. To what extent have the Japanese subsidiaries implemented industrial relations practices typically considered "Japanese" in origin? What have been the experiences in this regard?
2. To what extent have Japanese-owned subsidiaries benefitted, in ways germane to their industrial relations, because of their Japanese MNE parentage? What have been the experiences in this regard?
3. How have competitive pressures and strategies affected these subsidiaries' approaches to American workers and unions? In terms of influence, how do they compare to Japanese management philosophy?

THE CASE STUDY COMPANIES

Profiles of the nine Japanese-owned subsidiaries that participated in the case-study research are presented in Table 1. The U.S-owned firms were Ampex Corporation, Cessna Aircraft Company, Dow Chemical Company, Harley-Davidson Motor Co., Inc., Harris Corporation, Jones & Laughlin Steel Corporation (J & L), National Semiconductor Corporation, Pennwalt Corporation and Quanex Corporation. In addition, six non-Japanese foreign-owned subsidiaries also participated: Aerospatiale Helicopter Corporation, Badische Corporation; CIBA-GEIGY Corporation, Georgetown Steel Corporation, Raritan River Steel Co. and Volkswagen of America, Inc. (In this study, comparisons will be made mainly between the U.S.-owned firms and the Japanese subsidiaries. In a few places, the non-Japanese foreign-owned subsidiaries will be referenced.) Collection of the case-study data spanned the period from 1980 to 1983 and all the companies participated on a "named" basis.

The U.S. and non-Japanese foreign-owned firms were generally larger than the Japanese and had been in business (in the United States) longer. They were in the same four industries—chemicals, electronic equipment and computers, steel, and transportation equipment. Notwithstanding size and age differences, there were some fairly well-matched pairs or groups within industries: Honda and Harley-Davidson in motorcycles; Mitsubishi and Cessna in general aviation aircraft; Auburn, New England, Georgetown, Raritan River, Quanex and J & L in steel; etc.

THE TRANSFER OF JAPANESE MANAGEMENT PRACTICES AND LABOR-MANAGEMENT RELATIONS IN JAPANESE SUBSIDIARIES

Topic areas typically identified with Japanese management practices at the worker level were investigated in the case studies. These included employment maintenance, job classification systems, compensation levels, compensation systems, fringe benefits, training, and union-management relations. Other topics were covered and these are discussed in other sections.

EMPLOYMENT MAINTENANCE (PERMANENT EMPLOYMENT)

Of the nine Japanese subsidiaries only one—Auburn Steel—had a published (but limited) commitment to employment maintenance. Auburn, KOHKOHU, and Honda were found to be the only subsidiaries deliberately implementing a worker-related Japanese management philosophy (discussed in more detail later). Neither KOHKOKU nor Honda, however, had a publicized, permanent employment policy. Of the three, only Auburn actually laid off workers—workers that had been reassigned to non-production jobs for eights weeks prior to a layoff that lasted ten more weeks. The layoff was approved in advance by the local "management conference," but not by the parent company.

Murata, New England and Sanyo were the only unionized subs diaries of the Japanese case-study companies. All three of these have experienced layoffs—two on several occasions. At all three, the subsidiary management took the layoff decision. However, Murata and Sanyo expressed a preference to adhere to the letter and concept of the union contract. Layoffs were provided for, and they had their place as a policy option. At New England, management felt the layoff experience, in retrospect, was not beneficial to either the company or the employees and was to be avoided in the future.

At the other three Japanese firms—Fujitsu, Mitsubishi, and Mt. Pleasant—only Mt. Pleasant reported no layoff experience. At Fujitsu, the layoff that did occur was approved in advance by the parent's board of directors; at Mitsubishi by the local executive committee.

The conclusions here are several: Employment maintenance at Japanese-owned subsidiaries is not ubiquitous in practice, nor is it generally valued as a policy option. A union contract, however, where evident, typically overrides any "philosophy-based" alternative. Nonetheless, in the non-unionized cases, half have yet to experience a layoff, and where layoffs have been experienced, Japanese management at either the parent or subsidiary level participated in the decision—certainly a not unexpected behavior.

Only the larger, more established firms in Japan profess a permanent employment policy—a policy that has been set aside even in the face of especially compelling (adverse) economic circumstances. Permanent em-

Table 1: The Japanese-Owned Case-Study Companies

U.S. Subsidiary	Ownership Structure	Location	Product(s)	Entry into U.S. Method	Entry into U.S. Year	Subsidiary Size (1980) Sales (Mil.)	Subsidiary Size (1980) Employm't
Auburn Steel Co., Inc.	Kyoel Steel Ltd.[a] A.C. & Co.[a]	Auburn, NY	Steel Bar and Rod	Start-up	1973	$60[b]	285[b]
Fujitsu America, Inc. (Fujitsu Micro-electronics, Inc.)	Fujitsu Limited (100%)	Santa Clara, CA (San Diego)	Electronic Equipment and Components (Semiconductor Devices)	Start-up (Start-up)	1976 (1980)	NA[c] (NA)	62[d] (129)
Honda of America Manufacturing, Inc.	American Honda Motor Co., Inc. (80%)[e] Honda Motor Co., Ltd. (20%)	Marysville, OH	Motorcycles	Start-up	1978	NA	180
KOHKOKU USA, Inc.	KOHKOKU Chemical Industry Co., Ltd.	Everett, WA	Poly-Vinyl-Chloride Sheet	Start-up	1974	$12	119
Mitsubishi Aircraft International, Inc.	Mitsubishi Heavy Industries Ltd. (97.3%) Mitsubishi Corp. (2.7%)	Dallas, TX	Turbo-Jet and Fan-Jet Aircraft	Takeover Takeover	1970 1970	$80 $80	361 361
Mt. Pleasant Chemical Co.	Sumitomo Chemical Company Ltd. (45%) Sumitomo Corporation (5%) Stauffer Chemical Co. (50%)	Mt. Pleasant, TN	Insecticide	Start-up	1974	NA	88

Table 1: The Japanese-Owned Case-Study Companies (Continued)

U.S. Subsidiary	Ownership Structure	Location	Product(s)	Entry into U.S. Method	Year	Subsidiary Size (1980) Sales (Mil.)	Employm't
Murata Corporation of America	Murata Manufacturing Company (100%)	Marietta, GA	Electronic Components	Start-up	1973	$48	300
New England Drawn Steel Company, Inc.	Oshima Seisen Co., Ltd. (40%) Ozuma Seiko Co., Ltd. Mittetsu Shosi Co., Ltd. (30%)	Mansfield, MA	Steel Bar and Rod	Takeover	1973	$5	34
Sanyo Manufacturing Corporation	Sanyo Electric Co., Ltd. (51%) Sears Roebuck & Co. (25%) Sanyo Electric Trading Co., Ltd. (22%)[f]	Forest City, AK	Television Sets, Microwave Ovens, Wood Products	Takeover	1977	$146	2,100

Notes: [a]Percentage ownership not given.
[b]Figure is for 1979.
[c]NA means not available.
[d]Employment figure is for the Santa Clara facility only.
[e]American Honda, in turn, is 100% owned by Honda Motor.
[f]Private (U.S.) investors hold the remaining 2%.

ployment is also typically not relevant to certain classes of employees in Japan, such as females, nor does it relate to smaller, vendor-type firms.

One could identify several subsidiary-level parallels here. Were the economic situations onerous and compelling in the Japanese subsidiaries' layoff cases? Yes, they were. Were the American workers viewed as a different class of (MNE) employees from those at the parent? Apparently so. Do the Japanese subsidiaries take the layoff decision seriously? Certainly. They indicated a culturally-based concern on this issue. Do they differ from U.S. firms in this regard? No, at least not regarding the practice. In terms of the "philosophy," though, the U.S. firms were substantially influenced because of the economics involved. Does unionization matter on this issue? Apparently so—in both the Japanese and U.S. cases. Is there a relevant rationale? (This point will be discussed later.)

Income maintenance, as a policy, is a derivative of employment maintenance. It can also be obtained via supplemental unemployment benefits, as in the J&L case, and, to some extent, via cross-training which qualifies workers for varied tasks and provides a cushion in the face of the elimination of a specific job. No Japanese subsidiary paid supplemental unemployment benefits, as did J & L. Cross-training, often seen as a typical Japanese management practice, was found at Auburn, Honda and KOHKOHU, the firms implementing a "Japanese approach" to workforce management, and at Mt. Pleasant Chemical—a 50/50 joint venture managed by the U.S. partner Stauffer Chemical—where cross-training and flexibility in task assignments were consistent with industry trends. Cross-training for certain types of production workers was also in evidence at Dow Chemical and J & L. These programs were developed and implemented in unionized plants with the cooperation of the unions involved. None of the unionized Japanese subsidiaries engaged in cross-training. These observations suggest a more flexible approach to income/employment maintenance by the U.S. firms than by the Japanese—especially in the unionized context.

JOB CLASSIFICATION SYSTEMS

"Japanese management philosophy" is seen as typically embracing broadly constituted work groups. Job classification systems which narrowly define workers' jobs have no place in this approach. Auburn, Honda and KOHKOKU had no written job descriptions for production (or any) workers. Honda had no job classifications; Auburn and KOHKOKU had but a few. These practices were professed to be consistent with their Japanese management philosophies. However, Fujitsu also had neither job descriptions nor classifications and Mt. Pleasant reported only six job "grades." Industry practices and competitive pressures were reported as the relevant determinants. The three unionized Japanese subsidiaries all reported written job descriptions and large numbers of job classifications (ranging from seventeen at New England to thirty-eight at Murata). All eight of the U.S. firms that reported on these topics were unionized and all reported comparatively large numbers of job categories. For the U.S. and the Japanese alike, the union contract was cited as the genesis of these detailed structures.

The data here suggest several things. One is that unionization is the overriding influence affecting workforce structuring. Another is that there are influences other than Japanese management philosophy that seek open structures accommodative of flexibility and are responsive to the competitive environment. (This point may well be lost, of course, if Japanese management philosophy itself is judged to be determined in turn by competitive pressures—a question that will be discussed later.)

COMPENSATION SYSTEMS AND LEVELS

Production workers were paid hourly at all the Japanese firms except Auburn, where everyone was on salary status. Auburn felt this policy was consistent with its operational objectives regarding flexibility in assignments, income/employment maintenance, etc. One might speculate that Honda's and KOHKOKU's decisions to stay with hourly-paid systems were flawed in light of their basic strategy to implement a Japanese workforce management system in an American industrial context. Nonetheless, those were their decisions and operationally they have been successful (business-wise). The other Japanese subsidiaries have all hourly-paid production workers. With the exception of Dow Chemical, production workers at all the U.S. firms were also paid hourly. At Dow, production workers covered by union contracts were hourly paid. Those that were not were salaried.

Performance-related compensation supplements for production workers or bonuses based on company profitability were more often found at the American firms than at the Japanese subsidiaries. In fact, only KOHKOKU had a profit-sharing plan. It linked company contributions to the employee pension plan to annual profitability—as did both Harris and National Semiconductor. In addition, Harley-Davidson had a production incentive system where workers could earn up to 125 percent of base pay. J & L used an equipment utilization bonus system where, for example, if the equipment utilization grew to 110 percent of design capacity, employees working the equipment could earn 149 percent of a base wage rate. At Quanex, a bonus fund based on tons of steel produced beyond a target minimum was distributed periodically among the workers.

There are several important points here. The larger firms in Japan traditionally pay periodic bonuses to employees based on profits. Annual bonuses equalling 30 to 50 percent of base pay are not unusual. None of the U.S. subsidiaries of Japanese firms paid such bonuses. KOHKOKU's profit-sharing method for pension funding is not nearly so substantial. It is not typically Japanese either. Note that both National Semiconductor and Harris have similar programs. One-third of the U.S. firms had incentive pay programs that were aimed at improving productivity by improving shop-floor practices. None of the Japanese had such programs. The conclusion here seems fairly straightforward: In Japanese subsidiaries, management did not use compensation-related approaches to encouraging improved productivity and did not opt to share, at least immediately, the benefits of improved productivity in any financially substantial way with employees. One rationale for this behavior is that productivity enhancement might be seen as a function of technology improvements originated at the parent in Japan. Productivity growth at the subsidiary then was parent-dependent and its benefits should accrue to the parent. How valid is this though for the three subsidiaries implementing Japanese management philosophies? Is not their productivity position substantially U.S. worker influenced?

Wages paid by the Japanese subsidiaries were generally at the lower end of the ranges identified by all the case-study companies, both un-ionized and non-unionized. Nonetheless, each subsidiary reported that it was competitive in recruiting and retaining workers, thus implying that relevant labor market conditions were addressed in setting wage policies. There were several reasons for the lower average wage levels paid by the Japanese. One is the composition of the workforce. The Japanese subsidiaries were generally newer than the U.S. firms and the workers generally younger, with fewer years on the job. Also, at Sanyo, Murata and Mitsubishi Aircraft, for instance, reasonable numbers of technical (non-managerial) Japanese expatriates are performing on-site technical coordination and maintenance tasks—work that might conceivably be done by more senior, but hourly-paid technicians in a larger U.S. firm. In Japan, larger firms tend to internalize their labor markets. Inter-firm worker mobility is low among these firms in Japan, and company-specific bonuses account for a large portion of total annual employee compensation. We might speculate, sensibly, that subsidiary management, laden as it is with parent-company nationals in the top executive slots, is pressed culturally, and perhaps even organizationally, to keep actual wages low.

FRINGE BENEFITS

That the Japanese were basically labor-market followers regarding wages would suggest a similar behavior regarding fringe benefits—and they were such, but with some interesting exceptions. There were essentially no differences between the American companies and the Japanese subsidiaries on the number of paid holidays per year, vacations, insurance programs (medical, life and dental), and pension programs. Cost-of-living wage-rate adjustments based on inflation formulas (COLAs) were generally not published commitments in non-unionized firms or plants, be they American or Japanese. In the unionized cases, however, only Ampex in the American group (one in nine) had no COLA formula spelled out in the labor contract. Neither Murata nor New England in the Japanese-owned group (two in three) had a COLA clause. This could suggest an enhanced concern by the Japanese for direct control over labor costs.

Ampex, Harley-Davidson, and Harris, all of which were unionized to one degree or another, paid severance benefits if a plant were closed. None of the Japanese had such a policy—whether unionized or not. In this instance, the relative newness of the Japanese subsidiaries could well be the explanation.

A few Japanese subsidiaries installed some minor, innovative fringe benefits. Auburn paid annual cash awards for perfect attendance, length of service, and Christmas. Fujitsu paid a Christmas bonus and was considering purchasing a vacation resort condo for employee use. Mitsubishi gave out Christmas gifts and KOHKOKU wedding and birth gifts. None of the U.S. companies did such things. How Japan-originated are these practices? In Auburn's case, deeply so. The annual cash award programs are deliberate adaptations of parent-company practices to fit the U.S. environment. At Fujitsu, Mitsubishi, and KOHKOKU, the practices were more subsidiary-initiated. At all four subsidiaries, there was heavy involvement by Japanese expatriate management in the decision-making that led to these programs. It would be fair to say that had Japanese expatriates not been involved, the practice never would have been initiated.

TRAINING

Employee training in Japan is typically done in-house or on-the-job (OJT). This was almost exclusively the case in the Japanese subsidiaries too. All the firms reported extensive OJT practices. Four—Auburn, Mt. Pleasant, Murata and Sanyo—also had tuition-reimbursement programs for courses taken outside the company. Only Sanyo reported supervisory and management training programs (in-house). No apprenticeship programs were reported, nor was any union-management cooperation on training.

In contrast, training at the U.S. firms was considerably more varied and extensive. Like the Japanese, there was substantial OJT. All the U.S. firms reported supervisory and management training of one form or another—Harris and National Semiconductor even sponsored in-house MBA programs conducted by nearby universities. All but two of the U.S. firms had tuition-reimbursement programs. Cessna and Harris periodically conducted employee surveys to pinpoint training needs. National Semiconductor achieved a similar, but more directive result by putting each employee through a training needs assessment program. At Quanex and J & L, apprenticeship training programs existed for the development of skilled trades personnel. Both Dow and J & L, with cooperation from their unions, implemented special training programs targeted on productivity improvement.

Cross-training, a practice typical to firms in Japan, was evident at only three of the Japanese subsidiaries—Auburn, Honda, and KOHKOKU. These were the three purposely implementing Japanese management philosophies. Dow and Pennwalt also had cross-training programs to provide for the skill-level diversification required for flexibility in job assignments. Also, at Dow, a union contract provision aimed at improving productivity necessitated cross-training.

On the training subject in general, the evidence supports the conclusion that Japanese subsidiaries are fairly "culture bound" regarding the locus and extent of their training activities—except for cross-training, a practice abandoned in the United States by two-thirds of the Japanese case-study companies. The evidence supports the contention too that training is a much more embracing concept in the U.S. firms than in the Japanese subsidiaries. The U.S. firms do more of it, in more varied forms, for more classes of employees, and, in some cases, with institutional participation by unions. Several foreign firms engaged in cross-training too.

Size differences among the U.S. and Japanese case-study companies may be one factor explaining why the U.S. firms had more developed and extensive training. The cultural dimension, however, provides a rationale not only for what the Japanese subsidiaries were found not to be doing, but also what they were doing. It cannot just be dismissed out of hand.

UNION-MANAGEMENT RELATIONS

Japanese and American industrial relations systems differ substantially. The stereotyped Japanese management philosophy suggests Japanese subsidiaries would prefer not to deal with unions—so that they could construct internal operating systems as similar as possible to those that work so well for them in Japan. This, in turn, suggests research into a variety of behaviors and practices, several of which were investigated in the present case studies. These include plant location decisions, management preferences regarding dealing with unions and recognition and decertification of unions. In addition, productivity improvement programs in unionized subsidiaries, strike experiences, and the role of parent-company management will also be discussed.

Location decisions of both Japanese and other foreign-owned firms (referred to subsequently as "foreign firms") were found not to turn on union-related considerations, but the availability of quality labor at the right price was one of several influences. Table 2 identifies these influences and reports on the incidence of their being mentioned by companies as affecting the plant location decision. None of the Japanese or foreign-owned subsidiaries reported that the potential for union organizing or "right-to-work" legislation influenced location decisions. None of the U.S. companies did either. Moreover, some subsidiaries located where unions have traditionally been strong; others did not. Some located in "right-to-work" states; others did not. Some bought out operations that were unionized; others did not. It is important to note, too, that none of the subsidiaries closed down or relocated plants because of problems with the cost, quality, or attitudes of their American workers or with their unions.

Managements at the majority of the Japanese subsidiaries preferred a non-union environment. They stated they wanted to be free to manage and to innovate at the shop level. While the origin of this preference may in these cases be Japanese, the position is certainly not distinctively Japanese. The majority of the American and foreign firms expressed similar views for similar reasons.

Table 2: The Location Decision
Summary of Case Study Findings

	Frequency of Occurrence (Number of Subsidiaries)	
Topic/Influence Factor	Japanese	Foreign-Owned
Number of Takeover Cases	3	1
Number of Start-Up Cases[a]	7	5
Product Market-Related Factors	2	3
Proximity to Customers	2	3
Resource Market-Related Factors	7	4[b]
Quality of Workforce Available	4	4
Proximity to Suppliers	4	4
Availability of Low-Cost Energy	2	0
Availability of Transportation	1	3
State Government Assistance and Subsidies	1	3
Tax Incentives	1	3
Training Assistance	0	3
State or City Government Promotion Efforts	5	3
"Quality of Life" Considerations	3	0
Potential for Union Organizing	0	0
"Right-to-Work" Legislation	0	0

Notes: [a]Fujitsu America and Fujitsu Microelectronics are considered as two separate cases. Hence, the Japanese-owned cases total ten—seven of which were start-up cases. [b]The interviewee at Badische was unaware of any influences other than product market-related influences, but acknowledged others certainly were relevant. The response group totalled four foreign-owned cases then regarded these other influences.

Union organizing attempts were opposed at Auburn (USW, 1977), Mitsibushi (IAM, 1972, 1975), Honda (UAW, 1980–), KOHKOKU (Teamsters, 1978) and Murata (IUE, 1980, Douglasville, Ga. plant only). This represents five out of nine cases. In three cases, unions were either recognized with no opposition by management (Murata) or pre-dated the Japanese takeover of a U.S. company (Sanyo and New England). The incidence of opposition to union recognition by Japanese subsidiaries is similar to that of the U.S. firms where seven of nine opposed recent union organizing attempts.

The case studies suggest majorities of both the Japanese subsidiaries and the U.S. firms opposed having to deal with unions. The data also suggest, however, that the U.S. firms were much more aggressive in their dealings with unions than were the Japanese subsidiaries. In two (New England and Sanyo) of the three Japanese unionized cases, the union-management relationship was quite stable, although, in both cases, it had not been tested by non-contiguous facilities expansions (as in Murata's union organizing attempts). Only one (Murata) of the Japanese did. Five of the U.S. firms had stated, publicized positions in opposition to having unions. None of the unionized Japanese did. Three of the unionized U.S. firms hired special legal counsel on labor relations. Only one (Murata) of the Japanese did.

Several hypotheses could be presented to help explain why the Japanese were less aggressive towards unions in their union-manage-ment relations than were the U.S. firms. Japanese management is less conflict-oriented than U.S. management. It is typically viewed as less confrontationist. Japanese management is less experienced than U.S. management in dealing with U.S. unions, and perhaps sees greater risks in being conflict-oriented or is less comfortable with its capability to manage aggressively against unions. The Japanese subsidiaries are not as large and diversified as the U.S. firms and may feel they have less power vis-à-vis the unions than the U.S. firms do.

None of the collective labor agreements at the Japanese subsidiaries contained any special provisions to enhance productivity or clauses that were Japanese in origin. Murata, New England, and Sanyo all professed to be content to follow industry standards as adjusted for local labor market conditions (e.g., regarding wages). Within a union-management context, the Japanese subsidiaries were truly not innovators in personnel matters. In contrast, several U.S. firms felt they were managing their union-management relationship with improved productivity resulting. Recall the earlier comments on the production pay incentive systems at J & L, Harley-Davidson, and Quanex that are provided for in union contracts. Ampex reported employees progress through pay ranges, established in its IAM contract, on the basis of merit (performance evalu-ation). Dow's contract with the USW recently provided for a "multi-craftsman" job classification to allow a single worker to perform tasks previously requiring several workers. At J & L, the USW contract called for "labor-management participation teams" at the plants to promote, among other things, efficient and economic operations and to discuss, consider and decide on means to improve the performance of work units.

Do these findings suggest a lack of experience, or perhaps maturity, by the Japanese subsidiaries in dealing creatively with U.S. unions?

What, if anything, might they portend regarding the long-term competitiveness of these companies?

Two of the three unionized Japanese subsidiaries (New England
and Sanyo) had experienced strikes. The issues were economic in both
instances. All eight of the unionized U.S. firms had experienced strikes
in the past decade or so. The key issues were typically economic. The
Japanese and U.S. companies were not really different in terms of strike
experiences. In addition, parent-company management in Japan were
generally non-directive regarding the subsidiary's handling of strike issues and tactics, and during collective bargaining. Japanese expatriates
at the subsidiaries were involved in both collective bargaining and in
resolving strikes in varying degrees. At New England and Murata, they
participated directly. At Sanyo, they remained in the background but
provided advice and approvals when necessary.

Overall, the case studies confirm how difficult it is to accept the
stereotyped Japanese management philosophy as one that does not deal
with U.S. unions. True, most of the subsidiaries do not wish to have a
union relationship. But their location decisions subjugate this preference
to other concerns, as do their entry decisions that include a takeover of
a unionized firm. Also, where a union relationship exists, the Japanese
seem to be able to work with it to their own satisfaction. They appear
to be "environmental takers" in their union-related matters.

CONCLUSIONS ON THE TRANSFER OF
JAPANESE MANAGEMENT PRACTICES

Three Japanese subsidiaries (Auburn, Honda, and KOHKOKU) have
management practices that are unquestionably Japanese in origin. These
are practices that have deliberately been implemented at the instigation,
and with the approval, of top management. They include broad job
classifications, flexibility in work assignments, substantial cross-training,
etc. They exhibit some degree of modification, however, to accommodate
both labor markets and the U.S. environment. For example, wages and
fringe benefits are locally competitive. Compensation systems do not
include the typically Japanese annual bonus scheme. None of these three
subsidiaries are unionized. Each has opposed union organizing attempts.

We could argue that, with but few exceptions, the other six subsidiaries have preferred to acclimate themselves to the U.S. industrial—
relations environment. One, Mt. Pleasant, has opted to abandon direct
management responsibility for operating its subsidiary joint venture by
contracting to have Stauffer Chemical assume operation responsibility.

Another, Fujitsu, contended extremely tight labor markets forced it to behave as if it were a U.S. firm. Yet another, Mitsubishi, felt it wise to follow industry standards on job structures while paying competitive wages and benefits. Murata accepted a union relationship early-on, while New England and Sanyo took over U.S. firms that already had been unionized. None of the three have sought to influence its union relationship in ways that were Japan-originated. In fact, none of the three were at all innovative in this relationship.

PARENT SUBSIDIARY LINKAGES BENEFITTING SUBSIDIARIES AND THEIR INDUSTRIAL RELATIONS

Capital and technology are typically viewed as the two most important parent-company contributions of benefit to workers. This is certainly true in the macroeconomic perspective, but case-study research is microeconomic and firm-specific. Capital transfers were not investigated in the present study. Technology transfers were, however. They were found to be related more to competitive strategies and are discussed more fully later. Other, more detailed linkages are discussed here as they benefitted U.S. workers by making them more productive and their jobs more secure.

PRODUCTIVITY COMPARISONS INVOLVING U.S. WORKERS

Six of the nine Japanese subsidiaries maintained productivity comparisons between their operations and those of the parent organization. KOHKOKU, Mitsubishi, and New England did so to provide improvement targets. Sanyo and Mt. Pleasant did it for this reason, but also to identify distinct training needs. Comparisons were equipment and/or process stage specific. Murata maintained detailed data on equipment output and compared them with data generated via the use of the same type equipment at parent-company plants outside the United States. At one point the subsidiary's output was so deficient that Japanese personnel responsible for managing the operation of the equipment at a plant in Asia were temporarily assigned to the U.S. subsidiary in order to increase productivity. They eventually were successful.

Being able to compare U.S. operations with similar ones elsewhere allows a Japanese subsidiary to be more productive than otherwise, or perhaps sooner than otherwise. The case studies support such a conclusion.

INTERNATIONAL TRADE

American labor's stake in international trade, within the context of the present study, stems from several considerations. These range from "justifying" the subsidiary plant investment, to enhancing subsidiary competitiveness, to facilitating workforce development, and to ensuring employment stability.

Five of the Japanese firms exported to the United States to develop a market presence sufficient to justify direct investment. These were Fujitsu (Microelectronics), Honda, KOHKOKU, Mitsubishi, and Murata. Export success was one point on a continuum that led eventually to a U.S. plant and jobs for American workers.

At six of the Japanese subsidiaries, products and/or components were imported from the parent company. The reasons varied. Fujitsu, Honda, KOHKOKU, Murata and Sanyo imported products complimentary to those produced in the United States in order to expand product lines and to allow for important system-wide efficiencies in marketing, distribution, and general administration. This not only benefitted each subsidiary's own production cost effectiveness but could lead to expanded domestic production as the markets for these products themselves were developed.

Honda and Sanyo noted that they imported key components from Japan to maintain stringent quality control, while developing workforce competencies eventually capable of justifying locating production of such components at the subsidiary. Sanyo originally imported chassis frames and yokes. Both are now manufactuted at the subsidiary. Honda imported engines. Subsequent to this study, engine production was transferred to the subsidiary. Honda also transferred production of the smaller "Elsinor" model motorcycle to its U.S. subsidiary on a temporary basis to train U.S. workers to produce a product simpler than the heavy-duty, more complex models they would eventually produce. International trade, in these instances, facilitated workforce development while sustaining product quality and, ostensibly, sales.

Fujitsu, Murata, KOHKOKU, and Sanyo imported products similar to those made in the United States in order to smooth production at the subsidiary. Each noted imports occurred (or would occur) during peak demand periods—thus implying that the subsidiary production base would not be expanded until market size stabilized at a higher sales plateau. For example, Murata continues to import ceramic capacitors because its sales growth has been too rapid for it to reach its original goal of 100 percent U.S.-based production. Looking at the other side of the coin, not one Japanese subsidiary reported that it exported, or would export, in the face of a decline in the demand for U.S.-based production. The smoothing of production is only on the import, market-growth side.

In general, the Japanese subsidiaries were not big exporters. Several (e.g., Honda, Auburn, and Sanyo) exported to Canada on a regular basis. Mt. Pleasant sold all its output to its parent company while awaiting U.S. Goverment approval of its product for sale domestically. Only Mitsubishi produced for global markets on a regular basis. It appears subsidiary growth will not be related to export growth. Workers' employment growth and stability will relate to domestic sales in most cases.

PERSONNEL TRANSFERS

Substantial numbers of parent-company technical specialists have been assigned to the Japanese subsidiaries to facilitate technology transfers, to train U.S. workers, and to monitor production systems. This has been true in every case. In some, however, the assignments have become permanent (even though specific personnel on assignment have rotated). In addition, both Honda and Mt. Pleasant reported sending workers to Japan for training purposes.

CONCLUSIONS REGARDING PARENT-SUBSIDIARY LINKAGES

The case studies evidenced substantial and varied ways in which positive synergies can be implemented to enhance subsidiary operations in ways beneficial to American labor. Activities of relevance here include prior market development via exports to justify local production, contunued importation of complimentary products, etc. to enhance domestic competitivenesss, temporary importation of key components to support workforce development while maintaining product quality and the market franchise, production allocation and productivity comparisons on an international basis to facilitate training, importing for production and employment smoothing purposes, and the transfer of personnel internationally for training and development purposes.

In one way or another, all nine Japanese subsidiaries were identified with these activities—contrary to the Japanese management practices transfer inquiry, which found only three firms involved. It is interesting to note, too, that substantial trade creation occurs following direct investment—in ways, and for reasons, different from before. These findings suggest that Kojima's earlier referenced conclusions are too static at best.

The dynamics of international industrial development can result even in expanded trade following direct investment that results from trade barriers. The ultimate answer is not so readily obtainable as Kojima suggests, and it may involve trade comparisons across simultaneously expanding and contracting industries or industry sectors.

COMPETITIVE STRATEGIES OF THE JAPANESE SUBSIDIARIES

Analysis of the competitive strategies of the Japanese firms leads to several important conclusions. It answers why these firms are in the United States, how they are able to compete, and the extent to which they want, or need to rely on, Japanese management practices.

Mitsubishi excepted, the Japanese subsidiaries operating in the United States are basically "market seekers." They are outlets for products developed by the parent. There was no subsidiary-to-parent flow of product technology. Some subsidiaries reported on market trends, but product definition and development were the parent's task. Process technology development was also most often accomplished solely by the parent.

By and large, the products, or product cores, were mature. The Japanese competed then on the basis of quality and, perhaps surprisingly, not on price. To a firm, each Japanese subsidiary reported its product prices were market-based but at the higher end of the price range because of product quality. This contrasted with the U.S. firms, which generally reported a preference for abandoning mature products in favor of innovating and bringing new products to a market over which there was some price control. Figure 1 presents a representation of the Japanese and U.S. firms' preferred operating zones.

The curves in Figure 1 are not unlike those of the familiar product-life-cycle. As time goes by, products mature as markets become more competitive and firms lose control over product price. Process technology improvements, for whatever the reason, are more difficult to define and implement, or perhaps even to justify (e.g., exit barriers may be relevant here). Costs of production continue to expand, however. This is presented in Figure 1, where the sales and costs curves are shown as nearly converging. As this convergence appears, American firms prefer to abandon the product, to innovate by bringing new products to market, and to move back to the left side of Figure 1. Not so the Japanese subsidiaries!

Through their quality-based franchises and premium-pricing strategies, the Japanese are able to expand sales revenues above what

Figure 1:
Operating Preference Zones

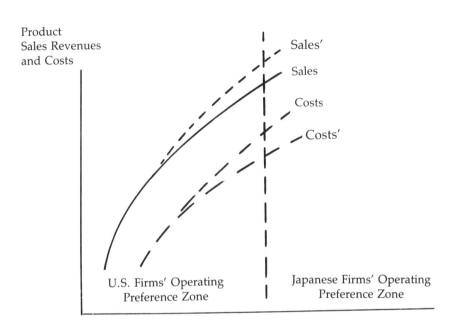

Time (After Product Introduction)

would otherwise occur. By controlling or lowering costs via process technology improvements, and, as the current research also suggests, by keeping labor input costs low, the Japanese are able to lower the product costs curve at the mature end. These actions are represented in Figure 1 as the Sales' and Costs' curves respectively. Note how the difference between these two curves, which is the operating profit margin, is superior to that experienced by the American firms.

One interesting sidelight here is that the behaviors depicted in Figure 1 put a rational perspective around the often-heard complaint that U.S. firms are too short-term oriented, while the Japanese take, and prosper with, the longer term commitment. Both are rational behaviors! The U.S. firms prefer innovative, growth markets; the Japanese, mature markets. The former's strategy is inherently more risk-laden; short-term success is a necessary objective. The latter's is more dependent on stable markets and can justify a longer-term payout. To compare Japanese "winners" with American "losers" means both firms are competing in the mature ends of their product markets—and the Americans face costly exit or adjustment barriers.

For the Japanese subsidiaries, the key to success is being the quality producer and the low-cost producer. They accomplish this via their technology strategies. If they can accomplish both via product or process control, which results in their being different, or better than the competition, they do it. If not, or as added insurance, they then seek to implement a "management-centered" strategy dependent upon the successful transfer of Japanese management practices. But this is a riskier strategy and is to be avoided if at all possible. The case studies suggest that where Japanese subsidiaries were able to secure a competitive presence via product or process-centered strategies, they did so. The management-centered strategy was more risk-laden than the others.[3] Note that the three firms that sought to transfer Japanese management practices to their U.S. subsidiaries were dealing with mature products—steel bar (Auburn), PVC sheets (KOHKOKU), and motorcycles (Honda). Did they have any better competitive alternatives?

CONCLUSIONS

What, if anything, does this all mean for American labor and for Japanese MNEs? For American labor, it's a mixed bag. Jobs are important. The quality of those jobs in terms of income-growth prospects appears questionable. How many of the better slots will be filled with Japanese expatriates? Will the Japanese subsidiaries be only production-oriented? Will improved operating margins be eroded eventually? If so, what happens then?

Japanese subsidiaries that rely on management-centered strategies do not want unions. What happens if they are unionized? Can the union be flexible enough to accommodate the competitive needs of the subsidiaries? These questions are all too real in these cases.

For the Japanese companies, the case studies demonstrate the tremendous absorption capacity of American labor—including the union movement. The Japanese subsidiaries have a challenge in front of them: If they want to be competitive over a sustained period, they will need to become comfortable with either working with, or managing, their union relationship for sustaining enhanced productivity. The data suggest Japanese management prefers to avoid this challenge and the American firms are much more comfortable with it. It may be easier than the Japanese think!

NOTES

1. Kiyoshi Kojima, *Direct Foreign Investment: A Japanese Model of Multinational Business Operations* (New York: Praeger Publishers, Inc., 1978), especially pp. 83–96.
2. The Japan Institute of Labor, "Overseas Investment and Its Impact on Domestic Employment," May 1981 (mimeographed).
3. Duane Kujawa, "Technology Strategy and Industrial Relations: Case Studies of Japanese Multinationals in the United States," *Journal of International Business Studies*, Vol. XIV, No. 3 (Winter 1983), pp. 9–22.

6
Japan's "Secret" Weapon
John A. Cicco, Jr.
and Richard D. Snyder

The success of Japanese business has intrigued managers. The authors offer here one essential ingredient in the armory of Japanese management techniques.

MURRAYSVILLE, PA—With American corporations' almost sycophantic admiration of Japanese business techniques, it is interesting that what may well be the most subtle, but most powerful, weapon in Japan's management arsenal has gone largely unnoticed.

It's so basic and simple, it can't be copyrighted or patented. And it's so uncomplicated that consultants can't make money teaching it. Yet it seduces our businessmen and trade negotiators. This beautifully plain—but critically important—secret is nothing more than simple courtesy. Not the plastic politeness retailers too often show customers in America. Not the pandering attitude that service types too often show clients. And certainly not the perfunctory "have a nice d..." that phone operators squeeze into rushed responses to callers.

In Japan, lack of courtesy is the one unforgivable sin—it can cause almost immediate banishment from the Garden of Lifetime Employment. Deeply ingrained courtesy is not limited to sales clerks, waitresses and taxi drivers. Even the most senior executive, phoning an associate, will patiently spend several minutes asking how he is, how the family is or how his back feels, before dealing with whatever business reason may have prompted the call—regardless of its seeming urgency. As the Japanese explain it, whatever the problem may be, it's the relationship with the other person that will be the basis of its solution. So the relationship, not the problem, deserves primary attention.

By contrast, perhaps the greatest weakness in American organizations' structure and their dealings with customers and constituencies is nothing more than a lack of simple courtesy. We have all dealt with companies and bureaucracies that, after going to great efforts to get us to use their products or services, give us an obnoxious sales clerk, waitress or someone else who leaves us feeling we have somehow intruded on their day. This discourtesy not only threatens the intended transaction so carefully encouraged by marketing and public-affairs personnel but also it discourages future transactions.

The problem runs far deeper than the obvious "get good people to deal with the public." It rests basically with an aloof managerial class that avoids personal contact except under the most controlled conditions. It is a class well-schooled in good manners but woefully illiterate in basic civility. As Inazo Nitobe, in "Bushido: The Soul of Japan," differentiates: "Politeness is a poor virture if it is actuated only by a fear of offending good taste, whereas it should be the outward manifestation of a sympathetic regard for the feelings of others."

Our managerial training grounds have failed miserably to instill the necessary "sympathetic regard for the feelings of others." As in the court of Louis XIV, while there is constant dwelling on proper etiquette and manners, the lack of coutesy spawns corrosive resentment and hostility.

So our influential institutions install elaborate communications systems to improve personal contact—only to have them stopped up by executives who have learned never to return calls too quickly. They develop expensive advertising programs only to have them break down because an impatient $4-an-hour sales clerk is rude. And they schedule tedious behavior-modification seminars that teach clever manipulation rather than the value of simple respect.

Fortunately, our lack of courtesy does not arise from some natural flaw in the American personality. We are normally a very friendly people. Rather, the problem seems to derive from the large size of institutions and the prescribed technocratic management persona of busy importance that requires aloof inaccessibility.

There is hope, however. Not too long ago, there was a brief flush of healthy courtesy among even the most pompous of organizations. As firms floundered during the last recession, organizational pretense broke down and basic cameraderie emerged. But as crises pass and old habits slowly return, an important economics lesson may be too quickly forgotten: discourtesy is not only not very nice, it is an intolerably inefficient luxury that no business nor society can long afford.

7
Management Trends
in Europe
Ivor Kenny

Considerable change has taken place in Europe since the end of World War II,
particularly in the last decade. In this article, the author, who is the Chancellor
of the International Academy of Management, provides a philosophical yet realis-
tic discussion of this transition and of the current status of business in Europe,
as well as a management perspective for the future.

THE ERA OF LOW GROWTH

Western Europe is still suffering from the fact that the post-war era
was, in the literal sense of that word, an extraordinary time. In no other
period of history was there such rapid economic growth or such an
expansion in world trade—the result of a happy combination of relative
political stability, economic integration, technological innovation, and
cheap energy. In the Western democracies, the standard of living doubled. There was relatively full employment. There was wide access to
secondary and higher education. There was social security from the
cradle to the grave. At the same time, there was an enormous expansion
in communications and travel. The world became a global village.

With affluence and improved communications came higher expectations. Full employment, social security and ever-higher wages became
the norm. People then began to look for improvements in the quality
of life—better conditions of work, a cleaner, less polluted, environment,
higher quality products and services, greater involvement in the decisions affecting their lives, more satisfaction on the job, more leisure and
holidays.

This era of prosperity and growth came to an end for the Western

Reprinted from *Management Japan*, Vol. 18, No. 2, 1985, published by the
International Management Association of Japan, Inc.

democracies in the early Seventies. Some countries, including my own, found this very hard to accept—even to the point of denial. For example, continuous economic growth had concealed the fact that governments were taking an increasing share of gross national product. When the growth stopped and government spending went on, it could be financed in only two ways: by increased taxation or increased borrowing, both leading to an oppressive growth of the state and to a crowding out of the enterprise sector. This growth in the state was, of course, spread unevenly throughout Western Europe. Some countries, such as Germany, with its justifiable paranoia about inflation (defined as the destruction of wealth by governments), were more disciplined than others. Still the same general trend in the growth of the state was discernible throughout Western Europe.

The characteristics of the new era of low growth are:

• Higher energy prices—a point that hardly needs to be made in Japan, where there is absolute dependence on imports. Notwithstanding present marginal reductions, the multiple increases in oil prices had very significant effects on energy and hydrocarbon-based industries.
• Lower economic growth—resulting in stagnation in world markets, accompanied by intense competition, particularly from Japan and from the newly industrialized countries. Both productivity and profitablity in OECD countries declined.
• The decline of basic industries, such as steel, textiles and shipbuilding, in which Western Europe is no longer competitive with the Third World.
• Protectionism—in the form of subsidies to domestic producers, anti-dumping duties, voluntary restrictions on exports, import quotas and various administrative and non-fiscal barriers, again something about which I do not have to remind a Japanese audience.
• Higher levels of inflation—the fact that inflation has been reduced should not blind us to its malign effects. It resulted from higher energy prices, higher (unearned) wages, higher taxation and the inability to pay for them through higher production and a greater share of international markets.
• Higher levels of unemployment—now the highest ever, caused by a rising demand from an increasing number of young people and working women, accompanied by a fall in the number of jobs available; this, in turn, caused by a decline of traditional industries and the

tendency to replace labor with capital equipment. Not only are there fewer jobs, but there is a wide gap between the quality of the jobs expected by a more highly educated workforce and the de-skilled, repetitive jobs being offered. Furthermore, there are still shortages of workers with the right skills.

With this emerging gap between the supply and demand for jobs, there is a growing disillusionment, particularly, among young people.

BIG BUSINESS

In the last thirty years, the structure of business has grown both in size and complexity. Businessess have expanded through internal growth and by merger and acquisition. They have diversified into related and unrelated products and markets. They have expanded internationally. The original owners have widened their shareholdings and brought in professional managers. A discussion of the role of business in modern society has to include businesses which are very large—even oligopolistic—which are multi-product and international in scope, which have thousands of individual shareholders and a smaller number of powerful institutional shareholders, and which are run by professional managers and technologists.

Of particular concern is the concentration of power in a few very large enterprises. This is a general trend in most industrialized countries, but large firms are particularly dominant in the United States, Britain and the Benelux countries. Other developed nations, such as this country, Italy, West Germany, Denmark and Ireland have managed to maintain a larger, thriving small business sector.

Merger and rationalization are seen as a normal development in a mature market, when growth has slowed down and profitability is largely a function of economies of scale in both manufacture and distribution. This is to be expected when competitors see barriers to entry, such as access to technology or finance, the need for a substantial investment in research and development, and in production facilities or marketing. Indeed, mergers appear vital to survival when producers are competing in regional, or even global, markets—as is the case with aircraft, cars, electronics, telecommunications and pharmaceuticals. In certain instances, however, e.g., the news media, this increasing concentration is of special concern because of their opinion-forming power.

The rise of multinational conglomerates with the power to distribute films, television programs, journal and newspaper articles, has given rise to the fear that a "new information order" is being created on a global scale.

A concern to businessmen is that officials in governments and international agencies still tend to discuss Competition Policy in terms of monopoly or oligopoly in a national or domestic market when many markets have become international.

The modern multinational multi-business corporation may have a budget similar to the government of a medium-sized state. The size and diversity of its resources are intimidating.

The role of big companies in influencing foreign policy and changing global relationships has been given attention in recent years because of the exhaustive investigation by the Multinational Subcommittee of the U.S. Foreign Relations Committee under Senator Church, and other similar hearings held in the early Seventies.

The detailed testimony, the subpoenaed memos, secret agreements and cable traffic, that emerged from these hearings provided the public with detailed information on the activities of management in ITT, Lockheed and some of the major oil companies.

In the same period, academic investigations such as the Harvard Project on Multinationals also drew attention to the growing power of international business. Responding to these promptings, national governments and international agencies have attempted to put legal constraints on the activities of international businesses and to improve codes of conduct.

A strong criticism of the modern corporation is that professional managers have now taken over from owners. They cannot be held accountable by the thousands of individual shareholders.

The contention is that the managers of mature corporations are primarily concerned with growth and security. It is only by growth that they can improve their personal position. The security of the corporation is the only way to enhance their own security.

Because of public concern about the increasing power of management in large corporations, steps have been taken by European governments, and by individual companies, to reform, boards of directors, and to ensure that operating managers are held accountable for their actions.

One solution has been sought in the two-tier board, i.e., an executive board which is responsible for the day-to-day running of the company and a supervisory board which determines or approves corporate policy, holds the executives accountable, and has certain ultimate powers, e.g., to appoint and dismiss the chief executive and to approve or veto major capital investments.

The two-tier structure has the advantage of separating the political debate from executive decision-making. The supervisory board provides a forum in which conflicts of interest between the representatives of various interested parties may be reconciled.

However, the distribution of power among the various stakeholders is still in the process of being worked out.

The growth of industry over the post-war period has been accompanied in Western Europe by demands for employee participation. In a broad sense the term is used to cover all the means employees and their representatives use in influencing the decision-making process of enterprise.

Works councils are the most pervasive form of employee participation. They are established by law in many EEC countries.

The powers of the Works Council usually include the right to consultation on all decisions affecting staff, the right to inspect the company's financial data, and the right to veto certain appointments e.g., the Personnel Director.

Since the war, there has also been a growth in trade union membership, first in the skilled crafts, then among unskilled workers, and more recently among clerical and managerial staff. There is a view in the UK that trade union power has "peaked" and is now on the decline. Trade unions are strong during periods of high employment. They are not so strong during periods of high unemployment. It would be premature to say whether their power is growing or declining.

THE RISE OF INTEREST GROUPS

There has been a growth in the activities of interest groups to protect rights or to fight for a particular cause.

The Consumer Protection movement has followed a classic pattern:

- The development of voluntary associations to provide comparative testing and product information and to act as political pressure groups;
- government legislation on health and safety, product information and fair trading with national and local regulatory agencies to follow up legislation through legal acts, codes of conduct and consumer advice;
- "an attempt to involve the consumer in decisions which affect him" nationally, e.g., via a National Consumer Council and in the business enterprise by seeking representation on the Board of Directors and through Consumer Councils.

We are now in the early stages of the Product Liability movement which aims to make producers strictly liable for damage caused by a defective product or service. The European Commission has produced a preliminary program. The German Pharmaceutical Act (1976) and the French Civil Code already make manufacturers strictly liable for defects in their products.

Environmental protection groups have influenced all OECD governments to enact legislation concerned with air and water pollution, dumping of wastes, etc. The governments of the United States, Japan, Sweden, Britain, West Germany, France and the Netherlands lead the way.

In many cases the results have been dramatic. In Britain, for instance, the Clean Air Acts have completely eliminated the notorious London fog and the Thames, which had no fish in 1957, now supports over a hundred species.

The movement seeking equal opportunity and equal pay for women has also developed world-wide.

The main effect on labor markets is that more women have re-entered the work force after having children. However, there are wide variations between different parts of Europe. In Denmark and Britain, at the age of 40, about 70 percent of women are working, but in the Netherlands and Ireland, in the same age group, only about 20 percent are working.

Women, many of them working part-time, will soon account for about a half of the European work-force. Yet unemployment laws and practices are still largely designed around the concept of the full-time male employee.

The post-war period has seen the migration of over ten million foreign workers into Western Europe from Southern Europe, from Africa and Asia. One result of the dissolution of the colonial empires was the immigration of large numbers of former colonial citizens, particularly into the "mother countries" of Britain, France and Portugal.

In addition, large numbers of "guest workers" migrated from southern to northern Europe and many stayed. By 1970, Western Europe had gained 10 million and Southern Europe had lost 7 million by migration.

THE GROWTH OF GOVERNMENT

The growth of government activity during the twentieth century has been a continuous process in all Western democracies. Government activity is measured by the size of budget, the number of public servants and the volume of legislation. Democratically-elected governments have responded to their voters' demands for more public services, more social benefits and more regulation.

Government activity is reflected in taxes. In Western Europe, income tax and social security (including the employers' contribution) now account for around half, and in the case of Sweden three-quarters, of an employee's salary. In Sweden, between 1971 and 1978, total taxes as a percentage of Gross Domestic Product rose by a fifth and they now represent 52.9 percent of Gross Domestic Product. In my own country, it has risen in recent years to almost two-thirds, a level at which it stubbornly stays.

The post-war period saw a remarkable development of free trade arrangements—not just in the EEC but internationally. This free trade régime was based on three principal agreements:

- The Bretton-Woods Agreement (1944)
- The General Agreement on Tariffs and Trade (1948)
- The European Economic Community (1957)

During the Seventies the free trade movement suffered some setbacks. The main pillars of the Free Trade structure are still intact but moves towards economic nationalism still have some strength.

Since the Second World War most West European government have been committed to the "mixed economy," i.e., an economy which has both publicly-owned and privately-owned enterprises.

Among the reasons for the growth of public ownership in industry are:

- a desire of government to have control over key industries which represent "the commanding heights of the economy," and the rise of a socialist dogma to this effect;
- the belief that certain firms are so heavily dependent on government finance that they ought to be under government control; and
- concern that certain sectors will survive in international competition only with government support.

The public sector played an important role in providing for the survival of European industries at a time when tariff barriers were being eliminated or reduced and European industry was not yet strong enough to match the superior performance of American-based multinationals which had come through the war unscathed.

A wide range of products and services is now provided by the public sector in Western Europe. These activities usually include: post and telecommunications, energy, transportation, export finance, and banking and, increasingly, basic industries such as steel, shipbuilding and even parts of the motor industry. In Italy, the public sector is particularly extensive, including both electrical and mining industries, as well as heavy mechanical engineering and food processing. A number of problems has arisen with the development of public enterprise:

- political interference has tended to hamper management in developing an economically efficient operation, particularly in trying to take a longterm view.
- statutory limitations have prevented businesses from diversifying into new technologies and from competing for international markets.
- government financing has enabled powerful trade unions to push up their wages in the knowledge that the business was not likely to go bankrupt.
- their monopoly status has inhibited the development of products and services that meet the real and changing needs of consumers.
- governments have failed to support profitable public enterprises with investment funds for developing new technology.

On the other hand, public enterprise has ensured:

- national control of essential services;
- the survival of public services which might otherwise have failed to obtain finance on the free market; and
- the provision of at least minimal services to communities which are remote and inaccessible.

A consistent development in West European countries has been the tendency for governments to intervene more directly in industry.

First, in France, under the Third Plan, and subsequently in Great Britain, Holland, Germany and Italy, governments sought to develop an industrial policy. In particular, they tried to re-structure their major industries by arranging for the establishment of a quasi-monopoly to act as a "national champion" in competing for markets at home and overseas. Attempts were made to create large national companies in each significant industry, e.g., in computers, aluminium, motor cars, shipbuilding and aircraft production.

The Seventies also saw attempts by government to control inflation by establishing Prices and Incomes Policies. This frequently involved negotiation with employers and unions, and promoted a further move towards "corporatism," i.e., the arrangement of bargains between the representatives of the manpower groups—the governnment, the employers and the trade unions.

European governments have also been tempted to intervene to promote the introduction of new technologies, such as aerospace, nuclear power, telecommunications and computers and to support declining businesses, e.g., steel, shipbuilding, textiles and automobiles.

For international business, political risks are increasing and host governments are becoming more demanding. The United Nations Committee on Multinational Corporations is recommending substantial extensions in government regulation, including free access to patents, fuller disclosure of financial information and tighter controls on new product introduction. International businesses are having difficulties imposing central coordination and control through corporate headquarters, regional headquarters and world-wide product divisions. To quote a Conference Board report:

"In a world of nations and nationalism, many business leaders affirm that the global economy is a myth, and efforts to organise at the global level which do not pay sufficient attention to the demands of individual nationals are likely to hinder, not help, the corporation in the longer run. Where national logics clash with the logic of global industrial enterprise, it is predictable that the latter, not the former, will have to give way."

THE CHALLENGE TO MANAGEMENT

The developments that I have outlined have had a cumulative impact on top management. People demand their rights:

• to full employment
• to job satisfaction
• to real wage increases
• to better job opportunities for women and ethnic minorities
• to better public services, better schools, improved medical facilities, clean and efficient public transport systems, etc.

In practice, such "rights" have to be earned by the individual. Or, someone else must earn the benefits for them in a world where resources are scarce and competition is intense.

Meanwhile, the motors of economic growth—the expansion in world trade, the rate of capital investment, the increase in consumption, the rise in government spending—have all slowed down.

Thus, a major challenge to both business and government is to help to change expectations, to convince people that their expectations for more jobs, higher wages , better public services, all at the same time—are unrealistic. The number of jobs in large companies is likely to go down, not up. The money available for government spending is likely to be reduced, not increased.

But an even more fundamental challenge lies in the redefinition of the role of business enterprises in present-day Western societies. The foundations of Western capitalism were laid at the end of the eighteenth century in the American Revolution, the French Revolution and the British Industrial Revolution. It is from this time that we have inherited our ideas about democracy, the role of the state and the free market system. These ideas have served us well. They are embodied in our laws and in our institutions.

But they are now badly in need of up-dating. They must take account of the emergence of power groups never envisaged by the early reformers—giant international businesses, large and powerful unions, huge government bureaucracies, and pressure groups able to work through the mass media. If business enterprises are to survive these changes, businessmen must understand, and play a leading role in, the social and political debate. If Western democracies are to prosper in the final decades of the twentieth century, the role of business in society needs to be re-thought to provide a vision of the future which people can be proud to work for.

The alternative, as the complex developments in this brief overview show, is increasing political and economic instability and an inability to meet the needs of an increasingly articulate and expectant population. Business is only one participant in the process, but it is a critical one.

CONCLUSION

I have set as an objective for the Academy that it should make its contribution to breaking down the social, political, economic and, above all, cultural barriers that so divide our world—barriers that, at worst, lead to so much bloodshed and human misery; at best, lead to so much wasted effort. I believe the old colonist-type manager is a dying breed, the man who moved into a strange country and said, "We shall now do things my way." He is a dying breed simply because his ways no longer work. Hand in hand with the internationalization of business is an increasing sensitivity to national cultures with their histories, traditions and values. Hand in hand with our duty as business managers continuously to innovate, to increase efficiency and eliminate waste, is, I hope a growing realization that we have no right to do violence to the deeply held beliefs of the people for whom we bear some responsibility.

At the time of the Industrial Revolution in Britain, workers were called "hands." Now at least there is some respect for the fact that attached to those hands is a mind, a spirit, a unique identity.

Management has been defined as a search for excellence—as have many other human endeavors. Management is part art, part science. It is also part confusion, blundering and self-correction. But it is, above all, practice. Practice is a continuous, a never-ending process. I would describe management at its best as a search for truth, a continuous striving to do what is right. But then only a man who has himself gone in search of truth knows how deceptive is the blaze of evidence with which a proposition may suddenly dazzle his eyes. The light soon fails and the hunt is on again.

In every country, at every time, it happens that the handling of public affairs gets entrusted to a class that stands in physical need of certitudes and takes dubious truths to its bosom with an almost religious fanaticism.

Our freedom lies in the knowledge that there are very few certitudes.

Chapter Three:
International Finance and Banking

A COMPANY OPERATING domestically is not exposed to as many different risks as are encountered by a multinational firm. One such risk is currency appreciation or depreciation. At a more serious level, the risk of a particular currency becoming non-convertible is something with which multinationals must contend.

It is difficult to predict either appreciation or devaluation of a currency. Correct guesses can lead to enormous profits for many multinationals, and an incorrect assessment can result in severe losses. During the last decade, the major shift from fixed to floating exchange rates has revolutionized the international finance function.

Financing, i.e., the sources of funds, is another major variable with which to contend. Complex equity markets world-wide, as well as the enormous Euro-dollar and Euro-bond markets world-wide, are significant variables within the financing function. Given the size and efficiency of these markets, multinationals must pay special attention to the lowest-cost capital markets and their salient characteristics.

Within the context of international finance, international banking plays an indispensable role. The growth and influence of large multinational banks cannot be understated. They provide very large amounts of capital and also play an important role in the financing of trade. It is impossible to conceive of export/import trade without letters of credit and drafts.

International monetary reform, OPEC's influence on past and future international financial structure, and external currency banking have made financing a complex function. Debt crises in many developing and newly industrialized countries have made the financial environment even more strained and complicated. These external factors have a profound impact upon the ability of a multinational company's ability to raise funds and affect its cost of capital. As such, the trend toward international project financing is becoming increasingly important.

8
Global Challenge
to Corporate Treasuries

William D. Turner and Stephen K. Green

The financial planning function in MNCs, already complex, has become even more so in an era of trade interdependence and government involvement in economic affairs. The role of the corporate treasury can be adjusted to enable the MNC to more effectively cope with such complexities. A mix of treasury centralization and integration with operations, and treasury involvement in corporate planning and management, will lead to more realistic operating objectives and standards within the context of the international financial environment.

FEW LARGE COMPANIES today can afford to disregard the growing importance of overseas markets as a source of corporate growth. During the 1970s alone, exports as a proportion of gross national product in the OECD (Organization for Economic Cooperation and Development) nations rose by better than half, and in the United States—historically less trade-oriented than the nations of Europe—they nearly doubled, from 5.5 percent to 9 percent of GNP. And the rapid economic growth of Third World nations compared to that of the major industrialized nations where most of the world's multinational corporations (MNCs) are based reinforces the message: for more and more of today's major corporations, the best prospects for growth lie overseas.

In a world of high inflation, increasingly interdependent trade flows, and growing government involvement in economic affairs, this means a quantum jump in the complexity of the financial management function, and specifically in the role of the corporate treasury. The volatility of exchange rates, even after adjustment for the effects of different rates of inflation (Exhibit I), has added a further dimension of uncertainty to the treasurer's task. Yet despite the deep involvement of corporate control-

Reprinted, with permission, from *The McKinsey Quarterly*, Spring 1982. This article is adapted by special permission from the July 1981 issue of *Euromoney*. Copyright © 1981 by Euromoney Publications Ltd.

Exhibit I: Inflation-adjusted Currency Changes vs. U.S. Dollar*

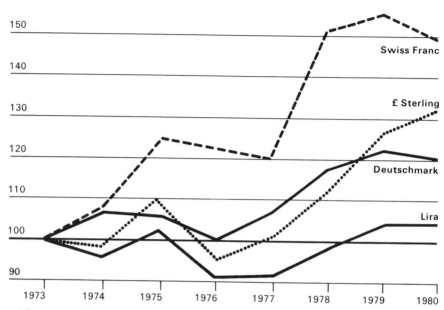

* Percentage increase in exchange rate against the dollar minus the excess of the U.S. inflation rate over the inflation rate in the country concerned.

SOURCE: IMF; McKinsey analysis.

lers in budgeting and business analysis—a consequence of their profit planning responsibilities—the role of the corporate treasury in many multinational corporations is still limited primarily to fund raising, tax planning, and cash and currency exposure management. Apart from capital investment appraisal, few corporate treasurers have much influence on substantive business planning.

Quite clearly, this has got to change. The complex international business environment of the 1980s demands close integration of international treasury management with corporate-wide planning and business management, and this cannot come about without some centralization of treasury functions.

PROBLEMS OF POSITIONING

The disadvantages of a decentralized treasury are well known. Without adequate central treasury control and coordination, local managements will lack guidance on overall corporate financial objectives and constraints. For instance, a subsidiary in one country may be placing surplus cash on the market, while another is raising short-term working capital that could be obtained more cheaply from within the corporation. Local financial managers may not have the expertise or required over-view to maximize the return on their surplus cash: cash balances that might easily have been placed on the money market for short periods may be left in demand deposit or low interest-bearing bank accounts or be inappropriately invested in long-term, fixed-rate securities.

Without strong coordination from the center, moreover, the inde-pendent actions of local financial managers may lead to excessive funds transfer and hedging costs. A strong, centralized treasury can ensure efficient funds mobilization and transfer across the corporation and limit hedging to net currency exposure.

Responding to these considerations, many MNCs have thought to resolve the whole problem at a stroke by centralizing their treasury functions. In doing so, they have usually improved the quality of finan-cial decision making. Just as often, however, they have stumbled into serious problems. In many companies the treasury remains isolated both from the business planning process and from line management. Typi-cally, the central corporate controller has strong links with the local subsidiary manager through the budgeting process. But the treasury may have few or no direct links with local operating units, dealing largely with the corporate controller and top corporate management on financial policy.

Such isolation can have two adverse consequences, as Exhibit II shows. On the one hand, subjects dealt with by the treasury may be considered separate from—and less important than—the company's day-to-day line operating decisions, and may be considered only as a final part of the budgeting process. Operations-related objectives, such as inventory management and investment, will be geared primarily to achieving operating unit profit objectives and cash and asset manage-ment will suffer. On the other hand, the corporate treasury may wield a great deal of power at the center, but be uninformed about the operating and marketing needs in overseas locations. As a result, major business-direction and day-to-day control decisions may be based on inappro-priate, inflexible financial mandates. Two fictionalized case examples illustrate these contrasting pitfalls.

CASE EXAMPLE 1

This example is of a treasury function so highly centralized that foreign operating units have no responsibility at all for working capital management. Two part depots in different countries were working to performance criteria relating to the proportion of orders that could be filled from stock, and to the overall inventory turnover. Inevitably, controlling parts stocks against such nonfinancial performance criteria resulted in each depot carrying excess inventory.

In theory, performance criteria of this kind should have enabled the depots to minimize working capital requirements. In practice, however, such criteria would have had to be very complex. The absence of a functional relationship or shared responsibility between the central treasury and the parts depots, together with no depot responsibility for minimizing the interest costs associated with financing excess inventory, resulted in no incentive for the depots to consider the tradeoff between their performance on delivering ex-stock and the level of inventory for any particular item.

CASE EXAMPLE 2

The second example demonstrates how the absence of a close relationship or shared responsibility between the corporate treasury and local

Exhibit II: Adverse Consequences of Treasury Isolation

Central finance function   **Local operating management**

| Treasury | Controller | | Marketing | Distribution | Production | Purchasing |

Profit plan targets

| | | Sales plan | Delivery ex stock targets | Volume productivity targets, capital investment | Sourcing strategy |

Profit plan and budget

Financial asset management

| | | Receivables costs | Working capital costs of inventory | Working capital costs, capital investments funding sources | Working capital costs of stockholding |

Financial asset management implications

Primary focus of business planning process

☐ Control bias: cash and asset management suffer

▦ Treasury bias: local operating and marketing needs are overlooked operating management can be detrimental to local business perform-ance. In the wake of the OPEC oil price rises in 1973, one multinational company decided that the deteriorating economy of a Third World coun-try in which an important subsidiary operated was leading to an over-valuation of that country's currency. The company decided to extract large cash dividends from the subsidiary and to ask it to substitute local currency borrowing for off-shore borrowing in an effort to minimize the corporation's exposure in the event of a predicted devaluation.

In carrying out these instructions, the subsidiary had to borrow at a greatly increased interest cost in order to maintain its planned sales growth. The resulting pressure on the subsidiary's profits led to several harmful decisions in trying to compensate for the higher costs. Service levels deteriorated as a result of severely cut inventories and, in turn, customer demand began to decline. In a further attempt to boost sales volume, the company gave its sales force more flexibility to offer price discounts. Profitability during the period fell dramatically.

This series of events resulted from the corporation applying policies that were not based on a careful analysis of the local economic environ-ment and close coordination between financial and operating initiatives. The parent took what it saw as a temporary financial decision, based on temporary economic conditions—i.e., the perceived overvaluation of a currency. The subsidiary responded by taking business decisions that amounted to a cash generation and contraction strategy, implying that the market was no longer attractive enough to justify maintaining the company's competitive position in it.

INTEGRATION WITH OPERATIONS

To avoid such pitfalls, the MNC needs to ensure that its operating units and the central treasury are well-integrated. But achieving integra-tion is not simply a matter of designing the proper organization struc-ture and reporting relationships. No single formula for the degree of financial centralization will suit all companies. A company's treasury function must be tailored to its unique situation, and will depend on such factors as the nature and geographic diversity of the business, the size and pattern of investments, and the caliber of local overseas trea-sury management. Whatever the appropriate division of respon-sibilities, the corporation's management approach must take into ac-count the overall financial position and objectives, as well as the busi-ness strategies and objectives of the individual operating units. It should encourage the application of expertise available in the units—e.g., on local international financial trends and investment opportunities—to all major issues, both operating and financial.

To meet these requirements, the treasury needs to be a primary participant in the process of directing and controlling the operating units—that is, in business planning. Such integration offers three major benefits: first, each operating unit appreciates the implications of the corporation's financial objectives for its own business strategy; second, treasury learns first-hand the business conditions and challenges facing the operating units and, cumulatively, their impact on corporate-wide performance and financial requirements; and third, corporate-wide strategies, plans and expectations can take account of the economic and financial environments in which the company competes. Let us see how these benefits can be achieved.

DEVELOPING BUSINESS PLANS

Business planning can be broadly described as having three phases: situation analysis, strategy development, and operations planning. For the MNC, situation analysis involves a systematic assessment of the country environment, those market sectors in which the MNC competes, its current operations and performance in the country, and its needs and capabilities outside the country that may affect the unit. Such an analysis enables the corporation to develop a clear understanding of the business opportunities available in the local market; development needs—i.e., bottlenecks requiring investment or commitment of technical expertise; and key challenges—i.e., two or three major business tasks that are identified by analysis of the company and its competitive situation.

Throughout the situation analysis, treasury input is critical (Exhibit III). However, in many companies, the business plan is developed under the aegis of the corporate planning function and may be assembled for top management review without receiving input from corporate treasury, an approach rather like looking through a pair of binoculars with one eye closed.

The situation analysis provides the basis for an overall strategy. The strategy has four key ingredients. First, a statement of overall direction, which should be explicit about whether the company is seeking, for example, to grow, maintain position, or divest in the market. Second, individual market-sector strategies for each business within the country in which the MNC is involved, covering target customer groups, products to be developed and provided, and distribution channels. Third, investment programs and funds commitments should be specified. Finally, performance targets need to be set that reflect a mix of market-

Exhibit III: Treasury Contributions to Situation Analysis

	Inputs from subsidiary managers	Illustrative corporate treasury inputs
Country environment	• Regulatory/legal trends • Expropriation risk • Long-term growth of economy	• Knowledge of international economic and financial trends
Market sectors	• Size/growth • Profitability • Competition • Product requirements	• Analysis of treasury opportunities – e.g. : – investment of surplus cash – capital markets as a source of funds
Country business	• Business volume and nature • Cost base • Capacity • Product quality • Financial position	• Analysis of current trends in – e.g. : – balance-sheet structure – cash flow – currency movements
Ex-country needs and capabilities	• Products • Financial position • Technical expertise	• Knowledge of : – financial position – technical financial expertise available

ing, production and financial objectives, rather than merely net financial results, such as return on capital or equity. Here, too, treasury has a vital role to play in supplying a broader view to business strategy development (Exhibit IV).

SUPERVISION AND CONTROL

Corporate management—including the treasury—should find the resulting business plan useful for focusing on the fundamental determinants of a subsidiary's economic performance.

When supervising and controlling overseas operations, companies often use a return on investment (ROI) measure to evaluate their profitability. This can give a misleading impression of management and subsidiary performance. For one thing, the return can look very different in the company's home currency. American MNCs, for example, have found that the performance of their European subsidiaries has looked very strong in recent years when translated into U.S. dollars. But in local currencies, after adjustment for inflation, the returns have in many cases been mediocre, while the subsidiaries' ability to finance themselves locally has probably declined. Moreover, a system for evaluating performance that is based largely on factors outside management's control is of little value. Assessing the extent to which man-

Exhibit IV: Corporate Treasury Contribution to Business Strategies

	Illustrative inputs
Overall strategic thrust	• Overall resource commitment (growing? declining?) • Ownership policy • Extent of equity commitment • Currency premium/penalty

Sector strategies	• Local treasury strategy on:
	  – excess cash
	  – exposure management
	• Sourcing strategy for operating sectors

Investment programs	• Evaluation of investment programs:
	  – net cash flows (local currency, home-base currency)
	  – repatriated flows
	  – hurdle rate

Target results	• Overall financial performance and profit planning • Exposure management targets (e.g., total hedging expense) • Excess funds management targets

agement decisions—as opposed to factors beyond control such as currency fluctuations—have contributed to eventual performance can be difficult unless original assumptions about currency movements and inflation rates are documented at the outset.

However, subsidiary managers can better be held accountable for their performance if the treasury has been involved in developing the country strategy to ensure that performance targets are set in the context of currency movement and inflation forecasts. The corporation can then more readily assess, for example, the justification for a subsidiary deviating from agreed priorities by investing more of its surplus cash in the money market and less in further business expansion.

Success for a multinational corporation requires the continual involvement of the treasury in most aspects of planning and managing the business. The appropriate degree of treasury centralization and its position in the corporate hierarchy will vary from company to company and over time. Proper integration will allow the corporation to set objectives for subsidiaries in the context of the international financial environment and will allow subsidiary performance to be measured against more controllable and realistic standards. This will allow corporate top management to focus on the fundamental determinants of economic performance overseas and to separate clearly the impacts of short- and long-term currency and inflation patterns from the operating performance of the subsidiary.

9

The American Depository Receipt as an Alternative Source of Funds for Multinational Firms

Alex Anckonie III
and Samer Mecattaf

The wide fluctuations of interest rates and the worldwide recession of the early 1980s have given ample reason for caution in the extensive use of debt financing by the growing multinational firm. This is especially true in countries with limited endogenous capital markets. Among the responsible alternative sources of funds to meet the needs of the expanding multinational firm, The Depository Receipt mechanism is perhaps the least understood and most underutilized. The following analysis is focused on the American Depository Receipt mechanism to illustrate the costs and benefits associated with this alternative source of multinational equity funding.

THE "DEBT CRISES," which have plagued international finance since the early 1980s, have given rise to concern by all elements of the global business community that excessive use of floating rate credit as a source of funds to satisfy the expanding capital budget and other requirements of a growing multinational firm places the firm's future solvency at too great a level of risk. Private firms and private providers of capital are relearning the value of a well diversified set of balance sheet liabilities and the importance of moderation in the debt to equity ratio associated with the firm's capital structure. The reluctance of international banks to lend to firms (especially in developing countries), which have heavy floating rate debt, has caused the management of these firms to seek alternative sources of funds to support the firm's growth plans.

As a diversified source of debt, many multinational firms have found banks more than willing to provide deferred and confirmed letter of credit trade financing by arranging the discounting of the resultant banker's acceptance into the capital markets of the confirming bank's country. The short-term, secured and "off-balance sheet" nature of the bankers acceptance makes it an interesting working capital financing tool to both the multinational firm and the "lending" bank.[1]

However, in meeting their long-term capital needs, many multinational firms in developing countries have seen uncontrollable debt service requirements as a major risk to the future solvency of their organization. They have begun recently to look with much greater favor on alternative forms of equity, as a method of financing long-term business expansion, which do not add to cash flow requirements during times of poor business conditions and/or high interest rates. One method of obtaining equity funds that has experienced considerable interest and application of late has been the joint venture mechanism.[2] A second method of obtaining equity funds that has had only limited application, but that could be much more broadly applied by knowledgeable multinational corporate managers, is the Depository Receipt mechanism. This mechanism allows well managed publicly traded firms in one country to reach into the capital market of another country to obtain equity funding.

How this financial strategy may be applied can be illustrated by the American Depository Receipt (ADR), which is a mechanism used by non-U.S. firms to access the U.S. equity capital markets. Of course, similar mechanisms either exist or could be developed in other "open" capital markets with the assistance of competent investment bankers. The purpose of this article is to increase the awareness of multinational executives of the existence of the Depository Receipt mechanism and to provide information concerning those management activites which enhance the ability of a multinational firm to utilize this equity funding source.

THE ADR MECHANISM

FUNDAMENTALS

An ADR is a certificate, denominated in shares, representing proof of ownership of foreign securities on deposit with a large (non-U.S.) home-country bank which is affiliated with a major U.S. bank. Ownership of equity shares, of a firm in a country outside the U.S., may be obtained by the U.S. bank. These shares are deposited in trust in the U.S. bank's large affiliate in the home country of the share-issuing firm.

The U.S. bank (using the services of an investment banking organization), then arranges for a primary U.S. issue of U.S. dollar demominated ADRs representing ownership in the deposited foreign shares. ADR holders are normally provided with the right to convert their U.S. dollar denominated ADRs into the underlying foreign currency denominated shares at any time. Hence, arbitrage operations keep the U.S. dollar price of the ADR very close to the foreign currency price of the underlying shares times the spot foreign exchange rate.

As elements of the normal ADR concept, the servicing U.S. bank provides ADR holders with English language summaries of the annual reports of the non-U.S. firm which issued the underlying shares. The U.S. bank also provides (for a small fee) a number of other service operations for ADR holders, such as the conversion of foreign currency dividends to U.S. dollars as well as the notice of and economic disposition of rights, warrants, and other financial interests in the underlying shares which accrue to ADR holders.

After their primary issue, ADRs are traded as U.S. dollar numeraire instruments on the U.S. secondary markets. Various ADRs trade on the New York Stock Exchange, on the American Stock Exchange and on the over-the-counter markets. Thus, the ADR functions like a warehouse receipt for commodities, enabling its holder to transfer ownership in the underlying shares without having to deliver the underlying securities.[3]

ADRs can be either sponsored or unsponsored. In the case where a foreign company approaches the bank and requests that ADRs be issued for company stock, the resulting ADRs are sponsored and all the costs of creating and administering the ADRs are often paid for by the company itself. For unsponsored accounts, U.S. brokers who consider that a sufficient market for the securities of a specific foreign company exists, approach a bank with a branch or a correspondent in the country of issue. The bank then contacts the company for a "no objection letter."[4] It is possible that such an expansion of interest could lead to a sponsored account, but more likely, the account will be unsponsored.[5]

Holding ADRs provides investors with several advantages over holding ordinary equity shares from another country. Valuable services are provided by the bank, which services the ADR in the U.S. capital market. The ADR has much better Transferability (liquidity) properties in the U.S. than would the foreign equity shares. They provide for lower wholesale foreign exchange rates for initial procurement and for dividend distributions instead of the less-advantageous retail rates which otherwise must be used by many investors in foreign equities. The ADR servicing bank keeps abreast of all corporate activities that affect the ADR holder and mails English language summaries of important information to holders of ADRs, supplies periodic financial reports and news releases, and sends proxy forms upon specific request.[6]

HISTORY OF AMERICAN DEPOSITORY RECEIPTS

The concept of ADRs is not new. They were first introduced in 1927 by the Guaranty Trust Company of New York.[7] In the late 1920s, sophisticated U.S. brokers had recognized the potential of dealing in foreign securities, and expenses. ADRs were developed to overcome such difficulties.[8]

As of November 1985, American investors, or foreign investors in the U.S. stock markets, could buy more than 550 foreign issues by means of ADRs, compared with fewer than 400 in 1978 and a mere 150 in 1961. During late 1985, ADRs for Japanese shares number 132; for Australian shares, 109; for British shares, 100; and for South African shares, 90. Other ADRs represent shares originally issued in West Germany, Sweden, Italy, Holland, France, Mexico, Norway, Jamaica, Zambia, Israel, Belgium, Hong Kong, Malaysia, Ireland, Singapore, and Bermuda. The list includes many developing countries, most developed countries and a number of newly industrialized countries. Of the issues, 18 are listed on the New York Stock Exchange, seven on the American Stock Exchange, and the rest are traded over the counter.[9] U.S. security information forms provide standard information on a large number of ADRs.[10]

HOW ADR ARBITRAGE WORKS

Large international brokers act as professional arbitragers between the underlying foreign currency denominated shares and the U.S. dollar denominated ADRs.[11] When the ADR price exceeds the cost of purchasing the underlying securities in dollar terms plus the ADR issuance expenses, arbitragers will buy the underlying securities and deposit them at the ADR servicing bank's foreign depository. In return, ADRs will be issued in the U.S., which will then be sold to American investors for a profit. The sale of the new ADRs will continue until the ADR price decreases and is no longer greater than the cost of creating them to the brokers-arbitragers.

Conversely, if the ADR price falls below the price of the underlying security in the foreign market, arbitragers will purchase the ADRs in the U.S., return them to the servicing bank, receive the underlying shares from the foreign depository and sell them at the higher foreign price. This will in turn drive up the depressed price of the ADRs because of the increased demand for them.

Thus, by necessity, the U.S. dollar price of the ADR follows closely the exchange rate adjusted price of the foreign currency denominated foreign share. It should be noted that the ADR price is closely tied to the exchange rate between the dollar and the currency of the underlying security.

The authors have conducted research on the efficiency of the ADR arbitrage process using data from ADRs issued by firms from four countries. Using monthly (U.S. dollar) ADR closing prices, closing prices of the underlying shares, appropriate closing exchange rates and ADR to underlying share ratios, common numeraire price difference time series were developed covering the period from January 1980 to January 1985.

Using standard statistical methods, the null hypothesis of efficient arbitrage between the group of ADRs and the group of underlying shares could not be rejected at reasonable significance levels. One concludes that the arbitrage process is effective in keeping the ADR price in line with the exchange rate adjusted price of the underlying foreign currency denominated share. Interestingly, the mean difference between the ADR prices and the corresponding price of the underlying shares was less than one-quarter of one percent; this is indeed a small "fee" to pay for the valuable services provided to the ADR holder through the ADR mechanism.

THE GLOBAL EQUITY MARKET[12]

Existing stock exchanges, as well as electronic network operators, are competing hard to form links that will extend trading hours, make domestic markets accessible to foreign investors across national frontiers and secure a piece of the emerging market in cross-border equity investments. Many stock markets have established bilateral links with markets abroad through which they trade an ever-increasing range of financial instruments: equities, options, financial futures, commodities and foreign exchange. Banks, brokers, and other financial intermediaries, regardless of their domicile, can now trade with ease across borders. This has, in turn, resulted in a gradual harmonization of rules, trading practices and accounting standards. With the desire to trade the same issue in many markets clearly evident, the ADR mechanism is a viable alternative available to meet this need.

BENEFITS TO THE INVESTOR

U.S. investors choose to invest in foreign equities for two reasons. First, they believe that specific foreign stocks, or even specific foreign markets, yield higher returns than the investment alternatives available in domestic markets. Second, an internationally diversified portfolio is likely to exhibit a lower overall total yield volatility than a similar portfolio limited to only domestic issues.[13]

A study by H. Levy and M. Sarnat[14] analyzes gains achieved through international diversification. The gain can be measured either by the increase in the average rate of return on the portfolio for a given level of risk or by the portfolio risk reduction attainable for a given mean rate of return.

Holding risk constant at the average level of domestic investment equity portfolio standard deviation of yield (6.62 percent and 9.05 percent in 1960–69 and 1970–79, respectively), a substantial increase in average return could have been earned on an efficient internationally diversified portfolio without incurring additional risk. The increment in the mean quarterly return for 1960–69 is 0.36 percent per quarter, while the relevant figure for 1970–79 is 2.38 percent per quarter.

The greater increase in the 1970s reflects the very poor performance of the U.S. stock market during this period. Hence, permitting U.S. investors to diversify their portfolios internationally leads to the possibility of gaining a very substantial increase in mean total portfolio returns. Alternatively, if one holds the level of total portfolio returns constant at the mean returns on domestic investment, one can measure the degree of risk reduction from international diversification.

Thus, the gain from international diversification, as measured by the reduction of the standard deviation of portfolio total yield was substantial in both periods. Efficient international diversification reduced the standard deviation in 1960–69 by 2.05 percentage points while the relevant figure for 1970–79 was a reduction of 1.27 percentage points.

The investment and portfolio management literature shows that the relationship between asset yields and asset yield correlations (as measured in the numeraire currency of the investor) determines the relative desirability of holding any given asset in a portfolio. The low correlations between the macroeconomies of various nations contributes significantly to the desirability of holding foreign assets in a given portfolio of financial assets. The relevant question at this point is whether or not the ADRs provide a low correlation with nominal domestic equity shares issued by U.S. firms in the U.S. capital markets.

Research by the authors of this study, using monthly total yield data for 19 ADRs and for the Standard and Poor's 500 index over the period from January 1979 to June 1985, shows an average correlation of ADR yields with the yields of a broadly based U.S. market index (the S&P 500 of 0.37 with correlation values below 0.30 being exhibited by six of these assets.[15] These low correlation values fully support consideration of ADR assets by U.S. portfolio managers. Using a qadratic programming asset allocation algorithm,[16] further research by ther authors has shown the clear desirability of holding ADRs in U.S. dollar denominated financial asset portfolios.

It is believed that the case for holding additional ADRs in U.S. dollar denominated portfolios has been clearly established. As these results become more widely known to portfolio managers, the demand for ADRs by U.S. investors should increase significantly.[17]

BENEFITS OF ADRs TO THE FOREIGN CURRENCY SHARE ISSUING FIRM

The issuing company can benefit from the ADR mechanism in many respects. By internationalizing its sources of capital, the issuing company can take advantage of a lower cost of capital. It is very important for a company to lower its cost of capital to the lowest possible level if it is to be a long-run profit maximizing firm. In addition to gaining a lower cost of equity through accessing the larger U.S. capital markets, a company in a country with small capital markets compared to the U.S. can also benefit from an improvement in its relative cost of debt. This results from the ability to improve its debt to equity ratio through the taking in of equity funds through application of the ADR mechanism.

Companies from developing countries are more affected than others by the size of their national capital markets. In some developing countries, trading volume is small and it is difficult to raise new capital without depressing existing security prices. There is simply a lack of investment capital in some markets. Also, national capital markets can be segmented from other capital markets.

The potential effect of segmented capital markets on a firm's cost of capital was investigated by Stapleton and Subrahmanyam.[18] They concluded: "In most cases, the effects of segmented capital markets is to depress security prices and also to produce an incentive for corporations to increase the diversification opportunities available to investors. Three corporate financial policies that effectively reduce the effects of segmented markers are: a) foreign portfolio/direct investment by firms; b) mergers with foreign firms; c) dual listing of the securities of the firm on foreign capital markets." Therefore, the listing of the shares of the firm in foreign markets using the ADR mechanism can help a company reduce the effects of national market segmentation, thereby reducing their overall cost of capital.

The net result of a well planned use of the ADR mechanism by firms in smaller-capital-market countries is a significant reduction in their overall cost of capital.[19] The following table contains selections from a list of developing country firms which have ADRs trading in the U.S. capital markets. The list is provided to show the diversity of firms which have been successful in using the ADR mechanism.

Table
Selected Firms Having ADRs Traded in U.S. Capital Markets

From the Bahamas: Worldwide.

From Botswana: Botswana RST.

From Malaysia:
Bandar Raya Development Berhad.
Genting Berhad.
Kuala Lumpur Kepong Berhad.
Malayan United Industries Berhad.
Parlis Plantations Berhad.
Selanger Properties.
Sime Darby Berhad.
Supreme Corp.

From Mexico: IEM S.A.

From Papua New Guinea: Bougainville Copper.

DEVELOPMENT BANKS AND NATIONAL CAPITAL MARKETS

By making investments in emerging markets, development banks help the expansion of those markets. Further, when underwriting new issues of securities, some development banks have cooperated with other financial institutions such as commercial banks, insurance companies and pension funds to give an implicit additional boost to the growth of domestic stock exchanges.[20]

The managers of the International Finance Corporation (IFC), The World Bank unit specializing in private sector development, believe that investments in emerging markets offer lucrative opportunities for sophisticated investors seeking to diversify their holdings geographically.[21] The IFC's capital market division is playing the role of a catalyst in stimulating the growth of developing country capital markets.

Two IFC-backed closed-end investment trusts are traded on the New York Stock Exchange and have attracted institutional investors. The $60 million Korea Fund and the $150 million Mexico Fund are both considered to be well managed, conservative vehicles. IFC management concedes that there is a great deal of apprehension about investing in emerging markets but maintain that it is due to unfamiliar economic and political environments and a lack of information.

Use of the ADR mechanism is an appropriate method of working to reduce the unfamiliarity associated with investing in well managed firms in developing countries. Developing countries should also be interested in their private sector firms achieving increased use of the ADR mechanism to raise equity funds because of the complimentary reduction in the need for aggregate external debt within the country.

STEPS LEADING TO SUCCESSFUL USE OF THE ADR MECHANISM

A developing-country firm desiring to develop access to the U.S. equity markets through the ADR mechanism can take a number of positive early steps to facilitate successful eventual use of this mechanism.

First, it must be recognized that major language and/or accounting differences between the firm's home country and the U.S. can be a significant hurdle to successful application of the ADR mechanism. This may be overcome if the firm has established a practice of preparing English versions of their financial reports which contain schedules quantifying the differences between home country accounting conventions and the generally accepted accounting principles in the U.S. or is willing to do so.

Second, the firm interested in learning more about the ADR process should review the articles and sources cited in this paper and then obtain the appropriate ADR mechanism literature from a number of large U.S. banks for further study.

Third, a firm contemplating the issuing of ADRs in the U.S. capital market would then do well to engage a major U.S. bank to assist in the development of a plan of action necessary to maximize the acceptability of its ADR in the U.S. market. Such a plan frequently involves increasing the visibility of the firm in the U.S. This visibility may be increased by arranging for senior officers of the firm to speak to appropriate U.S. financial analysts and portfolio managers or by more conventional media-related methods. For some firms, it may be desirable to establish some form of branch office in the U.S. or some other structure to facilitate an ongoing investor relations program.

When the necessary background work is done, and when the timing is appropriate (this may be as long as one to two years after initial contact with the advising U.S. bank), the U.S. bank can provide the necessary legal and administrative support for the initial offering (the bank may recommend a U.S. investment bank and an outside counsel to participate in the overall effort). Since U.S. security law and regulations are often more complex than corresponding laws and regulations in developing countries, these advisors must serve the dual function of ensuring all U.S. security laws and disclosure requirements are satisfied while simultaneously ensuring that the foreign firm thoroughly understands these requirements. In this regard, it is often considered beneficial to select a U.S. bank, U.S. investment bank, and U.S. counsel that are experienced in the firm's line of business and that are experienced in doing business with clients in the firm's home country. This line of business and home country experience frequently improves the quality of the early recommendations made by these advisors to the firm contemplating an ADR issue.

Using the firm's knowledge of its home-country banks, and in conjunction with the advising U.S. bank, the depository bank in the home country (and other appropriate home country legal and investment banking advisors as appropriate to the home country's financial institutions structure) should be selected to facilitate the home-country security operations that are component parts of the application of the ADR mechanism.

CONCLUDING REMARKS

ADRs have been shown to be very useful in providing successful developing-country companies with capital at a lower cost than the cost of capital in their home market. For U.S. investors, ADRs are very attractive to include in an international portfolio because of the useful services provided by the servicing banks and because an internationally diversified portfolio is likely to yield a higher average rate of return and is likely to be less volatile than an otherwise similar portfolio limited to domestic issues. Large growing companies in developing countries should integrate the potential use of ADRs or ADR-like mechanisms into their overall financial plans as one alternative method of lowering their cost of capital and/or increasing the availability of capital budget funds.

Large financial institutions in developed countries should explore further development of the ADR mechanism as one method of increasing their non-interest income. With significant potential benefits to both foreign firms and to U.S. investors, further development of the ADR mechanism could allow it to become a much more important and more profitable service of such institutions.

Large financial institutions in developing countries should explore further development of the ADR mechanism as one method of increasing their non-interest income by the provision of additional useful services to their established home-country clients. The established correspondent linkages between major banks in developing countries and major banks in the U.S. would appear to be one existing institutional linkage that could be used to facilitate the use of the ADR mechanism as a more appropriate, profitable and cost-efficient means of financing economic expansion.

Additional research and publication of such research concerning the appropriate application and the operation of the ADR mechanism is necessary to increase the understanding and awareness of the full potential of this financial intermediation scheme which has significant additional applications benefit for third-world companies, industrial country investors and existing financial intermediation institutions in both developed and developing economies.

NOTES

1. See "Banker's Acceptances Revisited" by Jack L. Hervey in the *Federal Reserve Bank of Chicago Economic Perspectives*, May/June 1983, pp. 21–31 and "Middle Market Firms Have New Enthusiasm for Using Banker's Acceptances" in *Cashflow*, May 1984.
2. For a recent analysis of a number of alternative methods of capitalizing new productive investments in a developing country, see "Foreign Investment in the People's Republic of China: A Study of Investment Incentives and Environment in the Shenzen Special Economic Zone" by Phillip D. Grub and Jian-Hai-Lin, Monograph number 85–3 published by the Office of Research Support and Continuing Professional Education, School of Government and Business Administration, The George Washington University, Washington, D.C. 20052.
3. Memorandum on ADRs prepared by the Office of International Corporate Finance, Securities and Exchange Commission, September 1983.

4. A "no objection" letter is the legal device by which the U.S. bank obtains the right to act as a limited agent of the firm for such matters as the establishment of the information-supplying exemption required by Rule 12g3–2(b) of Section 12(g) of the Exchange Act of 1934 as outlined in the Securities and Exchange Commission document "Memorandum on American Depository Receipts" dated September 1983.

5. "American Depository Receipts," Chapter 2, in Gerald Warfield, *How to Buy Foreign Stocks and Bonds*, New York, Harper & Row, 1985.

6. Timothy Tomlinson, "Federal Regulation of Secondary Trading in Foreign Securities," *Business Lawyer*, January 1977.

7. The Guaranty Trust Company of New York merged with J. P. Morgan in 1959 to form Morgan Guaranty Trust.

8. Anna Merjos, "Investors' Ticket Abroad," *Barron's*, April 30, 1984.

9. A recent listing of a large number of ADR issuing firms, their home country and the U.S. exchange on which they are traded is contained in the article "Investors' Ticket Abroad," in the April 30, 1984 issue of *Barron's*.

10. See for instance the information covering the Sony Corporation ADRs in the Standard and Poor's latest issue of their *Stock Reports: New York Stock Exchange Issues*.

11. Timothy Tomlinson, "Federal Regulation of Secondary Trading in Foreign Securities," *Business Lawyer*, January 1977.

12. See "The Global Equity Market," *Euromoney*, May 1985 and "Equities Enter the Eurobond Age," "Clearing the Way to Globalization" and "One Step Beyond Clearing" in the October 1985 issue of the same journal.

13. Richard K. Abrams and Donald V. Kimbell, "U.S. Investments in Foreign Equity Markets," *Economic Review*, Federal Reserve Bank of Kansas City, April 1981.

14. H. Levy and M. Sarnat, "International Diversification," *Portfolio Investment Selection*, Prentice Hall, 1984.

15. A subject suitable for further research would be to investigate whether or not the correlation of the total returns from holding ADRs and the total returns on the U.S. "market" are a function of the fraction of the foreign firm's equity which is traded on the U.S. market as an ADR.

16. Alex Anckonie III, "A Quadratic Program for Determining Efficient Portfolio Compositions Using the SAS Language," *Proceedings of the Tenth Annual SAS Users Group International*, SAS Institute, Cary, NC, 1985.

17. An additional source of ADR demand could be developed from two separate observations. First, it is noted that 32 countries currently peg their currencies to the U.S. dollar (See table I.1 of the 1985 Annual Report of the International Monetary Fund). Second, a study by D. R. Lessard entitled "International Portfolio Diversification: A Multivariate Analysis for a Group of Latin-American Countries" (in the May 1977 issue of the *Journal of Finance*) has shown that, contrary to a common assumption, a great deal of beneficial portfolio diversification by facilitating their holding assets, which have the significant portfolio benefits described in the Lessard study.

18. R. C. Stapleton and M. G. Subrahmanyam, "Market Imperfections, Capital Market Equilibrium, and Corporate Finance," *Journal of Finance*, May 1977.

19. For an excellent analytical history of a well conceived application of the ADR mechanism to reduce the overall cost of capital of a foreign firm while simultaneously providing a needed increase in the firm's capital budget, see: Arthur I. Stonehill and Kare B. Dullum, *Internationalizing the Cost of Capital. The Novo Experience and National Policy Implications*, John Wiley & Sons, 1982.

20. Karel Holbic, "Development Finance and Financial Intermediation in Developing Countries," *Journal of Economic Development*, July 1979.

21. Jonathan Friedland, "Will Anyone Bet on Third-World Stocks?" *Institutional Investor*, July 1985.

10
International Project Financing: Practices and Problems

Dara Khambata

International project financing is the only means by which many host countries can raise the funds necessary for essential development projects. By pooling resources, reputations, and experience of multiple organizations, including possibly the World Bank, leverage can be provided not only to spread the risk, but to prevent nationalization of project assets. While there is no standard package, the process is to identify the needs and goals of the parties involved and to design a package that best meets those requisites.

INTRODUCTION

Scenario: A manufacturer of durable consumer goods is interested in building a plant in a poor Third-World country because of cheaper labor costs and tax advantages, as well as the potential for entering a new regional market. Two factors, however, are hampering the plan: One is that the host-country government wants the company to locate the plant in a remote, underdeveloped corner of the country. That requirement poses all sorts of additional risks and costs. Second is that the company is at the tail-end of a major program of expansion and is not likely to be able to raise all the money it needs to construct the facility, which is highly capital-intensive. Even if it could do so, the company would not be able to repay the loan until the plant became operational and generated some revenue.

For its part, the host-country government very much wants the plant. It has promised to help that area achieve economic growth to further the legitimate social aspirations of the local citizenry. Equally important, the area is on the border of an expansionist neighbor that is

144

fomenting discontent by focusing on the inequitable treatment of the area and promising reform should the area secede. There is also the prestige factor of having a modern consumer goods plant that would at the same time help the country meet locally the growing demand for durable consumables. However, the company has said it will not locate there unless the government agrees to provide the necessary infrastructure and to help train the unskilled local labor pool. At present, interest payments on its foreign debt and declining receipts from primary exports have left the country with minimal domestic funds for development. Its failure to implement fully an IMF austerity program and structural adjustments have made an already jittery commercial lending market even more reluctant to extend further credit.

Other sources of assistance look equally bleak. A major donor country would like to help, but the budget of its development agency is tight because of its own austerity program, while the legislature is upset over alleged human rights violations. The regional development bank will provide some financing and guarantees, but not enough to fund the balance of what is needed. And so on.

It appears as though it will be impossible to build the manufacturing plant. However, a banker in the manufacturing company's home country learns of the sutiation and proposes a novel approach to raise the necessary funds. Recognizing that a number of parties are interested in participating in the project but cannot do so alone because of various constraints, and that conventional financing will not be forthcoming because of the repayment problems and risks involved, the banker puts together a project financing package. This approach is tailored to meet the problems often found in highly capital-intensive, risky projects. It does so by pooling the resources of different institutions that have a stake in getting the project underway, while at the same time including various types of assurances against the major risks. In addition, it permits the project sponsor to repay the loan out of the income generated by the facility once operating.

The above scenario, while fictitious, is not unlike many encountered in the world today. The same types of opportunities—and constraints—are faced by project owners, sponsors, lenders and governments. In an effort to address these facts of business, banks have been resorting to a creative approach to lending and borrowing known as project financing. Project financing takes a multitude of forms, but generally is characterized by the willingness of the lender(s) to be repaid out of the eventual earnings of the project and by the participation of several different parties in different capacities. As with other lending, the lenders look for security, and the borrower must be able to show a strong likelihood of repayment.

What advantages does project financing offer? First and foremost, it makes financing possible by pooling the resources, reputations, security, and experience of multiple organizations. Second, the risk can be spread over several parties. The package can, for example, be structured to include parties, such as the World Bank, that can provide leverage against certain risks, such as the nationalization of project assets. Third, a local party may be chosen to provide access to a country otherwise hostile to foreigners. Fourth, if structured astutely, the venture can yield valuable tax and other benefits to the participants. Fifth, this financing alternative may be the only way the host country can raise the revenue needed for a development project. The bank not only earns a healthy fee for putting the deal together, but it also becomes involved in a potentially profitable endeavor with minimum risk. And, project financing is also a good way for the bank to enter new fields in which it will want to operate at a later date.

It should be emphasized that there is no standard package. The players and their objectives vary, as do the types of funding and the structures of the packages, and hence of the projects themselves. It is necessary to identify the needs of the project and goals of the parties involved, and then to design a package that best meets those requisites. Obviously, the two basic objectives are 1) to pull together the desired amount of funds on terms acceptable to all parties and 2) to minimize the risks to all parties.

I. THE PARTIES TO PROJECT FINANCING

Four parties to project financing can be distinguished, although each can play more than one role: the project, the sponsor, the third party, and the lender.

The project itself may be a new entity, such as a corporation, or part of an existing one, such as a subsidiary. The long-term goal may be simply: to make a profit; to provide the parent corporation a market for an output or a supply of an input; to obtain for the parent corporation certain benefits, such as tax advantages; or to enable a parent to develop operations in a certain location that might otherwise be closed to it. The structure of the project, which can take a number of forms, is to a large extent dictated by the goals of the various participants and the nature of the financing package.

The project's immediate goal, however, is to obtain the funds needed to make it operational on the best possible terms—a fixed low interest rate, long maturity, minimum equity contribution, and minimum potential liability.

The *sponsor* may be the project itself or another party that wants the project implemented, such as the project owner. Frequently, there are multiple sponsors, such as a parent company requiring a reliable supply of an input or service, a government wanting to develop a backward region, and an international development agency looking for an optimal project to which to channel funds. Multiple sponsorship is one technique for avoiding certain regulatory or legal restrictions that the project might be subject to on its own, particularly in terms of further borrowing or of operating in a certain location.

As to actual financing, the sponsor will also want the funds at fixed, favorable terms, with minimal capital outlay and liability. It also looks for financing that has a finite cost budget. In addition, it wants no-recourse lending, that is, lending that does not affect its own credit standing or subject it to any borrowing restrictions and that does not show up anywhere on its balance sheet. Most likely, it is also interested in obtaining maximum tax benefits (for example, less income tax, more tax credits for investments, depreciation and depletion allowances, and interest deductions), to be achieved by structuring the financing package a certain way. Last, it wants to minimize its personal liability.

A *third party* might become involved in a number of ways. One would be as a conduit for, or to facilitate, the financing. A third party can be an existing entity or be set up solely to meet the requirements of the financing package. Another role a third party plays is to guarantee the credit by committing itself to purchase the project's output. In return for its participation, the third party might be looking for a profitable investment, a market for its own products, a source of inputs for its own operations, certain tax advantages, or, in the case of government or international development agency, the achievement of certain ecomomic and social objectives.

The *lender*, depending on who it is, may be interested in the project's implementation in the most cost-effective manner (the case with the project owner) or in purely risk-free profit (a syndicate of banks). Commercial lenders only want credit risk; they are not interested in equity or venture capital risk. Moreover, they very likely want to lend short-term maturities at a floating interest rate. A very major concern is the security of their investment, and they will require a range of assurances against potential risks to the investment (discussed later). Typical lenders are banks, government agencies, international and regional development agencies, export credit agencies, leasing companies, interested third parties, sponsors, insurance companies and pension funds.

Clearly, there may be a lot of overlap among these parties and who is involved. In simplest form, the package involves just the project and a parent company. At the other extreme, it might include the project, several sponsors with varying degrees and types of participation, several lenders such as a syndicate of banks, an area development bank and one or more governments, a nominee corporation set up to receive the loans, and a casualty insurance company. The lender may be the sponsor, while the sponsor might also be a third party, with another organization acting as lender.

II. THE LENDING OPTIONS

There are several types of financing: equity contribution, debt (straight loans); capital (owner's); stock—common or preferred (notes/debentures, bonds, commercial paper); leases (operating, capital, leveraged or unleveraged); sales, acquisitions, and mergers; and advance payments. With few exceptions, the sponsor or owner of the project will have to make *an equity contribution* to qualify for credit. The rule of thumb is 40 percent owner equity.

Debt, which is defined as loans, may be secured or unsecured, but is generally the former. In project financing, the facilities, equipment, real property, and other resources may serve as collateral, or the parent company may have to provide the security on the basis of its assets. Other options are unconditional take-or-pay contracts, in which some party guarantees to buy, on a prearranged schedule, the output of the project, regardless of whether it is delivered. Generally, the payments are equal to the obligated periodic debt payments (principal, interest, commitment fees, and other costs, plus an amount to cover contingencies). With production payments, the creditor is guaranteed a set share of the proceeds of the project. An unsecured loan is backed by the general credit and reputation of the borrower, but typically it has ratio covenants attached to it, as well as provisions that accelerate repayment or that trigger certain contingency arrangements. Some covenants may preclude the borrower from incurring further debt or from making other investments until the loan is repaid. Only the most creditworthy customers can obtain unsecured loans, although where the project owner is also the lender, it may choose that option.

The other important aspect of a loan is its maturity. As noted, commercial lenders generally lend only short-term loans (one to six or seven years). By contrast, certain international financing organizations or development banks offer only long-term loans (ten to fifteen years). As such, the project financing package might be structured to include various lenders of different types in order to cover the desired loan period. One problem is medium-term loans, for which little financing is available. One institution that does offer medium-term funds is the Private Export Funding Corporation (PEFCO), which was set up by a consortium of over 60 banks and export companies. PEFCO can raise capital and receives indirect guarantees from the U.S. government.

An increasingly popular form of project financing, particularly in the United States, is *leasing*—because of the tax advantages it offers. The option can be designed to cover both equipment and services. The main advantages of leasing are:

- Someone else makes the equity payments;
- The fees are fixed over the life of the lease;
- The result is equivalent to 100 percent financing;
- Other sources of financing may not be available;
- Payments come from pre-tax earnings;
- Payments can be coordinated with the project's cash flow;
- The project or sponsor can retain its capital for use elsewhere; and
- The terms may be better.

On the other hand,

- There is no residual value to show for the payments at the end of the lease;
- The project has less flexibility in terms of maintenance, servicing and use of the equipment or service;
- The lease is a senior fixed obligation against the project;
- There is no prestige of ownership;
- The tax breaks that make leasing popular in the United States may not be available elsewhere; and
- In the United States, only certain forms of leasing qualify for tax breaks, for example, a true lease, where ownership of the equipment rests with the lessor at the beginning and end of the lease, a requirement that precludes options such as a lease/purchase plan.

More obvious sources of financing are *sales of assets, acquisitions, or mergers*. In the first case, a key question is whether investing the proceeds of a sale in the new project yields more than the existing operation. When calculating the return from a sale, not only the sales price, but also the savings in operating the asset should be included.

Acquisitions and mergers offer a cost-effective way to obtain assets with little lead time. They are particularly useful options where a sponsor does not have a borrowing capacity: using these approaches, it may acquire resources needed for the project (equipment, technology, labor, and management), as well as capital and credit capacity.

Finally, there is the *advance payment*, similar in many ways to the production payment. Here a lender, usually a company that uses output similar to that to be produced by the project, makes a cash payment to the project, in return for which it will get a set portion of the output and the right to purchase as much as it wants.

Export credit facilities afford partial funding as well as guarantees of loans or insurance. Most countries have export credit agencies to promote exports, and generally these agencies offer low-interest (subsidized) loans, loan guarantees, or insurance. They may also offer marketing services, information on trade matters, and technical assistance.

III. RISK COVERAGE

The risk of financing is critical from the lender's perspective; it will not make loans if the risk of forfeiture or loss is too high. A lender will consider more than merely the soundness of the project or creditworthiness of the sponsor(s). The risks considered will include:

- The viability of the project in terms of:
    Its ability to operate according to the specifications of the agreement, that is, a certain output at a certain price starting at a certain time;
    The reputation of the contractor handling the construction;
    The project's ability to handle contingencies, such as cost overruns, delays in start-up, or world-wide recessions;
    Stability of the market for it output; and
    The quality of the technology being used.
- The political environment of the host country, especially its stability the likelihood of expropriation (country risk);
- The labor environment in the host country;
- Currency issues such as devaluation or a freeze on the transfer of funds into and out of the country.

A borrower can cover these risks to the satisfaction of the lender in a number of ways; broadly, they are insurance, guarantees, cross-default clauses, and nature of the participants in the financing package. An important point about most risk coverage options is that they require no out-of-pocket costs unless, of course, the provisions of a risk agreement have to be met. Cofinancing with the World Bank or the Export-Import Bank may go a long way in alleviating the risk of financing.

Insurance

The most familiar type of risk coverage, insurance, generally covers only casualty losses, and is not available for most of the risks described above. Some government agencies, however, such as the U.S. Overseas Private Investment Corporation, provide coverage against political risk.

Project Participation

Participation in a project financing or in the project itself can be structured to minimize political risk. Basically, the aim is to structure participation in such a way that the consequences of delays, defaults, or increased costs resulting from actions by the host country are inacceptable. For example, a major international financing or development group, such as the World Bank, may be asked to join the project or the lenders. If that institution is providing other financing to the country, its participation affords considerable leverage against political risk. That leverage may be reinforced by including a cross-default provision, in which failure to repay the project loan places the host country in default on all other loans from the same institution.

In some cases the loan goes through a development bank that then sells a portion to a commercial syndicate. This approach both retains the leverage of the development bank's participation and facilitates access to the commercial market. Where the host country is a lender, the borrower may seek to have the participation of, for example, the World Bank, with the understanding that decisions relating to its participation will require a majority vote of its directors. That approach provides balance in decisionmaking, so that no single participant can bias the project.

Guarantees

The most common type of assurance in project financing falls into the category of guarantee, which can take many forms. The *direct guarantee* is relatively straightforward—the sponsor or a third party directly and unconditionally guarantees assumption of the debt of the borrower or project in the event of default.

There are several *indirect guarantees,* the most important being a take-or-pay or throughput contract (the latter where the project involves an oil pipeline). Here the guarantor agrees to make set payments on a specified date for the output of the project, whether or not delivery is made. The payments are usually large enough to cover the debt service and contingencies. Frequently, even these contracts are backed by an agreement to transfer the assets of the project to the lender. Other indirect guarantees are: price supports for the output, given by the host-country government; contingency contracts, in which the borrower or the guarantor agrees to take a certain action in the event that certain conditions arise; payment "carve-outs," in which the project agrees automatically to pay the lender a certain portion of the proceeds from the operation; or "comfort letters," in which a creditworthy, reputable sponsor or borrower states in a letter its intention to monitor the project closely, to allow it to use its reputable name, and to do all it can to ensure the project's success (other reassurances may also be included at the borrower's request). Conversion rights—the right to assume ownership of the project and its assets—may be attached to any guarantee.

Implied guarantees are more informal. They are based on several factors:

- The reputation of the sponsor and its unwillingness to sully it with a failure;
- The importance of the project to the sponsor, for example, as a reliable source for some input (this guarantee is called economic necessity);
- The importance of the project to the host-country government; and
- The association of a reputable name, for example, that of the sponsor, with the project.

Completion Contracts

Clearly, many of these guarantees assume an operational project. In fact, perhaps the most critical time in the life of the project is the construction and start-up phases. Here is where the potential is greatest for things going wrong and of costly delays and overruns being incurred that can affect subsequent cash flow and profitability. To guard against this risk, many lenders require *completion contracts.*They guarantee that the project will operate according to stated specifications (a set output of a certain quality at a certain price by some date and for some designated period). In some cases, the contractor handles the completion contract; otherwise, it is handled by the sponsor or a third party.

Guarantors

Guarantors include: the project owner; third parties such as suppliers to the project, e.g., U.S. or foreign manufacturers that provide inputs; sellers; users of the project's output; interested governments and international or regional development groups, such as the Eximbank or the International Finance Corporation; and any party with an equity interest in the project, such as a foreign government or its central bank.

IV. THE STRUCTURAL ALTERNATIVES

As noted, there are many ways to structure a project financing package, the driving force being the desire of each participant to meet its objectives. To summarize briefly, the project sponsors may be looking for: tax and other financial advantages; no-recourse borrowing that does not affect their credit standing; minimum capital expenditures; arrangements that will not limit its future borrowing or financial obligations; ways around restrictions and regulations that will not apply to the project, if properly structured; a pooling of resources (manpower, financial, experience, and technological) of multiple organizations; spreading the risk; and distance from the liabilities of the project. The importance of those objectives varies from project to project and among the participants, and juggling them requires creative and skillful designing and negotiating. From the lender's perspective, the main concern is to maximize the return on the loan and to minimize the risk of loss.

The options (several may be present within the same financing package) include: an independent corporation; a subsidiary; joint ownership/control (with the main forms being partnerships, trusts, and joint ventures); leasing companies; captive financing companies; turnkey operations; and management contracts.

Independent Corporation

Corporations are used in two different ways. One is to set the project itself up as a corporation, with the financing going through it with the support of sponsors or third parties. The advantage of this option is that it establishes distance from the sponsor. However, it also generally precludes other parties from gaining any tax advantages and may, depending on the nature of the risk coverage, still leave the sponsor or third party liable. Another commom technique is to establish a nominee corporation between the project and the sponsor. These undercapitalized entities, which are composed of trustees, have nominal ownership of the project and receive the financing. Clearly, nominee corporations must be supported by other institutions.

Subsidiary

The subsidiary is an option that affords good tax advantages. Moreover, where the sponsor is strong, the subsidiary is essentially backed by an implied guarantee. Subsidiaries can be restricted—limited to certain operations—or unrestricted.

Joint Ownership/Control

Joint ownership/control is a popular structure that allows interested parties to share the cost, risk, and management of the project, while benefiting from maximum tax advantages. Inclusion of a local participant or a party with extensive experience and a good reputation in the host country can facilitate launching a project at that location. This structure also allows a pooling of resources, minimizes the impact on the credit standing of individual participants, and frequently affords optimal borrowing terms.

Partnerships. Partnerships are a very common type of joint ownership. They can operate a project, hold property and enter into financing arrangements on their own. The familiar forms are general or limited partnerships, or a combination of the two. Partners in the general form have unlimited liability for the entire project, and all their personal assets can be attached. In the limited form, each partner is liable only up to the limit of his investment or a prestated amount. Mixed partnerships involve a dominant partner, such as the corporate sponsor, who is the general partner, and individual investors as limited partners. Whatever the form, partners are bound by a legal contract that spells out their rights, obligations, and liabilities.

One way to address the issue of liability is to set up a subsidiary to the partnership that enters into an agreement with the partnership to operate the project as a joint venture (see below). Partners can also assign the lender limited recourse to the assets of the partnership and project, although the lender in turn may require take-or-pay contracts or the like. Partners may also require that each memnber obtain the approval of the others before entering into any individual loan agreements or financial obligations, with cross-indemnification of the partners or the parent partnership. Finally, there is the option of insurance coverage.

Trusts. Trusts involve joint ownership but without a formal partnership contract. Trusts may own facilities jointly or solely and can lease the project to an operator or operators. Frequently, a trust is used just during construction of the project, at which time it holds title to the project. Generally, an independent, nominally-capitalized corporation or financial institution acts as trustee, with limited discretionary authority. Typically the rents are guaranteed by the users, the trust's parent, some responsible source of credit, or take-or-pay contracts. The trust, for example, may borrow short-term to finance the construction against an unconditional take-out guarantee of the sponsors, who may need to guarantee the short-term debt. The trust offers tax and management advantages, but can be a very cumbersome way to do business.

Joint Venture. The joint venture is a contractual ralationship whereby the participants minimize their individual duties and obligations by sharing them. Joint ventures, which are covered by an operating agreement, are set up for limited periods with limited objectives. If one party forfeits, the others can sell its interests, and they may also be liable for its obligations. The manager is usually the participant with the most experience. Alternatively, the parties can appoint a corporation to act for them. Parties to a joint venture do not have general agency for one another, but are only liable to the extent of their investment and advances to the project; they own property as tenants in common, with undivided interests (that is, the property cannot be divided); and they can sue one another for breach of contract. Given that joint ventures are not legal entities, borrowing is difficult. However, each party can borrow individually against its interest, which it pledges as security, or on its own account. Joint ventures may also enter into leasing arrangements, with each party a co-lessee with an undivided interest in the joint venture. This structure is often used with mining projects and gas and electricity utilities sharing a common source of energy.

Leasing Companies

Leasing, which was discussed earlier, may go through an existing leasing company that may or may not be connected to one of the sponsors, or may be set up specifically for the purposes of the project.

Captive Financing Companies

Less well-known is the captive financing company. For the most part, they have been used by corporations that sell merchandise on credit. A captive financing company buys the purchase contracts from the parent company and assumes responsibility for collection. Because it can borrow against its accounts receivable, it can be used in project financing. Sponsors with existing captive finance companies may use them or may set one up specifically for the project, with capital in the form of accounts receivable and whatever else is necessary for start-up.

Turnkey Operations

As the name suggests, in a "turnkey" operation, a company, frequently multinational, sets up a project and then turns it over (sells it) to another company or entity. A variation is for someone else to manage it. The ultimate owner avoids the hassle of the tricky construction stage and the financing requirements. While the developer does have to arrange the financing, with one option a project financing package, it may be able to turn the operation over for a handsome profit.

Management Contracts

The management contract involves a third party running the project after completion. The manager assumes much of the risk in terms of the operational requirements, thus freeing the sponsor from some liability.

V. PUTTING THE PROJECT FINANCING PACKAGE TOGETHER

Although this section describes the process of putting a project financing package together from the perspective of the commercial lender, it will be clear from the discussion what a potential borrower must do to obtain financing from that source. One point is worth noting at the outset: borrowers have leverage, although it does not always seem so. First, making loans is a lender's business and often a major source of its profits. Risky projects often yield more profits, and the risks can be minimized. Second, a lender may have hidden agendas that make it more inclined to lend. For example, it may be interested in expanding into new areas of lending—mineral resource development, for example—or into a new geographic region, and may see the project as an appropriate vehicle. These kinds of agendas may push the lender to come to terms. Finally, a well-prepared proposal that addresses a lender's concerns is a persuasive tool.

The Criteria for Project Financing

What does a lender look for in a project? One is viability, because project financing repayments come from the proceeds of the project. Viability will be judged on the basis of:

- Careful, independent, reputable and conservative feasibility and engineering of studies that address: the economics of the project; the contingencies and the potential risks and problems (particularly cost overruns, delays in project completion, and change in financial conditions on which the assessment of feasibility is based, such as local taxes, availability of infrastructure, and prices, transportation (for output as well), and markets and purchasers; and stability and friendliness of the host-country government.

- A detailed plan for the acquisition of equipment and materials, especially if export credit facilities are to be part of the project financing.
- Identification of, and commitment from, a reputable contractor.
- Qualifications of the managerial staff and any special labor needs (also during start-up), and a valid management and operational plan.
- Description and justification of the technology to be used, which typically should be a proven commercial one.
- Plans for handling risks and contingencies, both operationally and financially, and where the risk burden lies.
- A well-designed financing plan, to include: the availability and source of the required equity financing; strong backing in terms of credit/guarantees (sometimes the backing is limited to the construction and/or start-up phases; sources and tentative commitment of additional financing and other support, with any contingency requirements by potential lenders and how they will be met; the financial and credit standing of any sponsors and third parties providing guarantees or other support; the proposed repayment plan, which should be designed realistically in terms of the project's cash flow and operating expenses and any contingencies that result in additional costs; and the range and nature of any risk coverage. As commercial lenders are not interested in equity or venture capital risk, the loan request must involve credit.
- The range of options in designing the financing plan is wide. The key is understanding the objectives of the different parties and their priorities and then choosing options that best meet those needs. Successful use of a similar plan elsewhere strengthens the proposal.
- The value of the assets of the project, which should have reasonable worth.
- Compliance with local laws and regulations and availability of the required government approvals.

Risk Analysis

With this information in hand, the lender will then conduct its own feasibility study and risk analysis of both the project and the country. It may request additional information based on its studies. Larger lending institutions may conduct their own assessments, or may choose (and most likely will do so if they are small) to hire outside experts, an approach that has the value of affording an independent opinion.

Negotiating the Project Financing

If the lender is satisfied with the feasibility of the project, it will initiate negotiation of the loan. It will want to have all the terms and obligations of all parties spelled out clearly. The negotiating team should include a lawyer highly experienced in project financing, as well as loan officers and other experts. Among the items to be settled are the provisions for lender response to certain contingencies, such as non-payment or delays in payment. The agreement may also spell out a method of conflict resolution, such as arbitration, a commonly-used technique. Where the lender is a syndicate, negotiations will also be conducted among the parties as to their roles and obligations. The lender will also develop a plan for monitoring and auditing project implementation and for the collection of funds.

REFERENCES

Baum, W., "The Project Cycle," *Finance and Development* 7(2), June 1972.

Eiteman, David K., and Arthur I. Stonehill, *Multinational Business Finance,* 3rd ed., Menlo Park, Calif.: Addison-Wesley Publishing Co., 1982.

Emerson, Christopher, *Project Financing,* London: Financial Times Business Enterprises, 1983.

Hall, William, "The Fashionable World of Project Finance," *The Banker,* January 1976.

Hellawell, Robert, and Don Wallace, Jr., eds., *Negotiating Foreign Investments: for the Third World,* Vol. I, The International Law Institute, Georgetown University Law School, Washington, D.C.: Georgetown University Law School, 1982, Chapter 6.

Huston, Robert L., "Project Finance," Merrill Lynch White Weld Capital Markets Group, New York.

Chapter Four:
International Marketing Management

MULTINATIONAL MARKETING strategies are formulated in conjunction with other functional areas such as production, finance, and R&D. These strategies are formulated in response to consumer needs and demands and the characteristics of the environment in which the consumer demands are satisfied.

It follows, therefore, that multinational marketing planning is the task of top management, which cannot be delegated to either a staff group of executives at the regional or country-management levels. There are several areas where strategies need to be developed in multinational marketing: the nature of the product, the types of brands and quality lines that must be marketed, the expansion or contraction of product lines, new product development, and other product-related areas.

The promotion of the product in different nations is fraught with problems. Cultural differences, availability and cost of media, identification of target markets, and the determination of appropriate messages make the task of advertising quite complex and expensive. Pricing policies have a direct impact on the profitability of the product. Determining the appropriate overhead-cost allocation to foreign product lines can be both nebulous and erroneous. Governmental policies in the form of anti-dumping legislation or price controls can add another variable in determining a fair price.

Distribution channels or methods of penetration of a foreign market are an integral part of the international marketing process—whether it is simple exporting or licensing or manufacturing—and add new complexities to the method of moving the product from the producer to the consumer.

Additionally, packaging and labeling, as well as transportation and storage, are issues that must be atteneded to. If the product and promotion are extended world-wide, or if either of the above variables are modified for global use, the marketing strategy will assume even more importance.

With many nations facing balance of payments problems, the use of countertrade has become an important part of many sales agreements. A good example of this trend may be seen in the case of Mexico, the subject of the last article in this chapter.

11
Multinational Product Planning: Strategic Alternatives

Warren J. Keegan

Multinational marketing planning also hinges on the consideration of appropriate international product strategies. Depending upon the product, the markets served, and company capabilities, MNCs have a variety of strategies to choose from in determining the most profitable approach to international marketing.

INADEQUATE PRODUCT PLANNING is a major factor inhibiting growth and profitability in international business operations today. The purpose of this article is to identify five strategic alternatives available to international marketers, and to identify the factors which determine the strategy a company should use. Table 1 summarizes the proposed strategic alternatives.

STRATEGY ONE:
ONE PRODUCT, ONE MESSAGE, WORLDWIDE

When PepsiCo extends its operations internationally, it employs the easiest and in many cases the most profitable marketing strategy—that of product extension. In every country in which it operates, PepsiCo sells exactly the same product, and does it with the same advertising and promotional themes and appeals that it uses in the United States. Pep-

Reprinted with permission from the *Journal of Marketing,* "Multinational Product Planning: Strategic Alternatives," Vol. 4 (January 1969), pp. 224-231, by permission of the American Marketing Association.

siCo's outstanding international performance is perhaps the most eloquent and persuasive justification of this practice.

Unfortunately, PepsiCo's approach does not work for all products. When Campbell Soup tried to sell its U.S. tomato soup formulation to the British, it discovered, after considerable losses, that the English prefer a more bitter taste. Another U.S. company spent several million dollars in an unsuccessful effort to capture the British cake mix market with U.S. style fancy frosting and cake mixes only to discover that Britons consume their cake at tea time, and that the cake they prefer is dry, spongy, and suitable to being picked up with the left hand while the right manages a cup of tea. Another U.S. company that asked a panel of British housewives to bake their favorite cakes, discovered this important fact and has since acquired a major share of the British cake mix market with a dry, spongy cake mix.

Close to home, Philip Morris attempted to take advantage of U.S. television advertising campaigns which have a sizable Canadian audience in border areas. The Canadian cigarette market is a Virginia or straight tobacco market in contrast to the U.S. market, which is a blended tobacco market. Philip Morris officials decided to ignore market research evidence which indicated that Canadians would not accept a blended cigarette, and went ahead with programs which achieved retail distribution of U.S. blended brands in the Canadian border areas served by U.S. television. Unfortunately, the Canadian preference for the straight cigarette remained unchanged. American-style cigarettes sold right up to the border but no further. Philip Morris had to withdraw its U.S. brands.

The unfortunate experience of discovering consumer preferences that do not favor a product is not confined to U.S. products in foreign markets. Corn Products Company discovered this is an abortive attempt to popularize Knorr dry soups in the United States. Dry soups dominate the soup market in Europe, and Corn Products tried to transfer some of this success to the United States. Corn Products based its decision to push ahead with Knorr on reports of taste panel comparisons of Knorr dry soups with popular liquid soups. The results of these panel tests strongly favored the Knorr product. Unfortunately these taste panel tests did not stimulate the actual market environment for soup which includes not only eating but also preparation. Dry soups require 15 to 20 minutes cooking, whereas liquid soups are ready to serve as soon as heated. This difference is apparently a critical factor in the soup buyer's

Table 1: Multinational Product-Communications Mix Strategic Alternatives

Strategy	Product Function of Need Satisfied	Conditions of Product Use	Ability to Buy Product	Recom- mended Product Strategy	Recommended Communications Strategy	Relative Cost of Adjust- ments	Product Examples
1	Same	Same	Yes	Extension	Extension	1	Soft drinks
2	Different	Same	Yes	Extension	Adaptation	2	Bicycles, Motor- scooters
3	Same	Different	Yes	Adaptation	Extension	3	Gasoline, Detergents
4	Different	Different	Yes	Adaptation	Adaptation	4	Clothing, Greeting cards
5	Same		No	Invention	Develop New Communications	5	Hand- powered washing machine

choice, and it was the reason for another failure of the extension strategy.

The product-communications extension strategy has an enormous appeal to most multinational companies because of the cost savings associated with this approach. Two sources of savings, manufacturing economies of scale and elimination of product R&D costs, are well known and understood. Less well known, but still important, are the substantial economies associated with the standardization of marketing communications. For a company with worldwide operations, the cost of preparing separate print and TV cinema films for each market would be enormous. Pepsico international marketers have estimated, for example, that production costs for specially prepared advertising for foreign markets would cost them $8 million per annum, which is considerably more than the amounts now spent by PepsiCo International for advertising production in these markets. Although these cost savings are important, they should not distract executives from the more important objective of maximum profit performance, which may require the use of an adjustment or invention strategy. As shown above, product extension in spite of its immediate cost savings may in fact prove to be a financially disastrous undertaking.

STRATEGY TWO:
PRODUCT EXTENSION—COMMUNICATIONS ADAPTATION

When a product fills a different need or serves a different function under use conditions identical or similar to those in the domestic market, the only adjustment required is in marketing communications. Bicycles and motorscooters are illustrations of products in this category. They satisfy needs mainly for recreation in the United States but provide basic transportation in many foreign countries. Outboard motors are sold primarily to a recreation market in the United States, while the same motors in many foreign countries are sold mainly to fishing and transportation fleets.

In effect, when this approach is pursued (or, as is often the case, when it is stumbled upon quite by accident), a product transformation occurs. The same physical product ends up serving a different function or use than that for which it was originally designed. An actual example of a very successful transformation is provided by a U.S. farm machinery company which decided to market its U.S. line of suburban lawn and garden power equipment as agricultural implements in less developed countries. The company's line of garden equipment was ideally suited to the farming task in many less-developed countries, and most importantly, it was priced at almost a third less than competing equipment especially designed for small acreage farming offered by various foreign manufacturers.

There are many examples of food product transformation. Many dry soup powders, for example, are sold mainly as soups in Europe but as sauces or cocktail dips in the United States. The products are identical: the only change is in marketing communications. In this case, the main communications adjustment is in the labeling of the powder. In Europe, the label illustrates and describes how to make soup out of the powder. In the United States, the label illustrates and describes how to make sauce and dip as well as soup.

The appeal of the product extension communications adaptation strategy is its relatively low cost of implementation. Since the product in this strategy is unchanged, R&D, tooling, manufacturing setup, and inventory costs associated with additions to the product line are avoided. The only costs of this approach are in identifying different product functions and reformulating marketing communications (advertising, sales promotion, point-of-sale material, and so on) around the newly identified function.

STRATEGY THREE:
PRODUCT ADAPTATION—COMMUNICATIONS EXTENSION

A third approach to international product planning is to extend without change the basic communications strategy developed for the

U.S. or home market, but to adapt the U.S. or home product to local use conditions. The product adaptation-communications extension strategy assumes that the product will serve the same function in foreign markets under different use conditions.

Esso followed this approach when it adapted its gasoline formulations to meet the weather conditions prevailing in foreign market areas, but employed without change its basic communications appeal, "Put a Tiger in Your Tank." There are many other examples of products that have been adjusted to perform the same function internationally under different environmental conditions. International soap and detergent manufacturers have adjusted their product formulations to meet local water conditions and the characteristics of washing equipment with no change in their basic communications approach. Agricultural chemicals have been adjusted to meet different soil conditions as well as different types and levels of insect resistance. Household appliances have been scaled to sizes appropriate to different use environments, and clothing has been adapted to meet fashion criteria.

STRATEGY FOUR: DUAL ADAPTATION

Market conditions indicate a strategy of adaptation of both the product and communications when diffferences exist in environmental conditions of use and in the function which a product serves. In essence, this is a combination of the market conditions of strategies two and three. U.S. greeting card manufacturers have faced these circumstances in Europe where the conditions under which greeting cards are purchased are different than in the United States. In Europe, the function of a greeting card is to provide a space for the sender to write his own message in contrast to the U.S. card which contains a prepared message or what is known in the greeting card industry as "sentiment." European greeting cards are cellophane wrapped, necessitating a product alteration by American greeting card manufacturers selling in the European market. American manufacturers pursuing an adjustment strategy have changed both their product and their marketing communications in response to this set of environmental differences.

STRATEGY FIVE: PRODUCT INVENTION

The adaptation and adjustment strategies are effective approaches to international marketing when potential customers have the ability, or purchasing power, to buy the product. When potential customers cannot afford a product, the strategy indicated is invention or the development of an entirely new product designed to satisfy the identified need or function at a price within reach of the potential customer. This is a demanding but, if product development costs are not excessive, a potentially rewarding product strategy for the mass markets in the middle and less-developed countries of the world.

Although potential opportunities for the utilization of the invention strategy in international marketing are legion, the number of instances where companies have responded is disappointingly small. For example, there are an estimated 600 million women in the world who still scrub their clothes by hand. These women have been served by multinational soap and detergent companies for decades, yet until this year not one of these companies had attempted to develop an inexpensive manual washing device.

Robert Young, Vice President of Marketing Worldwide of Colgate-Palmolive, has shown what can be done when product development efforts are focused upon market needs. He asked the leading inventor of modern mechanical washing processes to consider "inventing backwards"—to apply his knowledge not to a better mechanical washing device, but to a much better manual device. The device developed by the inventor is an inexpensive (under $10), all-plastic, hand-powdered washer that has the tumbling action of a modern automatic machine. The response to this washer in a Mexican test market is reported to be enthusiastic.

HOW TO CHOOSE A STRATEGY

The best product strategy is one which optimizes company profits over the long term, or, stated more precisely, it is one which maximizes the present value of cash flows associated with business operations. Which strategy for international markets best achieves this goal? There is, unfortunately, no general answer to this question. Rather, the answer depends upon the specific product-market-company mix.

Some products demand adaptation, others lend themselves to adaptation, and others are best left unchanged. The same is true of markets. Some are so similar to the U.S. markets as to require little adaptation. No country's markets, however, are exactly like the U.S., Canada's included. Indeed, even within the United States, for some products regional and ethnic differences are sufficiently important to require product adaptation. Other markets are moderately different and lend themselves to adaptation, and still others are so different as to require adaptation of the majority of products. Finally, companies differ not only in their manufacturing costs, but also in their capability to identify and produce profitable product adaptations.

PRODUCT-MARKET ANALYSIS

The first step in formulating international product policy is to apply the systems analysis technique to each product in question. How is the product used? Does it require power sources, linkage to other systems, maintenance, preparation, style matching, and so on? Examples of almost mandatory adaptation situations are products designed for 60-cycle power going into products which require maintenance going into markets where maintenance standards and practices differ from the original design market, and products which might be used under different conditions than those for which they were originally designed. Renault discovered this latter factor too late with the ill-fated Dauphine, which acquired a notorious reputation for break-down frequency in the United States. Renault executives attribute the frequent mechanical failure of the Dauphine in the United States to the highspeed turnpike driving and relatively infrequent U.S. maintenance. These turned out to be critical differences for the product, which was designed for the roads of France and the almost daily maintenance which a Frenchman lavishes upon his car.

Even more difficult are the product adaptations which are clearly not mandatory, but which are of critical importance in determining whether the product will appeal to a narrow market segment rather than a broad mass market. The most frequent offender in this category is price. Too often, U.S. companies believe they have adequately adapted their international product offering by making adaptations to the physical features of products (for example, converting 120 volts to 220 volts) but they extend U.S. prices. The effect of such practice in most markets of the world where average incomes are lower than those in the United States is to put the U.S. product in a specialty market for the relatively wealthy consumers rather than in the mass market. An extreme case of this occurs when the product for the foreign market is exported from the United States and undergoes the often substantial price escalation that occurs when products are sold via multi-layer export channels and exposed to import duties. When price constraints are considered in international marketing, the result can range from margin reduction and feature elimination to the "inventing backwards" approach used by Colgate.

COMPANY ANALYSIS

Even if product-market analysis indicates an adaptation opportunity, each company must examine its own product/communication development and manufacturing costs. Clearly, any product or communication adaptation strategy must survive the test of profit effectiveness. The often-repeated exhortation that in international marketing a company should always adapt its products' advertising and promotion is clearly superficial, for its does not take into account the cost of adjusting or adapting products and communications programs.

WHAT ARE ADAPTATION COSTS?

They fall under two broad categories—development and production. Development costs will vary depending on the cost effectiveness of product/communications development groups within the company. The range in costs from company to company and product to product is great. Often the company with international product development facilities has a strategic cost advantage. The vice-president of a leading U.S. machinery company told recently of an example of this kind of advantage:

We have a machinery development group both here in the States and also in Europe. I tried to get our U.S. group to develop a machine for making the elliptical cigars that dominate the European market. At first they said, "who would want an elliptical cigar machine?" Then they gradually admitted that they could produce such a machine for $500,000. I went to our Italian product development group with the same proposal, and they developed the machine I wanted for $50,000. The differences were partly relative wage costs but very importantly they were psychological. The Europeans see elliptical cigars every day, and they do not find the elliptical cigar unusual. Our American engineers were negative on elliptical cigars at the outset and I think this affected their overall response.

Analysis of a company's manufacturing costs is essentially a matter of identifying potential opportunity losses. If a company is reaping economies of scale from large scale production of a single product, then any shift to variations of the single product will raise manufacturing costs. In general, the more decentralized a company's manufacturing setup, the smaller the manufacturing cost of producing different versions of the basic product. Indeed, in the company with local manufacturing facilities for each international market, the additional *manufacturing* cost of producing an adapted product for each market is zero.

A more fundamental form of company analysis occurs when a firm is considering in general whether or not to pursue explicitly a strategy of product adaptation. At this level, analysis must focus not only on the manufacturing cost structure of the firm, but also on the basic capability of the firm to identify product adaptation opportunities and to convert these perceptions into profitable products. The ability to identify preferences will depend to an important degree on the creativity of people in the organization and the effectiveness of information systems in this organization. The latter capability is as important as the former. For example, the existence of salesmen who are creative in identifying profitable product adaptation opportunities is no assurance that their ideas will be translated into reality by the organization. Information, in the form of their ideas and perceptions, must move through the organization to those who are involved in the product development decision-making process; and this movement, as any student of information systems in organizations will attest, is not automatic. Companies which lack perceptual and information system capabilities are not well equipped to pursue a product adaptation strategy, and should either concentrate on products which can be extended or should develop these capabilities before turning to a product adaptation strategy.

SUMMARY

The choice of product and communications strategy in international marketing is a function of three key fctors: (1) the product itself defined in terms of the function or need it serves; (2) the market defined in terms of the conditions under which the product is used, including the preferences of potential customers and the ability to buy the products in question; and (3) the costs of adaptation and manufacture to the company considering these product-communications approaches. Only after analysis of the product-market fit and of company capabilities and costs can executives choose the most profitable international strategy.

12
Negotiating Compensation in International Licensing Agreements

Franklin R. Root and Farok J. Contractor

Little is known about how compensation is negotiated between parties engaging in agreements licensing technology. The methodology used in negotiation of licensing compensation is neither explicit nor systematic. Maturing technologies, more intense rivalry among technology suppliers, growing sophistication of technology recipients, and greater involvement of governments are together creating a more competitive international technology market.

THE LICENSING OF technology is one of the fastest growing areas of international business. In 1978 global licensing payments were approximately $14 billion, and U.S. companies alone received nearly $6 billion in that year.[1] Yet little is known about how payments are determined in the negotiations between licensors and licensees, despite the long standing debate on "technology pricing" in international forums.[2] In this article we begin to remedy this oversight by comparing actual behavior in licensing negotiations, based on an investigation of licensing agreements made by thirty-nine U.S. firms with independent licensees in forty-one countries, against a *normative* model of licensing negotiations. More specifically, the following questions are addressed: What are the returns to licensors from international licensing agreements? How do these returns compare to licensing costs? What factors do U.S. managers consider in negotiating licensing compensation? What factors are empirically associated with licensing compensation? How *should* managers negotiate licensing agreements?

REVENUES AND COSTS IN LICENSING

A licensing agreement transfers industrial property rights (patents and trademarks) and technical know-how to an unaffiliated licensee in return for compensation paid to the licensor.[3] The licensee enters the agreement because the possession of the property rights and know-how will provide a competitive advantage in the local market and, therefore, will ensure higher profits. Thus the source of licensing revenue is the exploitation of proprietary technology by the licensee. Revenues from the sale of the licensed product (or cost savings from the use of the licensed industrial process) are shared with the licensor during the agreement's life. The excess of all licensing revenues over all costs may be considered the economic rent of the agreement. Figure 1 depicts the allocation of the licensee's revenues from the product market to the cost of both parties and to their shares of economic rent. While this depiction is somewhat tautological, it will enable us to formulate a negotiating model.

The economic rent of the licensing agreement is defined as the licensee's total revenue from the sale (or use) of the licensed product minus the sum of the licensee's production and marketing costs and the licensor's transfer costs: $(a + b + c + d + e + f) - (a + f) = (b + c + d + e)$. The agreement's economic rent is divided into the licensee's share (b) and the licensor's share ($c + d + e$).

Figure 1: Allocation of Total Revenue to Costs and Economic Rent

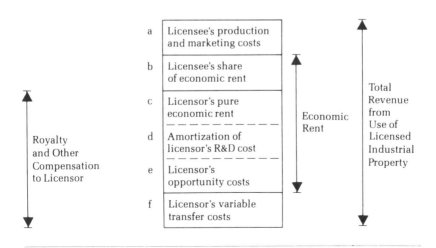

The licensor's compensation has to be allocated to three types of costs before we can describe the remainder as pure rent accruing to the licensor from the technology. The licensor's transfer costs are all the variable costs incurred in transferring technology to the licensee and all the on-going costs of maintaining the agreement—technical services, legal services, marketing assistance, travel and personnel costs, and other direct costs of executing the agreement. In addition to these transfer costs, two other kinds of costs are borne by the licensor: (1) the R&D cost of the licensed technology and (2) opportunity costs arising from the foreclosure of other sources of profit, such as exports or direct investment in the licensee's territory or in other countries. Figure 1 includes R&D costs in the licensor's share of the economic rent to indicate the possibility that licensing revenues may be used to amortize R&D expenditures of the licensor.[4] The sum $(c + d + e)$ therefore is designated more properly as the licensor's "contribution margin." The size of this margin in relation to transfer costs is of empirical interest.

A NORMATIVE MODEL OF LICENSING NEGOTIATIONS

THE LICENSOR'S OFFER PRICE RANGE

The model postulates that the licensor enters negotiations with a range of possible *offer prices* that the licensor is prepared to accept as compensation. Figure 2 shows one possible configuration of the model. The licensor's *offer floor price* is the sum of the present values of the transfer costs and opportunity costs. The licensor's *ceiling offer price* is the lower of two present values: (1) the value of the technology package to the licensee as perceived by the licensor and (2) the cost to the licensee of obtaining the same technology package from another source, as perceived by the licensor. The licensor will refuse to enter an agreement if the compensation does not cover the transfer and opportunity costs and will not expect to get more compensation than the ceiling price. The licensor's floor price does not account for R&D costs, but by securing a compensation higher than the floor, a contribution will be made toward this cost category.

THE LICENSEE'S BID PRICE RANGE

The licensor's offer price range is confronted by the licensee's bid price range. The licensee's *bid floor price* is the licensee's estimate of the licensor's transfer costs, but it omits any allowance for the licensor's opportunity cost which does not concern the licensee. The licensee's *bid ceiling*

Figure 2: A Configuration of the Normative Model of Licensing Negotiations

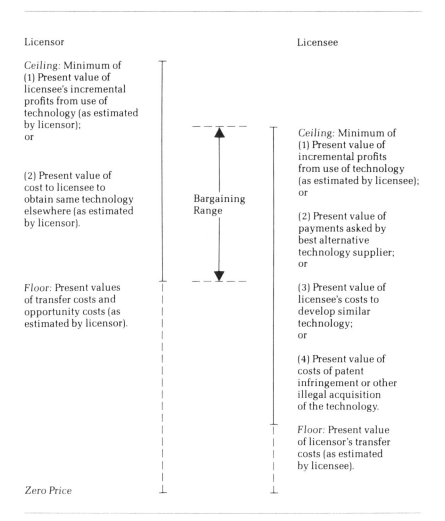

Licensor

Licensee

Ceiling: Minimum of
(1) Present value of
licensee's incremental
profits from use of
technology (as estimated
by licensor);
or

(2) Present value of
cost to licensee to
obtain same technology
elsewhere (as estimated
by licensor).

Floor: Present values
of transfer costs and
opportunity costs (as
estimated by licensor).

Zero Price

Bargaining
Range

Ceiling: Minimum of
(1) Present value of
incremental profits
from use of technology
(as estimated by licensee);
or

(2) Present value of
payments asked by
best alternative
technology supplier;
or

(3) Present value of
licensee's costs to
develop similar
technology;
or

(4) Present value of
costs of patent
infringement or other
illegal acquisition
of the technology.

Floor: Present value
of licensor's transfer
costs (as estimated
by licensee).

price is the lowest of four present values: (1) the licensee's incremental profits from the use of the technology package, (2) the cost of the technology package from the best alternative supplier, (3) the full cost to develop the technology package independently, and (4) the cost of obtaining the technology through illicit means, such as theft, illegal copying, or deliberate patent infringement.

The overlap of the licensor's and licensee's bid ranges—the distance between the licensor's floor price and the licensee's ceiling price—determines the bargaining range. Negotiations are possible only if the licensee's ceiling price is higher than the licensor's floor price. This condition is easily met in territories such as Eastern Europe. With exporting or direct investment precluded, opportunity costs are likely to be zero; the licensor's floor price is equal to the transfer costs. However, if expert or other business opportunities are attractive, the licensor's floor price may be greater than the licensee's ceiling price; licensing is not desirable in that country for the technology holder. Another reason for high opportunity costs is the threat that the licensee will become a competitor in third markets. This explains why many multinational firms regard arm's length licensing as a second or third best strategy option—to be resorted to only when investment and competitive threat is minimal.

THE NEGOTIATING PRICE

The final negotiated price is a point within the bargaining range. Each part seeks to negotiate a price that increases its share of the agreement's economic rent. At the licensor's floor price, the licensee gains all the pure economic rent. But at the licensee's ceiling price, the licensor gains all the pure economic rent only if that ceiling price equals the licensee's incremental profits from the use of the technology package. If the licensee's ceiling price lies below its incremental profits, then both parties share in the economic rent. Hence, the licensor can gain all the pure economic rent only if it is the sole supplier of a technology package and if the licensee's cost of duplicating that package exceeds the incremental profits to be gained from its use. A priori, there is no reason to assume that either party can obtain the full economic rent or any particular share of it.

Does this normative model explain the actual behavior of the two parties in negotiating the price of a technology package? To answer that question, we would need to make an empirical investigation of both licensors and licensees. Since our research is confined to the licensors, we can only ascertain if licensors behave in accordance with the model.

FACTORS CONSIDERED BY U.S. MANAGERS

Managers in the thirty-nine sample companies were asked to rank by importance the factors they considered in negotiating compensation in licensing agreements with independent foreign licensees.[5] These factors, derived from the normative model and the licensing literature, were presented in random order to executives. Responses are shown in

Table 1: Factors Considered by U.S. Managers in Negotiating Compensation [a]

Rank	Factors[b]	Score[c]
1	Amount of technical and other services provided to licensee	127
2	Industry norms	105
3	Licensee's market size and profitability	102
4	Take what's available	61
5	R&D expenditure	50
6	Returns must at least equal returns from exporting or direct investment	28
7	Less for old or obsolescent technology	27
8	Less when patent is expiring	10
9	Grantbacks	5
10	Patent coverage	3

a—The sample size was thirty-seven companies.
b—Factors from the model as well as other factors found in licensing literature were supplied in random order to executives.
c—Managers were asked to pick five of the nine factors, assigning "5" to the most important, "4" to the next most important, and so on. Factors not chosen were assigned a value of "0."

Table 1. The focus of the empirical investigation was on arm's-length negotiation, even though all the factors shown would apply to agreements with foreign affiliates as well. However, several studies have shown that in intracorporate licensing these factors may be overshadowed by tax minimization and other considerations.[6]

The low ranking of R&D expenditure sustains the normative model, which postulates that the R&D cost of the technology package is not considered by the licensor in determining the offer price range. Preliminary interviews in twelve companies revealed that managers seldom refer to R&D costs in licensing negotiations and then only as a negotiating ploy or as an estimate of what it may cost the licensee to develop the technology independently. One reason for this is the difficulty in assigning R&D costs to a particular agreement in multiproduct firms with joint R&D costs, especially when these costs are usually incurred several years before the agreement in question. A second reason is that firms usually amortize R&D expenditures only over domestic and foreign-affiliate sales.

The low ranking of opportunity cost ("returns must at least equal returns from exporting or direct investment") departs from the normative model. In the preliminary interviews, most managers said that they did not explicitly calculate the opportunity costs of licensing agreements;

they cited reasons ranging from ignorance of such costs to a belief that the calculations would be at best tenuous or hypothetical. Apparently, opportunity costs do not formally enter the licensor's floor price in negotiating practice. The expectation that licensing revenues from a proposed agreement would be a large multiple of transfer costs was adequate assurance to many negotiators that opportunity costs were being "covered."

The top-ranked factor is the amount of technical and other services provided to the licensee. If we interpret this factor as transfer costs, then its ranking supports the importance of transfer cost in the normative model.[7] But for the present, this finding can be regarded only as tentative.

DETERMINANTS OF CEILING PRICES

"Industry norms" can be regarded as a proxy for the cost to the licensee of obtaining the technology package from another licensor. Industry norms are most prevalent in cases where there are several licensors and licensee firms worldwide.[8] The licensor asks for a royalty rate or for other compensation that is believed to be in line with what other licensors would demand for the same technology package. Probing this question revealed that industry norms may apply either to royalty rates or to total revenues expected from an agreement. Executives in some industries reported that licensees pay quite uniform rates on a unit or percentage basis for standardized, mature technologies, such as electroplating or galvanizing. Other executives indicated that licensees throughout the world are becoming concerned about their total payment for technology, including lump-sum fees, royalties, and technical assistance fees.

"Licensee's market size and profitability" may be viewed as a proxy for the licensee's incremental profits from the use of the technology package. The high ranking therefore appears to agree with the normative model. The preliminary interviews, however, did not uncover any evidence that licensors make systematic market investigations to determine the value of their technology to licensees, as called for in the model. While a majority of interviewed executives indicated that they do study the licensee's market, less than a quarter indicated the possibility or desirability of a quantitative estimate of the licensee's incremental profit.

These responses tell us the relative importance that managers assign to several factors in negotiating compensation in licensing agreements. But what do actual data from licensing agreements tell us about compensation and the factors that influence it?

A SAMPLE OF INTERNATIONAL LICENSING AGREEMENTS

Our data on returns and costs to licensors are drawn from a sample of 102 recent licensing agreements in forty-one countries, negotiated by thirty-nine U.S. companies. The distribution of these agreements by region and product is presented in Table 2. The regional distribution conforms roughly to the universe of U.S. licensing agreements as estimated by the U.S. Department of Commerce from form BE-93, which is filed by all U.S. firms receiving licensing income from nonaffiliated foreign licensees. As in that universe, about three-quarters of the sample agreements are with licensees in the industrial countries. Unfortunately, there is no way of knowing if the sample distribution matches that of the universe with regard to product or to licensor size, since the Department of Commerce does not provide product or size breakdowns for receipts from nonaffiliated licensees. The data represent a little over one percent of the known universe. The sample licensing agreements are confined to agreements with foreign firms which are not affiliated with the licensors. They are all arm's-length agreements. The mean life of the sample licensing agreements is 12.6 years, and all but seven were in force in 1978.

Table 2: Distribution of 102 Licensing Agreements by Region and Product Type.

Product type	Industrial Countries	Developing Countries	Communist Countries	Total
Consumer Products	3	10	0	13
Industrial Equipment	18	5	1	24
Semi-Finished and Intermediate Components and Processes	29	5	2	36
Chemicals	19	3	2	24
Pharmaceuticals	3	1	0	4
Other	1	0	0	1
Total	73	24	5	102

The product types include the following United Nations category numbers: consumer products (11, 12, 61, and 63); industrial equipment (41, 51, and 52); and semi-finished and intermediate components and processes (21, 22, 42, and 53).
SOURCE: United Nations. *Classification by Broad Economic Categories* (New York: ECOSOC Statistical Paper Series M, No. 52, Rev. 1, 1976).

The licensor's contribution margin is defined as the total returns from the licensing agreement minus the transfer costs to effect and maintain the agreement. The contribution margin is not synonymous with profit or pure economic rent because some of it may be allocable to opportunity cost and R&D cost. The average contribution margins by industrial, developing, and Communist countries are shown in Table 3.

Table 3 indicates that the average transfer costs of licensing agreements are substantial. Like an earlier investigation by Teece, this finding does not support the assertion that transfer costs are zero or inconsequential.[9] But it is true that average returns are far higher than transfer costs, which results in very sizable contribution margins. When we average the return/cost ratios of the individual agreements, we obtain a multiple of 45.9 for agreements with licensees in industrial countries and significantly lower multiples for licensees in the developing and Communist countries. These differences do not concern us here, but we may note in passing that they do not support the allegation that licensors discriminate against the developing countries.

Table 3: Arithmetic Means of Total Returns and Transfer Costs
of 102 Licensing Agreements

	Industrial Countries	Developing Countries	Communist Countries
Total Returns to Licensor	$3,912,000	$3,284,000	$2,066,000
Transfer Costs of Licensor	192,000	280,000	349,000
Licensor's Contribution Margin	3,720,000	3,004,000	1,717,000
Mean Return/Cost Ratio of the Agreements	45.9	9.1	12.7

The returns and transfer cost totals represent the undiscounted totals over each agreement life. The return/cost ratio is the mean of the ratios of the individual agreements. Therefore, it does not equal the ratio of the aggregate returns and costs shown for the country groups.

If transfer costs occur mainly in the early years of an agreement and the returns come mainly in the later years, then discounting returns and costs should reduce the return/cost ratios. This is indeed the case for the industrial and developing countries, as shown in Table 4.

STATISTICAL ANALYSIS OF LICENSING AGREEMENT DATA

Regression analysis was used to identify those variables that systematically influence licensing compensation. Several regressions were attempted, using different measures of licensor compensation as the dependent variable and several features of an agreement's cost, technology, and limitations as independent variables. These variables are shown in Table 5.

Only equations 2 and 3, which use *total royalties* and *total returns* as the dependent variables show significant correlations.[10] The overlap in the sample between total returns and total royalties is considerable; royalties, usually a percentage of the licensee's sales, occur in four-fifths of the sample agreements, and when they occur they account for an average of 85 percent of the licensor's total returns. In equations 2 and 3, the greatest increment to the R^2 values comes from total transfer costs; the greater the transfer costs, the greater the total returns or total royalties. The other important independent variable is the recipient's plant scale; the greater the plant scale, the greater the total returns or total royalties. None of the other independent variables is significant at the 1 percent level and only one—technical transfer costs, as distinguished from other transfer costs—is significant at the 5 percent level.

IMPLICATIONS OF THE REGRESSION RESULTS

HOW LICENSOR COMPENSATION IS DETERMINED

What are we to make of these regression results? They suggest that managers negotiate for target *total returns* (which in the majority of

Table 4: Means of Total Returns and Transfer Costs of 102 Licensing Agreements Discounted at 15 Percent

	Industrial Countries	Developing Countries	Communist Countries
Total Returns to Licensor	$411,000	$422,000	$382,000
Transfer Costs of Licensor	85,000	138,000	156,000
Licensor's Contribution Margin	326,000	284,000	226,000
Mean Return/Cost Ratio of the Agreements	35.0	8.0	13.7

agreements are mainly royalties) rather than for target royalty rates, target contribution margins, or target return/cost ratios. There is no *a priori* or empirical reason for believing that the royalty rate bears any relationship to total royalty compensation which is determined by the royalty compensation, which is determined by the royalty rate and the licensee's sales or production volume. The regression results for equation 2 and for equation 3 suggest that licensors target total returns by estimating, however crudely, the sales or output of licensees. Several interviews support the proposition that licensors make "ball park" estimates of expected licensee output further supported by the significance of the "plant scale" variable in equations 2 and 3. If we interpret this variable as an indirect measure of the licensee's sales of the licensed

Table 5: Dependent and Independent Variables Used in Regression Analysis

Dependent Variable (Measure of Licensor Compensation)	Independent Variables	Unit Measure for Independent Variables
1. The royalty rate as a percentage of licensee sales	Total transfer costs of licensor	Total $ value over agreement life
	Technical service costs of licensor	Total $ value over agreement life[a]
2. Total $ value of royalty receipts over agreement life	Agreement life	In years
	Remaining patent life	In years; zero if not applicable
	Trademark dummy	1 when trademark right transferred; zero otherwise
3. Total $ value of all compensation types over agreement life		
	Export dummy	1 when licensee export permitted; zero otherwise
4. Total $ value of "contribution margin" over agreement life	Licensor R&D	$ 1976
	Recipient firm plant scale	Ratio of licensee's plant size to licensor's typical plant
5. The ratio of total returns to total transfer costs	Degree of supplier competition	Estimate number of alternative global suppliers for technology
	Technology adapted or not	1: yes; 2: somewhat; 3: no
	Commercial age of technology	Years from commercial inception anywhere till agreement start-up

a—This variable has a low correlation with total transfer costs. In general, multicollinearity among independent variables is not a problem.

product, or at least as positively correlated with those sales, then this finding also agrees with the high ranking given by managers to the licensee's market size.

THE IMPORTANCE OF TRANSFER COSTS

In deciding on target total returns, managers are influenced strongly by an agreement's transfer costs. This finding coincides with the top ranking given by managers to the amount of technical and other services provided to the licensee, as shown in Table 1. The influence of transfer costs on total returns does not imply that licensors negotiate for compensation as a mark-up on transfer costs. In view of the high return/cost ratios, it is evident that licensors do not practice cost-plus or cost-competitive pricing strategies. On the other hand, neither do licensors practice pure monopoly pricing strategies by charging "what the traffic will bear." Pure monopoly pricing would not be influenced by transfer costs (except as a floor price). Instead, pricing strategy appears to be based on the assumption that higher transfer costs "deserve" a higher compensation. But how much higher? The target compensation apparently reflects the manager's judgment of the value of the technology package to the licensee (as partly indicated by the licensee's plant scale) and of the costs of transferring the technology to the licensee. Regression analysis does not indicate a systematic influence of "industry norms" on compensation. The high ranking given to this factor in Table 1 may merely reflect a desire by executives to appear to conform to industry practices. Licensors are engaging in "satisficing" rather than in maximizing behavior. This finding is consistent with the literature on the subject.[11]

SATISFICING RATHER THAN MAXIMIZING

Satisficing behavior on the part of licensors is suggested by several findings of this study. Managers do not make systematic assessments of opportunity costs, and they do not assign R&D costs to particular licensing agreements. Furthermore, managers seldom make quantitative estimates of a licensee's prospective incremental profits in order to calculate a ceiling price prior to negotiations. Indeed, our interviews reveal that licensors do not want to obtain a ceiling price because they believe that efforts to maximize licensing revenues would be counterproductive. Instead, they stated a willingness to accept a minority share of economic rent for several reasons: the entrepreneurial risk borne by the licensee, the dependence of a successful agreement on a good relationship (royalties are dependent on the licensee's performance and therefore on his incentive to perform), and the ability of a licensee to "cheat" on an agreement if he becomes dissatisfied with it. As long as there is a wide margin between total compensation and transfer costs, managers are satisfied that there is also adequate coverage of R&D and opportunity costs.

CONCLUSIONS

Actual negotiation of licensing compensation differs from the normative model in two important respects: (1) the practice of satisficing rather than maximizing behavior, and (2) the lack of any explicit or systematic attention to opportunity costs.

As they do not seek to maximize contribution margins, managers may obtain a lower share of an agreement's economic rent than they would obtain with more information about the value of the technology package to the recipient firm. In the preliminary interviews, only one-fourth of the managers indicated that their companies customarily make a formal assessment of the licensee's sales potential to get an estimate of the licensee's incremental profits. Although managers fail to maximize returns, our investigation reveals high return/cost ratios in licensing agreements. When returns cover transfer costs (for which licensors believe thay have good estimates) many times over, managers feel no need to maximize their share of the economic rent.

Perhaps a more serious drawback of negotiating practice compared to the normative model is the failure to consider opportunity cost. Ordinarily, a company can exploit a foreign market through exports and direct investment as well as through licensing . But if a company chooses to license a foreign firm, it is then usually prevented from exploiting the foreign market in any other way. A licensing agreement almost always grants the licensee the exclusive right to use the technology (including trademarks) in his own country, and it is seldom easy for the licensor to break a licensing agreement. Licensing may also create a competitor for the licensor if the licensee enters third markets or the licensor's home market. The literature on international licensing cites many instances of opportunity costs that were not considered by licensors in negotiating agreements. Opportunity costs can be safely ignored only when licensing is the sole way a company can enter a foreign market and when the licensee poses no competitive threat in other markets.

In the past the technological dominance of U.S. companies has made it easy for them to obtain licensing returns substantially above their transfer costs. But the future may be different. Maturing technologies, more intense rivalry among technology suppliers, growing sophistication of technology recipients, and greater involvement of governments are together creating a more competitive international technology market. To prosper in that market, U.S. companies may well be forced to bring their negotiating practice closer to the normative model.

REFERENCES

1. Sources of these estimates are respectively the United Nations Center on Transnational Corporations and the U.S. Department of Commerce.
2. Opinion on the subject has ranged from a "cost-related" concept to a "monopoly-price" concept. For contrasting views, see: J. Bache and M. Duerr, *International Transfer of Technology: A Worldwide Survey of Chief Executives* (New York: The Conference Board, 1975); United Nations, *The Acquisition of Technology from Multinational Corporations by Developing Countries* (New York: United Nations, 1974).
3. It is not the purpose of this article to describe the nature of technology transfer, a subject which has an extensive literature. See, for example, J. Baranson and A. Harrington, *Industrial Transfer of Technology by U.S. Firms under Licensing Arrangements* (Washington, D.C.: Developing World Industry and Technology, Inc., 1977).
4. It is questionable that licensors view income from *independent* licensees as partly an amortization of R&D expenditures. Several scholars assert that international managers view direct foreign investment as the preferred strategy even though licensing may be a superior strategy in some countries. Hence R&D expenditures are motivated by opportunities in the home market and in the principal foreign markets in which an international company has manufacturing subsidiaries. See, for example: P. Buckley and M. Casson, *The Future of the Multinational Enterprise* (New York: Holmes and Meier, 1977); J. Baranson, *Technology and the Multinationals* (Cambridge, Ma.: Lexington Books, 1978).
5. The thirty-nine sample companies were selected to achieve a country distribution of licensing agreements that matched the country distribution of U.S. nonaffiliate licensing receipts. Thirty-one of the thirty-nine sample panies are in the *Fortune 500* list. The sample firms cover all the broad product categories with the exception of petroleum.
6. Compensation from agreements with affiliated licensees is often biased by taxes and nonmarket factors. See G. Kopits, "Intra-Firm Royalties Crossing Frontiers and Transfer-Pricing Behavior," *The Economic Journal* (December 1975): 791-805.
7. There was no way to explain the concept of transfer costs to the respondents without biasing the results.
8. In extreme cases, there may be a "most favored licensee" clause under which the licensor is obligated to grant a licensee the same terms he grants

to any other licensee. See M. Finnegan and H. Mints, "Determination of a Reasonable Royalty in Negotiating a License Agreement: Practical Pricing for Successful Technology Transfer," *Licensing Law and Business Report* (June 1978): 24.

9. See D. Teece, *The Multinational Corporation and the Resource Cost of International Technology Transfer* (Cambridge, MA: Ballinger, 1977). For the view that transfer costs are minimal, see R. Caves, "International Corporations: The Industrial Economics of Foreign Investment," *Economica*, February 1971, pp. 1-27.

10. Equation 2:

$$R_2 = -.195 + .297C_1^{**} - .191C_2^{*} - .236L + .349P + .257K + .622E - .194D + .135S^{**} - .175T_1 + .301T_2 - .759T_3$$

$df = (11, 38); R^2 = .63; R^{-2} = .52;$ overall F value = 5.894

Equation 3:

$$R_2 = -.142 + .325C_1^{**} - .216C_2^{*} - .241L + .368P + .341K - .766D + .125S^{**} - .109T_1 + .324T_2 - .138T_3$$

$df = (10, 39); R^2 = .66; R^{-2} = .57;$ overall F value = 7.415

**	= significant at 1 percent or better
*	= significant at 5 percent or better
R_2	= total royalties
R_3	= total compensation
C_1	= total transfer costs
C_2	= total technical costs
L	= agreement life
P	= remaining patent life
K	= trademark dummy
E	= export dummy
D	= licensor R&D in 1976
S	= plant scale ratio
T_1	= degree of supplier competition
T_2	= technology adapted or not
T_3	= commercial age of technology.

11. See, for example, J. Behrman and W. Schmidt, "Royalty Provisions in Foreign Licensing Contracts," *Patent, Trademark, and Copyright Journal of Research and Education* (Fall 1959): 272-299. Business International, *Opportunities and Challenges in Worldwide Technology Management* (New York, 1977).

13
Countertrade Options and Economic Development: Mexico Under the PROFIEX

Ann Elizabeth Robinson

This study is based on a series of interviews with over 50 representatives of the public and private sectors in Mexico City and the United States. It examines the use of linked trade arrangements, and how they could be applied to achieve the goals of national economic development. The focal point for the discussion is the Programa Fomento Integral a las Exportaciones (PROFIEX), which establishes the policy context for the use of countertrade options. Within the context of Mexico's attempts to reorient its policies of economic development towards the exploitation of external forces, the De la Madrid administration has turned to countertrade to obtain commercial, industrial, and social goals.

BACKGROUND

The basis for this article is a series of 28 interviews, which were conducted in May, 1985, with representatives of the public and private sectors in Mexico. The question that was foremost in my mind was: Can countertrade—or, more broadly, compensatory arrangements—be a valid tool in achieving the economic development goals of a country: in this case, Mexico.

The Mexican government announced a general program to promote trade and industrial development in July, 1984—the PRONAFICE, or Programa Nacional de Fomento Industrial y Comercio Exterior, aims to create structural changes in the Mexican national economy that will permit self-sustained growth.

Ideally, Mexico would like to generate its own foreign currency requirements through an industrialization process which "progressively reduces the demand for imports, promotes exports, and selectively substitutes imports." Although industrialization had been Mexico's engine for economic growth for four decades and a diversified manufacturing sector had developed, industry was not integrated. Inputs for industry were either imported or purchased from inefficient and protected domestic producers at higher than world market prices. The result was an industrial base that was dependent upon imports and that could not compete internationally.

Further, Mexico's economy had alternated between "boom and bust" cycles during the administration of former President Lopez Portillo (1976–82). By 1982 the economic picture was once again bleak. Therefore, President Miguel de la Madrid Hurtado, whose administration began in December, 1982, determined that a different approach was needed to overcome this economic volatility and the accompanying crisis mentality. This was especially true, given the continuing drop in oil prices and the shortage of international credit.[1] The only alternative was to refocus the Mexican economy outwardly, financing imports with resources from national industry.[2] The new approach included reducing the public and private sector debt, freezing borrowing, and turning the trade deficit into a surplus. In other words, Mexico decided to develop and rely on its capacity to produce, rather than to depend upon external sources of funds, and to diversify exports, rather than to base economic planning upon expected revenues from a single commodity—i.e., oil.

PRONAFICE and PROFIEX were the two major programs set up to realize these objectives and to move Mexico out of the grips of the debt crisis it had entered in 1982. They both emphasize foreign direct investment in Mexico and export promotion. Although Mexico was a domestic-oriented economy prior to 1982, today the public and private sectors believe it is essential for Mexico to become a diversified exporter and to enter the international marketplace.

RECENT EVENTS

Events in Mexico since the beginning of 1985 are making the PRO-NAFICE a reality. On February 7, 1985, the Government presented a new scheme of fiscal austerity, which included an across-the-board cut in public spending by 4 percent; the selling or liquidation of over 200 parastatals; and a shift in import-control policies, from regulation by permits to regulation by tariffs. On March 5, 1985, a policy of "desliz"—a daily devaluation of the peso—was begun to even out the periodic drops in the value of the peso. Then, in July, both the "controlled rate" and the "free rate" peso were devalued significantly (about 20 percent for the controlled rate and 43 percent for the free rate). In early April, PROFIEX was established, followed in June by its much-debated companion policy, DIMEX.

DIMEX—or Import Rights for Exporters—became effective June 7, 1985. It allows exporters to import up to 30 percent of the value of their exports without import licenses. To be eligible for this right, the product must have at least 30 percent Mexican value added. Further, the imports must be used as inputs for final products, or they may be sold to suppliers—i.e., the imports must contribute to the integration of the production process and lead to the generation of export revenues. Items which are excluded represent 28.7 percent of the value of 1984 imports.[3]

The DIMEX was originally to have been released with PROFIEX and to have been much more liberal. As conceived, it would have allowed imports of up to 40 percent of the value of exports and would not have required that they be used in the productive process. Further, the exclusions were more limited.

In addition to these measures, two other liberalization developments occurred; these events will facilitate countertrade and barter deals as well as trade in general. On May 8, 1985, SECOFI, the Mexican Ministry of Trade and Industrial Development, announced that imported materials which are used in the production of exports can be treated as "temporary imports" and are not subject to import duty.[4]

Secondly, on July 25, and on August 1, of 1985, the *Diario Oficial* announced the elimination of import permits on products, which represented 61.4 percent of the value of Mexico's 1984 imports. In most cases, the import permits are being replaced by an increase in the import duty so that most duties now fall within the 15–25 percent range, according to the Government of Mexico. At the same time, the minimum 25 percent tariff which was part of the June 6 DIMEX announcement was reduced to a minimum 10 percent tariff as part of the liberalization process.[5]

How this liberalization will affect the commercial trade balance is unclear, although it is possible that in the beginning the percentage of additional imports could exceed the percentage of additonal exports. This new external competition is expected to speed up the process of weeding out inefficient industries. The Banco de Mexico *Indicadores Economicos* cites the following figures for the commercial trade balance (see Figure 1).

Figure 1

1984 NET COMMERCIAL TRADE BALANCE

(in Billions US$)

	PUBLIC	PRIVATE	TOTAL
1984 Imports	4.790	6.465	11.255
1984 Exports	17.804	6.250	24.054
1984 Net			
Trade Balance	13.804	(0.215)	12.799

SOURCE: Banco de Mexico, Indicadores Economicos.

Although there is a general consensus that Mexico should enter the international marketplace, such an entry has painful costs to many industries which have been protected or subsidized in the past. The controversy over how this change should be effected focused in the early summer on DIMEX.

DIMEX, however, has no direct effect on the use of countertrade arrangements; the indirect effects will be as a result of the overall liberalization of the Mexican economy. Neither are PROFIEX nor DIMEX expected to affect the maquiladoras, due to the structure of those companies. Maquiladoras operate under the controlled rate of exchange; any currency brought in must be converted to pesos; also they operate as a cost center rather than a profit center.[6]

COUNTERTRADE OPTIONS

PRONAFICE explicitly mentions the use of non-conventional forms of trade for export promotion (*PRONAFICE*, 14). Likewise, under section 3.2 E of *PROFIEX*, published by the Ministry of Trade and Industrial Development (Secretaria de Comercio y Fomento Industrial, or SECOFI), non-conventional forms of foreign trade are discussed, specifically "intercambio compensado" (literally, "compensated exchange") and "trueque" (or "barter").

Export products, which are eligible for countertrade under PROFIEX, are those presenting marketing problems: non-traditional exports; traditional exports destined for new markets; and products with excess inventories. Specific lists of approved exports and approved imports are drawn up on a case-by-case basis by the Mexican government, with input from the private sector on their supply and demand positions. The types of products that probably will be excluded from importation to Mexico are luxury items or final consumer products.

The most active mechanism under PROFIEX is the Programa de Intercambio Compensado, referred to in Mexico as the "PIC Program." The well-publicized Mexico-Argentina Bilateral Agreement is the operational prototype for such programs. It is basically a counterpurchase agreement that is realized under the umbrella clearing arrangement established by ALADI—the Latin American Integration Association. The program has been in operation for one year and has increased bilateral trade significantly from 27 products worth approximately U.S. $40 million (1982) to about 100 products with a total export value of approximately U.S. $150 million (cumulative in this year of operation). This type of program is under consideration with Venezuela, Colombia, and Brazil. The next such agreement should be with Brazil in the early fall of 1985; the lists of products, interested exporters and importers, and values have been determined; a decision on the dollar limit is pending.

The appeal to the private sector of such arrangements is that payment is guaranteed by the Central Banks of each country through established credit lines; payment is in the local currency, is speedy, and is made on site; and, risk is reduced. The major difficulties are that many of the countries involved to date (i.e., other Latin American countries with payment problems) have similar products, effort is doubled in that two lists of exporters and importers must be developed, and government has the final say on approved products, adding another administrative layer. Exporters would also prefer to be paid in dollars.

Another example of a recent countertrade arrangement in Mexico is one that began in November 1984. Mexico sold U.S. $20 million worth of peripheral computer equipment to Brazil in exchange for Brazilian inflatable silos, later used to preserve grain at points of cultivation. As of May 1985, deliveries of U.S. $14 million have been made, with U.S. $6 million remaining to complete the contract. The contract is set by value, not by time; there is no swing value. However, there is a minimum 95 percent accomplishment requirement, set by a performance bond.

One example of barter is the purchase of raw materials for the pharmaceutical industry from Germany in exchange for agricultural products, such as cocoa and coffee. Another approved deal is the export of Mexican metallic yarns for Spanish mohair.[7] Comments from the private sector, based on interviews conducted in May 1985, suggest that few possibilities exist for conducting "trueque" or barter, because companies want to be paid in hard currency, not products. Trueque is conducted on a case-by-case basis and has become an alternative only due to the country's shortage of foreign exchange.

Some other developments are: 1) Discussion is under way whether or not to give points in the government bidding process to companies who offer to export Mexican products; 2) Pressure from outside banks is being applied to open escrow accounts to promote foreign trade; 3) the San Jose Agreement between Mexico and Venezuela allows the opening of a line of credit for development projects in the Caribbean equal to 20 percent of the value of oil payments from Central American and Caribbean countries; and 4) Latin Equip, a new public-private sector joint venture sponsored by the Central Banks of Mexico, Argentina, and Brazil, will permit countertrade arrangements to finance capital goods if traditional financing is not available. In addition, switch arrangements are sometimes authorized, as in the case of Peru, which has been unable to pay its debt to the U.S.S.R., whereby Mexico is making payments to the U.S.S.R. and will receive exports from Peru.

Two factors discourage countertrade practices in Mexico: 1) The IMF's disapproval of trading arrangements that do not increase foreign exchange and lead to the reduction of external debt; and 2) The perception that the U.S. Department of Commerce holds the position that this form of trade is restrictive and non-competitive, and, therefore, not encouraged. The recent "Understanding between the United States and Mexico regarding Subsidies and Countervailing Duties" (April 23, 1985) demonstrates Mexico's sensitivity to engaging in trade practices, like countertrade, which could be considered trade restrictive. Since the United States is Mexico's primary market, Mexico is contemplating the possibility of entry into the GATT arrangement.

Countertrade arrangements were used in a prior period in Mexican history—the 1950s and 1960s. Under the Mecanismo de Intercambio Compensado, the Banco Nacional de Comercio Exterior (BNCE) developed sales of raw materials and commodities and purchased machinery from Europe. The program was not very successful in terms of foreign exchange earned, but at that time Mexico had a balance of payments surplus. The present Programa de Intercambio Compensado, outlined by SECOFI, promotes the expansion of goods that are difficult to place in the global market and helps alleviate the foreign exchange deficit.

Countertrade arrangements, although only a small percentage of total trade in Mexico, will continue to be utilized while there are liquidity problems and the capacity to produce. The emphasis on export promotion and the backing of the De la Madrid administration have provided these programs with the political leverage to realize these alternative forms of trade, if only as an interim measure until Mexico enters the global marketplace as a competitor able to challenge even the best of the world's present suppliers.

COUNTERTRADE AND ECONOMIC DEVELOPMENT

Now to return to the original question, can countertrade be a valid tool in achieving the economic development goals of a country? I would say "yes," but one must consider the caveats of effectiveness and appropriateness, based on the development criteria of the specific country and the environment in which the country operates.

Mexico stated its strategies for structural change in the PRONAFICE (*PRONAFICE*, 11–12). They include:

- A new pattern of industrialization and specialization of foreign trade;
- A new technological pattern;
- A rationalization of the industrial organization;
- A strategy of industrial location, emphasizing balanced regional development;
- A social dimension, emphasizing employment, skills, basic needs, and income distribution; and
- A strategy for participation of public, social, and private sectors in industry, based on complementarity.

Given Mexico's present situation, countertrade options—including long-term arrangements such as co-production, involving technology transfer—can be used both defensively and proactively. Defensively, such arrangements can be used to protect and develop Mexico's industrial base and to accumulate export revenues. Proactively, they can be used as incentives, or requirements, for companies (or countries) who desire to compete in the Mexican market or engage in joint ventures there, in order to obtain technology, training, or specialized industries which fit in with development goals.

However, the following "Big If's" will influence the effectiveness of these countertrade options:

- If such options lead to trade creation rather than trade diversion;
- If the percentage of total trade and investment of such options can significantly affect the economy;
- If the gaps which need to be filled in the economic development process are actually filled;
- If the Mexican economy can use such incentives to gain access to first-rate technology, and then, establish a market niche; and
- If Mexico can provide the skilled, technical, and professional support to maintain the economy they desire to build, at each step in the process.

Finally, one must ask about the appropriateness of countertrade by questioning not only the use of the tool itself, but also the assumptions upon which its use is based. The questions which come to mind are: Do countertrade options introduce more rigidity or more flexibility into the national and global economies? Is there sufficient cooperation among industrializing countries, particularly of the Southern hemisphere, such that comparative advantage can be encouraged among themselves until such time as the industries of these countries can be more internationally competitive? And, how valid and successful in the late 1980s are policies that seek to attract high technology and focus on export generation—in light of shrinking export markets for value-added goods; rising un-employment; and a widening gap between haves and have-nots?

Although a nation may have no alternative other than some form of countertrade, there are many choices as to how to use it as a tool to achieve development goals. The final result will be determined not only by the objective facts, but also by the values of the policy-makers, politics, and wisdom—or the lack of it. Herein lies the pitfall or the promise.

NOTES

1. Midway through Portillo's regime in 1979, the annual percentage increase in real GDP had more than doubled over that of 1978 (about 9 percent compared

to about 3 percent); this growth followed a major foreign exchange and payments crisis. Growth remained high (above 7 percent annual increase in GDP)
through 1981—the year of the infamous interest rate crisis. Negative GDP
was registered for 1982 and 1983 (approximately "–2" and "–5" percent, respectively. *Business Mexico*, 6, quoting *Indicadores Economicos*, Banco de Mexico.

2. Sector plans have been developed to achieve this end. The Mexican government hopes that by 1988, 50 percent of the manufacturing sector's imports
will be covered by export revenues, compared to 25 percent in 1980 (*PRO-
NAFICE*, 4).

3. Exclusions include: luxury goods (such as Persian carpets and automobiles);
various inputs for the pharmaceutical, automotive, and forestry industries;
and products which are also produced by the domestic metal-working sector.

4. The new law also applies to goods used in the fabrication process (e.g.,
lubricants); inputs; machinery and equipment used to make the product, do
research, and maintain quality and safety control; and packaging materials
used for exporting the product.

5. According to U.S. Embassy information from Mexico, the other 38.6 percent
which still require permits, are 909 items of the 8077-item Mexican tariff code;
they include agricultural products, telecommunications and computer products, chemicals, clothing, inputs for pharmaceuticals, intermediate goods
(such as champagne). There had been licenses on about 4,000 items; the range
of tariffs is 0–50 percent.

6. According to a *Wall Street Journal* article of August 15, 1985 ("Mexico Finally
Acts Serious About Revamping Economy" by Mary Williams Walsh), about
80 percent of all Mexican businesses operate using the controlled rate of
exchange. Tourism is an exception.

7. This was a counterpurchase arrangement.

REFERENCES

The American Chamber of Commerce, "Mexico's Economy: A Turning Point in
Business Mexico, Mexico City, Mexico Vol. II, No. 3 (May 1985), 5–31.

The News, "'Temporary Imports' Ruled Exempt from Duty," Mexico City, Mexico
(May 9, 1985), 4.

Secretaria de Comercio y Fomento Industrial (SECOFI), *National Program for
Industrial and Foreign and Trade Promotion (PRONAFICE): Executive Summary*,
Mexico City, Mexico. (Sept. 1984)

Walsh, Mary W., "Mexico Finally Acts Serious About Revamping the Economy,"
Wall Street Journal, New York, New York (Aug. 15, 1985), 30.

INTERVIEWS

Representative, Association Nacional de Companias de Comercio Exterior
(ANCE) and Consejo Nacional de Comercio Exterior (CONACEX), May 23,
Mexico City.

Representative, Associacion Nacional de Importadores y Exportadores de la
Mexicana (ANIERM), May 16, 1985, Mexico City.

Representative, Bilateral Commission For Mexico-Argentina, Consejo Empresarial Mexicano para Asuntos Internacionales (CEMAI), May 15, 1985, Mexico
City.

Canalizo H., Lic. Andres, Adjunct Commercial Counselor, Instituto Mexicano
Comercio Exterior (IMCE), Aug. 16, 1985, Washington, D.C.

Representative, Consejo Empresarial Mexicano para Auntos Internacionales
(CEMAI), May 15, 1985, Mexico City.

Representative for the State of Mexico, Consejo Nacional de las Industrias
Maquiladoras de Exportacion, A.C., May 16, 1985, Naucalpan de Juarez,
Mexico.

Hockstein, Linda, Bureau of Intelligence and Research, Office of Economic
Analysis, U.S. Dept. of State, Aug. 14, 1985, Washington, D.C.

Representative, Instituto de comercio Exterior (IMCE), May 21, 1985, Mexico
City, Mexico.

Jacobs, Steve, Mexican Affairs Division, U.S. Dept. of Commerce, Aug. 14, 1985,
Washington, D.C.

Representative, Industrial and Trade Planning Division, SECOFI, May 21, 1985,
Mexico City.

Villareal Arrambide, Dr. Rene, Undersecretary of Industrial and Trade Planning,
SECOFI, May 21, 1985, Mexico City.

Chapter Five:
International Personnel Management

THIS CHAPTER FOCUSES on the selection and training of employees for assignment in an international setting. Developing an adequate and competent pool of workers is a crucial task for top management of a multinational corporation.

The choice of personnel needed to work in overseas postings, and the training they need, are matters quite different from the selection and training of domestic workers. For those workers to be sent abroad, the selection process needs to take into account other criteria. Over and above technical competence and managerial skills, the employee needs to portray cultural empathy and diplomatic skills. Emotional stability and involvement of the candidate's family would be more important in the case of an overseas posting.

Whether managers abroad should be citizens of the country in which operations are conducted, or whether they should be expatriates from other countries, will have an impact on the managerial style as well as the methods of motivation and communication.

Training and management development to ensure a supply of capable managers would also need to be geared to a multinational perspective. This would entail training in culture differences, knowledge of world-wide company operations, language training, and so forth. These programs may be expensive, but they will most certainly prove to be worthwhile.

Besides staffing and training, the international executive would need to possess skills in wage and salary administration, union relations, contract negotiations, government-business relations, and performance appraisal, as well as the differences that may exist from country to country in which operations are conducted.

Finally, little attention has been placed on one facet of international operations—viz.,how to deal with personnel returning home after their foreign assignment. For those employees who have been overseas for prolonged periods of time, the cultural change of returning home can be most significant, especially for their families. How to handle this transition successfully is a major task for corporate management.

14

Criteria for Selecting an International Manager

Jean E. Heller

Personnel management, particularly for overseas assignments, is yet another critical variable in the success equation for MNC operations. Just as international management differs from the management of domestic operations, so too must the criteria for international managers reflect the demands of the international, as opposed to the domestic, environment. Although many firms continue to use the same selection process for both domestic and overseas postings, MNCs are learning that the successful domestic executive will not automatically be a successful international executive.

NO ONE FAMILIAR with business and trade statistics can dispute that the international business scene has been the most impressive area of business growth since World War II. World trade went from $110 billion in 1949 to $2.3 trillion in 1978, with U.S. exports climbing from $12.5 billion in 1948 to $143.4 billion in 1978 and U.S. imports increasing from $7.2 billion to $172.0 billion. Then there is the tremendous growth of U.S. direct investment abroad, the impressive increase in the overseas assets of foreign affiliates of U.S. multinationals, and the sales of those U.S. affiliates—not to mention the spectacular jump of foreign investment in the United States.

Largely responsible for this growth were the multinational corporations and at their head, of course, the engine that powered them— modern management, management of resources, management of facilities, management of capital, management of people. Although much has been written about the multinational or international corpora-

Reprinted, by permission of the publisher, from *Personnel*, May/June 1980, © 1980 by AMACOM, a division of American Management Associations. All rights reserved.

tion, very little has been written about the multinational manager—this in spite of the fact that the international executive is of great importance in the scheme of things.

What kind of man or woman should this international manager be? What distinguishes international management from management per se? According to the Advisory Committee on Business and International Education of the U.S. National Commission for UNESCO, it is this:

Management initiates, organizes, mans, directs, [and] controls the scope and nature of an enterprise in all of its multiple internal and external relationships; international management includes all of this, and, as well, the added complexities of quite different cultures, economics, politics, and the levels of responsibility to fellow humans. In short, it is a management per se—plus!

It would seem then that an international manager must possess all of the usual managerial skills and then some. One author on the subject wrote:

Ideally, it seems, he should have the stamina of an Olympic runner, the mental agility of an Einstein, the conversational skill of a professor of languages, the detachment of a judge, the tact of a diplomat, and the perseverance of an Egyptian pyramid builder. . . . And if he is going to measure up to the demands of living and working in a foreign country he should also have a feeling for culture; his moral judgements should not be too rigid; he should be able to merge with the local environment with chameleon-like ease; and he should show no signs of prejudice.

Another idealized version of a candidate for an international executive post put it this way. He must have:

a flexible personality, with broad intellectual horizons, attitudinal values of cultural empathy, general friendliness, patience and prudence, impeccable educational and professional (or technical) credentials—all topped off with immaculate health, creative resourcefulness, and respect of his peers. If his family is equally well endowed, all the better.

DESIRABLE TRAITS: FROM THE IDEAL TO THE REAL

Well, now that we've gotten that out of the way, let's get down to reality. Almost everyone agrees that foremost among the many traits an international manager must possess is the ability to do the job. This may seem to be stating the obvious, but it cannot be stressed too strongly. As one study put it: "Resident nationals will overlook qualities in an American they believe are abrasive—if he is efficient and knowledgeable and can get results for them."

CULTURAL EMPATHY

Ideally, of course, we would hope to eliminate or at any rate soften any "abrasive" qualities such a manager might have. All authorities agree that high on the list of desirable traits is what is called "cultural empathy"—an awareness of and a willingness to probe for the reasons people of another culture behave the way they do. Thomas Aitken has pointed out that while sensitivity is accepted as an essential attribute of the international manager, not everyone has it to the same degree and that, meantime, "awareness is an *attitude* and this can be assumed even when sensitivity comes in short supply."

ADAPTABILITY

Closely allied to awareness and sensitivity is adaptability—a key personality trait for the international manager. In a 1970 survey by Business International of 70 companies, adaptability—along with its twin, flexibility—was listed as the second most important criterion for overseas executives. Specific types of adaptability and flexibility are listed in an American Management Association's research study written in 1965, and they are just as valid today. Among them are:

1. A high degree of ability to integrate with other people, with other cultures, and with other types of business operations.
2. Adaptability to change: being able to sense developments in the host country; recognizing differences, being able to evaluate them, and being able to qualitatively and quantitatively express the factors affecting the operations with which he is entrusted.
3. Ability to solve problems within different frameworks and from different perspectives.
4. Sensitivity to the fine print of differences in culture, politics, religion, and ethics, in addition to industrial differences.
5. Flexibility in managing operations on a continuous basis, despite lack of assistance and gaps in information rationale.

All of the above imply a person with great breadth. The international manager must not only know his job, his company, and his business; he must know and understand the history, cultural background, economic achievements, and social and political life of the country he works in, and of other countries as well. He must be "geocentric" in his attitude; he must think in world terms and see differences as opportunities rather than constraints.

LANGUAGE SKILLS

Language skills or capability are also significant. In fact, Exxon has said of international management candidates that "we have only one test that has proven successful, and that is language aptitude." Many other corporations also put great emphasis on language skills or, at any rate, the ability to acquire them easily. One American expatriate, formerly with Univac, noted that:

language facility is a fundamental prerequisite. As is the case with missionaries, one just cannot sell religion unless he is able to talk the language of the local people. Nor can he sell successfully if he is unable to take the local pulse, if he remains a country boy amid a sophisticated business environment.

Nevertheless, in the 1970 Business International Survey of 70 companies, language skills/ability was indicated by only 11 percent of the companies that checked off the criteria they considered important in selecting executives for overseas operations. And there are some companies that, although they feel sure language ability is helpful, don't rank it as an important feature to be sought in appraising international management development.

EDUCATION

Education—that is, a good academic degree and preferably a graduate degree—is considered of critical importance in an international executive. By far the biggest source of senior management staff is the university graduate. The familiar story of the messenger boy who rises to the president's chair never was very common, but today it is virtually unheard of—although, to be sure, a company may take its future management staff through a number of lowly training steps.

Corporations disagree on type of degree preferred. Companies with highly technical products tend to prefer science degrees. Other firms feel that successful management requires depth, drive, imagination, creativity, and character—and that the type of person exemplified by these traits is more likely to be produced by a liberal arts education. But the overall prize-winning combination seems to be an undergraduate degree combined with a graduate business degree from a recognized business school.

It goes without saying that an overseas manager must possess "managerial qualities"—in particular, such traits as supervisory ability, training ability, and the ability to organize. These traits are always important, but particularly so overseas where the manager must operate more on his own and, as an essential part of the job, build an effective overseas team. This requires a tremendous breadth of understanding of other people, other ways of thinking, other ways of doing things.

LEADERSHIP AND OTHER INDIVIDUAL TRAITS

Picking the right people to head subordinate functions or to train employees to take over top spots is also difficult. The ones who speak English are the ones who stand out in the minds of most Americans, but they may not be the natural leaders. What's more, local criteria for leadership may be quite different from American standards. They may in fact be based on the position of the employee's father in the community, tribal orgins, various family connections, and other criteria that would not be immediately apparent to an American.

Many other desirable traits come to mind in connection with an international manager. Besides what we have already discussed, he or she should be mature and creative, show independence and initiative, possess emotional stability, and have a high tolerance for frustration. That such a manager should also possess excellent health goes without saying. Some very effective domestic executives must have access to highly sophisticated medical facilities. This doesn't impair their effectiveness at home, but could be a problem in some overseas locations.

MATURITY

What about age? Should younger people be sent because they "make the necessary adjustments better?" Some corporations believe this to be true. But others prefer middle-aged people for overseas assignments. In fact, one New York corporation specified a minimum age of 35 years. Another multinational manufacturer established a prerequisite of at least 16 years business experience, five of them in key supervisory positions, and fixed the minimum age at 40.

Certainly some of the criteria considered necessary for an international manager—such as experience, ability to do the job, breadth, and broad horizons—are most apt to be found in a mature person. Then too, of course, certain cultural factors might enter into the decision. Some foreign cultures might not accept young people in authority; some companies want a more established, "mature" image. On the other hand, some firms might decide they want a young look. So it is a complex question.

MOTIVATION

In the end, much of it boils down to the candidate's interest in international work—vital to his motivation. Does he really want to work overseas? Many Americans (and this phenomenon has greatly increased in the last few years) are very reluctant to go overseas. This is a result, to a large degree, of value reorientation. It used to be "the organization first," but now employees in increasing numbers are putting their children's education, their spouses' careers, their enjoyment of their leisure time, and many other elements ahead of the lure of an international assignment. And unless a strong interest, a strong desire, is there, the risk of failure overseas escalates. As one U.S. executive put it:

Many of the failures overseas are of people who were shoved into something, rather than going into it on their own initiative. . . . In our company, the casualty list has been extremely large in the group where we said, "go" as compared [with] the people who said, 'I want to go. I don't give a damn about living conditions or language problems. I'm technically qualified and I want that job."

But nevertheless, motivation alone is not enough in a psychological profile. One personnel executive tried to build his cadre of international managers on their willingness and desire to work abroad. But he found after a short time that "a wish to go overseas may not reflect the ability to adapt to a foreign way of life. It may, indeed, reflect only an inability to adjust successfully to the social and work structure in one's own country." Since one of the key criteria we have been discussing is the ability to adapt or adjust anywhere, clearly the absence of this trait could be disastrous.

ADAPTABILITY OF THE CANDIDATE'S FAMILY

We have so far omitted another critical factor: The adaptability of the executive's family. Family, in this case, almost always refers to wife and children, since women are only just beginning to be given overseas assignments. In a 1978 survey of 25 U.S. firms by Business International, only one cited the assignment of women employees to international overseas positions. In a survey that was recently conducted by the American Graduate School of International Management among 33 companies that regularly come to the school to recruit, we asked if they felt that the international field was opening up for women. Twelve companies replied, "Yes," while five said, "It already has." But it should be noted that those five replies were from banks, which added that they generally didn't have a problem placing women overseas. Eight of the firms pointed out that the response depended on the country. Women were simply not accepted everywhere, especially in the sales and marketing area. Other replies (one each) included: "Opening up," "Firm has no bias," "Actively seeking women," and "I see the Equal Employment Opportunity Commission doing that; more and more women are coming into the international field because of it."

According to the 1978 Business International survey, however, most multinational companies do not accept the practice of assigning women overseas. The primary reasons given include the one we found (women are simply not always accepted by the host countries) and another that we also encountered (the difficulty of finding a position for the woman's husband). In fact, one firm told us that it had to bring back a young woman from her overseas position because she wanted to get married and her fiancé had a good position in the United States. So there are problems with such assignments for women. Again according to the Business International survey, however, European firms are using women expatriates to a great degree and they are operating harmoniously and successfully with government officials in such unexpected locations as Brazil and Egypt, where professional women are not so readily accepted.

In general, then, since it is men who are usually offered international assignments, the adaptability of wives and children is of critical importance. Some companies will go to great length in the initial screening process to make sure the attitude of the candidate's family is favorable—even to the point of testing and interviewing them as well as the candidate—but others feel, as most European firms seem to, that the adjustment of the family is the husband's concern.

METHODS OF SELECTION

Given such criteria, just how do multinational companies (MNCs) go about finding and selecting these paragons who are to operate as international managers? Most human resources executives agree that the selection of the candidate for an overseas position is *the* deciding factor in the assignments' success or failure. So, do the MNCs have some elaborate procedure, some foolproof method of testing potential international executives? Alas, no. In fact, the selection procedure in most firms varies little from that used for domestic manpower posting. However, enlightened companies are aware that in addition to an employee's professional qualifications, it is necessary to examine his psychological and emotional stability, family situation, language skills, and cultural awareness if he is to be considered for an international assignment.

Does this mean that personnel screening can be accomplished through a battery of tests? Some firms believe it can be, at least as a help in screening candidates for overseas assignments. But others do not believe that the tests designed by industrial psychologists provide the predictive measures needed.

It is generally agreed that extensive interviews of candidates (and their wives) by senior executives still ultimately provide the best method of selection. And although there is no agreement concerning the positive features that differentiate an international manager from a domestic one, two negative norms appear: (1) The executive who likes to go abroad for short trips but doesn't want to live outside his home country should not be selected, and (2) the executive who says he would love to go to the French or German subsidiary, but not to the Tanzanian or Peruvian one, appears less than truly internationally minded. As Honeywell puts, "Corporations should be alert to weed out those candidates who feel they are primarily interested in a Cook's tour abroad."

But, at best, this point of view is negative. It indicates what should *not* be done—not what should be done. Why then are corporations so negligent in setting up criteria for the selection of managers to head those critical overseas operations? Why do many use the same selection method for international managers that they use for domestic personnel, even though it is known that the business situation overseas is compounded by an infinite number of variables? Why do some ignore the language factor? Perhaps the answer here is that they subcribe to one American executive's emphatic sentiment: "To hell with the local language. They can understand me in English if I talk loud enough." Various authorities have suggested that use of the same policies arises from a need for expediency and cost effectiveness, and that furthermore, the picture is not likely to change as long as companies feel that their foreign market penetration and their overseas profits are adequate.

FOUR KINDS OF APPROACHES

Basically there are four approaches to international management development, and a particular company's selection methods depend on which approach it adopts. These four distinct approaches are as follows:

1. Colonialism—parent-company nationals only.
2. Bilateralism—local nationals only.

3. Regionalism—limited use of third-country nationals.
4. Internationalism—unrestricted use of any nationals.

Both colonialism and bilateralism reject the view that the best person for the job should be chosen. The regional approach is a compromise between bilateralism and internationalism, providing a gradual shifting of third-country nationals into executive positions. If carried further, it blends into internationalism, according to which executives are chosen on the basis of their ability, regardless of the country of their origin. They may be posted anywhere in the world, so their management training is aimed not at preparing them for a particular foreign location, but for global assignments.

THE ULTIMATE GOAL

Some companies have a cadre of seasoned international executives who have served in a number of foreign operations and attained a high degree of mobility and adaptability. They are often called the "Foreign Legion" of their companies. This appelation is similar to what another authority has dubbed the "Supranational Executive Corps"—a management pool:

composed of individuals from many national backgrounds who are thoroughly imbued by cosmopolitan corporate culture, which both balances and expands their national and international normative orientation, and who are available for assignment wherever their skills are required throughout the world.

No company is known to have reached this stage, but many have set this model as their ultimate goal.

No matter what the philosophy of the company, however, the selection of international managers remains a difficult one, suffering from imperfect testing and screening techniques and complicated by the fact that success in domestic operations is no guarantee of success in foreign assignments. Business International drew up a checklist ten years ago of certain personal qualifications that a candidate should have—such as motivation, independence, resourcefulness, resilience, intelligence, tolerance, and so on—in addition to technical competence and business expertise. The American Graduate School of International Management, which trains future International managers, found in a survey that companies recruiting at the school tend to agree with Business International's checklist. In particular, they cited the motivation, maturity, and adaptability of students.

Of course, recruiting at a graduate business school of international management is one way to find an international manager—though it is by no means the only way. But no matter which route a company takes, one point seems clear: The prosperity if not the very survival of any business depends on the performance of its managers, and this is even more critical when we are talking about that very special person—the international manager.

15
Selection and Training of Personnel for Overseas Assignments

Rosalie L. Tung

The selection process of overseas assignments can be refined through the adoption of a contingency approach, which would match managerial qualities to the variables of each foreign assignment. Using such a strategy, the MNC can more clearly relate existing skills to required skills. This approach would also facilitate the development of training programs to better prepare employees for foreign assignments.

IN THE AGE of supersonic travel, the contacts between people of different cultures and nations are widespread. With the increasing cooperation among nations in the fields of commerce, education, health, and development, cross-national contacts are likely to be even more numerous and extensive in the future. This implies that there will be a further increase in the demand for individuals who can function effectively and efficiently in a foreign environment.

According to statistics compiled by Henry (1965) on U.S. multinational corporations, approximately 30 percent of overseas assignments have been mistakes. These "casualties" not only represent substantial costs to the companies involved, but also constitute a waste of human resources because most of those who "failed" had good track records in the home office prior to assignment overseas. In light of the increased demand for people who can operate effectively abroad, and the relatively high failure rate among expatriates, the need for programs to identify possible misfits, and training procedures to ensure better performance abroad, presents itself with great urgency.

Reprinted, with permission, from *The Columbia Journal of World Business*, "Selection and Training of Personnel for Overseas Assignments" (Spring 1981).

Research in the area of selection of personnel for overseas assignments has been few and fragmented. In the main, research has been focused on generating lists of criteria or personal qualifications that a prospective candidate should possess, and identifying psychometric devices that could be used to measure such personality traits (Borrmann, 1968; Howard, 1974). The identification of relevant personality characteristics is undoubtedly important, but research has so far failed to integrate such variables into a comprehensive framework for conceptualizing and analyzing the selection process. A selection paradigm entails, at the very least, the identification of 1, variables or factors that are crucial to success or failure on the job; 2, relationships between these different sets of variables; and 3, the weight that should be assigned to each factor in a given situation. It is especially crucial to identify the latter, because assignments, and hence selection, vary on the bases of the task to be performed and the environment (country) to which the individual is sent. Different job assignments require varying degrees of contact with the local culture, which may be very different from or similar to the home culture. A selection paradigm has to take these situational variables into consideration.

In the broader field of organizational theory and management, theorists and researchers who advocate a contingency approach to management have provided evidence to demonstrate the fallacy of applying universal principles or the "one best way" to management practices, regardless of the situation. In essence, contingency theorists argue that the most effective management technique depends upon the set of circumstances at a particular point in time. In the area of selection and training of personnel for expatriate assignments, this approach essentially says that depending upon the country of foreign assignment and the task that is to be performed, the selection process should attribute varying importance to the factors (e.g., technical competence, relational abilities, etc.) that contribute to success or failure on the job; and candidates for different assignments should undergo different types of training programs to prepare them for such cross-cultural encounters.

Because of the dearth of literature and research in this area, and the absence of a comprehensive framework for analyzing the selection process, the objectives of this articles are twofold: 1, to develop a contingency framework which would identify the factors crucial to success in a particular job assignment and the type(s) of training programs that a candidate should be exposed to enhance the probability of success; and 2, to present the results of an empirical study on selection and training procedures adopted by a sample of 80 U.S. international corporations. The study was designed to test the validity of the hypothesized contingency framework.

A CONTINGENCY APPROACH TO SELECTION AND TRAINING

Before presenting the framework, the variables included in the model will be briefly discussed. This requires an identification of the different categories of overseas job assignments; the factors crucial to success and failure in an overseas assignment; and the different types of training programs currently available to prepare candidates for cross-cultural encounters.

CATEGORIES OF OVERSEAS JOB ASSIGNMENTS

Hays (1974) classified overseas job assignments into four major categories: 1, chief executive officer—whose responsibility is to oversee and direct the entire operation; 2, structure reproducer or functional head—whose job is to establish functional departments in a foreign affiliate; 3, trouble shooter—whose function is to analyze and solve specific operational problems; 4, element, or the rank and file members.

Each of these job categories requires varying degrees of contact with, knowledge of, and duration of stay in the foreign country. In general, job assignments in the first two categories require more extensive interaction with members of the local community and a longer stay in the foreign country than job assignments in the last two categories. Hence it would be appropriate to emphasize different criteria for selecting candidates for each of these job categories.

FACTORS CRUCIAL TO SUCCESS

Research in the area of selection of personnel for overseas assignments has suggested a list of variables that contribute to success or failure on the job (Ivancevich, 1969; Hays, 1971; Miller, 1972; Howard, 1974). These variables may be grouped into four general areas:

Technical competence on the job: As in the selection and placement of personnel in domestic operations, this factor is one of the primary determinants of success (Hays, 1971). In overseas assignment, this factor may be even more important because the individual is located some distance from headquarters, the hub of technical expertise, and cannot consult as readily with his peers and superiors at headquarters on matters related to his job.

Personality traits or relational abilities: This refers to the ability of the individual to deal effectively with his superiors, peers, subordinates, business associates, and clients. In overseas assignments, this variable greatly influences the probability of successful performance. This factor is not limited to knowledge of another culture, but includes the ability to relate to, live with, and work among people whose value systems, beliefs, customs, manners, and ways of conducting business may be greatly different from one's own.

Environmental variables: In domestic operations, the ability to identify and cope with environmental constraints, such as governments, labor unions, competitors, and customers, is crucial to effective performance (Tung, 1979). In overseas assignments, this same requirement holds but with one important distinction—environmental constraints are "now variables in the sense that obviously constant factors at home are now different abroad" (Farmer and Richman, 1965, p. 373). The political, legal, and socioeconomic structures which constitute the macroenvironment in the host country, may be very different from the systems with which the expatriate is familiar. This poses problems of adjustment. The expatriate has to understand these systems and operate within them.

Family situation: This refers to the ability of the expatriate's family (the spouse, in particular) to adjust to living in a foreign environment. Researchers and practitioners are becoming increasingly cognizant of the importance of this factor to effective performance abroad (Borrmann, 1968; Karras and McMillan, 1971; Harris and Harris, 1972; Hayes, 1974; Miller and Hill, 1978).

Researchers and practitioners are generally agreed that these factors, properly identified and measured, are the determinants of success or failure on the job. Despite the recognition that success or failure in an expatriate job assignment is a function of a complex of four sets of variables, most personnel administrators have, in practice, based their selection decision primarily on the technical competence. The reasons behind their decisions are twofold.

Many have reasoned that since task requirements are usually easily identifiable, whereas attitudes which are appropriate for cross-cultural interaction are not always identifiable and measurable, they should focus on the task requirement factor. As Dr. Francis J. McCabe, chief of executive personnel at ITT, put it: "Ability at his job is the *sine qua non* abroad, as it is here" (Howard, 1974, p. 138). McCabe's view is shared by most personnel administrators who are engaged in the multinational staffing function (Miller, 1972). In most instances, ability to perform the task under consideration was used as the *primary* criterion for selection in an overseas assignment. This was supplemented by interview and/or other psychometric devices to determine the candidate's so-called abil-ity to empathize with foreign cultures, but this factor was perceived as secondary to task requirements. Personnel administrators who adopt this approach justify it by optimism that proper training can give the candidate the appropriate attitudes for cross-cultural interaction. This is in line with the conventional wisdom, shared by many personnel agencies throughout the country, that training can bring about remark-able changes in the attitudes and hence behavior of individuals, as evi-denced by the millions of dollars invested annually in training sessions. In the words of Lynton and Pereek (1967, p. 3), "Training has become a tax levied on willing and unwilling alike." This should not be construed as a belittling of training programs. Rather, the present researcher con-tends that the selection procedure, appropriately used, can weed out the so-called "diehards," i.e., people who would not benefit from any type of training program.

A second and perhaps more compelling reason for focusing on the technical competence criterion stems from the self interest of the selec-tors. Miller (1972) found that almost all of the personnel administrators he interviewed adopted a "minimax" decision strategy, i.e., one which would minimize the personal risks involved in selecting a candidate who might fail on the job. Since technical competence almost always pre-vents immediate failure on the job, particularly in high pressure situa-tions, the selectors play safe by placing a heavy emphasis on technical qualifications and little on the individual's ability to adapt to a foreign environment.

This practice of basing the selection decision on the technical com-petence criterion, regardless of the country of foreign assignment, may account for the high failure rate among expatriates (Hays, 1971; Howard, 1974). This practice should not be continued when research findings indicate that other factors may increase the chances of successful per-formance abroad. Hays (1971) found that although technical expertise or competence was most often identified as the most important factor in the overall determination of success, relational abilities appeared to in-crease the probability of successful performance considerably. This led Hays to propose that deficiency in relational skills may be the chief cause of failure on the job. In subsequent research (1974), Hays found that most of the so-called "failures" had good track records prior to foreign assignment. Hays' assertion tends to be supported by other research findings (Ivancevich, 1969; Karras and McMillan, 1971; Harris and Harris, 1972; Howard, 1974). If deficiency in relational abilities, coupled with a "family situation" factor, are a frequent source of "failure," then the selection decision should give due consideration to these factors and not merely "sweep them under the rug," as was often found to be the case in Miller's (1972) study of personnel administrators.

TRAINING PROGRAMS FOR CROSS-CULTURAL ENCOUNTERS

This paper will review only the training programs that are designed to improve relational skills which are crucial to effective performance in expatriate job assignments.

Training programs or procedures currently employed by agencies active in assigning people abroad may be divided into the following five categories. These are presented in ascending order of rigor.

1—*Area studies programs:* These include environmental briefing and cultural orientation programs. They are designed to provide the trainee with information about a particular country's sociopolitical history, geography, stage of economic development, and cultural institutions. The content is factual in nature, and they prepare the individual for the particular environment to which he has been assigned.

The basic assumption behind this approach is that "Knowledge will increase empathy, and empathy will modify behavior in such a way as to improve intercultural relationships" (Campbell, 1969, p. 3). Although there is some indication that increased knowledge will remove some of the fear and aggression that tend to be aroused by the unknown, the evidence that knowledge will invariably result in increased empathy is sparse and usually not the result of rigorous experimental control. Besides, there is evidence to indicate that "understanding" and "endorsement" of a different culture are not necessarily linked (Useem, Useem and Donoghue, 1963; Deutsch, 1970).

When used alone, area studies programs are inadequate for preparing trainees for assignments which require extensive contact with the local community overseas (Textor, 1966; Harrison and Hopkins, 1967; Lynton and Pareek, 1967). Furthermore, since cultural differences between any two countries could be innumerable, training programs of an area studies nature could not possibly pass on to the trainee all the knowledge that would be required over the duration of his overseas assignment.

2—*Culture assimilator:* This consists of a series of 75 to 100 short episodes briefly describing an intercultural encounter. Encounters which are judged (by a panel of experts, including returned expatriates) to be critical to the interaction situations between members of two different cultures are included.

Studies designed to test the validity and effectiveness of this training device have usually shown that in general "These programs provide an apparently effective method for assisting members of one culture to interact and adjust successfully with members of another culture" (Fiedler and Mitchell, 1971, p. 95). The technique, however, was designed specifically for people who had to be assigned overseas on short notice. Consequently, where time is not a critical factor, and in assignments which require extensive contact with members of the local community, this technique should be supplemented by the more rigorous training programs discussed below.

3—*Language training:* The candidate is taught the language of the country to which he is assigned. This often involves months, or sometimes years, before a candidate can master the foreign language.

4—*Sensitivity training:* These programs focus upon learning at the affective level and are designed to develop an attitudinal flexibility within the individual so that he can become aware of and eventually accept that "unfamiliar" modes of behavior and value systems can also be valid ways of doing things in a different culture.

Although the effectiveness of sensitivity training sessions have been questioned, there is some indication that "Sensitivity training may well be a powerful technique in the reduction of ethnic prejudice, particularly among those who are low in psychological anomy" (Rubin, 1967, p. 30). The Peace Corps is by far the most ardent advocate of this type of training program. To enhance the effectiveness of sensitivity training sessions, the Peace Corps developed a strategy whereby such sessions were supplemented with field experiences, discussed below.

5—*Field experience:* These involve sending the candidate to the country of assignment or "microcultures" nearby (e.g., Indian reservations, urban black ghettoes) where the trainees may undergo some of the emotional stress that can be expected while living and working with people from a different subculture. Research indicates that even though differences in cultural content exist between these microcultures and the country to which the trainee is ultimately assigned, trainees seem to benefit from an encounter with people whose way of life is different from their own, since "The process problems that grow out of confrontation are similar" (Harris and Harris, 1972, p. 9).

Given the financial resources available to international corporations and the ready accessibility to microcultures at home, it appears that international companies could easily introduce their candidates for overseas assignments to such types of training programs. The field experience of living and working with members of a microculture need not involve months, or even several weeks, away from the company. Often a full week's "live-in" experience would expose the candidate to the emotional stress of living with members of a different culture. Many of the other training programs that are designed to improve technical or human relations skills involve week-long sessions. Consequently, such field experiences of living in a microculture could not be dismissed as a waste of scarce executive time.

The five types of training programs outlined above focus upon different kinds of learning—cognitive versus affective—and vary in terms of medium of instruction, information content, and time and resources required. These five types of programs are by no means mutually exclusive and should not be construed as such. Rather, they should be complementary and seen as part of a continuum ranging from low rigor (area studies type) to highly rigorous training programs (sensitivity training and field experiences). Depending upon the type of job and the country of foreign assignment, the individual should be exposed to one or several of these programs. This proposal will be elaborated further in the subsequent section.

A CONTINGENCY FRAMEWORK

In light of the different categories of overseas job assignments and the contributions of various factors to success on the job, any comprehensive selection paradigm has to incorporate this complex of variables and allow for their interaction and for a systematic analysis. However, because of the variability of each situation in terms of the country of foreign assignment and the task to be performed, constant weights applicable to all instances could not be assigned to each of these factors. A more feasible strategy is to adopt a contingency approach to the selection of personnel for overseas assignment.

This approach requires a clear identification of the task, the environment, and the psychological characteristics of the individual under consideration. A first step in the selection process is to identify the job in question. Here the administrator should assess the amount of interaction with the local community called for by the position. As pointed out previously, jobs in the "chief executive officer" and "functional head" categories generally involve more extensive contacts with the community. Hence jobs in these categories would rank high on the scale in terms of degree of interaction required with the local community. A second set of factors relates to the "environmental variables." In considering the environment, the magnitude of differences between the political, legal, socioeconomic, and cultural systems of the home country vis-à-vis the host country should be assessed and rank-ordered. Data on such differences are readily available from information banks located at various research and educational institutions in the United States, such as the International Data Library and Reference Service at the University of California at Berkeley, and the Cross-National Data Archive Holdings at Indiana University, Bloomington.

An indication should always be obtained as to whether a candidate is willing to serve abroad. If the individual is opposed to serving abroad, then no training program is capable of changing this basic attitude. If the individual is willing to live and work in a foreign environment, an indication of the extent to which he is tolerant of cultural differences and his ability to work towards intercultural cooperation should be obtained. Howard (1974, pp. 140-41) presents a list of appraisal methods (including psychometric devices) that could be used for assessing such personality traits. These include the Minnesota Multiphasic Personality Inventory, the Guilford-Zimmerman Temperament Survey, the Allport-Vernon Study of Values, the F-test, a psychiatric evaluation, and evaluations from superiors, subordinates, friends, and acquaintances to determine the individual's ability to be tolerant of foreign customs, cultures, and business practices.

In addition, personnel administrators should consider an alternative source of worker supply—namely, local nationals who have the technical competence required to carry out the job successfully. Results of the study reported here indicate that most of the 80 international corporations surveyed appeared to realize the advantages to be gained by staffing overseas subsidiaries with local nationals, wherever possible. The most important reasons cited for doing this were: familiarity with the culture, knowledge of the language, reduced costs, and good public relations. However, there were variations in the extent to which local nationals were used at various levels of management in the developed versus the Less-Developed countries (LDCs). Local nationals were used to a much greater extent at all levels of management in developed countries than in LDCs. This is not surprising, as one would expect the more developed nations to have a larger pool of personnel having the necessary management and technical skills to staff management level positions. Unfortunately, the countries which are staffed by a smaller percentage of local nationals at management levels of U.S. subsidiaries, tend to be the ones whose culture, values and business practices are more different from the U.S. For example, one would expect the culture, values, and business practices of the U.S. to be more similar to those of the U.K. (in that they have both evolved from the Protestant-capitalist ethic) than to Thailand. Consequently, the issue of selecting a candidate who would be able to live and work in a very dissimilar cultural environment still constitutes a pressing problem to U.S. international corporations.

The selection decision process can be illustrated diagrammatically by means of a flow chart (see Fig. 1).

Before headquarters launches a search (at home) for an appropriate individual to fill an overseas job, it should consider if the job in question could be filled by a local national. If the answer is yes, this alternative source of workers should certainly be considered. This paper will not discuss the problems and opportunities of staffing overseas subsidiaries with local nationals because these alone would constitute a separate topic for analysis. If the position cannot be filled by a local national, then a search must be conducted among those who are already with domestic operations or within competing industries.

The first step in the decision process is the identification of the degree of interaction with the local community that is required by the job. In positions involving extensive contact with the culture and an understanding of the local value system, "relational abilities" and "environmental variables" become more critical and should become dominant factors in the selection decision. The selector should then proceed to examine the degree to which the foreign environment differs from the home environment. If the differences are insignificant, selection should be on the basis of task variables primarily. Where the differences are great, the selection decision should focus on the "relational abilities" and "family situation" factors. In Fig. 1, the "family situation" factor is categorized with the "relational abilities" factor. Although these are distinct categories, research is still needed to determine exactly how much effect the spouse has upon the employee's performance. In any case, each situation has to be treated separately because for some people, the "family situation" factor may have little bearing on everyday activities, whereas for others its impact may be critical.

The rest of the flow chart is self explanatory. Training programs to prepare candidates for cross-cultural encounters vary according to the degree of rigor with which the program seeks to inculcate within the

Figure 1: Flow Chart of the Selection-Decision Process

START THE SELECTION PROCESS

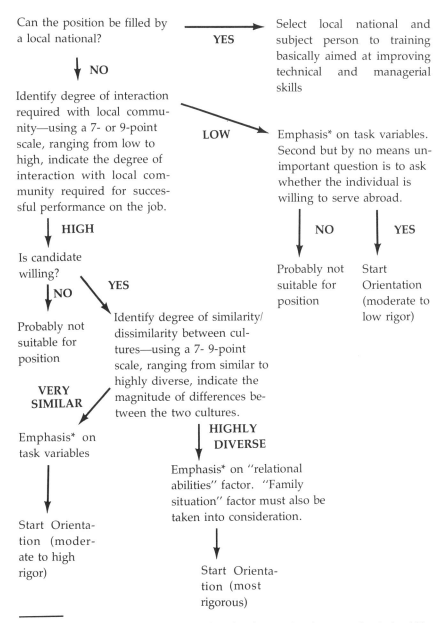

Can the position be filled by a local national? **YES** → Select local national and subject person to training basically aimed at improving technical and managerial skills

↓ **NO**

Identify degree of interaction required with local community—using a 7- or 9-point scale, ranging from low to high, indicate the degree of interaction with local community required for successful performance on the job.

LOW → Emphasis* on task variables. Second but by no means unimportant question is to ask whether the individual is willing to serve abroad.

↓ **HIGH**

Is candidate willing?

YES

↓ **NO**

NO ↓ Probably not suitable for position

YES ↓ Start Orientation (moderate to low rigor)

Probably not suitable for position

Identify degree of similarity/dissimilarity between cultures—using a 7- 9-point scale, ranging from similar to highly diverse, indicate the magnitude of differences between the two cultures.

VERY SIMILAR

Emphasis* on task variables

↓

Start Orientation (moderate to high rigor)

↓ **HIGHLY DIVERSE**

Emphasis* on "relational abilities" factor. "Family situation" factor must also be taken into consideration.

↓

Start Orientation (most rigorous)

* "Emphasis" does not mean ignoring the other factors. It only means that it should be the dominant factor.

individual the ability to relate to foreigners. If the job requires a great deal of interaction with the local community, and if the differences between the two cultures are great, the candidate should be subjected to all five types of training programs, with particular emphasis on Types 4 and 5. If contact with the local community is minimal (e.g., a trouble shooter's job) and where the differences between cultures are small, the area studies program would probably be sufficient. Between these extremes is a continuum of situations requiring varying degrees of contact with the local culture and involving varying magnitudes of difference between the cultures. Personnel administrators should locate the job under consideration along this continuum, and determine the type of training program that would be suitable for the expatriate in question.

PROCEDURE

SURVEY DESIGN

A questionnaire was developed to study the selection and training policies and procedures for staffing overseas affiliates. The questionnaire was pre-tested with a sample of 12 personnel administrators of U.S. international corporations. As a result of the pilot study, certain terminologies and items in the questionnaire were revised to improve readability of the questionnaire and facilitate response on the part of the administrators.

The revised questionnaire was sent to a sample of 300 of the largest firms listed in Angel's *Directory of American Firms Operating Abroad*. One hundred five questionnaires were returned. Of these, 80 were usable The questionnaires were completed by the vice president, foreign operations (or some similar designation) of each firm.

All the firms included in the survey had affiliate operations in at least nine other countries. Locations of overseas affiliate operations were categorized into one of seven regions: Western Europe, Canada, the Middle and Near East, Eastern Europe, Latin and South America, the Far East, and Africa. Respondents were asked to identify the regions in which they had affiliate operations. The percentage of firms that had affiliate operations in Western Europe, Canada, the Middle and Near East, Eastern Europe, Latin and South America, the Far East and Africa, were 95 percent, 86 percent, 66 percent, 19 percent, 88 percent, and 71 percent respectively.

ANALYSIS AND FINDINGS

CRITERIA FOR SELECTION DECISION

Respondents were asked to identify the criteria they would consider important in selecting personnel for each of the four major job categories (Hays, 1974) which were described previously. Table 1 presents a breakdown of the responses by the four job categories.

From Table 1, it is evident that for each job category, certain criteria were considered more important than others. In jobs which require more extensive contact with the local community (e.g., Chief Executive Officer and Functional Head), attributes like "adaptability, flexibility in new environmental settings," and "communication" were more frequently cited as being "very important" than in jobs that were more technically oriented (e.g., Trouble Shooter).

The study then proceeded to analyze the procedures undertaken by the firm to determine the candidate's suitability for the overseas position. In response to the question: "Are tests administered to determine candidate's technical competence?", only 3 percent replied in the affirmative. This was not surprising, since the majority of expatriates had been with the company for some time and had already demonstrated their technical competence. In response to the question: "Are tests administered to determine the candidate's relational abilities?", only 5 percent replied in the affirmative. The firms who do test the candidate's relational abilities described the nature of such tests to be: judgment by seniors, psychological appraisal, interview of candidate and spouse by a consulting psychologist. It is surprising that an overwhelming majority of the firms included in the study failed to assess the candidate's relational abilities when they clearly recognize that relational abilities are important for overseas work (as evidenced by responses exhibited in Table 1) and when research (Ivancevich, 1969; Hays, 1971; Miller, 1972; Hays, 1974) has shown "relational abilities" to be crucial to success in overseas assignments. Given the increasing demand for personnel who could function effectively abroad and the relatively high incidence of "failure," there certainly appears to be room for improvement in this area.

The respondents were then asked to indicate whether interviews were conducted only with the candidate, or with the candidate and spouse, for management-type positions and technically-oriented positions. For management positions, 52 percent of the companies interviewed both candidate and spouse, 47 percent of the companies interviewed the candidate only, and the remaining 1 percent did not conduct interviews at all. For technically-oriented positions, 40 percent of the companies interviewed both candidate and spouse, 59 percent of the companies interviewed the candidate only, and 1 percent conducted no interviews. These figures suggest that in management positions which involve more extensive contact with the local community, as compared to technically-oriented positions, the adaptability of the spouse to living in a foreign environment is perceived as important for successful performance abroad. However, even for technically-oriented positions, a full 40 percent of the companies did conduct interviews with both candidate and spouse. This lends support to the contention of other researchers (Borrmann, 1968; Harris and Harris, 1972; Hayes, 1974) that multinational corporations are becoming increasingly cognizant of the importance of this factor to effective performance abroad.

TRAINING PROGRAMS

Respondents were asked to identify the types of training programs their company used to prepare candidates for cross-cultural encounters. Only 32 percent of the respondents (or 26 firms) indicated that their company had formal training programs of some sort to prepare candidates for overseas work. A full 68 percent of the respondents had no training program whatsoever. The reasons and the relative frequencies with which the reasons were cited for omitting training programs were: (1) trend toward employment of local nationals (45 percent); (2) temporary nature of such assignments (28 percent); (3) doubt effectiveness of such training programs (20 percent); and (4) lack time (7 percent).

The 26 firms that had training programs were asked to indicate the types of programs they used for training personnel in each of the four job categories. Table 2 presents the relative frequency with which a type of program was used for each job category in these 26 firms.

Results indicate that most of the 26 firms recognized the need for "more rigorous" training programs for "Chief Executive Officer" and "Functional Head" job categories than for the "Trouble Shooter" and "Operative" job categories.

The firms that used training programs were asked whether they evaluated the effectiveness of such training programs, and if so, to enumerate the types of evaluation techniques used. Only 32 percent of the 26 firms adopted some form of evaluation process. Procedures used

Table 1: Selection Criteria Used for Different Job Categories

Criteria	Chief Executive Officer % Used, very important	Used, not important	Criterion not used	Functional head % Used, very important	Used, not important	Criterion not used	Trouble shooter % Used, very important	Used, not important	Criterion not used	Operative % Used, very important	Used, not important	Criterion not used
Experience in company	83	16	1	68	31	1	58	31	11	37	24	39
Technical knowledge of business	79	21	0	91	8	1	89	11	0	68	21	11
Knowledge of language of host country	26	50	24	42	51	7	25	62	13	46	38	16
Overall experience and education	87	12	1	81	17	2	69	21	10	52	41	7
Managerial talent	96	4	0	86	14	0	16	54	30	18	41	41
Interest in overseas work	65	29	6	62	28	10	40	43	17	59	25	16
Initiative, creativity	84	11	5	82	13	5	82	14	4	52	32	16
Independence	64	25	11	48	37	16	57	33	10	22	48	30
Previous overseas experience	25	51	24	22	55	23	13	56	31	12	43	45
Respect for culture of host country	68	8	24	70	8	22	50	25	25	71	11	18
Sex	14	19	68	9	22	69	2	23	75	7	19	74
Age	10	20	70	5	31	64	6	14	80	10	20	70
Stability of marital relationship	35	32	33	34	24	42	16	25	59	29	22	49
Spouse's and family's adaptability	61	28	11	63	24	13	40	23	37	49	29	22
Adaptability, flexibility in new environment	83	12	5	76	19	5	46	38	16	62	31	7
Maturity, emotional stability	94	9	1	98	1	1	75	17	8	86	11	1
Communicative ability	97	8	5	85	8	7	59	32	9	53	42	5
Same criteria as other comparable jobs at home	76	16	8	88	16	6	49	20	12	71	24	5

Table 2: Frequencies of Training Programs Used for Each Job Category (n = 26)

	CEO	Functional Head	Trouble Shooter	Operative
Environmental briefing	52%	54%	44%	31%
Cultural orientation	42%	41%	31%	24%
Culture assimilator	10%	10%	7%	9%
Language training	60%	59%	36%	24%
Sensitivity training	3%	1%	1%	0%
Field experience	6%	6%	4%	1%

to evaluate the effectiveness of such training programs include trainees' and supervisors' subjective evaluations.

FAILURE OVERSEAS

The respondents were asked to indicate the most important reasons for an expatriate's failure to function effectively in a foreign environment. The reasons given, in descending order of importance, were: (1) the inability of the manager's spouse to adjust to a different physical or cultural environment; (2) the manager's inability to adapt to a different physical or cultural environment; (3) other family related problems; (4) the manager's personality or emotional immaturity; (5) the manager's inability to cope with the responsibilities posed by the overseas work; (6) the manager's lack of technical competence; and (7) the manager's lack of motivation to work overseas. These findings are in line with Hays' (1974) assertion that the "family situation" and "relational abilities" factors were responsible, in the main, for "failure" or "poor performance" abroad. In light of these findings, it is all the more surprising that even though most personnel administrators recognize the importance of these factors, few companies have developed procedures for assessing and developing these abilities in their expatriate personnel.

Respondents were asked to indicate the percentage of expatriates who have to be recalled or dismissed because of inability to function effectively in a foreign assignment. Seven percent of the respondents indicated that the recall or failure rate was between 20 and 40 percent; 69 percent of the firms had a recall rate between 10 and 20 percent; and the remainder had recall rates below 10 percent.

The study then sought to analyze the relationship between the type of selection and training procedure used and the "failure rate." Because of the qualitative nature of the responses with respect to selection and training procedures, it was not possible to use sophisticated statistical techniques, and the researcher had to settle for less sophisticated assessment devices. Each respondent firm received an overall score from

1 to 5 on the degree of rigor of their selection and training procedures. A low score indicates that the respondent did not use rigorous procedures in their selection and training. A high score indicates that the respondent adopted very rigorous selection and training procedures. An overall score for each respondent was arrived at through the raters' assessment of the appropriateness of the criteria used in selecting candidates for the different job categories, the procedures (tests, interviews, etc.) undertaken by the firm to determine the candidate's suitability for the foreign position, and training programs (the type and evaluation of effectiveness of such programs) used. A firm which received a high score was one that (1) used appropriate criteria for selecting candidates in each of the four job categories (e.g., emphasizing "relational abilities" for management type positions and "technical competence" for the more technically oriented positions; (2) adopted rigorous procedures for determining the candidate's suitability for the position (e.g., tests administered to determine the candidate's relational abilities for management type positions, interviews with both candidate and spouse); (3) sponsored appropriate training programs that would better prepare the candidate for the overseas assignment. For example, for a "Chief Executive Officer" position, more rigorous techniques (such as sensitivity training and field experiences) were used; and (4) evaluated the effectiveness of the training programs used.

Two raters were used. Each rater independently evaluated the procedures and criteria used by each firm and assigned a score accordingly. The two raters' assessments were correlated as an indicator of inter-rater reliability. The r was .81. This showed that in general there was agreement between the two raters in their assessment of the degree of rigor in the procedures used by the firms. These overall scores were then correlated with the failure rates of the respective firms. The r was .63. This means that the more rigorous the selection and training procedures used, the lower the failure rate.

CONCLUSION AND DISCUSSION

This study shows that international corporations with lower "failure" rates tend to adopt different criteria for selecting candidates and sponsor different types of training programs for personnel in each of the job categories. This is a result of their recognition that different jobs involve varying degrees of contact with other cultures and varying durations of stay in a foreign country. It appears that there is no one best selection criterion or training program that would be appropriate for all job categories. There is a need to adopt a contingency approach to selection and training. The findings of the study with respect to failure rate and degree of vigor of selection and training procedures provide support for the contingency framework presented in the first half of this paper.

The contingency approach to management was developed in response to the complexities of organizational environments and as a result of the inadequacy of universal principles in solving the diversity of problems confronting management. In the area of selection of personnel for overseas assignments, it is little wonder that selection strategies which emphasize one particular criterion, regardless of the task and environment in question, have met with little success. A contingency framework which allows for the systematic analysis of variations in task and environmental factors appears to be a sensible solution to the problem. A contingency framework states that in practice there is no one criterion that could be used in all situations. Rather, each assignment should be viewed on its own. In each instance, the selection of the "right" person to fill the position should be made only after a careful analysis of the task (in terms of the extent of interaction with the local community), the country of assignment (in terms of the degree to which it is similar/dissimilar to that of the home country), and the personality characteristics of the candidate (in terms of the candidate's and spouse's ability to live and work in a different cultural environment).

In the area of training programs for cross-cultural encounters, the same holds true. Since different jobs call for different degrees of expertise in relating to members of another culture, it would not be appropriate to prescribe the same training program for all expatriates.

Contemplating the mixed blessings of the contingency approach to management, Wooton (1977) noted that the contingency paradigm emphasized a passive response to the environment—namely, one of coping and adaptation. He advocated a paradigm which would allow for active manipulation of the environment. In the area of international management, however, such a strategy is clearly not feasible for at least two reasons: (1) no single foreign agency or even collection of agencies possesses the "clout" to alter the environment of the host nation; and (2) extensive change in the sociocultural environment in any country is usually an evolutionary process, taking years or even generations. Thus a contingency approach to the selection and training of personnel for overseas assignments appears to be the best course of action to promote and adopt in practice.

REFERENCES

1. Borrmann, W. A., "The problem of expatriate personnel and their selection in international business," *Management International Review*, Vol. 8, No. 4/5 (1968), pp. 37-48.

2. Campbell, R. D., "United States military training for cross-cultural interaction," *Office of Naval Research*, June 4, 1969.
3. Deutsch, S. E., *International Education and Exchange: A Sociological Analysis.* Cleveland: Case Western Reserve University Press, 1970.
4. Farmer, R. N., and B. M. Richman., *Comparative Management and Economic Progress.* Homewood, Ill.: Richard D. Irwin, Inc., 1965.
5. Fiedler, F. E., and T. Mitchell., "The culture assimilator: an approach to cross-cultural training," *Journal of Applied Psychology*, Vol. 55, No. 2 (1971), pp. 95-102.
6. Hapgood, D. *Agents of Change: A Close Look at the Peace Corps.* Boston: Little, Brown & Co., 1968.
7. Harris, P. R., and D. L. Harris., "Training for cultural understanding," *Training and Development Journal*, May 1972, pp. 8-10.
8. Harrison, R., and R. L. Hopkins., "The design of cross-cultural training," *Journal of Applied Behavioral Science*, Vol. 3, No. 4 (1967), pp. 431-460.
9. Hays, R. D., "Ascribed behavioral determinants of success-failure among U.S. expatriate managers," *Journal of International Business Studies*, Vol. 2 (1971), pp. 40-46.
10. Hays, R. D., "Expatriate selection: insuring success and avoiding failure," *Journal of International Business Studies*, Vol. 5 (1974), pp. 25-37.
11. Henry, E. R., "What business can learn from Peace Corps selection and training," *Personnel*, Vol. 41, July-August 1965.
12. Howard, C. G., "Model for the design of a selection program for multinational executives," *Public Personnel Management*, March-April, 1974, pp. 138-145.
13. Ivancevich, J. M., "Selection of American managers for overseas assignment," *Personnel Journal*, Vol. 18, March, 1969.
14. Karras, E. J., and R. J. McMillan., "Interviewing for a cultural match," *Personnel Journal*, Vol. 18, March, 1971.
15. Lynton, R. P., and U. Pareek. *Training for Development.* Ill.: Dorsey Press, 1967.
16. Miller, E. L., "The selection decision for an international assignment: a study of the decision maker's behavior," *Journal of International Business Studies*, Vol. 3 (1972), pp. 49-65.
17. Miller, E. K., and R. E. Hill., "A comparative study of the job change decision for managers selecting domestic and overseas assignments," *Proceedings, Academy of Management*, 1978.
18. Rubin, I., "The reduction of prejudice through laboratory training," *Journal of Applied Behavioral Science*, Vol. 3 (1967), pp. 29-50.
19. Textor, R. B. (ed.) *Cultural Frontiers of the Peace Corps.* Cambridge, Mass.: M.I.T. Press, 1966.
20. Tung, R. L., "Dimensions of organizational environments: An exploratory study of their impact on organization structure," *Academy of Management Journal*, Volume 22 (1979), pp. 672-693.
21. Useem, J., R. Useem, and J. Donoghue., "Men in the middle of the third culture," *Human Organization*, Vol. 22 (1963), pp. 169-179.
22. Wooton, L. M., "The mixed blessings of contingency management," *Academy of Management Review*, Vol. 2 (1977), pp. 431-441.

16

The Other Side of Foreign Assignments: Dealing with the Repatriation Dilemma

Michael C. Harvey

The other side of the coin of international personnel management is the future role of employees selected for foreign assignments once the assignment is terminated. Most firms, and thus employees, are inadequately prepared in both planning and practical terms for the return of executives from overseas positions. It is all too often the case that the short-term objective of filling the overseas position outweighs the longer-term problem of employee fit in domestic operations upon returning to headquarters. Systematic planning for repatriation may minimize the costs of high executive turnover, resistance to overseas assignments by other employees, and lower morale and productivity associated with such a short-term perspective.

IN DEALING WITH international personnel issues, the subject of training executives for overseas assignments is frequently mentioned. Many multinational corporations (MNCs) have formal programs designed to prepare the executive, and to a lesser extent the executive's family, for overseas assignments. But what can executives expect when their foreign assignment ends and they return to the domestic organization? Few corporations have dealt directly with the problems of repatriation (*Business Week*, 1979).

And indeed there is a reentry crisis for the returnee. The areas of concern frequently cited by repatriates are: personal finances, reacclimation to life in the United States (or other home country), and read-

Reprinted with permission from *The Columbia Journal of World Business*. "The Other side of Foreign Assignments: Dealing with the Repatriation Dilemma" (Spring 1981).

justment to the domestic corporate structure. The problems of personal finances and re-acclimation to U.S. culture may be rather short-term, but how an executive fits into the domestic organization after returning can have wide-ranging effects on career and productivity. This concern for career paths causes stress and anxiety both in the decision to accept an international position and when the foreign assignment expires (Howard, 1980; Hamner et al, 1978; Kendall, 1981).

Therefore, because of the potential long-range impact on the individual and the MNC, this article focuses on the executive's readjustment to the domestic corporate structure. Possible solutions to the problems will also be presented, as well as a process by which the MNC can create a repatriation program or examine the usefulness of its present program.

REPATRIATION PROBLEMS

The complexity of the repatriation problem varies, of course, from corporation to corporation and from returnee to returnee. The situation is also affected by such factors as the number of years spent abroad, the purpose of the overseas assignment, the foreign location, and the executive's age (Clague, 1978). However, the following problems are consistently mentioned by expatriates and are common to most returnees.

INTERNATIONAL ASSIGNMENTS ARE OFTEN A ONE-WAY STREET

All too often a position opens up overseas or a problem occurs, so the MNC hurriedly seeks out the best person to fill this immediate need. The chosen executive and family are trained for overseas duty, make the move overseas, and the MNC has solved its problem. The executive then falls into the category of "out of sight, out of mind" (Clague, 1978; Howard, 1979). The MNC does not worry about this employee until the foreign assignment is over. In other words, little or no planning is done for the repatriation of the executive or for how the foreign arrangements fit into the career path of the individual.

ISOLATION OF THE EXILE

Lack of communication between the domestic office and its foreign subsidiaries makes the expatriate feel personal and professional isolation from the domestic operations. Many times the foreign offices are not even aware of the overall policies of the MNC (Hill, 1979). Not only does this cause problems when the executive is overseas (he or she feels ignored and may unknowingly act in conflict with corporate policy), but it also makes it difficult to readjust to the corporate mainstream, especially if some major changes have been made in management or policy.

EXPATRIATE IS OUT OF THE MAINSTREAM OF ADVANCEMENT

While overseas, the expatriate is less likely to be considered for domestic promotions. This brings up the question of, "Does an overseas stint really lead to the top?" Too often a returnee finds that the peers left behind have been promoted to superior positions. A *Dun's Review* survey indicated that 69 of the top 87 executives of major MNCs had no overseas experience (Smith, 1975). As one management consultant says, "International experience is great. Make sure you get it in the international division at headquarters, right down the corridor from the chairman of the board" (Smith, 1975).

LACK OF CLEAR CAREER PATHS

Executives may take a foreign assignment without knowing where it will lead careerwise. This causes a great deal of anxiety both before and during the international assignment. This problem ties in with the MNC's attitude that foreign assignments are a one-way street. The executive does not know what position to expect on returning to the domestic organization (Howard, 1979).

REPATRIATE CAUGHT IN HOLDING PATTERN UPON RETURN

If the MNC hasn't made plans for the return of its executive, all of a sudden it may realize that the executive's three-year overseas stint is over. The MNC brings the executive back into the organization without a position being open. This puts the repatriate into an uncomfortable holding pattern, until a suitable position becomes available. The repatriate may even have to prove himself all over again to the domestic organization (*Business Week*, 1979).

INTERNATIONAL EXPERIENCE MAY BE MORE VALUABLE OUTSIDE THE COMPANY

The managerial experience gained in international service may be more valuable to another corporation, so they may be willing to pay more for the repatriate's services and expertise. This is especially attractive to the repatriate who is forced into a holding pattern for perhaps as long as a year. This repatriate is likely to leave the MNC for both motivational and monetary reasons (Kendall, 1981).

LACK OF MOTIVATION CAUSED BY THE LOSS OF AUTONOMY

There is also the problem of how to keep the repatriate motivated after returning to the domestic organization. Overseas, the repatriate was likely to have been in a fairly autonomous position. Foreign positions tend to be professionally challenging, with the foreign manager acting almost as an entrepreneur. The more outstanding the performer, the more difficult it will be to adjust to the domestic organizational climate. Instead of being the leader, the repatriate is just another member of the organization, and must measure his steps carefully. "One minute he is Patton roaring across the desert, the next he is on Eisenhower's staff where the moves must be made an inch at a time" (Smith, 1975).

MULTINATIONAL CORPORATIONS CONSIDERATIONS

The MNC should be interested in solving the repatriation problems for two important reasons. First, if an executive who has previously been motivated is no longer motivated by a new domestic position, he or she is likely to leave the organization. Thus, the MNC will be losing a valuable employee, as well as the time and money invested in that employee.

Secondly, if other employees recognize the problems experienced by those who take international positions and see that the MNC does not pay any attention to those problems, there is likely to be resistance to accepting overseas positions. This can have long-range effects on the international operations of the MNC.

The costs of ignoring repatriation problems can be high. But the costs of solving some of these problems are relatively low. It's not just a monetary matter, but more a matter of planning and some additional staff time. Many problems can be avoided if MNCs developed a repatriation plan before the executive took the overseas position.

SYSTEMATIC PLANNING FOR REPATRIATION

Little has been written about formal repatriation programs of MNCs (Clague, 1978; *Business Week*, 1979; Howard, 1979). Few MNCs recognize the problems, let alone develop a formal program to assist repatriates. Approaches described in the literature are *ad hoc* and usually only address a single aspect of the repatriation problem (Howard, 1979; 1980; Kendall, 1981).

According to Herzberg's theory of motivation, the factors that motivate employees are achievement, recognition, responsibility, intrinsic interest in work, and nature of the task (Hamner, 1978). The lack of some of these motivational factors seems to be behind many of the repatriation problems. For instance, the executive in an overseas position ("out of sight, out of mind") often suffers from a lack of recognition. The goal of repatriation should be to bring back an overseas employee who will be a valuable addition to the domestic organization. In order to do this and avoid many of the repatriation problems, MNCs should concentrate on solutions that incorporate motivational factors, as opposed to hygiene factors such as living allowance, increased pay, and living accommodations.

The problems associated with the repatriation of executives must be systematically approached during various phases of the move overseas and the reentry. The following time frames would help in the development of a systematic approach to preparing expatriates to reenter the domestic organization: (1) planning expatriations; (2) pre-expatriation; (3) expatriation; and (4) repatriation. Figure 1 illustrates the planning process and the major objectives to be accomplished in each phase. Each of the phases will be discussed in detail in the following sections.

PLANNING EXPATRIATIONS

The initial step in the development of a system to deal with expatriation/repatriation problems is an assessment of the organizational commitments of the MNC. The organization must develop a procedure for dealing with the anticipated problems of expatriates reentering: (1) analysis of foreign environments; (2) classification of foreign assignments and likely duration; (3) assessment of potential expatriates' problem-solving styles; and (4) development of a feedback mechanism to permit modifications in dealing with repatriation problems.

To ascertain potential hardships to expatriates due to environmental conditions, MNCs must develop an assessment and classification system for foreign environments (Gilbertson, 1976). The classification system might assess such factors as: (1) geographic isolation; (2) degree of urbanization; (3) level of economic development; (4) length of time the organization has conducted business in the country; (5) cultural dissimilarity (business and social); (6) political/economic stability; and (7) legal constraints. Such a classification scheme develops the parameters of the foreign environment illustrating the difficulty of adjusting to the environment. This system has two advantages. First, the MNC can determine the relative hardship of various foreign assignments and can

Figure 1: Systematic Analysis of Repatriation Objectives

I. Planning expatriation

- Development of foreign assignment with specific objectives in mind, i.e., corporate and career path
- Development of assessment procedure of various environments
- Modification of objectives performance measures

II. Pre-expatriation phase

- Clear delineation/communication of executives' objectives in foreign assignments
- Developing a consensus on evaluation criteria for foreign assignments
- Information/awareness of repatriation problems
- Necessary training for family and executive for foreign assignment

III. Expatriation phase

- Establishing/maintaining formal communication channels to expatriate
- Supply of data on domestic activities and the importance of expatriates' assignments
- Systematic/periodic review of expatriates' foreign assignments
- Performance/evaluation of expatriate and adequate recognition/money
- Assessment of domestic job opportunities and their fit into career path of expatriate

IV. Repatriation phase

- Intensive organization/environment update for executive
- Redefinition of motivation for domestic position
- Assistance with family reorientation

---

analyze the conflict an expatriate would encounter. And secondly, it can judge the level of readjustment an expatriate will have to make on returning to the United States. The information obtained from this type of analysis is helpful in the design of a repatriation system for expatriates with varying degrees of overseas hardship.

The second area that the MNC needs to assess is the nature of the assignment and length of time in the foreign environment (Sieveking, 1978). The type of foreign assignment, i.e., managerial/supervisory, new responsibilities, number of subordinates, and the like, will influence the expatriate on returning to his domestic position. For example, if an expatriate is totally in charge of a foreign subsidiary and has to return to a position of assistant district manager, this individual will experience greater repatriation anxiety. Conversely, a plant manager assigned to a foreign operation for a trouble-shooting assignment would probably not have as much reentry adjustment on returning to a plant management position.

The length of time anticipated for the foreign assignment should be considered. The longer the expatriate remains in the foreign country the greater the likelihood of problems of reentry. The repatriation planning team (which will be discussed later in this article) would need to assess the length of stay in conjunction with the type of assignment to determine the potential difficulty in repatriation.

The planning process for repatriation should also include an assessment of the executive's problem-solving style (Hellriegal, 1979) This kind of analysis provides valuable insight into the anticipated behavior patterns of potential expatriate employees. It indicates the degree of flexibility and need for organizational support and participation in organizational teams. The expatriate will also reenter the domestic organization with the same problem-solving imprint and therefore will provide the domestic management with a means of accurately selecting a reentry position.

An essential aspect of the expatriation/repatriation planning process would be to assimilate data on the expatriates in the field, the environment in which they are working, and the problems they encounter on reentry. This data could be used to modify other phases of the repatriation process and to continuously update the procedures used to prepare executives for repatriation.

PRE-EXPATRIATION PHASE

The first phase of preparing for repatriation of executives that directly involves the executives is pre-expatriation. Prior to the departure of the executive and family, the concept of repatriation should be addressed. This phase of indoctrination should include: (1) communication of specific objectives of the international assignment; (2) expatriate mentor programs; (3) education of the executive in potential repatriation problems; and (4) appropriate training for the executive and family.

The expatriate executive must have a complete understanding of the purpose of the foreign assignment. The personal and organizational objectives of the foreign assignment must be carefully delineated. One of the executive's major concerns will be the career path.

Much anxiety can be eliminated if the executive knows, before accepting a foreign assignment, how it will contribute to his or her career at the MNC. Is the assignment for training purposes or will it lead to a promotion immediately upon return? How long can the executive expect to remain an international? These are questions to which the executive must have answers before accepting a position.

One alternative is to have a repatriation agreement (*Business Week*, 1979). Before an executive accepts a foreign position, the MNC will make a general promise as to the length of the assignment and the position to which the executive will probably return in the domestic organization.

This type of agreement has a favorable psychological effect, in that it alleviates possible career anxieties. However, this agreement may also cause problems for the MNC, if it is not made clear that the agreement indicates the corporation's intentions and is not a written guarantee. The executive must realize that the MNC must remain somewhat flexible in its planning. It may be impossible to honor an agreement made five years before, because of organizational structure changes, the need for an experienced international person in another area, or changes in the external environment. These objectives must be reviewed periodically during the foreign assignment. This allows room for changes in both the corporation's and the expatriate's thinking.

Organizational objectives must also be determined in advance to provide assurance to the departing executive. The organizational goals provide standards for performance evaluations and give some indication of the difficulty of the assignment. The degree of personal and professional adjustment required will also be illustrated, giving an indication of the problems that may be associated with repatriation.

All too often, the responsibility for international employees is either nonexistent, spread among several departments, or included in the personnel department's duties. Depending on the number of international personnel, one person or department can better coordinate the domestic organization's efforts to watch out for international employees' concerns. This single source will coordinate expatriate training programs, communications about the domestic organization to expatriates, and will design a specific reentry plan for the expatriate. Although this may add to the corporate bureaucracy, it can be valuable in communicating the MNC's concern for its international employees and in reducing the ambivalence associated with repatriation.

At the same time that the organization establishes a center control point for expatriates, an individual executive mentor program can be devised. This mentor program (McGill, 1980) can provide the expatriate with a personal "link" to the operations of the domestic organization during his absence. In addition, the mentor can evaluate job opportunities that will exist when the expatriate returns to the United States. It will be preferable for each mentor to be personally acquainted with the expatriate and to have had a foreign assignment also. The mentor program will provide the needed feeling of continuity with the domestic operation for the expatriate.

The most important aspect of the pre-expatriation phase is as complete an education of the expatriate as possible on potential problems of reentry. The entire litany of personal, professional, and family problems should be examined in detail (see Figure 2). The MNC must be as forthright with the expatriate as possible, and at the same time not completely discourage him or her from taking the foreign assignment. Again, this education process is a solution based on communication. If the executive is aware of the potential repatriation problems, he or she can take steps to avoid them. This education process will be a part of the expatriation training program. It will not hurt to refresh the expatriate's memory at least a year before he returns to the domestic organization.

EXPATRIATION PHASE

The period when the expatriate is involved in a foreign assignment is an appropriate time to continue planning the repatriation process, which can provide a form of "security blanket" and may help to improve morale and, possibly, productivity. The specific tasks to accomplish during the expatriation phase are: (1) development of formal communication channels concerning reentry; (2) in-field counseling of expatriate and family; (3) development of a reentry evaluation team; and (4) career counseling on various options open to the expatriate.

One of the first elements of the repatriation process to be undertaken during the foreign assignment is the development of formal communications channels concerning reentry. The expatriate's performance during the foreign assignment should be evaluated and an attempt made to keep the executive informed about the domestic operation. It is important for the expatriate to know what is happening at the domestic level, in order to feel a part of the MNC. Not only does this reduce the expatriate's anxiety level while overseas, it makes readjustment to the domestic organization easier.

Figure 2: Anticipated/Potential Problems on Repatriation

Problem area	Expatriate executive	Spouse	Children	Company
A. Financial				
• return to domestic compensation level	MI/LD	MI/LD	Mini/SD	
• loss of allowances, i.e., housing, education, travel, C.O.L.A.	MI/LD	MI/LD	Mini/SD	
• start-up cost, i.e., housing, auto	MI/LD	MI/LD	Mini/SD	
• rate of advancement	MI/LD	MI/LD		Mini/LD
B. Career/Professional Adjustment				
• availability of position	MI/LD	Mini/SD		MI/LD
• adjustment to lower level management position	MI/LD			
• loss of track record domestically	MI/LD			
• reduced productivity	Mini/SD			MI/LD
• tendency to want to leave MNC	MI/LD	Mini/SD		MI/LD
C. Psychological/Family				
• reduction in life style	Mini/SD	MI/LD	MI/LD	
• increased family stress	Mini/SD	Mini/LD	Mini/SD	
• disorientation and dissatisfaction	Mini/SD	MI/LD	Mini/SD	Mini/SD

MI = Major Impact; Mini = Minor Impact; SD = Short Duration; LD = Long Duration.

The performance review is an excellent communication tool. During the expatriate's review, career paths can be reviewed and discussed (Hill, 1979). Changes can be made in the original objectives of the assignment, if necessary. The review should reemphasize the purpose of the foreign assignment and what the executive can expect on returning.

The performance review allows for two-way communication. It can also serve as a motivational factor, in that the employee's efforts can be recognized and rewarded.

The MNC should form a team of experts to counsel expatriates during their tour of duty. This counseling will provide insight into problems of expatriation and guidance on how to prepare for repatriation. The in-field team should be composed of a domestic executive from the MNC, a psychologist and, if possible, the spouse of an expatriate who has recently returned to the United States. These individuals will provide information and counseling on problems of foreign assignments, i.e., dealing with language and cultural problems, development of meaningful activities for other members of the family, separation from loved ones, and the like. At the same time the in-field team can provide valuable insights on planning for reentry, i.e., finances, gradual adjustment from a foreign life style, and the timing of reentry.

Although costly, an annual trip back to the domestic organization will permit the expatriate to catch up on management and operating changes. Ties with the domestic corporate staff can be maintained. If possible, performance reviews can be done at the home office.

The mentor program mentioned earlier in this article should be augmented with a repatriation evaluation committee (International Personnel Review Committee). This committee will monitor expatriates while on foreign assignment and will attempt to match their skills and new experience with domestic positions that become open. The expatriate's mentor can provide the repatriation committee with information on the expatriate's interests and expectations on reentry. This standing committee will help to reduce delays in repatriation and the problem of placing expatriates in "holding positions" until appropriate positions can be found.

When the expatriate is within six to nine months of repatriation, the mentor and a member of the International Personnel Review Committee should visit the expatriate in the field. This visit will provide the forum to discuss career options. This visit with the mentor will also provide the opportunity to evaluate open positions within the MNC. The International Personnel Review Committee member can also be helpful in discussing the options and resulting career path modifications relative to the expatriate's options.

REPATRIATION PHASE

The pressure of repatriation is at its highest point when the executive and family return to the domestic environment. The lack of orientation to both the organization and the social/economic environment will increase the stress in the executive and the family unit. The major areas of assistance in repatriation should be: (1) organizational policy and position definition; (2) financial counseling; (3) professional adjustment time; and (4) family reorientation programs.

The returning executive will require an intensive organizational reorientation program. This program will provide data on policy/procedure change, shifts in corporate strategy, new personnel and new responsibility of existing personnel, and a detailed description of the repatriate's new position. The expatriate should be provided with a reorientation period of at least a month as an observer of meetings before taking on full responsibility for a new position. This phase-in period will permit the executive to readjust to the organization and to differences from the foreign position.

The MNC must provide financial counseling and some assistance to the repatriate (Howard, 1980). The counseling should be for the entire family, to illustate the reduced income (because of the elimination of the foreign allowance) and the resulting adjustment in lifestyle. It is imperative to include the entire family in the income flow so that they will have an appreciation of the income difference for discretionary spending.

Due to the inflation rate and the increased cost of housing, the MNC should provide creative financing for repatriated executives. Their financing options may include a low-interest rate for home purchase, pay-down mortgages (three- to five-year corporate loans to qualify employees for desired housing), second mortgages, participation mortgages, i.e., lower than market-level interest rates, with the MNC participating in the appreciation of the house when sold. For the MNC that has instituted a planning process for repatriation, the company may want to manage expatriates' house rentals while they are out of the country. An alternative to managing the property could be to purchase the house and resell it to the executive at a modest rate of increase on repatriation. The family tension concerning housing makes the MNC's obligation even more crucial, and a solution to the problem must be developed.

Professional adjustment time and family reorientation programs should provide an adequate period for both to become acculturated to their "new environment" (Kendall, 1981). Some flex-time for the executive will permit acquisition of the organizational skills to fit into a new position. The family also needs attention during the first six months after repatriation, to aid them in adjusting to the domestic environment. Professional counseling should be encouraged and paid for by the MNC to help insure as smooth a repatriation as possible.

CONCLUSIONS

MNCs have begun to experience difficulty in attracting executives to accept foreign assignments. One of the contributing factors in this reluctance to go abroad is the ambiguity that surrounds the executive's career upon repatriation. Just as the MNCs have recognized the need to train executives for foreign assignments, they must also develop a plan or process for facilitating the reentry of executives into domestic operations.

The MNC must act to solve repatriation problems in order to retain valuable employees and to encourage the acceptance of international positions. Most of the solutions have relatively low costs, and involve better communication and organizational sensitivity to the stress and the pressures involved in the return of expatriates to an unfamiliar domestic environment.

Most of the repatriation problems can be solved through planning and better communication. Probably the most effective, yet easiest to implement, solution is that of communicating the objectives of the foreign assignment before the executive accepts the position.

The problems and their solutions seem relatively simple, but many MNCs have not yet considered that the repatriate may have some adjustments to make. It is assumed that "They're home, aren't they?" As MNCs recognize some of the potential repatriation problems, the solutions will be near at hand.

REFERENCES

Clague, Llewellyn and Neil B. Krupp, "International Personnel: The Repatriation Problem," *The Personnel Administrator*, April, 1978, pp. 29-33.

Gilbertson, D. W., "Cross Cultural Intervention: A Case for Preintervention Strategy," *Organizational Renewal Newsletter*, Vol. VI, No. 3, March-April, 1976, pp. 2-3.

Hamner, W. Clay and Dennis W. Organ, *Organizational Behavior: An Applied Psychological Approach*. Dallas, Texas: Business Publications, Inc., 1978.

Hellriegal, D. and J. Slocum, *Organizational Behavior: Contingency Views*. St. Paul: West Publishing Company, 1979, pp. 239-45.

Hill, Roy, "Overseas and Overlooked?", *International Management*, August, 1979, pp. 20-21.

"How to Ease Reentry after Overseas Duty," *Business Week*, June 11, 1979, pp. 82-83.

Howard, Cecil G., "Integrating Returning Expatriates into the Domestic Organization," *The Personnel Administrator*, January, 1979, pp. 62-65.

Howard Cecil G., "How Relocation Abroad Affects Expatriate's Family Life," *The Personnel Administrator*, November, 1980, pp. 71-78.

Kendall, D. W., "Repatriation: An Ending and a Beginning," *Business Horizons*, November/December, 1981, pp. 21-25.

McGill, Michael E., "Mentors and Managers," *Working Paper 80-103*, Edwin L. Cox School of Business, Southern Methodist University, 1980, pp. 1-35.

Sieveking, Nicholas, and Ronald C. Martson, "Critical Selection and Orientation of Expatriates," *The Personnel Administrator*, April, 1978, pp. 20-23.

Smith, Lee, "The Hazards of Coming Home," *Dun's Review*, October, 1975, pp. 71-73.

Chapter Six:
International Accounting and Control

ACCOUNTING AND CONTROL are complicated issues facing a multinational corporation. Accounting systems established by foreign subsidiaries must meet the rules and guidelines established by the foreign government and the parent company's government. Because of the wide array of national accounting systems required all over the world, this task is much more complicated than might be presumed. Not only are accounting systems different, but views on what is important may be different. For example, American companies may emphasize income statements whereas Europeans, being more wealth-oriented, may emphasize balance sheets.

Consolidated financial systems as presented by the parent company are most significant for the management of a multinational. Not only do they portray the image of the firm but also are very important in raising funds and determining tax liabilities. Furthermore, they serve as crucial tools for evaluating the performance of subsidiaries and calculating their cash contribution to the cash flow of the parent company.

Other variables that may have a large impact on the financial statements' preparation may include the degree of disclosure required, the extent and type of auditing required, and the numerous accounting methods used in the calculation of depreciation, inventory valuation, allowable expenses, and reserve levels.

Equally important and possibly more complex is the function of tax planning. Tax laws in the countries of operation, as well as tax treaties between countries, may have a significant influence on the calculation of tax liabilities. In particular, tax credits and tax deferrals allowed to corporations that meet specific requirements may require detailed attention. The executive in a multinational corporation must, therefore, understand how the parent country taxes foreign-source income and also be acquainted with the national-tax environments in the host countries in which the firm operates.

Perhaps the most complex task facing corporate management is in establishing sound information and control systems for their multinational operations. Reporting standards must be developed at all levels of the corporation to ensure accuracy as well as to identify problem areas where additional support is required. Where decentralization was once advocated, management is now realizing that centralized control is essential to sound performance, along with uniformity of reporting procedures.

The most recent controls placed on multinational corporations have been in the area of transborder data flows (TBDSs). This issue is undergoing a radical shift in emphasis, which will become more pronounced in the remainder of this decade. Now that Germany has ratified the OECD Declaration on TBDFs, greater focus will be placed upon the type of information that can be transmitted by multinationals concerning personnel, operations, and technology. Furthermore, restrictions are also being extended to the methods of transmission and equipment that corporations use within a nation's borders. Also, the data flows issue is rapidly evolving into concern about the direction of telecommunications policy as well as trade in services.

17
Strategic Considerations in Financing of International Investment
Fariborz Ghadar

The dynamic nature of the international investment environment has significant implications for successful multinational operations. Increasing competition, host-government policies, and level of technology are some of the factors that may contribute to the erosion of MNC control in any given investment. In view of the possibility of less than total control, the selected international financial package takes on strategic importance.

THE FOREIGN-INVESTMENT decision is usually motivated by a complex set of strategic considerations, and it is in this light that the financing of foreign investment is evaluated in this paper. Foreign investments (from a joint-venture refinery project in a developing, oil-consuming nation to a TV assembly plant in the U.S.) are usually motivated by strategic considerations that are wider and more complicated in scope than domestic-investment decisions. The traditional financial evaluation methods used, such as the discounted cash-flow technique, do not easily capture the business, political, and foreign-exchange risks associated with these investments. Therefore, the international financial package ultimately used must reflect these considerations and give the firm the necessary flexibility it requires.

But before we can talk about the financing of international investment, we should be able to identify the firm's strategic motivation for its non-domestic investments.

STRATEGIC MOTIVES BEHIND NON-DOMESTIC INVESTMENTS

In the study of multinational corporations, researchers categorize five motivations[1] behind foreign direct investment. Companies can be categorized as pursuing the following:

1. Markets
2. Raw Materials
3. Product Efficiency
4. Knowledge
5. Oligopolistic Control

MARKET SEEKERS

Multinational corporations (MNCs) that pursue markets undertake foreign investments to satisfy local or export markets that they may not be able to satisfy from their home operations (e.g., Japanese TV assembly plants in the U.S. or U.S. automobile assembly operations abroad).

RAW MATERIALS SEEKERS

Firms that pursue investments internationally to assure sources of raw materials such as oil, coal, or forest products can be categorized as raw materials seekers.

PRODUCTION EFFICIENCY SEEKERS

Firms that are competing on price and must rely on production efficiency can be categorized as Production Efficiency Seekers. Examples of such firms are electronic component plants in Taiwan, which rely on the labor-intensive production that is involved in this industry.

KNOWLEDGE SEEKERS

Firms attempting to gain access to knowledge may pursue investments to obtain technical or managerial expertise and are categorized as Knowledge Seekers.

OLIGOPOLISTIC CONTROL SEEKERS

Direct investments to protect an existing oligopolistic market position or moves that tend to follow oligopolistic competitors are indicative of a strategy to maintain oligopolistic control. Examples are: cross-investments, such as Lever Brothers' investments in the U.S. as a defense against Proctor & Gamble's investment in the U.K., or band wagon behavior, where automobile manufacturers follow each other into Argentina.

As previously suggested, these strategic motives, at least in U.S.-based MNCs, tend to follow a sequence predicted by the International Product Life Cycle. However, at any given time the motivations may not be mutually exclusive. A direct investment may be taken to satisfy only one motive or a number of these motives simultaneously.

CONTROL OF ELEMENTS OF SUCCESS

Prior to discussing the financial packaging of a project, the strengths of the MNC involved in this investment must be identified. In other words, the next phase of strategic formulation is to assess the MNC's capability within its operating environment. Does the MNC control the elements that are important in the product/market category or the industry in which it is operating? This assessment could be undertaken by evaluating which entity (the MNC, the local partner, the government, etc.) has control over the following crucial elements of success:

• Technology
• Management Expertise
• Market Distribution
• Raw Materials
• Capital
• Economies of Scale

In each industry or for each investment, the significance of these elements of control varies. Therefore, it is impractical to give detailed strategic recommendations for general MNC operations. It is feasible, however, to sketch the main dimensions of a few strategic models.

COMPREHENSIVE CONTROL—THE IBM EXAMPLE

A leading MNC that has control over all of the above parameters commands significant control and power. An example is IBM, which two decades ago had a continuing high level of technology, high R&D expenditures to maintain a technological edge, control of management expertise, markets, raw materials, possession of capital, and economies of scale. Such a firm has close to total control over its operations.

DIMINISHING CONTROL: THE OIL INDUSTRY EXAMPLE

A different example is the case of an MNC conducting onshore drilling in an oil-consuming nation where the technology is fairly standardized (i.e., R&D expenditures in this section have remained low over the years). Management expertise can be acquired; the natural market for the oil, once discovered, will be the domestic market; and once the fields are operating, capital requirements are not significant. The MNC may have some control prior to discovery, but very little control after oil has been discovered.

A third type of strategic position would be that of a firm that manufactures products in a country where labor costs are low but sells those products through its international markets in other regions of the world. The firm possesses certain elements of control in the producing country, and controls another set of parameters in the country or countries where it markets the products.

ASSESSING CONTROL: FORMULATING STRATEGY

If the MNC does not possess certain crucial elements of control, others may. Examples would be: a direct foreign investment made to access the domestic market; a government that may give the MNC some type of tariff protection, or some other entity presently in the market place. In many instances, instead of competition, coordination of effort is undertaken, e.g., joint ventures, management contracts, or sale of certain elements of control, such as patents. The entity that possesses the greatest control no doubt will reap the most benefit. Control, however, changes over time as the significance of various parameters changes (e.g., technology may become standardized and thus no longer of paramount importance).

Within this framework, one can understand IBM's resistance to entering the Japanese market over ten years ago. At that time, IBM possessed all elements of control, yet the Japanese government insisted on a joint venture with local manufacturers. No doubt IBM was hesitant to share its technology, sensing that even if it did not manufacture in Japan, IBM computers would still command a major market share there. As computer technology became more readily available, IBM changed its position, and a decade later did enter the Japanese market on a joint venture basis, to protect its share of that market.

Similarly, one can understand the hesitancy of MNCs in the oil industry that are reluctant to drill for onshore oil fields in oil-consuming nations. They correctly assess what their position will be once oil is discovered. At that time, not possessing any elements of control, the benefits they will reap will be marginal. Therefore, they will not invest their funds in such areas, labeling them as "risky investments."

Add to this strategic analysis the elements of business and political risk associated with foreign investments, and we begin to see international financial strategy that is somewhat different from traditional investment financing considerations.

Traditionally, the sources of funds ideally involve minimizing cost of external funds after adjusting for foreign-exchange risk and using internal sources to minimize worldwide taxes—all this while ensuring managerial-motivation and reducing political risk. Theoretically this should be analyzed with an eye to minimizing the MNC's world-wide cost of capital. Numerous models have been put forward, one of the simplest being the Capital Asset Pricing Model. In real life, however, the complications make any kind of optimization almost impossible. Thus, guidelines are used which emphasize one variable over the other and, in essence, suboptimize. One such sub-optimization is the common guideline to minimize the cost of new long-term external funds after adjusting for possible foreign-exchange risks.

The above methods of financing are most useful in an investment where the MNC is in possession of all the crucial elements of control. These instances, however, are not the most common occurrences in international finance. What, then, should the financial package look like if the MNC does not control the crucial parameters? Furthermore, what flexibility should the financial package possess, given the changing importance of the elements of control over time?

Since in each industry the significance of the elements of control vary, it is impractical to give detailed strategic recommendations for general MNC operations. However, let us return to our three strategic models.

THE IBM EXAMPLE

It becomes clear that in the IBM example of ten years ago, the traditional financial analysis and its recommended international financial package are at first adequate. As the computer industry becomes more standardized, companies such as IBM will then have to either upgrade the technology (via R&D expenditures) or gradually shift from international financing to local borrowing so that once all elements of control are gradually lost, their exposure in that environment is reduced.

THE OIL-INDUSTRY EXAMPLE

In our example of onshore petroleum investment in an oil consuming nation, once oil is found the MNC will not control any crucial parameter of success. Thus the MNC will probably not invest its own funds, and financing must be arranged from other sources. Given the uncertainty of striking oil and the business risk of losing control if oil is found, these investments require local financing which in many cases is not available. Thus, these investments usually are not undertaken.

THE INTERNATIONAL LOGISTICAL CONTROL EXAMPLE

In the third strategic example, the manner of financing varies according to the level of technology as well as the importance of the production and marketing affiliate to the success of the operation. For example, car assembly operations in developing nations geared to local markets in many instances have the government or local partners and local banks involved for both equity and debt financing. Case studies indicate that the larger the local market, the greater the amount of financing from local sources. Interestingly enough, as the plant becomes more and more of an export operation, the role of local equity and financing once again is reduced.

The erosion over time of the importance of certain elements of control indicates how equity and debt financing is likely to change. For example, changes in the equity and debt financing of a refinery/fertilizer project involving the Indian government, AMOCO, and the National Iranian Oil Company (NIOC) reflected the change in the elements of control. In this example, NIOC controlled the crude, AMOCO the technology, and the Indian government the local markets. Once the plant was built and operational, the refining and fertilizer technology was fairly standardized, and thus was no longer a crucial control element. NIOC and the Indian government, controlling the raw materials and the markets respectively, then "bought out" the interests of AMOCO.

IMPLICATIONS FOR PARTICIPANTS IN INTERNATIONAL INVESTMENTS

These repeated financial occurrences in the international environment indicate that the international financial package should have flexibility to adjust to the erosion of control by the various entities involved in a project. What are the implications of these findings for the MNC, the local partners, the local governments, and the international financial institutions?

IMPLICATIONS FOR THE MNC

The implications for the MNC are quite significant. For example, assume a given type of technology is an element of control. As it becomes more readily available over time, its importance as an element of control erodes. Therefore, the MNC's role in that industry declines. The MNC will then have to either inject a newer type of technology (e.g., move from radios to black-and-white televisions to color televisions) or gradually prepare for divestiture. If the MNC does not have access to additional elements of control (in this case, higher technology), its financial strategy must change to one that increases local debt and equity financing, while gradually reducing its exposure in that environment by various methods such as transfer pricing, fees, and even dividends.

IMPLICATIONS FOR LOCAL PARTNERS

In many cases, the financial structure pursued indicates the overall strategic choice of the foreign partner. Studying this will assist the local partner not only in understanding what the foreign partner plans to do, but also in evaluating the tradeoffs. Arrangements can be made that will encourage the foreign partner to invest in newer technology or, alternatively, that will allow for the buying out of the foreign investor if, in fact, it no longer contributes to the joint venture. Needless to say, at this point the buy-out will be quite nominal. Therefore, the financial package should be consistent with the overall strategic choices.

IMPLICATIONS FOR LOCAL GOVERNMENTS

Traditionally, local governments have used their tariff and tax policies to control local markets, thus offering these markets as an incentive for local investment (e.g., import-substitution investment) to the MNCs. However, tariff, tax, and credit policies can also be used to encourage MNCs to constantly upgrade the level of technology employed, increase exports, and get involved in the economy of the nation. Conversely, if the firm no longer has a technological edge or access to markets or control over some other crucial area, the government can eventually, via taxes, regulation, and/or the encouragement of local ownership, replace the role of the MNC in the local market. Of course, the government should be sensitive to the impact of such actions on the perceived investment climate of the nation.

IMPLICATIONS FOR FINANCIAL INSTITUTIONS

As the elements of control in each investment shift from one entity to another, it is expected that the benefits accrued from the investment will likely shift as well. Therefore, the financial institution must be aware of who, in fact, is in control and whether the entity that is doing the borrowing can return the funds or whether control is shifting to another entity. For example, if the elements of control will soon be in the hands of the local marketers, the producing firm may not be the proper entity to which funds should be lent. In other words, as a local banker one does not want to finance a firm which should, strategically, withdraw from that environment.

THE ROLE OF INTERNATIONAL FINANCIAL INSTITUTIONS

In our example of oil exploration in an oil-consuming nation, once oil is found, it is, in fact, very likely that the benefits to the MNC petroleum firm will be reduced significantly. A survey of oil operations in numerous LDCs and developing, oil-consuming nations verifies this occurrence. Therefore, a peculiar situation arises where neither the oil companies, nor the consuming nation, nor the local marketers will borrow due to the risky nature of oil exploration. The oil companies correctly envision that they will be nationalized. The consuming nation has neither the foreign exchange nor the expertise to evaluate data. The local marketers are also worried that their revenues may be taken by the government. Thus the investment will not be undertaken.

In such instances, international financial institutions (such as the World Bank, IFC, ADR, etc.) can play a useful role by stepping in themselves and, by so doing, reducing the risk of both parties. The MNC will feel more confident since the participation of the International Financial Institution (IFI) will reduce the financial commitment required by the MNC and increase the likelihood that the MNC will get a fair return—and the oil-consuming nation will feel assured that the IFI will review the technical data and contracts and insure a fair return to the country. Basically, in this case, the MNC and the IFI are counting on the nation's continued dependence on the IFI to keep its agreed-upon terms. And the nation is counting on the IFI to keep the country's interest in mind.

STRATEGY AND FOREIGN INVESTMENT

The foreign-investment decision is a strategic consideration, and the thrust of this paper is that the international financial package should be viewed in that light. The financial package ought to be designed by examining the strategic motive of the MNC and analyzing which entity is in possession of the crucial parameters of success ("the elements of control") in that industry. As the control over the parameters shifts, the financial package should be modified.

To the extent that the MNC controls all crucial parameters of success, the traditional financial models adequately recommend a financial structure. However, if there occurs an erosion of "elements of control" in the traditional financial models, then the MNC is left financially exposed in environments in which it has no control over its investments and little potential benefit from them.

FOOTNOTE

1. Eiteman & Stonehill categorized foreign investment decisions into four motives, but the work of Aharoni (1966) and that of Knickerbocker (1973) suggest there is also a fifth—that of oligopolistic response. Raymond Vernon, in his works in explaining U.S. direct investment patterns, "International Investment and Industrial Trade in the Product Cycle" (1966) and *Sovereignty at Bay* (1971), suggests a sequence of events that evolves as products mature. The sequence begins with a new product manufactured in the U.S. and introduced to foreign markets through exports. When the product matures, technology becomes fairly routine, and the firm, to protect its foreign markets, produces abroad. Finally, when the product is completely standardized, production shifts to a low-cost location and is re-exported to the home country. Although the motivation for direct investment changes over time, the above categories can be used to describe the range of motives.

BIBLIOGRAPHY

Aharoni, Yair. *The Foreign Investment Decision Process.* Boston: Division of Research, Harvard Business School, 1966.

Eiteman, David and Arthur Stonehill. *International Business Finance.* Reading, Mass: Addision-Wesley Publishing Co., Inc., 1973.

Fayerweather, John and Ashok Kapoor. *Strategy and Negotiation for the International Corporation.* Cambridge, Mass.: Ballinger Publishing Co., 1976.

Ghadar, Fariborz. *The Evolution of OPEC Strategy.* Lexington, Mass.: D.C. Heath and Co., 1977.

Knickerbocker, Frederick T. *Oligopolistic Reaction and Multinational Enterprise.* Boston: Division of Research, Harvard Business School, 1973.

Lessard, Donald. "World Country and Industry Relationships in Equity Returns: Implications for Risk Reduction through International Diversification," *Financial Analyst Journal.* January-February 1976, pp. 32-38.

Mikesell, Raymond F. *Foreign Investment in the Petroleum and Mineral Industries.* Baltimore: The Johns Hopkins University Press, 1971.

Robbins, Sidney M. and Robert B. Stobaugh. *Money in the Multinational Enterprise.* New York: Basic Books, 1973.

Robock, Stefan and Kenneth Simmonds. *International Business and Multinational Enterprise.* Homewood, Ill.: Richard D. Irwin, 1973.

Rodriquez, Rita and Eugene Carter. *International Financial Management.* Englewood Cliffs, N.J.: Prentice-Hall, Inc., 1976.

Schelling, Thomas C. *The Strategy of Conflict.* Cambridge, Mass.: Harvard University Press 1960.

Stopford, John M. and T. Wells. *Managing the Multinational Enterprise.* New York: Basic Books, 1972.

Vernon, Raymond. "International Investment and International Trade in the Product Life Cycle," *Quarterly Journal of Economics*, May 1966, pp. 190-207; *Sovereignty at Bay*, New York: Basic Books, 1971, pp. 65-112.

Zenoff, David and Jack Zwick. *International Financial Management.* Englewood Cliffs, N.J.: Prentice-Hall, Inc., 1969.

18

Accounting Standards and Multinational Corporations

S. J. Gray, J. C. Shaw, and L. B. McSweeney

Recent trends toward the formulation of international standards of MNC accountability raise some important questions as to the necessity, scope, and force of such standards. While the goal of harmonizing different national disclosure requirments may be appreciated by MNC management in terms of reducing the current multiplicity of reporting requirements, the diversity of interest reflected in the movement supporting international standards suggests that other goals, less beneficial to the MNC, are to be served by an international set of standards.

INTRODUCTION

Accounting standard-setting is controversial and problematic at the national level, but at the international and multinational level it becomes even more complex, multidimensional, and dynamic. This paper attempts to identify and evaluate emerging issues and trends relating to accounting standards and multinational corporations. This is likely to be an area of growing importance to accountants not least because of the economic significance of MNCs and the sensitive political issues generated by their activities.

Multinational corporations are significant economic entities, both in aggregate worldwide situations and within most individual countries[1] where they operate. Their distinctive economic, social, and political im-

Reprinted, with permission, from the *Journal of International Business Studies*, Summer, 1981.

pact arises from their power to control and move resources internationally and has resulted in growing pressures for higher levels of accountability. Such pressures are exerted by host governments (the governments of countries which are recipients of foreign direct investments) and others, in part from a desire for information which may be the means of regulating, constraining, or analyzing the local activities of MNCs. It would appear that the dissolution of political imperialism during the last quarter century (for example: the Belgian, British, French, Portuguese, and Netherlands Empires and Colonies) has given rise to a deeply felt and sometimes strongly expressed eco-has given rise to a deeply felt and sometimes strongly expressed economic nationalism.[2] The host governments that are apparently most vociferous in the pressure toward greater accountability by MNCs are those of the developing nations. These pressures complement attempts by home governments[3] to control large companies—operating and particularly headquartered or based in their territories—many of which are the center of multinational operations.

Information about corporate behavior is recognized increasingly as an essential prerequisite to policy making at the national level. At the supranational and intergovernmental level, forms of accountability by MNCs are now being actively promoted, for example, by the United Nations (UN) by the Organization for Economic Cooperation and Development (OECD), and by the European Economic Community (EEC).[4] These activities are a relatively recent phenomenon with most of the developments taking place since 1975 and in the case of the UN and OECD within the broader framework of Codes of Conduct. Each of these organizations, of course, is constituted differently and has different objectives and varying powers of enforcement. All, however, demonstrate the political sensitivity and significance of MNC accountability and of questions concerning financial and nonfinancial disclosure. The development of such political pressures has been spurred by both the relative lack of comparability of corporate reporting in an international context and the apparent deficiencies in the information usually provided.[5]

These pressures for increased MNC accountability and disclosures have also been supported by international trade unions—such as, the International Confederation of Free Trade Unions, European Trade Union Confederation, World Confederation of Labour, and the International Metal Workers Federation.[6] The international investment and banking community and the accounting profession (for example: International Accounting Standards Committee) also appear to be anxious to improve the comparability of corporate reporting at the international level.[7] Managements of MNCs are naturally sensitive to these developments, with responses varying according to their perception of the costs and benefits involved.[8] Many are aware of the potential benefits of greater harmonization in terms of removing the current multiplicity of reporting requirements,[9] however, there is a proliferation of bodies claiming to have authority as standard-setting agencies—national and supranational, political, and professional. Hence, the managerial response to or acceptance of the need for harmonization of standards is to some extent confused and perhaps inhibited by these multiple claims to authority.

SOME FUNDAMENTAL QUESTIONS

It would seem useful to pose some fundamental questions, which, incidentally, are relevant in the national context just as much as in the multinational, as a means of structuring this inquiry into emerging issues and trends relating to accounting standards and MNCs. Questions which would appear to concern all interested parties include the following: Should there be standards for MNCs? What should be required by standards? Who should set standards? Before addressing these questions, however, we must first define the terms used in the analysis because they are subject to many interpretations.

What are standards? What are MNCs? The term "standard" may be used in a variety of ways but here it is used broadly to mean a set of statements which may include reference to disclosure or measurement issues to be dealt with by MNCs. Such statements may range from those intended to achieve strict uniformity to those capable of more flexible interpretation; from those derived from statutory authority, to those which are effectively advisory. The fact that they exist as guidelines or criteria against which MNC accountability can be assessed qualifies such statements to be described as "standards" in the context of this discussion. The relevant questions are thus concerned not only with the rationale for standards but also with their scope and force. The discussion is not restricted to standards which are associated exclusively with mechanisms to monitor compliance or impose penalties for noncompliance. A major problem in the international context is that the scope of standards is not always clearly specified, posing consequent potential for confusion.

The term "multinational corporation," or alternatives such as "transnational" corporation, may also be used in a variety of ways; but here it is defined broadly to mean any corporation that controls economic resources, in terms of production or service facilities, in two or more countries.[10] If MNCs are to be affected by standards set exclusively for them, then clearly questions of definition become crucial and will involve criteria such as overall size, relative economic significance in countries of operation, number of geographical locations, and the extent of foreign as compared to domestic operations. In this regard, it is instructive to note the focus of existing proposals/requirements. In the UN proposals [1977][11] the emphasis is on all large MNCs (broadly defined as above) but application to uninational companies is recommended. The OECD guidelines[12] [1976] refer to all MNCs irrespective of size but again wider application is expected. The EEC deals in the main with all corporate activities within the EEC territories, including those by MNCs, but with the emphasis on large companies. The accounting profession, through the International Accounting Standards Committee (IASC), attempts to prescribe for all companies without distinguishing between those that are uninational and multinational. Any attempt to evaluate the relevance of international standards requires specification of those enterprises for which such standards are primarily intended. The definition of the enterprise will indicate the range and nature of user groups involved and hence the rationale for the standards. It is only by reference to user groups and to their decision requirements that the effectiveness and relevance of standards can be judged.

SHOULD THERE BE STANDARDS FOR MNCs?

In the context of reporting financial information, it has to be recognized that there have been significant changes in the perceptions of the use to which accounts are put. In the past the emphasis was on legal concepts—accounts demonstrated the ability of the enterprise to satisfy those who had legally enforceable claims on its resources. Accounts were referred to primarily as a means of confirming that legally defined constraints on the disposition of resources and allocation of results had been complied with. Currently, a widely held view of the use of financial statements is that they serve as a basis for economic decisions. These decisions include not just the legality but also the fairness and effectiveness of managerial actions. The wide community of stakeholders interested in the modern corporate enterprise demands information not only about the conduct of the enterprise as a whole, but about the ways

in which any particular sectional stakeholders' interests in the enterprise
have been dealt with relative to the treatment afforded to other sectional
interests. If there are difficulties in discerning how best to provide for
the information needs of those varied stakeholder interests in the context of single-state, uninational enterprise, there are added degrees of
complexity in confronting the problem of standards for MNCs.

Traditionally, ideas of information disclosure and in particular financial reporting have been developed within the concept of the legal
entity—the corporation—whose boundaries coincided with those of an
economic entity. Increasingly the boundaries of the economic entity do
not coincide with those of a legal entity: the economic activity may be
within only a part of the legal entity (for example: the "group") or may
extend beyond the boundaries of an individual legal entity (for example:
single company). This problem is sharply demonstrated by the nature,
structure, and organization of the MNC.

It may be, of course, that there is no case for standards of any kind;
for example, where the content of existing published annual reports
satisfies the needs of the community of users without the intervention of
a standard-setting body. To some extent at least, the arguments of the
agency-theorists may be relevant here.[13] If the management of an MNC
perceives it to be in the interests of either the MNC as an entity or its
management to respond to the information demands of users, then
management will strive to assure satisfaction of those demands. Such a
line of argument leads to the proposition that no separate standard-
setting mechanism are needed; the normal pressures of demand and
supply will operate to achieve equilibrium.[14] If those who demand information from MNCs also exert influence over the environment within
which the MNC operates, then there will be a strong influence on the
MNC to move toward satisfying these information demands in exchange
for the maintenance of existing rights or the avoidance of potential constraints to the operations of the enterprise. If those responsible for meeting demands for information (that is, the management) conclude that
the information requirement is unreasonable or inimical to the interests
of the MNC, they have to achieve some compromise with the interest
group exerting pressure for disclosure. On this basis, the actual level of
accountability achieved is a constant shifting compromise between the
perception of user needs on the one hand and the view taken about the
interests of the corporate enterprise as a whole on the other hand. In this
context it can be suggested that where MNC managements respond to
pressures for increased disclosure then this demonstrates their recogni-

tion of the need to maintain reasonable operating environments in the face of political pressures for legal and economic constraints on MNC operations in many countries. Similarly they may recognize that the investor in the MNC, in national and international capital markets, seeks information about differential risks within the MNC and that labor relations in any locality may be affected by a local trade union's response to international trade union views or pressures.

It would seem, however, that the perception of some users and organizations such as the UN, OECD, and EEC is that market forces cannot be relied upon to ensure the provision of sufficient comparable information about MNCs. The emphasis in the UN proposals on more extensive disclosure by large MNCs[15] is directed toward a wide range of users but appears strongly influenced nevertheless by the needs of individual national governments, particularly in developing countries, for information about the economic, social, and political impact of MNCs.[16] A similar demand for information is expressed by trade union organizations, who would appear to support strongly the UN initiatives, both at national and international levels.

The OECD seems to have a range of users in mind similar to the UN. But in contrast to the UN proposals, which are detailed and cover individual subsidiary as well as group accounts, the OECD guidelines are limited to group accounts and incorporate disclosure requirements which are more general in nature.[17] This probably reflects the OECD's greater concern with and sensitivity to business interests.

It is perhaps not unfair to suggest that within the UN the influence of developing Third World nations appears to be relatively powerful as compared to the largely developed and substantially westernized membership of OECD. To date, neither the UN nor the OECD statements appear to have achieved much in the way of encouraging MNCs to provide additional information disclosures in practice; but these developments are, of course, still at an early stage. They do, however, provide powerful indications of expectations at the supranational political level, and within the terms set for the present discussion these statements do constitute standards against which to measure the performance of MNCs with regard to information disclosure and corporate conduct.

The position of the European Economic Community (EEC) and of EEC Directives is distinguishable. The EEC is what its name says—a supranational community; moreover, it is a community of nations committed to achieving, ultimately, political and economic union.[18] Member states have accepted treaty obligations to enact local legislation giving effect to the decisions of the Council of Ministers as reflected in the Directives approved by the Council. As regards company laws, the object of the EEC harmonization program is to facilitate freedom of establishment of companies within member countries and to protect the interests of shareholders, employees, and third parties. The company law harmonization program is seen as an important contribution to an economic environment within which finance and investment can move freely and where equality of competition is achieved. It is also seen as a means by which proper supervision of corporate activity can be attained. Observation of the consequences in the United States of fragmented, state-based company legislation suggested that individual states might seek to encourage corporations to establish headquarters in their territory by imposing only minimal regulatory and disclosure requirements. EEC harmonization is intended to achieve the highest common factor of disclosure and corporate conduct generally—not the lowest common denominator. The EEC company law directives are substantially prescriptive and become embodied in statutorily defined requirements.

In practice, the EEC directives and proposals relating to accounting achieve some degree of compromise between a perspective of legal prescription and one related to economic decision making; for example, the Fourth Directive[19] adopts the predominantly U.K. concept of a "true and fair view" but in the context of a rigorously defined financial reporting framework. The EEC Directives apply to all large companies and extend to those whose operations are restricted to the territories of the member states as well as MNCs which are based within one or other of the member states, but whose operations extend well beyond EEC boundaries. The proposed Seventh Directive[20] dealing with group accounts is particularly relevant to MNCs based outside but with operations within EEC territorial limits. This particular directive, if approved, would require the same disclosure for such MNCs with regard to their EEC activities as would be required from EEC-based MNCs. The important difference, of course, is that the latter must meet EEC reporting requirements with regard to their worldwide activities but the MNC based outside the EEC must report only those aspects of its operations relating to its business entities based in the EEC. Such MNCs will, however, be required to provide subgroup consolidations for each holding company within the EEC or, alternatively, a consolidation of its EEC operations as a whole.

Apart from such legislative harmonization within the relatively narrow confines of the EEC, there are other potent influences on most MNCs toward harmonization, indeed uniformity, through the medium of Stock Exchanges—perhaps the strongest influences being the U.K. and U.S. Stock Exchanges.[21] In the U.K. for example, it is obvious that any British-based MNC has to comply with U.K.-defined disclosure requirements with respect to its worldwide activities. The significance of the disclosure requirements of the U.K. Stock Exchange is that these will apply to any non-U.K.-based MNC which seeks a listing for its shares in the U.K.—either to provide access to U.K. capital markets for its existing shareholders or to raise funds through the U.K. capital markets; for example, a Japanese-based MNC seeking a U.K. listing for its share capital must report in the U.K. as if it were U.K.-based including worldwide consolidation of results and translation of accounts into the U.K. domestic currency. Recent years indicate growth of the transnationality of sources of capital and increasing numbers of MNCs seeking Stock Exchange listings outside the country of their base or headquarters.

Such influence tends to achieve a restricted uniformity rather than harmony because the prescription of Stock Exchange requirements in any individual country depends upon the local national legislative arrangements and professional accountancy influences in defining appropriate financial disclosure. The trend, noted earlier, toward multiple stock exchange listings demonstrates the problem of achieving harmonization. Philips, a Netherlands-based MNC, reports, for example, in terms of replacement values, a basis of measurement not accepted by regulatory agencies in the United States and, thus, to support its New York Stock Exchange listing, Philips has to provide a reconciliation translating its Netherlands figures into the U.S.-required historical cost equivalent. Senior executives of Royal Dutch Shell, a Netherlands-U.K.-based MNC, have commented publicly on the consequences of the present U.S. prescription for foreign currency translation—FAS No. 8 for the U.S. and, say, closing rate for the U.K.—or to maintain the use, for reporting outside the U.S., of a method of currency translation that may not be the most appropriate representation of Shell's financial performance.

Other areas of particular interest and concern to MNCs with regard to financial performance and measurement, besides inflation accounting and foreign currency translation, include consolidation techniques and the identification of groups, segmental reporting, accounting for taxation, and the treatment of provisions and reserves. These are areas where significant differences exist in national practice and prescription.[22] The managements of many MNCs certainly seem anxious to eliminate such differences and achieve harmonization without the need for complex supplementary or reconciliation statements to meet differently defined reporting requirements.

The problem is, of course, that the perception of the management of an MNC as to what is the most appropriate reporting or measurement formula will be very strongly influenced by the social and professional perceptions of the country in which the MNC is headquartered. At least in the English-speaking world, detailed perceptions of disclosure and of reporting tend to be developed through social mechanisms, and legislation gives expression to what should be disclosed. Questions of how disclosure should be made and the measurement methods adopted for reporting events and transactions in financial terms have been left, in the main, to the professional accountancy bodies—with greater or less advice from and control by nonaccountants. Non-English-speaking traditions are, of course, somewhat different and developments within the EEC touched on previously demonstrate these; that is, a more prescriptive, legalistic approach is evident.

Harmonization of legislatively defined disclosure can perhaps be achieved only at the political level. The need in the U.S. to create an SEC to deal at the federal level with the lack of harmonization in individual states' legislation can be pointed to in support of such a suggestion. Within the EEC it seems to have been recognized that political structures are needed to deal with legislatively defined matters. The professional accountancy-oriented views about how to measure and how to disclose reflect less immediately the concerns of trade unions, consumers, and governments. But to the extent to which all such questions relating to the use to which information is put by users of financial statements, even the accountancy professional bodies are responsive to such "external," nonaccountant pressures. Harmonization bodies are responsive to such "external," nonaccountant pressures. Harmonization of such local standards defined by professional accountancy societies need not necessarily involve political mechanisms—the self-regulatory stock exchange in the U.K. demonstrates this.

Transnational groupings of accountancy bodies—for example: IASC, IFAC, UEC, CAPA, IAA, and AFA[23]—are also seeking to make progress in this area. Perhaps the major organization involved is the International Accounting Standards Committee (IASC),[24] where the aim is to improve the comparability of measurement and reporting by all enterprises, worldwide. But there is very much less emphasis at IASC on extensions in disclosure and virtually no concern specifically with the problems of MNCs as distinct from uninational enterprises.

Professionally-developed IASC standards would seem to be influenced very largely by the needs of the investment and banking community, with special reference to best practice in developed equity markets such as the U.K. and U.S.[25] The specific interests of governments and of trade unions, on the other hand, are not directly recognized. Little real progress has been achieved toward harmonization, for example, on foreign currency translation, on inflation accounting, on research and development, or consolidations, because IASC has to accommodate the different established laws and professional practices of the United States and of Western Europe. It is not surprising, therefore, that IASC standards tend to be somewhat bland compromises which are generally ignored either because they are easily accommodated or cannot be enforced.

It continues to be difficult to provide a simple answer to the question, "should there be standards for MNCs?" Many MNCs are already subject to standards—imposed by legislation and defined by professional accountancy organizations—because MNCs based in any country have to follow at least the same degree of disclosure and accountability as any other domestic enterprise based in that same country. One set of problems arising from the lack of consistency of accountability among MNCs based in different countries is not really related to MNCs at all; they derive from the lack of consistency or harmonization of national standards and apply to the lack of comparability of disclosure by all large companies based in different countries. For MNCs there might be problems arising from substantially different disclosure requirements. There are difficulties for governments and for elements within domestic societies in relating information about the local units of an MNC to that provided about the worldwide activities of locally-based MNCs. For the governments and societies of host countries, there are problems in relating information about local units to the aggregated information of the worldwide MNC activities, particularly when there is no consistency in the provision of the aggregated data for MNCs based in different countries. For the MNCs themselves, or at least their management, there is the complication of maintaining records and providing information to satisfy distinguishable local demands as well as being able to provide the level of accountability expected in their home base. There is also an arguable case for international standards to the extent that MNCs are not providing information demanded and apparently needed by users. The demands from organizations such as the UN, OECD, EEC, International Trade Unions, and IASC indicate the quantity and quality of information currently disclosed by MNCs is less than satisfactory and warrants some form of standard-setting; however, whether or not the precise content of the demands identified can be justified in that the benefits outweigh the costs involved is a question which has yet to be answered despite the convictions of the groups involved.

Perhaps there is a case for standards applicable to MNCs only as opposed to all large companies worldwide, at least in the short term. The present lack of consistency in MNC accountability and the proliferation of national standards may lead to the conclusion that worldwide harmonization of MNC reporting—disclosure and measurement—is needed. Equally, there may be a supportable argument that international harmonization should not be considered a major priority for uninational (domestic) enterprises with no foreign operations, because the needs of the international investment community, the main group involved and relatively expert, could be met to a large extent by accounting policy disclosures. It is only when uninational companies become units of a supranational economic entity, the MNC, that arguments of consistency and comparability in the interests of international constituencies of users become persuasive. If this line of argument is to be pursued, then it would seem that the UN and OECD have embarked on a potentially more fruitful path than has the IASC—the important point being to emphasize and develop supranational standards for MNCs rather than to seek at this stage the ideal of a harmonization of national standards for all corporations.

WHAT SHOULD BE REQUIRED BY THE STANDARDS?

Ideally the answer to this question would seem to depend on the decision requirements of the user groups involved, taking into consideration the costs and benefits arising. In practice, the outcome is likely to result from a political process involving both MNC managements and the accounting profession as suppliers and verifiers of information in addition to international groups of users such as investors, creditors, trade unions, governments, and society at-large.

There is, of course, a fundamental problem, as in the national context, of defining user information needs. A positive approach would be to ask users what they need—with the danger, however, that responses may well be conditioned by experience, and hence less than imaginative in dealing with new situations. There is also the danger that users may be encouraged to compile shopping lists of information, including anything that might conceivably be useful, especially when they do not bear the cost, at least directly, of providing the information. Can users then be trusted to articulate their needs, and are MNCs to respond unquestioningly to stated needs without challenging the relevance of the information demanded? An alternative normative approach to defining user needs is to attempt to construct models of the decision processes of users and thereby deduce what information they should need to satisfy their objectives. It may be that more attention should be paid to this approach in the MNC context where new situations have arisen with the corresponding potential for new forms of reporting to be developed and for information needs to be shaped by policy-makers at the supranational level.

An important issue in the supranational context is the extent to which the separate needs of users are to be satisfied by general purpose reports or by special purpose reports.[26] It appears at present that the UN, with special reference to the developing nations and trade unions, at the national and international levels, is concerned to obtain as much information as possible in a general purpose report. The interests of these groups appear to be initially to obtain information as a step toward developing policies and strategies for dealing with and regulating MNCs. The governments of developing countries and those involved in trade unions (nationally and internationally) feel themselves to be at a severe disadvantage in their dealings with MNCs. The relative transnational freedom of MNCs and the mechanisms available to them, especially transfer pricing, to modify the impact of national economic, fiscal, and social policies have been discussed extensively elsewhere.[27]

Those who seek to constrain and regulate, or at the very least to influence, the activities of MNCs, tend to suspect the existence of abuse by MNCs in their supranational powers and flexibility. Part of the pressure for MNC accountability is to assist the perception of the existence of abuse or, more positively, to confirm its absence. In the context of the single company, the various stakeholders (investors, creditors, employees, customers) are concerned to preserve their own individual interests; with the MNCs, individual governments are concerned to protect the interests of their own nationals as against other nationals; at the trade union level, there is ideological commitment to eliminate exploitation of any one group of employees in favor of another, or in favor of other stakeholders.

"Special" reports, however, may be more pertinent to specific needs and these could be tailored to meet the requirements of individual countries or individual interest groups. In this case, the onus of specification is shifted directly to the user group seeking information; there has to be definition of the data needed, and desirably an explanation of why it is needed.

A key element of the UN emphasis on general purpose reports is the provision of nonfinancial information relating to employment, production, investment, social policies, and pollution,[28] which would seem to be relevant mainly to governments. If so, then there is the question of whether some of this information could be presented better in special reports.

Other disclosure and measurement issues which are regarded as especially significant (and often sensitive) in the context of MNCs include: (a) segmental information, particularly on a geographical basis, or multianalysis by activity and by country[29]; (b) transfer pricing policies and their impact[30]; (c) employment conditions and prospects[31]; (d) foreign currency transactions and the translation of foreign currency financial statements.[32] Additional MNC financial reporting issues, which are nonetheless controversial, include accounting for groups and the consolidation of financial statements, accounting for inflation, and accounting for taxation.[33] Consideration also needs to be given to the form of presentation of financial information.

It may be that the conventional Income Statement and Balance Sheet for consolidated groups or for individual companies is not the most appropriate, say, for government and employee users. Statements of Value Added[34]—segmented as required—might be a more useful method of presentation. Statements of funds or cash flow may also be useful—again segmented. The present perception of the bases on which governments and trade unions are seeking additional disclosure certainly suggests that such forms of accounting are worthy of further investigation in that they might meet more fully the needs of these groups for information from MNCs. Both the UN and the OECD are at the moment striving for acceptance of their ideas with regard to a minimum list of items of disclosure but, at this early stage of their activities, have given relatively little attention to issues concerning classification, presentation, and measurement; thus, there is much work to be done if standards for MNCs are to be developed. This effort will require cooperation from the accountancy profession and a substantial research effort, as well as political will.

The very fact that one has to discuss the need for standards of MNC disclosure and measurement implies that the definition of such standards cannot be left to the MNCs themselves. Reference was made earlier to the proposition that standards as such would be unnecessary if the process of enlightened self-interest, in the long run, assured that managements of MNCs meet the information needs of all the multinational interest groups who establish claims to disclosure by the MNC about its worldwide and/or local activities. On the one hand, there is the local community—whether host or home government, or national elements of employees, investors, consumers, or others within the nation—anxious to supervise, influence, or at least be informed about the MNC's operations. On the other hand, there is the management of the MNC, anxious to achieve the most congenial operational environment possible and to minimize costs of preparing and producing information for external (to the management) consumption. This assures that there are two strong parties to the bargaining process by which equilibrium may be achieved.

If one rejects the argument that natural balance will be achieved and accepts the argument that MNCs themselves cannot be relied on or expected to develop appropriate standards, one is forced to consider the two alternative agencies referred to earlier—the political or the professional. This choice, or tension, between these two types of agency exists, of course, at the national level. As with so many other aspects of this discussion it may be that there are few new problems with MNCs; many similar problems can be found at the domestic level, but with MNCs there is an extra multinational dimension of complexity.

On the whole, accountants prefer the professionally-oriented IASC type of approach whereby auditors and, to a lesser extent, financial executives agree on procedures of measurement and disclosure. The weaknesses of this approach have already been touched on. Accountancy bodies cannot legitimately claim to identify exclusively the effect of accounting reports on the decision-making behavior of users nor the sole right to choose between reporting alternatives which may influence actions by some users to the detriment of others.

The auditing bias of many of the professional accountancy organizations also leads to preoccupation with the validation aspects of disclosure and a reluctance to develop ideas for disclosure of information which cannot be validated other than by the passage of time. There is a tendency for such efforts also to concentrate on how to achieve disclosure rather than to examine ideas of what should be disclosed to meet the needs of users. Further, the needs of users other than shareholders and creditors have received little attention. Ideas for alternative methods of disclosure are not examined enthusiastically; alternative measurement bases—for example: current cost accounting in the U.K.—are seldom initiated except under "encouragement" from political agencies. As noted earlier, only very limited progress has been made with difficult technical issues—for example: foreign currency translation—and very little harmonization has been attained. Last, the close relationships between professional firms, which are increasingly multinational, and their clients (the MNCs) together with the apparent acquiescence of management generally in any professionally-based program is seen by some, at least, as a valid basis for challenging the validity of such an approach. Perhaps self-regulation is too suspect to succeed.

It may be then that a political approach is inevitable. In the United States, a political solution in the creation of the SEC was seen as the only way of achieving harmonization at an acceptably high level of disclosure. Until recently the SEC was content to leave to professional accountancy agencies the determination of technical accountancy matters. Now the accounting standard-setting agencies (notably FASB) involve directly many more influences other than accountants, and the SEC itself has challenged and even reversed procedures approved by FASB; for example: oil and gas accounting.[35] Matters of accountancy appear to have become too important to be left to accountancy bodies. If the levels of accountability are to be defined at the national level in the first instance and ultimately some form of supranational harmonization is to be achieved, then it is difficult to see any alternative to political agencies. At this stage, it also seems likely that such agencies will concentrate on the philosophy of information disclosure—why information is needed and in what form it is required—leaving detailed aspects to be worked out in cooperation with professional accountancy organizations.[36]

Whereas the UN and OECD approach to MNC standards seems inevitable, it may well succeed only in the long term because it is difficult to see how anything other than "guidelines" as opposed to "requirements" can be provided at this stage.[37] Mechanisms for reviewing and enforcing compliance can operate only at the national level—applicable to corporations within the jurisdiction of nation-states and exercised by

local regulatory, legislative, and judicial agencies. If different supranational agencies issue competing guidelines then individual nation-states
have to decide which, if any, set of guidelines matches their information
needs; the harmonization sought by the management of MNCs is frustrated and they have to respond to differently defined information
needs. Even if guidelines emanate from only one supranational agency,
unless a sufficient degree of commonality is achieved in the specification
of information, it is likely that nation-states will individually vary the
guidelines, again arriving at the frustration of the desire for simple,
unequivocal, and uniform disclosure. The relative success of the EEC in
achieving enforceable standards with a fair degree of commonality cannot be expected to be repeated worldwide. As has already been noted,
the EEC is a relatively homogeneous, cultural grouping of nations committed (even if less than wholeheartedly in some instances) to ultimate
total political and economic unity. But presumably from the standpoint
of the UN and OECD some attempt at standards is better than none at
all. Nevertheless, the paradox remains: supranational requirements
cannot be enforced; supranational guidelines may lead to so many national variants that standardization will be frustrated. There may be
more rapid progress to be made by achieving initially some degree of
harmonization among smaller, perhaps regional groupings of nations
sharing at least some common cultural and economic characteristics and
ultimately achieving harmonization of that smaller number of regionally
defined standards.

Such a regional approach could also simplify the attainment of adequate representation of various user groups. The better the user representation, the more confident one could be that the information being
sought was relevant to user needs, and the easier it would be to distinguish what should be conveyed in general purpose reports from that
confined to special reports.

In practice, a gradualist approach may therefore be preferable to the
attempt to arrive at a total solution for MNC standards, though clearly
there are some aspects of MNC activities which may lend themselves to
universal solutions; such as, transfer pricing, segmental information,
and foreign currency translation.

CONCLUSIONS

The power of MNCs and corresponding pressures, especially from
governments and trade unions, for higher levels of accountability has
brought into focus the need for more information about MNCs as a basis

for policy making at national and international levels. To some extent the conflict expresses the shift in the balance between the economic power of MNCs, still largely based in developed nations, and the growing political influence of developing nations. It is generally recognized that calls for greater accountability must be accompanied by consideration of what and how disclosure is to be made; some degree of consistency or standardization is needed. However, the problem of developing accounting standards of disclosure and measurement for MNCs is complex, multidimensional, and dynamic.

An attempt has been made in this paper to clarify some of the issues involved and to identify trends. The analysis has centered on three fundamental questions: Should there be standards for MNCs? What should be required by the standards? Who should set standards? Some tentative conclusions follow.

Despite the many similarities in the problems associated with accounting standards for MNCs and those restricted to wholly domestic companies, MNC problems are more complex, in terms of identifying user groups involved, in defining their information needs, and in considering the factors determining the standard-setting process. The confusion of boundaries between economic, legal, and political entities raises special issues when considering standards for MNCs.

If the bargaining processes between MNCs and users were to result in the provision of information which was acceptable, in terms of quantity and quality, both to management and the user groups concerned—such as, governments, trade unions, investors, lenders/bankers—there might be no need to consider further the issue of standard setting.

Where MNCs are unwilling (or unable because of difficulties in defining user needs) to meet the demands of governments, trade unions, investors, and others for information there is an arguable case for MNC standards at the supranational level. The current activities of the UN, OECD, EEC, International Trade Unions, IASC, and others indicate a strongly perceived need for improvements in information disclosure and the comparability of reporting by MNCs.

The content of MNC standards will depend on the user groups involved, their decision requirements, and their need for general purpose or special reports. It may be that special reports would be more pertinent in some instances to the specific needs of individual governments and interest groups; however, the problem of identifying and validating user needs and resolving conflicts, where they exist, between these needs is unsettled and warrants further investigation.

The fears and problems of management concerning the effects of government interference, better informed competition, and changes in employee relations must also be evaluated, together with the costs and complexities believed to be associated with implementing standards.

Significant disclosure and measurement issues in the context of the development of MNC accounting standards are: (a) nonfinancial information relating to employment conditions and prospects, organization, production, investment, and the environment; (b) segmental information, particularly on a geographical basis, or multianalysis by activity and country; (c) transfer pricing policies and their impact; (d) foreign currency transactions and the translation of foreign currency financial statements. Additional MNC financial reporting issues include accounting for groups and the consolidation of financial statements, accounting for inflation, and accounting for taxation.

The setting of MNC standards is essentially a political process and it seems inevitable that corporate reporting objectives and standards of disclosure will be harmonized only at the supranational or inter-governmental level; for example, the UN, OECD, and EEC. The accounting profession and the IASC are likely to play a more supportive role in terms of providing the detailed development and assisting practical implementation of desired standards of disclosure and measurement.

The development of MNC standards by the UN, OECD, and other supranational political agencies seems likely to be both more supportable, at least in the short term, and to have better prospects for success than the professional IASC attempt to seek the ideal of international harmonization of national standards for all corporations. The relative preference for the UN and OECD approach is due, at least in part, to the emphasis on MNCs which are in many important respects distinguishable from domestic corporations.

MNC standards may be developed as "requirements" or as indicative "guidelines." It is difficult to see them as anything other than guidelines because compliance can be enforced only at the national level or in regional groupings equivalent to the national level such as the EEC. The paradox is that supranational "requirements" cannot be enforced without national adoption, and supranational "guidelines" may lead to so many national variants that simple specification of universally relevant MNC standards is frustrated. A gradualist approach may be preferable with MNC standards implemented initially on a regional basis.

FOOTNOTES

1. The relative importance of MNCs to individual country economies is not confined to developing nations. There is a high level of MNC penetration of many developed countries which accounts for nearly three quarters of the MNCs' foreign activities. See OECD [1977], UN Economic and Social Council [1978].

2. See Turner [1974]; Wallace [1976]; and Vernon [1977].

3. By home government is meant the government of a country from which ultimate control is exercised. Home and host countries are not discrete catagories because the major home countries are also major host countries. The extent to which MNCs are centralized or decentralized is discussed extensively in the literature but is not considered here. See Stopford and Wells, Jr. [1972]; Robbins and Stobaugh [1974]; Vernon and Wells, Jr. [1976]; and Vernon[1977].

4. The principal statements are: OECD [1976]; UN [1977]; and Commission of the European Communities [1976 and 1978].

5. See for example Lea [1971]; UN Economic and Social Council [1975]; Choi and Mueller [1978]; and Fitzgerald and Kelley [1979].

6. For an account of the role of international trade union organizations and international trade union centers, see, for example, Northrup and Rowan [1974]; Roberts and Liebhaberg [1977]; and Wilms-Wright [1977].

7. The object of the International Accounting Standards Committee (IASC) is " . . . to formulate and publish interest standards to be observed in the presentation of audited financial statements and to promote their world-wide acceptance and observance." [IASC 1977].

8. Resistance to increased disclosure by many MNCs is based on a variety of objections including the cost, the limited comprehension of recipients, and the possible utilization of the additional disclosure by others to the detriment of the MNC. (From private interviews with a number of UK and U.S.-based MNCs. Also USA-Business Industry and Advisory Committee [1974]; Behrman [1976]; Mautz and May [1978]; International Chamber of Commerce [1978]; and OECD [1979].)

9. See for example de Bruyne [1980].

10. There is an extensive literature on defining MNCs. See for example American Accounting Association [1973]; Confederation of British Industry [1975]; and Wallace [1976].

11. The UN proposals—UN [1977]—are contained in a report prepared for the Commission on Transnational Corporations by an Expert Group on "International Standards of Accounting and Reporting." The Group, serving in their individual capacities, came from various disciplines (accounting, law, social sciences) and backgrounds (including the accounting profession, home and host government, trade unions, and MNCs).

12. The OECD guidelines referred to here are those relating to information disclosure in the OECD's wide-ranging code of conduct: "Guidelines for Multinationals" in OECD [1976].

13. An agency relationship between managers and shareholders is postulated whereby managers in their capacity as agents have market incentives to disclose information consistent with their own shareholders' interests. See Jensen and Meckling [1976]; Watts [1977]; and Watts and Zimmerman [1978].

14. Watts [1977]; Watts and Zimmerman [1978]; and Benston [1969].

15. UN Economic and Social Council [1977] recommends that smaller companies be excluded from its proposed reporting requirements. The requirement for consolidated reports of the MNC as a whole would apply if it met two of the three specified criteria (p. 47). No criteria for size are stated for individual subsidiaries or intermediate parent companies.

16. The UN proposals refer to a number of different user groups including "governments," "the general public," "the international community," consumer groups, labor, trade unions and company employees, investors, creditors, local authorities. They have been criticized for neither specifying nor justifying their perception of the information needs of these users nor relating their proposals to these needs. See International Chamber of Commerce [1978].

17. OECD [1976] refers primarily to "the enterprise as a whole" thereby avoiding a major source of tension: the extent to which an MNC's subsidiaries' reports may be influenced by or reflect its relationship with the group as a whole, see Robbins and Stobaugh [1974] and Vernon [1979].

18. Treaty establishing the European Economic Community, signed at Rome, 25th March 1957.

19. Commission of the European Communities [1978]. The Fourth Directive has as its object the harmonization of the content and format of annual accounts (Art. 2) of individual companies. This directive does not require absolute uniformity because options are provided in certain clearly defined areas.

20. Commission of the European Communities [1976], amended [1979].

21. See for example Watson [1974]; AISG [1975]; and Zeff [1979].

22. See for example Fitzgerald, Stickler, and Watts [1979] and Gray [1980].

23. International Accounting Standards Committee, International Federation of Accountants, Union Europeene des Experts Comptables, Confederation of Asian and Pacific Accountants, Inter-American Accounting Association and Asean Federation of Accountants. See Choi and Mueller [1978].

24. The International Accounting Standards Committee was founded in 1973 by accounting bodies from Australia, Canada, France, the Federal Republic of Germany, Japan, Mexico, Netherlands, the U.K., Ireland, and the U.S. Fifty-six accounting bodies from 43 countries are represented in the Committee. Its controlling board is composed of the founders plus Nigeria and South Africa.

25. The narrowness and relatively minor role of the equity markets in most developing countries and in some developed countries restricts the relevance of the IASC's current work even further. See Scott [1970] and Lowe [1974].

26. Special purpose reports may be confidential or publicly available but are tailored to the information needs of a single user. See for example Confeder-

ation of British Industry [1975]; International Chamber of Commerce [1978]; and UN Economic and Social Council [1977].

27. Robbins and Stobaugh [1973]; UN Economic and Social Council [1974]; Barnet and Mueller [1975]; and UN Conference on Trade and Development [1978].

28. UN Economic and Social Council [1977] suggests a wide range of nonfinancial disclosures at both individual company and group levels but states "that this aspect of general purpose reporting requires further study (p. 27). OECD [1976] requests disclosure of only one item of nonfinancial information, the average number of employees in each geographical area (p. 15). The IASC has not considered nonfinancial information.

29. U.S. Business Industry and Advisory Committee [1976]; Gray [1978]; OECD [1979]; and IASC [1980].

30. The Monopolies Commission [1973]; U.S. Business Industry and Advisory Committee [1976]; UN Economic and Social Council [1977]; UN Conference on Trade and Development [1978]; and OECD [1979].

31. UN Economic and Social Council [1976]; International Labour Office [1977]; International Confederation of Free Trade Unions; European Trade Union Confederation, World Confederation of Labour [1977]; and International Chamber of Commerce [1978].

32. FASB [1975]; and Choi and Mueller [1978].

33. Choi and Mueller [1978]; Center for International Education and Research in Accounting [1977 and 1979]; and Scott and Drapalik [1978].

34. By a "value added" statement is meant a statement which reports, in financial terms, the output of an enterprise less external inputs (that is, its value added) and the distribution of the value added to the various stakeholders. See for example Gray and Maunders [1980] and UN Economic and Social Council [1976].

35. Zeff [1978].

36. In identifying complementary but separate roles for political and professional agencies in the development of standards for MNCs we are rejecting the view of some commentators who consider the political and the professional to be mutually exclusive alternatives and who usually favor the professional. See for example International Chamber of Commerce [1978] and Fitzgerald and Kelley [1979].

37. This conclusion is based on the recognition of a number of political and technical constraints including: the divergent interests of the involved parties; the difficulty of defining MNCs; the diversity of existing national laws/ requirements; the experience of agreeing and implementing existing multilateral conventions.

REFERENCES

Accountants International Study Group. *International Financial Reporting*. New York, 1975.

American Accounting Association. "Report of the Committee on International Accounting." *The Accounting Review*, Supplement, 1973.

Barnet, R. J., and Mueller, R. E. *Global Reach: The Power of the Multinational Corporation.* London: Jonathan Cape, 1975.

Behrman, J. N. *Demand for Information from Multinational Enterprises.* New York: Fund for Multinational Management Education/Council of the Americas, 1976.

Benston, G. J. "The Value of the SEC's Accounting Disclosure Requirements." *Accounting Review,* July 1969.

Center for International Education and Research in Accounting. *The Multinational Corporation: Accounting and Social Implications.* University of Illinois, 1977.

———. *The Impact of Inflation on Accounting: A Global View.* University of Illinois, 1979.

Choi, F. D. S., and Mueller, G. G. *An Introduction to Multinational Accounting.* Englewood Cliffs: Prentice-Hall, 1978.

Commission of the European Communities. *Proposal for a Seventh Directive on Group Accounts.* Brussels, 1976, amended 1979.

———. *Fourth Council Directive for Co-Ordination of National Legislation Regarding the Annual Accounts of Limited Liability Companies.* Brussels, 1978.

Confederation of British Industry. *The Provision of Information by Multinational Enterprises in the UK.* London, 1975.

de Bruyne, D. "Global Standards: A Tower of Babel." *Financial Executive,* February 1980.

Financial Accounting Standards Board. *Statement of Financial Accounting Standards No. 8, Accounting for the Translation of Foreign Currency Transactions and Foreign Currency Financial Statements.* Stamford, CT, 1975.

Fitzgerald, R. D., and Kelley, E. M. "International Disclosure Standards—the United Nations Position." *Journal of Accounting, Auditing and Finance,* Fall 1979.

Fitzgerald, R. D.; Stickler, A. D.; and Watts, T. R. *International Survey of Accounting Principles and Reporting Practices.* Butterworths and Price Waterhouse International, 1979.

Gray, S. J. "Segment Reporting and the EEC Multinationals." *Journal of Accounting Research.* Autumn 1978.

———. "The Impact of International Accounting Differences from a Security Analysis Perspective: Some European Evidence." *Journal of Accounting Research,* Spring 1980.

———, and Maunders, K. T. *Value Added Reporting: Uses and Measurement.* London: Association of Certified Accountants, 1980.

International Accounting Standard No. 1, Disclosure of Accounting Policies, London, 1975.

———. *The Work and Purpose of the International Accounting Standards Committee,* London, 1977.

———. *International Accounting Standard No. 3, Consolidated Financial Statements,* London, 1976.

———. *Exposure Draft 15, Reporting Financial Information by Segment.* London, 1980. International Chamber of Commerce. *ICC Comments on the Report of the UN Expert Group on Accounting Standards and Reporting.* Paris, 1978.

International Confederation of Free Trade Unions, World Confederation of Labour, European Trade Union Confederation. *Trade Union Requirements for Accounting and Publication by Undertakings and Groups of Companies.* Brussels, 1977.

International Labour Office. *Tripartite Declaration of Principles Concerning Multinational Enterprises and Social Policy.* Geneva: ILO, 1977.

Jensen, M. C., and Meckling, W. H. "Theory of the Firm: Managerial Behavior, Agency Costs and Ownership Structure." *Journal of Financial Economics,* October 1976.

Lea, D. "International Companies and Trade Union Interests." In *The Multinational Enterprise,* edited by J. H. Dunning, London: Allen and Unwin, 1971.

Lowe, J. W. "Financial Markets in Developing Countries." *Finance and Development,* December 1974.

Mautz, R. K., and May, R. G. *Financial Disclosure in a Competitive Economy.* New York: Research Foundation of the Financial Executives Institute, 1978.

The Monopolies Commission (UK). *Chlordiazepoxide and Diazepam.* London: HMSO, 1973.

Morris, R. C. "The Financial Reporting Problems of Multinational Companies." *The Accountant's Magazine,* September 1975.

Northrup, H. R., and Rowan, R. C. "Multinational Collective Bargaining Activity: The Factual Record in Chemicals, Glass and Rubber Tyres." *Columbia Journal of World Business,* Spring and Summer 1974.

Organization for Economic Co-Operation and Development. *International Investment and Multinational Enterprises.* Paris, 1976, revised 1979.

————. *Penetration of Multinational Enterprises in Manufacturing Industry in Member Countries.* Paris, 1977.

————. *International Investment and Multinational Enterprises–Review of the 1976 Declaration and Decisions.* Paris, 1979.

Robbins, S. M., and Stobaugh, R. B. "The Bent Measuring Stick for Foreign Subsidiaries." *Harvard Business Review,* September/October 1973.

————. *Money in the Multinational Enterprise.* New York: Basic Books, 1974.

Roberts, B. C., and Liebhaberg, B. "International Regulation of Multinational Enterprises: Trade Union and Management Concerns." *British Journal of Industrial Relations,* November 1977.

Scott, G. M. *Accounting and Developing Nations.* Washington, DC: International Accounting Studies Institute, 1970.

————., and Drapalik, J. F. "Financial Control and Reporting in Multinational Enterprises." In *Accounting for Multinational Corporations,* edited by D. D. Al Hashim and J. W. Robertson. Indianapolis: Bobb-Merrill, 1978.

Stopford, J. M., and Wells, L. T., Jr. *Managing the Multinational Enterprise.* London: Longman, 1972.

Turner, L. *Multinational Companies and the Third World.* London: Allen Lane, 1974.

United Nations Conference on Trade and Development. *Dominant Positions of Market Power of Transnational Corporations—Use of the Transfer Pricing Mechanism.* New York: UN, 1978.

United Nations Economic and Social Council. *The Impact of Multinational Corporations on the Development Process and on International Relations—Report of the Group of Eminent Persons*. New York: UN, 1976.

———. *Some Aspects of Corporate Accounting and Reporting of Special Interest to Developing Countries*. New York: UN, 1976.

———. *International Standards of Accounting and Reporting for Transnational Corporations*. New York: UN, 1977.

———. *Transnational Corporations in World Development: A Re-Examination*. New York: UN, 1978.

United States of America—Business and Industry Advisory Committee, Committee on International Investment and Multinational Enterprise. *A Discussion of Provision of Data on MNC Operations*. New York: USA-BIAC, 1974.

———. *A Review of the OECD Guidelines for Multinational Enterprises: Disclosure of Information*. New York, USA-BIAC, 1976.

Vernon, R. *Storm Over the Multinationals—the Real Issues*. London: Macmillan Press, 1977.

———., and Wells, L. T., Jr., *Economic Environment of International Business*. 2nd ed. Englewood Cliffs: Prentice Hall, 1976.

Wallace, D. *International Regulation of Multinational Corporations*. New York, Praeger, 1976.

Watson, W. H., Jr. "Global Role for US Stock Exchange." *Columbia Journal of World Business,* Spring 1974.

Watts, R. L. "Corporate Financial Statements, A Product of the Market and Political Processes." *Australian Journal of Management*, April 1977.

———., and Zimmerman, J. L. "Towards a Positive Theory of the Determination of Accounting Standards." *Accounting Review,* January 1978.

Wilms-Wright, C. *Transnational Corporations: A Strategy for Control*. London: Fabian Society, 1977.

Zeff, S. A. "The Rise of 'Economic Consequences.' " *Journal of Accountancy,* December 1978.

———. "Greater Disclosure Fever Spreading Across the Globe." *World Accounting Report*. February 1979.

19

Transborder
Data Flows:
An Endangered Species?

Phillip D. Grub
and Suzanne R. Settle

A vivid example of the emerging restrictive trend toward multinational firms may be found in the transborder data flow (TBDF) issue. Once relatively free of government interference, international flows of information are currently subject to a variety of restrictions. The implications of such restrictions for MNCs are significant, since virtually all international operations are dependent upon the timely and efficient transfer of information. In order to avoid the expensive shock of unexpected laws, high costs for compliance, and perhaps even market loss, the top management of MNCs needs to devote attention to the variety of foreign measures threatening the free flow of information.

INFORMATION TECHNOLOGY AND NATIONAL SOVEREIGNTY: A NEW PROBLEM FOR MNcs

THE EXPLOSIVE GROWTH in information resources, and increasing reliance on them, in both developed and developing countries during the past decade, has prompted governments to focus more attention on the complex array of associated public policy issues. One consequence of such attention has been a shift from unquestioning acceptance of the advantages of technological advances in the information field to a search for effective social, economic, and political controls over the application and use of such technologies.

Although the United States may be leading the trend toward information societies, it does not have a monopoly on awareness of the costs and benefits of information technologies. Many other governments have recognized the value of information; indeed, some have identified information as a resource of paramount national importance:

Information is power, and economic information is economic power. Information has an economic value, and the ability to store and process certain types of data may well give one country political and technological advantage over other countries. This, in turn, leads to a loss of national sovereignty through supranational data flows.[1]

Among developed and developing countries alike, the protection of national sovereignty constitutes the highest priority on the national agenda. Global interdependence, and its primary agents, multinational enterprises, have served to heighten national sensitivities in this regard and to reinforce general goals of governmental autonomy. The following excerpt from a government-commissioned report on the implications of telecommunications technologies illustrates the perceived link between transborder data flows and national sovereignty:

Of all the technologies that are developing so rapidly today, that of informatics (computer communications) poses possibly the most dangerous threat to Canadian sovereignty, in both its cultural and commercial aspects.... the government should act immediately to regulate transborder data flows to ensure that we do not lose control of information vital to the maintenance of national sovereignty.[2]

For many countries, the lack of control over information in- and out-flows reflects a corresponding lack of sovereignty by the extent of their control over local resources—including information—marketed for domestic and world consumption. TBDF, to the degree it is unfettered by local regulation, diminishes national sovereignty according to this standard.[3]

Closely related to national sovereignty is the concept of vulnerability to foreign influence, decision-making or, indeed, interference in national affairs. Within the particular context of computer/communications reliant societies, TBDF refers to the storage of data outside the country, ready access to critical information from a foreign location, and the potential for flooding a country with inaccurate or misleading information. In response to the discovery that personal data on Swedish citizens was stored or processed in some two thousand systems outside the country, Sweden passed its Data Act in 1973, which required approval for the export or transmission of personal data files outside the country.[4]

Vulnerability takes on an added dimension for developing countries since TBDFs have served to reinforce existing economic disparities between developed and developing countries in general and the unequal bargaining position between host governments and MNEs in particular.[5] The concerns of developing countries regarding undue reliance on foreign computer/communications systems are best understood within the context of the goal of self-reliant development. The prospects for achieving that goal have been dimmed by the lack of sovereign control over information systems and technologies. Developing countries view their dependence on foreign firms for telecommunications and computer resources as evidence that "an important basis for national decision-making is now extra-territorially located with some private firms."[6]

Vulnerability has also been associated with the possible erosion of local cultures through the use of foreign media programming and data banks. Many countries (particularly the developing and Eastern block states) resent the intrusion of foreign values and ideas, considering them to be elements of cultural imperialism. Even some industrialized states have become apprehensive about losing their national identities.

The last, but certainly not least in order of significance, factor underlying the trend toward government regulations on TBDF can be given the broad label of economic nationalism. As noted earlier, an ever-growing number of governments have recognized both the importance of information technologies and the need to develop a corresponding national policy. The combined perceptions that telecommunications and information resources are increasingly essential to national survival and that the U.S. plays an almost larger-than-life role in the global computer/communications systems market, have resulted in rather nationalistic (some would say protectionist) policies vis-à-vis TBDF.

The clearest articulation of such a policy orientation may be found in a report to the French government, which made the following points:

1. The "informatization" of society will have serious consequences for France, socially, economically, and culturally.

2. Foreign firms (particularly IBM) must not be allowed to be instruments of foreign (primarily U.S.) dominance.

3. Post, Telephone and Telegraph Administration (PTTs) should be restructured so that the telecommunications portion can be redirected to work more closely with other high technology agencies.

4. Mastery of component technology is as important as nuclear mastery for national independence.[7]

The message delivered to the French government was very direct: a strong information policy will be the critical element in controlling the future direction of the country, resisting foreign domination of French markets and ensuring greater autonomy.

At the same time, governments have begun to express concern regarding the social implications of further advances in information-related technologies. Much of this concern has been directed toward the protection of personal privacy and individual rights. As data collection, processing, and storage have grown to become an integral part of daily life, so has uneasiness regarding the accuracy and use of such data, particularly in terms of potential abuses of individual privacy.

Transborder data flows have both heightened government concern in these areas and stimulated government response in the form of data protection legislation.

In what has become known as a data protection movement, many countries have either enacted or are considering legislation to restrict flows of information across their borders in support of certain national interests. Due to the dominant role the United States has played in the use and supply of information resources, it is not surprising that American firms have become caught in the cross-fire of this data protection movement.

Industry has responded, but many firms do not realize the impact that this legislation may have on their operation. It is not only the fact that vast quantities of data, the content of which may be highly sensitive, are regularly transmitted throughout the world in total disregard of national boundaries, but that the principal agents of data transmission are non-national, usually American, entities. Although privacy issues appear to be the most compelling reasons for the imposition of controls on transborder flows, there are a number of other less visible factors contributing to the regulatory trend.

The spectrum of purposes served by data protection legislation is broad and extends from the protection of privacy to "protection of national sovereignty, balance of payments, employment, technology, social and cultural values, telecommunications policy and national defense."[8]

National regulatory challenges to the free flow of information have significant consequences for the operations of multinationals, primarily in terms of increasing costs and decreasing flexibility. Since transborder data flows have an impact on most corporate functions—production planning, inventory control, standardization and coordinations, financial planning and control, R&D, customer and purchasing questions, legal reporting, and employee relations—it follows that restrictions on transborder data flows have both actual and potential implications for the planning and implementation of corporate strategies. The results of a series of interviews by the authors with corporate executives certainly bear this out.

DATA PROTECTION LEGISLATION

Throughout the 1970s, legislative initiatives geared toward the "protection of the rights, freedoms and essential interests of persons vis-à-vis the processing of personal information relating to them"[9] were proposed, debated, and, in some cases, passed by the parliaments of a number of countries. Sweden was the first to enact a national privacy protection law (1973) but has since been joined by the United States, the Federal Republic of Germany, France, Austria, Norway, Denmark, Canada, Luxembourg, and New Zealand. Recognizing the need for national action, the countries of Australia, Belgium, Finland, Iceland, Italy, the Netherlands, Portugal, Spain, Switzerland, and the United Kingdom, have either prepared draft legislation or governmental reports on the subject.

The objective of national data protection laws is the protection of personal privacy, which, in the context of automated data record-keeping systems, refers to the rights of individuals in relation to the collection, processing, storage, dissemination, and use in decision making of personal data. Hence much of the language in these laws is directed toward record-keeping practices. One noted observer has characterized the record-keeping requirements found in these laws as extensions of the essential principles of privacy:

1. The Social Justification Principle—the collection of personal data should be for a general purpose and specific uses which are socially acceptable.

2. The Collection Limitation Principle—the collection of personal data should be restricted to the minimum necessary and such data should not be obtained by unlawful or unfair means but only with the knowledge or consent of the data subject or with the authority of law.

3. The Information Quality Principle—personal data should, for the purposes for which they are to be used, be accurate, complete and kept up to date.

4. The Purpose Specification Principle—the purpose for which personal data are collected should be specified to the data subject not later than at the time of data collection and the subsequent use limited to those purposes or such others as are not incompatible with those purposes and as are specified on each occasion of change of purpose.

5. The Disclosure Limitation Principle—personal data should not be disclosed or made available except with the consent of the data subject, the authority of law, or pursuant to a publicly known usage of common and routine practice.

6. The Security Safeguards Principle—personal data should be protected by security safeguards which are reasonable and appropriate to prevent the loss of, destruction of, unauthorized access to use, modify, or disclose the data.

7. The Openness Principle—there should be a general policy of openness about developments, practices, and policies with respect to personal data. In

particular, means should be readily available to establish the existence, purposes, policies, and practices associated with personal data as well as the identity and residence of the data controller.

8. The Time Limitation Principle—personal data in a form that permits identification of the data subject should, once their purposes have expired, be destroyed, archived or de-identified.

9. The Accountability Principle—there should be, in respect of any personal data record, an identifiable data controller who should be accountable in law for giving effect to these principles.

10. The Individual Participation Principle—an individual should have the right (a) to obtain from a data controller, or otherwise, confirmation of whether or not the data controller has data relating to him; (b) to have communicated to him, data relating to him (i) within a reasonable time, (ii) at a charge, if any, that is not excessive, (iii) in a reasonable manner, and (iv) in a form that is readily intelligible to him; (c) to challenge data relating to him and (i) during such challenge to have the record annotated concerning the challenge, and (ii) if the challenge is successful, to have the data corrected, completed, amended, annotated or, if appropriate, erased; and (d) to be notified of the reasons if a request made under paragraphs (a) and (b) is denied and to be able to challenge such denial.[10]

The above principles, which may either be totally or partially (i.e., some combination thereof) represented in each national data protection law, are indicative of the common philosophy shared by most privacy legislation. The widespread recognition and acceptance of what may be called the "basic rules" of privacy protection has not, however, resulted in an identifiable body of uniform protection standards. Rather, there are some important differences between national privacy protection laws in terms of the dimensions of those laws, which include (1) the scope of coverage (e.g., public sector, private sector, or some combination of both); (2) data subjects covered (physical persons, associations of physical persons, legal persons); (3) types of record-keeping systems covered (automated, manual); (4) privacy rights granted to individuals; (5) privacy protection requirements placed on record-keeper; (6) mechanisms and authorities for enforcement (licensing, self-regulation, national commissions); and (7) types of penalties.[11]

The European laws reflect an omnibus approach to regulation, covering both public and private sector recordkeeping. The privacy laws in the United States and Canada, on the other hand, are directed primarily toward the public sector and only selected parts of the private sector are regulated. Some laws include both manual and automated data files (such as Sweden, Germany, Canada, the U.S.) while others do not, perhaps because the distinction between the two has been blurred due to advances in informational technologies.[12] The inclusion of legal persons as data subjects is found in the laws of at least four European countries (Austria, Denmark, Norway, Luxembourg) but the laws of most other states apply only to physical persons. This question of coverage remains a source of controversy; rather than protecting their rights, many business entities fear an infringement upon the rules of fair competition, since customers, competitors, and suppliers would have access to corporate files and information.

Significant differences between national privacy laws are also found in the methods of controlling (1) internal record-keeping and (2) external data transmissions. The laws of most European states and Canada provide for an independent, data protection enforcement body charged with certain responsibilities, which may include "inspections, consultations with data users, advising government and data users about data protection, the conciliation of data users and data subjects, and the issuance of operations licenses.[13] These data authorities, inspectorates, or commissions also have the power to bring legal actions and impose administrative sanctions against data record-keepers found in violation of the law.

In contrast, the United States relies on the courts and sectoral oversight agencies in a more corrective approach to regulation, whereby failures to comply with the law are subject to prosecution. Nor does the United States apply controls on the transmission of information abroad, beyond those imposed for national security reasons.[14] Under the laws of a number of other countries, however, certain data may either be barred from export, or require prior approval for transmission outside the country.

Although somewhat limited in scope, the foregoing treatment of some data protection laws suggests that apart from similarities in the underlying objectives, these laws represent discreet national interests, legal systems, regulatory mechanisms, and cultural settings. As such, they do not offer a body of mutually acceptable data protection standards that all states could subscribe to and that all affected record-keepers could recognize and comply with on an international basis. It is precisely because national standards are uneven that certain international organizations have undertaken efforts to harmonize differing data protection standards as they pertain to TBDF. Thus, prior to a discussion of the actual and potential ramifications involving transnational data regulation, these international efforts will be examined to shed more light on the scope of the regulatory trend.

MULTILATERAL ACTIONS

The stimulus for multilateral action with regard to international regulation of transborder data flows of personal information can be traced to a growing recognition of two inherent problem areas: different levels of data protection and conflicts or uncertainty about applicable law. Central to both is the sensitive issue of high versus lesser standards of data protection.

Attempts to address these issues have been most notably made by the Organization for Economic Cooperation and Development (OECD) and the Council of Europe. The central goal in the efforts of each organization has been the reconciliation of the competing values of free information flows and privacy protection.

Realizing that the imposition by many countries of restrictions on the outward flow of data to countries without equivalent data protection (often called "data havens") was creating future impediments to transborder data flows, the OECD and the Council of Europe felt that positive action was needed to encourage the adoption of common national procedures for the protection of personal data and the exchange of relevant data.

In 1980, after considerable study[15] and often intense intra-organization negotiations, the OECD adopted a recommendation and a set of "Guidelines Governing the Protection of Privacy and Transborder Flows of Personal Data" and the Committee of Ministers of the Council of Europe adopted the "Convention for the Protection of Individuals with Regard to Automatic Processing of Personal Data."[16]

The OECD Guidelines are designed to provide both governments and companies with basic principles for handling personal information. Simultaneously, governments are called on to agree to accept internationally established minimum standards of privacy protection and to avoid creating obstacles to personal data flows that would exceed these common standards. The Council of Europe Convention is similar in many respects, particularly with regard to the balance to be struck between legitimate privacy protection interests and excessive barriers to transborder personal data flows. Differences between the two international instruments revolve around "(1) their legal nature—the Guidelines are voluntary, the Convention, if ratified, will be legally binding; (2) their scope—the Guidelines apply to the privacy of personal data irrespective of the manner in which they are handled, the Convention focuses on automatic processing; and (3) their follow-up machinery—the Guidelines do not contain institutional provisions and the Convention envisages a Consultative Committee."[17]

Thus, there is currently in place among the industrialized countries a privacy-related TBDF regulatory framework, composed of these two multilateral instruments and individual national laws.

Work in the OECD has now shifted to the economic and legal aspects of non-personal transborder data flows. A questionnaire is currently being circulated to firms by the Business Industry Advisory Committees (BIACs) of the OECD member countries as a means of (1) reviewing the current state of TBDF; (2) determining the views of the private sector on their uses of transborder data flows; and (3) obtaining information on the nature of obstacles to TBDF.

The interests of developing countries are reflected in the activities of three other international organizations. The U.N. Center on Transnational Corporations issued an overview report on Transnational corporations (TBCs) and transborder data flows in 1981 and has embarked on a five-year study program addressing the impact of commercially-generated TBDF on less-developed countries.

UNESCO was instrumental in the Third World call for a New World Information Order, which reflects developing country concerns about global disparities in information resources and capabilities. It is felt that continuous improvements in information technology have created a new element of inequality between North and South.

The Intergovernmental Bureau of Informatics (IBI) was established for the express purpose of providing assistance to developing countries in the application of information technology. This predominantly Third World organization considers computer-based information processing and transmission to be a "key to national survival" and is concerned with the impact of transborder data flows on the international division of labor and technological concentration. IBI has initiated studies on codes of conduct for information technology transfer and on the development of information law.

Either independently or under the auspices of a variety of international organizations, developing countries are demanding greater access to existing telecommunications networks, particularly satellite systems, as well as assistance in the development of local telecommunications, broadcasting and data processing systems.

DATA PROTECTION REGULATIONS AND MNCs

The immediate implications for multinational firms of the expanding

TBDF regulatory framework are clear: those firms transmitting name-linked data, as opposed to anonymous data, are confronted and must comply with a variety of national data protection laws and standards. This patchwork of laws serves as a barrier to the free flow of information through multinational computer systems, which may increase the costs and decrease the efficiency of multinational operations. As one representative of an American multinational firm has observed:

With the advent of more and more complex and sometimes conflicting new laws governing data files and the confusion that is developing, we are experiencing delays in system design. Planning is becoming increasingly difficult and administrative costs are starting to increase. . . . The increased difficulty of managing the company, increased delays in reporting vital operating data, reduced market information, less effective means of evaluating personnel for promotion—all will be far more disruptive to productivity and effective operation than the added out-of-pocket costs.[18]

Multinational computer/communications systems must often be redesigned or restructured in accordance with the new nationally-imposed procedures for handling information. Requirements may include all or some combination of the following: (1) the registration of personal data files with a central regulatory authority; (2) limits on data collection to clearly defined purposes; (3) access to data files by subjects and/or governmental authorities for purposes of inspection; and (4) sufficient security precautions to prevent unauthorized access to data bases.

While some firms may already have a mechanism in place, others may need to establish "an effective arm of organization to set and implement data security and privacy policy."[19]

Multinational firms generally accept the central objective of data privacy protection legislation, which many feel is simply an extension of existing corporate policy. Their major concern involves the effects of overlapping (often conflicting) national laws, as well as the wider impact the new regulations will have on corporate information flows. Because multinationals operate on a global basis, they are highly visible and, as a consequence, feel more vulnerable for the following reasons:

1. MNCs operating in *any* country with data protection laws may be obliged to extend compliance to *every* country where they have operations, resulting in communications with a much higher degree of transparancey than would otherwise be normal or acceptable for the firm.

2. Licensing or registration requirements legitimize government supervision and scrutiny of corporate information systems. Further, registering the patterns and destinations of flows within their organizations to comply with privacy rules may expose much wider corporate policies and practices.

3. The right of access by data authorities to corporate data processing operations for security safeguards checks may lead to disclosure of non-personal data, since name-linked data may not be segregated from other types of data; even the disclosure of personal information may involve a great deal of related collateral information of a proprietary nature.[20]

While some industries, such as banking and insurance, would appear to be more heavily impacted by laws regulating the flow of personal information by virture of their organization, geographic dispersion, products and services offered, and the volume and types of data they process, the fact that TBDF can so easily be disrupted poses potential problems for the producers of data processing and telecommunications goods and services and manufacturing firms as well.

These problems can be magnified in the event countries impose trade restrictions on the flow of information under the guise of, or in addition to, their data privacy laws. A number of the subordinate issues of TBDF are actually hidden trade issues which have little to do with the protection of privacy. Some examples include (1) requirements for local data processing; (2) local equipment specifications and interface standards; (3) increased tariffs on private leased lines and a denial of service of those lines in favor of PTT networks; (4) refusal to allow connection between internal (domestic) networks and international carriers; (5) denial of market access to foreign firms for reasons of inadequate security procedures; and (6) denial of access by foreign vendors to regional computer/communications networks (such as EURONET).[21]

Discussions with a number of corporate executives indicate that such trade-related restrictions are indeed being imposed, with effects ranging from a loss of business at the extreme to higher costs in doing business at a minimum.

One U.S. information services firm indicated that Canadian banking laws were responsible for the loss of at least two clients, due to requirements for the local storage of data. As the company maintains storage facilities in the U.S., its only option was to place equipment on the bank site, thus increasing up-front costs. The company has not yet decided whether data-storage facilities will be placed in Canada. The same firm has been threatened with limits on ports of entry in Mexico and thus anticipates difficulty in expanding its market share.

A major American bank has encountered problems in Germany and Brazil. A new German law requiring that private international leased lines coming into the country terminate in a single computer system and that incoming data be processed locally prior to distribution within Germany literally forced the bank's subsidiary to switch from its private line to the local PTT network.

In Brazil, the bank has had to "donate" American check-processing equipment to its local branch; the government denied approval to purchase the equipment for balance-of-payments reasons. The result for the bank was a 31 percent increase in costs. In another instance, the bank was denied approval for the purchase of a U.S.-made computer which would have resulted in considerable savings. Instead, they were forced to purchase a Brazilian computer with capacity beyond the bank's needs, resulting in a reduction of expected savings by several hundred thousand dollars.

Two American computer companies, Control Data and Tymshare, have encountered regulatory difficulties in Japan. In both cases, restriction imposed by the Japanese international record carrier, KDD, on lines leased from KDD had the effect of delaying operations for five years and limiting the types of services each U.S. firm could offer to Japanese customers. Both companies have expressed concern that the new KDD usage sensitive network, known as VENUS, will preclude the use of private fixed-cost leased lines. Tymshare expects the new service to cost ten times more than their existing network.

Eaton Corporation has voiced concern that the forced use of national PTT services may have the effect of limiting access by international firms to adequate information networks, thus giving local firms an unfair competitive advantage. Further, the costs of using PTT services are much higher than those for private lines. U.S. carriers charge approximately $4,100 per month for their portion of private lines between the U.S. and Europe while the Europeans charge nearly $5,800 and the Japanese charge approximately $11,000. A shift from flat-rate charges to usage-based charges would also escalate communications costs, as would the imposition of tariffs on data transmissions. Easton has estimated that the company's communications costs in the United Kingdom will increase by 85 percent due to tariffs.

Those companies with decentralized international operations have had an easier time of complying with data privacy and local storage and processing requirements, but they are by no means immune to other TBDF-related problems. A major United States MNC, for example, has been required to purchase locally-manufactured computers at two- to three-hundred percent higher cost.

Other areas of corporate concern revolve around the interoperability of equipment, security in the transmission of confidential data, the reliability of the public PTT services as opposed to private services, and the question of liability in the transmission of data via the PTT networks. This latter issue is particularly important for the banking industry. One banker made the point that if PTTs insist that U.S. firms use their facilities, they should be willing to assume more of the financial liability for transfer problems, such as delays or missed payments.

The interviews indicated that while some companies have begun to include data-flow considerations in their marketing and strategic planning, the vast majority of multinationals have yet to do so. According to two executives, TBDF problems are poorly understood or, indeed, barely recognized because many firms have paid inadequate attention to their internal computer/telecommunications needs. A better understanding of the nature, frequency, and volume of information flows in support of business activity is a prerequisite to understanding the impact of TBDF restrictions on international operations.

As all international operations are dependent on the timely and efficient transfer of information, it is imperative that business devote top-level management attention to the variety of foreign measures threatening the free flow of information. In addition to monitoring the specific actions of governments on a country-by-country basis, companies must assess their information requirements within the context of a changing, and more restrictive, global environment. Finally, companies must factor this assessment into their strategic planning to be better able to deal with future problems or prospects.

CONCLUDING REMARKS

Prognostications as to the future nature of transborder data flows are premature. The ink with which the various national data protection laws were, and are being, written is only just drying and the principal international instruments on the subject are in their infancy. Furthermore, corporate experience with both the obvious and hidden restrictions on the transnational transmission of data has been uneven and rather limited to date.

It is possible, however, to draw at least one conclusion from the foregoing discussion. The debate over the free flow of information is a fact of contemporary international life. Most countries have given the question of data flows high priority on their national agendas and a growing number of states have formulated national information policies to enable them to cope more effectively with the challenges presented by steadily advancing information technologies.[22] Interdependence, economic nationalism, and cultural sovereignty have combined to steadily elevate the issues surrounding transborder data flows to a level of considerable international significance.

NOTES

1. Statement by Louis Joinet, French Magistrate of Justice, before the Organization for Economic Cooperation and Development Symposium on Trans-

border Data Flows and the Protection of Privacy in Vienna, Austria, in September 1977. Cited by John Eger, "Emerging Restrictions," *Law and Policy in International Business*.

2. Clyne Report to the Canadian Government in 1979; quoted in William Fishman, "Introduction to Transborder Data Flow," *Stanford Journal of International Law*, pp. 9-10.

3. Robert E. Jacobson, "The Hidden Issues: What Kind of Order," *Journal of Communications*, Summer 1979, p. 152.

4. John M. Eger, "Emerging Restrictions," *Law and Policy in International Business*, p. 1067.

5. For a discussion of the impact of the uneven access to information on the bargaining capacity of developing countries, see Rita Cruise O'Brien and G. K. Helleiner, "The Political Economy of Information in Changing World Order," *International Organization*, Autumn 1980, p. 445.

6. United Nations, *Transnational Corporations*, p. 61.

7. Cees J. Hamelink, "Informatics: Third World Call for New Order," *Journal of Communications*, Summer 1979, p. 147.

8. Alden Heitz, "The Dangers of Regulation," *Journal of Communication*, Summer 1979, p. 129.

9. Frits Hondius, "Data Law in Europe," *Stamford Journal of International Law*, Summer 1980, p. 89.

10. Justice Michael Kirby, "Transborder Data Flows and the 'Basic Rules' of Data Privacy," *Stanford Journal of International Law*, Summer 1980, pp. 46-64.

11. Rein Turn, "Privacy Protection and Security in Transnational Data Processing Systems," *Stanford Journal of International Law*, Summer 1980, p. 101.

12. See R. Stadlen, "Survey of National Data Protection Legislation," *Computer Networks*, 3, 1979, p. 174.

13. Frits Hondius, "Data Law in Europe," *Stanford Journal of International Law*, Summer 1980, p. 101.

14. An example would be export controls on information pertaining to national defense or information on high or critical technologies going to the Soviet Union or other Eastern bloc countries.

15. The OECD initiated computer-utilization studies as early as 1969, and a treaty on data protection was first proposed by the Council of Europe in 1972.

16. See, respectively, Organization for Economic Cooperation and Development, *Recommendation Concerning Guidelines Governing the Protection of Privacy and Transborder Flows of Personal Data*, C (80) 58 (final) of 1 October 1980 and *Annex* (Guidelines); Council of Europe, "Convention for the Protection of Individuals with Regard to Automatic Processing of Personal Data," *European Treaty Series*, no. 108.

17. United Nations, Center on Transnational Corporations, *Transnational Corporations and Transborder Data Flows: A Technical Paper* (Geneva: UN, 1981), p. 8.

18. See prepared statement by Earl Kendle, Vice President for Information Systems, Eaton Corporation, in *International Data Flow*, Hearings before the Subcommittee on Government Information and Individual Rights, March 10, 1980, pp. 139-42.

19. Peter L. P. Rooms and John Dexter, "Problems of Data Protection Law for Private Multinational Communication Networks," *Computer Networks*, 3, 1979, p. 213.

20. See prepared statement by G. Russell Pipe, President of Transnational Data Reporting Service, in *International Data Flow*, Hearings before the Subcommittee on Government Information and Individual Rights, March 27, 1980, p. 399-421.

21. Represents a synthesis of the views presented by private sector representatives in *International Data Flow*, Hearings.

22. According to a UN study, approximately 60 countries have adopted some form of official informatics policies. For a discussion of U.S. policy (or rather, the lack thereof), see John M. Eger, "Emerging Restrictions on Transnational Data Flows: Privacy Protection or Non-Tariff Barriers?", *Law and Policy in International Business*, Vol. 10, 1978, p. 1055; and *International Data Flow*, Hearings.

Chapter Seven:
International Manufacturing and Production

POLICY PERTAINING TO manufacturing and R&D is very important for corporate success both at home and overseas. The domestic policy of a company is determined by a combination of corporate resources available and market conditions. In international operations, the market conditions a company faces may be completely different, as will its manufacturing abilities.

Manufacturing abroad entails not only a detailed analysis of resources available to a company but also the prevalent conditions pertaining to manufacture. Variables that may be relevant are the availability of labor, technology, infra-structure raw materials, transport services, and so forth. Other factors pertinent in decision-making for manufacturing abroad include political risk, degree of unionization of workers and their wages, proximity to world markets, and the like.

R&D strategy in an MNE involves a consideration of national interests both at home and abroad. The degree of centralization of this function may be crucial in determining where the R&D is actually done. Such factors as extent of duplication of research, control of patents, and secrets may all be crucial to competitive advantage.

The transmission of superior skills and efficiency is the major contribution of international firms. Given the substantial scientific lead of a few countries, a flow of skills and the dependency by more countries on those very skills seem inevitable for the forseeable future. However, we are also witnessing a trend by some of the newly-industrialized contries, particularly South Korea, to establish subsidiaries abroad, both as a means of serving a local market as well as enhancing their technological lead in home markets.

20
Shaping a Global Product Organization

William H. Davidson
and Philippe Haspeslagh

Achieving the proper balance between subsidiary independence and headquarters control remains one of the more persistent of MNC organizational problems. In recent years, the need to respond to global rather than simply local competition has prompted MNCs to consider implementing a global-product structure. This structure is only one of a variety of organizational options, however, and companies must weigh the inherent difficulties in the global-product structure against its potential benefits. Still, a global structure can backfire if a company blindly follows organizational fashion.

AFTER YEARS OF pitting their wits against local competitors in single markets, many international companies now find themselves competing *globally* against other U.S., European, and Japanese multinationals. While there are many ways to respond to the pressure of this competition, top management has often turned to an organizational shake-up as the tool most useful for focusing internal decision making.

During the 1970s a large number of multinational companies shifted from a traditional organizational structure with an independent international division to one built around worldwide or global product divisions. (See the Appendix for a definition of the various types of structures used to manage international operations.) Among the 180 companies in the Harvard Multinational Enterprise Project sample, for example, 32 percent had switched to a global product structure by 1980.[1]

In another recent survey of 105 U.S.-based multinationals, more than one-third of the respondents adhered to a global product structure while only 22 percent maintained an international division.[2]

A closer look reveals that the companies adopting global product structures vary widely in size, diversity, and international experience and are drawn from all major industrial sectors. Such transition in structure can have unintended results if organizational change follows fashion and not strategy.

To understand the problems with, and prospects for, global product division organizations, we examined the records of several U.S. multinational corporations in detail, as well as aggregate statistics on the performances of 57 other MNCs. We discovered several common pitfalls that are inherent to the global product structure, and several others that result from faulty implementation. Companies should recognize these difficulties as well as the potential benefits if they are to succeed with organizational change. Our research shows that the global product structure:

- Promotes cost efficiency in existing products for existing markets;
- Helps companies consolidate their positions in mature and stable markets; *but*
- Seems to retard, rather than facilitate, the transfer of resources abroad—especially technology;
- Forces the company into a defensive competitive position;
- Results in lower foreign sales performance; and
- Requires extensive attention to the need for international experience, responsiveness, and advocacy.

THE IMPERIAL CASE

To help illustrate how companies adopt global product structures, let's first take a look at Imperial Corporation, a pseudonym for a large, diversified industrial company based in the United States. Imperial has an extensive record of foreign activities, which were developed and managed through an international division, Imperial Overseas (IO), beginning after World War II.

In the early 1960s, IO expanded aggressively abroad, moving from exports and licensing into foreign manufacturing. By 1970, as a result, IO accounted for more than one-third of corporate profits on less than 25 percent of its sales.

The impressive rise in IO's profitability began at the same time to spell its demise. Its direct manufacturing investments spurred the need for technology transfer from domestic product divisions as well as for corporate funding. Resentful of IO's "star" performance, domestic divisions began slowly to take advantage of IO's increased dependence to gradually assert their control over international operations.

Dotted lines of responsibility between IO and the parent grew more solid on the organizational chart. First, domestic groups became responsible for engineering and technical assistance, but soon international line personnel reported directly to their domestic counterparts. Only international staff functions, like treasury, market research, field personnel administration, and licensing remained at IO headquarters.

In 1971, the parent formally dissolved IO and made each of the four company sectors responsible for their worldwide businesses. The stated aims were to simplify a complex corporate organization, to improve efficiency, and to make the company more responsive to the world market. Though it was the company's intention to retain them, many senior IO managers left or retired during this period.

Imperial took the final step to a global product structure in 1974; it adopted portfolio planning in response to resource constraints and increased competition. Businesses were grouped into 35 strategic business units (SBUs). Imperial gave the management of each SBU worldwide responsibility over its product lines. Most of the new SBU general manager positions went to former U.S. division managers, who, besides being close to operations, were thought to be good planners.

POTENTIAL BENEFITS FROM GLOBAL PRODUCTS

The Imperial case illustrates not only the benefits companies hope to achieve with a move to global product divisions but also the internal forces behind the transition. We found that companies typically expect three benefits from the transition to global product structure. The first is improved cost efficiency through rationalization of manufacturing facilities and centralization of capacity management. These activities are imperative in industries like television, tires, trucks, and automobiles where cost position is determined by world market share and the extent to which manufacturing is rationalized.

The second benefit is improved communication and resource transfer through closer ties between the domestic product divisions and international operations. And the third and perhaps most important benefit is the development of a global strategic focus in response to the new global competition.

These expected benefits provide the logic behind the widely based move to adopt global product structures. But, as important, may be the political pressures that give rise to the decision. Domestic product managers, eager to claim control over international revenues, earnings, and growth opportunities in their lines of business, typically are strong advocates of transition. Domestic managers often think that the success of an international division is gained on the back of their own technological, marketing, and managerial efforts.

The widespread use of analytical planning tools such as experience curve analysis and portfolio planning often leads corporate staff to support the introduction of a global product structure.[3] These planning tools typically start with an analysis of the value-added structure of the business. In all but a few consumer products, the value added by product costs (such as manufacturing and R&D) exceeds that added by market costs (such as distribution and marketing). As a result, planning invariably emphasizes product-based units. Once planning units have been defined along global product lines, we found that there are, in practice, strong pressures to align the organizational structure in the same way. Only 7 percent of the companies that introduce portfolio planning define planning and operating units differently.

Whatever the combination of forces that cause a company to replace its international division with a global product structure, we found that the expected benefits are seldom realized. Companies achieve improved cost efficiency but at the expense of increased risk and rigidity. Resource transfer to foreign affiliates actually diminished for the companies we examined. In most cases, the company's strategy began to emphasize a defense of its domestic position. These shortcomings can be attributed partly to faulty implementation, but they also appear to be inherent in the global product structure itself.

COST-EFFICIENCY: SHORT-LIVED & DEARLY PAID

Companies universally cite improved cost efficiency as the global product structure's single most important advantage. Centralization of capacity and sourcing management creates a significant impetus for cost reduction. At Imperial, for instance, the capital spending targeted at cost reduction increased dramatically as the new global business unit managers—clearly more concerned by their competitive cost position —established offshore facilities in Puerto Rico, Ireland, and the Far East.

Yet, this improved cost efficiency has a price. To the extent that it results in single-plant sourcing, it makes a company more vulnerable to such risks as transportation problems and labor disputes.

In moving from an international division organization to a global product structure, for example, International Harvester created a new group that centralized sourcing for components such as axles, engines, and transmissions in single plants. When the UAW struck the company in 1979 over the issue of voluntary overtime, the company was pushed to the brink of bankruptcy.

The strategy also runs afoul of the import restrictions that LDC governments impose to solve balance-of-payments problems. Competitors who are willing to produce within foreign markets can preempt companies that serve markets by export from centralized plants. Centralized manufacturing may be an inferior approach in a world of rising protectionism.

Volatile foreign exchange rates also disrupt centralized sourcing systems. Sales and profits can be affected dramatically by changes in exchange rates, causing pricing, planning, and financial problems for local managers. S. C. Johnson & Son, Inc., which used a central sourcing strategy in Europe, lost ground to competitors who sourced locally when exchange rates began to float in the 1970s.

Most impotant, the benefits, when they do appear, may not last long. Rationalization provides an optimal production configuration only in a static market. Shifts make existing production facilities outmoded. Philip Caldwell, CEO, of Ford Motor Co., admitted that the company's shift to single-model assembly lines for world markets seriously reduced its ability to adapt to fluctuations in demand.[4] Changes in the geographic composition of the demand can also reduce benefits.

TRANSFER OF RESOURCES

Some global companies declare that the move to a global product structure removes the international division as a "barrier" to the transfer of technology to foreign markets. They contend that global business units, by avoiding the "proprietary" reflexes of domestic divisions, facilitate direct communication between the source and foreign users of the new technology.

Our study of 57 large U.S. multinationals found that technologies (as embodied in new products) in fact spread abroad more slowly in companies organized along worldwide product lines.[5] We examined this issue by first identifying all commercially and technically significant new products introduced by these 57 companies between 1945 and 1978.

Exhibit I classifies the sample of 954 new products by their speed and level of foreign introduction for companies in different structures.

We found that global product companies transferred fewer new products abroad than companies in the matrix structure. That result is not unexpected, although the magnitude of the differential in speed and level of activity is striking. Perhaps more important, companies with an international division also transfer more new products abroad at a faster pace. Products introduced by companies organized along global product lines spread abroad more slowly and infrequently than the products of companies in other structures.

Critics can argue that the findings are inconclusive because they may reflect the unsettled aftermath of any organizational transition, in which ideas flow slowly. Or that companies in global product structures operate in industries where rates of technology transfer are generally low. Neither argument is supported by our in-depth analysis. More importantly, when viewed individually, companies moving to the global product structure show a significant decline in the number of product transfers made after the transition (see Exhibit 2). This reduction occurs despite a pervasive tendency for transfer activity to accelerate over time.

Exhibit 1: International Transfer Patterns for New Products by Structure of Parent at U.S. Introduction

Parent's Organizational structure	Number of new products	Percent first appearing abroad		
		Within one year	Within five years	By Jan. 1978
Domestic product divisions*	128	13.8%	40.1%	69.5%
Domestic functional divisions*	84	19.1%	41.9%	73.8%
Domestic product divisions with international division	403	19.6%	45.5%	81.6%
Domestic functional divisions with international division	93	20.7%	44.4%	72.1%
Global product divisions	140	8.1%	30.2%	64.3%
Global matrix	106	23.6%	57.5%	85.9%
Total	954	17.7%	43.5%	76.3%

*No formal international structure. Foreign units typically report directly to the chief executive officer as autonomous units.

Exhibit 2: International Transfer Patterns for New Products:
For 12 Companies Before and After Transition to the Global Product Structure

Organizational structure of parent at time of transfer	Number of new products	Percent first appearing abroad		
		Within one year	Within five years	By Jan. 1978
Global product structure	140	8.1%	30.2%	64.3%
Previous structure	101	13.9%	39.7%	84.4%
Total	241	10.5%	34.1%	72.0%

Could the reduction in transfer activity for companies in the global product structure be a reflection of success in rationalizing overseas production facilities? On the surface, that interpretation is consistent with the data. However, a more detailed examination of transfer patterns refutes this view.

It is widely believed that companies pursuing a strategy of global rationalization will be extremely averse to permitting outside ownership in their manufacturing affiliates.[6] The benefits of outside ownership are negligible in such cases, because markets are internal and host governments welcome such export-oriented facilities with generous financial incentives. In addition, the costs of outside ownership are relatively high. The risk of potential conflicts with outside owners over operating policies encourages the company to maintain complete ownership and control of manufacturing affiliates.

If companies organized by global product lines are pursuing rationalization of production, little or no outside ownership of manufacturing affiliates can be expected. In fact, the group of companies organized along global product lines exhibits the highest level of outside ownership in the sample. Particularly striking is the rate of licensing by such companies. Exhibit 3 shows that these companies use licensing in slightly more than 30 percent of all transfers, compared to a rate of only 5 percent for companies in the matrix structure. Why such a dramatic difference? The answer focuses on several inherent shortcomings of the global product structure.

In most companies, the change to a global product organization has significantly reduced the scope of international commitment. Attention shifts from reliance on investment to emphasis on licensing. Global product companies view licensing more favorably than other forms of investment. The reason is that the new organizational structure affects

Exhibit 3: Licensing Rates for Companies with Different Organizational Structures

Organizational structure of Parent at time of transfer	Percent of transfers to independent licensees
Domestic divisions·only	30 %
International division	24.8%
Global product structure	30.3%
Global matrix	5.1%
Average for total sample	25.9%

the value of foreign projects both through its impact on the economics of these projects, and through a change in the decision-making environment of the managers who must make international commitments.

Fragmentation of international experience

The profitability of any foreign investment project is directly related to the company's ability to apply shared resources and bring prior experience to it. Resource sharing, in the form of joint manufacturing, materials management, marketing, or administrative overhead, for example, can significantly reduce project costs. Experience in the form of information and expertise also reduces costs and risks and results in faster and greater levels of foreign activity.

The transition to global product divisions systematically erodes the company's ability to realize these benefits. The global product structure fragments the international resources of the company previously embodied in the central management of the international division and in the foreign affiliates. The result is an increase in the cost and uncertainty of foreign projects. As each division pays for infrastructure and peripheral investments in its own projects, the parent duplicates overhead at the host-country level.

A manager at Imperial commented after the change to product division responsibilities for foreign operations: "Our divisions duplicated efforts in each country. At a certain point, we had several product groups in Brazil running around, reinventing the wheel with respect to government contracts and know-how, when another division was already well established."

The global product system also erodes the value of central headquarters support systems as each division or group develops its own. At Imperial, several product divisions even began to set up their own internal international units! A manager in one of the companies we studied described the extent of this fragmentation:

"The worldwide responsibility of our SBUs led, with few exceptions, to an unbelievably bad administrative situation and yet an unawareness of the consequences. I could tell a story about 17 decision makers from different product divisions in our country who had to agree on a common financial policy. The idea was that we could realize the benefits of a technological base in the business units, but the splintering of presences in national markets led to administrative nightmares."

Discriminating decision environment

Compounding the impact of fragmented administrative structures on the economics of foreign project evaluation is the change in the managerial setting in which foreign projects are evaluated. Foreign investment projects, like all others, are shaped largely by the perceptions and career stakes of the managers who define, propose, and support them. The dissolution of the international division leads to a decline in manager support for foreign projects. One reason is that experienced international personnel are lost once the company decides to adopt a global product structure. Even though Imperial's original plan for organizational change did not include the collapse of the international division, it became inevitable as managers engaged in trench warfare over authority and preferred to leave rather than accept diminished status in the new structure.

In practice, the choice of managers for the new global business units tends to aggravate this problem. In most U.S. MNCs, worldwide business unit managers are usually former domestic division managers whose domestic business represented between 60 percent to 80 percent of worldwide product sales. Few have had foreign assignments at any point in their careers. The decision to assign these domestic-minded managers to head international operations is usually a mistake. With this single decision, companies have managed to negate the years they've spent in developing foreign operating expertise.

Reducing the power of experienced international management may cause the company to revert to risk-averse patterns common in the early stages of international expansion. The new managers are often not well-versed in foreign matters, but these individuals now hold the decision-making reins. When these managers compare a set of investments that could be made domestically (and which are less uncertain in terms of cost reduction and market penetration) with foreign investment projects (which involve greater uncertainty), they will often be biased against the latter projects.

Of course, the outlook and actions of individual business managers vary widely. At Imperial a few business unit managers felt comfortable enough doing business abroad—on the basis of experience—to expand their reach overseas. Others did so because opportunities at home were limited. Most of these farsighted executives, however, were less interested in developing foreign markets than they were in reducing domestic costs to counter inroads by foreign competitors. Caution won out; after one Imperial division had weakened a strong domestic position by spending too much time and corporate resources on an international venture, its example was seen as typical of a division "sacrificing itself on the altar of the worldwide charter."

GLOBAL STRATEGIC ORIENTATION

Perhaps the argument in favor of a global product structure that holds the greatest attraction for most companies is its promise of the introduction of a worldwide perspective on competition. This perspective supposedly improves competitive monitoring and response, ultimately making the company a more effective and aggressive international contender.

Reality, however, undermines these expectations. A heightened sense of competition has to start in the field, with the awareness of local administrators. While "old style" country managers may have been unable to fashion the integrated response that is supposedly second nature to a worldwide business manager, they were quick to perceive changes in the competitive environment. Even in industries where the economics of competition are completely global, there is always a need for local adaptability. One rival of Caterpillar commented:

"The company is a formidable competitor. Yet it is so centralized, the worldwide price of any piece is set in Peoria, Illinois. In certain markets, like the Middle East, the policy allows us to be much more responsive to local opportunities and conditions."

In addition to problems of local responsiveness, the risk is great that global business unit managers will in fact become increasingly risk-averse and defensive in their strategic outlook on foreign operations. Where the strategic intent is to grow and be more aggressive internationally, the worldwide product structure tends to be counterproductive for economic and behavioral reasons. Many MNCs lose foreign market share and see the rate of international growth slowed after their transition. For example, Corning's foreign sales grew from $35 million in 1965 to $336 million in 1974. After partially dismantling the international division in 1975, foreign sales actually declined over the next three years.

The results for Imperial have been equally disappointing. The export growth rate for its major product lines was less than 6 percent from 1971 to 1978, versus growth rates for total OECD exports in those product lines of 13 percent. From 1976 to 1978, Imperial's exports actually declined at a rate of 10 percent, while U.S. competitors' exports grew 5.5 percent.

Our larger sample confirms this deterioration of foreign sales after introduction of the global product structure (see Exhibit 4). While there are no fundamental differences (besides organizational structure) between the companies organized by global product divisions and those organized with an international division, there is a marked difference in foreign sales performance. Of the 85 companies in the Harvard Multinational Enterprise Project sample that remained in the same structure from 1970 to 1980, companies with an international division increased foreign sales by an average of 435 percent; those with a global matrix structure saw international revenues rise by 371 percent. But the foreign sales of companies organized by global product divisions grew only 259 percent——even though they started from a lower base of sales.

Exhibit 4: International Sales Growth for Companies
With Different Organizational Structures
(in millions)

Structure 1970-1980	Number of Companies	Average percent increase in foreign sales 1970-1979	Average foreign sales 1970 (millions)
International division	34	435%	$424.35
Global product divisions	27	259%	$354.7
Global matrix	24	371%	$600.17

SOURCE: Annual reports.

WHAT TO DO?

If a company wants to expand internationally, it should think twice before taking on a global product structure. While the format results in improved cost efficiency for existing products sold in established markets, it can undermine the transfer of resources abroad and fosters a defensive global outlook.

Companies considering the adoption of a global product structure should weigh two other organizational options. For example, companies that base their strategies on a worldwide exploitation of technology can benefit from a matrix organization that facilitates the transfer of resources to foreign operations. Effective transfer requires a "push" from domestic managers and a "pull" from host-country management—two forces the matrix structure uniquely combines. Another sound option for most companies is to retain and rejuvenate an existing international division. Our statistical findings support recent research that shows international divisions are capable of handling complex global strategies.[7]

We do not want to suggest that companies can ignore the underlying problems leading them to the global product structure. Needs for cost efficiency and a more unified worldwide strategic focus are very real. Companies with these critical needs may find that the global product structure is the best organizational solution if it is modified to address the problems we have identified. In fact it appears to be most appropriate for harvesting a mature or declining business. American Standard's global business unit planning facilitated its systematic withdrawal from the European plumbing and heating business. Union Carbide's divestment of its European chemical operations was conducted in an orderly manner partially because of a product-based planning system and organization.

The choice of structure is largely a function of the nature of the company's businesses, its strategic intentions, and its administrative capabilities. For companies considering the transition to a global product structure, several critical issues should be addressed.

ASK THE RIGHT QUESTIONS

To determine the effectiveness of the global product organization, managers should not simply ask whether their businesses are global. Instead they should ask whether their strategy is offensive or defensive. More importantly, managers need to examine how well the company's administration can implement the structure effectively. As a guide to this last assessment we have formulated the following five questions:

1. Are foreign operations equally important to each individual business? (Managers who do not depend on foreign operations for a large part of net income are not likely to generate global strategies.)

2. Can the company staff the worldwide business unit manager positions with people who are cosmopolitan in outlook and administrative background? (Previous international exposure among business unit managers is a key ingredient in generating global strategies. Unfortunately, the pool of such people in most U.S. companies is very small.)

3. Does the corporate climate permit risk taking? (Corporate attitudes toward risk have a big influence on the way in which business unit managers treat their more uncertain foreign ventures.)

4. Can the company reduce the loss of foreign experience resulting from the transition to a global product structure? (Many companies have

lost experienced international executives and left each worldwide business to learn from its own mistakes.)

5. Is there someone in the company who will continue to strongly promote foreign expansion? (Typically, such advocacy disappears with the international division.)

If, after answering these questions, top management decides to move to a global product structure, it should take any one of several possible steps to reduce the loss of advocacy, experience, and resource sharing once the international division disbands. These steps might include ensuring that career paths remain open for former international executives. In addition, the company must establish mechanisms for resource sharing, and exchange of information. At the host country level, well-established product divisions in each country can become innkeepers for other divisions. At headquarters, planning staff can play a key role in ensuring coordination and resource sharing.

Above all, the core of the international division can be kept intact to assist the efforts of worldwide product managers. Retaining the unit helps the company hold on to key personnel. The international division provides a focal point for communication and accumulation of information and can play a critical role in introducing "infant" divisions to international operations. Most importantly, the unit will ensure that corporate decision making doesn't neglect the area dimension of the organization. One of the most important objectives in designing a global organization is to achieve the proper balance between product, area, and functional dimensions in the company's administrative processes. Giving area managers responsibility for problems such as host government and labor relations, for example, can improve corporate performance.

Any organization constantly evolves, and a good one will keep the best characteristics of the old system at the same time it attempts to realize the benefits of a new structure. Companies currently in global product structures can augment their organization in order to enjoy its benefits without falling into any of its traps. For other companies, managers can make a rational choice among enriching their existing international divisions, introducing a global product structure, or moving all the way to a formal matrix structure.

Whatever the structure chosen, the most important thing to remember is the necessity of creating a decision pattern that can allow either functional, product, or area ideas to surface when needed—at an administrative cost the company can bear. The approach used by each company in attempting to achieve the objective should and will remain unique to its own culture.

APPENDIX

Although many forms and combinations of structures are used by multinational corporations, three principal types of organization predominate.

The first formal structure companies use to manage foreign activities is the international division, with responsibility for foreign operations centered in a distinct unit. While companies can organize international divisions internally along product, functional, or area lines, in practice they grant primary authority to regional and national managers, whose responsibilities are defined in graphic terms.

Companies can outgrow their international divisions as they expand in size, diversity, and complexity of international operations. New problems and needs create pressures for more "sophisticated" structures. At this point, two organizational options exist:

● One alternative is the global product structure, which takes power out of the hands of international division managers at headquarters and in foreign affiliates and gives it to central product-division managers. Two changes in the administrative structure result: authority shifts from affiliates and regional managers to headquarters, and headquarters' responsibility for international operations shifts from a single line of authority to multiple lines.

● The other alternative is the matrix format, which attempts to balance the roles of central-product managers and foreign area-based managers in the administrative structure, offering them shared responsibility—and authority.

Although most corporate structures contain elements of all three formats, these broad categories describe the principal approaches to managing multinational operations.

NOTES

1. The project is described in Raymond Vernon, *Storm Over the Multinationals* (Cambridge: Harvard University Press, 1979), and in Joan P. Curhan, William H. Davidson, and Suri Rajan, *Tracing the Multinationals* (Cambridge, Mass.: Ballinger Publishing Co., 1977).
2. M. E. Wicks, "A Comparative Analysis of the Foreign Investment Evaluation Practices of U.S.-based Multinational Companies" (New York: McKinsey & Co., 1980).
3. Philippe Haspeslagh, "Portfolio Planning: Uses and Limits," *Harvard Business Review* (January-February, 1982), p. 58.
4. In a speech at the Harvard Business School, May 1980.
5. William H. Davidson, *Experience Effects in International Investment and Technology Transfer* (Ann Arbor, Mich.: UMI Research Press, 1980).
6. See John M. Stopford and Louis T. Wells, Jr., *Managing the Multinational Enterprise* (New York: Basic Books, 1972), especially pp. 113-17.
7. See Christopher A. Bartlett, "Multinational Structural Evolution: The Changing Decision Environment in International Divisions," Ph.D. diss., Harvard Business School, 1979.

21
Productivity: Learning from the Japanese

Hirotaka Takeuchi

One of the many variables that contributes to the success of international manu-facturing operations is a high level of productivity. Thus, indications of lagging productivity deserve prompt investigation. In the U.S., where productivity has declined in recent years, considerable attention has been directed to macro-economic reasons as a cause for the decline. For U.S. multinationals, however, the productivity problem is more pressing at the micro- (or internal) management level.

In many cases, the introduction of a corporate productivity-improvement program would help MNC management address those micro-level problems. Given the success of the Japanese productivity system, an examination of the implementation and nature of the Japanese system may provide U.S. firms with some valuable insights in the event those companies contemplate establishing similar systems.

EVERYONE SEEMS TO agree that lagging productivity is a serious problem in the U.S. Everyone seems to agree that something ought to be done about it soon. After three decades of diminishing growth rate, productivity of the private economy actually declined in the first three quarters of 1979. But no one seems to agree on what is causing the slowdown or who should be taking responsibility. The bulk of the blame has been placed, rightly or wrongly, on the following:

* the government, for increasing the number of federal, state, and local regulations, for enacting equal opportunity rules, for maintaining

large military spendings, and for not providing tax incentives to boost investment;

• unions, for being responsible for featherbedding and for spiraling wage costs;

• OPEC, for creating a sharp rise in energy costs;

• environmentalists, for demanding stringent pollution control measures;

• the worker, for taking days off from work, for being inexperienced and undereducated, and for being "more interested in the 'me' in his life than in keeping his nose to the grindstone";[1] and

• corporate managers, for making workers feel alienated and for not investing more in long-term research and development.[2]

Given the long list of possible "suspects," productivity experts have been struggling to determine from where to start the investigation. These experts, who are mostly comprised of economists, have tended to concentrate their investigative efforts at the macro-economic level. As a consequence, relatively little has been said thus far on what corporate managers or workers could do to improve the productivity problem.

The prevailing view among corporate managers has been to treat productivity as "someone else's problem." Those who hold such a view would point out that many of the causes of the productivity slowdown cited by experts are beyond their own control. Some managers would go a step further to argue that they have been the victims of actions taken by the government, union, and others.

There may be other reasons why corporate managers have opted to take a noncommittal attitude towards the productivity problem. For one thing, corporate managers are sensitive to the tradition in the U.S. of dismissing concern for productivity as "right-wing patter." They fear that a call for steps to improve productivity would be linked to work speed-ups and layoffs. Yet another reason may be rooted in the fact that the U.S. is still ahead of other countries in terms of the absolute level of productivity. In 1977, the output per employee hour of Japan, which recorded the fastest productivity growth rate in recent years, stood at about 62 percent of the U.S.'s.[3] A plausible response to the U.S. decline could be: "Don't panic—we're still the most productive nation."

In recent years, more and more corporate managers in the U.S. are beginning to realize the direct impact of declining productivity on their business. Productivity, these managers argue, is very much "their problem." These managers see productivity as playing some part in the loss of U.S. companies' share in the domestic and world markets to foreign competition. Others are alarmed by a report published by the New York Stock Exchange suggesting that a small productivity decline may have a large "multiplier" effect on inflation.[4] Still others are concerned with empirical results that show productivity as a significant determinant of profits.[5] To the extent that these concerns—loss of market share, inflation, and profits—are of pivotal importance to everyday business, it seems logical that corporate managers are beginning to show much more than a casual interest in productivity.

Some U.S. companies—Westinghouse, General Motors, IBM, General Electric, Honeywell, TRW, and Nashua Corporation, to name a few—have put their productivity concerns into action by adopting various productivity improvement programs. Westinghouse has recently started a multimillion-dollar project to study how robots, computer-aided systems, office and paperwork systems, energy conservation, value engineering, quality-control teams, and reorganization can improve productivity in the plant and the office. The companies named above have been enthusiastic about the results of such programs—namely, an improved rate of productivity growth for the company and improved morale among the workers.

One of the characteristics common to all these U.S. companies has been their willingness to learn from how Japanese companies manage productivity. Many Japanese companies have been testing and implementing productivity improvement programs for almost three decades. These long years of experimental efforts have now produced a unique way of thinking about and managing productivity, which I call the "Japanese productivity system" in this article.

This article addresses three questions regarding the Japanese productivity system:

• What is unique about the Japanese productivity system?

• Can a management technique developed within the context of Japanese companies be transferred to U.S. companies?

• What can U.S. managers interested in initiating successful productivity programs learn from past experiences?

I believe that corporate managers can do something about the productivity problem perplexing the U.S. I invite managers to evaluate, for themselves, whether the Japanese productivity system can deliver to them the kinds of benefits currently enjoyed by a small number of U.S. companies and their workers.

Words of Caution

A casual observer may note that Japanese companies must be doing something right to post a rate of productivity growth more than three times faster than their own in the past decade. According to the Bureau of Labor Statistics, output per hour of manufacturing worker rose 9.9 percent annually in Japan between 1967 and 1977, compared to 2.7 percent in the U.S. for the same period.[6]

A casual observer may also note that the Japanese have been able to record a higher level of productivity in some key industries. Take the automobile and steel industries. According to the latest census data, an average Japanese auto worker produces 50 cars per year, compared to 25 cars for an average U.S. worker. An average Japanese steelworker turns out 420 tons of output per year, compared to 250 tons in the U.S.

Some words of caution are in order. First of all, an unwary use of readily available raw data may render comparisons meaningless. Taking the auto industry comparison, an informed observer may respond: "How can you call that a legitimate comparison when you know that differences in the size of the car produced, the length of the work days, the level of automation, the degree of participation by outside suppliers, the attitude and skills of the workers, and a host of other factors distort the understanding of what's really happening in the two countries?" An informed observer may also explain that the difference in the annual growth rates may be largely due to the differences in the stages of industrial development in the two countries.

Second, there is a danger of obscuring the focus of the Japanese productivity system if corporate managers in the U.S. become too preoccupied with numbers. The focus should be more on the process by which productivity programs are implemented and less on the results of having implemented them. To the extent that productivity programs are implemented by people, managers should be concerned primarily about people and secondarily about numbers. There is already some criticism that U.S. managers have become too preoccupied with short-term performance results (such as returns on sales and investment, earnings per share, and equity ratios) at the risk of becoming myopic in their thinking. Translated within our context, a myopic manager may possible run the risk of going to the extreme in thinking, "What we need to do is to get those 'automatons' to crank out more products, even at the expense of increased defective rates."

The digression was needed to strike a sense of balance. We should be cautious of unqualified claims made by overly eager advocates of the Japanese productivity system. We should also be cautious of becoming too preoccupied with playing the numbers game. On the other hand, we should guard ourselves against becoming overly critical of the advocates' claims because differences between the two countries have not been accounted for entirely, and against shunning all comparative numbers that show differences between the two countries. An appropriate frame of mind to maintain is to recognize that differences do exist and to see if something can be learned from them.

Japanese Productivity System

Some U.S. managers seem to feel that Japanese companies must have developed secret formulas for dealing with the productivity problem. There is nothing secret or magical about the productivity improvement programs (such as the suggestion box or quality control program), or the measures of productivity that they employ. In fact, most of the programs and measures were developed in the U.S. and subsequently borrowed by the Japanese (more on this topic later).

There are also no major gaps in the resources employed in the two countries. As the manager of a Japanese consumer electronics company aptly observed, "Our workers are no smarter (than U.S. workers); our technology is no more advanced; our materials are no different; and our energy is less abundant."

What is unique about the Japanese productivity system is not the ingredients or pieces that go into the system, but how the pieces are put together. Productivity is like a jigsaw puzzle—all the pieces must be fitted together before the entire picture can be seen. Japanese companies seem to have mastered the art of putting together a workable productivity system.

The following describes five major idiosyncrasies of the Japanese productivity system. These idiosyncrasies are the key factors for success. Each is indispensable because without one the entire picture cannot be appreciated.

Product Quality Control: Productivity improvement came about among Japanese companies as a by-product of the emphasis placed on product quality control. The most urgent problem that most export-minded Japanese companies faced in the 1950s was the "cheap and shoddy" image associated with made-in-Japan products. In order to compete in the world market, these companies placed their top priority in improving the quality of their products.

One of the first steps taken was to invite American experts to lecture on statistical quality-control techniques. Visits by W. Edwards Deming, a statistician, in 1950 and J. M. Juran, a consultant, in 1954, helped to spread the use of the methodology and practice needed in carrying out quality-control programs. Every new technique subsequently developed in the U.S.—such as Zero Defects or Value Engineering—has been studied and adopted by Japanese manufacturers. By the 1970s, quality control had almost become a religion.

This religious dedication towards quality control seems to have paid off for the Japanese. Taking the television industry as an example, J. M. Juran observes:

● Between 1.5 to 1.8 defects per television set were discovered at the Motorola TV factory before Matsushita Electric took over in 1974. In 1978, under new management but virtually the same employees, the new Quasar brand had a defective rate of 0.03 to 0.04 per set. In the Japanese parent company, the defective rate at the factory averages 0.005 per set.

● Once on the market, Japanese televisions have from one-half to one-fourth the failure rates as compared to U.S. and European sets.[7]

Of the computer industry, a representative from Hewlett-Packard recently reported the test results conducted on three hundred thousand 16K RAMs (random access memory microcomponents) supplied by three Japanese vendors and three U.S. vendors. The incoming inspection failure rates of the 16K RAMs supplied by the three Japanese vendors were all 0.00 percent, compared to the range between 0.11 percent to 0.19 percent for the three U.S. vendors. Similarly, the field failure rates of the 16K RAMs supplied by the three Japanese vendors ranged from 0.010 percent to 0.019 percent, compared to a range between 0.090 percent to 0.267 percent for the three U.S. vendors.[8] Although considerable caution must be taken in interpreting these results and in generalizing these findings to other industries, the fact still remains that made-in Japan products no longer suffer from the stigma that was attached to them up to a decade ago.

What does quality control have to do with productivity? Quality control affects both output and input. On the output side, Louis P. Bucklin notes, "If television sets that move off the assembly line fail to function, then there is no real output, even though the physical presence of something that would otherwise be described as a television undeniably exists."[9] From a marketing perspective, lower defective rates in the factory and on the market are likely to be translated into higher trial rates and repeat purchase rates—higher sales, in other words. On the input side, a large number of rejected items means: more human resources required to repair them; duplicated use of materials; and more energy consumed per unit produced.

Grassroots Involvement: With such dedication to quality, it was natural for technical experts to assume a leadership role in promoting productivity in Japan. But the major driving force behind its productivity movement came from millions of rank-and-file workers who have taken the initiative to suggest changes to their superiors. This "bottom-up" process constitutes the backbone of the Japanese productivity system.

The number of suggestions reported by some companies is astonishingly high:

• In the past few years, both Toyota Motor Company and Mitsubishi Motors have been averaging close to twenty suggestions per worker a year at their factories.

• In the ten months ending October 1976, Matsushita Electric averaged fifty suggestions for each of the fifteen-hundred production workers in its Ibaragi television factory.[10] The company as a whole has been averaging over ten suggestions per worker (factory and office workers combined) per year in the last few years. These numbers should be treated with discretion because they include all suggestions for change. But a Matsushita manager points out, "All these suggestions somehow relate to making the product better, the job easier, or the worker happier. Wouldn't that lead to better productivity?"

Once the suggestions are submitted in writing, using preprinted forms in most cases, a suggestion committee evaluates the ideas, and if necessary, hands over the acceptable set to technical experts for further evaluation. At Matsushita, the acceptance rate has been averaging about 10 percent.

One interesting feature of the suggestion program is its rapid increase since the mid-1960s. Toyota averaged only one suggestion per worker in 1965 and Matsushita averaged 1.1 suggestion per worker in 1966. The rapid increase in worker involvement since the mid-1960s corresponds directly with the rise of small-group activities discussed next in the same time period.

Another interesting feature of the suggestion system is the heavy promotional effort directed towards the newcomers to the company. Slogans such as "Make Every Worker a Manager" and "Make Every Worker an Engineer" are emphasized to encourage initiative taking on the part of even the lowest ranked workers. Some companies put the program into practice by offering newcomers small incentives (such as a meal ticket) in exchange for suggestions, whether used or not. If accepted, the name of the contributor is publicized through a company newspaper or a bulletin board. In such a way, workers are conditioned early in their career to thinking that there is room for creativity even within the routine operations of the factory, and to thinking that "giving is rewarding."

A personnel manager at Toshiba Electric asked a twenty-one-year-old factory worker what prompted her to make seventy technical suggestions a year, half of which were accepted. "Her answer was simply, 'It makes me feel good,' " said the manager. "Our strength lies in the fact that we can mix the scientific management approach and the behavioral approach (self-actualization, job enrichment) together and come up with rank-and-file workers with a very constructive frame of mind."

Quality-Control (QC) Circles: Quality-control circles are a natural outgrowth of the suggestion program. As in the suggestions program, workers offer solutions towards job-related problems, but the problems addressed by QC Circles are often more complex and less obvious to uncover. Also, the solutions no longer consist of untested ideas, which may or may not work. Members of QC Circles devote a considerable amount of their time toward testing their recommendations and putting them into practice. QC Circles thus serve to further enhance worker involvement.

Although the QC Circle is well-known in Japan, the concept as it is understood in Japan is still relatively unknown in the U.S. A quality-control circle is a voluntary study group dedicated to solving job-related problems. Two commonly held misconceptions need to be dispelled. First, the study group does not consist of quality-control specialists with extensive prior technical training. QC Circle members are mostly rank-and-file workers and foremen who receive virtually all of their technical training once they join the study group. Some see the inclusion and training of foremen, who usually serve as circle leaders, as the most innovative characteristic of the Japanese approach to quality control.[11] Second, problem solving is not restricted to the area of product quality control. According to a 1979 survey, the kinds of projects being conducted by over five hundred of the QC Circles in Japan include (in order of importance) cost reduction, product quality control, improvement of workshop facilities, safety precautions, employee morale improvement, pollution control, and continued employee education.[12] Directly or indirectly, these projects become instrumental in improving productivity and quality of work life.

QC Circles have grown explosively in Japan since their establishment in 1962. In 1965, fewer than 5,000 QC Circles were registered with Japan Union of Scientists and Engineers (JUSE), a nonprofit association serving as the QC Circle coordinator. By the end of 1979, there were over 100,000 circles. Membership of these registered circles totalled 980,000 in

1979, with an average of nine members per QC Circle. A high-ranking JUSE official estimates the number of unregistered and quasi-QC Circles in Japan to reach as high as eight times the number of registered circles. Assuming the same number of members per group, as many as one out of five employees in the entire Japanese labor force (thirty-seven million) could be taking part in some form of job-related group activities today.

This rapid diffusion of QC Circles in Japan is credited largely to JUSE's pioneering efforts. Among other activities, JUSE has been responsible for:

• Holding training sessions for managers and foremen. In 1979, more than thirty such sessions, usually lasting from two to six days, were held in its Tokyo headquarters and its eight regional offices. In addition, close to thirty-five hundred foremen took two training courses conducted via radio and TV.

• Publishing a monthly trade journal called *FQC* (Quality Control for the Foreman, whose subscription reached over one hundred thousand in 1979. In addition, it publishes numerous textbooks and training manuals.

• Sponsoring a series of conferences and visitor programs. In 1979, a total of 107 coferences, in which some two thousand successful case stories were presented by QC Circle members, were held throughout Japan. Exchange visits among different Japanese companies active in QC Circles (initiated in 1963) and exchange visits with foreign countries (initiated in 1968) are increasing every year.

Table 1

Managers

1. Improved worker morale
2. Improved safety
3. Strengthened teamwork
4. Improved product quality
5. Led to better human relations

Circle Leaders

1. Provided good opportunity for learning
2. Improved communication with superior
3. Heightened problem awareness
4. Heightened consciousness to improve status quo
5. Improved working environment

JUSE's activities are financed through nominal fees charged for these training programs, publications, and conferences. It does not, however, charge membership fees. "It's a voluntary movement," said a JUSE official. "This movement will grow as long as we can continue to deliver the hoped-for benefits to member companies and their workers."

According to the 1979 survey cited earlier, the QC movement delivered different benefits to company managers and circle members. The intangible benefits cited most often by the two groups are shown in Table 1. The survey also tried to ascertain the extent of tangible monetary benefits enjoyed by both groups. About 80 percent of the managers reported that the company gained annual monetary benefits ranging from $12,000 to $1.2 million per business unit.[13] Taking the mode, the ratio of these benefits to incremental, out-of-pocket costs was ten to one per business unit.[14] On a company-wide basis, one large Japanese electronics company with forty-six thousand employees interviewed by the author estimated its benefits at $13.3 million a year and its incremental costs at $2.7 million in 1978 (a benefit-cost ratio of five to one). Monetary benefits to QC Circle members, on the other hand, appear to be relatively insignificant. As an indication, only 2.7 percent of over five hundred QC Circle leaders surveyed mentioned higher pay as one of the benefits of participating in QC Circles (more on this topic later).

Of course, companies will not be able to amass such large benefits by simply providing moral encouragement. Active company support is a necessary condition for the successful operation of QC Circles. First, workers are encouraged to use company facilities to test out their ideas or to develop prototypes. Second, workers are encouraged to conduct QC Circle meetings during working hours—two-thirds of the circles surveyed did so in 1979. On the average QC Circles met twice a month for more than an hour per session. Third, even if meetings are held outside of regular working hours, most companies (69 percent in 1979) offer some financial support. For the most part, such support consists of nominal overtime pay. Fourth, almost all the companies bear the costs associated with putting together intercompany QC Circle contests. These intercompany contests, usually held two or three times a year regionally and once a year nationally, can turn into fiercely competitive events. QC Circle members spend long hours rehearsing their case study presentation, oftentimes on stage. The presentations are often accompanied by skits or music to make the potentially dry technical content as appealing as possible. "Sometimes these contests turn into talent shows," said one manager. "It can also become as thrilling and exciting as an Academy Award when the time for selecting the winner is reached. I've seen many winners in tears."

The case study method has been used very effectively within QC Circles. In the early stage of the case study, much of the effort of the study group is directed towards identifying crucial problems that may have a far-reaching impact if resolved. This search process tests the creativity of QC Circle members and heightens their sense of mission. In the analytical stage, QC Circle members make extensive use of basic statistical and graphical techniques that they've learned in the training program. The major objective of the analysis is to derive meaningful relationships and inferences from the raw data that have been collected. The most frequently utilized analytical tools include histograms, Pareto analysis (similar to "80-20" analysis), cause-and-effect diagrams, and flow charts. This analytical process conditions QC Circle members to argue with facts rather than with intuitions. In the recommendation stage of the case study, QC Circle members try to convince their superiors that the solution makes a positive contribution to the company. The number of case studies that reach this stage is low (an average of 2.4 per QC Circle in 1979), but the rewards are high for the workers.

Nonfinancial Rewards: The reward that seems to work best within the Japanese productivity system is the pat on the back. The success of many Japanese companies in applying positive reinforcement, such as praise and recognition, suggests that rewards do not necessarily have to take the form of a fat check.

Some Japanese companies, to be sure, are offering cash rewards to individual workers and QC Circles, but payments appear to be nominal. A worker at Matsushita Electric's TV factory suggested a device to stop solder from dripping down the endplates of television sets and causing short circuits.[15] His suggestion, which was designated as a fifth-grade award under Matsushita's eight-grade system, earned him thirteen dollars. Another worker received a total of one hundred dollars for sixty suggestions that were accepted in a year. The cash reward came out to sixty cents per suggestion. At Mitsubishi Electric, ten members of a QC Circle jointly received a cash reward of two hundred dollars for suggesting the best cost-reduction idea of the year. According to Robert E. Cole, "Symbolic payments are common, with rewards for even the best suggestion, leading to say a patent, seldom exceeding $600."[16]

Most companies prefer to rely on some form of nonfinancial reward. At a Honda Motor company plant small rectangular cards are hung from the ceiling directly above some of its workers. These cards are the most visible rewards that Honda's workers receive for contributing to the suggestion program. Under the system, workers can receive up to a hundred points per suggestion, depending on the value of the suggestion made. A cumulative record is kept of the points earned by each worker and a gold-colored car is awarded once he or she reaches fifty points.

Extensive use is also made of trophies, plaques, medals, diplomas, and other commemorative items to honor the contributors. According to the 1979 survey of QC Circles, 93 percent of the companies handed out some variations of the above awards in their intercompany contests. For some QC Circles fortunate enough to be selected to attend the national contest, positive reinforcement may result from something less tangible than a trophy or a medal. The opportunity to visit the corporate headquarters, to present their case studies to top management, and for a presidential handshake have been mentioned by QC Circle members as morale boosters.

Another positive reinforcement tool, within a broader context, is the posting of performance results—such as defective rate, output per employee hour, number of suggestions, attendance rate, and repair rate—on the factory bulletin board. The results are charted and updated on a regular basis. Performance results of other factories or the norm for the entire company are frequently charted to provide a basis for comparison. Workers are praised for internal improvements and for superior performance over others.

Are cards hanging from the ceiling, trophies, presidential handshakes, and performance charts too sophomoric as mechanisms for reward? Call it whatever you please, but the Skinnerian principle of offering positive rewards in the form of praise and recognition has become an integral part of the Japanese productivity system.

Maternalistic Management: The missing link in understanding the Japanese productivity system is the role the company plays in making the worker become closely involved with productivity. The answer lies in the "maternalistic" way in which the company relates to the worker on a day-to-day basis. Maternalistic management is characterized by the close, caring, nurturing type of relationship that companies build in trying to motivate, guide, and develop their workers.

Many readers may be puzzled at this point with the seemingly perverse use of the word *maternalistic* to describe a management style traditionally called *paternalistic*. As M. Y. Yoshino observes, "The [Japanese] company was regarded as one vast family, with management playing the benevolent 'father' role and the workers accepting the sub-missive role of 'children.' "[17] To be sure, Japanese companies still adhere to a paternalistic style of management in building enduring employer-employee relationships. A paternalistic system—which connotes secur-ity, solidarity, loyalty, and authority—is reflected in their personnel practices, such as the "guarantee against dismissal, regularized wage increases to meet the rising needs of a growing family, and fringe benefits."[18]

But many Japanese companies switch over to a more maternalistic style when managing the short-run execution of specific programs. Within the context of productivity improvement programs, this style is reflected in the following practices:

• Presence of top managers: frequent visits of top managers to the factory and their participation in training programs or in companywide events (such as sports competition or QC Circle contests) help to convey the message that "top managers care." Taking QC Circle contests as an example, 89 percent of the five hundred or so companies interviewed in 1979 responded that their presidents regularly attended these contests.

• Guidance and support provided by middle managers: 98 percent of QC Circle leaders interviewed acknowledged receiving some form of guidance and support from their immediate supervisors (mostly section or department managers).

• Daily contacts with productivity "facilitators": all the companies interviewed assigned one or more full-time administrative staff mem-bers to serve as facilitators between the company and QC Circle mem-bers. Workers are on "equal" terms with these facilitators, unlike the "submissive" role suggested within paternalistic system.

• Support of QC activities: as seen earlier, the company supports QC activities by providing materials and equipment necessary for work-ers to conduct experiments, arranging QC Circle meetings on company premises and during working hours, sponsoring contests, organizing visits to other companies, and sending its managers and foremen to training sessions conducted by JUSE. Company expenditure for these activities averaged thirty dollars per QC Circle member annually, ac-cording to the 1979 JUSE survey.

Attempts to motivate and nurture the workers start as soon as the workers join the company. As cited earlier, the seeds for an active sug-gestion program are planted during the first few days of training when the workers are encouraged to stretch their creative thinking. The seeds for teamwork are also planted during the initial training program in which the new employees are organized into study groups. Some companies go so far as sending their new recruits to Zen temples, farms, camps, or even the Self-Defense Force. "By eating together, sleeping together, and organizing daytime activities around groups, we want the trainees to have a first-hand experience in what teamwork means and what it can accomplish," said the personnel manager of a company which recently incorporated climbing Mt. Fuji into the training program.

The company enables workers to feel like "part of the system" by providing a constant flow of information from different sources. Mention was made earlier of the use of charts to disseminate information regarding worker performance. In addition, general information on the financial status of the company, industry and competitive trends, long-run corporate strategy, and other areas is shared with everyone in the organization via formal channels (such as company newspapers or routine morning gatherings) and informal channels (social gatherings, company clubs).[19] Information about QC Circle activities is also disseminated in some companies. According to the 1979 survey, 40 percent of the companies published intercompany QC Circle newsletters; 60 percent of these companies published such newsletters over six times a year.

The bottom-up nature of the Japanese productivity system does not come about simply as a result of positive-thinking workers becoming personally "turned on" with solving problems. Considerable effort is expended by the company in laying out the necessary network of people and communication to support the workers. The maternalistic nature in which the day-to-day programs are executed, combined with a paternalistic framework, helps to foster the belief among workers that "the best interests of my company are also my own best interests."

Regarding the key factors of the Japanese productivity system just discussed, U.S. managers may legitimately raise the question, "So, what's new?" Suggestion boxes, for example, have been around for a long time in many companies. Statistical quality control, work groups, positive reinforcements, and human relations (a broader concept encompassing maternalistic management) are not unheard of either. In fact, many of the original ideas date back to the experiments conducted at Western Electric Company's Hawthorne plant in the late 1920s.

Again, the distinguishing feature of the Japanese program lies in how the pieces are put together. In planning and organizing productivity improvement programs, Japanese companies rely on almost a fanatic dedication to details. In implementing and controlling the programs, they resort to tender loving care. In re-orchestrating the entire effort, they mobilize managers from different levels and staff members from different departments. And at all times, they keep sight of why productivity is being pursued—to benefit the workers, the company, and the product simultaneously.

Is It Transferable?

The discussion thus far has centered on the successful implementation of a productivity system in a country several thousand miles away that shares little, culturally, with the U.S. Before discussing what lessons can be drawn from the Japanese experience one must ask whether its success is endemic to Japan or whether it could be transferred across cultural boundaries.

Managers who hold a negative view (it will never work in the U.S.) would argue that the differences in the business culture between the two countries are too many for any meaningful transfer to take place. They would call the idiosyncrasies of the Japanese business culture—close government-business ties, company-based unions (which play a less adversary role than in the U.S.), commitment to a lifetime employment, and innate group orientation—barriers to entry. Their arguments could run as follows:[20]

• Under the cozy government-business partnership known as "Japan, Inc.," the government gives companies direct and indirect support for productivity improvement. For companies in selected growth industries, the government provides direct support in the form of tax breaks, technology transfer, and preferential financing. The government also provides indirect support to all companies by funding the Japan Productivity Center (JPC), which it established in 1955 as a means of involving management and labor unions in a national movement towards achieving higher productivity. In the U.S., a nonprofit organization similar to the JPC (last known as the National Center for Productivity and Quality of Working Life) was established by the U.S. Government in 1970, but was closed in 1978.

• Although the percentage of the work force participating in labor unions is somewhat higher in Japan, the locus of union power does not reside at the industry level, but resides within the company. Unlike local trade unions in the U.S., which are "outside" unions, the so-called enterprise unions in Japan (sometimes referred to as home unions) are based "inside" the company. Most Japanese companies consider their unions as friends, not as adversaries. Company managers involve union leaders in key decisions, socialize with them, and regard "bringing up good union leaders" as part of their responsibility. Such practices are unheard of, if not illegal, in the U.S.

- The lifetime employment practice of Japanese companies has dual benefits for productivity. Knowing that the employees will be around until they retire at age fifty-five or sixty, companies can make substantial investment in training programs and efforts directed at human resources development. Knowing that their personal well-being hinges on how well the company performs, workers are induced to making as much contribution to the company as possible. In the U.S., several companies—IBM, Hewlett-Packard, and Eli Lilly, among others—are committed to job security (a no-layoff policy). These companies, however, are the exceptions rather than the rule.

- Japanese workers are prone to working in groups and teams, given the emphasis placed on traditional values of cooperation, harmony, and group consensus within the culture. Companies foster this group spirit by having their own uniforms, badges, mottos, and songs, and by organizing training programs, sports competition, and social events around groups. In the U.S., work teams are still a novelty. Although experiments with work teams have been conducted in General Foods' Topeka, Kansas plant, in Procter and Gamble's Lima, Ohio plant, in four Donnelly Mirrors plants in Holland, Michigan, and more recently in Sherwin-Williams' Richmond, Kentucky plant, they are still the exceptions rather than the rule.[21]

Although these arguments may support Kipling's contention that "East is East, and West is West, and never the twain shall meet," recent developments indicate that the twains are beginning to meet. We now turn to two groups of companies—U.S. subsidiaries of Japanese companies and U.S. companies that have established QC Circles—to present the view that the ideas basic to the Japanese productivity system can be transferred to the U.S.

Japanese Companies in the U.S.

Japanese companies that have established subsidiaries in the U.S. are finding that American workers are responding very positively towards concerns for product quality and human resources development. Mention was made earlier of how Matushita was able to improve the factory defective rate of its TV sets by a factor of almost fifty to one in the four years since it took over the Motorola factory in Chicago. Other examples abound.

Sanyo Electric Company took over a unionized Forrest City, Arkansas television factory of Whirlpool-controlled Warwick Electronics in December 1976, and in less than a year reduced the retail failure rate of its TV sets from 10 percent to less than 2 percent. In the computer industry, Fujitsu American reduced the factory defective rate of its subassemblies by a factor of ten to one in the past two years. Its president describes the process as follows:

I conducted a meeting once every week and had the American managers discuss their work openly. I encouraged everyone to think through problems together, to an eventual solution. Working together, we found these problems: carelessness, poor handling of delicate parts, inaccurate testing equipment, improper placement of parts to be tested and, most important, failure of managers to act on the foregoing.[22]

Japanese companies in the U.S. are as committed to people building and team building as they are to product quality. Concern for the workers is best reflected in the words of the Fujitsu America president: "We Japanese managers consider our employees to be our greatest asset. We treat them as treasures, and they respond with loyalty and hard work."[23] This commitment is put into practice by the chairman of Hitachi Magnetics Corporation in Edmore, Michigan, who organizes and personally attends softball games and weekend picnics; by the president of NTN Bearing in Des Plaines, Illinois, who works as a manual laborer in the warehouse during the semiannual physical inventory count; and by the plant managers of Sony Corporation of America's San Diego plant, who hold monthly meetings with all its workers (over twelve hundred) to keep them abreast of relevant information related to marketing, production, and personnel matters.

These efforts seem to be paying off, as many companies are reporting superior performance records in absenteeism, employee turnover, and productivity. Sony's San Diego plant's absenteeism and turnover rates were 25 percent to 50 percent below those of other electronics companies in that area. Output per unit of labor was 22 percent higher than that of a U.S. counterpart.[24]

To be sure, Japanese companies are not free of problems in their U.S. subsidiaries:

• A dispute over wages led to a strike by the United Auto Workers at the Ann Arbor, Michigan plant of Nippon Seiko, a bearing manufacturer. In general, Japanese companies are discovering that a pat on the back and trophies alone do not provide adequate incentives for American workers.

• Charges of discrimination over promotion, wages, and fringe benefits has led three American workers to file a law suit against C. Itoh and Company, a large trading company. Charges of sexism and racism led women employees of Sumitomo Bank to demonstrate in front of its San Francisco office. Japanese companies are discovering the penchant for American workers to put their complaints into immediate action.

• Japanese companies in the service areas see the high turnover among middle managers as a major problem. They are discovering the difficulty of preventing American workers from job hopping.

• When the Forrest City, Arkansas plant of Sanyo constructed a softball field for employee and community use, one employee's reaction was the following: "When I leave here, my interest is on my things, not Sanyo's. I am a Christian, and I put my non-company time into serving the Lord."[25] Japanese companies are discovering a clear-cut distinction of company time from personal time.

Japanese companies are generally confident that those problems can be worked out in the long run. According to the manager of a Japanese bank in New York, "It is going to take time for us to learn about how American workers think and behave. It is also going to take some time for American workers to understand how we operate. If both sides are willing to adapt, the learning curve will be steep."

U.S. Companies with QC Circles

Japanese quality-control circles, or work groups modelled after them, are beginning to spread among U.S. companies. QC Circles were first "imported" to the U.S. in 1974 by Lockheed Missiles and Space Company, which had sent its manufacturing manager to Japan to visit JUSE and eight companies actively involved in QC Circles. Lockheed adopted training programs developed by JUSE and followed suggestions from Japanese companies on how to organize and implement QC Circles. After two years, the company had some fifteen QC Circles and had accumulated savings of almost $3 million from problems solved by circle members. In one operation, the manufacturing defective rate declined from twenty-five to thirty per thousand hours of work to less than six per thousand hours.[26]

Other aerospace companies soon followed Lockheed's steps in installing QC Circles (or whatever names the companies decided to call them). These companies provided an ideal setting for QC Circle activities to expand since their work environment is characterized by acute sensitivity towards product quality, nonroutine jobs that often require group involvement, and a cooperative relationship between management and workers. Similar characteristics also helped the diffusion of QC Circle activities among such electronics companies as Tektronix, Hewlett-Packard, and IBM. These companies were also better prepared than others to install QC Circles due to their prior commitments to people-building and quality-improvement programs.

Companies in other industries have also incorporated QC Circles. General Motors' Buick Division spearheaded the introduction of QC Circles in the automobile industry in late 1977. QC Circles soon spread to a number of other divisions within General Motors and to other automobile manufacturers as well. The enthusiasm of these companies can be seen in the fact that circle activities are continuing to expand despite sales declines and worker layoffs. Automobile companies join several diversified manufacturers that have actively pursued QC Circle activities—Westinghouse, General Electric, the 3M Company—in emphasizing that a QC Circle program should be looked upon primarily as a people-building tool and secondarily as a means to realize savings and quality improvements.

Application of QC Circles is not limited to the production line alone. QC Circles can now be found in the offices as well. Lincoln National Life Insurance Company of Fort Wayne, Indiana has found that circles have been able to make improvements in job structure, work flow, paper flow, and service quality to customers. Experiments are also underway to establish QC Circles in retail stores and in other service-oriented workplaces.

Assistance in setting up a QC Circle program appears to be readily available in the U.S. Companies can turn to nonprofit organizations, such as the American Productivity Center, the American Society for Quality control, and the International Association of Quality Circles, to gain a better understanding of the QC Circle concept. They can also turn to a number of consultants in California who specialize in organizing training sessions and conducting pilot programs within the company.

Several U.S. companies have modified the Japanese version of the QC Circle program to fit their own needs. One company incorporated a hefty financial incentive program into the QC Circle program, offering one-sixth of the savings (up to twenty-five hundred dollars) as cash reward. Another company paid overtime wage rates for the extra time that workers put in after work on QC Circle activities. Another created QC Circles that operated on a revolving basis: A QC Circle worked on solving job-related problems, but once its recommendations were presented to management (usually between six to eight months after its inception), the circle was dissolved automatically. Another company made participation in QC Circle meetings mandatory because they were being held during working hours. The company assigned first-line managers as QC Circle leaders, rather than allowing circle members to elect their leaders, as is the case in Japan. Yet another company significantly curtailed the training period to thirty minutes because "the workers preferred solving problems rather than sitting down for twenty hours of lecture." Although some are concerned that too liberal a deviation from the Japanese model may cause the basic philosophy behind QC Circles to be misconstrued, most believe that adaptations have to be made to suit the American work environment. As one manager put it, "After all, didn't the Japanese adapt ideas that originated in the U.S. to develop what is today called QC Circles?"

Some observers are starting to voice other concerns over the development of QC Circle activities in the U.S. Are QC Circles being sold as an instant panacea? As one U.S. manager aptly remarked, "It takes extreme patience and painstaking regularity to make QC Circles work. It's one thing to come up with buzz words, but it's another thing to make QC Circles a 'way of life.' " Why is the attrition rate of QC Circles in some companies so high? In one company, for example, 20 percent of the circles ceased to function in the last two years. The common thread among companies facing these situations is the lack of commitment and support from both middle and top management. Are cost savings resulting from QC Circle activities being overemphasized? Excerpts from recent articles include the following:

• An assembly line circle at the solar-turbines division of International Harvester found a way to simplify the production of a compression disc for a turbine. As a result, several production steps were eliminated and $8,700 a year was saved.[27]

• The circle at a GM plant in Michigan decided it should do something about the large number of automobiles leaving the assembly line with flat tires. Their analysis eventually traced the problem to a defective tire stem. The part was replaced and the company's annual savings turned out to be $225,000.[28]

• A purchasing department circle [of Westinghouse] noted that when supplies were ordered, many vendors routinely sent more than requested. The company either paid the bill or shipped the parts back at its own expense. The solution was to inform suppliers that the company would either keep the extra material or charge for returning it. The saving: $636,000 a year.[29]

Fortunately, the articles quoted above give a balanced view, as does the following quotation of a factory worker: "It's the best thing that's happened in a long time around here. We've saved the company a lot of money. It gives you a feeling of accomplishment when a solution your circle thought up is enacted by management."[30] The concern is on whether overemphasizing cost savings may lead U.S. managers to become further preoccupied with end results rather than the process.

Whatever concerns observers may have, QC Circles generally receive high marks from companies that are actually implementing the program. The number of U.S. companies that have already implemented QC Circles has reached over two hundred as of this writing. Some of these companies—General Motors, General Electric, Hewlett-Packard, IBM, TRW, and Eaton Corporation—have also been active in pursuing quality of work-life programs. The basis concerns of such programs—humanization of work, job enrichment, and participative management—are integral parts of QC Circle activities as well.[31] QC Circles are also receiving high marks from the workers. "I feel like I've put in my two cents worth," said one worker. "I'm discovering that I can solve lots of problems if several of us get together," said another. The unions have generally been supportive of QC Circle activities. Some companies have invited union representatives to participate during pilot programs; others have assigned union representatives as QC Circle leaders or trainers.

Enough evidence has been accumulated to suggest that the underlying principles of the Japanese productivity system have taken root in the U.S. The East and West have met in a number of U.S. subsidiaries of leading Japanese companies and in a number of U.S. companies described above. The question to be addressed now is whether the current momentum behind productivity improvement programs can be sustained in the U.S. Will the productivity improvement program become a way of life or will it whither away as just another fad?

Conclusion

The fate of productivity improvement programs in the U.S. rests on the shoulders of managers. Growth will be sustained if managers can provide the leadership required to tap the reservoir of productivity improvement potential within the company. To begin with, managers need a proper frame of mind. The Japanese productivity system has taught us that productivity should not be looked upon as someone else's problem or as a right-wing pattern, but as something that managers can have control over and something that can benefit the company, workers, and products.

The Japanese productivity system has also taught us where to tap the reservoir of productivity improvement potential and how to tap it. The first and most obvious place for managers to look is at themselves, because without top management commitment and support, productivity improvement programs are doomed to failure. In some U.S. companies, top managers have demonstrated their commitment and support by establishing productivity seed-money funds, visiting Japan as members of the productivity task force, participating in productivity training seminars, attending QC Circle meetings, or presenting awards in productivity contests. In implementing productivity improvement programs, they should not expect an overnight success nor a panacea. After all, it has taken almost three decades of trial and error for the Japanese productivity system to reach where it is now. A Japanese saying best describes how managers should view the process: "When dust accumulates, it makes a mountain."

Second, managers should solicit assistance from a wide variety of departments within the company to facilitate productivity improvement programs. To "make every worker an engineer" managers should rely on the support of departments such as production, research and development, quality control, and others. To "make every worker a manager" they should turn to departments such as employee relations and personnel for education and training, and to data processing, finance, accounting, and marketing for relevant managerial information. At the same time, managers should solicit support from appropriate outside constituents, especially labor unions. The Japanese experience has shown that a broad-based internal support system and an early involvement of outside constituents are indispensable to the success of productivity improvement programs.

Third, managers should draw substantially more from their own workers, who are probably one of the most untapped and undervalued resources available. Managers should start with the premise that workers know best when it comes to identifying problems that exist in their workplace. The Japanese experience has shown that managers should go a step further in challenging workers to actually solve those problems. In trying to crack the problems, workers should be encouraged to resort to practices followed by many management consulting firms—working in teams, analyzing issues in depth, searching for creative solutions, and presenting the analyses and solutions in graphical form. Workers should also be asked to implement the solutions, which allows them to see what they have been able to accomplish and "feel mighty good" about it. One U.S. manager warned that "you should not try to 'nickel and dime' on savings or try to set minimum ROI requirements because, you have to remember, the primary focus throughout the exercise is on people building." Shouldn't human resources deserve as much attention and care from managers as financial resources?

Fourth, managers should utilize product-quality control as a catalyst toward improving productivity. One of the most innovative characteristics of the Japanese productivity system has been the infusion of quality-control consciousness into the blood of everyone in the organization, including the president, foremen, and rank-and-file workers. Quality control became a grassroots activity, rather than "a little room adjacent to the factory floor, whose occupants make a nuisance of themselves to everyone else."[32] Through the formation of QC Circles, quality control has been pursued within a cooperative environment. This dedication to quality control has been instrumental in bringing about greater acceptance of made-in-Japan products in the world market. At the same time, improved product quality and improved market performance has instilled a sense of craftsmanlike pride among Japanese rank-and-file workers.

Managers in the U.S. should realize that the Japanese originally learned about advanced quality-control techniques from the U.S. They first invited leading American authorities in the field to Japan and later sent study teams to leading companies in the U.S. that were practicing new quality-control programs (such as Zero Defects and Value Engineering). In general, sending study teams to the U.S. appears to be a prevalent mode of learning for the Japanese, as exemplified by the fact that the Japan Productivity Center has commissioned about a thousand productivity study teams to this country in the last twenty-five years. The Japan Union of Scientists and Engineers also initiated a similar program in 1968. Based on the belief that "there is so much to be learned in the U.S.," numerous Japanese companies have been sending study teams to this country. Several companies in the U.S. have reciprocated in recent years by sending task forces to study the quality-control circle movement in Japan. These companies are finding that "seeing is believing."

Ten years ago, Peter Drucker warned that it would be folly for managers in the U.S. to attempt to imitate the Japanese management system.[33] The same could be said today about the Japanese productivity system. But, it would be folly not to attempt to learn from other people's successes, especially when lagging productivity is one of the most pressing problems facing the U.S. today. Success should be contagious.

REFERENCES

1. *The New York Times* (26 January 1979), p. 28.
2. For a more detailed description of what is causing productivity to slow down, see Campbell R. McConnell, "Why is U.S. Productivity Slowing Down?", *Harvard Business Review* (March-April 1979), pp. 36-60.
3. U.S National Center for Productivity and Quality of Working Life, *Productivity in the Changing World of the 1980s* (U.S. Government Printing Office, September 1978), p. 24.
4. The New York Stock Exchange, *Reaching A Higher Standard of Living* (The New York Stock Exchange, January 1979).
5. Hirotaka Takeuchi, *Productivity Analysis as a Resource Management Tool in the Retail Trade* (Ph.D. diss., University of California, 1977).
6. *Monthly Labor Review* (November 1978), p. 15.
7. J. M. Juran, "Japanese and Western Quality: A contrast in Methods and Results," *Management Review* (November 1978), pp. 27-45.
8. *The Rosen Electronic Letter* (31 March 1980), 4.
9. Louis P. Bucklin, *Productivity in Marketing* (Chicago: American Marketing Association, 1978), p. 20.
10. *International Management* (February 1977), pp. 36-39.
11. See Robert E. Cole, *Work, Mobility, and Participation: A Comparative Study of American and Japanese Industry* (Berkeley, California: University of California Press, 1979).
12. Japan Union of Scientists and Engineers (JUSE), *Current Status of QC Circle Activities* (Tokyo: JUSE, 1979), in Japanese.
13. These benefits took the forms of savings in labor hours, capital expenditures, energy, or materials, as well as quantifiable improvements in quality or output rate.
14. This benefit-cost ratio is inflated to the extent that wages and overtime pay of the workers and expenses for materials and energy utilized in carrying out the projects are not included.
15. Example taken from *International Management*, op. cit.
16. Cole, op. cit., p. 140.
17. M. Y. Yoshino, *Japan's Managerial system* (Cambridge, Massachusetts: The MIT Press, 1978), p. 78.
18. Ibid.
19. Employee-initiated clubs are strongly supported by most Japanese companies. One of the divisions of Matsushita Electric, for example, has over twenty sports, cultural, and other company clubs. According to a Mat-

sushita manager, "These clubs serve to counterbalance the intensity and pressure the work place may create. Our intent is to develop a 'total' person."

20. For more details on these idiosyncrasies, see M. Y. Yoshino, op. cit.; and Ezra F. Vogel, *Japan as No. 1: Lessons for America* (Cambridge, Massachusetts: Harvard University Press, 1979).

21. See Richard E. Walton, "How to Counter Alienation in the Plant," *Harvard Business Review* (November-December 1972); Louis E. Davis and Albert B. Cherns (eds.), *The Quality of Working Life, Volume II* (New York: The Free Press, 1975); Edward M. Claser, *Productivity Gains Through Worklike Improvement* (New York: Harcourt Brace Jovanovich, 1975); Ernesto J. Poza and M. Lynne Marjus, "Success Story: The Team Approach to Work Structuring," *Organizational dynamics* (Winter 1980), pp. 3-25.

22. *The New York Times* (20 March 1980), p. 16ff.

23. Ibid.

24. Richard T. Johnson and William G. Ouchi, "Made in America (Under Japanese Management)," *Harvard Business Review* (September-October 1974), p. 63, and "Are Japanese Managers Really Better?" *International Management* (July 1976), p. 35.

25. *Industry Week* (19 February 1979), p. 74.

26. Ed Yager, "Examining the Quality Control Circle," *Personnel Journal* (October 1979), p. 684.

27. *Wall Street Journal* (21 February 1980), p. 48.

28. Ibid.

29. "The Workers Know Best," *Time* (28 January 1980), p. 65.

30. *Wall Street Journal*, op. cit.

31. For further readings on quality of work-life programs, see Robert H. Guest, "Quality of Work-Life-Learning from Tarrytown," *Harvard Business Review* (July-August 1979); and Richard E. Walton, "Work Innovations in the United States," *Harvard Business Review* (July-August 1979).

32. *The New York Times*, op. cit.

33. Peter F. Drucker, "What We Can Learn from Japanese Management," *Harvard Business Review* (March-April 1971).

22

Transnational Corporations: Market Orientations and R&D Abroad

Jack N. Behrman and William A. Fischer

The tendency for U.S. MNCs to concentrate R&D activities in the parent-company location has changed in the past decade, with a greater proportion of R&D expenditures occurring abroad. A firm's market orientation, whether home, host, or global, is often the determining factor in the MNC decision to undertake R&D abroad.

OVER THE PAST several decades, the transfer of technology, in its various guises, has become an accepted part of doing business for transnational corporations and has been profitable for many of them. Other things being equal, most transnational corporations would be reluctant to transfer abroad the origins of their technology—their research and development (R&D) activities. Since other things are not equal in reality, however, the transnationals have increasingly found themselves considering where and how they will do their R&D. For many of them this is a relatively new situation, but, given expectations in the developing countries, one which will become more common in the near future.

R&D activities of American firms abroad have increased over the past decade. The 1966 foreign R&D expenditures of American companies were estimated to be $537 million.[1] By 1979:

Expenditures of U.S. firms for research and development performed abroad reached $1.5 billion, increasing 41 percent from 1974 to 1977, compared to a 32 percent increase for industrial research and development performed within the United States.[2]

Reprinted, with permission, from *The Columbia Journal of World Business*, "Transnational Corporations: Market Orientations and R&D Abroad" (1980).

Yet it was further noted that "the vast majority of U.S. firms do not conduct any research and development abroad. According to the Census Bureau, only an estimated 15 percent of the major U.S. industrial performers maintain foreign laboratories. These firms, however, account for nearly one-half of total U.S. company-funded R&D expenditures."[3]

In order to formulate effective policies, officials in developing and developed countries, and in the transnational corporations, need to understand why certain firms choose to pursue R&D abroad while others don't, and what the consequences of such activities are. None of this information is available from the statistics.

Recently, several studies of multinational R&D behavior have chronicled the experiences of transnational firms performing R&D abroad.[4] While these case studies improve our understanding of this phenomenon by supplying more information, they tend to lack a framework enabling them to go beyond mere data collection to a fuller understanding of the dynamics involved in the foreign R&D location decision. On the basis of a substantial amount of interviewing among transnational corporations, we believe that a rather simple taxonomy based upon market orientations can be quite useful in explaining the decision to do R&D abroad.

MARKET ORIENTATIONS

The market orientation of a transnational corporation refers to the market it is primarily interested in serving. There are three possible primary market orientations: home market, host market, and world market. While it is possible for a firm to appear to have several market orientations, they are often mutually exclusive for a given product line.

HOME MARKET FIRMS

"Home market" firms are primarily concerned with investing abroad for the purpose of serving their domestic market through imports of materials and components. It is unusual for them to have international R&D operations. To the extent that such firms do R&D abroad, it usually is in support of their domestic market objectives. Typical firms of this type are the extractive industries and offshore component assemblers taking advantage of resource availability or low-wage labor in foreign locations to improve their ability to compete domestically. These firms can be expected to have few durable foreign scientific and technical commitments, a highly ethnocentric managerial style, low external orientation on the part of management, and an organizational structure that is largely unaffected by the firm's foreign operations. The products of these firms tend to be highly standardized, often because of their commodity nature, needing no diversified R&D effort.

HOST MARKET FIRMS

Foreign affiliates of "host market" firms are oriented to the markets of the place where they are located. Included among these firms are industries spanning a range of technical sophistication from chemicals and pharmaceuticals, to food and tobacco, to services. The products of the firms in this category typically exhibit a high degree of standardization within a market but not necessarily between markets. The management style of these firms can be characterized as polycentric, since a relatively low level of control is exerted by corporate headquarters over a decentralized organizational structure. Their need for R&D abroad is dictated by the diversity of market demands on their products.

WORLD MARKET FIRMS

"World market" firms are those whose foreign affiliates are integrated to serve a standardized international market. These firms are typically organized to achieve economies of scale based upon high technology and a high degree of worldwide product standardization, and guided by a geocentric management style and a highly centralized corporate structure. They also have diverse R&D needs reflecting the range of markets they serve and the sources of ideas they must monitor.

THE SAMPLE STUDIED

The utility of these market orientations in explaining foreign R&D behavior among transnational corporations was demonstrated in a study of 35 American and 18 European transnational corporations, undertaken during 1978. The purpose of the study was to determine: what type of R&D is being performed abroad by transnational corporations; how they have come to select their foreign sites; how they manage their foreign R&D activities; what sort of collaborative R&D activities they are engaged in; and the nature of their relationship with host-country governments.[5]

Data collection for the study consisted of structured interviews conducted with top R&D executives in each firm. The average interview lasted approximately two and one-half hours, ranging from one hour in the few firms with little foreign R&D experience to a full day with those with extensive experience. Most of the firms interviewed were chosen because of their foreign R&D experience.

FOREIGN R&D ACTIVITIES OF THE FIRMS STUDIED

Although the firms were selected because of their foreign R&D experiences, the volume of activity discovered was surprising. Among the 31 American transnationals reporting foreign R&D activities, 106 active foreign R&D groups were identified. Furthermore, the European transnationals appeared even more active, with the 18 firms interviewed reporting 100 distinct foreign R&D activities. While most of these foreign activities were smaller in size and more restricted in scope than the R&D activities pursued at home, they were distinctly involved with R&D and were not technical services or quality control.

The firms included in this study were typically large firms (*Fortune 500* members) whose relatively strong commitment to R&D was evidenced by their membership in the Industrial Research Institute in the U.S. or the European Industrial Research Managers Association. Although they exhibited significant foreign R&D activities, their international manufacturing and marketing operations were far more numerous and dispersed than their R&D activities. Although the firms we shall describe are clearly among the largest in the world in terms of both sales and geographic spread, they are representative of firms pursuing R&D activities in foreign locations, since such activities, by their very nature, are the domain of large multinational organizations.

The large majority of the foreign R&D activities identified among the American transnational corporations belonged to firms with a "host market" orientation (96 out of the 106 foreign R&D activities identified, or 91 percent). While this reflects, to some extent, the preponderance of "host market" firms in the sample, 23 of the 34 American firms (68 percent) had "host market" orientations; it thus goes beyond a simple proportional relationship. The "host market" companies averaged more than four foreign R&D activities per firm, compared with less than two among the four American "world market" companies, and slightly less than one-half of a foreign R&D activity for each of the seven American "home market" companies (Table 1). All of the European firms, but one, had "host market" orientations. Thus, a comparison of their propensity to pursue R&D abroad cannot be made with their counterparts, who favor other market orientations. However, when the European R&D activities are considered along with those of the American firms, the combined 38 "host market" firms account for 184 foreign R&D activities, or 89 percent of those identified.

Among the American transnational corporations it was possible to discern the nature of the R&D mission assigned to most of the foreign R&D activities. Thirty of the 106 foreign R&D activities (28 percent) had missions which included new product research, and of these 30 facilities, 25 belonged to "host market" firms and five belonged to "world market" companies (Table 2). Three of the five foreign laboratories of American corporations dedicated to exploratory research belonged to "world market" firms.

Table 1: Foreign R&D Activities of Transnational Corporations

	American firms	
Market orientation	Number of firms	Number of foreign R&D activities
Home market	7	3
Host market	23	96
World market	4	7
Not included	1	—
	European firms	
Home market	0	0
Host market	15	88
World market	1	12
Not included	2	—

Table 2: Inclusion of New Product: Research Responsibilities in the Missions of Foreign Laboratories (American Firms Only)

Market orientation	Number of foreign laboratories with a new product research mission	Percentage of foreign laboratories with a new product research mission
World market	5	71%
Host market	25	26%
Home market	0	0%

LOCATION OF FOREIGN R&D ACTIVITIES

Over thirty different countries were identified in our interviews as hosting the foreign R&D activities of the firms in the sample. Both American and European firms indicated that their foreign R&D activities were predominantly located in developed countries, such as the U.S., France, the U.K., Japan, Canada, Australia, and Germany, and in advanced developing countries, such as Mexico, Brazil, and India (Table 3).

The "host market" firms appeared most likely to establish R&D activities in developing countries.

Table 3: Most Popular Sites for Foreign R&D Activities

American firms		European firms	
U.K.	(11)	U.S.	(14)
Australia	(8)	France	(10)
Canada	(8)	Germany	(9)
Japan	(8)	India	(6)
France	(7)	Brazil	(5)
Germany	(6)	U.K.	(5)
Mexico	(6)		
Brazil	(5)		

NOTE: Numbers in parentheses refer to the number of corporations reporting an R&D presence in a particular country.

As it was important to them to get as close to the markets they were serving as possible, they would favorably consider developing country locations when necessary, if the market was an attractive one and if the R&D group could be supported both financially and technically.

THE MOTIVATION TO DO R&D ABROAD

The propensity of various firms to do R&D in the developing countries highlights the topic of motivation to do R&D abroad. "Home market" firms typically have little or no sales in foreign markets. When they do sell to foreign customers, they view it as a direct extension of their domestic business, not requiring any further R&D beyond that which has already been performed for the original (domestic) market. Because of their extractive operations, and their employment of low-wage workers for assembly operations, "home market" firms tend to have high exposure in the developing world. They have not, however, located much R&D activity in these countries because they typically do not refine raw materials or sell components or finished products in these markets. Accordingly, in those few instances when "home market" companies did consider doing R&D abroad they were most interested in being close to their foreign operations in order to provide technical support.

Firms involved in the international marketing of goods and services designed to satisfy local styles and tastes have a more compelling reason to do R&D abroad. These firms need to be as close to their markets as possible. Illustrative of such motivation is the agricultural chemical firm that needs to test its products in the markets they are intended for and, hence, has facilities in South America to treat South American pest problems, facilities in the Far East to address problems of tropical climates, and facilities in the Philippines to provide market conditions indicative of Japan. Similarly, all of the American pharmaceutical firms interviewed had European formulation laboratories as a result of European preferences for drug administration practices which differ from those in the U.S.

"Host market" firms also tend to endorse the proposition that their foreign affiliates often serve distinctive markets and, as such, are autonomous business entities requiring R&D of their own. Rosemarie Van Rumker's experience with Chemagro Corporation explains just such a philosophy:

Attempts to establish *direct* links between research in one country and technology and the market place in another country have largely been unsuccessful. In my experience, the barriers of distance and language can be overcome reasonably well by scientists working within the same discipline, but scientists in one country are not good at answering the specific market needs of another country. . . .

We believe that the best way to overcome this problem is to have subsidiaries in important markets away from the parent company develop their own complete R&D organizations, to enable them to take full and direct advantage of the opportunities peculiar to their environment, and to be full-fledged practicing members of the scientific and technological community in their country.[6]

While all of the firms interviewed expressed an interest in enhancing their relationship with host-country governments, the "host market" firms, with their national market focus, were particularly sensitive to the importance of such relationships. In a number of cases, this sensitivity resulted in the establishment of foreign R&D activities, some of which have become particularly productive.

The "world market" firms are concerned with the availability abroad of specific types of skills in particular technical areas. This, of course, is in keeping with their propensity to assign new product development responsibility to foreign R&D groups. More than one of the foreign R&D laboratories of the "world market" firms was characterized as having achieved a level of competence in a technical area which far surpassed the capabilities of other research groups in the corporation. Accordingly, "world market" firms typically establish their R&D abroad without regard for the location of their existing international manufacturing and marketing operations. They are much more attracted to the concentration of knowledge and talent than to market size in a foreign country.

A summary of the important criteria for considering or not considering overseas R&D locations by firms in the various market orientation categories is presented in Table 4.

THE CRITICAL MASS OF FOREIGN R&D GROUPS

As Table 4 reveals, one of the principal deterrents to the performance of R&D abroad by transnational firms is their perception that they will be unable to assemble an R&D group large enough and diverse enough to be productive. While the size of an R&D group is a function of many variables, there is substantial agreement within the R&D community that a "critical mass" of R&D professionals must be reached if a laboratory is to be a worthwhile investment. This "critical mass" is the size necessary to ensure rich communications both within the group and between the group and its environment, to allow the degree of scientific and technical interaction among the group's personnel necessary to fulfill its mission, and to acquire whatever instrumentation and organization are necessary for acceptable performance. There is considerable variation in the estimates of "critical mass" for specific situations, but in general, R&D laboratories in industries serving consumer markets (i.e., "host market" firms) require a smaller R&D staff to reach "critical mass" than do laboratories in science-based industries. Furthermore, R&D groups in consumer-oriented industries require less sophisticated personnel and less variety in personnel specialization than do R&D groups in science-based industries. These observations suggest that "host mar-

Table 4: Important Criteria for Considering or Not Considering Overseas R&D Locations.

	Home market firms	Host market firms	Worldwide market firms
Important criteria for considering an overseas R&D location	1. Proximity to operations 2. Availability of universities	1. Proximity to markets 2. Concept of overseas operations as full-scale business entities	1. Availability of pockets of skills in particular technical areas 2. Access to foreign scientific and technical communities 3. Availability of adequate infrastructure and universities
Important criteria for not considering overseas R&D locations	1. Products sold in the developing countries are not sophisticated 2. Lack of qualified scientists and engineers 3. Economics of centralized R&D	1. Increasing costs of doing R&D overseas 2. Economics of centralized R&D	1. Economics of centralized R&D 2. Difficulties in assembling R&D teams

ket" firms are more likely than their counterparts to be in a position to establish R&D in a developing country.

THE ESTABLISHMENT OF R&D ABROAD

There are several ways in which a transnational corporation can establish R&D activities abroad: it can allow R&D to evolve from technical support activities for marketing or manufacturing it; it can directly establish R&D activities abroad with the intention of doing R&D right

Table 5: Methods of Establishing Foreign R&D Activities

Market Orientation	Evolution from Technical Service	Direct Placement	Acquisition
"Home market"	2	0	0
"Host market"	33	11	18
"World market"	2	5	0

NOTE: The data in this table represent only those instances where the means of establishing the foreign laboratory could be ascertained. All data in this table comes from American corporations.

from the start; it can acquire some other corporation's R&D activities; it can enter into some form of collaborative R&D arrangement with another partner. Just as market orientation appears to affect the location and mission of foreign R&D activities, it influences the means of establishing these activities.

In 71 of the foreign R&D activities of American firms it was possible to ascertain the means of establishment. In approximately one-half of these cases an evolutionary pattern where R&D originated from technical services was evident. Nearly all of these cases were found among "host market" firms and two of the three foreign "home market" laboratories were also in this group. In approximately 28 percent of the cases direct placement was the means of establishment and, while most of these were attributable to "host market" firms, more than 70 percent of the foreign laboratories of "world market" firms were established in this manner. Almost 25 percent of the laboratories were established through acquisition, all of them being by "host market" companies (Table 5).

The data collected on laboratory establishment appears to agree quite well with the findings reported earlier. "Home market" firms are not interested in R&D abroad and so what foreign R&D of theirs does exist is the result of an evolution of capabilities and missions among their technical support activities. Conversely, "world market" firms are interested in pursuing R&D abroad if they can gain access to particular technological skills or communities. Accordingly, they tend to rely more upon direct placement of their foreign R&D activities, as their other foreign commercial operations are not necessarily related to their R&D activities. "Host market" firms need to be close to the markets they serve and they will utilize a variety of methods to get there.

COLLABORATIVE R&D ARRANGEMENTS

At least 28 specific manufacturing joint ventures between parent companies of different nationalities, which required R&D support in some form, were reported in the interviews. All but four of these belonged to "host market" companies. Our interviews indicated quite clearly that the key determinant of *active* R&D participation by a transnational firm in such a venture is the ownership position it commands. Foreign joint ventures will bring forth *new* R&D only when the transnational firm can maintain control over that R&D, namely, when it possesses a majority interest in the joint venture.

HOST-GOVERNMENT RELATIONS

As noted earlier, although all firms professed an interest in maintaining good relationships with host-country governments, "host market" firms appeared particularly sensitive to pressure from their hosts. During our interviews, fourteen American and five European firms indicated having received some form of pressure from host-country governments hoping to influence their foreign R&D location decisions. Sixteen of these firms had "host market" orientations. Furthermore, 19 foreign R&D laboratories were identified as having their origins in host-government pressure, three of these being joint ventures, and in four other cases the pressure resulted in the acquisition of R&D results without a laboratory. The countries most active in attempting to influence transnational corporations were Brazil, France, India, and Japan.

CONCLUSIONS

The data presented in this study argue strongly for the usefulness of a simple taxonomy of transnational corporations, based upon market-orientations. The location and operations of foreign R&D laboratories of transnational corporations can be explained by referring to the market orientations of the firms in question.

The data presented indicated that a considerable amount of R&D is presently being performed abroad by both American and European transnational corporations. While most of this R&D is located in developed countries, there is diversity among the locations selected. This diversity, in part, reflects the varying market orientations of the firms. Market orientation also appears to be an important determinant of the means by which a transnational corporation establishes R&D activities abroad.

The evidence presented suggests that transnational corporations with "host market" orientations are generally most likely to pursue R&D abroad, particularly when developing countries are at issue. They are, however, less likely than their "world market" counterparts to delegate new product research responsibilities to their foreign laboratories, and they also rely heavily upon evolution from technical services as a means of establishing foreign R&D groups.

REFERENCES

1. D. Creamer, *Overseas Research and Development by United States Multinationals*, 1966-1975, New York, The Conference Board, 1976, pp. 3-4.
2. "U.S. Industrial R&D Spending Abroad," Industry Studies Group, Division of Science Studies, U.S. National Science Foundation, *Review of Data on Science Resources*, NSF 79-304, No. 33, April 1979, p. 1.
3. *Ibid*, p. 3.
4. W. T. Hanson, "Multinational R&D in Practice: Eastman Kodak Corporation," *Research management*, Jan. 1971, 47-50; M. Papo, "How to Establish and Operate a Multinational Lab," *Research Management*, Jan. 1971, 12-19; R. Van. Rumker, "Multinational R&D in Practice: Chemagro Corporation," *Research Management*, Jan. 1971, 50-54; R. C. Ronstadt, "International R&D: The Establishment and Evolution of Research and Development Abroad by Seven U.S. Multinationals," *Journal of International Business Studies*, 9, 1978, 7-24.
5. For a more complete report on this study the reader is advised to see: J. N. Behrman and W. A. Fischer, *Overseas R&D Activities of Transnational Corporations*, Cambridge, Mass.; Oelgeschlager, Gunn & Hain, 1980.
6. Van Rumker, *op. cit.*, p. 54. Emphasis added.

Chapter Eight:
MNC/Host-Government Relations

WITH THE INCREASING internationalization of business enter-prises, the geographic base of their operations has widened con-siderably. Concomitant with this growth of multinational operations, each foreign nation-state has its own nationalistic spirit and set of national goals that are often directly opposite of other nation-states or the large multinational corporations. Because a corporation's goals may well differ from those of a nation-state or host government, some conflict is inevitable.

Host governments have felt the need to control the flow of goods and funds across national boundaries. Such controls include: re-quiring the use of local personnel; requiring the use of local component parts; restricting the transfer of funds; tariffs and taxes; and so forth. In extreme cases, when the political philosophy of the host govern-ment and the government of the parent company are opposed, serious conflict has resulted. Cuba and Iran are poignant examples of such conflicts.

The importance of the foreign investment and the host govern-ment's dependence on the project may be crucial variables that set the tone for the MNE's relations with the host government. In particu-lar, technology transfer and the requirements for vitally-needed foreign exchange (hard currency) and jobs for workers may influence the inter-action between a foreign government and a multinational corporation.

In the remainder of this century, much of the focus and expansion by multinational corporations will be on the emerging newly-industrialized nations of the world, particularly in the Pacific Rim and Latin America, with emphasis on economic development. However, if one looks at studies on economic development, developing nations all too often are lumped together under a single classification. Although they do indeed have common problems, these countries cannot and should not be so easily categorized. Not only does per capita income vary greatly, but there is a wide range of differences in all of the things that are essential to the development process: political philosophy, sta-bility of the economy, natural resources, educational levels, demo-graphic distribution, culture, climate, and institutions—each of which has an impact on how these nations can and should develop.

As a consequence, multinational corporations will be working with host governments in the planning process and, more than ever, will be attempting to demonstrate the contribution that their firm(s) will make to the overall growth and development of the respective economy. The relationships developed, and the nature of the firm's operations within each economy, will differ depending upon the environment of the economy. Multinational corporations must balance initiative and entrepreneurship, their greatest assets, with the controls, policies and goals that national governments at home and abroad deem essential for their own political and economic interest. Executives of these corporations must be concerned not only whether their firms are productive, efficient and profitable in an economic sense, but whether they are socially constructive and fulfilling a need for the various societies in which they function, including the impact that they will have on each nation's goals, devleopment objectives, and balance of payments.

23
Evaluating Foreign Investment

Dennis J. Encarnation
and Louis T. Wells, Jr.

When multinationals locate their investments in developing countries, their investment decisions are affected by public policies and strategies for economic development. This chapter discusses how governments of these countries organize their negotiations with foreign investors and screen foreign investment proposals.

FEW DEVELOPING COUNTRIES permit multinational enterprises to locate investment inside their borders unencumbered by public policies and government agencies designed to screen would-be investors. While the effectiveness of specific policies in shaping investment decisions is hotly debated,[1] few doubt that the ways governments organize for negotiation with mutlinationals is critical to that final decision.[2] Recognizing this, government officials, international organizations, academic researchers, and consultants galore have made innumerable proposals concerning how governments should organize themselves to negotiate with foreign investors.[3] The centralization of negotiation and decision making is the theme common to most such recommendations. Yet the conventional advice, regardless of the source, has frequently gone unimplemented or, when implemented, has turned out to lead to results quite different from those intended. The patterns of variation are not random; as we shall see below, they are the result of identifiable variables. A country's general strategy for economic development is one of these variables.

Prior to addressing how their country should organize to screen foreign investment proposals, policymakers must address why negotia-

This article will be published in *Investing in Development: New Roles for Private Capital*, by Theodore H. Moran, for the Overseas Development Council, Transaction Books, 1986.

tions with foreign investors are necessary at all. Often the answer lies in the country's development strategy. Some strategies are quite hostile to foreign investment; others lead governments to attract multinationals. Most developing countries vacillate in their attitudes over time and across industries. As a result, how they organize to screen and negotiate with foreign investors also varies. And so too does the likelihood of attracting foreign investment beneficial to economic development.

Policymakers' attitudes toward foreign investment, and the policies and structures that these attitudes spawn, are typically based on implicit assumptions about the effects of foreign investment on economic development. These assumptions, in turn, are usually based on a great deal of faith. Less frequently, they have been informed by a development literature that offers little unambiguous guidance for policymakers. To date, the empirical evidence for determining the impact of foreign investment on economic development remains rather weak. What little is known supports the implicit assumptions of government policymakers: the portfolio of would-be investments can best be characterized as a mixed bag in the prevailing policy environment. That is, in countries with limited domestic markets, high protection, and subsidized inputs, the incidence of economically harmful proposals from prospective investors is likely to be high—comprising a sizeable minority of import-substituting projects. For policymakers in many developing countries this means that current development policy makes the screening of foreign investment essential.

WHY SCREEN FOREIGN INVESTMENT

In the development literature, the multinational enterprise has been attacked by some as a hindrance to development, while it has been praised by others as an important engine to pull countries out of their poverty.[4] Often that debate has been waged at a pedantic level by both supporters and detractors of multinationals; others also unencumbered by rigorous empirical research have been equally emotional if less pedantic.[5]

Among empirical studies, this debate has continued at several levels of analysis. Cross-national studies of the world capitalist system, for example, often conclude that foreign investment has a deleterious effect on the economic development of semi-industrialized countries; the principal beneficiaries of that system are the United States and other countries that are the primary sources of investment outflows.[6] With equal frequency, cross-national studies employing quantitative data find that national income is positively correlated with inflows of foreign investment—either foreign investment is a cause of better performance, or foreign investors are attracted to better performing countries.[7]

Equally cross-national but more narrowly defined, numerous studies have examined the impact of foreign investment on certain aspects of development. These studies have attempted to weigh data, for example, on the propensity of foreign firms to export, to use imported technology and other inputs, to invest in local R&D, to hire local workers, to concentrate markets, and to collude with local producers.[8] This research has both sharpened and intensified the debate.

Focusing on many of the same indicators but less global in scope, case studies of national economies have similarly offered competing perspectives on the development effects of foreign investment. And again, some conclude that development is ultimately hindered by that dependence on foreign investment,[9] while others conclude that development will be bolstered by that same interdependence.[10]

Finally, interpretative works that have drawn on the full range of empirical studies have subjected their conclusions to numerous qualifications.[11] Indeed, one of the principal problems with the empirical studies cited above has been their reliance on bits and pieces of largely idiosyncratic data that could be combined only with considerable faith into a broad judgment. Given their multifarious origins, these earlier studies have not attempted to capture in a single, consistent set of measures the economic impacts of foreign-owned projects.

This weakness has been partially overcome in two studies of particular usefulness to policymakers, studies that utilized variations of social cost-benefit analysis to measure the overall effect of foreign investment on economic development. One of these studies was done for UNCTAD in the early 1970s by Lall and Streeten, two critics of the role of multinationals in development.[12] At roughly the same time, Grant Reuber completed another study under the auspices of OECD.[13] Although the ideological predispositions of the two studies differed, as did their methodologies and data, the results of the two were surprisingly consistent: both the UNCTAD and OECD studies concluded that upwards of 30 percent of proposed import-substituting projects were harmful for the domestic economy. Understanding the reasons for this conclusion is critical to policy makers charged with screening foreign investment proposals.

THE UNCTAD AND OECD STUDIES

Lall and Streeten examined 133 foreign-owned and locally-owned projects operating in six countries. For 88 of these firms they were able to calculate national income effects, using a social cost-benefit methodology. For two-thirds of these 88 firms, the effect of foreign investment on national income was positive; for the other one-third, negative. This pattern did not vary by the foreign or domestic ownership of the project; that is, Lall and Streeten found no statistically significant differences between the effects of locally-owned projects on the economy and those of foreign-owned projects.

Although the lack of a significant difference between foreign and domestic projects might at first seem surprising, it is easily understood when one considers the principal reason that explained the private profitability of socially unattractive projects. High rates of protection from import competition facilitating high private but not social rates of return regardless of whether the investor was foreign or local. Indeed, the competitiveness of sales had the greatest impact on Lall and Streeten's calculation of social rates of return.[14]

Reuber's OECD study arrived at similar conclusions, but employed a different methodology and database from those used by Lall and Streeten. Reuber examined 45 foreign-owned projects from a sample that covered 30 host countries. Rather than utilize a conventional social cost-benefit model to evaluate the impact of each project on generating national income, Reuber compared (among other calculations) the production costs of the subsidiaries to the production costs of their parent operations. The results were a crude approximation of social cost-benefit calculations that rely on market price assumptions.[15] Using this simpler method, Reuber concluded that upwards of one-quarter of the subsidiaries had production costs that were equal to or lower than the production costs of the parent operations; the remainder—nearly three-quarters of the 45 subsidiaries he examined—had higher production costs.

Reuber subsequently separated projects according to whether their output was destined largely for the domestic, host market or for export. For the 14 export projects he identified, the aforementioned relationship reversed: that is, over three-quarters of these 14 subsidiaries had production costs that were equal to or lower than the production costs of the parent operations; less than one-quarter had higher costs. As for the 31 projects that were not export-oriented, Reuber calculated that the host country could have imported equivalent products at a 30 percent savings over local production. In other words, Reuber found that export-oriented projects had lower production costs and, by inference, higher social profitability than the average projects that were import-substituting. Again, like Lall and Streeten, Reuber concluded that the competitiveness of sales had a major impact on production costs. For import-substituting projects, protection from import competition put little pressure on managers to cut production costs; the absence of such protection in export markets brought a subsidiary's production costs more in line with its parent's.

In conclusion, for both the UNCTAD and OECD studies, government policies shaping the market for a project's output were important predictors of the social profitability of that project. And among these policies, tariffs figured prominently. But no mention was paid to other policies shaping the input markets of these projects. This would await later research, research that would build on these two studies.

NEW DATA, OLD CONCLUSIONS

METHODOLOGY

A more recent study conducted by the present authors attempted to improve on the data and methodology employed in the pioneering work commissioned by UNCTAD and OECD. Like Lall and Streeten, the new study employed a more standard social cost-benefit analysis, but this time one modeled on the work of Roemer and Stern.[16] We defined the benefits of a proposed project to be its contributuion to national income— the value of goods and services produced by that project for domestic consumption or investment, plus additional earnings generated from exports. In our calculation of the domestic value of goods and services subsequently consumed or invested, we substituted world market prices for the sales prices assumed by the prospective investors. As for export sales, we assumed that they were consummated at world market prices.

While the benefits of the proposed project show up in increased consumption, investment, and exports, the costs to the national economy consist of the resources used in the project. These include domestic labor, local capital, locally purchased goods and services, plus a range of foreign exchange costs—imported raw materials, components, and machinery as well as the foreign share of dividends, royalties, interest, debt repayment, and technology fees. Where there were reasons to suspect that market prices underestimated or overestimated the value to the economy of local resources used by the project, we substituted shadow prices for the prices reported by the would-be investor. In this way our study departed from the UNCTAD and OECD studies. The shadow prices were intended to reflect the opportunity cost of the resources to the national economy. Thus, if energy could be exported at a price greater than the project paid given government price policies, the shadow price would be above the market price. If labor would be unemployed in the absence of the project, its shadow price would be lower than its market price. In various calculations, we used shadow prices for labor, energy, foreign exchange, and domestic capital.

We did not attempt, however, to estimate any impact a project might have on other concerns of a would-be host country, aside from the project's direct contribution to the country's national product. For example, we did not capture at all any economic effects external to the project itself. These might include a range of costs to society, including pollution from a manufacturing plant, or investment by local producers idled by fear of foreign competition. These external economic effects may also include benefits for the economy, including the training of workers and managers who leave these projects and apply their new-found skills elsewhere. We also did not capture a wide range of social effects—effects on local consumption, income distribution, and defense procurement, to mention just a few. These and other effects not captured by our indicators could make some seemingly attractive projects unattractive. And some projects that do not contribute directly to national product might become attractive if these other criteria are taken into account.

While recognizing the potential importance of these other criteria, we suspect that the direct positive impact on the national product is the contribution most sought by countries when they accept foreign investment. Of course, this appraisal of a project's benefits should take into account the alternative uses of domestic resources employed directly by the project. Below, we assume that domestic capital if employed alternatively would yield at least a 10 percent return to society, and that future benefits should be discounted at the same rate. Given this criterion, if the social rate of return of the project is less than 10 percent, the host country's screening board should reject the project in the belief that a better, alternative use can be made of local project inputs.

As we shall see below, few projects yielded rates of return close to this cutoff point. The vast majority yielded either very positive or very negative returns. Therefore, we doubt that project externalities and other criteria for project evaluation noted above would result in dramatic shifts in our overall evaluation of beneficial and costly projects, even though these other criteria may alter the rank ordering of projects.

DATA

An added benefit of our methodology was the relative ease of gathering requisite data from local sources. Our calculation of shadow prices, for example, reflected the informed opinion of local analysts. We collected all other data from application forms submitted by prospective foreign investors to the investment screening board of a large developing country. The sample of 50 foreign manufacturing firms was drawn from the pool of all foreign investment proposals completed and submitted to that board during a recent five-year period. These applications generally contained ten-year forecasts of income statements and balance sheets for the proposed project. We extended the forecasts to twenty years using common financial techniques. Thirty-one of the would-be investors sought to supply the domestic market of the country, where they invested in industries typically protected by the government against import competition. In these cases, the investment screening board asked prospective investors to estimate the costs of imports equivalent to their proposed production. The remaining fourteen projects proposed to sell most of their output to export markets.

Since private investors submitted the data for projects not yet in existence, we had no way to verify independently the accuracy of these data. Some investors may have submitted biased figures that made their projects look better than the actual results might indicate. The investor, for example, may have understated the project's capital requirements or overstated the value of foreign exchange saved through the local manufacture of goods previously imported. If so, the results summarized below underestimate the social costs of these projects. The reporting bias could also push in the opposite direction given the peculiarities of local government policies. The host country's investment board granted exemptions from import duty on capital equipment according to a list of equipment needs submitted by the investor; fearing that the total list would not be approved or seeking profits from duty-free imports, the investor might hedge and overstate the project's capital requirements. Even if the board approved the entire sum, the items subsequently imported duty-free could be sold at a premium in the local economy. Undoubtedly, both sets of biases existed, but there was little indication that they were systematic or recurrent. Indeed, each of the checks employed could discern no such pattern. [17]

FINDINGS

Like Reuber and Lall and Streeten before us, we found that a majority (ranging from 55 percent to 75 percent depending on our assumptions) of the projects increased the hosts country's national income. (See Table 1.) And like our predecessors, we also found that a sizeable minority of investments proposed by foreigners would have had a deleterious effect on that country's national product if they were accepted. That is, anywhere from 25 percent to 45 percent of the would-be projects proposed to use resources in ways that yielded less goods and services for the host country than those resources cost the country. This sizeable minority was therefore unattractive to the host country even though the projects were profitable to private investors.

According to Table 1, the proportion of unattractive projects increased if the project was a sizeable consumer of government-subsidized energy, or if the project was a significant user of officially overvalued (our assumption) foreign exchange. As noted above, such large foreign exchange costs may reflect the prices of imported raw materials, components, and machinery, as well as the foreign share and timing of dividends, royalties, interest, debt repayments, and technology fees. As for the proportion of attractive projects, only small increases were recorded when we assumed that 30 percent of the wage bill went to workers who otherwise would have been un- or underemployed in the absence of the project. Similarly, small shifts occurred when social rates of return for energy costs and foreign exchange were substituted for market rates.

Differences between social profitability and private profitability, however, were not limited to different views of the costs of energy, raw materials, labor, and other inputs. Much more important were the results of government policies affecting prices in output markets. As noted above, the competitiveness of sales had the greatest impact on Lall and Streeten's calculation of social rates of return; the greater the protection from import competition, the lower the social rate of return. Reinforcing this conclusion, Reuber found that export-oriented projects had lower average production costs and, by inference, higher social rates of return than did import-substituting projects protected by tariffs.

Both sets of conclusions find support in Table 2. As one moves from industries with low rates of protection to those with higher rates of protection, the proportion of would-be projects deleterious to the host economy correspondingly increased; indeed, the rank-order correlation was perfect. Investors in protected industries can build plants that do not contribute (net) to the local economy, but which do generate adequate private rates of return to make them attractive to the firm. Conversely, where protection was low, most projects were beneficial to the economy

Table 1:
Social Cost-Benefit Analysis

Assumptions of the Model	Distribution of 50 Projects by Social Rate of Return		
	Less Than 10%		10% or Greater
	Total	Of Which, % Negative	Total
No Tariff on Foreign Inputs[a]			
1. Market Prices Reported by Investor[b]	40%	(85%)	60%
2. Market Prices Except Labor[c]	36%	(94%)	64%
3. Market Prices Except Energy[d]	44%	(91%)	56%
4. Market Prices Except Labor, Energy, and Foreign Exchange Costs[c,d,e]	32%	(81%)	68%
20% Tariff on Foreign Inputs[f]			
5. Market Prices Reported by Investor[b]	28%	(100%)	72%
6. Market Prices Except Labor, Energy, and Foreign Exchange Costs[c,d,e]	26%	(85%)	74%

[a]Assumes that prices for imported inputs as reported by the investor did not include a hypothetical 20% duty imposed by government.
[b]Assumes that prices paid by the investor for all inputs reflected the value of the input to the economy; that is, market prices equal shadow prices.
[c]Assumes that the shadow price of labor was 70% of its market price; that is, some 30% of the project's wage bill went to workers who would be un- or underemployed in the project's absence; for all other inputs, market prices equal shadow prices.
[d]Assumes that the shadow price of energy was twice its market price; that is, energy utilized by the project could be sold on world markets at a price 100% higher than its domestic price; for all other inputs, market prices equal shadow prices.
[e]Assumes that the shadow foreign exchange rate relative to the U.S. dollar was 120% of the official rate; that is, the effective foreign exchange cost of the project was greater than reported because the host country's currency relative to the dollar was overvalued by 20%; for all other inputs, market prices equal shadow prices.
[f]Assumes that prices for imported inputs as reported by the investor included a 20% duty; the recalculated price of imported inputs equals 80% of the reported price.

as well as to the investor. The extreme case was made up of export projects; all eight firms here had to compete without any protection on the world market, and all eight were beneficial to the economy.

POLICY IMPLICATIONS

The implications of these findings for government policymakers are significant. The rewards for eliminating bad projects appear to be quite

Table 2:
Protectionism and Social Profitability

Industry	Tariff Rate on Competing Imports		Proportion of Projects Whose Social Rate of Return was Less than 10%[c]
	Nominal[a]	Effective[b]	
Export-Oriented[d]	0%	0% or Less	0%
Import-Substituting, of Which:[e]			
Chemicals[f]	about 10%	26%	30%
Pharmaceuticals	20-25%	150%	33%
Textiles	50-100%	191%	50%
Autos	about 100%	717%	70%

[a]Derived from government sources.
[b]Derived from a World Bank report on effective protection in the country.
[c]Assumes that prices paid by the investor for all inputs reflected the value of the input to the economy; that is, market prices equal shadow prices. Also assumes that prices for imported inputs included a 20% duty; the recalculated price of imported inputs equals 80% of the reported price.
[d]Includes all projects that export a majority of their output.
[e]Includes industries with three or more projects selling the majority of their output in the domestic market.
[f]Excluding pharmaceuticals.

large: of the projects that were unattractive when measured by their contribution to national product, most yielded negative returns to the economy on the resources that they used.

The elimination of these "bad" projects could be achieved in either of two ways. First, policies can be changed so that the price signals given the investor for project inputs and outputs match their relevant social costs. Alternatively, the host country can administratively screen out or reshape through negotiations the projects that are likely to be harmful to the economy.

The most important step to bring market prices in line with social prices would be for the country to lower its effective rates of protection. If investors, local or foreign, had to compete with imports, virtually all socially unattractive projects in our sample would also have been unattractive to private investors. Less government protection from imports might be a necessary but not a sufficient step to match private and social returns. The need for further steps would be especially important when the internal prices of labor, energy, foreign exchange, and other inputs depart even more significantly from social values than in the country we studied. In such an instance, major subsidies for energy and other resources would have to be eliminated before investors themselves would reject socially "bad" projects. But the data for the country that we studied strongly suggested that lower protection alone would go a long way toward leading investors to be interested only in socially attractive projects in most developing countries.

Western economists would generally consider the reduction of effective protection, changes in the pricing of domestic resources, and effective domestic competition in both product and resource markets to be the first-best solution to the problem of eliminating unattractive investments. Yet, despite the recommendations of these economists, few countries with high rates of protection are likely to eliminate tariffs and other trade barriers quickly. And few find it politically easy to eliminate generous subsidies. Consequently, policymakers in developing countries are left with admittedly second-best alternatives: administratively screening proposals to eliminate those that are likely to be harmful to the economy, negotiating with other foreign investors to bring social rates of return above a minimum cut-off, and simultaneously promoting those investments with adequate social rates of return.

SCREENING, NEGOTIATING, AND PROMOTING FOREIGN INVESTMENT

While this second-best alternative may be easier to implement than the first, establishing an effective mechanism for screening, negotiating, and promoting foreign investment has, nevertheless, proved exceedingly difficult. The task poses frustrating choices for policymakers in host countries.

First, policymakers must decide how centralized to make the negotiating process. There are a number of possibilities, and each has its advantages and disadvantages. Some government organizations, for example, that might be particularly effective in negotiating with investors for the most favorable terms and in screening unattractive proposals are likely to discourage would-be investors. Few countries have established a single organization that was effective both in screening out "bad" proposals and in promoting foreign investment.

In a separate study of the organizations used by government to evaluate proposals, negotiate with foreigners, and promote investment, we found considerable variation across countries, across industries, and over time in the organizational choices of governments.[18] The same country was likely to use different approaches for different industries at any one time; its approach for the same industry might well change over time; and different countries may adopt similar approaches to deal with investors in the same industries. These patterns of choice were not random, but were influenced primarily by three identifiable variables. The choices reflected a country's general development strategy and the role of foreign investment in that strategy; the salience of a particular industry in the development plans of that country; and the degree of competition that the country faced in attracting particular kinds of investors.

THE CHOICES

In our in-depth study of four countries (plus a quick review of several others), we observed four basic ways of handling the tasks of promoting foreign investment, screening subsequent foreign investment proposals, and negotiating the terms under which projects would be accepted.

The first option, an unusual one for developing countries, was a "policy approach." Countries following this approach did not, in fact, conduct individual negotiations with investors over important issues. Rather, they had determined in advance general policies that specified, at least for the majority of investors, the industries in which they would be accepted or excluded, and the terms under which they could operate. Such policies might be lenient toward foreign investment, excluding few potential projects, or they might be very restrictive, virtually closing the country to foreign investment. Hong Kong and the United States federal government illustrated the first type; Burma was an example of the second.

For those Western economists who prefer "getting the prices right" as their first-best solution, a simplified "policy approach" that reduces government discretion may seem like the best of the second-best, especially if it encourages foreign investment. Among the benefits of non-negotiation is the greater predictability of the outcome for both government and investor compared to the inevitably more ambiguous negotiations associated with selective policies. Consequently, the potential costs for the firm considering entry are likely to be low. But in the presence of price distortions resulting from tariffs, subsidies, and limited competition, a very "open door" policy will result in the entry of those investments identified above that were not socially profitable. Moreover, a government's fear of these social costs may generate simple exclusionary rules that keep out many investments that would be beneficial to the country. Short of adopting simple rules that either promote or discourage investment indiscriminantly, project-by-project screening may be necessary if the host country is to extract all the potential social benefits from each prospective investment.

Once a government adopts public policies that require negotiations with prospective foreign investors, the government's approach to negotiating with these investors is likely to fall on a continuum that has a decentralized approach at one extreme and a centralized one at the other. Under a decentralized regime, a foreign investor typically must conduct a series of difficult negotiations dispersed across several ministries, agencies, and enterprises whose operations and interests would be affected by the investment—for example, the ministries of industry, trade or finance, the central bank, and perhaps a state enterprise in the sector. Virtually all developing countries adopted this approach at some point in their histories, and for many it still continues in some industries. On the other extreme, authority to negotiate with an investor is concentrated in one organization that has the full authority to accept or reject an applicant and to conclude the terms that will govern the investor's sojourn in the country. Along the continuum between centralized and decentralized structures lie various coordinating mechanisms.

ADVANTAGES AND DISADVANTAGES

The extremes of this continuum offer quite different advantages and disadvantages to the host country. (See Table 3.)

A decentralized approach, for example, is attractive for several reasons. First, enterprises can muster the technical expertise necessary to evaluate proposals for a specific industry. Tax expertise is likely to be concentrated in the finance ministry; knowledge of labor laws and issues, in the labor ministry; technical skills for the relevant industry, in the ministry of industries; and so on. Second, these units of government are likely to be the same agencies that will eventually have to administer the terms of any agreements that might be reached. Having these agencies conduct the relevant part of the negotiations is likely to generate terms that can be effectively administered with available resources. Further, if the administrators are the negotiators, there is a reasonable chance for learning from past successes and mistakes. Indeed, when the same people are regularly assigned to foreign investment negotiations, technical skills and in some case longevity of employment enable such specialized units to learn and retain lessons that may enhance the government's negotiating skills in the future.

At the same time, a decentralized approach may cause serious problems. First, the involved agencies and ministries are likely to have little

Table 3:
Strengths and Weaknesses of Patterns and Structures of Decision Making

Patterns and Structures of Decision Making	Strengths/Benefits	Weaknesses/Costs
A. Abstention: no structures or procedures	• Predictability for investors • No administrative costs • Speed of response	• Unrestricted entry: entry of firms inconsistent with national interest • Autarchy: excludes socially beneficial investments
B. Decentralization 1. Government functional agencies 2. State-owned enterprises	• Can muster technical expertise for specific industry • Results in high organizational learning on part of government • Agencies that negotiate often same that implement policies	• Little evaluation of overall net benefits: focus on technical feasibility • Little consideration of larger policy issues • Little consideration of impact of decisions on other investors • Little promotion of national investment opportunities • High negotiating costs to investors • Disjuncture between policy as negotiated and policy as implemented since implementers are multiple
C. Coordination 1. Permanent interagency board 2. Ad hoc interagency committee	• Both: reduce investor's negotiating costs • Both: reduce interministerial conflict • Both: improve monitoring of international environment • Permanent: considers larger policy issues and issues' impact on other investors • Permanent: greater promotion of investment opportunities • Ad hoc: masters industry expertise	• Permanent: little in-depth industry knowledge • Permanent: disjuncture between policy as negotiated and policy as implemented since implementation occurs outside the new structure • Ad hoc: little organizational learning • Ad hoc: little consideration of impact on other investors or larger policy issues • Ad hoc: little promotion of investment opportunities

Table 3:
Strengths and Weaknesses of Patterns and Structures of Decision Making (Continued)

Patterns and Structures of Decision Making	Strengths/Benefits	Weaknesses/Costs
D. Delegation 1. Industry-specific agencies and state-owned enterprises 2. Broadly defined development authorities	• Both: reduce investors negotiation costs • Both: policy negotiated is policy implemented • Both: greater promotion of investment and greater scanning of environment • Both: improved organizational learning • Broad authority: consider larger policy issues and impact on other investors	• Industry agency: larger policy issues and impact on other investors ignored • Broad authority: little in-depth industry knowledge • Broad authority: loss of personnel to industry • Both: ignore interests of other agencies and their constituents

SOURCE: Dennis J. Encarnation and Louis T. Wells, Jr., "Sovereignty en Garde: Negotiating with Foreign Investors," *International Organization* 39 (Winter 1985): 76-77.

technical knowledge or limited experience with the industry or with foreign investors generally. They may insist on performance requirements that repel an otherwise desirable investor, for example, without even caring about or understanding the full implications of their demands. Second, diffuse units operating autonomously also have little ability to evaluate overall net benefits in light of larger policy issues. For example, a ministry of labor is likely to support a project for the employment it generates whatever the cost in terms of foreign exchange or foregone tax revenues. As a consequence, too little or too much may be offered to the potential investor. Moreover, an individual government unit has no incentive or mechanism to consider the wider implications of its actions on potential foreign investors in other industries. As a result, inappropriate precedents may be established.

Finally, a decentralized approach is likely to be costly to the foreign investor. The period of negotiation is likely to be longer and the results unpredictable at the outset. The potential investor with only marginal interests is likely to go elsewhere. In fact, the pool of investors applying to a country with a decentralized process might well be less than for a similar country that is quicker and promises more predictable outcomes for the investor. In the countries that we studied, it was the effect on investors that led governments to abandon the decentralized process for a more centralized approach.

Centralized bodies are of two distinct types, each with its own peculiar benefits and disadvantages. Both have a common objective to reduce the high costs to potential foreign investors otherwise associated with decentralized approaches.

The first type of centralized body can be found in Singapore and a few other countries that have centralized in one autonomous body negotiations with the vast majority of foreign investors. This approach directly addressed the problem of greatest concern to most countries that abandoned a decentralized approach: negotiate quickly and have a predictable pattern of outcomes. It also offers other advantages. An autonomous body that covers a wide range of negotiations can consider the overall impact of a project on the country and it can weigh the total package of incentives and performance requirements to determine what is required to attract a desired investor. Moreover, it is very likely to consider carefully issues of precedent in its negotiations and decisions.

Still, such a centralized body has its problems. It leads to a separation of negotiation from implementation. Implementation usually remains the problem of the relevant technical ministries. The distance between negotiator and administrator can lead to terms that may well be difficult to administer. Moreover, broad autonomous units pose one additional problem. The breadth of the task assigned to such an agency almost assures that it will not have in-depth expertise in industry-specific issues.

To overcome this latter problem, governments have established a second type of centralized body with specialized expertise, a body that covers only a single industry or a single type of investment. For example, all agreements might be negotiated by a particular state enterprise. Or agreements with potential exporters might be the sole responsibility of an export-processing zone authority. Like the autonomous unit with authority for a wide range of industries, this more specialized agency was also likely to conduct quick and reasonably predictable negotiations. But unlike its more broadly-defined counterpart, industry-specific organizations rarely took into account the impacts of their agreements on the other investment negotiations outside of their area of authority. This created problems. State oil companies, for example, were unlikely to worry about the impact that the terms of their petroleum agreements had on discussions with mining or manufacturing firms. Moreover, the single-industry organization was likely to ignore other larger policy issues, including the net national benefit of the investment.

Finally, both types of centralized organizations also imposed a major political cost on the host country. Establishing such organizations required the government to "disenfranchise" agencies which expressed interest in the outcome of negotiations and sought to participate. Centralization meant, for example, that tax matters were decided outside the ministry of finance; foreign exchange issues, outside the central bank; and so on. It was this reason that made broad-based, autonomous agencies for foreign investment so unusual. Governments were not willing to incur the political costs of centralization without strong reason.

Unwilling to incur the political costs associated with the imposition of centralized structures, and displeased with the operation of decentralized approaches, many countries have tried to combine some of the advantages of each. In particular, they have attempted to coordinate the activities of various government agencies involved earlier in a decentralized negotiation process. They do this without going to the extremes of centralization.

This intermediate step of coordinating government screening and negotiation also took at least two forms. Most common was the investment coordinating board, which was run jointly by a number of ministries whose interests were typically affected by foreign investment. Like other organizational responses to foreign investment, coordinating boards have had their advantages and disadvantages as well. Unlike industry-specific bodies, they did provide a mechanism for examining the overall benefits and costs of proposed projects and for weighing the total package of incentives and performance requirements. Moreover, coordinating boards considered the precedents that were generated by individual negotiations. Particularly important, they did, when they worked well, reduce the costs of negotiation for the investor.

Rarely, however, did coordinating bodies work as well as intended. First, they typically developed little expertise in particular industries or policy areas. Even worse, powerful ministries often refused to cooperate in the coordination effort. Those ministries might not honor the agreements reached by the coordinating board, or they might slow down the negotiating process by sending low-level personnel, or no one at all, to meetings. Wise investors then learned to negotiate with the separate ministries regardless of the descriptions of the power of the boards. Those that did depend on the coordinating board found their agreements not honored; the experience of these investors further damaged the investment climate of the host country.

In an effort to overcome these weaknesses of interministerial boards, governments sometimes took another approach to coordination. They formed special ad-hoc coordinating committees to deal with particular investments. Except for their duration, these project-specific committees were quite similar to the industry-specific centralized bodies noted above. Politically, these ad-hoc bodies sought to minimize through co-opting a ministry's possible effort to sabotage negotiations; administratively, they sought to assemble a special team with in-depth knowledge of the industry involved. Like their centralized counterparts, such committees generally paid little attention to matters of precedent and overall policy; even worse, they could rely little on institutional learning.

Given these several problems with each approach to screening and negotiation, few countries adopted a single approach for all industries. Most established a portfolio of approaches that reflected the various types of investment under consideration. Thus, in the 1970s, Indonesia negotiated with most investors through the BKPM, a coordinating board that represented such ministries as trade, industry, and finance. At the same time, however, a state enterprise, Pertamina, had almost full effective authority to negotiate oil and gas agreements. Simultaneously, negotiations for a large petrochemical project were handled by an ad-hoc committee with representation from several government agencies, including Pertamina and the Ministry of Industries. Moreover, some consideration was being given to the creation of new export processing zones where the authority for negotiation might, like other countries in the region, be centralized in an organization solely responsible for the operation of the zone. Indonesia's experience was not unique; our research saw it replicated in various ways in India and the Philippines, for example.

FACTORS AFFECTING THE CHOICES

The choices that countries made when they established negotiating structures followed quite regular patterns influenced by three sets of variables. First, a country's general development strategy and, thereby, its attitude toward foreign investment determined the approach that would govern its negotiations with most would-be investors. Countries that were not eager to attract foreign investment tended to choose more decentralized approaches. On the other hand, countries that desired more foreign investment tended to establish more centralized organizations; this typically meant some kind of coordinating body. In making its choice, the country had to weigh the political cost incurred by centralizing the negotiation process against the high costs that decentralized processes imposed on would-be investors. Only countries that evidenced a strong desire for more investment were willing to pay the costs of disenfranchising ministries otherwise involved in more decentralized negotiations.

This relationship between strategy and structure was also apparent within a single country. Changes in attitude toward foreign investment frequently preceded changes in a country's screening processes. Indonesia required investors to negotiate with a large number of government agencies in the Sukarno days, when it was particularly suspicious of the supposed benefits from foreign investment. Under the Suharto regime, however, attitudes changed. Eager to attract foreign investment, the government moved toward coordinating the negotiation process. Complaints about the effectiveness of coordinating efforts led to an increase in the role of the coordinating board in the mid-1970s. And by the 1980s, the desire to promote exports led to consideration of a centralized, autonomous authority to handle investments entering a proposed export processing zone.

Whatever the choices countries make for negotiating with the majority of investors, they tend to make special arrangements when the industry is particularly important, or "salient." In that event, countries have been unwilling to live with the possibility that a decentralized approach would result in a poor agreement, or none at all. And they have not been willing to live with the lack of industry expertise that typically characterizes a broad coordinating board or investment authority. The most suitable approach for countries facing a particularly salient project has been to vest power to negotiate in a specialized state enterprise or to create a special ad-hoc coordinating committee if no relevant state firm existed. Either approach offered the prospect of speedy negotiations, the possibility of weighing the incentives and performance requirements as a package, and, most important, the potential for bringing to bear a good deal of industry expertise in the negotiations.

There were other special cases when the countries that we examined decided not to use the negotiating approach that they used for most investors. These special arrangements were generally established when the competition among countries for particular kinds of investors was quite intense. Examples commonly involved export-oriented projects. Although a country, especially one with a large domestic market, could attract foreign investors for the local market by offering protection from import competition, this most effective incentive was not available for firms that wanted to set up facilities for export. Such firms could locate their plants in any of a number of countries that offered cheap production resources. In most cases, they needed only inexpensive labor, sufficient infrastructure, and good transportation and communication facilities. Many countries viewed this kind of investment as attractive; indeed, our own research (see Table 1 above) shows that this investment consistently increased national income. Given this common perception, the competition for these "footloose" investors was usually quite intense. Fearful of losing the battle for such investors, many countries have centralized in one unit negotiations for such firms. The goal of centralization was to create an organization that could act quickly and decisively, thereby increasing the attractiveness of the country to investors. Accordingly, in many countries, such as the Philippines and India, potential investors for export plants have had the option of investing in export processing zones. Not only do these zones offer infrastructure, but they generally are run by an organization that is fully vested with authority to reach agreements quickly.

THE OPERATION OF SCREENING BODIES

The first problem facing policymakers in developing countries has been to choose from the aforementioned organizational portfolio. The next problem has been to balance the accomplishment of one or more of the following, often competing objectives: attract potential investors, screen their proposals, negotiate entry terms, and administer the agreements just negotiated. Some observers would add an additional task: determining when the terms under which investors operate should be re-negotiated.

None of the countries we examined adequately resolved the apparent dilemma posed by the dual objectives of first attracting potential investors and subsequently reviewing their proposals to screen out projects that were not socially attractive. Most organizations placed almost all of their emphasis on one or the other of these two functions, but never the two together. The Economic Development Board (EDB) of Singapore, for example, put most of its effort into promotion. EDB rewarded its personnel according to their success in attracting investment. Those same employees typically moved into the private sector after their short tenure with EDB. In contrast, the BKPM in Indonesia devoted little of its resources to investment promotion. Screening appeared to be its principal function, evidenced by its long application form and lengthy approval procedures.

Even when screening appeared to be the major function, the effectiveness of that screening was often in doubt. This was especially true in the large developing country where we performed the social cost-benefit analyses summarized above. There, the head of that country's investment board expressed his unwillingness to perform relevant social cost-benefit analysis on investor proposals, as follows: the possibility of rejecting "bad" proposals using this methodology would have a negative impact on the number of potential investors that would subsequently apply to the board. The dilemma had, in this particular case, especially unfortunate consequences. The board did little to attract investment. At the same time, it did not screen out bad proposals . In our own analysis we were not able to find any relationship between a proposed project's contribution to national income and that project's acceptance or rejection by the investment board. In other words, the board neither screened nor promoted investment effectively.

Even if the investment board more effectively screened projects, there typically was not a close relationship between the terms negotiated and the terms implemented. We have encountered frequent discrepancies between the seeming intent of an agreement negotiated by one organization and the implementation of that agreement done by another body. For example, ministries of finance would occasionally not honor tariff exemptions granted by investment authorities. In other cases, tax authorities would later renegotiate tax terms more or less favorable to the investor than those that had been negotiated with the investment authority. These differences usually arose during the implementation stage, when practical problems of administering the original terms began to appear, when ministries needed to collect more revenue, or, we occasionally suspected, when unofficial payments were passed to particular officials. Regardless of its cause, this disjuncture between terms negotiated and terms implemented would have rendered meaningless earlier cost-benefit analyses.

IMPLICATIONS

What do the experiences of the developing countries that we studied suggest for other countries concerned with foreign investment?

The results clearly show that most developing countries cannot have confidence that projects that are attractive to foreign investors are attractive to the country. There is some assurance of a match between private and national interests only under certain conditions: (1) prices that face the investor must be good guides to the opportunity costs of inputs that the project will use, and (2) the prices for the output of the project must be close to those that indicate the social value of the product. In the projects that we studied, failure to satisfy one or both of these conditions resulted in investment proposals that were privately but not socially attractive. In the absence of policies that establish accurate price guidelines for managers, the government must seriously consider careful screening of proposals on their economic merits.

Existing research, all on market economies, says a great deal about where the emphasis should be placed in the screening process. When the proposals are for projects that would serve a domestic market that is protected from import competition, careful evaluation is most necessary to assess price distortions in output markets. On the other hand, such an evaluation is less essential when projects are to manufacture for export markets . . . all the better since competition among countries for this investment demands quick and predictable decisions.

Unfortunately, this generalization about export projects has an important caveat. One cannot be so sanguine about the effects of export projects in an economy where many domestic prices are administered rather than determined by market competition. We know of no research that evaluates a sample of proposals or projects in countries with a large number of administered prices for domestic resources, but some anecdotal evidence suggests that in such environments even export projects can easily be wasteful of national resources. One case is of an onion-drying plant which would import onions to a free trade zone, dry them with fuel oil that was priced below export value, and export the dried onions at world market prices. A study of the proposed project indicated that the country would be better off exporting the oil (or importing less oil) and rejecting the drying plant. A similar study of a metal smelter in a non-OPEC oil-producing country concluded that the country would have earned more foreign exchange by exporting the fuel oil and the ore concentrate than it did by processing the ore in the country in an inefficient (by world standards) plant. These examples suggest that screening may be necessary even for export projects in countries with administered prices that depart considerably from opportunity costs. And as Table 1 shows, such distortions in prices must also be considered for domestic-oriented projects.

Although the potential benefits of screening foreign investment are clear for a country with import protection and with price distortions in the internal market, the experience of other countries suggests that those benefits are in fact quite difficult to achieve.

First, the screening process is not an easy one. Of all the organizations that we studied, none actually performed careful economic cost/ benefit calculations. The reasons were numerous. Scarcity of skilled personnel was certainly one factor. Another was the diffculty in assembling adequate data. Moreover, the failure was, on occasion, blamed on the supposed incompatibility of screening and investment promotion.

The problems in undertaking economic analysis suggest that efforts should be made to concentrate analytical skills on those areas of investment where economic and private profits are most likely to differ. One approach, suboptimal from a theoretical point of view but perhaps necessary as a practical matter, is to make crude classifications of types of investment proposals. This enables the screening bodies to devote scarce resources to the most likely trouble areas. Such a classification system might, for example, separate out export projects for a very simple, quick test. In the country which we studied, a simple test of the ratio of energy used (underpriced to the investor) to labor employed (overpriced to the investor) could be used. A ratio above a certain figure would separate out proposals for special attention. Since the vast majority of projects with lower ratios would be beneficial, they could be approved virtually automatically.

Similarly, proposals for serving the local market might be divided into industries categorized according to priority and according to effective protection. Scarce analytical resources might be devoted first to high-priority sectors, with special attention subsequently paid to those industries with high rates of effective protection. Model terms might be prepared to improve predictability for would-be investors. Some poor projects might slip through such a screening process, but the increased speed of analysis is likely to generate more proposals for consideration. Proposals for low-priority sectors might have to wait for evaluation and negotiation until time is available. Some potential investments might, of course, be lost due to slow processing, but the losses are likely to be unimportant if the sectors are indeed low priority.

The second set of lessons derives from the difficulties posed by the organizational issues. If negotiations were decentralized, they were particularly likely to be ineffective and to discourage potential investment. On the other hand, centralization came at a high political cost. Only when the stakes seemed particularly high were governments willing to disenfranchise ministries in order to centralize the negotiating function. Coordination was, because of the lack of political commitment at the top, often ineffective and, in some cases, deteriorated into decentralized negotiations soon after the initial attempts at coordination. Coordination can work only if government is actually willing to remove authority from departments with legitimate interests in the outcome of negotiations with potential investors.

The experiences of various countries indicate where the problems lie. Understanding the likely sources of problems in different structures is an important step in designing effective organization.

FOOTNOTES

1. Stephen Guisinger and Associates, *Investment Incentives and Performance Requirements* (New York: Praeger, 1985), Chapter 1.
2. When managers of foreign firms are asked to rank-order those factors which were important to their investment decision, one consistent conclusion emerges. Irrespective of host country or manufacturing industry, managers consistently rank political and administrative concerns as more important than government incentives. These general concerns figure prominently in managers' appraisals of the overall "investment climate" of the host country. For a summary of and addition to this research, see Stephen J. Kobrin, *Managing Political Risk Assessment* (Berkeley: University of California Press, 1982), pp. 114–20.

3. See, for example, United Nations, Department of Economic and Social Affairs, *The Impact of Multinational Corporations on Development and International Relations* (New York, 1974), p. 38ff.
4. Most of the important studies are summarized in Richard E. Caves, *Multinational Enterprise and Economic Analysis* (Cambridge: Cambridge University Press, 1982), Chapter 9; T.J. Bierstaker, *Distortion or Development: Contending Perspectives on Multinational Corporations* (Cambridge: MIT Press, 1978).
5. Both detractors and supporters engaged in this level of debate have relied on piecemeal studies, anecdotal evidence, some plausible if unsubstantiated arguments, and several major leaps of faith. Among the best known of the detractors is Richard J. Barnett and Ronald Mueller, *Global Reach: The Power of the Multinational Corporations* (New York: Simon and Schuster, 1974); for a rejoinder to this book, see *A Comment on Global Reach* (Washington: The Center for Multinational Studies, 1975). Within this same genre, support for the role of multinational in economic development can be found in the following: Orville L. Freeman, *The Multinational Company: Instrument for World Growth* (New York: Praeger, 1981); Arthur McCormack, *Multinational Investment: Boon or Burden for the Developing Countries?* (New York: W.R.Grace and Company, 1980).
6. Constantine Vaitsos, *Intercountry Income Distribution and Transnational Enterprises* (Oxford: Clarendon Press, 1974); for a critical review of these studies, see V. Bornschier, "Multinational Corporations and Economic Growth: A Cross-National Test of the Decapitalization Theory," *Journal of Development Economics* (June 1980), pp. 191–210.
7. For a critical review of these studies, see C. Stoneman, "Foreign Capital and Economic Growth," *World Development* (January 1975),pp. 11–26; Stephen F. Kobrin, *Foreign Direct Investment, Industrialization, and Social Change* (Greenwich, Conn.: JAI Press, 1977).
8. For multinational and technology, see Robert Stobaugh and Louis T. Wells, Jr. (eds.), *Technology Crossing Borders* (Boston: Harvard Business School Press, 1984). For multinationals and exports, see Vaitsos in fn. 6 above and Gerald K. Helleiner, "Manufactured Exports from Less Developed Countries and Multinational Firms," *The Economics Journal* (March 1973), pp. 21–47. For multinationals and industrial structure, see Sanjaya Lall, "Transnationals, Domestic Enterprises, and Industrial Structure in Host LDCs: A Survey," *Oxford Economic Papers* (July 1978), pp. 217-48.
9. Peter Evans, *Dependent Development: The Alliance of Multinational, State and Local Capital in Brazil* (Princeton: Princeton University Press, 1979); Gary Gereffi, "Drug Firms and Dependency in Mexico: The Case of the Steroid Hormone Industry," *International Organization* 32 (Winter 1978): 237–86.
10. Helen Hughes and P.S. You (eds.), *Foreign Investment and Industrialization in Singapore* (Canberra: Australian National University, 1969); David W. Carr, *Foreign Investment and Development in Egypt* (New York: Praeger, 1979).
11. See the separate works of Caves and Bierstaker in fn 4 above; also see Raymond Vernon, *Storm Over the Multinationals* (Cambridge: Harvard University Press, 1977).

12. Sanjaya Lall and Paul Streeten, *Foreign Investment, Transnationals and Developing Countries* (Boulder, CO: Westview, 1977).
13. Grant L. Reuber, Foreign Investment in Development (Oxford: Clarendon Press, 1973).
14. Lall and Streeten, *Foreign Investment,* p.174.
15. That is, Reuber's results approximate the results of a social cost-benefit analysis that assumes that all inputs are charged at local market prices , and that all outputs are valued at world market prices. For summary table, see Reuber, *Investment,* p.179.
16. Michael Roemer and Joseph J. Stern, *The Appraisal of Development Projects* (New York: Praeger, 1975). There are differences between this and other methods, such as the so-called Little and Mirrlees approach; see, I.M.D. Little and James A. Mirrlees, *Project Appraisal and Planning for Development* (New York: Basic Books, 1974). The variations can yield different rank-orderings for projects, but do not yield different cutoffs for selecting projects. Moreover, these differences in analytical techniques are far less important than biases in the data analyzed.
17. For example, overstating the project's capital requirements would lower the projected return for the private investor. Consequently, by separating the sample into two sets of firms—one for which the income statements indicated a relatively high rate of return and another where the projected private return was low—we could test to see whether there was a difference in reporting by the two groups. This test yielded no indication of such a reporting bias.
18. See Dennis J. Encarnation and Louis T. Wells, Jr., "Sovereignty en Garde: Negotiating with Foreign Investors," *International Organization* 39 (Winter 1985); 47–78; and Encarnation and Wells, "Competitive Strategies in Global Industries: A View from the Host Country," in Michael Porter, ed., *Competitive Strategies in Global Industries* (Boston: Harvard Business School, forthcoming, 1986).

24

Multinational Codes of Conduct and Corporate Accountability: New Opportunities for Corporate Counsel

George W. Coombe, Jr.

National efforts by host governments to monitor and control the activities of MNCs have stimulated similar efforts at the international level. The goal of corporate accountability is now embodied in a variety of international proposals, which may collectively be termed multinational codes of conduct. The fact that these codes of conduct are not uniform in either language, scope, standards, interpretation, or implementation is a source of concern and uncertainty for MNCs.

As the principal targets of such codes, U.S. MNCs need to increase their awareness of, and familiarity with, the codes themselves and their implications. Experience with the issues of domestic corporate accountability may be useful for management and corporate counsel in developing an appreciation of the mounting pressures on corporations found in the multinational codes of conduct.

THE CONDUCT OF U.S. corporations, at home and abroad, provides an important point of reference in the ongoing appraisal of corporate accountability. Domestic criticism of corporate conduct has focused upon proposed corporate governance reform, i.e., reallocation of corporate legal responsiblity among directors, officers, and stockholders. The U.S. multinational corporation, however, must account, further, to expanding appraisal of its business objectives by host governments concerned with specific social and economic goals.[1] That appraisal has been

---

effected through several proposed multinational codes prescribing
multinational conduct. Placed within broad political, economic, and
social objectives, these prescriptions seek to address every aspect of a
multinational's business activities: general policies and procedures;
disclosure, competition and antitrust; financing; taxation; employment;
personnel and industrial relations; transborder data flow; transfer of
technology; and accounting practices.

Multinational code negotiations provide corporate counsel in the
United States a new and helpful perspective to assist management in
addressing public expectations of corporate conduct. These expectations
were augmented significantly in the wake of corporate transgressions
associated with illicit payments overseas and violation of the federal
election laws at home. Corporate counsel assumed an important role in
the development of responsive corporate policies and procedures.
Enhancement of corporate accountability in the United States, however,
has been accompanied by an increase in expectations by host
governments of U.S. multinational behavior abroad. This important
development will have a profound future effect upon the business affairs and activities of U.S. multinationals. Accordingly, it will prove
helpful to consider specific preventive law opportunities afforded corporate counsel to assure management understanding and corporate accommodation to government and public expectations abroad.

Corporate conduct and the governance of U.S. corporations provide a familiar domestic point of reference. Multinational code proposals
present a less familiar prospect. Yet their influence upon U.S. corporate
behavior, at home or overseas, may prove significant.[2] The more important contemporary code negotiation activity is summarized in the Appendix to provide a convenient general background for discussion of
specific code provisions. Sponsorship of a particular code may well provide critical insights to predictions underlying code effectiveness, the
prospect for eventual adoption or enactment, and ultimate application
and enforcement.

Further, code deliberations often are accompanied by the efforts of
individual foreign states to address similar concerns through domestic
law. Those deliberations may also reflect regional concerns and the intention of states similarly situated, such as the developing nations or
"Group of 77," to apply code principles on a broad geographical basis.
Finally, code negotiation and the particular substantive issues addressed
will continue to reflect worldwide multinational conduct as well as the
aspirations of individual states. Ironically, the perceptions abroad of

U.S. multinational behavior may be conditioned and influenced by U.S. domestic criticism of corporations, generally. Thus, public expectations at home may affect appraisal of U.S. multinational conduct abroad. In turn, corporate criticism here will reflect overseas performance of U.S. multinationals. Indeed, foreign multinationals doing business in the United States already have evidenced a growing awareness of the need to conduct business operations here in light of increased public expectations regarding corporate conduct. There is every reason to believe timely and constructive domestic response by U.S. multinationals to those expectations will strengthen the efforts of the U.S. private sector to meet evolving standards of corporate accountability throughout the world.

Appraisal of the subject here begins with identification of certain underlying issues of major concern to U.S. multinationals addressed throughout code negotiations. Consideration is then given to problems faced by U.S. multinationals required to approach those negotiations during a period of expanding corporate criticism at home. Corporate response which might prove efficacious at home and abroad—voluntary disclosure and the implementation of a company code of conduct—is then reviewed. The paper concludes with a discussion of the role of corporate counsel in support of management efforts to understand the implications associated with code negotiation and the need for counsel encouragement of necessary corporate initiatives.

I. EVOLVING CODE PROPOSALS: A POINT OF DEPARTURE

In 1974, a distinguished observer of the multinational enterprise concluded: "Surveillance and restriction are in the air. The multinational finds itself under steady assault from host and home government alike. In addition, a congeries of international, not entirely friendly, examinations are in progress."[3] Those examinations have accelerated and expanded since 1974 and, today, provide relevant criteria for U.S. multinationals in the conduct of business activities throughout the world. Accordingly, corporate awareness of those criteria, the circumstances surrounding appraisal of multinational conduct, and attendant public and governmental expectations will be required. Evolving multinational code proposals represent an important manifestation of those expectations.

Some, such as the Rules of Conduct (and Guidelines for Implementation) to Combat Extortion and Bribery adopted by the International Chamber of Commerce (ICC),[4] represent a studied attempt by a private business group to involve both multinationals and governments in a voluntary effort to address corporate behavior in an important but limited area. Others, such as the Declaration on International Investment and Multinational Enterprises adopted by the Organisation for Economic Co-operation and Development (OECD),[5] encourage voluntary corporate response within comprehensive guidelines created and adopted by international agreement among the industrialized nations. Still others, in particular the U.N. Commission on Transnational Corporations and the United Nations Conference on Trade and Development (UNCTAD), seek mandated international standards with specific provisions to identify corporate transgression. Corporate concern for behavioral constraints mandated by international agencies is understandable, particularly in light of the wide philosophical divergence between developing and industrialized nations and the attempts of governmental representatives to rationalize the difference.

Significantly, implications associated with the existence of voluntary codes or guidelines (discussed *infra*) are not fully appreciated by the U.S. corporate community. A reasonable corporate concern can be raised regarding the manner in which the negotiation of multinational codes proceeds in a given international forum. The State Department Advisory Committee on International Investment, Technology and Development represents a meaningful attempt by the U.S. Government to assure purposeful corporate involvement. But the nature and extent of that involvement is limited by the absence of a significant corporate awareness in the United States of the several evolving code activities. U.S. business should understand that the result of code negotiation may lead directly to new and expansive sanctions and increased government regulation of corporate conduct throughout the world.

A second major consideration for corporate attention in addressing code proposals is the absence of preciseness or clarity of underlying terms and their application. Indeed, it has become evident during the negotiation of some codes that imprecision represents a studied attempt to obscure possibilities for abuse and discrimination in ultimate code application. The serious implications presented to U.S. multinationals by the draft international code concerning restrictive business practices, now in an advanced stage of negotiation by UNCTAD,[6] aptly illustrates the problem. This code proposal, from its inception, has failed to state clearly that it is intended to be voluntary in nature, has set forth vague definitions of restrictive business practices, and has provided no explicit assurances that application will be nondiscriminatory in nature. Similar problems are presented by another UNCTAD code proposal pertaining to the transfer of technology[7] which, after several drafts, still contains no definition for such terms as "control," "affiliate," or even for the term "technology." No attempt has been made to define these terms, and the expert negotiators appear to have avoided the question. As a consequence, neither the text of the draft nor the negotiating history yet provides adequate guidance as to the subject matter or scope of the code.[8]

Code interpretation and implementation present a third major issue for corporate concern, an issue closely related to Group of 77 (developing countries) pressure for mandated application. U.S. negotiators, at the urging of U.S. advisory groups actively monitoring the codes, have sought to maintain the principle, set forth in the OECD Decision on Intergovernmental Consultation Procedures on the Guidelines for Multinational Enterprises, that any consultative committee "shall not reach conclusions on the conduct of individual enterprises."[9]

By contrast, details of implementation of the proposed U.N. Code for Transnational Corporations have become a hotly debated topic in the Intergovernmental Working Group of the Commission on Transnational Corporations.[10] A Secretariat Paper suggests the Code may be "implemented" by some U.N. body with authority to review specific cases.[11] Indeed, at several negotiating sessions the United States has been singled out as intransigent for insisting that implementation could not properly be discussed until the Group knew what was going to be implemented. The Group cannot agree on whether there is a need for a body to clarify or interpret the Code nor whether there is a distinction between clarification and interpretation. Nevertheless, the Group's Chairman has drafted formulations which include an elaborate set of international procedures.[12]

Similarly, the UNCTAD code concerning restrictive business practices calls for "international measures" and "international institutional machinery" which could lead to the establishment of an international bureaucracy within UNCTAD to oversee the Principles and Rules and their implementation and to annual reporting and publication activities in furtherance thereof. Further, the UNCTAD text includes specific implementation mechanisms including consultation, international institutional machinery within UNCTAD, formal review procedure and the adoption of a "General Assembly Resolution," suggesting the code may cease to be a voluntary set of principles.[13] It would appear the UNCTAD code on restrictive business practices is in the same anomalous position as the companion code on transfer of technology where representatives of the developing nations (Group of 77) have warned that within four to six years a review Conference will be summoned to discuss the adoption of the so-called voluntary principles as a binding code.

The very existence of code mechanisms to monitor compliance and address interpretive problems relates directly to other serious issues requiring U.S. corporate attention: the right of governments and third parties to access a given code review mechanism and the attendant demands for compliance levelled at an alleged corporate transgressor. The opportunity for such access and creation of some forum to consider such demands may be facilitated through periodic comprehensive reviews of experience under the code by code sponsors. In this regard, two examples already are provided: one, by the OECD formal review of experience under the Guidelines effectuated by the OECD Committee on International Investment and Multinational Enterprises (CIME) and the 1979 action of the OECD Council of Ministers reaffirming the 1976 OECD Declaration;[14] and the other, by the express action of the ICC Council in adopting By-laws of an International Panel on Extortion and Bribery in Business Transactions which encourage Panel interpretation, promotion and oversight of the Rules of Conduct.[15] Self-initiation of review procedures by code sponsors, however, will not obviate demands for hearings on complaints by third parties, a conclusion well illustrated by the *Badger* and *Batco* experience.[16] In *Badger*,[17] trade unions representing dismissed employees of a bankrupt Belgium corporate subsidiary joined with the Belgian government to invoke, before the CIME Committee of OECD, application of the OECD Guidelines on employment and industrial relations against the U.S. multinational parent. The parent ultimately agreed to share, in part, responsibility for severance payments due to the subsidiary's employees under Belgian law. The Belgian government characterized as a "moral responsibility" of the parent such liabilities of subsidiaries, a characterization arrived at shortly after the government's meeting with the OECD Committee. In *Batco*,[18] both the Dutch government and trade unions representing employees of a Dutch subsidiary requested the OECD Committee to interpret the application of the Guidelines to the attempt of a multinational parent to close down a subsidiary in one country and transfer its production to a subsidiary in another country. Relief ultimately was obtained in a Dutch court which applied Dutch law and did not rely upon the OECD Guidelines. The actions of the Belgian and Dutch governments in these particular cases suggest that governments may rely upon the experience gained through code negotiation and implementation in their direct dealings with multinationals.

A final important consideration for corporate concern relates to problems associated with the potential impact of codes on the principle of national treatment and the need for nondiscrimination in code application. National treatment, or equal treatment by a government of all enterprises qualified to do business in a foreign country, continues to be a professed objective of U.S. code negotiators. Any code reference to the national treatment standard should state, as does the OECD Declaration, that the standard of treatment is "consistent with international law."[19] U.S. corporate concern will increse justifiably should any code standard proposed appear to set a different test for national treatment than that set in the OECD Declaration. The several principles set forth in the OECD Guidelines were acceptable to the business community because the OECD approach, unlike most other code proposals, included broad and balanced provisions in areas of concern to both business and governments among generally like-minded countries. They were combined with the acceptance by the signatory governments of the obligation to grant national treatment coupled with a minimum international law standard.

In contrast, the proposed UNCTAD Principles and Rules relating to restrictive business practices provide the less specific assurance that states "should ensure treatment of enterprises which is fair, equitable, on the same basis to all enterprises and in accordance with established procedures of law." During recent negotiations, the less developed countries refused to accept the developed country proposal that the said standard of treatment must explicitly be "nondiscriminatory." Initially, spokesmen for socialist countries insisted that state owned or controlled enterprises be exempted from the Rules entirely. U.S. observers emphasized the futility of a United States agreement with the Soviet Union and other socialist countries to a "universal" set of rules applicable to our enterprises but not to theirs. The UNCTAD Principles and Rules on restrictive business practices do appear to lay a foundation for favoritism by developing countries in the regulation of their domestic enterprises and possible acceptance by the developed countries of denials of national treatment to foreign multinationals by the developing countries. The text contemplates exceptions where "conduct of enterprises, whether or not created or controlled by States, is accepted under applicable legislation or regulations," terminology that could be used to justify discriminatory treatment by developing countries in favor of their domestic enterprises.[20]

It is still not clear whether the proposed U.N. Code for Transnational Corporations will apply in a nondiscriminatory way to state-owned and domestic enterprises as well as to transnational corporations. The term "transnational corporations" was reportedly proposed by the socialist countries with the avowed intent of excluding application to state-owned enterprises. Nevertheless, the U.S. negotiating position insists the U.N. Code be appropriately balanced in reference to the responsibilities of governments as well as corporations, that it not be used as a basis for discriminatory action against multinationals and in favor of domestic firms, that it apply to all enterprises whether their ownership is private, government or mixed, and that multinationals receive equitable treatment in accordance with international law.[21] The U.S. negotiating position here is similar to its position regarding the nature and scope of the proposed UNCTAD Code of Conduct for the Transfer of Technology: the Code should be appropriately balanced in reference to the responsibilities of governments as well as firms and ensure that national laws regulating the transfer of technology should be in accordance with international law.

Despite these objectives, the negotiating experience to date permits the conclusion that international principles and rules under negotiation by UNCTAD and the Intergovernmental Working Group of the U.N. Commission on Transnational Corporations are not aimed at anticompetitive practices as much as at the political goal of the less developed and socialist countries to increase their leverage in dealing with multinational enterprises from the OECD countries. By mischaracterizing the UNCTAD Principles and Rules as rules on competition, their promoters have acquired unwarranted U.S. and other developed country support for a code which may well be used by less developed and Eastern bloc countries to discriminate against western, primarily United States based, multinationals.

The uncertainties for U.S. corporations are compounded by the fact that many of their representatives continue to participate actively in code negotiations, directly and through U.S. government agencies, without any clearly defined domestic point of reference. At the same time, U.S. domestic political realities, influenced by rising public expectations of corporate conduct, portend unique problems for U.S. multinationals. Those political realities, next addressed, provide a useful context within which to explore implications related to adherence by U.S. corporations to proposed multinational code standards.

II. CORPORATE ACCOUNTABILITY IN THE UNITED STATES: A CURRENT APPRAISAL OF PUBLIC EXPECTATIONS

U.S. multinationals, perhaps more intensely than their foreign counterparts, have been subjected to public scrutiny and criticism evolving over an extended period. However, the nature and extent of that criticism have changed significantly. The dimension of that change, in turn, should shape and condition U.S. multinational attitudes toward code provisions affecting their operations. Unitl the 1960s, public attention in the United States focused upon corporations in economic terms with particular emphasis upon job creation, new consumer goods and services, expansion of eonomic opportunity, and increase in economic growth. During the 1960s, public attention, assisted by growing numbers of special interest groups, focused upon corporations as a means to address perceived social problems (environmental concerns, product safety, equal employment opportunity) augmenting government regulation. The public attitudes of the 1960s and 1970s derived from growing disillusionment with government (related directly to Vietnam), a heightened awareness of the social and economic effect of corporate policy and conduct upon the quality of life, concern with corporate size and power, and misunderstanding of the essential underlying economic function and purpose of the private corporation. Further, there was little public understanding of corporate governance (the allocation of legal responsibility among stockholders, management, and the board of directors) or the nature of the corporate decision-making process. Public expectations of corporate conduct in the 1960s and 1970s were manifested through the concept of corporate "social responsibility," a concept carefully nurtured by corporate critics to assure public judgment of corporate response. That concept, analogous to the provisions of multinational code proposals, included corporate legal compliance, the impact of corporate behavior upon the community, corporate relationships with stockholders, employees, customers, and suppliers, and voluntary corporate change in governance, increased disclosure, and the adoption of internal codes of conduct. Voluntary change was encouraged through stockholder proposals submitted pursuant to the SEC proxy rules, annual meeting activity, and persistent criticism by special interest groups demanding corporate reappraisal of internal systems and priorities.

Contemporary corporate criticism has evolved from demands for corporate social responsibility to identification of "corporate account-ability" as a focus for public reference in the 1980s. Several manifesta-tions of U.S. public expectations underlying corporate accountability have emerged, again closely related to government expectations abroad with respect to U.S. multinational activities:

- Growing criticism of big business and the remote and impersonal nature of the corporate decision-making processes;
- Demands for corporate legal compliance and accountability in the wake of corporate transgressions;
- New opportunities for special interest groups to access the corpo-rate decision-making process as an important means to their self-appointed ends;
- Increasing attention to the manner in which corporations govern themselves and the contrast between corporate and political systems of governance;
- The effect of business decision-making upon individuals and communities accentuated by the growth of multinationals.

Criticism of the corporate governance of U.S. corporations, implicit in several multinational code proposals, insists that fundamental changes in the corporate decision-making process must occur. Such changes would include board independence, special interest directors, a viable board committee system, cumulative voting, stockholder democ-racy, increased corporate disclosure, community impact analysis, ex-pansive rights for employees, increased reporting responsibilities for corporate counsel and auditors, and drastic criminal sanctions and penalties for corporate transgression. All of this is coupled with renewed demands for comprehensive federal chartering of corporations. Con-temporary criticism in the U.S. may or may not result in future legisla-tive or regulatory change. However, U.S. multinationals, unlike their overseas competitors, already must face existing constraints affecting corporate conduct in the form of the Foreign Corrupt Practices Act and the Securities and Exchange Commission proposals for enforcement of the Act's internal accounting control requirements.[22]

The familiar circumstances surrounding passage of the Foreign Corrupt Practices Act (FCPA), in December, 1977, need no repetition.[23] U.S. corporate response mandated by the Act, proposed by the Securities and Exchange Commission and anticipated by public opinion should provide a convenient and important precedent for U.S. corporate consideration of multinational code proposals. Provisions of the FCPA include the requirement that all corporations subject to the Act maintain adequate books and records and devise and maintain a system of internal accounting control sufficient to provide reasonable assurances that:

(i) transactions are executed in accordance with management's general or specific authorization;

(ii) transactions are recorded as necessary (a) to permit preparation of financial statements in conformity with generally accepted accounting principles or other criteria applicable to such statements, and (b) to maintain accountability for assets;

(iii) access to assets is permitted only in accordance with management's general or specific authorization; and

(iv) the recorded accountability for assets is compared with the existing assets at reasonable intervals and appropriate action is taken with respect to any differences.[24]

Public attention preceding passage of the FCPA had focused on questionable corporate foreign payments. Thus, little attention was directed to the internal accounting control provisions of the FCPA. The SEC, however, quickly focused corporate attention on the latter when it proposed for comments, in April, 1979, rules which would require inclusion of a statement of management on internal accounting control in the corporation's 10-K report filed with the Commission and in the annual report to shareholders furnished pursuant to the proxy rules.[25] It also revealed a Commission intention to follow closely the further initiatives of the private sector and consider the need to propose additional rules relating to matters other than internal accounting control that might be included in a management report. Most important, the Commission's proposal provided an expansive view of its expectations regarding management determination of whether a system of internal accounting control provides reasonable assurances that the broad objectives of internal accounting control are achieved. In that regard, the Commission identified, as the first element of such a determination, evaluations of the overall control environment and recognized that:

such evaluations will require a careful exercise of management's judgment, generally involving consideration of matters such as the organizational structure, including the role of the board of directors; communication of corporate procedures, policies and related codes of conduct; communication of authority and responsibility; competence and integrity of personnel; accountability for performance; and the objectivity and effectiveness of the internal audit function. The role of the board of directors in overseeing the establishment and maintenance of a strong control environment, and in overseeing the procedures for evaluating a system of internal accounting control, is particularly important.[26]

Corporate management and the corporate bar properly questioned the extremely broad corporate statement called for by the Commission proposal. And the Commission recently announced its support of a staff recommendation to withdraw that proposal[27] "and look instead to the corporate community and accounting profession voluntarily to develop management reporting and auditor review techniques in this area."[28] Further, the Commission continues to emphasize the desirability of an internal code of conduct as an important corporate mechanism to achieve legal compliance. Voluntary constructive response to this Commission suggestion will provide helpful experience and insight to U.S. multinational consideration and appreciation of multinational code activity.

Much of that code activity pertains directly to illicit payments, the same subject matter which preoccupied the attention of the Congress in its consideration of the Foreign Corrupt Practices Act.[29] Thus, the U.N. Economic and Social Council established the Ad Hoc Intergovernmental Working Group on the Problem of Corrupt Practices to address corrupt practices in international commercial transactions. Those same problems have been investigated by the International Chamber of Commerce, resulting in the adoption of voluntary corporate observation of Guidelines which include the statement that enterprises should "not render—and they should not be solicited or expected to render—any bribe or other improper benefit, direct or indirect, to any public servant or holder of public office."[30] Other efforts, such as that of the U.N. Commission on Transnational Corporations to formulate a code of conduct relating to transnational corporations, seek to define broad concepts of acceptable corporate behavior in various substantive areas. It is submitted that a thorough corporate understanding of the described SEC "control environment" and the adaptation of internal corporate policies and procedures to assure the existence of such environment will assist U.S. corporations in their ultimate response to expectations heightened by multinational code activity.

The need for corporate preparation is close at hand. Those expectations already have resulted in inquiry by sponsors concerning the intention of U.S. multinationals to announce their adoption code proposals and exhortation by third parties citing such adoption in support of their particular demands. The practical realities associated with such inquiry and exhortation require corporate understanding of attendant implications. Can the U.S. multinational manifest its support for and adherence to multinational code effort without first putting its domestic house in order pursuant to SEC and U.S. public expectations? Once safely embarked on the requisite FCPA compliance program within a carefully constructed control environment, what shoals lie ahead in international waters for the U.S. multinational which endorses and supports voluntary code efforts to address broad aspects of multinational operations? Phrased another way, what international opportunities may enure to the advantage of U.S. multinationals as a result of their constructive response to the U.S. domestic corporate constraints associated with Foreign Practices Act compliance?

III. VOLUNTARY ADOPTION OF CODE PROPOSALS:
IMPLICATIONS FOR THE MULTINATIONAL CORPORATION

The Introduction to the Rules of Conduct to Combat Extortion and Bribery adopted by the International Chamber of Commerce presents the case for multinational support of voluntary codes:

These Rules of Conduct are intended as a method of self-regulation. Their voluntary acceptance by business enterprises will not only promote high standards of integrity in business transactions, whether between enterprises and public bodies or between enterprises themselves, but will also form a valuable defensive protection to those enterprises which are subjected to attempts at extortion.[31]

Another rationale appears in the OECD Guidelines For Multinational Enterprises:

Observance of the guidelines is voluntary and not legally enforceable. However, they should help to ensure that the operations of these enterprises are in harmony with national policies of the countries where they operate and to strengthen the basis of mutual confidence between enterprises and states.[32]

The foregoing provisions addressed to multinational conduct undertaken on a voluntary basis find a domestic counterpart in the observations of Chairman Williams of the SEC in urging U.S. corporations to develop constructive voluntary responses to the dictates of the Foreign Corrupt Practices Act and to public expectations for corporate accountability (discussed *supra*):

I hope, however, that there would be little disagreement with the propositions that we need to strengthen public trust in our business sector and that the issue is very much open as to whether government's role in that process will be one of oversight or intervention.[33]

Domestic or international, the proposition before the corporate community is the same: conduct corporate affairs in a manner responsive to public expectations or be prepared for additional, and more severe, governmental constraints.[34] Placed in this context, the proposition is reasonable enough. Indeed, the most effective domestic response to contemporary corporate criticism remains extensive strengthening in the governance of corporations voluntarily achieved through guidelines such as those developed by The Business Roundtable and the Corporation, Banking and Business Law Section of the American Bar Association.[35] That change, of course, will not deter persistent demands of certain corporate critics for expansive federal legislative constraints, but it appears convincing to more objective public consideration of corporate conduct. Absent further revelations of corporate transgression, evolving standards, voluntarily obtained, may suffice.

Domestic measures to enhance public perceptions of corporate conduct should assist corporations in the perception of their conduct overseas. Whatever voluntary action is undertaken, and whatever the efficacy of the corporate policies and procedures adopted, the possibility remains such undertakings may not result in timely response to rising expectations of some governments. Perhaps the very knowledge of multinational code activity will heighten public awareness and attendant expectations leading government negotiators to conclude that code application must be mandatory to assure uniform multinational conduct and a fair competitive environment for all.

Public understanding of multinational conduct is certain to be increased with regard to those corporations which expand voluntary disclosure of corporate information responding to code provisions. Thus, the OECD Guidelines state:

Enterprises should, having due regard to their nature and relative size in the economic context of their operations and to requirements of business confidentially and to cost, publish in a form suited to improve public understanding a sufficient body of factual information on the structure, activities and policies of the enterprises as a whole, as a supplement, in so far as is necessary for this purpose, to information to be disclosed under the national law of the individual countries in which they operate.[36]

Assuming good faith corporate response through more expansive disclosure pursuant to the OECD Guidelines, will improved "public understanding" necessarily follow? The dictates of the OECD Guidelines aside, increased corporate disclosure is likely to address public uncertainty regarding the corporate decision-making process and could have a healthy internal effect upon that process, causing management to approach corporate policy decisions with the realization that many will become publicly available; accordingly, more corporate decisions will be arrived at with heightened management appreciation of potential public impact.

An important corporate disclosure subject which might present the multinational in a most favorable light overseas is an internal company code of conduct. The ICC, in the Guideline for Implementation of its Rules of Conduct to Combat Extortion and Bribery, included company codes as an integral part of voluntary multinational conduct:

> These Rules of Conduct being of a general nature, enterprises should, where appropriate, draw up their codes of conduct consistent with the ICC Rules and apply them to the particular circumstances in which their business is carried out. Such codes may usefully include examples and should enjoin employees or agents who find themselves subjected to any form of extortion or bribery immediately to report the same to senior management.[37]

Voluntary corporate codes of conduct can provide a much needed manifestation of corporate intent to engage in ethical behavior and obey the law. Again, voluntary disclosure appears to be an essential element in any such code and publication and distribution of the code itself, wherever the multinational engages in business activity, a desirable objective. Any such company code should include many of the substantive matters sought to be addressed by the several proposed multinational codes now under negotiation. In addition to disclosure and employee behavior, a typical code might address corporate governance, functioning of the Board, integrity of accounting and records, responsibility as an employer, description of business activities, general rules of business behavior, responsibility to customers, and responsibility as a corporate member of the community. Appropriate code guidelines will respond directly to the SEC and to Chairman Williams in their characterization of a code and its voluntary enforcement as the heart of the corporate internal control environment (discussed *supra*). Such a code also would address similar concerns overseas.

It is, of course, unrealistic to assume that preparation and adoption of voluntary codes by individual multinationals will forestall evolving international efforts to mandate multinational conduct. At the very least, however, a voluntary effort by a given multinational should place its management in a far better position to perceive the implications of the described multinational code negotiations and to contribute to their successful resolution. Perhaps most important of all, such an endeavor on the part of corporate management will provide meaningful opportunities to anticipate public and government expectations and to accommodate business transactions and activities accordingly.

Voluntary multinational codes may or may not obviate ultimate mandatory application. More certain is the likelihood that failure on the part of a multinational to comply with a voluntary code will have serious implications.[38] At best, any such transgression will create an unfavorable public impression. At worst, it may lead directly to attempted retaliation by the host government. Apart from affecting a given commercial relationship, failure to respect voluntary code guidelines may encourage a host government to enact legislative constraints enforcing the code prescription disregarded by the multinational. Further, it is not difficult to foresee the alacrity with which a host government would seek to attack the credibility of the multinational involved in a given transaction to the government's bargaining advantage. The very existence of voluntary codes may enhance the bargaining power of developing nations, quite apart from any failure on the part of multinationals to respect code provisions, by encouraging them to interpret and apply, in concert, code compliance provisions applicable to the multinational activities addressed. Consideration of potential sanctions for noncompliance and the use of noncompliance as an affirmative opportunity for governments and third parties to exact penalties provides a convenient opportunity to appraise the effect, if any, of current code negotiations upon multinational conduct.

Any consideration of the possible effect evolving development of multinational codes has had, or continues to have, upon multinational conduct and accountability is conjectural at best. Nevertheless, an enumeration of logical possibilities provides a helpful point of reference for continuing observation of the relationship between multinationals and foreign governments:

(1) Has there been discernible change in contemporary multinational conduct? If so, can that change be related to evolving code proposals?

(2) Has any such change proved beneficial to the host governments in terms of economic development or related social-cultural considerations?

(3) Has code negotiation influenced municipal or regional legislation or regulation pertaining to multinationals?

(4) What discernible effect, if any, has the requirement, set forth in several code proposals, for increased voluntary corporate disclosure had upon multinational conduct?

(5) Will the periodic review of code provisions, such as that recently concluded by OECD, mandate subsequent change in the constraints placed upon multinationals?[39]

(6) Consider the attendant, perhaps indirect, effect resulting from the intensification of code activity. Is there a better understanding today of the several underlying issues? Has public awareness been heightened? Have public and government expectations of multinational conduct increased?

(7) Regardless of the negotiation outcome in a given codification effort, has the very fact of the negotiation itself influenced multinationals and their perception of corporate accountability? Will changing attitudes, if any, result in greater accommodation between multinationals and governments and between industrialized and developing states?

(8) What has been the effect upon the sensitivity of multinational corporate management with respect to evolving issues addressed through code negotiation?

(9) Have governments relied upon the experience and precedent provided by evolving code negotiations in their dealings with mulinationals?

(10) Have multinationals evidenced an increasing inclination to consult directly with governments to avoid potential economic and social-cultural problems in substantive areas addressed by proposed codes?

U.S. corporations have indeed evidenced an increasing awareness of domestic implications associated with corporate conduct. It is reasonable to asume that overseas activities of U.S. multinationals will reflect an early appreciation of the several implications herein discussed. But corporate awareness and appreciation, and constructive and timely response, require a continuing effort by corporate management. Any such effort will require a major contribution by corporate counsel.

IV. CORPORATE RESPONSE TO MULTINATIONAL CODE PROPOSALS:
NEW OPPORTUNITIES FOR CORPORATE COUNSEL

Several recent developments in the United States have focused increased attention upon the role of Corporate General Counsels in matters pertaining to corporate accountability. A summary of these developments will provide a helpful insight to counsel opportunities in assisting the multinational client to address the several concerns above described and to encourage purposeful corporate initiatives:

(1) The responsibilities of the Office of General Counsel have increased dramatically, accompanied by public and governmental concern for professional conduct responsive to demands for corporate accountability.

(2) Those seeking increased regulation of corporate governance also insist government place increasing responsibility upon lawyers to assist in the creation of internal discipline essential to effective corporate accountability.

(3) As perceived by the public, lawyers have societal responsiblities to assure the conduct of their clients anticipates increasingly stringent societal expectations.

(4) The American Bar Association, through a special Commission on Evaluation of Professional Standards, has begun a comprehensive reexamination of the Code of Professional Responsibility. That commission, among other things, is addressing the responsibilities of the corporate bar to assure its counsel reaches appropriate levels of management and, where necessary, the board of directors.

(5) The role of corporate counsel in the corporate implementation of the Foreign Corrupt Practices Act has focused SEC attention upon counsel responsibility to recommend written policies, assist in the introduction of proper procedures, and monitor their implementation. The Commission has concluded the Office of General Counsel is in a special position to define the requirements of a viable internal control environment.

These developments strongly suggest corporations need to enunciate their policies on legal compliance and effectuate internal legal support through close cooperation among the General Counsel, the Chief Executive Officer and the Board. The perceptions of Chairman Williams of the SEC reflect rising public expectations of the performance and responsibilities of the Corporate Office of General Counsel:

Because they are corporate insiders, internal attorneys are in a unique position to help the companies which they serve, and through them the corporate community as a whole: to focus attention on the issues of corporate responsibility; to assess the consequences of alternative courses of conduct; to weigh the short- and long-term costs and benefits; and to decide on positive steps which, in the context of the objectives of each particular corporation, can help to promote accountability and thus retard the pressure for federal restraints. . . . The inside attorney should also be concerned with the process by which the company evaluates the potential impact on itself of conduct which could be construed to be unethical, albeit technically legal. And a fundamental task is to sensitize and inform management and directors regarding the implications of the public's expanding perceptions of corporate responsibilities. Finally, inside counsel is in a unique position to implement a program of preventive law. On the scene and in intimate conduct with the management, he can help avoid many corporate decisions which fail to take into account those perceptions and their implications.[40]

All of the foregoing, of course, applies also to management and counsel consideration of public expectations overseas regarding conduct of U.S. multinationals. Any such consideration will require counsel attention beyond the traditional formulation of legal support for business activities within an international setting. Even traditional legal analyses in that regard may require considerable judgmental skill. It is one thing to address familiar jurisdiction, choice of law, choice of forum and remedy principles presented by transactional relationships involved in U.S. multinational business activity abroad. It will be quite another to resolve prospective legal conflict resulting from possible adoption of various codes and guidelines all potentially applicable to a given multinational or a particular business transaction: some voluntary and some mandatory; some outlining legal norms reflective of municipal law; others representing broad substantive accommodations among states with attendant uncertainty of application within a given jurisdiction. Accordingly, counsel, reflecting reasonable corporate concerns, should play an active role in professional support of efforts to assure development and declaration of coherent national policies underlying code issues. Those efforts will succeed only if counsel provides the corporate client timely information and analyses of code development to assist the client in recognition and understanding of attendant implications.

Counsel initiatives to achieve desirable corporate understanding and participation in the formulation and negotiation of desirable national policy positions addressing code proposals might include the following:

(1) Monitoring of all code activity to anticipate possible future code application;

(2) Identification of the several substantive issues addressed by proposed code provisions relating to the client's overseas business activities, present or contemplated;

(3) Periodic reports to senior management and the board regarding evolving code negotiation and the attendant implications for the client;

(4) Participation in business and professional advisory and support

efforts to assure U.S. government appreciation of business concerns
during code negotiations;

(5) Internal coordination of client response to third party inquiry
regarding application of code provisions to client business activities;

(6) Preparation of a corporate legal compliance system including
multinational code requirements;

(7) Timely discussions with government representatives abroad to
determine overseas expectations of multinational codes and their intended application to the client's business activities;

(8) Encouragement of purposeful voluntary corporate response
(voluntary disclosure; corporate code of conduct) to accommodate anticipated resolution of evolving issues addressed through code negotiation.

Counsel can be particularly helpful to management in appraising
implications to the client arising from periodic requests, such as those of
the ICC and OECD, seeking voluntary corporate response. Such
requests manifest a continuing effort to encourage and publicize business support for voluntary codes as an alternative to mandatory provisions. Nevertheless, any such request requires careful corporate attention prior to any corporate action. Recently, the ICC sought information
through its United States Council regarding U.S. business awareness of
the ICC Rules of Conduct to Combat Extortion and Bribery in Business
Transactions.[41] In turn, the United States Council enquired of its members "whether, during the past year, your company has either prepared
or updated its code of conduct."[42] Copies of any such code were
requested by the Council for forwarding to Paris headquarters of the
ICC. Further, the Council enquired of its members "if your company has
endorsed the ICC Rules, and if your company's name can be used publicly in further efforts to promote them." Considerations of these
requests should reflect the several concerns, discussed above, regarding
code proliferation, generally, and the manner in which any particular
code provision might be applied against the corporate client in a given
situation. Again, these legitimate concerns should in no way detract
from the constructive ICC effort to lead or the particular route chosen.

Accordingly, counsel and management might seek additional information pertaining to the activities and experience of the ICC Panel in
addressing its charter "to intepret, promote and oversee the application" of the Rules of Conduct. Management will be interested to learn
from counsel that the By-laws pertaining to the competence and functions of the Panel encourage Panel receipt of "information concerning

practices contrary to the ICC recommendations to governments or to the Rules," and "on the basis of its review of such information" to report to the ICC Executive Board. Further, "the Panel in its discretion may, upon the request of any member or National Committee of the ICC, or of any other enterprise or public authority which, in the opinion of the Panel, has a bona fide commercial or other legitimate interest, examine any alleged infringement of the Rules by any party, including nonmembers of the ICC . . . ." The By-laws preclude the Panel proceeding with the examination of a case absent "explicit consent by the party alleged to have infringed the Rules." But those same By-laws permit the Panel to recommend to the ICC Executive Board publication of the "general nature of the alleged infringement and of any reply or comment by the respondent (with or without identification of the parties)" when, in the Panel's opinion "the purpose of the Rules would be served thereby." Any application of the By-laws should prove of considerable interest to counsel and client already engaged in addressing the need for a company code of conduct responsive to the realities of the Foreign Corrupt Practices Act and SEC expectations. And their application will provide an important continuing reference point for those U.S. corporations which have endorsed the ICC rules and permitted that endorsement to be used publicly in promotional efforts. [43]

Reaffirmation of the voluntary OECD Guidelines and Declaration in June, 1979, following CIME review and OECD Ministerial Council adoption of the CIME Report, [44] has encouraged additional efforts by the U.S. State Department and by the U.S.A.-Business and Industry Advisory Committee (USA-BIAC) and the OECD to obtain support for the Guidelines by U.S. mulinationals. USA-BIAC has requested chief executive officers of U.S. multinationals to obtain corporate consideration of a "statement supporting the Guidelines in, for example, your company's annual report, other publications or speeches" and a report to the Secretariat of USA-BIAC "on any actions which you may take in support of the OECD Declaration and Guidelines." [45] Here, too, prospective application of the Guidelines to the conduct of a multinational requires careful review by counsel and understanding of possible future implications by the client.

CIME is expressly precluded from reaching "conclusions on the conduct of individual enterprises" [46] but is obligated "periodically or at the request of a member country" to "hold an exchange of views on matters related to the Guidelines and the experience gained in their application" and to report to the Council on such matters. CIME must also invite BIAC and the Trade Union Advisory Committee (TUAC) "to express their views on matters related to the Guidelines and shall take account of such views in its reports to the Council." The OECD Decision, as amended by the June, 1979[47] Council action, now expressly grants an individual enterprise "if it so wishes... the opportunity to express its views orally or in writing on issues concerning the Guidelines involving its interests," and it strengthens the obligation of CIME to exchange views with advisory bodies by granting the latter the right to request such an exchange.

Finally, the Decision, as amended, expressly assigns CIME responsibility "for clarification of the Guidelines" to be provided. The document provides important "legislative history" on the Guidelines. The U.S. position is that the Report itself in no way amends the Guidelines and that CIME's future role in issuing Guidelines "clarifications" should be used sparingly. Nevertheless, it may be anticipated that some member countries and TUAC will occasionally press for such clarifications. Although the Guidelines are voluntary and do not supersede national laws governing corporate liability, they are said to "introduce, where relevant, supplementary standards of a nonlegal character." In view of the likelihood that TUAC or member countries will make increased resort to the Guidelines for "clarifications" therof, counsel and management of U.S. multinationals are well adivsed to review the probable Guidelines status of proposed corporate actions likely to be controversial.

CONCLUSION

Experience of U.S. multinationals at home in addressing corporate governance and accountability issues should provide helpful insight to management and counsel alike in the appreciation of evolving multinational code proposals. That same experience should heighten awareness of the implications associated with proposed voluntary corporate response encouraged by ICC and OECD efforts. The threatened advent of mandatory provisions applicable to corporate conduct through codification efforts of the several U.N. agencies portends increased pressures on the U.S. multinational. Accordingly, U.S. business must assume a more emphatic role in manifesting legitimate concerns to government negotiators. At the same time, U.S. multinationals must conduct their activities abroad in a manner that will not undercut the support of U.S. Government negotiators. Future transgressions by multinationals anywhere in the world will influence significantly evolving standards of corporate conduct reflected in national or regional legislation or regulation.

In the wake of earlier corporate transgressions leading directly to passage of the Foreign Corrupt Practices Act, public criticism predictably focused upon the failure of the corporate bar to insist that the corporate client obey the law. Today, in light of the several concerns and uncertainties associated with evolving code negotiations, and their potential effect upon business activity, the U.S. corporate bar, generally, and each General Counsel of a U.S. multinational, in particular, have unique opportunities to assist their clients in anticipating and understanding rising public expectations of corporate conduct. Carefully fashioned preventive policies and attendant internal legal compliance practices can assist the U.S. multinational to respond in a constructive and timely manner at home and abroad.

APPENDIX

I. INTERNATIONAL CHAMBER OF COMMERCE (ICC)
RULES OF CONDUCT TO COMBAT EXTORTION AND BRIBERY

The international business community, primarily through the International Chamber of Commerce, has addressed the issues of extortion and bribery in business transactions and the need of the business community voluntarily to apply high standards of business ethics to assure growth of international commerce within a framework of fair competition.

The ICC, in December, 1975, created an Ad Hoc Commission, under the chairmanship of Lord Shawcross, to investigate the existence and effectiveness of legislation enacted by individual countries to prohibit extortion and bribery. The results of the Shawcross Commission effort convinced the ICC that such laws do exist but their enforcement varies considerably. The ICC concluded that neither governments nor business alone can effectively address the problem and, therefore, complementary and mutually reinforcing action by both governments and the business community is essential.

Accordingly, the Council of the ICC, in November, 1977, adopted a report[48] recommending to governments the adoption and administrative enforcement of laws prohibiting and punishing all forms of corruption and support for an inter-governmental treaty on corruption of the type now being addressed by a U.N. Intergovernmental Working Group.

The report emphasizes the responsibility of the international business community to make its own contribution toward effective elimination of extortion and bribery. To this end, the ICC adopted voluntary Rules of Conduct and guidelines for implementation by individual companies. The Report called for the establishment by the ICC of a Panel to interpret, promote and oversee the application of the Rules of Conduct. In June of 1978, the Council adopted By-laws of the International Panel on Extortion and Bribery in Business Transactions.[49]

The Panel recently invited ICC National Committees to "disseminate the Rules . . . to companies . . . in their countries which are engaged in international trade calling upon them to obtain endorsement of the Rules by their...Board of Directors" and "to inquire of individual companies whether they have themselves introduced codes of conduct reflecting the principles underlying the ICC rules and in the event of a negative response, to encourage them to do do."[50]

The U.S. Council Committee on Multinational Enterprises, in a recently prepared study on "Guiding Principles for Codes of Conduct," concludes: "The adoption of nonbinding and flexible codes of conduct for MNEs can be a positive development in creating a stable investment climate."[51] The Council concluded certain principles should be incorporated into any code of conduct:

(1) Responsibilities of both governments and MNEs should be recognized.

(2) Codes should apply to all international investors, including private, government or mixed.

(3) MNEs should receive "national treatment,"i.e, the same treatment accorded local firms, in accordance with international law.

(4) Codes should be nonbinding and flexible.

(5) Principles of international law should be respected in areas ranging from fair and equitable treatment to sanctity of contracts.

Not discussed here, but an important reference point for any consideration of voluntary multinational code proposals, are the *Guidelines for International Investment* adopted by the ICC in 1972.[52] The Guidelines, consisting of practical recommendations based upon experience, address multinational corporations, home governments and host country governments and are designed to facilitate consultation between investors and governments and to promote a better understanding of the needs and objectives of the respective parties.

II. ORGANIZATION FOR ECONOMIC COOPERATION AND DEVELOPMENT (OECD) THE DECLARATION OF INTERNATIONAL INVESTMENT AND MULTINATIONAL ENTERPRISES

The OECD, in June, 1976, adopted a Declaration and Associated Decisions on International Investment and Multinational Enterprises consisting of four elements: a Declaration and annexed voluntary Guidelines for Multinational Enterprises; a Decision on National Treatment; a Decision on International Investment Incentives and Disincentives; and a Decision on Intergovernmental Consultations among member governments on matters related to the Guidelines.[53] These agreements on principles reflect the basic orientation of OECD member governments towards an open international investment system stressing the beneficial aspects of such investment, affirm their obligations to provide national treatment for multinational enterprises *vis-à-vis* domestic firms, recommend that multinationals in OECD countries voluntarily observe the Guidelines reflecting standards of good business practice, and manifest an intention to achieve closer cooperation and consultation on international investment issues. The Declaration called for a formal review of experience under the 1976 instruments within three years with a view to strengthening cooperation among OECD member countries. This review, concluded in June, 1979, focused primarily on certain areas of the OECD investment package, in particular the Guidelines for Multinational Enterprises. At its June, 1979 meeting, the OECD

Ministerial Council adopted the Report of the Committee on International Investment and Multinational Enterprises (CIME) on its review of the Declaration.[54] The review process resulted in one minor change in the Guidelines provisions on Employment and Industrial Relations (aimed at transfer of staff from one country to another to break the strike), a number of technical changes in the various Decisions, and reaffirmation of the revised OECD documents for another five years.

The CIME Report is useful review of a wide range of investment issues on the OECD region and identifies a number of areas that may become more critical in multinational government relations or a subject of further CIME attention:

(1) Increased CIME attention on departure from national treatment, particularly through administrative practices. Initially, CIME will press for greater "transparency" (i.e., reporting of discriminatory measures whether or not justified as permissible exceptions to national treatment);

(2) New CIME projects including an analysis of the effects of investment incentives and disincentives and comparison of the scope of, and experience of member governments with, bilateral investment treaties;

(3) CIME anticipates that significant further efforts will be necessary to encourage wide observance of the recommended disclosure standards and is exploring ways to harmonize national accounting standards to promote this goal;

(4) CIME takes the view that "the restrictive business practices of multinational enterprises do not differ in form from those operated by purely national enterprises but may have a more significant impact on trade and competition . . . ." In this connection it draws attention to the 1978 OECD Council recommendation (Annex II) of more active programs against multinational restrictive business practices;

(5) Enterprises that have not already done so are asked to state publicly, preferably in their annual reports, their acceptance of the Guidelines;

(6) OECD member governments are asked to "provide appropriate facilities and arrangements for handling matters and problems arising with regard to the Guidelines" ("With respect to specific matters arising under the Guidelines, the Committee urges that such matters first be raised, discussed, and, if possible, resolved at the national level and, when appropriate, such efforts be pursued at the bilateral level between the states involved");

(7) BIAC and TUAC are encouraged to continue their active programs of consultation with CIME with respect to matters arising under the Guidelines.

III. UNITED NATIONS ECONOMIC AND SOCIAL COUNCIL—COMMISSION ON TRANSNATIONAL CORPORATIONS, INTERGOVERNMENTAL WORKING GROUP ON A CODE OF CONDUCT RELATING TO TRANSNATIONAL CORPORATIONS

The U.N. Commission on Transnational Corporations, in March, 1976, agreed to give highest priority among its various tasks to the formulation of a code of conduct.[55] The Commission established an Intergovernmental Working

Group which has held substantive discussions and identified a wide range of issues but without agreement. In March, 1978, a working paper was submitted by the U.N. Centre on Transnational Corporations in which common elements that emerged during the earlier Working Group discussions were identified and formulated in language designed to assist the Working Group in its deliberations on the formulations of a code of conduct, without prejudice to the position of governments.[56] Subsequently, in September, 1978, the Chairman of the Working Group, Sten Niklasson of Sweden, was requested to prepare formulations on the basis of the Group discussions and the Centre was requested to prepare a paper presenting possible modalities for implementation of the code, taking into account various options regarding its legal nature. The Chairman's formulations and the Centre's paper on Modalities for Implementation of a Code of Conduct in Relation to its Possible Legal Nature was submitted for Working Group consideration in January, 1979.[57] The U.N. Code, now in "composite text" (i.e., complete with proposed Preamble, Provisions on Activities of Transnational Corporations and Treatment of Transnational Corporations, Intergovernmental Cooperation, and Implementation), will be discussed at U.N. Working Group sessions throughout 1980.[58]

The proposed U.N. Code addresses a broad range of considerations underlying activities of transnational corporations including: respect for national sovereignty and observance of domestic laws, regulations and administrative practices; adherence to the economic goals and development objectives, policies and priorities of the countries in which they operate; adherence to the sociocultural objectives and values of those countries; respect for human rights and fundamental freedoms; noninterference in internal political affairs and intergovernmental relations; and abstention from corrupt practices. Specific code provisions pertain to: the ownership and control of transnational corporations; balance of payments and financing; transfer pricing; taxation; competition and restrictive business practices; transfer of technology; employment and labor; environmental protection; consumer protection; and disclosure of information. The code will also consider the treatment of transnational corporations by the countries in which they operate. In this regard, nationalization and compensation and jurisdiction are included within the subject matter addressed. Finally, the code places considerable emphasis upon the need for intergovernmental cooperation to effectuate code objectives.[59]

Concerns of U.S. business regarding the proposed code and its application to U.S. multinationals have been manifested to a State Department Advisory Committee. These concerns derive from the language of the November, 1979, *Composite Text of Formulations by the Chairman and Elements Prepared by the Centre on Transnational Corporations.* The Composite Text contains numerous instances where it may be impossible to arrive in the near future at language which does not intensify multinational/host-country controversies, cloud the legitimacy of customary business practice, and undercut reasonable expectations that governmental actions with respect to multinationals will be fair, nondiscriminatory, and in accord with international law.

(1) CONFLICTING PROVISIONS AS TO LEGAL NATURE OF CODE

There is no statement that the Code is voluntary. Paragraphs 58 and 62 suggest that "application of the Code of Conduct at the national level is essential for its effectiveness." Beyond this, however, paragraph 63 commits governments "to take no action contrary to the objectives and principles set forth in this Code, and to undertake national measures and make institutional arrangements necessary for this purpose." Paragraph 64(c) invites governments to "use the Code as a source of law in their administrative and judicial processes." Clause (g.) and (h.) of the Preamble fo further and refer to the Code as "establishing widely accepted international standards" and set the goal of "establishment and effective implementation of an international code of conduct." In short, the present draft appears in part to negate the concept of a voluntary code.

(2) ABSENCE OF PROVISIONS ON EQUAL APPLICATION TO STATE-OWNED ENTERPRISES

There continues to be an absence of any provision on application of the Code to state-owned enterprises. The recent negotiating session in Geneva on an UNCTAD Code on Restrictive Business Practices (which in turn would be incorporated by reference at paragraph 33 of the UN Code) provided the Soviet Union with an opportunity to object to application of such codes to state-owned enterprises. The United States takes the position that any code must be equally applicable to private and state-owned enterprises and this position was ultimately accepted in the UNCTAD text.

(3) NEGATIVE IMPLICATIONS AND LACK OF BALANCE

Both the added text and Chairman Niklasson's previous formulations are replete with negative implications with respect to multinational corporate behavior and treatment by governments. Paragraph "a" of the Preamble expresses a "determination to promote the establishment of a New International Economic Order," and paragraph "g" refers to the need for "controlling and eliminating . . . negative effects" of transnational corporations. Paragraphs 1-3 imply that such enterprises fail to respect the sovereignty, laws, or regulations of nations, and paragraphs 10-11 imply interference in nations' internal political affairs. New paragraph 32(b) implies that tax avoidance by legal methods is no longer permissible. Paragraphs 46 and 52 imply that the force of international law is limited to those "international obligations and contractual undertakings to which States have . . . subscribed." Thus, the Code contains numerous erroneous and trouble-some negative implications which will be difficult to eliminate. If the obligations of governments to treat multinational enterprises fairly (addressed in paragraphs 45-56 of the Chairman's draft) are also cut back from even the present unsatisfactory text, the draft Code will not have the "balance" U.S. representatives said would be essential to any Code.

(4) IMPLEMENTATION PROBLEMS

The new sections in the draft Code on implementations are an invitation to decisions by the UN Commission on specific cases involving multinational enterprises (see paragraph 66[b]), to media events about multinationals in highly political UN forums (see paragraph 67), and to attempts by the UN Commission or the Centre on Transnational Corporations to become a supranational Corporations Commission, gathering data and reporting on multinationals worldwide (*see* paragraphs 68 and 69). These proposals conflict with the position taken by the U.S. on the OECD Guidelines, and go well beyond the mandate and capacities of the UN Commission and the Centre on Transnational Corporations. U.S. business spokesmen have consistently concluded the relationships between a multinational and the governments of the states where it operates should be left to them and not to a UN overseer.

In light of the foregoing concerns, business representatives to the State Department Advisory Committee question whether it will be possible during forthcoming meetings of the UN Commission to obtain the substantial revisions necessary to present a voluntary, nondiscriminatory and balanced document. Accordingly, those representatives have urged the State Department to make clear to the participants in the discussion of a Code the seriousness of the problems in the present text, the desirability of avoiding a product that impairs the contribution of multinational enterprises to national economic growth and exacerbates relations between multinationals and host governments, and the necessity of taking whatever time is required to arrive at an appropriate consensus statement along the lines of that reached in the OECD Declaration of 1976.

IV. UNITED NATIONS CONFERENCE ON TRADE AND DEVELOPMENT (UNCTAD)

(1) PRINCIPLES AND RULES FOR THE CONTROL OF RESTRICTIVE BUSINESS PRACTICES

An Ad Hoc Group of Experts on Restrictive Business Practices was formed pursuant to a 1976 UNCTAD Resolution.[60] The Group's mandate included the formulation of principles and rules for the control of restrictive business practices likely to adversely affect international trade and economic development of developing countries and the drafting of a model law. Concerning the principles and rules, the Experts produced a final report containing a text, as to which agreement has now been reached, with approximately fifty provisions, including objectives, definitions and scope of application, general principles, principles for enterprises, principles for states, and principles for implementation at the international level.[61] Several portions of the text raise important and difficult issues such as the scope of application of the principles and rules, the extent to which transactions among affiliated enterprises should be subject to the principles and rules, and whether developing-country enterprises should enmjoy special treatment.[62]

The two diplomatic Conferences to negotiate the UNCTAD Principles and Rules took place in December, 1979 and April, 1980. As a result of these Conferences, the text of the principles and rules is now complete.[63] Two issues that remained unresolved until the final days of the April negotiations were the applicability of rules to State-owned enterprises and their voluntary nature. In the end it was agreed that the "enterprises" covered include state-created or controlled enterprises. While there is no express statement that the rules are voluntary, they are characterized as "recommendations."

Three other basic issues remained to be resolved in the second diplomatic Conference: the issue of preferential as opposed to nondiscriminatory treatment;

whether the activities of affiliated enterprises and the concept of "shared monopoly" should be dealt with in the code; and the extent to which UNCTAD will be involved in implementation of the code:

Nondiscriminatory vs. Preferential Treatment

Some members of Group B (the developed countries), particularly the United Kingdom and the Netherlands, had requested a text that excepts flatly all restrictive business practices which are exempted or accepted under national legislation. The Sanchis-Munoz draft (a compromise text proposed by the Argentinian Conference President) took a milder form, suggesting only that nations "should take into account that certain restrictive business practices are 'exempted' or 'accepted' by national legislation." The Group of 77 wanted all LDC enterprises exempted from the code. Group B countered with a proposal for a combination of the "take into account" language accompanied by a provision that special attention should be given to small- and medium-size enterprises. The Sanchis-Munoz draft, in the section on Preferential and Differential Treatment, prescribed that states, in enforcing their own antitrust laws, should take into account the interest of LDCs. The final text with respect to exceptions (§C(b)(6)) provides that States "should take due account of the extent to which the conduct of enterprises, whether or not created or controlled by States, is accepted under applicable legislation or regulations." On the issue of nondiscrimination, the text (§E)(3) calls for "treatment of enterprises which is fair, equitable, on the same basis to all enterprises, and in accordance with established procedures of law."

Intra-enterprise Activity Exclusion

Section D(3) of the text which identifies various horizontal restraints excludes arrangements between enterprises "dealing with each other in the context of an economic entity wherein they are under common control, including through ownership, or otherwise not able to act independently of each other . . . ." The restraints identified in section D(4) are qualified by a footnote to the effect they must be evaluated "in the light of the organizational, managerial, and legal relationships among the enterprises concerned, such as in the context of relations within an economic entity and not having restrictive effects outside the related enterprises."

Code Implementation

Consultations on implementation under the Code are to be handled directly between countries and not by UNCTAD. States may jointly request use of UNCTAD conference facilities.

(2) UNCTAD CODE OF CONDUCT ON TRANSFER OF TECHNOLOGY

An Intergovernmental Group of Experts was formed in 1975 for the purpose of drafting an UNCTAD code of conduct on the transfer of technology. Since 1975, several meetings of the Intergovernmental Group have addressed code proposals submitted by developing and developed countries. Those proposals differ substantially in their philosophical foundation, legal nature and actual content. The issue of the code's legal nature has been debated at length.[64] UNCTAD directed the Group of Experts to proceed with drafting the provisions of a code but to leave the question of the code's legal status to decision by a UN Conference. In July, 1978, the Group completed work on a text which continues to reflect serious differences. UN Conferences held in 1978 and 1979 to address those differences failed to reach overall agreement. Extensive discussions on the code's legal nature were held at UNCTAD V in Manila in May, 1979.[65] The Group B (developed) countries were united in their view that the code should be voluntary. The Group of 77, on the other hand, maintained its position that the code be legally binding. Group B outlined its view on the institutional arrangements to implement the code and argued that a voluntary code coupled with an effective follow-up institution would address the primary concerns of the Group of 77. Conference discussions on the code in late 1979 focused on the code's legal character and the chapters covering restrictive business practices and guarantees. The Conference agreed the code will be voluntary during its first four years of application. Its legal status then will be reviewed. Conference sessions are continuing in 1980.

The U.S. negotiating position regarding the nature and scope of the code insists the code:

- be voluntary in nature, though a follow-up machinery to review the Code may be possible;
- be appropriately balanced in reference to the responsibilities of governments as well as firms;
- ensure that national laws regulating the transfer of technology should be in accordance with international law;
- provide that provisions addressed to enterprises should be consistent with legal standards and practices commonly recognized among developed countries.

Other developed countries have advocated similar positions, and to date there have been no substantial differences among the developed countries (Group B).

The developing countries (Group of 77) advocate that:

- the code should be legally binding in all aspects;
- all transactions between affiliated enterprises should be subject to the code;
- responsibilities addressed to enterprises need not be balanced by responsibilities of governments;
- creation of a follow-up mechnaism to supervise and implement the code.

The State Department Advisory Committee's Working Group on the Transfer of Technology has reflected the concern of U.S. business since the inception of code negotiations. Several members of the Working Group have concluded the U.S. should not be disappointed if the effort to construct a code were indefinitely postponed so long as no Third World code on technology transfer is substituted for the UN effort.[66] Given the difficulties the Group of 77 is having in maintaining unanimity on specific issues, it may be unable to construct a Third World code that goes beyond broad generalities. Such a code might also lack credibility.

It has been pointed out by the Working Group that many of the issues covered by the technology transfer negotiations—industrial property, standards for commercial contract, choice of law, and restrictive business practices—are also at issue in other international negotiations. The current negotiations on technology transfer, however, may be a better forum for achieving recognition for developed countries' interests than other negotiations. The Working Group agreed this is certainly not the time for Group B to compromise on points of principle.

The Working Group also addressed problems of implementation. Although considerable attention has been focused on the question whether the code should be binding or voluntary, the Working Group believes that implementation and enforcement techniques might well overshadow this issue in practice. A "voluntary" code backed up by a quasi-judicial tribunal could have a major impact, while a "binding" code that is not enforced either by national implementation or by an international bureaucracy might well prove ineffective. The United States is firmly rejecting any effort to force technology-supplying countries to take an affirmative role in regulating private behavior. The United States has opposed a binding code that would require enforcement by individual nations, and it has also opposed any sort of quasi-judicial international body. It has, however, proposed some international administrative supervision of the effects of the code. The Working Group has suggested that creation of an administrative body to investigate transfers or to make reports on them might well slow the flow of technology to less developed countries. The State Department evidently thinks, however, that the greatest danger is from a quasi-judicial body; it is less willing to resist a bureaucracy with other functions. The value of a voluntary code to the Group of 77 has been questioned, but such a code could serve as a model for national laws on the subject, and it could be incorporated by reference in technology-transfer contracts.

FOOTNOTES

1. Vagts, *The Multinational Enterprise: A New Challenge for Transnational Law*, 83 Harv. L. Rev. 739 (1970).
2. *See* Schollhammer, *Ethics in an International Business Context*, 17 Management Int'l Rev. 23 (1977).
3. Rubin, *Developments in the Law and Institutions of International Economic Relations*, 68 The Am. J. of Int'l L. 475, 478-479 (1974).
4. International Chamber of Commerce, *Extortion and Bribery in Business Transactions*, ICC Publ. No. 315, 12-16; Part III: Rules of Conduct to Combat Extortion and Bribery (Report adopted by the 131st Sess., November 29, 1979) [hereinafter "Rules of Conduct"].
5. Organization for Economic Cooperation and Development (OECD), Declaration of International Investment and Multinational Enterprises (June 21,

1976) [hereinafter "Declaration"]; OECD, Guidelines for Multinational Enterprises (Annex to Declaration, *supra*) [hereinafter "Guidelines"] (June 21, 1976).

6. United Nations Conference on Trade and Development, The Set of Multilaterally Agreed Equitable Principles and Rules for the Control of Restrictive Business Practices (2d Sess., April 8-21, 1980), U.S. Doc. TD/RBP/CONF/ April 22, 1980) [hereinafter "Principles and Rules].

7. United Nations Conference on an International Code of Conduct on the Transfer of Technology, Draft International Code of Conduct on the Transfer of Technology (2d Sess., November 16, 1979), U.N. Doc. TD/CODE TOT/20 (November 6, 1979).

8. *See generally,* Finnegan, *Code of Conduct Regulating International Technology Transfer: Panacea or Pitfall?,* 60 J. of the Pat. Off. Soc'y 71 (February 1978).

9. OECD Council, Decision of the Council on Inter-governmental Consultation Procedures on the Guidelines for Multinational Enterprises §3 (June 1976).

10. United Nations Commission on Transnational Corporations, Intergovernmental Working Group on a Code of Conduct, Transnational Corporations: A Code of Conduct (8th Sess., January 7-8, 1980), Working Paper No. 10, November 5, 1979 (also known as Composite Text of Formulations by the Chairman and Elements Prepared by the Centre on Transnational Corporations) [herinafter "Composite Text"].

11. Commission on Transnational Corporations, Intergovernmental Working Group on a Code of Conduct, Transnational Corporations: Certain Modalities for Implementation of a Code of Conduct in Relation to Its Possible legal Nature (6th Sess., January 8-19), U.N. Doc. E/C.10AC.2/9 (December 18, 1978).

12. Commission on Transnational Corporations: Intergovernmental Working Group on a Code of Conduct, Transnational Corporations: Codes of Conduct; Formulations by the Chairman (6th Sess., January 8-19,. 1979, U.N. Doc. E/C.10/AC.2/8 (December 8, 1978).

13. Principles and Rules, *supra* n. 6.

14. Organisation for Economic Co-operation and Development (OECD), Committee on International Investment and Multinational Enterprises, Review of the 1976 Declaration and Decisions on International Investment and Multinational Enterprises (OECD Ministerial Council Meeting, June 13-14, 1979).

15. International Chamber of Commerce, The By-laws of the International Panel on Extortion and Bribery in Business Transactions (132d Session of the ICC Council on June 20, 1978) [hereinafter "By-laws"].

16. *See, How to Make Business Behave Better: Codes of Conduct for Business Will Have to Be Backed by Publicity if They Are Not to Be Backed by Law,* The Economist, 89 (October 8, 1977).

17. The matter was discussed in the CIME Committee on March 31, 1977. Meeting minutes are confidential. *See* Vogelaar, *Multinational Enterprises: The Guidelines in Practice,* OECD Observer, 7 (May 1977).

18. Hoff Amersterdam (Ondernemingskamer), 21 June 1979, N.J. 1980, No. 71.

19. Declaration, *supra* n. 5.

20. Principles and Rules, *supra* n. 6.

21. *See* Transnational Corporations—*The United Nations Code of Conduct,* 5 Brooklyn J. Int'l Law 129 (1979).

22. Atkeson, *The Foreign Corrupt Practices Act of 1977: An International Application of SEC's Corporate Governance Reforms,* 12 Int'l Law 703 (1978).

23. *See* Solmon and Linville, *Transnational Conduct of American Multinational Corporations: Questionable Payments Abroad,* 17 B.C. Indus. & Com. L. Rev. 303 (1976); *see also* Baumeister & Cohen, *Foreign Bribery by American Multinational Corporations: A Status Report,* 2 Delaware J. of Corp. L. 207 (1977).

24. Foreign Corrupt Practices Act of 1977 §102, Pub. L. No. 95-213, tit. I (91 Stat. 1494 (1977)) (amending 15 U.S.C. §§78q(b), 78dd, 78ff(a) (1976)).

25. SEC Rel. No. 34-15772 (April 30, 1979), 44 Fed. Reg. 26702 (May 4, 1979).

26. *Id.* at 26705.

27. SEC Rel. No. 34-16877 (June 6, 1980). The proposed rules of SEC Rel. No. 34-15772 (April 30, 1977) were withdrawn.

28. Statement by SEC Chairman Harold Williams, Opening Statement at the Commission's Consideration of Proposed Rules to Require a Management Statement on Internal Accounting Control (May 28, 1980 at Washington, D.C.).

29. Gustman *The Foreign Corrupt Practices Act of 1977: A Transnational Analysis,* 13 J. of Int'l L. & Econ 367 (1979).

30. Guidelines, *supra* n. 5, General Policies §7.

31. Rules of Conduct, *supra* n. 4, at 12.

32. Guidelines, *supra* n. 5, §6.

33. Speech by SEC Chairman Harold Williams, Implementation of The Foreign Corrupt Practices Act: An Intersection of Law and Management (August 14, 1979, before the American Bar Association, Dallas, Texas).

34. *See* Davidow & Chiles, *The United States and the Issue of the Binding or Voluntary Nature of International Codes of Conduct Regarding Restrictive Business Practices,* 72 Am. J. of Int'l L. 247 (1978).

35. Statement of the Business Roundtable, *The Role and Composition of the Board of Directors at Large Publicly Owned Corporations,* Bus. Law. (January 1978); *see also, Corporate Director's Guidebook* (Revised Edition, January 1978), 33 Bus. Law. 1595 (1978).

36. Guidelines, *supra* n. 5, Disclosure of Information.

37. Rules of Conduct, *supra* n. 4, at 15 (article 10).

38. Plaine, *The OECD Guidelines for Multinational Enterprise,* 11 Int'l Law. 339 (1977); *see* Chance, *Code of Conduct for Multinational Corporations,* 33 Bus. Law. 1799 (1978).

39. *See* Hawk, *The OECD Guidelines for Multinational Enterprises: Competition,* 46 Fordham L. Rev. 241, 248 (1977).

40. Speech by SEC Chairman Harold Williams, The Role of Inside Counsel in Corporate Accountability (October 4, 1979, before the Corporate Counsel Institute, Chicago).

41. Note to National Committees from ICC Secretary General's Office (November 11, 1979). (ICC Internal Document No. 192-22/8.)

42. Memorandum from Paxton T. Dunn, ICC Vice President—Policy, to Members of the United States Council (December 21, 1979).

43. By-laws, *supra* n. 15.
44. Review of the 1976 Declaration, *supra* n. 14, Appendix I (Revised Decision of the Council on Inter-Governmental Consultation Procedures on the Guidelines for Multinational Enterprises).
45. Letter from Alexander B. Trowbridge, Richard L. Lesher and David L. Grove to Alden W. Clausen (February 21, 1980).
46. Decision of the Council, *supra* n. 9.
47. *Id.*, §1.
48. Rules of Conduct, *supra* n. 4.
49. By-laws, *supra* n. 15, at 17.
50. Williams, *supra* n. 40.
51. United States Council (of the ICC), Committee on Multinational Enterprise, Guiding Principles for Codes of Conduct: The Business Viewpoint (February 25, 1980).
52. International Chamber of Commerce, Guidelines for International Investment (ICC Publication No. 272, 1972).
53. Declaration, *supra* n. 5.
54. Review of the 1976 Declaration, *supra* n. 14.
55. Rubin, *Developments in the Law and Institutions of International Economic Relations,* 70 Am. J. of Int'l L. 73 (1976).
56. Commission on Transnational Corporations, Intergovernmental Working Group on a Code of Conduct, Formulation of a Code of Conduct: Elaboration of the Chairman's Annotated Outline on the Basis of Discussion in the Intergovernmental Working Group on a Code of Conduct (4th Sess., March 20-31, 1978), Working Paper No. 2, March 24, 1978.
57. Composite Text, *supra* n. 10.
58. *Id.*
59. *See* Asante, *United Nations: International Regulation of Transnational Corporations,* 13 J. of World Trade L. 55 (1979); *see* Coonrod, *The United Nations Code of Conduct for Transnational Corporations,* 18 Harv. Int'l L. J. 273 (1977).
60. Joelson, *The Proposed International Codes of Conduct as Related to Restrictive Business Practices,* 8 L. & Policy in Int'l Bus. 837 (1976).
61. United Nations Conference on Trade and Development, Committee on Manufacturers, Report of the Third Ad Hoc Group of Experts on Restrictive Business Practices on its Fifth Session (July 10-21, 1978), U.N. Doc. TD/B/C.2/AC.6/18 (July 27, 1978).
62. Wex, *A Code of Conduct on Restrictive Business Practices: A Third Option,* 1977 Canadian Year Book of Int'l L. 198 (1977).
63. Principles and Rules, *supra* n. 6.
64. *See generally* Jeffries, *Regulation of Transfer of Technology: An Evaluation of the UNCTAD Code of Conduct,* 18 Harv. Int'l L. J. 309 (1977).
65. United Nations Conference on Trade and Development, Report of the Intergovernmental Group of Experts on an International Code of Conduct on Transfer of Technology to the United Nations Conference on an International Code of Conduct on Transfer and Technology (Meeting of June 26-July 7, 1978), U.N. Doc. TD/CODE TOT/1/Add.I, TD/AC.I/18/Add. 1, Annexes I, II, III (July 25, 1978).

66. United Nations Conference on an International Code of Conduct on the Transfer of Technology, Draft International Code of Conduct on the Transfer of Technology (2d Sess., November 16, 1979), U.N. Doc. TD/CODE TOT/20 (December 5, 1979).

25
The Multinational Corporation and Its Host-Country Environment
John S. Schwendiman

The role of the multinational corporation in the economic development of a country can take many forms. Involvement can range from direct investment in wholly-owned manufacturing facilities to joint ventures or licensing arrangements for technology. For an involvement to make a long-term contribution it must be of long-term benefit to both parties, the multinational corporation and the host country.

ALTHOUGH UNITED STATES natural resource companies (in mining and petroleum, for example) were heavily involved in resource-rich developing countries for many decades, the broad internationalization of U.S. business interests has come about since the 1950s. Many large U.S. companies have gone from virtually no involvement in international markets to half or more of their business now being done outside the country. This is somewhat in contrast to many European companies, which, because of relatively smaller home-country markets, have been much more internationally-oriented for a longer period of time.

Companies investing in other countries have always been concerned about relations in the host countries. For many years the potential problem of expropriation was a significant concern to investors. In recent years expropriation (in the traditional sense) has probably become less of a concern. However, other concerns have arisen to replace those of outright expropriation. The term "creeping expropriation" has sometimes been used to describe a process that is perceived by the investor as one in which the policies of the host country in effect strangle an enterprise, and accomplish over time, in a *de facto* sense, an expropriation.

A company is seen to have reached this point when it has no control of its capital resources or its profitability because of rules, regulations, or discriminatory policies, for example.

Companies have tried and are trying to be cognizant of the potential problems (or risks) which they face in a given host-country environment. Business strategies are developed to deal with potential risks. (Professor Louis Wells of Harvard has written much on this subject of building on a company's strengths in developing a strategy for dealing with a host country. See, for example, L. T. Wells, "Negotiating with Third World Governments," *Harvard Business Review*, January-February, 1977, pp. 72-80).

The events occurring in Iran late in 1978 and into 1979 with the overthrow of the Shah and subsequent negative experiences for many investing companies (especially many U.S. companies) spawned further emergence of a field that had begun years earlier. "Political risk analysis" became a new term that many companies talked about. Companies hired "experts," often people from the U.S. Foreign Service or the Central Intelligence Agency, to make political assessments of countries as a part of the strategic planning and management process.

The high-growth period of the use of "political risk analysis" by U.S. companies is over and the emphasis has subsided somewhat. There remains, however, a basic caution and sensitivity that was lacking for many companies previously. A wide range of consultant services has become somewhat institutionalized and professionalized with the establishment in 1980 of the Association of Political Risk Analysis, which has over 400 members in the United States and Europe.

This study aims to address the subject of "political risk assessment," which is broadened in concept to include economic, social, political and business environment factors. To aid in an understanding of this subject in a very specific way, the author uses many examples from the experiences and programs of The Dow Chemical Company to illustrate points which can be generalized to a large number of U.S. companies.

A clear understanding on the part of host-country officials and business people of the concerns, criteria, and priorities of potential private foreign investors can greatly help the negotiation process. It can help directly and in a positive way influence the positive role which foreign investment can play in the national development of a country, and in particular, China.

The remaining sections of this study will describe the international involvement of The Dow Chemical Company, and the experience of

Dow is then generalized to other companies. There follows an example of how host-country analysis can be done, with emphasis on the key factors that a foreign investor will consider. A description of information sources that multinational corporations use will also be given, followed by some conclusions.

INTERNATIONALIZATION AND EXPERIENCE
OF THE DOW CHEMICAL COMPANY

Rapid expansion in international marketing, through direct investments, licensing, joint ventures and export sales was the great engine of growth for The Dow Chemical Company in the 1960s and 1970s. From an international base of less than ten percent of sales in 1960, the company reached the point of having over one-half of its sales and profits come from outside the United States by 1980. In 1984 total worldwide sales were in excess of $11 billion. The company fully expects that for the future the non-U.S. business will provide over one-half and perhaps even a growing proportion of corporate sales and profits.

The Dow Chemical Company operates manufacturing plants in approximately thirty countries and sales offices in seventy. There is hardly any country in the world that is not the specific responsibility of a Dow manager. Being involved in Dow's international business has been a proving ground for many of the company's top corporate officers. Of the top twenty who are members of the company's management committee, fourteen have had significant international management experience.

Dow's experience with international growth is not untypical of the experiences of many companies. Investment followed export sales. Dow's first investment outside the United States was in Mexico in the early 1950s. At the time, the rapidly growing Texas manufacturing division considered the small Mexico market and the small investment there just a logical extension of their business. In 1952, Dow and the Asahi Chemical Company in Japan established a joint venture, Asahi-Dow, which was to grow and develop for thirty years. When Asahi-Dow split up by mutual agreement of the partners in 1982, it was an $800 million sales company in its own right.

These early investments were not followed by additional ones until the 1960s. In the meantime, a global sales organization, based on exports from the U.S., and an international division (Dow International) came into being. The first European plant, at Terneuzen in the Netherlands, was begun in 1962. At Terneuzen, Dow set out to do for the European market, under the beneficial trade arrangements of the European Economic Community, what it was best at doing in the U.S.—building a very large, world-scale, highly integrated and efficient chemical production complex for the manufacture of large-volume commodity chemicals and plastics. With that idea for a base, Dow became the largest U.S. participant in the European chemical market. In 1984, sales in Europe were approximately $4 billion.

The mid-1960s brought a change in the way the international business was managed. A regional management concept was introduced, and geographic "Areas" were established. These were Dow U.S.A., Canada, Latin America, Europe, and Pacific. Today, additionally, there are sub-Areas for Brazil, Middle East/Africa, and Japan. Regional headquarters were established, with the headquarters for Dow Chemical Pacific being in Hong Kong.

With the establishment of the Area concept came the first attempts to develop investment projects in the so-called "developing countries." It was at this point that Dow first confronted directly the challenge of country environment risk. Some early experiences pointed up the necessity of a more formal approach to risk assessment and management in Latin America and then in the Pacific Area. But for Canada, Europe, and the United States itself, there were no formal organizational procedures for assessment. Managers who had spent many years on the international side of the company continued to make basically intuitive judgments as far as managing enterprises and risks was concerned until the end of the 1970s.

Although the Area organization was overlaid in a matrix fashion with a centralized product management group called the "Corporate Product Department" (now the Global Product Management Unit), which had responsibility for global product strategies, in practice the power base in the company shifted from centralized to decentralized management, with the Area managers becoming very powerful in the company. At one point (in 1979) all Area presidents were also members of the company's Board of Directors.

The evolution is now in the direction of individual globally-managed businesses, the first of which are pharmaceuticals, agricultural products, and consumer products. There are now emerging centralized management and control over these major sectors of the company.

No two multinational companies have evolved in exactly the same way. However, patterns do exist and emerge, and can be studied. Basic issues such as organization, control, preferred ways of doing business, and personnel have to be handled no matter what product or technology is involved.

This brief historical look at Dow is useful to understand how the formal environment assessment program came into being.

In 1966 and 1967, The Dow Chemical Company was invited by the government of Chile to go to Chile and build a petrochemical complex. The project was to be a joint venture, but majority ownership would be in Dow's hands. The plants would produce basic plastics. The business outlook was good, a decision was made, and the company's Board of Directors authorized a $30 million investment (which would be over $100 million in today's dollars), of which a major portion would be by external borrowing.

As is the case with large capital-intensive petrochemical projects, the design and actual construction of the plants took more than three years. In 1970, with six months remaining before the plants were to be started up, Salvador Allende was elected president of Chile. His campaign promises had been to change completely the basis of the economy, expropriate foreign investors, and throw off foreign influences. The Dow project, although a joint venture with a Chilean government company, was a large, visible one. It was a time of decision, but Dow decided to finish the plants, run them, live up to the contracts, and be "a good corporate citizen."

Dow was expropriated about two years later. The legal term in Chile was "intervened." Dow was one of the last foreign companies to be taken over, but that was still six months before the coup that ousted Allende. In the meantime, business conditions had deteriorated rapidly in Chile. Inflation was runaway—over 900 percent in Allende's last year. The balance of payments was a disaster. There was no foreign exchange available. Dow costs went up faster than prices because there was an attempt to control chemical product prices, but not raw materials. Profits disappeared. The situation was dismal.

Several months after the coup that ousted Allende the new military regime approached Dow and asked the company to come back. That meant going back into a very shaky environment, but Dow went back and is still there in 1986.

It was during the same period that an even larger project was being developed for Bahia Blanca in Argentina. That project had already cost over two million dollars of development money with expenses for the project team to move to Argentina, when a government change occurred. The new government changed the rules for that kind of investment almost 180 degrees. Dow decided not to do anything further, dropped the project, and moved people home.

During this period both corporate and Area management asked a lot of tough questions. Was there any way to foresee these problems? Could Dow's strategies have been developed or adjusted to deal more explicitly with foreseen or unforeseen risks? What could be done differently for the future?

It was out of these difficult experiences that in 1971 an effort was begun in Dow Chemical Latin America, which resulted in Dow's Economic, Social, and Political Assessment Program (ESP Program). It is a systematic framework for analyzing the many factors in the country and business environment, which can impact on a foreign investment by Dow.

Other companies have had varied experiences. The oil companies had to cope at much earlier dates with problems of expropriations. Exxon Corporation, for example, had a well-developed program for environmental assessment both at their New York headquarters and in their regional operating companies by the late 1960s. Others, previously noted, did not formalize any assessment activities until they had been badly hurt in the aftermath of the ouster of the Shah of Iran.

BASES AND CONTENT OF COMPANY
ENVIRONMENTAL ASSESSMENT PROGRAMS

Companies approach the assessment of country environments with different methodologies, but the same kinds of issues appear for consideration, no matter what the methodology. Before considering the specifics of what is assessed, however, it is appropriate to define the concept of "risk." What does it mean to speak of "risk" in a host-country environment?

There are at least two broad categories of risk to be distinguished: First is "normal business risk," what might also be called "commercial risk" or "competitive risk." This risk is the natural consequence of being in business—the risk that one's competitors may come out with a better product, or a lower price, or better technology, terms, lower cost production, better delivery, or a completely new product that eliminates the need for the product being produced—and operative against a background of a basically stable business environment.

Second is "environmental risk"—arising out of economic, social, and political events, trends, or shocks, that can cause the business environment itself to change. The business environment changes, and oftentimes changes in the "rules," or ways of doing business, may either be favorable, unfavorable, or possibly neutral. But change brings uncertainty, and it is uncertainty that people regard as being important environmental risk.

Many analysts and students of business have used the term "investment climate" to refer to countries and their business environments. I do not believe that there is a single investment climate for a country. Rather, there is a whole range of investment climates, depending on the nature of the product, the project, the importance of the sector, and other factors (This is why Dow finds the reports of generalized country risk assessment services and consultants of little relevance or use in decision-making.

Two writers, Paul M. Sacks and Stephen Blank, in "Forecasting and Political Risk" (*The Corporate Director*, September/October, 1981, p. 10), have said:

For most companies, in fact, *countries don't have risks, projects have risks* [italics ours]. And the degree to which an individual project is at risk in a particular country will vary with such factors as the size of the fixed investment, the degree to which investment is bunched at one moment in time or strung out over a longer period, the stability of the project's basic technology, the extent to which the sector is divided among many smaller or a few larger firms, the extent of vertical integration and its importance to the project's economics.

Dow's experience in Brazil can be utilized to illustrate this point. Dow has major chlor-alkali production in Brazil—what is called basic chemicals. On the other hand, the company has a major pharmaceuticals business, which faces a completely different set of rules and regulations. Then there are commodity plastics like polystyrene, and specialty products like epoxy resins and styrene-butadiene latexes, not to mention agricultural chemicals. Every one of these businesses faces different challenges and risks.

For an industrial company, the project's economic, social, and political risks, in the context of the total country economic, social and political environment, are important. For example, at Dow, the economic evaluation (capital project analysis) for a major new manufacturing plant proposal generally projects ahead 12 to 14 years. From the time a decision is made to build a plan, it can take three to five years for engineering, construction and start-up. If the plant has been gauged properly to a growing market demand, it will be two to three years before full capacity utilization is reached. Profitability (with efficient full capacity production) thus peaks around seven years into the project.

The time horizon for Dow's economic, social, and political assessment studies therefore becomes five to seven years. If it is uncertain that the political and economic situation in the host country, and the rules under which the investment is to be made, are going to be stable seven years into the future, then it is very questionable whether the investment should be made. Alternatively, the company must find some way, or strategy, to hedge against the perceived risks. The problem of time horizon varies with the type of industry and company. The problem for a capital-intensive chemical company is much different than for a consumer products company. The focus of analysis is also different from that of a banking institution, which may look primarily at the ability of a country to repay its debts.

Most companies do not conduct risk analysis to reach "on" or "off" decisions regarding investments, but it is a very important part of the decision process. Once a worthwhile commerical opportunity has been found and proposed, risk analysis can be used to assess the non-commercial risks so that they can be understood and dealt with. Strategies can be developed to minimize the risks and maximize the opportunities. Ideally, only after a project has been developed and its risks analyzed and minimized can it be compared with other projects in the corporation, similarly developed, which compete for limited corporate resources and both capital and management time.

In the Dow Chemical program for environmental assessment (as in other multinational companies) there are four basic elements of structure. The four elements are: (1) a business condition checklist or index; (2) a checklist or index of basic pressures for change; (3) key factors and basic assumptions; and (4) a range of scenarios or "alternative futures."

The *business conditions checklist* is made up of approximately 40 key descriptors of business conditions in the country. These include:

- real economic growth rate
- availability of local capital
- price controls
- infrastructure
- profit repatriation rules
- freedom to reinvest
- skill levels of workforce
- labor stability

- investment incentives
- attitudes toward foreigners

When each factor is evaluated against a scale of "goodness" or "badness" (in terms of impact on a company or project), an *index* can be created. The checklist can be used in a retrospective, present, or prospective mode.

The concept of a *checklist or index of basic pressure for change* (those pressures building either for positive or negative change in the business environment) goes back to a book by Peter Drucker entitled *The Age of Discontinuity*. Discontinuities in trends are the things that give business planners the most headaches. Typical business forecasting looks for trends and postulates continuation of trends, perhaps with cyclical components added. But what is really dangerous to companies are discontinuities. Drucker pointed out that when discontinuities occur, the seeds of the discontinuity generally were there well before the event. Risk assessment analysts must find those seeds that are germinating, sprouting, growing, and perhaps even being fertilized, but that are not obvious in trend lines. The Dow checklist of over 40 types of potential pressures to watch includes:

- balance of payment structure and trends
- vulnerabilities for external shocks
- economic growth vs. expectations
- where opinion leaders are headed
- stability of leadership changes
- relations with neighboring countries
- terrorism, unrest
- balance of economic and social progress
- population composition and demographic trends
- attitudes toward foreigners and foreign investments

Considering all the various factors and potential pressures on the checklists, eight or ten key factors can be identified that lead to the success of a project or country involvement. These *key factors*, and *basic assumptions* that underlie them, become key indicators to be monitored on an ongoing basis. These become the basis for continuing country assessment and review.

A fourth element of structure in Dow's program, which is widely used among other companies as well, is *a range* of scenarios or "alternative futures." Key factors and assumptions must be generated before scenarios must be built upon them. Different types of scenarios can be created. In Dow's case, four country/project scenarios are normally developed. The first generated is a "most likely" scenario of key factors— economic, social, political, and business conditions—for seven years into the future. A second scenario postulates, "if things go better than expected, how much better might they be?" This is the basis for an "optimistic" scenario. A third scenario asks the question, "if things go worse, what might characterize the situation?" A "pessimistic" scenario is postulated. To focus on things of greatest importance to the company, a "disaster" scenario is also postulated. This does not necessarily mean a country disaster scenario, but what would constitute a "disaster" for the company. When scenarios have been developed, subjective probabilities can be assigned and compared by various people, if desired, to portray the results to the company's management.

RESOURCES FOR COUNTRY INFORMATION, INSIGHT, AND INTERPRETATION

In conducting business environment analyses, companies use many different sources of information. Outside of the country, analysts will use many of the following sources:

(1) *"Think-tank" specialists* such as those at Georgetown University's Center for Strategic and International Studies, the Hoover Institution, and the Council on Foreign Relations in New York City.

(2) The *U.S. Department of State* has country-desk officers and political and economic analysts who are well informed.

(3) The *U.S. Department of Commerce* likewise has country-desk people, but these people focus primarily on the commercial and business environment. Analysts find the Commerce Department an excellent source of trade and market data.

(4) The *World Bank (IBRD)* has people who are constantly conducting "missions" to various countries. These people are generally willing to talk about their views, though often their written reports are confidential.

(5) The *International Monetary Fund* has excellent publications, such as "International Financial Statistics," which are a key and consistent source of data.

(6) The officers of the *U.S. Export-Import Bank* may be able to offer helpful insights.

(7) *International banks* maintain extensive files of country data. Also,

officers and economic-political analysts are generally willing to share their views.

(8) *Other companies,* both in the same and in different industries, can relate their experiences and give first-hand impressions if they are operating in the country under consideration.

(9) *University Centers of International Studies* have many scholars and faculty who have spent lifetimes studying various countries and cultures. Examples are: the Institute of Latin American Studies at the University of Texas at Austin; the Middle East Research Institute at the University of Pennsylvania; the Center for Chinese Studies at the University of Michigan; the School of International Studies at the University of Washington; and the Center for African Studies at the University of California at Los Angeles.

(10) *Regional organizations,* such as the Organization of American States for Latin America, have many resources.

(1) *"Rating" organizations,* such as Business International, Frost and Sullivan, Business Environment Risk Index (BERI), and the Economist Intelligence Unit have built up large databases on countries.

(12) There are a large number of *consultants* who specialize in economic, social, and political environment studies for clients. Examples are: Probe International, Inc., Multinational Strategies, Inc., International Business-Government Counsellors, Inc.; firms such as Keller-Dorsey Associates and Oxford Analytica in the United Kingdom; and a host of individual cousultants, many of them former government people.

(13) *Journalists* can be helpful with observations also, although often they look for a current "story" rather than the historical context and meaning of events.

Key decision-makers and analysts should also visit the countries. In order to get a broad view of the local business environment and the pressure for change (discontinuities), the visitors should be involved with a wide cross-section of people. There are a number of local resources that can be investigated:

(1) *Bankers,* both locals and internationals "resident" in the country, can give an overview of the investment climate and problems.

(2) *Local businessmen* can give a feeling for how the foreign investor has been or will be received.

(3) *Foreign businessmen* operating in the country can give another viewpoint on essentially the same conditions. It is always good to com-

pare the perspectives of local and foreign businessmen and note the congruence or divergence of views on key issues.

(4) The *U.S. Embassy* has economic, political, and commercial people who can give an immediate "on-the-spot" review, which can be compared with the viewpoints in Washington, D.C.

(5) To the extent possible, conversations with university *students and professors* can yield important perspectives on emerging issues and conditions.

(6) *Customers* and potential customers are a good source of information on the key business conditions in the target market.

(7) *Political or government leaders* may be visited, but one generally does not learn anything more than what the people are saying and being quoted as saying in the press. In countries where an organized political opposition exists, members of the opposition may also be contacted.

(8) Local *publications and journalists* can indicate the beliefs of the "opinion leaders" and their viewpoints.

(9) To the extent possible, *labor leaders* may be consulted. If the project in question has a high labor content, it is important for the investor to know exactly what kind of labor needs it will be facing.

Neither of these lists is intended to be complete. They cover a range of resources, however, that can be investigated. And probably no two analysts will approach an assignment in the same way.

Environmental assessment ideally should not be just a one-time thing, which is done only when a major project is being developed. It should be a continuing part of a program of good relations with the host country. Evaluation needs to be on-going in order to cope with changes and contingencies. Over time, good relationships with local sources can be developed. But assessment specialists should always probe beyond the easy and obvious to get an early feeling for changes that may be coming.

CONCLUSIONS

In contrast to years past, multinational corporations today, particularly those that are U.S.-based, are much more sensitive to political, economic, and business conditions in their host-country environments. The experiences of Dow Chemical cited in this study are probably quite typical of those of many other companies as well.

More sensitivity to the issues raised has resulted in better business strategies being developed in more productive and definitive negotiations between multinational corporations and host countries. On the one hand, host-country negotiators are better prepared than ever before: They have more experience, expertise, and better understand how multinational corporations operate. On the other hand, the companies better understand the needs, concerns, and priorities of the host countries, and thus are more sensitive to going where they are wanted or desired.

The most important factors that companies consider in evaluating a host-country environment vary because of, among other things, planning horizon, nature of the business, capital and/or intensity. The specific "checklists" may differ in particulars but not in breadth. The use of internal evaluation systems or hired consultants will result in the same kinds of issues being investigated. Preeminent among concerns, however, is the necessity for the rules for foreign investments and the conduct of business to be stable—not necessarily unchanging, or unevolving, but nevertheless stable. It is the uncertainty of random change that causes companies to decline otherwise attractive opportunities.

This study has described the kinds of information sources to which a company will turn in making assessment of its host-country environment. Knowledge of how the country environment is viewed by such sources can be useful to the host country in developing its policies for, and negotiating stance toward, foreign investors.

BIBLIOGRAPHY

Books

Blank, Stephen, Basek et al., Assessing the Political Environment: An Emerging Function in International Companies, New York: The Conference Board, 1980.

Ensor, Richard, editor, Assessing Country Risk, London: Euromoney Publications Limited, 1981.

Ghadar, Kobrin, and Moran, editors, Managing International Political Risk: Strategies and Techniques, Washington, D.C.: Ghadar and Associates, 1983.

Ghadar, Fariborz, and Moran, editors, International Political Risk Management: New Dimensions, Washington, D.C.: Ghadar and Associates, 1984.

Haendel, Dan, Corporate Strategic Planning: The Political Dimension, Beverly Hills: Sage Publications, 1981.

Kobrin, Stephen J., Managing Political Risk Assessment, Berkeley: University of California Press, 1982.

Moran, Theodore H., editor, International Political Risk Assessment: The State of the Art, Washington, D.C.: Georgetown University, 1980.

Rogers, Jerry, editor, Global Risk Assessments: Issues, Concepts and Applications, Riverside, California: Global Risk Assessments, Inc., 1983.

Schwendiman, John S., Strategic and Long-Range Planning for the Multinational Corporation, New York: Praeger, 1973.

Articles

Alsop, Ronald, "More Firms are Hiring Own Political Analysts to Limit Risks Abroad," *Wall Street Journal,* March 30, 1981, p. 1.

Baily, Kathleen C., "Profiling an Effective Political Risk Assessment Team," *Risk Management,* February, 1983.

Brown, Alan S., "Handicapping the Foreign Investment Gamble," *Chemical Marketing Reporter,* September 21, 1981, pp. 30-35.

Byron, Christopher, "In Search of Stable Markets," *Time,* May 25, 1981, p. 69.

Haner, F. T., "Rating Investment Risks Abroad," *Business Horizons,* April, 1979, pp. 18-23.

Kobrin, Stephen J., "When Does Political Instability Result in Increased Investment Risk?" *Columbia Journal of World Business,* Fall, 1978, pp. 113-22.

Kobrin, Stephen J., "Assessing Political Risk Overseas," *The Wharton Magazine,* Winter 1981-1982, pp. 25-31.

Kraar, Louis, "The Multinationals Get Smarter About Political Risks," *Fortune,* March 24, 1980, pp. 86-100.

Laquer, Walter, "The Press, The Devil, and World Coverage," *The Washington Quarterly,* Vol. 5, No. 3, Summer, 1982, pp. 99-102.

Rummel, R. J., and David A. Heenan, "How Multinationals Analyze Political Risk," *Harvard Business Review,* January-February, 1978, pp. 67-76.

Sacks, Paul M., and Stephen Blank, "Forecasting Political Risk," *The Corporate Director,* September/October, 1981, pp. 9-14.

Shreeve, Thomas W., "Be Prepared for Political Changes Abroad," *Harvard Business Review,* July-August, 1984, pp. 111-18.

Vernon, Raymond, "Storm Over the Multinationals: Problems and Prospects," *Foreign Affairs,* January, 1977, pp. 243-62.

Wells, Louis T., "Negotiating With Third World Governments," *Harvard Business Review,* January-February, 1977, pp. 72-80.

Chapter Nine:
Political Risk

CULTURE, NATIONAL IDEOLOGY, political differences, and national sovereignty may lead to clashes between the investor and the recipient country's government. When relations reach a point where cooperative coexistence is no longer possible, host governments have resorted to expropriation or severe and strict operational controls. When legal redress is unavailable and remittance of profits is nonexistent, many multinationals have abandoned their investments.

Every foreign investor needs to be aware of political risk and its ramifications. Forecasting this political risk is a very difficult task. It entails not only a study of the political, social, and cultural climate, but also the economic variables involved. Such forecasting is quite misleading and arduous. Coping with such political risk entails several strategies ranging from procuring investment insurance to adapting to host-government goals.

With the revolution in Iran, war betwen Iran and Iraq, upheavals in El Salvador and elsewhere, the study of political risk has become more refined. But few companies have yet developed any systematic way of applying the assessment of political risk to their overseas operations.

Most "conventional risk" managers have had little involvement in decisions on how to handle corporate political risk. However, experts (usually consultants versed in forecasting political risk) can make this unfamiliar task somewhat easier.

A political risk to business can be simply defined as the possibility of any arbitrary and discriminatory government action that results in a financial loss. Common examples are: expropriation of assets; embargoes; cancelled licenses; nonconvertibility of local currency; and defaulting on contracts.

Strategies widely suggested for dealing with some of the above-mentioned risks include: more local participation in the ownership and management of the business; adapting to local government goals; buying insurance coverage; and having available contingency plans and a system of monitoring the political climate.

26

Assessing
Political Risk
Overseas
Stephen J. Kobrin

Political-risk assessment is a relatively new issue that has been incorporated into the management functions of most MNCs, albeit with varying degrees of success. Perhaps because of the dramatic nature of macro-political events, the risk-assessment function has tended to be a reactive rather than pro-active function. More significant for the multinational firm are the implications of micro changes in the political environment, such as changes in government policy.

To enhance the effectiveness of the firm's risk assessment function, the MNC should consider establishing a specialized internal corporate unit that draws on the expertise of local managers worldwide and is integrated into overall corporate planning and decision-making.

CORPORATE CONCERN WITH political risks abroad has increased significantly in recent years. Dramatic events such as the revolution in Iran and the spread of armed conflict in Central America have attracted widespread attention, but in most instances the causes of managerial concern are considerably more mundane—and considerably more pervasive. However, regardless of the nature of the risks, managerial perceptions of a new relationship between political environments and corporate strategy accurately reflect a new underlying reality. Political events are more likely than ever before to affect achievement of the international firm's objectives. There is no reason to believe that this is a temporary aberration: Political risk is going to be a major managerial concern for the foreseeable future.

Reprinted, with permission, from "Assessing Political Risk Overseas," *The Wharton Magazine*, Vol. 6, No. 2, Copyright © 1981 by The Wharton School of Pennsylvania.

This heightened concern has been reflected in an outpouring of articles in the business press, considerable academic attention, and—perhaps the most important indicator of legitimacy—the emergence of a large number of consulting firms offering services to help managers come to grips with political risks abroad. It has also been reflected in the commitment of significant corporate resources: Political risk assessment is emerging as a new managerial function in international firms. More than half of the companies contacted in a recent survey had taken at least some steps toward formal assignment of responsibility for the function, and more than one-third had established specialized political assessment units.

As one would expect at this stage, there is a great deal of variance in corporate practice. Political assessment "units" range from an assistant international treasurer involved on a part-time basis to a group of academically trained political scientists, ex-foreign service or intelligence officers, or other country specialists. The unit's analytical approach may involve no more than a checklist or an outline for a country study, or it may entail a relatively sophisticated "system" designed to formally elicit and process expert-generated opinion. However, regardless of how the function is organized, practice in this area represents a marked change from that of a decade and a half ago, when Franklin Root found no evidence of a systematic approach to political risk assessment in U.S. firms.

Corporate experience with specialized political risk assessment units has been mixed. Firms such as Eaton and United Technologies have disbanded groups formed in the relatively recent past and released the individuals who staffed them. Other companies have experienced considerable difficulty in integrating assessment units into the mainstream of corporate planning and decision making. However, in a considerable number of companies, such as Gulf and General Electric, the experience with specialized assessment units has been positive, and these units have provided valuable input into decision making and planning.

Experience has shown that the way in which the political risk assessment function is organized is *the* critical factor determining its success or failure. Thus, where the unit is located, its formal and informal relationships with the rest of the organization, and the support it receives from top management are possibly even more important than the quality and quantity of its substantive efforts. The two are, of course, related.

Situations such as the revolutions in Cuba and Iran produce what is known as "macro" risk. In such situations, impacts on a firm are almost totally determined by events in the external political environment, and organizational characteristics such as industrial sector and technology become largely irrelevant. Under these conditions, political events affect all firms in much the same way, and it is reasonable to talk about the "investment environment" in a given country. Nonetheless, it is rare for organizational characteristics to be totally immaterial. For example, in Allende's Chile, where mass expropriations took place and where ITT certainly was a "cause celebre," that company's Sheraton Hotel in Santiago was never touched.

While these dramatic "macro risks" tend to attract considerable managerial attention, their number is relatively limited. Most political risks are "micro" risks in that potential impacts are specific to an industry, firm, or project.

Micro risks generally result from situations that do not involve political conflict or even a change in regime, but rather a change in policy. They represent attempts by host-country governments to exert control over their economies to attain national objectives. Political environments can affect both the security of assets and the viability of operations; possible contingencies include nondiscriminatory measures, such as tax increases and price controls, and policies aimed directly at foreign firms, such as partial divestment of ownership, local content regulations, remittance restrictions, and limits on expatriate employment. "Catastrophic events," such as the mass expropriation of all foreign (or all private) investment, will continue to occur, but the trend is clearly toward micro risks that are firm or project specific, and toward impacts that affect operations rather than assets.

What is of concern to firms is not political events and processes per se, but the managerial contingencies they may generate. Political environments are of interest only to the extent that they produce impacts on the firm that affect either the security of assets or the viability of projects.

Assessing these potential impacts presents a formidable problem. Compared to most types of economic or business forecasting, political forecasting remains a very underdeveloped art. However, even more severe problems are encountered when managers attempt to use a political forecast to assess potential impacts on their firms.

We simply do not know a great deal about the nature of the relationship between political environments abroad and impacts on firms. While many companies have a long history of international involvement, widespread internationalization, especially in the manufacturing sector, is relatively recent. There is only a very limited body of experience with managerial contingencies resulting from political factors abroad, and, with the exception of expropriation, little has been documented. Furthermore, while many managers have had considerably more experience with politically generated risks than they would have preferred, few have had a broad enough range of experience to allow them to generalize and begin to conceptually model the process.

In sum, political assessment is hampered by both conceptual and operational problems. We have only a partial understanding of the relationship between environment and firm, and forecasting is severely constrained by a lack of historical data.

Nonetheless, the task must be undertaken, and every international firm performs some sort of political risk assessment; it is inherent in international operations. One cannot develop a strategic plan or consider an investment abroad without assessing the political environment, if only on the most intuitive and subjective basis. The assessment may involve no more than the expression of a feeling such as "Zork is okay" or "Zork is a lousy place to do business," or it may take the form of an unspoken consensus that the company does not even consider involvement in countries like Zork. However, while political risk assessment is universal in the international firm, there is a great deal of variation in its structure and performance.

Political risk assessment is normally a reactive rather than a proactive function. Assessments are motivated by a specific "trigger"—either an "event" within the firm such as an investment proposal or the strategic planning cycle or, less frequently, a major event in an important country. Eighty percent of the U.S.-based international firms responding to a recent Conference Board survey reported that they assess overseas political environments only "on demand," and only 34 percent reported routine monitoring. The result is that assessments of political environments are often not undertaken independently; they are done in conjunction with something that someone within the firm wants approved.

A number of studies have concluded that firms rely primarily on internal sources for information about external environments. That certainly applies to political environments abroad. According to the Conference Board survey, the single most important source of information is, as one would expect, managers of overseas subsidiaries. Regional managers and managers in headquarters with international responsibilities follow closely. Interestingly, no external information source is considered even relatively important by a majority of managers.

It would appear that a number of potentially valuable sources of information about political environments abroad are underutilized by U.S. firms. For example, only 28 percent of firms find consultants even a relatively important source of information about political environments abroad; only 17 percent so rate domestic agencies of the U.S. government (for example, the State Department); and only 9 percent so rate academic specialists. Thus, firms rely primarily on their global network of managers for information about political environments abroad, and only a small minority consider a number of potentially valuable sources of specialized information to be important.

THE ROLE OF LOCAL MANAGERS

The network of managers located around the world, many of whom are host country nationals, *is* the most important resource available to the international firm. Local managers are in a unique position at the junction of the firm and the host country political-economic environment, and they *should* be the firm's primary source of political information. However, information obtained from international managers reflects both their particular view of reality and the biases imparted by their position and their other objectives. Thus, improved political risk assessment requires that the firm exploit internal sources as effectively as possible and that it utilize external sources when necessary. Both of these ends are facilitated by a formally constituted political assessment unit within the firm.

A formal unit within the organization can contribute to more effective political assessment in three ways:

• Facilitating better utilization of a wider range of information sources;
• Enabling assessment specialists to fulfill a number of important educational roles;
• Improving patterns of communication within the firm through the coordination and control of information flows.

An assessment unit allows the firm to make better use of internal sources of information, particularly country and regional management. First, as the unit's analyses of political environments abroad are at least partially insulated from active interest in an investment proposal or a strategic plan, the unit can provide an independent point of view to top management. As was noted above, political assessments are often "triggered" by an investment proposal or the strategic planning cycle. Thus, country and regional managers may have an "oar in the water." They are being asked to evaluate the potential impact of the political environment on a project at the same time that they are recommending that the firm invest in it. It is unlikely that the two will be completely independent. Line management's political assessments are biased by their wider objectives.

In fact, the rationale for the establishment of a number of political assessment units was to provide top management with a source of political information that was relatively unconstrained by other business considerations. However, independence is a two-edged sword. Too often political assessment units have been located on the periphery of the organization, beyond the pale of the managerial process. The specialists in these units may never fully understand investment decision making or strategic planning, and their influence on outcomes may be limited. The combination of a peripheral existence and a high potential for staff-line conflict ("We don't need some 'expert' in headquarters telling us why we can't build a new plant here in Zork.") can be deadly and has resulted in the demise of more than one political assessment unit. I will return to this crucial topic when I discuss organizational issues.

A specialized political assessment unit can also help country management contact a much broader range of sources than might otherwise be possible. The range of sources accessible to subsidiary managers may well be limited by both their position in local society and the political realities of the host country. A subsidiary's managers are members of the local elite, and although that often provides the advantage of direct access to top-level officials of the current government, it may constrain contact with other important groups, such as student leaders, labor union officials, intellectuals, and the political opposition. Information obtained from line management may take the current government's view of the world too literally; it may understate the power of the opposition to influence policy or even to take control. Cuba under Batista, Portugal under Salazar, and Iran during the last years of the Shah provide obvious, if extreme, examples.

A political assessment specialist from headquarters, who does not personify the company in the host country and can often assume a low profile, may be able to engage a very broad range of opinion—including opposition political figures—without compromising the company's position. In fact, a political assessment specialist employed by a major U.S. oil company claims that his major asset is his ability to contact groups representing a relatively wide range of host-country opinion and to make the information he receives available to subsidiary management. Interestingly, the individual involved believes that it was this capability that overcame subsidiary management's initial resistance to his role as "an expert from headquarters."

Political assessment units can also make major contributions to more effective utilization of the firm's worldwide network of managers by coordinating and systematizing analytical procedures. Political assessment in most firms is a "bottoms up" process; it is the responsibility of country managers, who decide what to report and how it should be reported. Thus, it is often difficult, if not impossible, to compare political risks across countries or even across time within the same country.

Problems of comparability are exacerbated by the very subjective nature of this area. Political events do not have universal meaning; a coup in Washington or Mexico City, for example, would have very different implications from those of a coup in La Paz or Dacca. Rhetoric that involves hyperbole based on different value systems or assumptions may be misunderstood. One's perception is directly influenced by one's background and experience. In addition, most managers have not had a great deal of experience with the impact of political environments on their operations and find it difficult to generalize. Thus, one is not likely to encounter universal agreement about what a political event means in any given country, and far more importantly, about its potential impact on the business. In fact, one often hears the argument that it is impossible to compare countries.

For international firms, however, the bottom line is not a comparison of countries, but rather of investments; of risk and return. This can be greatly facilitated if some degree of structure is imposed on the assessment process. Such a structure need not entail "elegant and sophisticated" methodologies or even rigid analytical processes. It does require some attention to format and procedure. This may be as limited as establishing a basic outline for a country report or a checklist to guide the political assessment accompanying an appropriation request. It requires that some attempt be made to routinize the political assessment process; to ensure that managers' political reporting the world over can be utilized to provide comparable evaluations of investment risk.

Firms which employ political assessment specialists are more likely to value external sources of country expertise—such as the State Department and academics—than are those which do not. Political assessment specialists facilitate utilization of these external sources of information in two ways. First, they make it easier to locate appropriate and competent outside experts, and, second, they provide a "translation function" that allows rather generalized country expertise to be directly applied to evaluating potential impacts upon the firm. The latter, the translation function, is by far the more important of the two.

Although external sources of information such as State and academic specialists may be potentially valuable to the firm, they are difficult to use and even to locate. Foreign service officers, for example, change assignments very frequently, and the current country desk officer may well be new and inexperienced. The most competent source of information about that country may be in an unrelated assignment. It thus takes a reasonable knowledge of the informal organization of the State Department to use its resources effectively. Firms that do find the government to be a valuable source of information about political environments abroad are often those with a great deal of experience in dealing with the State Department, such as oil firms, or firms employing ex-foreign service officers or similar specialists.

Similarly, academic experts may be difficult to locate and evaluate without a knowledge of the "market." One needs to be tied in to the "invisible college" linking country specialists to locate appropriate sources of help.

Once an appropriate government official, academic, or consultant has been located, the firm has obtained only a source of raw information about a country. Although that certainly is important, it is not an assessment of political risk. As was discussed above, political risk involves the managerial contingencies that result from political events, and not the political events themselves.

Political risk assessment thus requires knowledge of both the country environment and factors such as the firm's technology and the nature of the industry. Government and academic country experts can provide the former but not the latter. Furthermore, it simply is not feasible—nor is it desirable—to turn country specialists into industry experts. An alternative is to frame the questions asked of country specialists in such a way as to elicit information relevant to impacts upon the firm. In other words, the country specialists' valuable but general expertise must be "translated" into assessments of firm-country interactions.

Political assessment specialists within the firm, who exist at the nexus of both worlds, can provide such a translation function. They are, or more correctly can be, in a unique position that enables them to understand both politics in general and their specific industry and firm in particular, and link the two in the assessment process.

Political assessment specialists in a number of firms, and not only those with political science or international relations backgrounds, have been able to locate appropriate and competent sources of expertise in government, in academia, and in consulting firms. However, the number of firms that successfully *use* the input provided by these specialists is much more limited. In most of the firms where outside sources contribute to meaningful assessments of political risk, the political assessment unit has developed a formal or informal system for eliciting information relevant to specific impacts on the firm. The unit has developed the capacity to translate general evaluations of the political environment into assessments of firm-specific political risk.

ORGANIZATIONAL LEARNING

Political risk assessment is differentiated from other managerial functions, such as marketing or finance, by its lack of a domestic counterpart. While marketing and finance require considerable adaptation to new problems when the firm expands abroad (for instance, there is a need to learn how to deal with exchange rate fluctuations), both are solidly grounded in a considerable body of domestic experience. In contrast, formal political assessment has generally not been required in the domestic U.S. context.

As a result, although many managers have had experience with politically generated impacts on their firms' operations, very few have had enough to be able to generalize. We do not know very much about how, and under what conditions, political events affect firms. We lack both data and models (in a basic conceptual sense) describing the relationship between the political environment and the firm.

In addition, most American managers do not have a formal understanding of politics as a process in the sense that they understand marketing, finance, or economics. Again, until the relatively recent expansion of U.S. firms abroad, politics did not have a major impact on managerial strategy. Most U.S. managers have not been exposed to formal political training; it is only in the last five years that even a few business schools have offered courses with any explicit political content.

Furthermore, as most U.S. managers were brought up and educated within the confines of a single political system that spans a continent, they have not had the advantage of their European colleagues of close contact with a wide range of governments in a very limited geographical area.

Political assessment specialists can help to alleviate these problems. To a large extent, the lack of historical data about political risks encountered abroad can only be remedied on a firm-by-firm basis. One of the most important steps that can be taken to improve the effectiveness of political risk assessment is for each firm to systematically review its own historical experience. What were the underlying environmental determinants of politically-generated contingencies, and how did they become apparent to the firm? Did the political evaluations undertaken in conjunction with investment proposals prove to be accurate? Perhaps most important, were political reasons for avoiding potentially attractive markets well grounded? Establishment of a formal political assessment unit within the firm can facilitate this kind of critically important organizational learning.

A LINE MANAGEMENT FUNCTION

As was noted above, managers abroad are the firm's most important source of information about political environments. I have argued that that is as it should be, and that political assessment is basically a line management function. Thus, an extremely important role of a formal political assessment unit, and of the specialists who staff it, is to help line managers improve their political assessment capabilities. I am certainly not suggesting a formal program, or that line managers be trained as political scientists. Rather, I would hope that, through informal and day-to-day interaction with specialists, managers would develop a better understanding of the underlying political environment and its relationship to the firm.

A unit can also provide a focal point for political assessment within the firm and a means for improving communication flows between those persons who are scanning political environments and those who are using political assessments in planning and decision making.

Political assessment in most firms can be characterized as a process in which multiple flows of information about political environments enter the organization informally and never converge until they are integrated into planning or decision making. Furthermore, and most critically, that integration is typically intuitive and subjective. Information about political environments abroad serves as a general background or context in which plans are drawn or decisions made. Instances in which political assessments are formally integrated into plans or investment proposals are the exception rather than the rule. The link between the assessment and its use is most often subjective and intuitive; it is implicit in the thought process of a manager. The net result is a loss of information and a loss of effectiveness in the planning and decision-making process.

Political information enters the firm from a number of sources, including country and regional managers, trips abroad by top management, the general media and the business press, bankers, colleagues in other companies, the government, consultants, and the political assessment unit if one exists. As the information comes from different sources with very different points of view, one would expect differences in perceptions.

While multiple sources of information are certainly an advantage under conditions of uncertainty, that advantage evaporates if differences are not reconciled. I am not suggesting that a consensus be forced where none exists—the resulting "average" may be meaningless. However, analyses must be formally compared in an attempt to understand the reasons for differences that may exist. A focal point where reconciliation can take place is necessary to fully exploit those differences. Clearly, a political assessment unit can provide a locus for that function.

In addition, a political assessment unit can provide the *potential* for improving communication flows between assessors and consumers of political analyses. Although part of the difficulty that firms encounter in using political assessments is a result of the current underdeveloped state of the art, a good part also results from limited communication between assessors and decision makers. Assessors' contacts with users of their output are often limited to formal information flows and are typically asymmetrical. There is little in the way of feedback; assessors are often unable to state with certainty how, or even whether, their output is used. The result is that political assessors often do not understand the information needs of strategic planners and decision makers and—the other side of the coin—planners and decision makers are not fully aware of the capabilities of the political assessment process.

Although it is unreasonable at this point in the development of the field to expect that assessments can be directly or mechanically integrated into capital budgeting calculations, for example, the assessments can be expressed in a form that allows decision makers to make explicit judgments about the effects on cash flows. This does not require quantification; it does require explicit and specific qualitative assessment of potential impacts on the firm's operations over time. It requires that the output of political assessment units be directly relevant to the input needed by decision makers, or in other instances, planners.

In sum, a formal political assessment unit can serve as a focal point that allows full advantage to be taken of multiple information flows, and it can provide the potential for improving patterns of communication. However, it does not inherently do so. Whether a political assessment unit is successful depends, to a large extent, on how well it is integrated into the organization. That in turn is often a function of how it is organized.

ORGANIZING ASSESSMENT UNITS

Although there is a good deal of variation in the organization of political assessment units, the vast majority can be categorized in terms of three basic types.

The first involves assignment of responsibilities to an individual in an existing staff group on a part-time basis. For example, at a large oil company, political assessment is one of a number of tasks performed by an analyst in the corporate economics department. Similarly, in a paper company, an assistant to the international treasurer is responsible for preparing extensive country studies, following an established outline, whenever a new investment abroad is considered.

A second organizational form can be characterized as a *political intelligence unit.* Typically, several specialists with international relations backgrounds form a quasi-independent political analysis unit at the corporate or divisional level. A major oil company has a staff of five regional specialists recruited from academia and the foreign service who report to a vice president for public affairs. In a large auto firm, a number of ex-foreign service officers staff a unit lodged in the international governmental affairs department. A number of firms have hired relatively senior individuals from the State Department or the intelligence community to develop similar political assessment units.

The third common organizational structure involves one or more individuals, typically lodged in the international strategic planning department, who have the responsibility for *coordinating* the firm's political assessment activities. This may entail the extensive use of outside consultants, or it may be limited to assisting business units in the preparation of their own political analyses. The assistance may involve substantive help; it often includes establishment of formats; and the unit usually coordinates flows of information within the firm. An example is provided by a large producer of electrical products and machinery. The manager of international environmental analysis is located in the international strategic planning department, and he works with the business units to develop social, political, and economic analyses of countries of major interest to the firm. The individual concerned initiates the analytical process and then "subcontracts" many of the actual analyses to appropriate outside consultants. He or she is directly involved in integrating the assessments into strategic plans.

While all three structures involve formal establishment of the political risk assessment function, only the last two are clear examples of a specialized unit or group. I will restrict discussion of organizational issues to political intelligence and coordinating-facilitating units. One caveat is necessary. The organizational structures summarized above are simplified representations of complex realities. In fact, in a number of firms there are multiple units doing political risk analysis on at least a part-time basis, at times competing with one another and, at times, unaware of one another's existence.

Each of these two modes of organization has its advantages. A political intelligence group staffed with specialists usually provides a greater concentration of expertise than does a coordinating-facilitating unit, and it is more likely to assess political environments independently from other managerial concerns. The coordinating-facilitating unit, on the other hand, is more likely to be integrated into the organization, and there is a greater probability that it will have an impact on planning and decision making. Thus, there is a clear trade-off between specialized expertise and independence on the one hand and integration into the organization and the larger managerial process on the other.

At this point in the development of the field I would argue that, in most cases, one should opt for the integration provided by a co-ordinating-facilitating unit. Two points discussed above are of importance in this regard. First, improved political risk assessment requires more effective exploitation of existing resources, especially the firm's network of international managers. Second, it appears that producing a political anaysis is easier than using it effectively in planning and decision making. If the political assessment unit is to deal productively with both of these issues, it must be fully integrated into the firm and not stand on the periphery.

It must serve as a true focal point for political assessment by establishing meaningful relationships within the organization.

This does not mean that all of the quasi-independent political intelligence groups stand alone at the margin of the company, nor do I mean to imply that all firms should choose a coordinating-facilitating type of unit. However, the goal of integration into the organization will be more difficult to achieve if one opts for a quasi-independent unit. In fact, while interviewing at firms, my colleagues and I found that in many cases where a political intelligence unit was well integrated into the company, there were special historical or personal considerations, such as strong links between the head of the assessment unit and top management.

I will close this article with some suggestions, and they are certainly no more than that, which are based on the preceding analysis. For a firm considering establishment of a political-risk assessment unit, the best course of action might be to avoid an independent staff of specialists at first and to assign responsibilities to an appropriate individual who is respected within the firm and who is attached to a centrally-located staff group. That individual can then begin by coordinating and systematizing corporate political-risk assessment activities. After the unit becomes firmly established within the organization, specialized expertise can be added as the need arises. Perhaps a reasonable initial configuration would be a small unit comprised of a relatively senior manager who understands the firm and its planning and decision-making process and a more junior specialist with an international relations background.

If there are reasons for preferring a political intelligence unit, it should be clear that substantive expertise alone will not be sufficient to ensure success. The unit must have the explicit support of top management, and pains must be taken to build links with the rest of the organization. The individuals who staff it must be more than specialists. To be effective, they must understand the business, its technology, and the structure of the industry. They must understand the managerial process, and, perhaps more importantly, they must understand the corporate culture. "I don't even understand their language" is a frequent complaint of even relatively senior political assessment specialists brought into the firm after successful careers in government.

While individuals who fulfill all of these conditions may be difficult to find, they certainly can be developed. This means that the firm opting for an independent unit must be prepared to devote considerable resources to the task of bringing the specialists it hires into the mainstream of the organization. I firmly believe that specialized political assessment personnel can make a valuable contribution to the firm. Their understanding of country environments and their ability to locate and effectively utilize external sources of information can be extremely useful, both for analysis and for planning and decision making. However, if they are to assess political risk rather than political environments, their expertise must be integrated into the firm.

27
Bargaining Power of Multinationals and Host Governments

Nathan Fagre and Louis T. Wells, Jr.

Negotiations between host governments and MNCs are a function of the bargaining power of the two sides. Ownership of the foreign subsidiary is a key variable, which is generally determined not only by the size of the investment but also by the level of technology, the diversity of products offered by the MNC, the extent of competition, and the generation of exports.

INTRODUCTION

As several scholars have pointed out, the relationship between host developing countries and multinational enterprises can be analyzed in terms of bargaining power.[1] The arrangement settled upon determines the distribution of benefits between the firm and the host government. Such framework is based on the assumption that there is some range of possible terms that might be acceptable to a government and to a potential investor. In a completely competitive world, there would of course be no room for bargaining; however, the industries in which U.S.-based multinationals operate are indeed oligopolistic.[2]

In a bargaining model, the deal that is eventually struck between foreign investors and host governments reflects the need for, and the scarcity of, the resources offered by the two parties as well as, perhaps, their bargaining skills. Thus, a multinational firm that can offer access to capital, technology, or marketing skills might be in a relatively strong bargaining position, especially if few other firms offer similar resources.

This study reports the results of the authors' efforts to measure the influence of U.S. multinationals' various resources on the outcome of

Reprinted with permission from the *Journal of International Business Studies*, (Fall 1982).

negotiations in Latin America through 1975. There is no attempt to measure other possible important variables: negotiating skills, home government support,[3] side payments, regional economic groups, and so on. Moreover, the study is static. No attempt is made to measure over time the effect of development, for example, even though a country's needs and what it can offer to an investor probably change with industrialization[4]; nor is an effort made to capture the fact that an investor's bargaining power deteriorates once its capital is sunk in a country.[5] Measuring changes in bargaining outcome over time is an important task that must be left to later study.

This study includes only one measure of the bargain struck between host and investor: equity ownership. Ideally, the bargain would be measured by all terms of the arrangement that affect ownership, control, and the allocation of economic benefits. No composite measure of the outcome of negotiations is available for a large number of firms. The skeptical reader would do well to interpret results of the study narrowly, as measuring only the impact of a firm's resources on the ownership that it is able to retain in developing countries. Ownership is a sufficiently important variable to both investors and governments so that even the skeptic should find the results of the study interesting. Nevertheless, the authors would argue that ownership is a proxy—albeit an imperfect one—for the overall outcome of negotiations.

If an economist were to consider the principal elements of an investment arrangement as classified under the rubrics of ownership, control, and economic benefits, he would probably rank ownership as the least important. After all, taxes and other financial provisions can assure the government economic benefits that are unrelated to its degree of ownership. Similarly, rights to name board members, special regulations from the government, and other approaches can assure that control is not linked directly to ownership as an important goal when they negotiate with foreign investors. Their concerns presumably arise from political motivations; thus, investment regulations typically emphasize joint venture requirements. At the same time, many managers of multinational enterprises also view ownership as an important variable. Most readers will be familar with the statements from executives of IBM and other multinationals as to why they cannot live with joint ventures. Whatever the facts about the relationship of ownership to control and economic benefits, both parties to negotiations seem to view the distribution of shares as an important outcome in its own right.[6] Moreover, in the authors' experience governments are hesitant to trade ownership for other kinds of benefits in an agreement. Admittedly, there is no hard evidence to support this contention. Thus, the reader may choose to view the results of this study narrowly: as an attempt to measure the effect of certain resources of the firm on its ability to control with ownership; or the reader may support the authors' belief that the study provides some evidence of the effect of a firm's resources on its overall bargaining power vis-à-vis its host government.

MEASURING THE DEGREE OF OWNERSHIP

If all multinational enterprises desired full ownership of their overseas subsidiaries, measuring the outcome of the negotiating process would present few problems, at least as far as ownership goes. The firm that gives up more equity to local investors would have come out worse in the bargain than the firm that gave up less equity. This simple approach is the one taken in Measure (Model) I. (See Table 1.)

Multinational enterprises do not in fact have such a uniform attitude toward ownership—some choose to include local partners, up to a certain fraction of ownership, even in the absence of host-government pressure. The differences in attitude toward local ownership are related in rational ways to the strategies of the enterprises.[7] Thus, the use of Measure I entails certain risks. If one multinational holds, say, 80 percent of the shares in its Mexican subsidiary and another holds only 40 percent in its venture, the one with 40 percent might well not have been in a weaker bargaining position: rather, it might have had a different attitude from the outset toward local ownership. To account for such differences, a second measure was developed. First, for each multinational enterprise an average ownership figure was calculated for its holdings in its subsidiaries in Europe. This measure, from a geographical area where ownership is usually left largely to the firm's discretion, was assumed to reflect the enterprise's preference in the absence of government intervention. The parent's ownership of a particular Latin American subsidiary was then compared to this ideal figure for the enterprise. Thus, Measure II is simply the ownership of a particular subsidiary in Latin America less the average ownership of its parent's subsidiaries in the EEC.

Still another measure was developed. This time an attempt was made to account for the different emphasis various countries in Latin America might place on ownership. Thus, Measure III is calculated by subtracting from the parent's ownership in a subsidiary the average U.S. ownership in all subsidiaries in the particular country.

Table 1: Three Measures of Ownership: Definitions of Dependent Variables

Model	Dependent Variable	Definition
I	Actual ownership	Percent equity ownership held by U.S. parent corporation
II	Firm-corrected ownership	Actual ownership minus the EEC average ownership for the parent
III	Country-corrected ownership	Actual ownership minus the average foreign ownership in all subsidiaries in that country

Table 2: R&D Expenditure as a Percentage of Sales and 3 Measures of Parent's Ownership

Percent of Sales Spent on R&D	Average Ownership Level (%)		
	Actual	Firm-corrected	Country-corrected
0-.75	88	18	−1
.75-2.5	86	15	−3
2.5-5	89	14	0
5 and over	99	20	10

NOTE: Any table with fewer than 50 observations in any category will contain an indication of the number. For subsidiaries active as of 1 January 1976, R&D and sales data are for 1975 by parent corporation.

SOURCE: All data on multinationals' operations in this and in later tables are from Harvard Business School's Multinational Enterprise Databank. For details about the underlying data see Curhan, Joan P.; Davidson, William H.; and Suri, Rajan, *Tracing the Multinationals* (Cambridge, MA: Ballinger Publishing Co., 1977).

Table 3: Level of Advertising and 3 Measures of Parent's Ownership

Percent of Sales Spent on R&D	Average Ownership Level (%)		
	Actual	Firm-corrected	Country-corrected
0-1	85	14	−3
1-7	89	17	0
Over 7	98	21	9

NOTE: Advertising is measured by the advertising expenditure as a percent of the total value of the shipments in the affiliate's 3-digit SIC industry. Lower bounds are inclusive, upper bounds are exclusive. For subsidiaries active as of 1 January 1976. Advertising expenditures from 1974 data are aggregated by 3-digit SIC category.

Each of these measures was used to test the effect of the independent variables. Table 1 summarizes these measures.

An attempt was made to determine the impact of 5 economic characteristics of foreign investors on the outcome of the bargaining process (or ownership alone, for the skeptical reader): the level of technology, the degree of product differentiation through advertising, the access provided to export markets, the amount of capital, and the diversity of the firm's product line. For clarity and ease of presentation, the variables are presented one at a time. Of course, a serious test of their impact requires multivariate analysis. The presentation of a multiple regression analysis is given in Table 4 after the variables are discussed individually. This table shows that multivariable analysis confirms the results of the more primitive (and dangerous) approach of treating the variables singly.

SOURCES OF BARGAINING POWER: TECHNOLOGY

Many writers have argued that the level of technology supplied by the foreign investor has a significant influence on the bargaining outcome. The results of this research are somewhat suprising because the relationship between level of technology and ownership appears to be somewhat more complicated than one might have anticipated.

The level of technology available from a multinational enterprise was aproximated by the percentage of sales spent by the parent corporation on R&D activities in 1974. (Other measures of technology were also used in this study, with roughly comparable results. They are not presented here.)

The bargaining power of a developing country is likely to be weak when it is faced with a high technology firm. The more an industry is characterized by rapid innovation, the more difficult it is for a developing country to enter the industry without the help of an established firm from an advanced nation. Conversely, the older a given technology is, the more opportunity a developing country will have to acquire and utilize it without the involvement of a foreign investor. Thus, the level of technology and the bargaining outcome are likely to be related. Evidence from the plastics industry and certain petrochemical industries supports this contention.[8]

The cross-sectional data used in this study are consistent with the conclusions of others. As Table 2 indicates, the percentage of parent corporation sales spent on R&D activities is positively associated with bargaining success. However, this relation is primarily a consequence of the major distinction between parent corporations spending 5 percent or more of sales on R&D and those parents spending less. For corporations in the lower categories of R&D expenditures, the relative level of expenditure seems to have no consistent impact on bargaining power. A parent corporation spending between 2.5 percent and 5 percent of sales on R&D, for example, achieved no more bargaining success than a parent corporation spending less than 0.75 percent on R&D.

Indeed, when firm-corrected ownership is examined for each level of parent R&D expenditure, the middle-range technology firms prove to have the least bargaining success of any group. Bradley found that this same group of corporations has also been the most vulnerable to expropriation in recent years.[9] Although developing nations seem to achieve some success with middle-range technology enterprises, they are unable to make headway against the high-range technology enterprise.

Only 17 parent corporations of the 178 studies spent more than 5 percent of sales in R&D in 1974. The degree of bargaining success achieved by these 17 corporations in the 98 subsidiaries and branches in Latin America is remarkable. In fact, the ownership patterns were uniform regardless of the industry, the number of affiliates held by the parent corporation, or the number of competing parent corporations in the same industry.

The data for Latin America suggest that the relation between technology and bargaining power is not a simple one. To be sure, at the high end of the range of technological skills, technology does seem to place the multinational in a strong position. In the middle range, the outcome appears much less certain. There is some risk, however, that the relationships are distorted because R&D as a percentage of sales is an imperfect measure of technological uniqueness.

PRODUCT DIFFERENTIATION

Multinational enterprises do seem to be in a comfortable position at the bargaining table when they are in an industry for which marketing skills are important. It has been established in earlier studies that firms that rely on product differentiation through advertising tend to desire a high degree of control over their foreign subsidiaries.[10] Such enterprises tend to see local partners as providing few resources but as bringing disagreements over their marketing policy. Product differentiation by multinational enterprises presents a formidable barrier to potential local enterprises in developing countries. Although the production technology needed to manufacture satisfactory ball-point pens and carbonated beverages is hardly secret, Parker pens and Coca Cola are still the preferred products in many developing countries.

This strength of U.S. multinationals is reflected in the data presented in Table 3. Multinationals that spend more than 7 percent of total sales revenues on advertising have attained a high level of ownership in Latin America in each of the measures. In fact, advertising seems to be related to bargaining power at all levels of expenditures. Almost all of the 202 operations that are in the highest advertising category are in the pharmaceutical or cosmetic industry (SIC 283,284): 95 percent of these operations were wholly owned. A breakdown between ethical and proprietary drug corporations in terms of bargaining success was impractical although a separate test of two groups would have been interesting. Given the mix of firms at the top of the advertising heap, separating the effects of advertising and technology becomes difficult. Nevertheless, the strength of the relationship between advertising and

Table 4: The Percentage of Affiliate's Output Transferred Within the Parent System and 3 Measures of Parent's Ownership

Percent Transferred	Average Ownership Level (%)		
	Actual	Firm-corrected	Country-corrected
0-10	80	15	−1
10-50*	91	21	2
50-100	96	23	8

NOTE: Lower bounds are inclusive, upper bounds are exclusive. For subsidiaries active as of 1 January 1976, based on 1975 sales activity.
*There are 49 observations in this category.

Table 5: The Percentage of Affiliate's Output Exported and 3 Measures of Parent's Ownership

Percent Exported	Average Ownership Level (%)		
	Actual	Firm-corrected	Country-corrected
0-10	88	15	−1
10-50	92	19	3
50-100	98	21	9

NOTE: Lower bounds are inclusive, upper bounds are exclusive. For subsidiaries active as of 1 January 1976, based on 1975 sales activity.

ownership at lower levels of advertising suggests that it is a significant variable in its own right. The advertising-oriented enterprises, it should be noted, have not obtained their high degree of ownership in Latin America by avoiding host nations that take a dim view of complete foreign ownership. Indeed, Mexico is the country with the largest number of pharmaceutical and cosmetics affiliates operating within its borders, although it is a country that emphasizes local ownership. None of the other independent variables studied that are associated with bargaining success provides even a partial explanation for the bargaining power held by the pharmaceutical and cosmetics firms.[11] The primary source of their bargaining strength appears to lie in the barriers to entry raised by the high degree of product differentiation.

MARKET ACCESS

Fundamental to the strategy of some multinational enterprises is an ability to rationalize production on a global scale and a capacity to acquire and utilize sophisticated knowledge of foreign markets. These qualities provide an important bargaining lever for U.S. firms operating in Latin America.

In situations where a large portion of a subsidiary's output is sold or transferred to another affiliate of the same parent corporation, the parent controls market access to a significant degree. Intrasystem transfers in manufacturing industries often consist of intermediate goods which may have value only when combined with other intermediate goods made by the same enterprise. Automotive parts that fit only one make and model would be an illustration. Since a host country would have great difficulty marketing such goods on its own, it depends on the international production system of the multinational firm.[12]

The value of control over market access is clear in Table 4. When more than 50 percent of the output from the local operation is transferred to other members of the same multinational system, the enterprise achieves high levels of ownership for all three measures. This method of control over market access is also an effective deterrent to expropriation. None of the 114 U.S. foreign manufacturing affiliates that have been seized since 1960 sold more than 10 percent of their output within the parent system.[13]

To obtain bargaining power, it is not necessary for the firm to export to affiliates. The overall exports of manufacturers from the host nation is also positively related to ownership for each measure. This relationship is presented in Table 5. The bargaining power afforded multinational enterprises by the ability to export 50 percent or more of their affiliate's output is remarkable. Of 54 such affiliates in Latin America, 51 were wholly owned. In no instance was the parent corporation a minority partner.

The two measures of market control are related. There are cases of affiliates that export 50 percent of more of their output and transfer 50 percent or more of their output within the parent systems. In these cases,the average ownership held by the parent corporation is more than 99 percent. A number of the 40 affiliates falling into this category are in the drugs and cosmetics industries (SIC 283,284); however, it is not certain that product differentiation or technology is not the source of their bargaining power. Many affiliates are in the television and electronic components industries (SIC 365,367); in those cases, product differentiation did not seem to be an important factor. In fact, the difference between outcomes of bargaining for the exporters and the nonexporters is quite noticeable. The difference established some degree of confidence that market access was an important variable.

The positive relationship between market access and ownership is consistent with other studies in the field.[14] The parent corporation will be particularly adamant in its desire for control over the activities of affiliates that transfer or export a large proportion of their output. Developing countries are in a weak position to deny multinational enterprise this control; many of these nations are eager to export manufactured goods but find that they must turn to multinational firms for help in implementing this strategy. On the other hand, firms seeking an export base have many alternative plant sites. The existence of such alternatives for these firms stands in contrast to the fact that a firm interested in the local market must usually build its plant in that market.

The dependence on multinationals for exporting is so real and immediate that it has been reflected in legislation regarding foreign investors in many Latin American countries, not simply in practice, which so often departs from the published regulations. Mexican law generally allows 100 percent foreign ownership only if the operation exports all its output. Andean Pact countries exclude foreign investors from the divestiture requirements if the operation exports more than 80 percent of its output outside of the area.

CAPITAL

` financial resources that a multinational enterprise offers to bring
   ︎developing country might be a source of bargaining strength. In
    ︎. the capital brought for the establishment and operation of a

Table 6: The Financial Size of the Affiliate and 3 Measures of Parent's Ownership

Assets (in millions of dollars)	Average Ownership Level (%)		
	Actual	Firm-corrected	Country-corrected
0-1	88	14	−1
1-10	89	17	0
10-25	88	17	−1
25-100	83	13	−5
Over 100*	94	24	3

NOTE: Lower bound of each category is inclusive, the upper bound is exclusive. For subsidiaries active as of 1 January 1976, based on total assets at the close of 1975.
*There are 25 observations in this category.

Table 7: Parent's Ownership, Size of Affiliate, and the GNP of the Host Nation

Size of Affiliate (assets in millions of dollars)	GNP Per Capita of Host Nation (%)		
	Below $400	$400-$800	Above $800
0-1	96	84	93
1-10	83	88	91
10-25	74*	88	89
25-100	—	83	84†
Over 100	—	89**	100***

NOTE: In this table, the lower bound of each category is inclusive, the upper bound is exclusive. For subsidiaries active as of 1 January 1976, based on total assets at the close of 1975. Host GNP per capita based on 1973 data from the Overseas Development Council.
*There are 4 observations in this category.
**There are 15 observations in this category.
***There are 10 observations in this category.
†There are 20 observations in this category.

foreign subsidiary or branch was estimated in two ways: the annual sales of the affiliate and the assets of the affiliate. Because the level of sales and the level of assets in each affiliate are closely correlated, only the results using assets as an independent variable are presented here.[15]

One might suspect that the parent corporation would desire much ownership and strong control in large investments: one could also anticipate that the host country would insist on ownership and control in particularly large projects, given their potentially great impact on the local economy. On the other hand, the host country may be so eager for the capital that it might have to retreat from its desired stance.

The facts are again somewhat complicated. For investments with assets up to $100 million, the financial resources of the multinational corporation provide little bargaining power, as is demonstrated in Table 6. In Table 7 the difference in average ownership for both actual and firm-corrected ownership between affiliates in the $25 million to $100 million range and those in the $100 million and over range is 11 percent, which is noticeably larger than the similar difference for country-corrected ownership. A close examination of these operations (in the $100 million and over category) reveals that they are generally located in host countries that have receptive attitudes toward foreign investors and few ownership restrictions. The seven countries with the most restrictive policies regarding foreign ownership contain 40 percent of all U.S. manufacturing affiliates in Latin America but only 20 percent of the largest investments.[16] Trinidad and the Bahamas, both with relatively lenient policies toward foreign investors, have as many of these giant operations as Mexico, a country with 40 times the population and 18 times the number of U.S. affiliates as those of the other two countries combined. The patterns may be the results of conscious decisions made by the parent corporations to locate their large projects in lenient countries, or they may be the consequence of the expropriation of these investments in very nationalistic countries. Most likely, both factors are involved.

In the relatively few instances when an investment in excess of $100 million was made in a Latin American country having a more critical policy toward foreign ownership of investments, the multinationals fared poorly in the bargain. The average parent corporation ownership for the 5 affiliates located in the 7 Latin American host nations with the most restrictive policies was 70 percent, well below the 100 percent ownership held in all other operations with large assets. Thus, a large capital investment does not appear to improve greatly the bargaining position of the firm.

It is important to note at this point that the fact that the largest investments are located in countries that allow more foreign ownership is not merely a result of the concentration of these investments in those countries. In other words, those "lenient" host nations do not have a high level of foreign ownership because they have so many of these giant investments. When investments over $100 million are excluded and the average U.S. parent ownership is recalculated for each Latin American country the same group of countries is still found to be the most lenient toward foreign investors.

In summary, the financial resources held by multinationals are not an important source of bargaining power in Latin America. Perhaps, because managers recognize that size does not give them power, they have tended to place very large projects in less nationalistic nations. Perhaps the primary explanation for the insignficance of capital for the multinational in the bargaining process lies in the increasing number of alternative sources of capital available to developing countries. One could also argue that the poorest countries might have the strongest need for capital and, thus, be willing to relax their insistence on local ownership. The data show that the poorest countries in Latin America do not end up with large projects. (See Table 7.) The reasons could have to do with their insistence on significant local ownership or on the small size of their home markets, or on both factors.

PRODUCT DIVERSITY

Thus far, the importance of 4 firm characteristics in the bargaining process has been discussed. Each of these variables has appeared in the literature and the findings are easily explained. However, one other firm characteristic, diversity of the product line of the subsidiary, appears to be important but less easily explained.

When subsidiaries are classified by the number of products (3-digit SIC) they produce, a quite strong relationship to ownership appears. The greater the number of products, the greater the apparent bargaining power of the firm, as Table 8 shows. It appears that firms have a choice of forming one subsidiary to produce several products or several subsidiaries to produce only a few products each. How this choice is resolved appears to be related to ownership.

In an effort to understand the phenomenon, the authors decided to examine one country in detail. Mexico was chosen because it provided the largest sample. The impact of the differing corporate strategies in Mexico is demonstrated in Table 9.

Each affiliate was placed into one of four categories, according to the total number of affiliates its parent had in Mexico. Then, within each grouping, the percentage of multiple product line affiliates and the percentage of wholly-owned affiliates was calculated. Enterprises that have only one affiliate in Mexico use it as a base for several product lines in 55 percent of the cases, roughly double the similar figure for corporations owning 5 or more affiliates in Mexico. Parent firms using the single affiliate strategy also wholly owned their affiliate in 64 percent of the cases, again roughly double the similar figure for corporations having 5 or more affiliates.

Table 8: The Number of Products Produced by the Affiliate
and 3 Measures of Parent's Ownership

| | Average Ownership Level (%) | | |
Number of Products	Actual	Firm-corrected	Country-corrected
1	88	14	0
2	87	17	−1
3-4	91	21	3
5 and over*	95	36	7

NOTE: For subsidiaries active as of 1 January 1976, based on the number of different 3-digit SIC product lines manufactured during 1975.
*There are 20 observations in this category.

Table 9: Corporate Strategy in Mexico: Percent of Multiproduct Affiliates and Percent of Wholly Owned Affiliates, Classified by the Number of Affiliates Per Parent Corporation

Number of Affiliates Per Parent	Percent of Multiple-product Affiliates	Percent of Wholly Owned Affiliates
1	55.0	64.0
2	40.0	59.8
3-4	32.8	58.7
5 and over*	26.9	35.7

NOTE: For subsidiaries active as of 1 January 1976, based on the number of subsidiaries and the major product lines of each in operations during 1975.
*There are 10 parents in this category.

Although the desire for control on the part of the firm with a multi-product affiliate could be a result of having "all its eggs in one basket," less clear is the reason why the product diversity of a subsidiary is a resource desired by the host nations. This relatively weak bargaining position of the Latin American nations is especially difficult to understand because product diversity is not correlated with any of the other corporation resources desired by the developing nations, with the exception of capital. (See Table 13.) The correlation between product diversity and financial size of an affiliate is not surprising because operations manufacturing a number of different products are likely to be larger in size. However, capital has proven to be relatively unimportant in the bargaining process, while product diversity appears to be quite important. (In fact, the relationships between product diversity and ownership in Europe appear to be the opposite!) There are several plausible explanations for these observations.

One possibility is that product diversity is related to management skills. One could speculate that larger plants, simultaneously manufacturing many goods in different lines, may require a higher level of management expertise. If this is indeed the case, then product diversity would reflect a resource needed by many developing countries. Another possibility is that multiproduct affiliates may fit into an import-substitution development strategy. Obviously, the greater the variety of goods produced, the greater the capacity the affiliate has to supply many goods formerly imported. There is no reason for a host nation with such a development strategy to prefer one foreign investment producing a variety of goods over a number of foreign investors, each producing one import-substituting good. However, developing nations are rarely faced with such an explicit choice. Instead, at any given time, their choice is more likely to be between a larger investment producing a number of goods or a smaller one producing just one good. In this case, the multiproduct investment may be strongly preferred.

A third explanation concerns the nature of the industries in which multiproduct affiliates are concentrated. Developing nations may desire investments in these industries more strongly than investments in other industries and thus be in a weaker bargaining position. More than 70 percent of all affiliates in Latin America that manufacture four or more different 3-digit SIC product lines are concentrated in just three major industries: chemicals (excluding drugs and cosmetics), nonelectrical machinery, and electrical machinery (SIC 28,35,36). If these industries play a special role in the development programs of the Latin American countries, then the relationship between product diversity and bargaining success may be a reflection of the need for these investors.

A fourth possibility (favored in this study) is that the observed relationship between ownership levels and product diversity is a result of the structure of governmental regulations in the host countries. Corporations may tend to create a separate subsidiary whenever they are dealing with a product line in which the government will insist upon some measures of local control. Firms in that situation would have more subsidiaries, fewer multiproduct affiliates, and few wholly-owned affiliates.

DEGREE OF COMPETITION

Not only firm-related variables are important in the bargaining process—one of the most important variables is the number of investors competing in the firm's industry. Generally, the greater the competition, the weaker the bargaining power of the multinational firm. If a developing country is forced to choose among a small number of multinationals in a particular industry, it seems that its ability to play one firm against another will be limited. The multinational, realizing that it is one of the few firms able to offer a certain technology or bundle of resources to host nations, will demand and probably receive more favorable terms.

The general nature of the relationship between number of competitors and ownership is apparent in Table 10. For this table, the number of U.S. multinationals operating in Latin America in each 3-digit SIC industry was calculated:[17] then, within each industry, the average level of bargaining success for the firms was determined for each bargaining measure. Only the summary findings are presented. The ownership patterns continued in the table indicate that a larger number of parent corporations per industry is associated with lower bargaining power for members of that industry relative to other industries. Multinationals that were the sole members of their industries operating in Latin America had exceptional bargaining success: 16 of the 18 industries

Table 10: The Number of Competing Parent Corporations in Each 3-digit SIC Industry and 3 Measures of Parent's Ownership

| Number of Parent Corporations | Average Ownership Level | | | Number of Industries |
	Actual	Firm-corrected	Country-corrected	
1	95%	25%	7%	24
2	90%	19%	2%	7
3-5	84%	11%	–4%	13
6 and over	87%	18%	–1%	9

NOTE: For subsidiaries active as of 1 January 1976. Parent corporation SIC classification from 1975 10-K report.

Table 11: The Number of Competing Parent Corporations in Each 3-digit SIC Industry and 3 Measures of Parent's Ownership

| Number of Parent Corporations | Average Ownership Level | | | Number of Industries |
	Actual	Firm-corrected	Country-corrected	
1	95%	25%	7%	24
2	90%	19%	2%	7
3-5	84%	11%	–4%	13
6 and over	83%	11%	–5%	6

NOTE: For subsidiaries active as of 1 January 1976. Parent corporation SIC classification from 1975 10-K report.
*Excluding SIC industries 283, 291, and 357.

in which all foreign investments were wholly owned contained only one corporation, and the average parent ownership of subsidiaries for the 24 single-corporation industries was 95 percent.

The general relationship is reversed in industries when six or more U.S. corporations are in the same industry. Three industries in this category account for the upturn. These three industries are pharmaceuticals (SIC 283), petroleum refining (SIC 291), and office machinery (SIC 357). When these three industries are excluded, the relationship between the number of corporations per industry and bargaining success is consistently negative for all three measures. (See Table 11.)

Since pharmaceuticals, petroleum refining, and office machinery are industries with special characteristics in Latin America, some readers might concur with their exclusion. The pharmaceutical industry was discussed in some detail in an earlier section; note here that those firms have the highest level of advertising and that the oligopoly strength is usually at the individual product level. Thus, industry measurements are misleading. The Latin American investments of the office machinery industry are dominated by those of two large computer corporations. Computer technology is extremely complex and, for the period under study, was generally unavailable to developing countries except through a very small number of computer firms. Three of the remaining investments are in the hand calculator business and are not really competing with the computer firms. The final investment is a plant actually engaged in producing office machinery. Thus, not only is the high level of technology in the computer firms special, but the arbitrary grouping of computer, hand calculator, and office machine corporations together in one industry leads to errors. The petroleum refining investments are particularly large, the majority with assets in excess of $100 million. As previously noted, operations this large appear to be located primarily in host countries with lenient investor policies. The investments are also owned by the five largest U.S. oil companies, a group that some writers have described as following noncompetitive behavior in foreign investments. These three industries, then, are all cases where other variables are important or where the measure of the level of competition is misleading. Although it is dangerous to drop the observations that are exceptions without a correspondingly thorough investigation of other observations, there does seem to be a somewhat convincing case for dismissing these three industries.

The approach to industrial concentration and bargaining power illustrated in Tables 10 and 11 is open to criticism on several grounds. First, the 3-digit SIC industry of the parent corporation and the subsidiary do not always coincide, making classification by parent industry inaccurate on occasion. Second, the number of U.S. multinationals operating in Latin America may not be a good measure of the range of options available to a host nation: firms in the same industry may have understandings among themselves concerning the regional distribution of their foreign investments. Certain enterprises may also be unwilling to invest in countries they deem politically unstable, allowing less risk-averse competitors to obtain better terms as a result. However, the same relationship is found when the analysis is repeated using the 3-digit SIC industry of the local affiliates, and when parent corporations operating in a single host nation (Mexico) are examined.[18]

The influence of competing multinational firms from home countries other than the United States was not taken into account. It seems unlikely that foreign multinationals would be concentrated in industries relatively unpopulated by U.S. multinationals. In fact, the opposite is probably the case. Moreover, the majority of foreign investments in Latin America come from U.S. firms. Thus, the inclusion of non-U.S. multinationals would probably not change the findings.

The preceeding analysis leads to the proposition that, just as domestic industrial concentration is related to domestic market power, so is "foreign-investor concentration" related to international bargaining power; but relative concentration at home does not adequately measure relative concentration abroad. Corporations in some highly concentrated industries in the United States do not necessarily find themselves in similarly advantageous positions in Latin America; instead, they are often companies facing a large number of competitors overseas. (See Table 12.) The negative relationship between concentration at home and

Table 12: U.S. Concentration Ratios for the Industry of Each Parent Corporation Classi-fied by the Number of Corporations in Each Industry Having Latin American Affiliates

Number of U.S. Parent Corporations in the Industry Active in Latin America	Average U.S. Concentration Ratio Industries of U.S. Parents (%)	Number of Industries*
1-2	35.9	30
3-4	40.6	9
5 and over	45.0	12

NOTE: For subsidiaries active as of 1 January 1976. The 4-firm concentration ratio for each 3-digit SIC industry was used, based on 1972 Commerce Department data. The first line is read as follows: For industries with one or two U.S. parent corporations active in Latin America, the average U.S. concentration ratio was 35.9 percent. There were 30 such indus-tries.

* Data not available for 2 of the 53 industries.

abroad is probably a result of investment reactions in the oligopolistic industries. Firms in a particular industry tend to react defensively to foreign investments by their competitors. According to research on this pattern, the more concentrated an industry is in the United States, the more likely are all members of that industry to react when one of their group makes a foreign investment.[19]

This investment pattern has significant implications for the bargaining processes between developing nations and multinationals. As soon as one firm from a concentrated industry established a subsidiary in a particular country, other members of that industry are eager to follow suit. Thus, by allowing one member of an industry to invest, the host country may acquire additional bargaining power vis-à-vis the others that come later.

MULTIVARIATE ANALYSIS

Many readers will, by this point, have become concerned about the analysis variable by variable. Table 13 demonstrates the generally low correlation among the independent variables. The principal exception, exports and intrasystem transfers is, of course, to be expected. Table 14 presents the results of multiple regression analysis for all Latin America and for Mexico. The low R^2's reflect the fact that the measures of both dependent and independent variables are imperfect, that the relations are not linear, that no account was taken of the degree of competition, and, probably, that there are other important variables that were not included in the regression—but the coefficients all bear signs consistent with the preceding analysis and all are significant. In such a complex field of study, that is probably as much as one could hope for.

SUMMARY AND CONCLUSIONS

This study provides some evidence to support the claim of others

Table 13: Correlation Matrix for the Independent Variables

	Assets	Intra-system	Exports	Adver-tising	R&D	Product Diversity
Assets	1.00					
Intrasystem	0.10	1.00				
Exports	0.05	0.60	1.00			
Advertising	–0.16	–0.09	–0.02	1.00		
R&D	–0.01	0.06	0.13	0.30	1.00	
Product diversity	0.29	–0.10	–0.05	–0.14	0.05	1.00

Table 14: *Regression Equations for All Latin American Affiliates and for Mexican Affiliates Only*

Dependent Variables	Size of Affiliate (assets)	Intra-system Transfers	Independent Variables: Beta Coefficients Advertising	R&D	Product Diversity	R^2	d.f.
ALL LATIN AMERICA							
Actual ownership	0.47	4.44*	1.25*	123.1*	1.93*	.14	648
	(0.51)	(3.03)	(6.18)	(3.55)	(2.28)		
Firm-corrected ownership	1.14	4.87*	0.65*	-5.57	5.59*	.13	648
	(0.98)	(2.61)	(2.43)	(0.12)	(5.25)		
Country-corrected ownership	0.26	4.09	1.10*	117.2*	2.00**	.12	648
	(0.29)	(2.86)*	(5.60)	(3.48)	(2.43)		
MEXICO ONLY							
Actual ownership	-0.99	6.70*	1.72*	152.4*	1.39	.25	192
	(0.55)	(2.67)	(4.09)	(2.61)	(0.93)		
Firm-corrected ownership	-0.16	6.03**	1.29**	55.7	4.83*	.19	192
	(0.07)	(2.01)	(2.38)	(0.80)	(2.65)		

NOTE: The t-statistics are in parentheses.
*Significant at 0.01 level.
**Significant at 0.05 level.

that the bargain struck between foreign investor and host country is influenced by the resources brought by the investor and by the number of firms offering similar resources. The ownership obtained by U.S. multinationals in Latin America has been related to the multinationals' level of technology, the degree of product differentiation, and the access to foreign markets. The study provided evidence that ownership is also influenced by the number of multinational competitors active in the industry. Further, a relationship was found between product-diversity of a subsidiary and its ownership: subsidiaries that produced a number of 3-digit SIC product lines had higher levels of ownership by the foreign firm than those produced a single line. Several explanations were proposed, although no convincing evidence was available to favor any particular interpretation.

This study leaves a great deal of work undone. Ownership is clearly an imperfect measure of bargaining power, even after adjusting for the firms' and countries' preferences; moreover, the relationships between government and firm change with time. Thus, work is called for that uses more complex measures of bargaining power (including, perhaps, licensing agreements) and that covers arrangements over a period of time. Further, the increasing importance and greater availability of data suggest that non-U.S. multinational firms ought to be included in future empirical studies of bargaining power.

Although a great deal of work remains to be done, this study provides the business manager and the government official with some evidence that the use of the concept of bargaining power is likely to be helpful in thinking about the probable course of negotiations between multinational firms and host governments. It is the first study of a large sample of firms that has attempted to test the impact of a firm's resources and industry competition on the outcome of negotiations between investor and host. The fact that the results are consistent with bargaining models proposed elsewhere, but heretofore largely untested, lends some credibility to managers or officials who might attempt to use the underlying concepts for making decisions about the complex problems that they face.

FOOTNOTES

1. See, for example, Raymond Vernon, *Sovereignty at Bay* (New York: Basic Books, 1971), chapter 2; R. B. McKern, *Multinational Enterprise and Natural Resources* (Sydney: McGraw-Hill, 1976); and David N. Smith and Louis T. Wells, Jr. *Negotiating Third World Mineral Agreements* (Cambridge: Ballinger, 1975), chapter 1.

2. Among many sources of evidence, see Vernon; and Stephen H. Hymer, *The International Operations of National Firms* (Cambridge: MIT Press, 1976).

3. The arguments of Magdoff, Baron, and Sweezy on this point are summarized in Benjamin Cohen, *The Question of Imperialism* (New York: Basic Books, 1973), chapters 4 and 5.

4. See John M. Stopford and Louis T. Wells, Jr., *Managing the Multinational Enterprise* (New York: Basic Books, 1972), pp. 155-156, for an effort to measure this factor.

5. See Smith and Wells, Jr.

6. For some evidence that ownership and control are typically linked in practice, see Simon Rottenberg, "U.S. Direct Investment in the Mexican Economy" (mimeograph, 1968); Edith Penrose, "Ownership and Control: Multinational Firms in Less Developed countries," in *A World Divided,* edited by G.K. Helleiner (Cambridge: Cambridge University Press, 1976); and Grant L. Reuber, *Private Foreign Investment in Development* (Oxford: Clarendon Press, 1973), p. 83.

7. See Stopford and Wells, chapter 5.

8. For example see Raymond Vernon, "Conflict and Resolution between Foreign Direct Investors and Less Developed Countries," *Public Policy,* Fall 1968, p. 346.

9. David G. Bradley, "Managing Against Expropriation," *Harvard Business Review,* July-August 1977, p. 81.

10. Stopford and Wells, pp. 108-113.

11. The firms represent a wide range of R&D expenditures and export orientation and there are a large number of parent corporations active in this industry.

12. See Jose de la Torré, "Marketing Factors in Manufactured Exports from Developing Countries," in *The Product Life Cycle and International Trade,* edited by Louis T. Wells, Jr. (Boston: Harvard Business School, Division of Research, 1972), pp. 227-259.

13. Bradley, p. 82.

14. Reuber, p. 83.

15. See Table 14 for the correlation.

16. The seven countries were Bolivia, Haiti, Jamaica, Nicaragua, Ecuador, Mexico, and Colombia.

17. The primary 3-digit SIC industry of the parent, as recorded in the 10-K report for 1975.

18. The results are not reported here.

19. See Frederick Knickerbocker, *Oligopolistic Reaction and the Multinational Enterprise* (Boston: Harvard University Press, 1973), pp. 192-196. Two of Knickerbocker's findings are of special interest. First, entry concentration exists: one half of U.S. foreign direct investments in any given industry and in any given country are established in three-year peak clusters. Second, the degree of entry concentration is positively related to domestic industry concentration, except at exceedingly high levels of industry concentration.

28
How to Insure
Against Political Risk
Lynn Brenner

Beyond developing internal risk assessment expertise, MNCs may either change their operating strategies to ensure greater adaptability to changing political conditions, or they may want to purchase political-risk insurance to cover unexpected events. The commercial market for risk coverage is growing and is often more flexible than government insurers, such as OPIC. Through commercial risk insurance, MNCs may obtain more extensive coverage in potentially unstable political environments.

ARMCO HAD SPENT THREE YEARS, and an estimated $2 million in lawyers' and engineers' fees, dickering with the Russians over its participation in a Soviet steel project. "We were still negotiating as our chairman was landing in Moscow to sign," recalls a company spokesman. But scarcely had the 1,800-page agreement to start work at the end of January 1980 been signed when Armco executives awoke to the news of the Soviet invasion of Afghanistan, almost immediately followed by the threat of U.S. trade sanctions on the Soviet Union.

Armco chairman William Verity immediately called President Carter and volunteered to pull out of the deal. And after taking two months to decide whether to accept this show of corporate patriotism, the administration finally did—leaving Armco $2 million poorer, since it was not insured for losses in the aborted deal. Meanwhile, the French company Creusot Loire, one of Armco's major competitors for the contract, leaped into its place—shortly thereafter to find a U.S. import ban imposed on some of its steel products, ostensibly because they contained nickel from Cuba.

No corporate executive needs his consciousness raised about the political risks in foreign business ventures these days. Indeed, what with revolution in Iran, a coup in South Korea, war between Iran and

Reprinted, with permission, from *Institutional Investor*, April 1981.

Iraq, upheavals in Ecuador, El Salvador, Angola, Liberia and elsewhere, that consciousness has been raised to new heights in the past two years. It has spawned dozens of new political analysis consultant firms, sharply increased the demand for political risk insurance, and prompted the expansion of the small commercial market for the coverage.

But few companies have yet developed any systematic way of assessing political risks to their overseas operations. For one thing, American businessmen have no real experience to draw on when it comes to political analysis of this sort. After all, points out Stephen Kobrin, associate professor at New York University's Graduate School of Business and co-author of a recent Conference Board study of political risk, compared to most of the rest of the world, "there haven't been any real changes in regime, ideology or business relationship with government in the U.S. in 200 years."

Corporations *can* turn, of course, to "experts": U.S. government agencies, banks, a host of new independent consultants, political scientists retained on staff and their own overseas employees, both foreign and American. But not surprisingly, each of these sources has a different perspective, and the sum of their opinions is as likely to confuse as to enlighten. The Delphic approach still prevails in political forecasting, and tackling a subject in which the answer to virtually any question is "it depends" can be very frustrating for corporations used to dealing in quantifiable data. "This information just isn't easily reducible to numbers," says John Sassi, manager of international studies for Gulf Oil.

Moreover, risk managers—who routinely deal with more conventional business risks—have to date had little involvement in decisions on how to handle corporate political risks (*Institutional Investor*, November 1979). While the method varies from company to company, those judgments are usually made by the international division manager, corporate treasurer, the legal staff or some combination of the above. But as the commercial political risk insurance market expands, more and more risk managers are likely to be fielding questions about expropriation and contract repudiation coverages from senior management and serving as the contact point for brokers and underwriters expanding into the field.

PARALLEL PRINCIPLES

The risk manager often feels uncomfortable in this unfamiliar role. After all, insuring against the risks inherent in a revolution is a far cry from placing fire and workers compensation coverages. But the newcomer can take heart: Political risk analysis and insurance are still in their infancy, and few experts will be very far ahead of him. And he will soon discover that accepted risk management principles can be applied even to political risks.

A political risk to business can be simply defined as the possibility of any arbitrary and discriminatory government action that results in a financial loss—which can mean anything from a shooting war to the U.S. boycott of the Moscow Olympics. Governments can, and have, expropriated assets, declared embargoes, cancelled import and export licenses, refused permission and export licenses, refused permission to convert and repatriate currency, and repudiated or defaulted on contracts. And it certainly doesn't take a revolution to set off trouble. A politically stable country encountering serious balance-of-payments problems may well impose currency convertibility restrictions, for example.

But underwriters and consultants agree that the extent to which any foreign venture is vulnerable to these risks depends as much, if not more, on the nature of the business its products and services as on the condition of the host country. A corporation with a consumer product, like food, for example, may function unscathed through a revolution. (It's worth noting that there are U.S. companies still doing business in Iran, insured for political risk, that haven't filed claims.) On the other hand, highly visible businesses involved in areas the host government is likely to consider vital to its political interests—like raw materials, finance and the infrastructure—are more vulnerable than others. Businesses engaged in mining, insurance, banking, transportation and electric power, for example, are likelier targets of expropriation than most manufacturing companies.

Insurers therefore agree that any good assessment of political dangers to a foreign operation must examine that operation *in conjunction* with the host-country's political, social, and economic stability. No company wants, can afford, or can even obtain coverage for all of its overseas risks. It must, therefore, concentrate its attention on investments it knows are vulnerable because of their liability to expropriation or other hostile acts and countries whose internal problems suggest trouble is brewing. And there are two basic rules for judging the situation: 1) get information from more than one source, because every source has its limitations as well as its advantages, and 2) make sure that no matter how many sources you use, the information they provide is evaluated at the home office. "Four of our five operating companies were in Iran [before the Shah fell]," a senior U.S. corporate executive told a recent Conference Board survey, "and no one knew what the others were doing. Each company was off on its own, talking to a limited circle of Iranians and advisers. No one had the responsibility to pull their various views together, to get a sense of where they agreed and disagreed, or to lay out possible scenarios of political developments that might affect the firm's interest—or even the safety of its employees."

Before moving to insure identifiable political risks, companies can do some things to reduce their exposure. Insurers and consultants advise a number of adaptable loss-control measures for the overseas investor:

• **Get a local partner.** A joint venture avoids the stigma of being a wholly-owned foreign operation and is therefore a less likely target of expropriation; in addition, a local partner's political influence can be helpful in maintaining a good rapport with the host government. One needs some luck in choosing the right partner, however. "The nephew of the present minister of finance is not going to be a help if the government falls," says David Avasthi, executive vice president of INAMIC, INA's political risk subsidiary.

But at least a company can be sensitive to local conditions. Benjamin Weiner, president of Probe International, an independent consulting firm, remembers steering a client away from an Iranian businessman who would have proved a most insubstantial ally. Says Weiner, "He was a multimillionaire who had represented many U.S. corporations." But in Weiner's view, the man has a real drawback: "He was a Bahai, a religious minority in Iran—and he was breaking the basic Middle Eastern rule for religious minorities, which is that it's okay to get rich as long as you aren't too visible. This man had built himself a duplicate of the Trianon, only bigger, and one of his art acquisitions had been written up in *Newsweek*."

• **Maintain contact with local authorities.** Governments change routinely more often than by revolution—and regulatory and administrative changes are a much more frequent cause of politically attributable loss than violent upheaval. ("It's rare that a country blows up in your face," says NYU's Kobrin.) A good rapport with a permanent undersecretary can be more valuable than a relationship with a President or a minister of finance. It's also important to be aware of the views of political parties not in power.

• **Be a good citizen of the host country.** The firm that's a local employer, borrows from local banks, and buys or leases local goods and equipment is less likely to be a target of inimical government action. And be sure local authorities *know* the ways in which you benefit the country's economy, says Hugh Sinclair, president of INAMIC. It's wise to have good citizenship documented and ready for presentation. Host governments are favorably impressed, for instance, with a track record of exports that has helped their country's balance of payments. Sinclair's associate David Avasthi also stresses the importance of sensitivity to local society. "It's important to be aware of how your operation is perceived by nationals," he says, adding, "If there's a strong 60/40 religious split in a country, your local hiring should probably follow that split." Weiner agrees, and sometimes recommends a census of local population, to determine tribal and religious affiliations, voting records, and opinions on labor issues.

• **Keep the subsidiary dependent on its home-country parent.** A government may hesitate to expropriate a business it lacks the technology to operate, especially if the firm's services or products are of national importance. Maintaining worldwide trademarks, so that nationalization would mean a reduced market for a plant's product, and keeping proprietary research and processing technology outside the host country, can minimize the chances of expropriation. (But some of these loss-control methods have negative as well as positive sides, cautions Avasthi. A nationally important business whose technology is withheld by foreign owners may be all the more resented by nationalists—and nationalist fervor often carries with it a willingness to sacrifice important goods or services provided by foreigners. By the same token, a joint venture may enjoy more goodwill, but entails the risk that local partners may learn the business well enough to make expropriation feasible.)

• **Keep a low profile.** Consultant Weiner says this is easier than might be supposed. "People often don't realize the nationality of a company doing business in their country," he says. "After all, how many Americans know that Good Humor is foreign owned?"

• **Install a system of ongoing monitoring.** Political and social climates and regulations are subject to constant change. So is the status of business operations. A foreign firm may win extremely favorable terms to drill for oil, for instance, but once the oil is found, the terms may change radically.

• **Have contingency plans.** Expropriation often leaves a corporation with a number of choices. "If it's asked to divest itself of 20 percent of ownership, for instance," says Avasthi, "it has a choice of whether to reduce the capital base by 20 percent or increase it to 120 percent." A demand that ownership be shared with native interests is a common occurrence, and companies that have strategies planned can minimize the impact of an expropriatory loss. And, adds Sinclair, if a country does blow up in your face, the confusion can actually help the company with contingency plans to put them into operation quickly and smoothly.

TWO MARKETS

Finally, for investments that management decides are still vulnerable to hostile acts of governments, there is insurance. There are really two political risk insurance markets for the U.S. corporation—a U.S. government-sponsored market and a commercial market. For several years, Lloyd's underwriters had a virtual corner on the latter market, but recently a handful of U.S. insurers have jumped in as well. They include American International Group, INA, Continental (through its subsidiary, the Swett & Crawford group) and, in the near future, Chubb.

The U.S. government's involvement in insuring these risks was prompted by a desire to spur exports and encourage investments in developing nations as a deterrent to the spread of Communism (not to mention the fact that expanding economies also provide attractive markets for its exporters). Export insurance is more or less the province of the Export-Import Bank and the Foreign Credit Insurance Association, an underwriting association of some 50 property and casualty insurers and reinsurers, whose policies are in turn reinsured by the Ex-Im Bank. Direct investment abroad is more the concern of the Overseas Private Investment Corp., established by Congress in 1969 and operative the following year. (Foreign subsidiaries of U.S. companies can also buy coverage from foreign government programs, available in most developed countries, that are the counterparts of OPIC.)

In many ways, OPIC is the Sears, Roebuck of the political-risk market, an insurer whose coverage is hard to compete with in terms of value and durability. Among its advantages:

• **War coverage.** Only OPIC covers physical damage caused by war—"but we're working on it," says AIG's assistant vice president Robert Svensk. (War damage has so far proved less costly than might be supposed. OPIC's losses for this coverage, although admittedly reduced by the fact that it had no insurance in Lebanon, have been less than 5¢ per premium dollar.)

• **Lower cost.** Premiums for expropriation coverage range from $^4/_{10}$ of 1 percent of assets covered up to a little more than 2 percent, depending on the project in question. (OPIC doesn't rate by country.) Incovertibility and war damage policies cost less than 1 percent of assets covered. Commercial market premiums, by contrast, range from less than 1 percent to close to 10 percent of assets covered at Lloyd's, from less than 1 percent to more than 3 percent of assets at AIG and from less than 1 percent to 14 percent of assets at INA, which has only been in the market since last fall. Continental, an even more recent seller of expropriation coverage, charges from less than 1 percent to about 5 percent of assets covered.

• **Greater capacity.** OPIC can write up to $150 million of coverage per project and tries to limit its exposure per country to about $300 million. AIG will generally write about $35 million of coverage per project per country and INA about $13 million per project, with varying country limits, although both companies can increase their limits per risk with facultative reinsurance. Lloyd's syndicates can provide capacity of $100 million (sometimes more) per country and $50 or $60 million per project. Continental has a top limit of $40 million per risk per country.

• **Longer policy terms.** OPIC policies are written up to twenty-year terms, at what is essentially a fixed rate. Commercial market policies, on the other hand, generally run from one to three years.

But OPIC has very definite limitations, the concomitant of its being a political instrument. Coverage, for example, is now only available for new investments in countries with per capita income of $1,000 or less a year whose governments have signed an appropriate bilateral agreement with the U.S. Also, OPIC must get host-government permission to sell the coverage, which can cause bureaucratic delay in obtaining the insurance. (Host-government knowledge of the existence of insurance makes some corporations nervous. Indeed, the commercial insurers require that the existence of a policy be kept confidential.) And since OPIC must act in accordance with U.S. foreign policy, it will not sell coverage for projects it deems harmful either to the host-country's economy or the U.S. economy.

Furthermore, OPIC coverage is only available for corporations owned by U.S. citizens, which means acquisition by a foreign buyer could cause termination of coverage. One can't even be sure OPIC will always be there. Its existence, and its rules of operation, are subject to change by Congress every three years, although in the event of change, or OPIC's elimination, existing policies would, of course, be honored. (Actually, OPIC's encouragement of the private sector in developing countries and the fact that it is self-sustaining—its net income last year was $65.8 million, though, of course, one major catastrophe could wipe out twenty year's premiums—seem likely to win strong support from the Reagan Administration and the new Congress.)

Even when a buyer qualifies for OPIC insurance, it may not provide the best coverage for him. An example is coverage for the on-demand financial guarantees often required of contractors who are hired by foreign governments. These are performance bonds or letters of credit posted as collateral against the contractor's advance payments in case the project is not completed satisfactorily. Since host governments have been known to seize these guarantees arbitrarily, some kind of insurance is needed. But Alexander & Alexander vice president Francis Boylan recommends that contractors use OPIC coverage for these guarantees only if the contract calls for international arbitration of disputes; if the contract demands local arbitration, he thinks commercial coverage is better.

Boylan points out that if the financial guarantee is called and arbitration decides in favor of the host government, OPIC will pay a claim only if the arbitration "record" shows the decision to have been unsupported by substantial evidence. On the other hand, he says, in many countries that insist on local arbitration, "it's virtually impossible to secure any 'record' from an arbitration proceeding," and the contractor might be unable to collect on OPIC coverage—even if the decision were totally unfounded.

A "BOUTIQUE"

While it is more expensive, the expanding commercial market for political risk coverage is far more flexible than the government insurers. It serves almost as a "boutique" where the insurance shopper can supplement his OPIC coverage with custom-designed products. Exporters and overseas investors and contractors can buy insurance in the commercial market against almost any conceivable disaster—excluding, again, war itself, although "war" is defined as one involving the "five great powers" or between the insurance buyer's country and the host country. And while it excludes physical damage, commercial coverage does include some losses indirectly caused by war.

The private market will insure against expropriation, confiscation, or nationalization without prompt and adequate compensation: "creeping" exporpriation (snowballing disciminatory acts whose end result is equivalent to expropriation); currency inconvertibility; contract repudiation; the arbitrary calling of on-demand financial guarantees; embargoes or license cancellations; and other like events. Private insurers can consider countries excluded by OPIC's restrictions and they can negotiate the terms of policies to meet a company's needs, while the government agencies issue "package" policies.

"The private sector is in many ways our godson," says Gerald West, acting president of OPIC. "We've helped build up their reserves with our premiums by sharing reinsurance, and our experience has given them good information." One piece of information private insurers have received is that underwriting political risk insurance can be profitable, which has been incentive enough to try the waters. "With increased economic interdependence and the thrust to nationalism coming simultaneously," says INAMIC's Sinclair, "political risk insurance is the wave of the future." INA estimates that the commercial market now generates about $20 million a year in premiums, and that cooperation between INA, AIG and Lloyd's can, with appropriate reinsurance, produce up to $200 million of coverage on a risk.

HOW TO CHARGE?

How do these insurers decide what to charge for their coverage? Unlike the political analysts, the underwriter doesn't attempt to forecast events. "You consider the project, the country, the competition and your portfolio," says AIG's Svensk. "If it's a country you have very little exposure in, the rate might be lower than in a 'safer' country you have a lot of exposure in." Writing any kind of catastrophic risk depends on breaking it into small pieces (through spread of risk and reinsurance) and generating enough premium "to cover at least one disaster," Svensk explains. "I price to fund my portfolio, and the country probably doesn't affect the decision on any one risk as much as how great an exposure I can afford in that country relative to my whole book." AIG, he says, collected twice as many new business premiums last year as in 1979, and although "we won't write currency inconvertibility coverage in Zaire, for instance, because we know there's a problem, we don't rule any single country out automatically for all coverages."

Given the smallness of the commercial market, how much real price competition is there? Broadly speaking, very little, says Charles Liotta, assistant vice president of March & McLennan. "But on specific placements, the underwriter's judgement can make a difference of up to two-and-a-half times the premium." Other brokers agree that underwriters are no more objective than anybody else about political risks; both their nationality and background influence their assessment. "A London underwriter and an American underwriter don't see a former British Colony the same way," points out one expert. Lloyd's seems to charge less for risks in Africa, says another broker, while AIG charges less for risks in South America. Adds Christine LaSala, assistant vice president of Johnson & Higgins: "It often happens that AIG is interested in a risk and Lloyd's isn't and vice versa. But I've never really found a discernable pattern to it."

How does a company determine how much of its exposure to cover? AIG advises corporations to take into account their equity contribution to the foreign enterprise, their share of retained earnings, their loans to it (including accrued but unpaid interest), their guarantees of its non-local obligations and to subtract whatever receivables they owe the foreign enterprise. "Essentially," says J&H's LaSala, "you have to ask yourself how it would affect the balance sheet if you stopped owning that plant. In real life, an underwriter will listen to whatever valuation you set forth—but underwriters are unlikely to include a ten-year stream of earnings as a component of the valuation." Underwriting expropriation risks depends in part on the insurer's expectations of recovery from the expropriating government—and, in fact, some compensation is usually made. "If the insurer covers you on a book value basis," says LaSala, "he may feel he could recover 60 percent from the host government. It's extremely unlikely a host government wil pay for a future stream of earnings."

A contractor's exposure at any given time is actually less than the total value of the contract, so a two-year, $10 million contract doesn't mean $10 million worth of insurance, points out Harvey Mallement, senior vice president of the brokerage firm JLS Group. "Your maximum exposure at any time during the life of a $10 million contract might be no more than $2 million," he says. Among the factors to be considered are cash advances and progress payments for goods or services delivered vs. cash outlay and legal commitments to buy goods from others (minus whatever salvage value could be recouped if the contract were repudiated), as well as the cost of letters of credit. The premium for contract frustration coverage, says Mallement, can fluctuate during the life of the contract, as the exposure and coverage change.

A COOLING-OFF PERIOD

The risk manager should be forewarned that all insurers, both public and commercial, insist on a waiting period after the loss occurs before they will pay a claim. "There's a delay to let the dust settle, see who's in power, give everyone a chance to cool off and appeal to reason," says Sinclair of INAMIC. Waiting periods vary depending on the insurer and the type of coverage. (AIG, for instance, delays one year after expropriation before paying a claim.) And, of course, unless they clearly specify

otherwise, policies only cover losses caused by "arbitrary and discriminatory" political events—which can leave plenty of room for
disagreement between insurer and insured and explains the existence of
an arbitration clause in all political risk policies. "There has to be real
trust between insurer and insured," says one broker. "A lot depends on
the sophistication and good faith of the carrier. Cases of expropriation or
unfair calling of on-demand financial guarantees aren't always
clear-cut."

In cases where a contractor claims his on-demand financial guarantee was unfairly called by the host government, says AIG's Svensk, the
insurer will use common sense: "In a macro situation like Iran, no one
will argue that it's a wrongful calling. In a micro situation—a friendly
country where one contractor has his bond called or his contract cancelled and 499 other contractors are still working happily—you have to ask
if maybe he simply didn't perform well. We have to be skeptics." In expropriation coverage, adds J&H's LaSala, a constitutionally-sanctioned
change in laws or regulations—a corporate tax increase, for instance—
won't be considered an insured political risk unless it entails a discriminatory change in the corporation's investment agreement with the
host government. "If there's a critical component in your investment
agreement," she advises, "identify it up front and present it to the
underwriters. Don't leave it to the gray areas."

In spite of the tremendous progress that has been made during the
past decade, there remain, inevitably, political risks that no market,
public or commercial, will write: new coverage in already hostile countries, for example (although renewals at hefty premium increases may be
available). Nor does anyone cover currency devaluation, although its
effects—the insolvency and default of a buyer of goods and services, for
instance—may be covered. Consequential losses—the long-range costs
to a food processor if a foreign crop vital to his product is no longer
exported, for instance—are not insurable. Nor, not too surprisingly, will
anyone cover losses caused by a major cutoff of oil from the Middle East.

But new coverages will most certainly emerge as the market expands. And an increased demand for political risk insurance and consequent increase in premium volume will no doubt result in lower rates
as well. One of the most hopeful signs of a better market is the predic-
tion by many in the field that buyers will soon be able to combine OPIC
and commercial coverage. OPIC's West says his agency has already
discussed joint undertakings with Lloyd's and AIG, as well as some of
its foreign government counterparts. The result would be far greater

flexibility in terms of the market capacity and terms and inclusiveness of the coverage. Concludes West: "It will happen. It's only a matter of time."

APPENDIX

WHEN POLITICAL RISK GETS PERSONAL

In an age of growing political terrorism, companies have another risk to worry about: that their overseas executives will be kidnapped. Since 1970, there have been approximately 370 identified kidnappings of corporate personnel, and no one knows how many have gone unreported. The executive who followed all the security precautions recommended to minimize the chance of being kidnapped—varying the route to work every day, keeping an unpredictable schedule (arriving late one day and early the next) and so one—would have little time for anything else. But experts do suggest some easy-to-follow precautions:
• Blend in locally. It's inadvisable, for instance, to drive a Mercedes with a licence plate bearing the company logo.
• Make sure the company knows how to raise funds on a weekend or a holiday.
• Make sure the person authorized to approve the payment of ransom money has a backup. One expert remembers a case in which the only executuve so authorized was himself the kidnap victim.

And, of course, have insurance—which is now readily available at competitive rates from several Lloyd's and U.S. underwriters. Indeed, after an initial reluctance to write the kidnap policies, "Underwriters are staying up nights figuring out how to broaden the coverage and lower the rates," says Ira Shapiro, senior vice president of the brokerage firm JLS Group. One benefit of such a policy, adds JLS senior vice president Harvey Mallement, "is that it removes some of the uncertainty of the situation and gives you a systematic program of what to do in the event of a kidnapping."

A million-dollar three-year policy for a small company might cost as little as $2,500, although most policies provide from $10 to $20 million of coverage. And the protection is now much broader than when the policies first became popular in the early 1970s. (Coverage has actually been available at Lloyd's since the Lindbergh kidnapping.) The typical policy covers either key executives or all employees (the price differential is small) on a worldwide basis. Included automatically are families (down to third cousins) and house guests of employees; personal as well as corporate assets; rewards for information; legal expenses of negotiating the victim's release; medical expenses; interest on loans taken out because of the kidnapping; and a death benefit. Some policies even cover "transit loss risk"—theft of the ransom money while it's en route to the kidnappers.

More recently, endorsements covering the victim's salary, a salary for his temporary replacement and lost corporate earnings because of the absence of key personnel have been available as well. (And companies can even cover the costs of a lawsuit by a disgruntled, albeit released, executive.) Endorsements or separate policies will also cover extortion payments made after a threat to blow up corporate facilities.

Interestingly, policy language has not specifically excluded detention by a government: Had the 52 U.S. hostages in Iran been corporate employees, held for corporate assets, says Richard Wagner, vice president of March & McLennan, "I don't believe anything in the old policy would have excluded coverage. Although it wouldn't have been the intent of the policy to cover such a case, I think underwriters would have been hardpressed to deny a claim." Wagner adds that insurers are now eliminating ambiguities here: They are working on endorsements that will specifically cover unfounded governmental detentions.

Chapter Ten:
Future Considerations

ALMOST TWENTY YEARS have passed since Jean Jacques Servan-Schreiber published *Le Defi Americane* (The American Challenge), in which he advocated that the future of international business would be dominated by American multinational corporations unless there was a reaction by foreign governments to meet this challenge. In the intervening years, however, we have seen not only the growth and development of European and Japanese multinational corporations across international boundaries, but a strong challenge from multinationals in developing countries, particularly South Korea, to MNCs originating in developed economies. Consequently, while U.S. multinationals still remain in the forefront in terms of advanced technology, multinational companies from other countries continue to expand and to demonstrate their ability to compete successfully in the world marketplace.

A major complication on the international scene—one that seriously affects multinational corporate activity—has been the foreign-debt problem of many of the less-developed countries (LDCs), as well as large trade surpluses accruing to Japan and major oil-exporting countries. Debt rescheduling of LDCs has arisen rapidly in the past few years, both in terms of frequency and the total amount involved. Furthermore, debt problems with major borrowing countries such as Poland, Mexico, and Argentina have severely shaken the confidence of the international banking community, particularly when there are rumors that some countries may even refuse to honor their international obligations. Even some of the oil-exporting countries, including Venezuela and Indonesia, have been forced to reschedule their external debt. There is every reason to believe that the number of countries forced to reschedule their external debt will increase in the near term, at least through 1990.

To complicate the issue further, the multinational corporation is buffeted by, and must respond to, constantly-changing environmental conditions around the world at both the micro and macro levels. Not only is the enterprise faced with new products and new companies, but it must also adapt to changes in technology, information systems, and personnel.

Global issues such as recessions and banking crises have already had a serious effect on the flow of goods, services, and capital. Protectionism by one country and direct retaliation by another alter traditional patterns of world trade. Transfers of technology and restrictions on transborder data flows significantly affect management's control of multinational enterprises in their global pursuits. Moreover, political embargoes and confiscation of assets by hostile governments are facts of life with which multinationals will need to contend. Rapid development of many Third World countries, and ensuing rising expectations, will affect the ownership and control of many multinationals abroad. As a consequence, corporate planners will need to pay close attention to the changing structure of world economic and political affairs if their companies are to remain competitive in the international marketplace. The impact of these forces will vary from industry to industry and country to country. However, the following factors will be of significance to corporations in dealing with host countries over the next decade:

- Increasing government involvement in economic planning and management, particularly in the LDCs.
- Closer government-private sector cooperation—following, in particular, the Japanese model of development.
- Increasing emphasis on national priorities and nationalism.
- Aggressive steps aimed at increasing the transfer of technology from the developed world to developing nations, in order to raise productivity and enhance development.
- Additional pressure to develop, train, and employ local nationals, particularly in senior positions.
- Renewed efforts to seek foreign capital from both public and private sectors for both industrial and economic development.
- Increasing competition in domestic markets from foreign firms of both developed and developing nations.
- Continuing restrictive legislation and regulation to preserve local markets and to increase local ownership in joint ventures.

Because of these important changes in the years ahead, multinational corporations will need to develop truly global management philosophies and systems. An awareness by multinational corporations of the changing environment will be essential so that corporate planners can mesh and adjust their corporate goals and objectives to meet the needs and objectives of the host countries in which they operate.

29
Soviet Natural Gas in Europe: The OPEC of the 1990s?

Fariborz Ghadar
and Robert J. Pelosky, Jr.

Energy has indeed been a major issue of the 1980s, and will continue throughout this century. Not only have there been many fluctuations in the price and supply of energy, primarily oil and natural gas, but many new players have entered the field as major suppliers, one of which is the Soviet Union. Within a few years, the Soviet Union will have positioned itself in the Western European market, as a supplier of natural gas, in such a way that it could indeed monopolize the market and thereby make Europe dependent upon the Soviet whims of market manipulation.

RECENT CHANGES in the European energy market, namely, a decline in oil consumption and an increased use of natural gas, have caused the West in general and West Europeans in particular to become vulnerable to the increasing importation of and dependence on Soviet natural gas. Although in some cases the Soviets have had to cut back the amount of gas contracted to Western European nations, Soviet exports of natural gas have steadily increased during the last few years, capturing a larger and larger market share in Europe. With substantial excess capacity in its gas export system, the Soviets have begun to price their gas below CIF (equivalent) oil prices. Soviet gas will thus gradually replace a portion of heavy fuel oil and residual fuel oil, as well as coal consumption. This will reduce the demand for these forms of energy in Europe. This shift is likely to put downward pressure on coal and fuel prices, and, in the

This article is based on a study by the authors, entitled "East West Energy: Natural Gas Supply and Demand in the Soviet Union, Afghanistan, Iran, Eastern and Western Europe" (1985).

near term, European heavy fuel oil and residual oil prices will decline. With lower gas prices, development of the more expensive alternative natural gas fields outside of the Soviet Union, such as those in Norway, may not be economical and Western Europe will become increasingly reliant on Soviet gas.

Although the West European gas market will remain competitive, one may expect that in the next five to eight years the Soviet Union will continue to be the most economic source of gas for Europe by virtue of geographical proximity, abundance of supply, existing gas infrastructure and transport system, foreign exchange needs, and price cutting ability. It is felt that the Soviet Union will solidify its position as Europe's primary gas supplier over the next decade. At present, gas is the growth fuel of both East and West Europe. The Soviet Union has positioned itself by means of the Urengoi pipeline to offer substantial gas flows to the region at prices that are sure to remain competitive.

Even in the event of a continuing energy oversupply in Europe, the Soviets are capable of price-cutting as a means of maintaining their market share. There can be little question that Soviet importance as an energy supplier for Western Europe will increase. This trend should be of concern to Europe and its allies. If unchecked, and if alternative sources are not developed, Europe may find itself in the early 1990s reliant not on an OPEC oliogopoly but on a Soviet gas monopoly. If energy markets tighten, the ramifications of that dependence may be more than economic.

SOVIET GAS AND THE URENGOI PIPELINE

A recent report prepared by Professor Fariborz Ghadar, Director of the International Business Programs at the George Washington University, and J. Pelosky of the European-American Bank investigates in detail the history and current and future impact of the Soviet Union's natural gas pipeline to Western Europe.[1] The original impetus for this study was the 1982 U.S. embargo on parts and technology destined for use on the pipeline. In order to put that event in perspective, the authors reexamined the complex natural gas relationships between the Soviet Union and those states which both influence and are affected by Soviet natural gas policy. The full report constitutes a comprehensive overview of the Soviet Union's domestic energy and gas reserves and of its energy relations with Afghanistan, Iran, Eastern Europe, Western Europe, and Japan.

The Soviet Union's gas reserves are by far the largest in the world.[2] Not only does the Soviet Union have more gas than any other single nation, it has the bulk of the world's economically exportable reserves—about 70 percent. The Urengoi field alone has reserves amounting to more than all proven U.S. reserves. Until recently, however, these reserves have not had a significant effect on the shape of the world's energy trading because the Soviet Union did not have the infrastructure necessary to get their gas from the Siberian fields to the West. The Urengoi pipeline changed all that. The Soviets are now able not only to meet their domestic needs and the needs of their Eastern Bloc allies but are able to significantly participate in the world energy market on many fronts.[3]

Since the Soviet Union is changing from an oil-intensive to a gas-intensive economy,[4] the infrastructure development represented by the Urengoi pipeline serves an important double purpose. Soviet gas reserves have been made available for domestic consumption[5] as well as for export to Eastern Bloc nations and Western Europe, exports which generate the hard currency earnings that go to pay for the gas distribution system.[6] Thus, with the successful completion of the Urengoi line the Soviets have simultaneously strengthened their own energy infrastructure and Western dependence on Soviet energy.

The availability of Soviet natural gas to the energy deficient Eastern European nations is also, from the Soviet point of view, strategically and economically beneficial. All four of the Western European nations profiled here—West Germany, France, Italy, and Great Britain—can be characterized by their need for increased natural gas imports in the ten-year period from 1955 to 1995. By virtue of its ability to supply and its need to sell natural gas, the Soviet Union will be the principal supplier of natural gas to these countries. For the next decade, at least, these supplies will flow through the Urengoi export line.

Urengoi, straddling the Arctic Circle, is the world's largest gas field and produces the gas that flows to Western Europe.[7] The Urengoi export line, stretching 2,800 miles from Western Siberia to Europe, puts the Soviet Union on line as a major natural gas exporter to the West. The controversial project, which was completed in the summer of 1984 and which is expected to reach full carrying capacity in 1986-87, will have a throughput of 40 to 50 bcm (billion cubic meters) per year. This will give the Soviets the opportunity to replace their lagging oil exports with natural gas exports, thus retaining vital flows of hard currency as well as providing the opportunity to develop their gas transport system further and exploit Siberian reserves even more effectively.

Construction on the Urengoi line began in 1981. *The New York Times* reported in July of 1983 that, according to the Soviets, the pipe laying for the entire line had been completed, connecting the Western Siberian gas field with Uzhgorod on the Czechoslovakian-Soviet border. (The Czechs themselves constructed 534 miles of 56-inch pipeline from Uzhgorod to the West European terminal at Waidhaus on the Czech-West German border, for which they receive 5.3 bcm/yr of natural gas from the Soviets for transit fees and as compensation for the pipeline construction.) Despite the completion of pipe-laying in the summer of 1983, the line did not become operational at that time because of a lack of compressors needed to power the gas through the pipe. The Soviets planned to use a new generation of 16,000 and 25,000 kw compressors on the Urengoi pipeline, and by September of 1983 had enough to complete only half the compressor stations on the line.[8] The Soviets probably pressed an older generation of compressors into service, but it is the availability and performance of the new GNT-25 units that will largely determine the rate at which the Urengoi line reaches full carrying capacity.

The most significant instance of Soviet-West European economic cooperation to date, the Urengoi export line was, of course, a source of serious conflict between the U.S. and its European allies since the late 1970s when the project was first conceived. The Reagan administration looked unfavorably on the development of the Urengoi line, contending from the start that it would make West Europe overly dependent on Soviet energy sources, particularly in the event of a major energy source disruption elsewhere. The West Europeans rejected this view, arguing that, in addition to improving their security by diversifying energy sources, the pipeline would also act as an incentive to rationalize Soviet behavior in Europe. In essence, the controversy which broke out between the United States and her Western allies stemmed from these contradictory—but not mutually exclusive—views of the pipeline's effect on the East-West balance of power. The U.S. also correctly perceived the pipeline as a significant hard currency earner for the Soviets, one which would provide them with substantial monies to pour into defense projects. For the U.S., therefore, the Urengoi pipeline seemed to be a destabilizing factor in U.S.-Soviet relations. For their part, the West Europeans, who have a historical trading relationship with the Soviet Union, view such trade as inherently stabilizing, both in the context of European-Russian and U.S.-Soviet relations.

The Reagan administration's imposition of sanctions on U.S. equipment, earmarked for use on the pipeline, escalated the controversy into a serious conflict among the Western allies. The embargo, in part a response to the Polish crisis of 1981, failed to sufficiently take into account West European attitudes and energy needs. Aside from the question of extraterritoriality,[9] West European officials strongly resented being told by American officials that they were jeopardizing the future freedom and security of their countries. However one looks at the ultimate legitimacy of the American rationale for the policy, the U.S. embargo proved a dubious undertaking from most points of view. It created a great deal of misunderstanding and ill will between the U.S. and its allies, some of which still remains. It had, at best, only a temporary effect on the construction and successful completion of the Urengoi line.

The New York Times noted that a study by the Office of Technology Assessment concluded that "while U.S. sanctions on energy equipment may have slowed work on [the] Siberian pipeline, [the] embargo's actual impact is extremely difficult to pinpoint in view of delays endemic to most Soviet construction projects."[10] In the end, the Reagan administration was forced to retreat slowly, and rather awkwardly, from its position in order to allow U.S. companies, such as Caterpillar Tractor Co., to sell pipeline-related equipment to the Soviets. Despite the untenability of the embargo policy, the enormous economic and political significance of Soviet gas exports to Western Europe is a development that, as we shall see, needs to be more carefully considered and completely understood by all parties.[11]

The Soviets reported the Urengoi pipeline operational as of January 1, 1984, with the first deliveries of natural gas to Gaz de France under their 25-year contract with the Soviets.[12] The West Germans, in the form of a consortium headed by Ruhrgas AG, began receiving gas from the Soviets on October 1, 1984, and deliveries to Italy, Austria, and Switzerland were slated to begin in 1985. The Urengoi line carried over 5 bcm to Western Europe in 1984 and is expected to move about 7 bcm in 1985. With a full carrying capacity of 40 bcm, which should be reached in early 1988, the Soviets have at present contracted for 21-24 bcm/yr of gas for delivery to Western Europe (see Table 1). In addition to sales to Eastern European countries, buyer states include West Germany, Great Britain, France, and Italy. The Netherlands and Belgium cancelled contracts with the Soviets, while Soviet negotiations with Spain were cancelled in 1982, apparently due to U.S. pressure. Sweden also rejected, because of costs, Soviet gas for the time being.

Eastern Europe was the first significant export market for Soviet gas.[13] Beginning with a joint Polish-Soviet project in 1966, the Soviet Union, working in conjunction with various Council for Mutual Economic Assistance (CMEA) nations, has constructed an extensive pipeline network to export gas to Poland, Bulgaria, East Germany, Czechoslovakia, and Hungary. The East European states will also benefit from the enlarged pipeline capacity the Soviet Union is constructing to boost gas exports to Western Europe. Declining demand in West Europe could result in surpluses which could be used to meet Eastern Europe's growing demand for gas.

The developing economies of the CMEA states generate a significant demand for liquid fuels. In 1961, the oil and gas accounted for 12 percent of East European energy consumption. By 1975, this figure had increased to 34 percent, and by 1981, oil and gas provided 39 percent of all energy consumed (gas 16 percent, oil 23 percent). Oil and gas demand will continue to rise as a consequence of industrial sector development and its need for a hydrocarbon energy base. From 1977 to 1982 East European primary energy consumption increased 1.5 percent/yr, gas consumption increasing 4 percent, oil 1.0 percent, coal 0.7 percent/year. If Eastern Europe is to industrialize, natural gas will have to be its fuel. Even during the economic slowdown between 1980 and 1983, gas consumption continued to increase, albeit modestly (3 percent). In 1983, the Soviets exported 34.4 bcm of natural gas to Eastern Europe. The Soviets thus have, in the CMEA states, an available back-up market for the export gas going to Western Europe.

WESTERN EUROPE'S CHANGING ENERGY MARKET

When the OPEC oil increase of 1973/74 and 1979/81 forced the Western European nations to seek ways of lessening their heavy dependence on Persian Gulf oil, the growing supply of natural gas from both Western European sources and the Soviet Union presented an attractive alternative.[14] In contrast to declining oil consumption, gas production, importation, and consumption all rose substantially from 1972 to 1982 (see Table 2 and Figure 1). During this period, oil as a percentage of overall West European energy demand fell from 60 percent to 49 percent, while gas consumption grew from 10 percent to 14 percent, despite the economic downturn of 1979/82, which depressed gas demand somewhat. The demand for gas again grew rapidly in 1983/84.

Natural gas production within Western Europe, primarily in the North Sea, was at first used to meet most of the increased demand. The

Table 1: 1985 Soviet Gas Exports

West Germany	371 bc ft	(10.4 bcm)
France	282 bc ft	(7.9 bcm)
Italy	—	—
Austria	53 bc ft	(1.5 bcm)
West Berlin	25 bc ft	(0.7 bcm)
Switzerland	14 bc ft	(0.4 bcm)

SOURCE: *Oil and Gas Journal*, 83:64-65 (1 January 1985).

Figure 1.

Natural Gas Consumption, Production and Imports

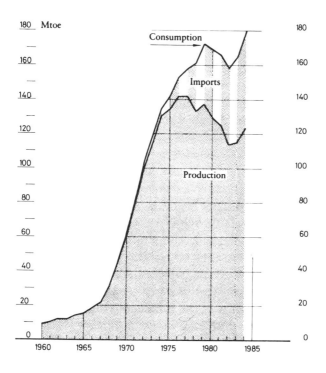

SOURCE: *Energy in Europe,* Commission of the European Community, No. 1 (April 1985).

Table 2: Western Europe, Oil and Gas

	Oil consumption % change/yr 1987-82	Gas consumption % change/yr 1972-82	Gas production % change/yr 1972-82
West Germany	− 2.2	+ 6.0	+ 1.0
France	− 2.1	+ 5.7	+ 1.1
Italy	− 0.8	+ 6.4	+ 0.1
Great Britain	− 3.7	+ 5.1	+ 3.3

SOURCE: Ghadar and Pelosky, p. 92.

Table 3: Western Europe, Gas as a Primary Energy

	% of primary energy consumption met by gas 1982
West Germany	15.0
France	11.7
Italy	17.4
Great Britain	21.1
Total for Western Europe	15.9

SOURCE: Petroleum Economist, 52:45 (February 1985).

Table 4: Western Europe as a Natural Gas Importer

	% of consumption met by imports in 1983
West Germany	66.3
France	74.5
Italy	52.4
Great Britain	18.2
Total for Western Europe	24.5

SOURCE: Petroleum Economist, 52-45 (February 1985).

remainder was met by imports from the Soviet Union, which grew rapidly during this period. Prior to the surge in demand following the oil shocks, domestic needs had been met largely through domestic supplies. The upsurge in demand following 1973/74 revealed the inability of domestic supply sources to meet the rise in demand. Between 1979 and 1983, natural gas production in the European Economic Community (EEC) fell 17 percent, making it clear that increased gas demand would have to be met by imports. The available or acceptable alternative energy sources for either East or West Europe are limited. Natural gas will increasingly play the role of the "swing" fuel, countering delayed nuclear programs, insufficient oil production or imports, and limits on coal usage due to environmental concern (see Table 3). By 1985, gas represented nearly 20 percent of Europe's primary energy demand.

Soviet gas plays a considerable and a crucial role in the West European energy picture. Western Europe imported 2 bcm of Soviet gas in 1973. By 1981 this figure had risen to 28 bcm. In contrast, West European production rose from 145 bcm in 1973 to 197 bcm in 1981 before declining to 179 bcm in 1982. Regional projections in 1980 estimate that total domestic gas production would decline from 190 bcm in 1980 to 172 bcm in 1990. The U.S. government has estimated that West European domestic gas production will meet only 60 percent of total domestic demand in 1990, as compared with 85 percent in 1981. Given these figures and trends, there can be no doubt that Western Europe will require significant imports of natural gas to meet future regional energy requirements (see Table 4).

Although Soviet, Algerian, Dutch, and Norwegian gas will compete for their shares of the European market, there is also no doubt that Soviet gas will continue to play a major role in meeting Western Europe's natural gas needs (see Table 5).[15] According to the *Oil and Gas Journal*,

Table 5: Gas Exporters to Western Europe
(billion cubic meters)

	1982
Netherlands	34.8
Norway	29.4
USSR	27.9
Algeria	8.4
Libya	1.0

SOURCE: *Petroleum Economist,* 52:45 (February 1985).

Table 6: Western Europe and Natural Gas, A Profile for 1990 (billion cubic meters)

	Total gas consumption	Indigenous production	Intra-Community trade	Total imports	USSR	Algeria	Norway
West Germany	68.0	17.5	22.5	28.0	20.0	—	8.0
France	42.9	3.1	6.5	33.3	12.0	9.2	2.9
Italy	45.5	7.8	6.5	31.2	8.0	13.0	—
Netherlands	38.0	75.8	39.8	2.0	—	—	2.0
Great Britain	61.5	45.0	39.8	16.5	—	—	16.5

SOURCE: Ghadar and Pelosky, p. 34).

Western European gas demand will grow to 4.68 million b/d (barrels per day) oil equivalent by the year 2000 from the current level of 3.63 million b/d. For the remainder of the century, the report continues, gas will account for 15.5 percent of Western Europe's total energy requirement. Prior to 1985, the Soviets had been delivering 22.5-26 bcm/yr of gas to Western Europe.

The Oil and Gas Journal predicts that "by 1990 about 45% of all continental western European gas demand will be met by imports. The Soviets will command about 45% of this market and Algeria 25%. Norway will supply about 30% after 1986, when gas production begins in Statfjord field in the North Sea."[16] To meet its natural gas needs the key factors in the eyes of the Western Europeans are availability, security of supply, and price. In general, they see the Soviet Union as a reliable producer of natural gas with excess capacity (which provides a measure of security) and a willingness to cut prices in order to boost exports and earnings (see Table 6).

The four Western European countries considered—West Germany, France, Italy, and Great Britain—all require increased natural gas imports to meet future energy needs.[17] Gas is the pivotal fuel in Western Europe for several reasons: being a liquid fuel it is more energy efficient; it is in plentiful supply and readily available; its fixed investment costs, aside from transportation, are limited; and demand for gas is rising sharply for residential use, one of the fastest growing sectors of energy consumption. As noted, gas assists in the general diversification away from oil dependence—a major energy policy goal. Finally, gas does not pose the difficult technological and political questions raised by nuclear power development and is cleaner, easier to exploit, and more energy efficient than coal.

Eager to cultivate both economic ties and a new gas market, the Soviets have provided West Europeans with additional incentives for cooperation on the Urengoi pipeline project in the form of subcontracts to West European firms for pipeline construction materials and technology. Energy relations between West Germany and the Soviet Union have been ongoing since the early 1960s. Trade in energy and energy-related materials remains of great importance in West Germany. Between 1973 and 1979, pipe was the largest single export item in West German-Soviet trade. During the 1970s, West Germans were active participants in the planning for IGAT-II, the trilateral Iran-Soviet-European pipeline consortium which would have supplied West Germany with an estimated 5 bcm/yr of Soviet gas.[18] In fact, from 1975 to present, West Germany has imported more Soviet gas annually than any other West European country. The cancellation of the IGAT-II project led to the development of the Urengoi export line for which several German firms are major subcontractors. West German firms also played a major role in the construction of the Orenburg (Soyez) pipeline. The Soviet use of West German firms as subcontractors provided it with a strong base of support within the country.

West Germany, the most highly industrialized state considered here, is extremely dependent on imported liquid fuels. In 1982 this dependence amounted to 67 percent of total energy consumed. At that time West Germany imported 96 percent of its oil and 62 percent of its needed gas. In its efforts to reduce reliance on imported oil, West Germany has looked to natural gas. Domestic gas production has stagnated, however; between 1977 and 1982, it increased only 0.3 percent per year. Total production was 14.6 mt, while consumption was 38.6 mt. The likelihood of increasing domestic production is bleak due to a lack of reserves. In order to meet the shortfall and the growth in demand expected as a result of economic recovery, West Germany will have to increase its imports. In the past, most of West Germany's gas shortfall has been met by Soviet or Dutch gas exports. In 1983, West Germany received 10.8 bcm from the Soviet Union, which represented 29 percent of its gas consumption. Prior to the economic recession, West Germany had imported as much as 12.4 bcm per year (in 1981) from the Soviets.

Due to uncertainty regarding Holland's desire to increase gas production levels and transport capacity problems inherent in boosting Norwegian gas flows, Soviet natural gas will undoubtedly be the fuel of growth for West Germany. In 1970 the first Soviet-West German gas deal was made, whereby Soyuzneftexport, the Soviet trading company, would sell 51.5 bcm of gas over twenty years to Ruhrgas. This gas began flowing into West Germany in 1973. Add-on deals since then have increased Soviet gas exports to the point where they supplied 29 percent of West Germany's gas demand. Under the new Urengoi agreements, Ruhrgas is committed to purchasing an additional 11.5 bcm per year for the next twenty-five years.[9] This virtually doubles Soviet gas exports to West Germany.

West German officials believe that Soviet gas aids in reducing energy dependence on Middle Eastern oil, although they are aware of the ever-present possibility of fluctuations in Soviet supplies (such as the reduction in gas deliveries to Bavaria in 1979). West Germany has taken steps to increase its own gas reserves, to improve back-up energy sources and changeover capabilities, to study alternative supply sources and to advocate a strengthened intra-regional pipeline system. The efficacy of these measures to ensure that a critical energy dependence on the Soviet Union does not replace the OPEC dependence of the 1970s will have to be carefully watched and evaluated.

France is also heavily dependent on external energy sources. In 1982, this dependence amounted to 82 percent of total energy consumption, down from 95 percent in 1979. Like West Germany, France has worked to reduce its dependence on Middle Eastern oil and has consequently increased its dependence on natural gas in general and on Soviet gas (and oil) in particular, though to a lesser extent than West Germany and Italy. France's 1979 imports of Soviet oil and oil products equalled 5 percent of all oil imports. By 1982, Soviet oil accounted for 8 percent of total French oil imports. Soviet gas exports to France began in 1976 and have since risen to approximately 6 bcm per year in 1981, before slumping to 4 bcm per year in 1982. 1979 Soviet gas exports amounted to 11 percent of total gas consumption and 16 percent of all French gas imports. French purchases of Soviet gas increased to 15 percent of total gas consumed and 22 percent of 1982 gas imports. Although France receives roughly 60 percent of its gas imports from the Dutch, its reliance on Soviet gas will increase. Based on an expectation of increased domestic gas demand into the 1990s, the French have contracted to purchase 8 bcm/yr for twenty-five years from the Urengoi export line, more than doubling current French imports of Soviet natural gas.[20]

Although well aware of the need for diversification, the French have rather limited options with regard to their sources of natural gas. The Netherlands, France's major supplier, has been frugal with its gas for export and, until recently, has sharply limited exports. A recent upward re-evaluation of gas reserves has influenced the government of the Netherlands to indicate its willingness to sell more gas, a policy that may, however, continue to fluctuate. Algeria, a recent supplier of natural gas to the French, poses special opportunities and difficulties because of the historical ties between the two countries. Although Algeria is a less than reliable trading partner, Gaz de France admits to paying above-market prices for Algerian gas, mainly for political reasons.

France's participation in the Urengoi project underscores its commit-ment to natural gas as the fuel of the future. Coal production and demand is predicted to fall, supply uncertainty clouds external oil sources, and demand uncertainty limits the further development of nuclear power. Natural gas is in abundant supply externally and is priced to fluctuate with specific oil prices. The French recognize that increased dependence on Soviet gas involves some risk, but they feel that with adequate pre-cautions such risks are acceptable.[21]

Although Italy's energy consumption has, like that of West Germany and France, dropped during the last five years—from 150 mt in 1979 to 141 mt in 1982—Italy's dependence on foreign energy sources has not decreased. Italy is not only heavily dependent on external sources for her energy supplies, but is also more energy dependent on the Soviet Union than any other Western European state. Much of that dependence is in the form of Soviet natural gas.

Italian natural gas consumption has been steadily increasing, from 22 bcm/yr in 1975 to 28 bcm/yr in 1982. This is a result of Italy's attempt to reduce its reliance on oil. Gas production has declined, however, from a peak of 19.2 bcm in 1976 to 15.1 bcm in 1982 (after having bottomed out at 14.3 bcm in 1981). To cover the divergence between domestic supply and demand, imports of Soviet gas rose considerably. In 1976, Soviet exports of natural gas to Italy equalled 4 bcm/yr. By 1982, this figure had more than doubled to 9.3 bcm/yr and represented approxi-mately 33 percent of total Italian gas consumption. This degree of depen-dence is greater than that of either France or West Germany and is destined to grow as gas increases its share of total energy consumed.

The current Italian energy plan projects that gas will supply approx-imately 20 percent of its total energy needs by 1990. Given the delays which have plagued the development of Italy's nuclear and coal indus-tries, this percentage will in fact, we expect, be even higher. In the context of these expectations, Soviet gas imports assume even greater importance. Italy's alternative natural gas supplies are problematic. In

1982, Italy imported approximately 4.8 bcm of natural gas from the Netherlands, a 29 percent decline from 1981 imports of 6.8 bcm. Italy's current gas contract with the Netherlands expires in 1992, and although at present the Dutch seem willing to sell more gas, their commitment to do so could very well change in coming years. Algeria, which began piping gas in mid-1983 after a two-year delay, has been an unreliable supplier of gas to Italy. Furthermore, the 1,070 km trans-Mediterranean pipeline from Algeria to Italy via Tunisia and Sicily will require additional work before it reaches its full carrying capacity of 12 bcm/yr.

In recognition that its gas imports will have to double to ensure an adequate gas supply in the 1990s, Italy had negotiated several agreements with the Soviet Union regarding the Urengoi export line. Currently, the Italian national oil company, Ente Nazionale Idrocarburi (ENI), seeks to purchase 4 bcm/yr for twenty-five years. Italy's renegotiated (as of October 1984) gas contract with the Soviets gives them some flexibility insofar as the new agreement provides for a longer build-up-to-peak periods—3 bcm/yr by 1989, 4-5.5 bcm/yr after 1990, and 4.8-6 bcm/yr after 1992/93.[22] In return, Italy is asking for increased Soviet purchases of Italian industrial equipment in order to reduce Italy's trade deficit with the Soviet Union. The new gas trade agreement results in substantial Italian reliance on Soviet natural gas imports well into the 1990s, the Soviets supplying as much as 35 percent of Italy's natural gas needs.

The United Kingdom is of special interest because its North Sea gas and oil reserves make it a potential major player in the West European energy market. Although Great Britain's gas production is slipping, (North Sea production equalled 32.4 mt in 1982, down from the 1977 peak of 35.2 mt), estimated gas reserves are rising. In March 1984, British Petroleum announced it had discovered four natural gas fields in the North Sea estimated to hold up to 70.80 bcm of recoverable reserves. The British government accordingly was able to revise its natural gas reserve estimate up 7.6 percent to 2,259.68 bcm.

Even given increasing reserves, however, rising domestic demand for natural gas will force Great Britain to increase imports by 1990. Although Britain's natural gas consumption fell slightly in 1982, it has exhibited an overall upward climb since 1972. In 1972, the U.K. produced 23 mt and consumed 25 mt, a shortfall of only 2 mt/yr, a gap that held through 1977. By 1982, however, production was 32 mt and consumption 42 mt, a gap of 10 mt. This disparity between natural gas production and consumption in Britain is expected to continue to widen, creating a need for increased gas imports.

The British negotiated with Norway on the purchase of gas from its North Sea Sliepner field, which is scheduled to come on-stream between 1990 and 1992, but ultimately rejected the proposed $26.7 billion agreement in favor of looking to its own reserves. (This will, says Statoil, Norway's state-run company, delay the development of the field.) The delays resulting from the conflicting views on the subject of whether Norwegian off-shore gas is required have clouded the prospects not only for Sleipner, but perhaps also for the much larger Norwegian Troll field.

According to a report by the Directorate General for Energy of the Commission of the European Community,[23] the development of the Troll field is pivotal to the structure of Community gas imports to the year 2000 and thereafter. Without its development, the Community must inevitably seek larger volumes from other non-OECD sources. Even with the possibility of Canadian or African LNG supplies reaching Europe by the turn of the century, the likelihood is that, without Troll, the Community would either have to cut imports or establish costly reserves storage or run indigenous production flat out, or some combination of all three, to maintain existing security levels. The British have also entered into talks with the Netherlands regarding the development of a gas pipeline between the two countries which would allow Great Britain to enter the European gas market. (Currently, North Sea gas exports from the U.K. are banned.) It appears likely, therefore, that the U.K., in the form of the British Gas Company, will purchase Norwegian gas, which at the moment is the least expensive source.

Recently, however, the British Treasury has made an arrangement for tying into the Soviet pipeline, a potentially attractive alternative given that it would assist the Soviets in paying back a $350 million British credit which was part of the financing for the Urengoi line. The Treasury seems to be responding to Soviet hints that they might otherwise have difficulty repaying the credit. In any event, British Gas has already determined that imports of Soviet gas would be the best alternative to Norwegian imports. The Soviets are anxious to sell their gas and may make a below market price offer to the U.K.

The general trend is clear. The major industrialized nations of Western Europe are now and will continue to be significantly dependent on gas imports from the Soviet Union to meet domestic energy needs. While in the short run these supplies appear to be secure—because of the Soviet need to sell their excess natural gas—there is no ironclad guarantee that they will remain so. Less dependent on OPEC than they were a decade ago, the major Western European states are now unquestionably more dependent on the Soviet Union for energy. Alternative sources of natural gas for Western European nations will remain somewhat problematic for the foreseeable future. As we have seen, Norway, the Netherlands, Nigeria, and Algeria are the countries most frequently mentioned as capable of filling the alternative supply function. A close examination shows, however, that while these countries are, to one degree or another, potential suppliers to Western Europe, the economics of their gas systems make it inevitable that Soviet supplies will gradually play a more and more prominent role in the European gas system.

Norway is perhaps the most likely long-term, complementary supplier, but is presently incapable of increasing production. According to the Norwegian government, all the gas it is technically able to produce has been contracted for, leaving no room for additional exports. Norway's new North Sea fields all require substantial investments and development that, at existing prices, is economically unfeasible.

The Netherlands has traditionally been Europe's largest gas supplier and is expected to continue playing a major role in gas supply. Until 1984, the Dutch government managed its gas resources conservatively, limiting sharply the number of gas export contracts signed. Partly as a result of a recent upward revision of its estimated reserves, and partly in response to Soviet market penetration, the Dutch government has lately adopted a more liberal exploitation policy, making more gas available for Western Europe.

Despite the size of Great Britain's North Sea gas reserves, actual production has never been sufficient to meet Britain's domestic needs, and this gap is widening. On first appearance Great Britain is a logical market for Norwegian gas, but British reluctance to buy and the Soviet's ability to undersell Norway adversely affect energy trade between the two countries. Nigeria, a country with significant associated gas reserves, is anxious to reduce its level of flaring and consequently increase its gas export potential. However, the unstable nature of its government and the country's uncertain monetary situation make it a questionable partner for a gas export project that could take five to ten years to reach fruition. An LNG project proposal aimed at the European market was scrapped in 1982 due in part to political and financial factors. Finally, there is the possibility of gas exports from the Middle East, but that region too suffers from endemic political instability and by shipping costs that push the price of gas to an estimated $5.25 per million btu (British thermal units).

OUTLOOK AND IMPLICATIONS

For the time being the increase of the Soviet presence in the international gas market has been slowed by the current energy glut. European energy consumption has declined and energy prices fallen accordingly. However, as the world economy improves the need for energy, and the need for natural gas as the choice alternative to oil, will pick up. Barring another severe economic downturn, demand is expected to grow on a 3 percent to 4 percent annual basis through 1990. The Soviet Union, having developed its gas infrastructure, is now perfectly positioned to become a major player—and perhaps the dominant figure—in world natural gas markets, particularly in Western Europe.

Assuming continued growth in the West European economies, we see natural gas demand rising substantially in the future. Those who speak confidently of an energy glut for the foreseeable future are simply waiting to repeat the mistakes of a decade ago. Energy supply and demand will always be volatile, and forecasting energy needs will never be an exact science—for political as well as economic reasons. Accepting this, and given the economic and strategic importance of energy, it seems best to err on the side of caution and not on the side of complacency.

Future demand projections are especially difficult to make with confidence because it is at the moment difficult to distinguish between the effects of recent energy conservation efforts and the effects of economic stagnation. In general, conservation, the strong U.S. dollar, the retirement of energy inefficient plants, and the move toward service economies will, no doubt, limit the rebound in energy demand.

Nevertheless, one can foresee substantial demand expansion from the artificially low levels of 1981 to 1983, particularly in gas consumption. Recent statistics bear this out. First quarter 1984 West European energy consumption figures show a 6 percent increase in total energy consumed. Notably, the 14 percent increase in natural gas consumption is the largest increase for any energy source. In contrast, oil consumption for the first six months of 1984 increased only 0.5 percent over the same period in 1983. Figures for the first half of 1984 show a substantial increase in gas consumption in Western Europe (see Table 7). This expanding demand will be boosted further by the declining real price of energy. Clearly, the direction of West European energy demand is toward increased natural gas consumption, and this trend will continue for the longer term. World Bank projections support this thinking. In its "World Development Report 1983," the World Bank forecast a 53 percent hike in

Table 7: Rising Western European Gas Consumption
(million cubic meters)

	1982	1983	1984 (1st half)
West Germany	48,710	52,670	30,233
France	25,930	26,055	16,160
Italy	26,809	27,443	17,969
Great Britain	45,720	48,580	28,870
Total for all Western Europe	203,386	214,680	128,520

SOURCE: Petroleum Economist, 52:45 (February 1985).

global natural gas consumption between 1980 and 1995. In comparison, oil consumption is predicted to increase by only 10 percent. The same report projected natural gas consumption among industrialized nations to rise by 20 percent (a somewhat conservative estimate) during the period 1980 to 1995, while oil consumption declines by 7 percent.

The Soviet role in this world of increasing natural gas demand is equally clear. The latest OECD projections of Soviet natural gas exports to OECD members put Soviet natural gas exports to OECD members at 60 bcm/yr by 1990, which represents a total utilization of the Urengoi export line. At $4.50 per million btus, this would net the Soviets $9.6 billion, more than double the $4 billion earned from gas exports in 1982.[24]

There is no question that the Soviets have a substantial economic stake in maintaining gas supplies to its Western European customers. There is also no question, however, that Western Europe's growing gas dependency on the Soviet Union, as the retiring director of the European Commission's Energy Directorate, Mr. Georges Brondel, recently noted, is the "next problem looming for the [European] Community."[25] With nearly half of the European Community's gas imports by 1990 dependent on Soviet sources, history should have at least taught all concerned that energy dependency is a liability that no nation or economy can afford to be complacent about.

NOTES

1. Fariborz Ghadar and J. Pelosky, *East-West Energy: Natural Gas Supply and Demand in the Soviet Union, Afghanistan, Iran, Eastern Europe and Western Europe* (1985).

2. As the full report points out, the Soviet Union leads the world in both energy production and energy reserves. In addition to holding the world's largest natural gas reserves, the Soviet Union is the world's largest oil producer; see Ghadar and Pelosky, p. 9.

3. The *Oil and Gas Journal* reported early in 1985 that the Soviet Union would easily surpass its gas production targets for 1981/85. In 1983, Soviet Union passed the United States in gas production with 536 bcm. In 1984 it produced 582 bcm. The Soviets are expected to produce 600-640 bcm in 1985, 630 bcm in 1986, and 825 bcm/yr in 1990. These expectations for 1990 double the 1980 Soviet gas production level of 435 bcm. The Soviets are expected to maintain world record gas flows through the year 2000. *Oil and Gas Journal*, 82:73-76 (1 October 1984) and 83:64-65 (28 January 1985).

4. This development is treated in more detail by the full report; see Ghadar and Pelosky, pp. 15, 18, 37-8. Gas will surpass oil by 1990.

5. The Soviets consume 85 percent of their gas production domestically; see Ghadar and Pelosky, p. 5.

6. Soviet energy exports currently account for 70 to 80 percent of the country's hard-currency earnings; see Ghadar and Pelosky, p. 13.

7. As Ghadar and Pelosky note on p. 33, Urengoi is by no means the only giant Siberian gas field waiting to produce for export. Eventually, all of the Soviet Siberian reserves will be tied into the export line system, a system of six lines emanating from Urengoi and totalling 12,350 miles of pipeline. The *Oil and Gas Journal* notes that this trunk system is substantially in place (*Oil and Gas Journal*, 82:75 [1 October 1984]). The Yamburg field, for example, just north of Urengoi, will come on stream to replace Urengoi in the 1990s, maintaining the flow of gas to Europe.

8. Perhaps an effect of the U.S. embargo on equipment and technology. But some have argued that the embargo, though it may have caused short-term delays in the completion of the line, forced the Soviets to improve and develop their own gas distribution technology and manufacturing—to their own long-term benefit.

9. The British Attorney General, Sir Michael Havers, argued that the U.S. embargo was an illegal interference in British affairs.

10. *The New York Times,* 9 May 1983, IV, 3:2.

11. In fairness to the justifiable fears behind the embargo policy, it should be noted that the Soviets announced (though they never put into effect) a suspension of fuel deliveries to Britain because of the coal strike there in the fall of 1984. The Reagan administration rightly pointed out at the time that this was an example of the kind of political, if not in this case strategic, use of energy "diplomacy" to which it feared its allies were becoming vulnerable. For a study of the politics of gas trading, see Jonathan P. Stern, *International Gas Trade in Europe: The Policies of Exporting and Importing Countries* (London: Heinemann, 1984). Stern sees importing countries as more likely to break contract agreements than exporters.

12. The actual beginning of the flow of Urengoi gas to Europe is shrouded in conflict and controversy. According to *The New York Times,* Gaz de France questioned whether the gas it received in January of 1984 had in fact come

from the Urengoi field through the new export pipeline or whether it had a more local point of origin. The Urengoi pipeline operation was significantly damaged by a fire at the largest of the pipeline substations. By mid-summer, however, it seems clear that the line was in fact operational though not yet at full capacity.

13. The Soviets currently export 55 percent of their energy to Eastern Europe. This is expected to decline as the Soviets expand their role in the world energy market, despite the need for natural gas in Eastern Europe.

14. Western Europe's reliance on Persian Gulf oil was shockingly high in 1973, with West Germany getting 49 percent, France 96 percent, and Great Britain 75 percent of their oil from Persian Gulf states. Ten years later, the lesson learned, these percentages were 13, 33, and 14 percent, respectively; see Ghadar and Pelosky, p. 90.

15. In the long run, the Netherlands is seen as the "swing" supplier, Norway as a "marginal supplier," and the Soviets as the "dominant supplier of baseload gas," with Algeria a potentially major supplier; *Petroleum Economist,* 52:47 (February 1985).

16. *Oil and Gas Journal,* 82:50 (8 October 1984). The DRI Europe report sees European gas imports as rising, slightly less dramatically, from 16 percent in 1983 to 35 percent by 1995; *Petroleum Economist,* 52:80 (March 1985).

17. It should be noted that other European nations are also becoming dependent on Soviet gas. Austria, which can only meet 25 percent of its gas demand, imports a significant percentage of its gas from the Soviet Union—1.4 bcm/yr by 1989 according to the *Oil and Gas Journal.* The *Journal* also reports that Switzerland will be taking 800 million cubic meters of gas from the Soviets by 1988. *Oil and Gas Journal,* 82:50 (8 October 1984).

18. For the history of the ill-fated IGAT-II agreement, see Ghadar and Pelosky, pp. 60-68.

19. Pricing policy is uncertain; the West Germans report a price of under $4.70 per million btus with an escalator formula tied to heating oil and other selected oil prices in West Germany.

20. The Soviets, for their part, have purchased increased amounts of goods from France. France has emerged as the third largest supplier of energy equipment to the Soviet Union and has strengthened its trade relationship with an economic cooperation agreement which calls for the Soviet purchase of $1.2 billion worth of French industrial goods. This agreement is most likely the *quid pro quo* to reduce France's trade deficit with the Soviet Union.

21. For example, Gaz de France has stated that it will not use Soviet gas for home heating purposes. Whether such a gesture addresses the issue of national security, which critics of energy dependence on the Soviet Union have raised, must remain to be seen.

22. *Oil and Gas Journal,* 82:50 (8 October 1984).

23. *Energy in Europe: Energy Policy and Trends in the European Community,* Commission of the European Communities, Directorate General for Energy, No. 1 (April 1985), p. 32.

24. Ghadar and Pelosky note that the Soviets also have their eye on the Japanese market; see pp. 124-41.

25. *Petroleum Economist,* 52:85 (March 1985).

30

The Rise
of Third World
Multinationals

David A. Heenan and
Warren J. Keegan

Long accustomed to playing the role of host to foreign multinationals, many developing countries are now home governments to their own MNCs. The phenomenon of Third World multinationals is significant as an indication of the increasing economic strength of developing countries and as a challenge to the dominance of Western MNCs in world markets.

On the international level, the rise of Third World multinationals can contribute to a lessening of tensions between the industrialized North and the developing South by striking a better balance in the global industrial system.

FEW OBSERVERS OF the international business scene were surprised when a Saudi Arabian businessman, Ghaith R. Pharaon, acquired a majority interest in the National Bank of Georgia from former Budget Director Bert Lance. Pharaon, after all, already had shown his muscle in U.S. banking circles by winning control of the Mainbank of Houston and its $60 million in deposits. Then, too, the multinational spread of wealthy Middle Easterners has been well publicized. Whether it is the alleged Arab takeover of London or Saudi Arabia's proposal to buy the Gaza Strip from Israel, another Middle Eastern investment overseas is no longer front-page news.

Far less publicized, however, is the fact that OPEC bloc nations are not the only developing countries that are practicing the art of global reach. From Brazil to South Korea, a major move is underway to indus-

trialize, and the engine of growth is that familiar institution, once confined to the developed world, the multinational corporation. Consider
the evidence:

• The explosion in international construction spearheaded by multinational corporations headquartered in South Korea, Taiwan, and the
Philippines. Korean companies are paving roads in Ecuador, while the
Taiwanese build steel-mills in Nigeria. Filipino companies span the
globe—from Indonesia, where they are restoring the fabled Borobudur
shrine, to the Persian Gulf, where they are developing deepwater port
facilities.

• The worldwide manufacturing and marketing strategy, announced
two years ago, of Stelux Manufacturing Company, the Hong Kong-
based watchmaker. At about the same time, Stelux underscored its international intentions by purchasing 29 percent of Bulova Watch Company. Stelux's C. P. Wong spent eighteen months as Bulova's chairman—to put the floundering American partner back on its feet. This
is only one of many inroads made by developing-country investors
in a superpower nation.

• On a regional level, the recent commitment of the 25-nation SELA
(the Latin American Economic System) to establish multinationals in
Central and South America. Special priority is being given to agribusiness, selected capital goods, low-cost housing, as well as an intra-
American data center.

• Even the poorest nations are getting into multinational economic
development. India is a prime example. The nation's Hindustan Machine and Tools Company is helping Algeria develop a machine tools industry, while other Indian multinationals are upgrading Iran's capacity
to manufacture detergents, building Libyan steel mills, and constructing electronics plants in Yugoslavia.

Many more examples could be cited. In fact, 34 of today's *Fortune*
"overseas 500" companies are headquartered in the developing
countries—and that represents a 48 percent increase over last year.

What is more, the scope and impact of the developing countries
extend far beyond the enterprise level. In fact, a growing number of
them are being placed among the strongest nations in the world. According to a ranking devised by Ray S. Cline of Georgetown University's
Center for Strategic and International Studies, 11 of the 20 most powerful countries are from the emerging world; 4 (Iran, Brazil, People's
Republic of China, and Egypt) are in the top 10.[1]

Consequently, the prevailing image of the developing countries as impoverished, unstable, and in a general state of disrepair deserves reconsideration. This is not to say that the Third World has solved its centuries-old socioeconomic problems. Nor is the multinational enterprise by itself the rags-to-riches answer to these problems. The multinational corporation, however, is an essential element in the gathering strength of the developing countries. And, what is most significant of all, the Third World multinational could play a key role in lessening the structural dualism that now exists between the haves and the have nots.

Like it or not, the days are numbered for the political and economic hegemony of a few major powers whose populations are a minority of our planet's membership. Today, developing nations comprise 70 percent of the world's population; by the turn of the century, this population figure will increase to 80 percent; and by the middle of the next century, 90 percent. History tells us that the will of a small minority cannot forever prevail to the detriment of the majority.

The rise of the Third World multinationals offers both developing and developed countries a unique opportunity to gain the benefits of a truly international economy. Indeed, it is the likelihood of restoring greater balance to our present global industrial system that has made even the strangest bedfellows staunch advocates of corporate multinationalism by the developing countries. Leading international businessmen, United Nations officials, even the hierarchy of the People's Republic of China are all openly supportive of this growing trend.

Let us emphasize that Third World corporate multinationalism is still a very young phenomenon. The cost of going global, as the multinationals in the developed countries have learned, is high. Consequently, there are few developing nations that seriously influence world business at the moment.

This article examines the emerging phenomenon of the Third World multinational corporation: where it has come from, where it is going, and why this new social institution is quite unlike its predecessor in more affluent parts of the world. Finally, it will explore the implications of the rise of Third World multinationals for corporate leaders in the developed countries.

ROUTES TO MULTINATIONALISM

There are three kinds of economic soil in which the Third World multinational is taking root. They may be categorized as follows:

1. *Resource-rich developing countries*

These nations, most notably the OPEC bloc, are eager to pursue accelerated programs of international expansion and are in a position to acquire the technology and managerial skills to do so. With tremendous export earnings, state-owned monoliths such as National Iranian Oil, Indonesia's Pertamina, and CODELCO/CHILE are fully capable of investing abroad.

To date, foreign direct investment by companies based in these countries has been modest. While traditionalists might question the "multinationality" of these enterprises, their potential for international expansion is clear.[2] Consider the example of First Arabian Corporation.

Recently, the Paris-based representative of this Arabian conglomerate submitted tentative proposals for the acquisition of major petroleum refineries in Newfoundland and Puerto Rico. This action marked the first serious attempt by the Arabs to improve their vertical position in energy projects outside the Middle East. Other developing countries with similar assets and aspirations are expected to follow the First Arabian Corporation's example.

2. *Labor-rich, rapidly industrializing countries*

With limited natural resources and narrow domestic markets, internationalism has long been synonymous with survival for areas such as Hong Kong, Singapore, and the Republics of China and Korea. Strict adherence to the watchwords "export or die" has triggered the economic miracle of these communities, which now exhibit real GNP growth rates four to five times higher than that of the United States.

Over time, these economies have moved away from their former emphasis on being intermediary centers of trade and into sophisticated manufacturing. Combining a cheap, but industrious and well-educated work force with astute political leadership, developing countries in this category have evolved from basic trading nations to more complex, production-based economies.

A significant step in this evolution occurred in the 1960s with a massive influx of "satellite plants" from the multinationals of developed countries. Singapore, for example, served as a major manufacturing base for many high-technology companies, including Hewlett-Packard, Fairchild, Litton Industries, Philips, and Hitachi. But by the 1970s, the more adventurous developing countries became net exporters of the labor, products, and ideas.

Witness, for instance, the invasion of the Middle East by South Korean construction companies and their army of 60,000 skilled expat-

riates. Competitors are particularly astounded by how swiftly the Koreans are extending their capabilities beyond civil construction and into
the more technical and lucrative engineering-related areas once dominated by major Western contractors.[3] For 1978, it was estimated that
Korean contractors would land more than $4 billion in foreign construc-
tion contracts.

Consequently, to the roster of such traditional corporate giants as
Jardine, Matheson & Co., Sime Darby Holdings, Swire Pacific Ltd., and
others must be added new names such as Daewoo, Samsung, and Yul-
san.

3. Market-rich, rapidly industrializing countries

Building success through their large, growing domestic markets has
been the favored route to multinationalism for several Third World
countries: Brazil, Mexico, the Philippines, and, to a lesser extent, Argentina, Venezuela, and Turkey. In many instances, of course, these same
nations are also resource rich, but it is their unique ability to gain manufacturing and marketing experience at home for subsequent re-export
abroad that sets them apart from the others.[4] Two leading Filipino
multinational corporations illustrate this category—

● The colors of the management services firm of SyCip, Gorres,
Velayo & Company (SGV) fly in every commercial capital in Asia. Following extended market dominance in the Philippines, the firm now
maintains a multinational staff of professionals in public accounting and
management services. In the Pacific Basin, SGV more than holds its own
against the "Big Eight" accounting firms or, for that matter, any other
professional group from the developed world.

● The international standing of San Miguel Corporation, a food
processing conglomerate, would not have occurred without its virtual
monopoly of the Philippine beer market. Success at home quickly led to
success abroad—first, through exports; then, through the sales of
foreign-manufactured products. As a result, today one finds San Miguel
breweries in such diverse locations as Spain, Hong Kong, and Papua
New Guinea.

There are significant differences among the three types of Third
World multinationals, but they share a common denominator: governments that are manifestly pro business and committed to enterprise
growth and development—especially, the expansion of overseas trade
and investment. This feature, perhaps more than anything else, differentiates the internationally-oriented developing country from the
rest of the pack.

Exhibit: Partial Listing of Major Third World Multinationals

Company	Country of incorporation	Industry	1977 sales in estimated millions of $
National Iranian Oil	Iran	Petroleum	$22,315.3
Petróleos de Venezuela	Venezuela	Petroleum	9,628.1
Petrobrás (Petróleo Brasileiro)	Brazil	Petroleum	8,284.3
Pemex (Petroleos Mexicanos)	Mexico	Petroleum	3,394.5
Haci Ömer Sabanci Holding	Turkey	Textiles	2,902.7
Hyundai Group	South Korea	Shipbuilding, transportation	2,590.7
Indian Oil	India	Petroleum	2,315.5
Schlumberger	Neth. Antilles	Measuring and scientific equipment	2,160.3
Chinese Petroleum	Taiwan	Petroleum	1,920.1
Zambia Industrial & Mining	Zambia	Mining and metal refining—copper	1,862.3
The Lucky Group	South Korea	Petroleum, electronics, appliances	1,744.3
Steel Authority of India	India	Metal refining—steel	1,447.6
Turkiye Petrolleri	Turkey	Petroleum	1,376.7
Kuwait National Petroleum	Kuwait	Petroleum	1,376.3
Korea Oil	South Korea	Petroleum	1,341.1
Samsung Group	South Korea	Industrial equipment, electronics, textiles	1,305.3
Thyssen-Bornemisza	Neth. Antilles	Shipbuilding, farm equipment	1,258.7
CODELCO-CHILE	Chile	Mining and metal refining—copper	1,231.2

Exhibit: Partial Listing of Major Third World Multinationals (Continued)

Company	Country of incorporation	Industry	1977 sales in estimated millions of $
Koç Holding	Turkey	Motor vehicles	1,207.6
Philippine National Oil	Philippines	Petroleum	986.2
Daewoo Industrial South	South Korea	Textiles	851.8
Siderúrgica Nacional	Brazil	Metal refining—steel	847.5
USIMINAS	Brazil	Metal refining—steel	826.4
General Motors do Brasil	Brazil	Motor vehicles	824.4
Vale do Rio Doce	Brazil	Mining—iron	824.0
Ford Brasil	Brazil	Motor vehicles	758.7
SANBRA	Brazil	Food products	707.3
Indústrias Reunidas F. Matarazzo	Brazil	Chemicals, food products, textiles	675.3
Grupo Industrial Alfa	Mexico	Metal refining—steel, chemicals	603.2
ICC	South Korea	Metal products, rubber, textiles	580.6
Bharat Heavy Electricals	India	Industrial equipment	525.4
Ssangyong Cement Industrial	South Korea	Chemicals	598.0
Sunkyong	South Korea	Textiles	467.6

SOURCE: "The 500 Largest Industrial Corporations Outside the U.S.," *Fortune*, August 14, 1978. p. 171. Includes only industrial companies that elected to officially report 1977 sales figures. Hence omitted are several MNCs, such as Hong Kong's Jardine, Matheson & Company, Algeria's Sonatrack, and Indonesia's Pertamina.

But two other critical factors have also aided the rise of multinational corporations in the developing countries:

Third World Solidarity. This decade has witnessed a ground swell supranationalism in the developing countries. Through such forums as the United Nations' Commission on Trade and Development "collective self-reliance" has become a byword of the times. To be sure, certain of the more impoverished nations still seek the fundamental human needs of nutrition, health, and education. But today, the goal of many other developing countries is a more equitable stake in this global economy.

One effect of greater Third World unity, Louis T. Wells, Jr. notes, is a strong preference in the developing countries for multinational corporations from like countries.[5] Regional success, it seems, tends to accompany Third World multinationalism. Take, for example, the recent agreements of Brazilian multinationals to assist Peru in the mining of its copper and Colombia its coal.

In many cases, developing countries appear to prefer investment from other like countries to investment from a major power. For one thing, such investment is less threatening. In wooing Hong Kong investors, Sri Lanka's trade minister made it clear that investors from smaller countries would receive a warmer welcome than those from the developed nations: "We favor investors from small places like Hong-Kong because nobody can talk about a sell-out to imperialism in the case of a country that is as small as or smaller than we are."[6]

Access to Technology. Since developing-country leaders are well aware of the importance of Western technology in their own industrialization and worldwide competitiveness, it is not surprising that they are demanding access to it. In fact, a complex network of national, regional, and international institutions has evolved to serve this end.

But even without legislated transfers of technology from the developed world, the more enterprising developing countries continue to astound the world with their resourcefulness. Many Third World multinationals have developed successful niches by exporting technology appropriate to labor-intensive environments. The most significant breakthroughs have been made in tropical agriculture, aquaculture, textiles, rural construction, and housing.

While most Third World companies have avoided capital-intensive industries, a few have proved that they need not be confined to bottom-of-the-line market segments. Through technological leapfrogging, they have been able to advance quickly into complex industrial areas.

Take, for example, South Korea's spectacular entry into shipbuilding. Its Hyundai Group had very limited experience in that industry
prior to the groundbreaking ceremonies of its shipyards in March 1972.
Less than two years later, Hyundai launched its first supertanker, the
260,000-ton Atlantic Baron. Today, it is able to construct 35 ships of
various sizes simultaneously.

Many other examples of increasing Third World involvement in
complex industries could be cited; to name a few: Taiwan's success in
electronics, Singapore's in oilrig construction, and Brazil's in light aircraft manufacturing.

Developing countries are also making up ground in sophisticated
service industries. For example, take banking. While the developing
countries are represented by only two banks, the Banco do Brasil and the
recently expanded Hong Kong & Shanghai Banking Corporation,
among the world's 50 largest financial institutions, several others,
including the Bank Melli Iran and the Philippines' Bancom Group, are
going multinational. Opportunities abound, particularly at the regional
level, for Third World banks with international ambitions and expertise.

IMPEDIMENTS TO EXPANSION

The road to multinationalism by the Third World is not without
barriers and dangers. There are the obvious growing pains that strain
the inner tissues of all countries in transition. From population control to
the latest food crisis, the developing countries must confront a host of
complex problems—each seemingly more difficult than the last. We
would like to single out four important countervailing forces that merit
special attention:

1. *Sluggish demand in the advanced nations*

The economies of the developing world depend on the health of the
Western nations. Without significant improvement in the economic
conditions of developed countries, which are the primary export markets for the developing countries, Third World industrialization will be
stalled—at least temporarily.

2. *Rising protectionism*

Growth in world trade means economic and political survival for
most emerging nations. Without steady export gains, the Third World
can expect economic stagnation and, eventually, political instability. For
the first half of 1978, however, the rate of export expansion barely exceeded 50 percent of the 1977 level, and future projections are even
gloomier.

Observers agree that a major factor responsible for the downturn is the rash of neomercantilism that now grips the world economy. There is no doubt that the recent import quotas imposed by the United States and the European Common Market's nontariff barriers will have serious implications for developing countries and their internationally ambitious companies.

3. *Growing public debt*

The bogeyman of the developing countries in 1977 was their swelling public indebtedness, estimated at a total of $200 billion. In recent months, however, the rate has slowed—especially for the more affluent developing countries that had healthy 1977 export earnings.

Unfortunately, this improvement in the balance-of-payments positions of the emerging nations does not appear to be either permanent or widespread. For the reasons just mentioned—stagflation and protectionism—the majority of developing countries should anticipate continued current account problems, requiring balance-of-payments loans. Debt-servicing difficulties, in turn, will reduce the international trade and investment opportunities of these nations.

As a result, we expect that most emerging nations will face massive debt repayments at precisely the time when their export earnings are likely to be under heavy pressure. Thus their ability to repay could be seriously threatened.

4. *Widening gap between rich and poor*

What political scientist Robert A. Scalapino of the University of California at Berkeley calls the "capital centrism problem" may outweigh all other factors in impact.[7] Simply stated, the economic and political power of most developing countries typically gravitates to the major urban centers—excluding the rural masses from adequate participation in decision making. Unless these distortions are eliminated or at least lessened, Scalapino warns, a nation's political stability will be endangered.

A MATTER OF PRIORITIES

"Dress me slowly, I'm in a hurry!" Napoleon once demanded. This paradoxical remark captures the double bind of the Third World: the demands of internal nation building and the simultaneous recognition of global interdependence. Domestic pressures must always outweigh any dreams of geographical adventurism. But for the balance of this century, a growing number of emerging nations will view the multinational corporation as an engine of economic growth both at home and abroad.

Yet in their excitement to become first-class trading nations, developing countries often sacrifice business sense for cosmetic attempts at commercial status. The Philippines' overbuilt hotel industry—now operating at 40 percent capacity—is symptomatic of a tendency to let wishful thinking sway hard-headed business judgment. Far more serious, however, is the preoccupation in some developing countries with excessive defense spending at the expense of industrialization. (The size of the military budget for some of them approaches 35 percent of GNP.) In the end, such short-sighted nations will have neither guns nor butter.

Thus leaders in the Third World must be mindful of the tug between "head" and "heart"—between what is realistic and what is fanciful. Selectivity is the key. Given their limited resources and shifting global conditions, Third World multinationals must carefully pick their spots if they are to survive and prosper.

LESSONS FROM JAPAN

In our discussions with executives from developing countries, one message emerges: the Japanese version of multinationalism stands as an ideal model. The envy of many nations, developed and developing, Japan is viewed as the economic pacesetter for good reasons—her rapid industrialization, rising currency, growing export surplus, productive work force, and overall leadership in international business. What is more, this process of economic achievement has occurred without disrupting Japan's social and cultural values. Quite the contrary, traditional Japanese norms (such as the work ethic) have tended to legitimatize her commercial accomplishments.

It is no wonder, then, that the emerging nations are eager to follow Japan's course. But in what directions? Above all, developing countries will opt for some version of "Japan Inc."—that strong coalition of business, government, and labor.[8] By the same token, they will seek to avoid the adversary posture that is often assumed in dealings between government and business in North America, Oceania, and some parts of Western Europe. As a black African leader, Gordon C. Chavenduka, put it, "We need mixed capitalism, modified socialism."[9]

Like Japan, the nations of the Third World quite clearly prefer the collaborative approach to industrialization. Among other things, this means considerable government intervention or "administrative guidance" in the economic affairs of nations on the rise.

"In a developing country, government initiative plays the leading role," argues Nam Duck Woo, South Korea's economic planning minister. "It's decisive. The government must give guidance, direction, stability."[10] Following Japan's lead, South Korea (often referred to as "the second Japan") and other emerging nations are calling on the public sector to plot their economic offensives.

Nowhere is this more noticeable than in the organizational characteristics of Third World multinationals. State-owned monopolies, trading companies, and new corporate coalitions all reflect the visible hand of government in international business.

STATE-OWNED MONOPOLIES

Encouraged by permissive legislation supporting public enterprise, the governments of many developing countries are building their own multinationals. "What stronger backing do you need than that of a rich, prospering nation?" asks the advertisements of Pernas, Malaysia's state-owned conglomerate. Pernas was created in 1969 to provide business opportunities and employment for the *bumiputra* (the term for ethnic Malays which means "sons of soil"). Today this conglomerate employs more than 4,000 workers in 50 subsidiaries. With interests in businesses ranging from mining to insurance, Pernas assures private investors of strong public commitment to their affairs.

TRADING COMPANIES

To a great extent, the overseas activities of Third World multinationals are being fueled by powerful trading corporations. The "general trading companies" of South Korea, fashioned in the image of Japanese *zaibatsus,* are a good example. Their charter is quite specific: (1) to penetrate domestic and foreign markets, (2) to establish a global distribution network, and (3) to finance smaller Korean companies that act as suppliers.

With proper guidance, these quasi-public monoliths have been directly responsible for the lion's share of Korea's economic success. The $1.3 billion Samsung Group, for example, maintains a competitive presence in 29 countries—building hotels, refining sugar, and overseeing many other businesses. Since 1970 it has averaged slightly less than 50 percent growth in annual revenues; and today Samsung accounts for approximately 4 percent of South Korea's gross national product.

CORPORATE COALITIONS

Developing countries are reluctant to "go it alone." Third World multinationals favor interdependence over independence. The value of building joint ventures has been recognized by enlightened developing country investors for many years: large-scale economies, resource pooling, improved access to foreign markets, and other signficant advantages of shared enterprise.

Take the case of the airlines industry. At various points in time, there have been long-standing agreements between Pan American and Air Afrique, Trans World Airlines and Ethiopian Airlines, Scandinavian Airlines System and Thai International, and KLM and Philippines Airlines. Whether for pilot training or aircraft maintenance, these linkages have been vital to the development of air transportation services around the world.

With many such precedents, we can anticipate a rise in new forms of shared enterprise: Third World conglomerates with *multiple* national identities. First spotted by Howard V. Perlmutter of the Wharton School, who called them "industrial systems constellations," these alliances permit nationally-oriented companies to join together to achieve a worldwide competitive advantage—without sacrificing their national identity.[11] Hence they are quite different from the single enterprise whose global strategy is managed from a single corporate headquarters.

In the developed world, the union of General Electric and Hitachi of Japan to form General Television of America, an innovative attempt to pool resources in the TV business, is one recent example of such a constellation. General Electric will provide plant, personnel, and—with Hitachi—technology. (Volvo-Norway, Dunlop-Pirelli, and American Motors-Renault are other harbingers of this evolving organizational form.)

Multinational marriage would seem to be especially attractive for the Third World. Several, in fact, are visible today.

● The PSA Group in Thailand represents a consolidation of many small-scale enterprises into one dominant force at the *national* level. With origins that go back to 1970, this constellation now claims more than 25 local companies. (Appropriately, Thais refer to PSA as "the management hospital.")

In much the same fashion, Bancomer S.A. became Mexico's largest private banking institution in November 1977 following the merger of 37 local banks. In addition to its 565 branches south of the border, this national giant is represented in New York, Tokyo, London, Madrid, and Los Angeles.

● As one of the many *regional* coalitions, the Triad Holding Corporation represents the first Arab-owned and managed conglomerate. Principal investors come from Egypt, Iran, Lebanon, Saudi Arabia, and Sudan. Included in Triad's portfolio are oil tankers in Indonesia, cattle feeding operations in Brazil, and fashion houses in Paris.

Similarly, on the heels of a United Nations study encouraging regional coalitions, the Association of South East Asian Nations is taking steps to build ASEAN multinationals. Early results are expected in banking, trading, and fertilizer production.

● On a *global* scale, the Saudi Arabians and the Dutch have established the Albank Alsaudi Alhollandi to be headquartered in Jeddah. Designed to offer worldwide banking services, this new coalition blends the substantial Arab influence of the Saudis with 150 years of international financial experience of the Dutch partner, Algemene Bank Nederland.

Like any marriage, the pressures of cohabitation will be demanding, especially when leading companies representing various nations are involved. Hence the challenge of managing these coalitions will be staggering.[12] Nevertheless, in our opinion, they will represent the favorite form of multinationalism for Third World investors.

IMPLICATIONS FOR CEOS

For executives in developed countries, our advice is: take the Third World multinational seriously. This evolving force is here to stay, and, on balance, its pluses outweigh its minuses.

These corporations bring important resources to the world of international business. Obviously they offer major contributions to those industries that can profit from skilled—and inexpensive—labor. Not so obvious is their resource of executive talent. Witness Bulova's improvement under the management of Stelux. In the years ahead, other enlightened investors from the rich nations will form coalitions with their counterparts in the emerging countries.

In fact, chief executive officers from wealthy countries should be mindful of possible "reverse takeovers"—that is, instances where a developing-country investor gains a controlling interest in an enterprise based in a developed nation. In addition to Stelux's influence on Bulova, there are other noteworthy instances:

● In 1973, Hong Kong's Jardine, Matheson & Co., Ltd. doubled its net worth with two such acquisitions—Theo. H. Davies & Co., Ltd., an old established Honolulu agribusiness company, and Reunion Properties Company, Ltd., a major British enterprise.

● Venezuela's Organisación Diego Cisueros not only bought out the Venezuelan subsidiary of the International Basic Economy Corporation (IBEC) but also acquired 20 percent of the parent company. Today, "mother and daughter" companies jointly run IBEC supermarkets in Ecuador and El Salvador.

• No doubt the Iranians' massive capital infusion into the then-faltering German conglomerate, Fried. Krupp GmbH, in 1976 also had a dramatic effect. It marked the arrival of Third World investors in the backyards of the superpowers.

• But more than any other case, the Hong Kong & Shanghai Bank's acquisition of a 51 percent controlling interest in Marine Midland Bank, the thirteenth largest in the United States, revealed the growing force of the Third World multinational. Though its top officials originally came from England, The Bank (as it is known in the colony) is owned primarily by local Chinese investors.

The foregoing is not to suggest that the developed world gird itself for a contemporary replay of David and Goliath. But these examples do point to the increasing competitiveness of Third World multinationals. Consequently we look for continuing Third World corporate intrusions into the domestic markets of even the most established multinationals.

Whether this competitiveness is viewed as a threat or an opportunity, there almost certainly will be long-term benefits from Third World multinationalism.

For one thing, we expect that the political leaders who are encouraging the formation of multinationals in their developing countries will reassess their existing expropriation or confiscation strategies. The increased risk of retaliation against their own investments overseas should caution political leaders in the Third World against discriminatory takeovers of foreign-owned properties at home.

For another thing, a more symmetrical exposure of assets abroad through Third World multinationalism should lessen hostilities around the world as well as restore the geopolitical balance. At the very least, it should enable Third World leaders to distinguish more clearly between the myth and reality of today's multinational enterprise.

CONCLUDING NOTE

The multinational corporation, long regarded by its opponents as the unique instrument of capitalist oppression against the impoverished world, could prove to be the tool by which the impoverished world builds prosperity. When properly guided, global companies can enable all nations to realize higher standards of living. Third World multinationalism, only yesterday an apparent contradiction in terms, is now a serious force in the development process.

For the past 100 years, observers have commented on the increasing competitiveness of world markets. But until the postwar emergence of Japan, we restricted our thinking to multinationals based in North America and Western Europe. Inevitably, though, one nation's competitive dominance passes to another. Today, the Japanese, tomorrow the Brazilians, the Mexicans, the Koreans, and others. *Plus ca change, plus c'est la même chose.*

NOTES

1. Ray S. Cline, *World Power Assessment 1977: A Calculus of Strategic Drift,* (Boulder, Colo.: Westview Press, 1977). His power equation includes such items as geography, population size, economic strength, military capability, and the critical but elusive factors of strategic purpose and national will.
2. We are using the United Nations definition that "the term 'multinational corporation'. . . in the broad sense [covers] all enterprises which control assets—factories, mines, sales offices and the like in two or more countries." See *Multinational Corporations in World Development* (New York: United Nations Department of Economic and Social Affairs, U.N. publication, No. E.73 II. A. 11, 1973), p. 5.
3. "Korean Contractors Invade the Mideast," *Business Week,* May 29, 1978, p. 34.
4. This process of international evolution through initial successes at home underlies the product life-cycle theory of international trade and investment; see Raymond Vernon, "International Investment and International Trade in the Product Life Cycle," *Quarterly Journal of Economics,* May 1966.
5. Louis T. Wells, Jr., "The Internationalization of Firms from Developing Countries," in *Multinationals from Small Countries,* ed. Tamir Agmon and Charles B. Kindleberger (Cambridge, Mass.: M.I.T. Press, 1977), p. 133.
6. "Preference for Investors from Small Countries," *Hong Kong Standard,* October 30, 1977, p. 6.
7. Robert A. Scalapino, "Emerging Trends in the Pacific-Asian Region," in *ASEAN and a Positive Strategy for Foreign Investment,* ed. Lloyd R. Vasey (Honolulu: The University Press of Hawaii, 1978), p. 32.
8. See Ezra F. Vogel, "Guided Free Enterprise in Japan," *Harvard Business Review,* May-June 1978, p. 170.
9. "Doing Business with a Blacker Africa," *Business Week,* February 14, 1977, p. 75.
10. See Roy Rowan, "There's Also Some Good News About South Korea," *Fortune,* September 1977, p. 174.
11. Howard V. Perlmutter, "The Multinational Firm and the Future," *The Annals of the American Academy of Political and Social Science,* September 1972, p. 141.
12. See my article (co-authored with Howard V. Perlmutter), *Multinational Organization Development: A Social Architectural Approach* (Reading, Mass.: Addison-Wesley, 1978), chapter 5.

31
Increasing Private Capital Flows to LDCs
Ibrahim F. I. Shihata

The share of developing countries in foreign direct investment is small, perhaps less than 30 percent of the total. The volume of this small share has also declined in recent years from more than $17 billion in 1981, according to the highest estimates, to some $10 billion in 1983. The higher financial returns that an investor often receives from investing in developing rather than developed countries have not changed this picture, due in part of the prevailing perceptions that investing in developing countries usually entails greater noncommercial risks. So important are these perceptions that quite often even investors from developing countries, when given the choice, tend to invest in developed countries despite awareness of the smaller profits and more complex regulatory requirements often encountered there. In this article, written by the Vice President and General Counsel of the World Bank, who is also the Secretary-General of the International Center for Settlement of Investment Disputes, the background of the Multilateral Investment Guarantee Agency is described. The Agency, which was approved by the Board of Governors at the annual meeting of the World Bank in October, 1985, is described in the update which follows.

THE EFFECTS OF the decline in the volume of foreign investment and the continued problem of capital flight have been aggravated by a serious fall in commercial bank lending to developing countries as a group (net transfers—a concept used by the World Bank to denote net flows less interest payments—dropped from $16 billion in 1981 to –$21 billion in 1983) and by a decline in official development assistance. More than at any previous time, there seems to be a need to improve the investment climate in developing countries and stimulate greater commercial flows to them. In addition, there has been a growing realization among de-

---

Reprinted by permission from *Finance and Development,* December 1984 and December 1985.

veloping countries that foreign private investment, under appropriate conditions and safeguards, can produce net gains. The complex relationship between investors and their hosts has become more balanced with the growing importance of developing countries in the world economy and the evolution of substantive and procedural rules for the treatment of foreign investment. It is in this context that the Bank has revived its proposal to establish a multilateral investment guarantee agency.

Governmental guarantees against noncommercial risks in foreign countries are not new; their origins lie in the export credit schemes that European countries adopted in the 1920s. The United States established a national program in 1948, guaranteeing U.S. investments in Western Europe against restrictions on the conversion of currencies (transfer risks), and gradually expanded it to cover investments in developing countries against all political risks. Similar programs have now been adopted by other industrial countries and some semi-industrial countries, with many of them combining these programns with their previously established systems of export credit insurance.

In the late 1950s a proposal was made to establish an international agency that would insure foreign investors against noncommerical risks. Although the Bank, at the request of the OECD's Development Assistance Committee, assumed responsibility for the matter in 1961 and produced a number of elaborate studies and draft conventions in the late 1960s and early 1970s, the establishment of such a multilateral agency did not materialize.

Citing the need "to improve the investment climate—for potential investors and potential recipients alike," A. W. Clausen, the President of the Bank, took the initiative to revive the proposal in his first address to the Fund-Bank Annual Meetings in 1981. As a result of detailed studies undertaken by the Bank and informal discussions by its Executive Directors, the management of the Bank formulated a new plan. This version differs in many respects from previous proposals in which the agency would have no share capital and would have conducted operations exclusively on behalf of sponsoring member countries. The new features—which include a primary reliance upon share capital, a willingness to leverage this capital, and a greater role for the host countries—should give the agency broader scope in which to operate and greater flexibility, thus making it of particular interest to developing countries. The Bank is currently in consultation with members prior to a formal presentation of this proposal to its Executive Board.

NATURE AND SCOPE

The basic objective of the proposed new multilateral agency is to encourage greater flows of resources to productive enterprises in developing member countries by guaranteeing foreign investments against noncommercial risks. The agency would, in addition, furnish information on investment opportunities, prepare studies, give advice to its members on formulating and implementing policies toward foreign investment, and cooperate with other international organizations engaged in related areas. The agency's operations would be broadly delineated in its convention, elaborated in its policy rules, and more precisely defined in its contracts of guarantee. This would permit it sufficient flexibility to adjust coverage to changes in investment arrangements and gradually expand operations as it built up financial reserves and gained experience.

Covered risks would encompass noncommercial events that affect an investor's rights, including the three traditionally recognized political risks: (1) the transfer risk resulting from host government restrictions and delays in converting and transferring local currency; (2) the risk of loss resulting from host government action or omission depriving investors of control over or substantial benefits from investments; and (3) the risk of loss resulting from armed conflict or civil unrest. (Other specific noncommercial risks may also be covered under the joint request of the investor and the host country.) General nondiscriminatory measures, such as those normally taken by states to regulate economic activity, are, however, not included unless they result in breach of legal commitments. In all cases, guarantees would be confined to measures introduced or events occurring after a contract had been concluded. Transfer risk seems the obvious candidate for wide coverage; under present circumstances it is the most relevant from the viewpoint of investors, and probably least likely to evoke political objections from the host countries.

Although the agency would focus primarily on direct investment, eligible investments could include any other transfer of assets, in monetary or nonmonetary form, for productive purposes. The scope of eligible investments could be expanded as the agency's resources increase and it becomes better able to develop its risk-measurement rules. At the outset the investment covered might include equity participation and equity-type loans; eventually, it could also encompass profit-sharing, service, management and turnkey contracts, arrangements concerning industrial property rights, international leasing arrangements, and arrangements for the transfer of know-how and technology. It might even cover straight project loans, portfolio investments, and some forms of export credits. Coverage would be limited to long- and medium-term arrangements that involve productive new investments, including new transfers of foreign exchange to modernize, expand, or develop existing enterprises. Reinvested earnings, which could otherwise be transferred abroad, could also be deemed new investments.

The agency would charge premiums and fees for its services, the structure and level of premiums to be determined by its board. Revenues would be allocated, in order of priority, to (1) cover administrative expenses; (2) pay claims of insured investors; and (3) a reserve fund. Initially, however, the agency would have to rely on its members in meeting its administrative expenditures and paying whatever claims might arise under contracts of guarantee.

There would eventually be separate windows for two types of operations: guarantees issued on the basis of the agency's own capital and reserves, and guarantees issued for investments sponsored by members. The latter would be issued by the agency on behalf of the sponsoring members who would carry the ultimate financial burden of the sponsored guarantees on a *pro rata* basis. The proposed $1 billion initial capital would be subscribed by all members, with only a small portion (10 percent) paid in and the remainder kept under call to meet obligations that could not otherwise be met through paid-in capital and retained earnings. The agency's operations would be financed through its capital and reserves until it reached the ceilings designated by its board. Such ceilings would include a general limitation of up to five times capital and reserves, as well as country ceilings related to the volume of investments originated from or carried out in one member country. Once a ceiling is reached, the agency could start the second window operations based on sponsorship; here the agency basically would act as the agent of the sponsoring countries and hold a separate sponsorship fund. This would receive the premiums of sponsored guarantees and pay for administrative costs and claims resulting from them, complemented in this respect by calls on sponsoring members.

ADDITIONALITY

One basic concern raised about the proposed agency is whether it would, in fact, increase investment flows. Additional flows would result when guarantees attract investments that would not have taken place otherwise. Although it is impossible to quantify potential additional investments, there are strong indications that multilateral guarantees would encourage otherwise hesitant investors by providing a better investment climate.

Investors' calculations to maximize profitability usually involve two components, risk and return. Any perceived improvement in the risk profile could lower the rate of return required by the investor to undertake the investment ("hurdle rate"). If noncommercial risk is associated with an investment, an investor can expect to reduce this hurdle rate in return for a guarantee that diminishes risk. As the premium that the investor would pay for such a guarantee would reduce the return from the investment, additionality could ensue whenever the reduction in the hurdle rate exceeded the premium.

Concern over noncommercial risks has been reflected in the creation of national investment guarantee schemes and underscored by the rapid growth of the private political risk insurance market and the political risk analysis profession over the last decade. A study for the U.S. Overseas Private Investment Corporation concluded that in about 25 percent of the cases it examined, investments would not have taken place without a guarantee; in 18 percent, investments would have proceeded without a guarantee; and in the remaining 57 percent, although there was no decisive evidence, a guarantee did appear essential in many instances.

"Qualitative additionality" can also occur when a guarantee offered by an international agency, even if not essential for the investment to be undertaken, has an impact on the structure of the investment. This would be the case when, as a result of the agency's evaluation, investments are made for longer periods of time or with greater benefits to the host country. It may also ensue from changes in the mix of foreign investors: if a guarantee plays a larger role for small- and medium-sized investors than for large transnational corporations, host countries might be able to gain more technology adapted to their needs and more labor-intensive investments.

Some developing countries could also benefit as home countries of investments, since an agency would accord their nationals investing abroad protection that is lacking at present. This aspect is gaining importance with increased investment flows among developing countries.

LINKS TO NATIONAL PROGRAMS

With all DAC member countries operating their own national investment guarantee programs, is an international agency necessary and would it increase effectiveness? It is estimated that less than 20 percent of net investment flows from DAC member countries to developing countries was guaranteed under national programs during 1977–1981. According to OECD sources, only an estimated 9 percent of the existing stock of investments was covered at the end of 1981. The various national programs are utilized in different degrees, varying from more than 50 percent (Japan, Austria, and possibly Korea) to less than 5 percent (most European programs). The small percentage of coverage by national agencies cannot be taken as evidence of the lack of need for guarantees. Recent contacts with investors prove the contrary; there is a potential demand for investment guarantees that is not met by the national programs, due mainly to constraints inherent in the national approach to investment insurance (lack of risk diversification, emphasis on nationality and national interests, and limited financial and appraisal capacities).

The proposed agency would complement national programs rather than compete with them. It would be designed to enhance risk diversification, contribute additional appraisal capacity, and overcome gaps resulting from different terms, conditions, and administrative practices of the various national agencies. To achieve this complementary role, it would focus on the following operations:

- Guarantee, or co-guarantee with national agencies, investments in countries where the national agency is already heavily exposed.
- Guarantee investments from member countries that do not have a national investment guarantee program.
- Guarantee types of investments (e.g., service contracts) or risks (e.g., breach of host-government undertakings) not covered under the respective national programs.
- Co-guarantee large investments with national agencies, multinationally financed investments, permitting uniform protection to all co-investors.
- Guarantee low-risk projects in high-risk countries (most national investment guarantee administrations are not fully equipped to assess risks on the basis of project-related criteria).
- Provide reinsurance of national investment guarantee agencies, in particular of transfers of large investments and part of large host-country exposures. In this way the agency could enhance its own risk diversification and that of the reinsured national agencies.

FINANCIAL VIABILITY

The agency must become self-sustaining over the medium term.

Administrative expenses and claims would have to be met through premium revenues and returns on invested reserves. The experience of national investment guarantee programs of OECD countries sustains this expectation: as of December 1983, their aggregate net payments on claims (claims not recovered from host countries) amounted to just 16.4 percent of their aggregate premium revenues. The dramatic expansion of private political risk underwriting over the last decade also indicates that it has been a profitable business.

Nonetheless, the agency might not quickly become self-sufficient, as the term is understood in insurance economics, because political risks cannot be readily calculated by conventional actuarial criteria. The proposed financial structure would ensure that claims would be paid even if losses exceeded premium revenues. These could be met through calls on shareholders or sponsors, as the case may be.

Obviously, the agency's ability to pay claims without recourse to such calls would largely depend on its premium structure. While a variation of premiums according to actual loss potential would serve the financial interests of the agency, differentiation by host countries might give rise to political difficulties. To reconcile these two aspects, the agency could differentiate by project rather than by host country. This would follow the practice of all major private U.S. political risk insurers and the Overseas Private Investment Corporation. Private insurers in the United States, for example, have quoted premiums ranging from 0.75 to 7 percent per annum for investments in the same host country. OPIC considers 12 different factors to rate expropriation risks and another 11 factors to rate armed conflict risks. Aspects such as the host government's attitude toward the guaranteed investment are also considered. While the transfer risk is normally associated with the foreign exchange of liquidity of the host country, investments generating export revenues might not be affected by the general balance of payment problems of a host country. Premiums would reflect a variety of considerations and most differences would relate to economic rather than political factors.

VOTING ARRANGEMENTS

Most international financial institutions, such as the World Bank, are donor agencies that transfer funds on their own account to developing countries. The proposed agency would, by contrast, only guarantee investments made by third parties in developing member countries. It would emphasize the importance of stable investment conditions rather than provide financial intermediation. As a consequence, its proposed voting structure differs from that of a typical financial institution where voting is primarily linked to capital contributions. Voting in this context would reflect an emphasis on building mutual confidence and policy cooperation with the agency.

The proposed allocation of equal voting power to home and host countries as groups is intended to reflect the focus on policy cooperation between host and home countries. A requirement of special majorities for decisions of particular financial significance would provide an advantage to larger contributors, reflecting the financial nature of the agency.

A distinction between home and host countries as groups would be confined to the allotment of voting rights. Votes would not be cast in groups but by individual governors or directors according to the merits of each case; in effect, it is expected that decisions would be taken by consensus in most cases. Home and host countries have a common interest in a well-balanced voting structure, since such a structure would ensure the agency's credibility and success.

RELATIONS WITH HOST COUNTRIES

Since the agency would underwrite only investments specifically approved by the host country for that purpose, any involvement or potential for a dispute with a host country would be confined to investments guaranteed by the agency with the full consent of the host country. Where the agency compensated an investor under the contract of guarantee, it would assume only the substantive rights that the investor had acquired. Subrogation, assumption of the legal rights of the compensated investor to collect damages, could thus achieve nothing more than the assignment of an existing claim from the investor to the agency.

Host-country approval could eventually result in international arbitration of a dispute between the agency and a member state related to a guaranteed investment. It would not endow a private investor with procedural rights under international law.

The convention establishing the agency would not include substantive rules with respect to the treatment of guaranteed investments. Any bilateral agreement between a member and the agency would be concluded by mutual consent and no member would be under obligation to enter into such an agreement. The convention could not conflict with the Code of Conduct of Transnational Corporations currently under negotiation within the framework of the United Nations, nor could it conflict with bilateral investment protection treaties whereby the contracting parties give reciprocal assurances on the treatment of the investments of the nationals of a party in the territory of the other. In particular, a multilateral guarantee would not affect the validity of an investment protection treaty; it would add to it.

Multilateral guarantees, though normally available for foreign investment only, would not in themselves discriminate against domestic investment, since they would protect only existing rights for the investor *vis-à-vis* the host country. A transfer risk occurs because a foreign investor must rely on the ability to repatriate invested capital. In an expropriation, the guarantee would assure the investor only adequate compensation in a foreign currency; it would not protect against host governmental actions as such. Foreign investment would remain subject to host governmental regulation, as would domestic investment.

THE AGENCY AND THE BANK

As proposed, the Bank would not have an institutional stake in the agency or assume responsibility for its operations. Although the agency would presumably enter into a cooperative agreement with the Bank to benefit from its services and cut down its own costs, the only direct role envisaged for the Bank is that its President would act as chairman of the agency's board of directors. The interest of Bank members that do not wish to join the agency would not be affected. The initiative to create a multilateral agency has, nonetheless, been taken by the Bank's management; it is being discussed by the Bank's Board, and its various aspects are being studied by Bank staff. This is consistent with the Bank's role as a catalyst in the promotion of foreign investment.

The experience of several national investment guarantee schemes in developed countries should point to the need for a multilateral agency to support and supplement their work through reinsurance and co-insurance activities and the provision of insurance where protection by national schemes is unavailable or inefficient. It is hoped that the mutual interests involved would enable the Bank to bring the proposed agency to fruition in the near future. Although not a substitute for concessional flows or for new lending by commercial banks, foreign direct investment from developed as well as from capital-exporting developing countries should be encouraged to promote development efforts. An adequate financial protection provided through a multilateral agency may well prove to be the most timely step required in this direction.

SALIENT FEATURES OF THE PROPOSED
MULTILATERAL INVESTMENT GUARANTEE AGENCY

Membership: open to all Bank members and Switzerland.

Entry into force: when 15 (10 developing) countries join and furnish part of initial capital subscriptions.

Organization: council of governors, board of directors, and president and staff. Council delegates general authority to board, but retains vote on admission, changes in capitalization, amendments, and suspension or liquidation of operations. President has responsibility for ordinary business.

Subscribed capital: share capital, initially $1 billion, is open-ended and increased with new membership. Individual subscriptions negotiated on the basis of ability to pay.

Sponsorship: in addition to operations based on share capital and reserves, members may sponsor investments for guarantee, incurring loss-sharing liability for them on a *pro rata* basis with other sponsoring members.

Relationship with national agencies: cooperative arrangements using their administrative support, facilitating communication between them.

Relationship with private risk insurers: cooperative arrangements to leverage underwriting capacity, diversify risks, maximize administrative efficiency. Reinsures some of its portfolio with private insurers and co-insures large investments.

Payment of claims: investor first required to seek administrative remedies in host country. Agency assesses claims, provides for prompt payment. Disputes submitted to arbitration, unless the parties agree on other methods.

Voting: Members classified for voting purposes only as home or host countries; each group allocated the same number of votes. Important decisions require approval by a special majority.

The Multilateral Investment Guarantee Agency: An Update

At its 1985 Annual Meeting the World Bank's Board of Governors approved the Convention Establishing the Multilateral Investment Guarantee Agency. The Convention will enter into force upon ratification by 5 capital-exporting countries and 15 capital-importing countries, if subscriptions of these countries total at least one third of MIGA's authorized capital. MIGA could begin operations as early as 1986.

MIGA's broad mandate is to stimulate capital flows to its member countries, particularly to its developing member countries. To this end it will issue guarantees for investments against noncommercial risk and, among other activities, conduct research and provide technical assistance and information on investment opportunities.

MIGA is not intended to displace national and private investment insurance programs already in effect in many developed and some developing countries. MIGA will be in a position to supplement these schemes through co-insurance and reinsurance. It will also concentrate on extending guarantees to investments not currently eligible for national or private coverage. Some of the salient features of MIGA are:

RISK COVERAGE

To discourage irresponsible behavior by investors, MIGA will not fully cover losses. It is envisaged that MIGA typically will cover 70-95 percent of the investment (similar to national programs). The following risks are covered:

- Risk of host government restrictions on currency conversion and transfer.
- Risk of loss resulting from legislative actions or administrative actions and omissions of the host government that have the effect of depriving foreign investors of ownership or control of, or substantial benefits from, their investments.
- Risk of repudiation of government contracts where investors have no access to a competent forum, face unreasonable judicial delays, or are unable to enforce rules issured in their favor.
- Risk of armed conflict or civil unrest.
- Other noncommercial risks, to be added on a case-by-case basis at the joint request of the investor and the host country and with the approval, by a special majority, of MIGA's Board.

ELIGIBILITY

Eligible investments: new investments, of a medium- to long-term nature, judged by MIGA to be both sound and in accordance with the declared development objectives of the host country, including equity and direct investments, as well as medium- or long-term loans made or guaranteed by owners of equity in the enterprise concerned. Direct investment may include franchising, licensing, leasing, and production-sharing. MIGA will not guarantee or reinsure any export credit provided, guaranteed, or reinsured by a government or an official export credit agency. Commercial loans may be covered if they are related to a specific investment otherwise covered, or to be covered, by the Agency.

Eligible investors: nationals or member countries, or corporations whose principal places of business are in member countries (or have the majority of their capital owned by nationals or member countries). Eligibility may be extended to nationals of developing countries who invest in their own countries, if invested assets are transferred from abroad. This is designed to help reverse capital flight.

Eligible host countries: except for sponsored investments (see below), MIGA is only able to guarantee investments in developing member countries, with priority given to lesser developed member countries.

ORGANIZATION

Membership: open to World Bank member countries and Switzerland. There is, however, no obligation upon any country to join.

Organizational structure: MIGA is an autonomous agency, with its own Council of Governors, Board of Directors, and President and staff. The President of the World Bank as *ex officio* Chairman of MIGA's Board nominates the Agency's President.

Voting rights: developing and developed member countries will have equal voting power as groups once all Bank members join MIGA. During MIGA's first three years the minority group will be guaranteed 40 percent of total votes and decisions will be taken by a two-third majority of the total votes representing not less than 55 percent of subscriptions to MIGA's capital. In the third year, MIGA's Council will review the voting structure with a view to assuring parity between the two groups.

MIGA AND HOST COUNTRIES

Host country approval: MIGA "shall not conclude any contract of guarantee before the host government has approved the issuance of the guarantee by the Agency against the risks designated for cover."

Subrogation: if MIGA pays a claim, it assumes the rights of the indemnified investor. (See following paragraph for procedures for settling disputes between MIGA and host countries with respect to such rights.)

Settlement of disputes: if negotiations between MIGA and the host country fail, either party will have access to international arbitration unless both agree to resort first to conciliation. However, MIGA will be authorized to agree with individual host countries on alternative dispute settlement procedures.

FINANCING

Capital base: SDR 1 billion initial share capital: 10 percent in cash; 10 percent in promissory notes; the remainder subject to call.

MIGA guarantees: initially totaling no more than one and a half times the capital plus reserves and a portion of MIGA's reinsurance coverage. This could increase, with experience and the formation of a balanced risk portfolio, to a maximum ratio of 5 to 1.

SPONSORSHIP

In addition to guarantee operations based on the Agency's capital and reserves, MIGA can cover investments sponsored by member countries as trustee for these countries. Revenues from these operations accumulate in a separate fund out of which claims and expenses are paid. (If this fund is totally depleted, liabilities would be shared proportionately by all sponsoring countries.)

APPENDIX I:

CROSS REFERENCES TO CHAPTERS IN STANDARD TEXTBOOKS

APPENDIX
The Multinational Enterprise in Transition

CHAPTERS IN STANDARD TEXTBOOKS

Chapters	Ball & McCulloch[1]	Daniels, Ogram & Radebaugh[2]	Kolde[3]	Korth[4]	Mason, Miller & Weigel[4]
1 The Multinational Enterprise in Transition	1	1, 12, 13	1, 9, 11	1	1
2 International Management	21, 22	18, 23	12, 13, 18	15	16
3 International Finance and Banking	2, 5 10, 18	2, 7 9, 10 11, 22	6,7,8	5,6 8,10 16,20,21	3, 4 5, 6 10, 13, 14
4 International Marketing Management	2, 12 14, 15, 16	19		11,17	9
5 International Personnel Management	7, 11 20, 22	4, 24	2,15	18	16
6 International Accounting and Control	9, 10, 18	20, 21	7, 8, 14	19,21	3
7 International Manufacturing and Production	19	15, 16	19		15
8 MNC/Host-Government Relations	3,8 9,13	3	13, 15, 16	12,13,14	7, 17
9 Political Risk	8,9			11	
10 Future Issues Affecting MNCs		25			11, 18

1. Donald A. Ball and Wendell H. McCulloch, Jr., *International Business: Introduction and Essentials* (Plano, TX: Business Publications, Inc., 2nd edition, 1985).

2. John D. Daniels, Ernest W. Ogram, Jr. and Lee H. Radebaugh, *International Business: Environments and Operations* (Reading, Mass.: Addison Wesley, 1982).

3. Endel-Jakob Kolde, *Enviroment of International Business* (Boston: Kent Publishing Co., 1982).

4. Christopher M. Korth, *International Business: Environment and Management* (Englewood Cliffs, NJ: Prentice-Hall, 2nd edition, 1985).

5. R. Hall Mason, Robert R. Miller, and Dale R. Weigel, *International Business*, New York, NY: John Wiley, 1981).

APPENDIX   CHAPTERS IN STANDARD TEXTBOOKS
The Multinational
Enterprise in
Transition

Chapters	Moyer[6]	Robinson[7]	Robock & Simmonds[7]	Roman & Puett[8]	Rugman, Lecraw & Booth[10]
1 The Multinational Enterprise in Perspective	Intro- duction 12,14	1	1, 2, 3	1	1,5
2 International Management	35	5	16, 17 21, 23	3, 12 15, 16	4,6 13,14
3 International Finance and Banking	24,26 28,29,30	7	4, 5 6, 22	2, 10	7,8 9,18
4 International Marketing and Management	40	2,3	18	3, 11, 14	
5 International Personnel Management		4,5	23	12, 16	17
6 International Accounting and Control		9	20	2, 14, 16	
7 International Manufacturing and Production	33,34	3		2	16
8 MNC/Host- Government Relations	13,15 18,19 35,36,37	6,8	10, 11, 12		12
9 Political Risk			15		11
10 Future Considerations	21,22	10	19, 24	6, 11, 17	

6. Reed Moyer, *International Business: Issues and Concept* (New York, NY: John Wiley, 1985).

7. Richard D. Robinson, *Internationalization of Business: An Introduction* (New York, NY: Dryden, 1984).

8. Stephen F. Robock and Kenneth Simmonds, *International Business and Multinational Enterprises* (Homewood, IL: Richard D. Irwin, Inc., 3rd edition, 1983).

9. Daniel D. Roman and Joseph F. Puett, Jr., *International Business and Technological Innovations* (New York, NY: North Holland, 1983).

10. Alan M. Rugman, Donald J. Lecraw and Lawrence D. Booth, *International Business: Firm and Environment* (New York, NY: McGraw-Hill, 1985).

APPENDIX   CHAPTERS IN STANDARD TEXTBOOKS

The Multinational Enterprise in Transition Chapters	Rutenberg[11]	Schnitzer, Liebrenz & Kubin[12]	Tsurmi[13]	Wortzel & Wortzel[14]
1 The Multinational Enterprise in Perspective		1,2	2	
2 International Management	1,11	4,5,14	4,8 9,12	4–9 32–35
3 International Finance and Banking	2,3	6,12	3,7,8	14–18
4 International Marketing Management	8,9	15	5,6	21–26
5 International Personnel Management		14	11	36–38
6 International Accounting and Control		16,17	10	19–20
7 International Manufacturing and Production	5,6 7,8,10		13	27–31
8 MNC/Host-Government Relations		10,11	4	
9 Political Risk		13	15	10–13
10 Future Considerations		21		

11. David P. Rutenberg, *Multinational Management* (Boston, MA: Little, Brown, 1982).

12. Martin C. Schnitzer, Marilyn L. Liebrenz and Konrad W. Kubin, *International Business* (Cincinnati, OH: Southwestern Publishing Co., 1985).

13. Yoshi Tsurmi, *Multinational management: Business Strategy and Government Policy* (Cambridge, MA: Ballinger, 2nd edition, 1985).

14. Heidi V. Wortzel and Lawrence H. Wortsel, *Strategic Management of Multinational Corporations: The Essentials* (New York, NY: John Wiley, 1985).